Fictions of the Irish Literary Revival

A CHANGELING ART

JOHN WILSON FOSTER

Syracuse University Press

First Paperback Edition 1993

93 94 95 96 97 98 99 6 5 4 3 2 1

Portions of the book have appeared in somewhat different form in *Ariel* (chapter four), *University of Toronto Quarterly* (chapter six), *Criticism* (chapter eight), *Eire-Ireland* (chapter ten), and *Irish Renaissance Annual* (chapter fifteen).

Extracts from "The Dead" from *Dubliners* by James Joyce. Copyright 1916 by B. W. Huebsch. Definitive text copyright © 1967 by The Estate of James Joyce. Reprinted by permission of Viking Penguin Inc.

Extract from Anatole Le Braz, *The Land of Pardons,* trans. Frances M. Gostling (London: Methuen & Co., 1906) reprinted by permission.

Extracts from Tomás Ó Crohan, *The Islandman,* trans. Robin Flower (Oxford: Clarendon Press, 1951) reprinted by permission.

Extract from Jack E. Reece, *The Bretons Against France: Ethnic Minority Nationalism in Twentieth-Century Brittany* (Chapel Hill: University of North Carolina Press, 1977) reprinted by permission.

Extracts from James Stephens, *The Charwoman's Daughter* and *Deirdre* reprinted by permission of the Society of Authors on behalf of the copyright owner, Mrs. Iris Wise.

Extracts from John M. Synge, *Collected Works 2: Prose,* ed. Alan Price (London: Oxford University Press, 1966) reprinted by permission.

The paper used in this publication meets the minimum requirements of American National Standard for Information Sciences—Permanence of Paper for Printed Library Materials, ANSI Z39.48-1984. ∞™

Library of Congress Cataloging-in-Publication Data

Foster, John Wilson.
Fictions of the Irish literary revival

(Irish studies)
Bibliography: p.
Includes index.
1. English fiction—Irish authors—History and criticism. 2. English fiction—19th century—History and criticism. 3. English fiction—20th century—History and criticism. 4. Ireland in literature. 5. Cuchulain (Legendary character) in literature. 6. Folklore in literature. I. Title. II. Series: Irish studies (Syracuse University Press)
PR8801.F6 1987 823′.8′099415 87-1916
ISBN 0-8156-2374-7 (alk. paper)
ISBN 0-8156-2588-X (pbk.)

Manufactured in the United States of America

I think that all happiness depends on the energy to assume the mask of some other self; that all joyous or creative life is a rebirth as something not oneself, something which has no memory and is created in a moment and perpetually renewed.

—W. B. Yeats, "The Death of Synge"

—*T*his race and this country and this life produced me, he said. I shall express myself as I am.

—James Joyce, *A Portrait of the Artist as a Young Man*

To the Memory
of my
Mother

Contents

Acknowledgments

For various kinds of help during the writing of this book, I am grateful to a number of people, especially Jocelyn Foster, Dr. Graham Good, Dr. Cormac O Grada, and Dr. Peter Taylor. I am indebted also, for their sound advice and encouraging assessments, to the two scholars who read a version of the study at the request of Syracuse University Press. Over the years, the University of British Columbia and the Social Sciences and Humanities Research Council (Canada) have awarded me useful travel grants, and I thank them. Lastly, I ought to have acknowledged before this the early encouragement given to me at Queen's University, Belfast by fine teachers, including Professor W. B. Gallie, Dr. Marjorie Grene, and Dr. Philip Hobsbaum.

Introduction

What follows is a study of the fiction of the Irish Literary Revival. It is a fiction written by those who revolutionized Irish perceptions and sensibilities, who produced an enduring body of literature, and who became dominant figures in contemporary Irish (and in several cases, British) literary culture. They were associated through their cultural nationalism, their romanticism, their preoccupation with heroism, their interest in folklore and the occult, their attention to the peasantry, their promotion of an ancient Gaelic polity and worldview, and by their repudiation of realism, democracy, individualism, modernization, the bourgeoisie, and cultural union with England. Irish writers had pursued the interests of the revivalists before the new movement, but not with such concentrated will, energy, and genius. Other European countries or regions before Ireland had followed the German example in engaging in cultural revival that was at once romantic and nationalistic, but few had produced a literature to equal that of Ireland's between the 1880s and 1920s.

Whereas the poetry and drama of the Irish literary revival have been studied broadly and in depth, the movement's achievements in fiction have been neglected. Perhaps this is because the fiction of the revival represents a highly diverse and uncooperative body of work. The movement did not begin or perpetuate a tradition of the novel, as literary critics customarily understand that word. (The sole major enterprise forsaken by the revival's chief writer, W. B. Yeats, was, tellingly, his only begotten novel.) Indeed, the Anglo-Irish novel, and the adjective is instructive, suffered with the onset of the revival. Because the revival encouraged other literary forms at its expense, the novel as a recognizable and autonomous form received a setback at the hands of the revival and its aims and aspirations. True, one of the greatest achievements of the revival years was a novel, but *Ulysses* was not a novel in the current accepted sense, nor was it written by a supporter of the revival. For several decades after the movement expired, a debate was waged as to whether we could refer honorifically to "the Irish novel" at all!

The talents of the revival supplanted extant Irish novelists as representers of significant Irish feeling and opinion. They did not dam the flow of native fiction; by forming an artistic mainstream themselves, they merely caused it to appear by comparison as a middlebrow tributary. Few would bemoan what happened. Here is a fairly representative list of novels and story collections (one per author) published between 1890 and the turn of the century by Irish writers, most of whom were unassociated, at least then, with a revival that was mustering its strength: *When We Were Boys* (1890) by William O'Brien, M.P.; *Irish Idylls* (1892) by Jane Barlow; *Grania: The Story of an Island* (1892) by Hon. Emily Lawless; *Pat O'Nine Tales* (1894) by M. McDonnell Bodkin, K.C.; *The Chain of Gold* (1895) by Standish James O'Grady; *By Thrasna River* (1895) by Shan F. Bullock; *Through the Turf Smoke* (1899) by Seumas MacManus; *Some Experiences of an Irish R.M.* (1899) by Somerville and Ross; *My New Curate* (1900) by Canon Sheehan; *A Girl of Galway* (1901) by Katharine Tynan. I have omitted from the list the novels George Moore published during the 1890s, none of which is set in Ireland, unlike his earlier *A Drama in Muslin* (1886). I could have added titles by Miss L. MacManus, Richard Ashe King (to whom Yeats dedicated *Early Poems and Stories,* 1925), Edmund Downey, Amanda McKittrick Ros ("the World's Worst Novelist"), M. E. Francis (the *nom-de-plume* of Mrs. Francis Blundell), H. A. Hinkson (who married Katharine Tynan in 1893), Frank Mathew, J. J. Moran, and three alarmingly prolific authors: James Murphy, who had written more than twenty-five novels by 1915, Rosa Mulholland (Lady Gilbert), who had published twenty-nine novels or collections of tales by the same date, and Mrs. Riddell (Charlotte E. Cowan), who published almost fifty novels. With the exceptions of Somerville and Ross and George Moore, these authors have sunk from readerly sight, many even (Stygian fate, indeed) from academic sight.

Yet many were immensely popular in their day: a ninth edition of Barlow's sketches appeared in 1908; an eighteenth edition of *My New Curate* came out in 1918 and the novel was translated into French, Dutch, German, Italian, Spanish, Hungarian, and other languages; Seumas MacManus' tales were published in London, Toronto, and New York; a 1919 reprinting of O'Brien's novel sold out in Ireland. Some fiction writers contemporary with Yeats, Synge, and Stephens were more prolific even than Murphy, Mulholland, and Mrs. Riddell: George A. Birmingham (Canon James O. Hannay) wrote scores of novels, and the combined total of all four barely matches the prodigious output of Katharine Tynan, who published one hundred and five novels and twelve short story collections. Since Tynan was a poet and memoirist of repute and ambition, she is only statistically put in the shade by L. T. Meade (pseudonym of Elizabeth Thomasina Toulmin Smith) who is credited with almost two hundred novels, many of them written for schoolgirls. The popular Irish novel (Irish in a way that permitted popularity in Britain) continued in blithe disregard of the revival. Tynan and Birmingham published novels in the middle 1920s not essentially different in kind from those they had published twenty years before, while Bullock's last and possibly best novel, *The Loughsiders* (1924), shows no detectable influence of the cultural ferment in Dublin.

This popular fiction would make a fascinating study in its own right. A majority of its authors were women, especially Protestant women of middle-class or upper middle-class (or even noble) background. Much of it is historical fiction, and much of it romance. There is a high incidence of humor of a quaint or picturesque kind that can betray its class or racial origins. It is what I would term Anglo-Irish fiction of the first type: a self-consciously Irish form written mainly but not exclusively by southern Protestants but for English readers. Occasionally it exhibits seriousness and achieves distinction. Katharine Tynan's *A Girl of Galway,* despite its Big House gothic romance, tries through its young, peacemaking heroine to reconcile the peasantry with the "quality" at the expense of the established and villainous land-agentry, but not at the expense of the new, modernizing bourgeoisie to whom Tynan allots a portion of the new Ireland while leaving a diminished aristocracy intact. Tynan was a Catholic, sympathetic to the nationalist cause, but essentially a unionist. William O'Brien was a Catholic, editor of the *United Ireland* journal, and a nationalist who went to jail periodically for his beliefs. *When We Were Boys,* written in jail, nevertheless has an English readership in mind. It is a remarkably dense and knowledgeable analysis of Fenian Ireland that exceeds in scope Moore's *A Drama in Muslin;* it is not as shapely as Moore's novel, and lapses into whimsy on more occasions, but it covers some of the same ground, yet with greater dash and more observations of the Irish reality.

What I would term Anglo-Irish fiction of the second type is much less common: the novel of broad appeal that happens to be set, unself-consciously, in Ireland. An example would be Canon Sheehan's *The Triumph of Failure,* which is in my opinion essential reading for anyone who seeks the entire picture of Irish fiction in the 1890s, and I will have occasion to return to it.

The reluctant welcome Tynan's heroine extends to the coal-mining interests would have given the writers of the revival pause. But it is not its countenance of modernizing capitalism that disqualifies *A Girl of Galway* from being a work of the revival; rather is it form: the novel embodies a tired, conventional form (social realism bowing to social romance) instead of impatient and refreshed necessities of intelligence, vision, and ideology. The Anglo-Irish novel could not, it seems, adapt to rapidly changing mental circumstances in Ireland; brittle in genre, inclined to humor and romance, it seemed ill-equipped to register the political gloom and cultural euphoria of post-Parnellite Ireland. The shunting of the Anglo-Irish novel into its middlebrow and popular sidings accompanied the increasing irrelevance of the Anglo-Irishry as Ireland entered the twentieth century and neared the brink of political and cultural home rule. Those members of the Anglo-Irish who did survive, and indeed who helped to gain Ireland its independence, included the leaders of the Irish literary revival. They survived by adapting in rather startling ways, one of which was to abandon the Anglo-Irish novel as a vehicle for their survival.

Despite, or because of, the fate of the Anglo-Irish novel, no one could dispute the fact that a copious amount of first-rate imaginative prose was written from the 1890s onwards. But it was written in furtherance of, or *in conscious reaction against,* the Irish literary revival. It is this imaginative prose that is the subject of my book, and I have found it wise as well as necessary to widen my implicit definition of fiction beyond novels and short stories to include autobiographies and also translations, collections, and adaptations, be they of folktales or ancient sagas and romances. During the revival, writers were in pursuit of a native prose tradition that would be a mingling of the old and the experimental. This pursuit did not succeed in concealing the need for a vigorous realist fiction in Ireland, a fiction which a handful of Catholic (or lapsed Catholic) writers tried to provide while the revival was under way and with whom I deal in the central part of my study. But it did result in a variegated body of prose that demands our attention if we would fully understand the Irish literary revival.

Grappling with a diversity of material has, in any case, been desirable, for it has enabled me to approach more closely the revival itself, which is my real subject. Synge the author of *The Aran Islands,* for instance, is an important figure in my study, and so too are Yeats the folklorist, and Lady Gregory the adapter of sagas. The storyteller-novelists Padraic Colum, James Stephens, and Lord Dunsany are here, as well as

Hyde the collector of tales, and AE the composer of *The Interpreters,* that singular novel-cum-symposium. Yeats and Patrick Pearse the short-story writers would have been eligible in any case, but I have treated them with rather more critical respect than they usually receive in this role. In short, no important figure of the Irish literary revival is absent, with the exception of Sean O'Casey, whose autobiographical volumes were published after the event (between 1939 and 1954) and which I deemed outside the historical scope of my investigation.

Fictions of the Irish Literary Revival, then, offers a perspective on the chief figures of this time: the range of authors is here, and the chronological spread, but not the range of genres. (Wider accounts of the literature of the revival can be found in Ernest Boyd's contemporary study, *Ireland's Literary Renaissance,* 1916, rev. 1922, and Richard Fallis' *The Irish Renaissance,* 1977.) My book also offers a perspective on some of the informing ideas of the revival. These ideas can be found among what according to most critical surveys of the movement are miscellaneous or marginal works, and possibly most vividly in prose, where ideas are closer to statement than in poetry and drama. If anything, I have broadened, not narrowed, the field of study by adding to the familiar revival canon writings either commonly neglected or uncommonly bracketed together for discussion.

This book, though, is not a history of revival prose, even though there is a roughly chronological arrangement. I begin with P. W. Joyce and Standish James O'Grady, whose first books appeared in the late 1870s, and close with a book by Tomás Ó Crohan published in 1929, but there are numerous backward sweeps in the story I have to tell, among them the consideration of Ó Crohan himself, who was born only ten years after O'Grady and nine before Yeats. I have tended to sacrifice a conventional survey of the fiction to an interpretation of its chief images, themes, and motifs. The importance I attach to these, as well as the kinship I believe them to share, is no doubt contestable. If *Fictions of the Irish Literary Revival* is a first look at the imaginative prose written during the period and at some of the social and cultural forces working through the prose, it is also a second look at a literary and cultural movement of significance for Ireland as profound today as when it occurred. The issue I take with much of the ideology of the Irish revival is reflected in my equivocal use of the word "fictions" in my title, meaning by it now prose narratives, now departures from reality (or, if we like, now fabulations, now fabrications).

Of as great an interest to me as chronology is setting, the role of place in the literature and thought of the revival. The West (more specifically the western island) is a key image in my study and it presides over a number of oppositions: island-mainland, west-east, country-city, Ireland-Europe. In turn, these sites and symbols connect with the variety of literary styles of the revival (and styles are also ways of seeing), and the connection is suggested in the patterning of my chapters. This variety resolves itself on one level into a contest between revival styles and fictional realism. I have set my discussion of realism (and of Dublin) in the center of the study surrounded by the rural romanticisms and fantasies of the revival, something of a stone in the midst of all. Both history and place are important to me as forces from which—with the aid of realism—the theme of self-realization can be seen emerging despite revival discountenance of it.

The realistic work of George Moore, James Joyce, Brinsley MacNamara, and others might tempt us to distinguish an Irish Literary Renaissance from the Irish Literary Revival. By the former (which more accurately might be termed a 'naissance') I would mean the tremendous release of literary energy in Ireland around the turn of the century, whatever its direction and ideology; to this Renaissance Moore and Joyce contributed hugely. By the Irish Literary Revival I would mean the work of those who sought to employ literature in a resuscitation of elder Irish values and culture that they hoped would transform the reality of the Ireland they inhabited. I have not, however, maintained this distinction pedantically in my book, and it may well be in practice untenable, given the critical, realistic, or ironic crosscurrents we find in some writers we deem "revivalist."

The appeal to ancient values was not the only transformation being essayed during the period. Metamorphosis is a key motif in my study and has suggested its subtitle. At bottom, the idea of metamorphosis in what follows refers to those shape-shiftings and enchantments that are imagination (a venerable Celtic equation) and lends a third meaning to the word "fictions" in my title, and one that bridges the other two. Above this meaning, however, there is all manner of shape-changing amenable to social and literary analysis. A bald summary of the argument underlying my discussion of the prose will suggest what I have in mind.

Most of the figures who dominated the revival were of Anglo-Irish background, but they chose to rebel against their racial, class, and religious heritage to don the mask of another identity. (They had had, of course, predecessors; indeed, almost enough to comprise over the years a subculture.) Their rebellion took the form of self-recruitment to the ranks of Catholic Ireland but shed of Catholicism; we would do better to call it "native Ireland," thereby evoking the Gaelic language, pagan belief, ancient literature in the native tongue, and nationalism. Certainly the time was overdue for the Anglo-Irish to admit their own Irishness. But this was no gradual self-perception; it was a conversion so rapid that it could not be other than unrealistic. Besides, to a great extent the leaders of the revival were inventing a native Ireland into which they could comfortably fit with room nevertheless to accommodate some unjettisonable and desirable Anglo-Irish values and characteristics. At first, Catholic intellectuals and writers were suspicious of the renegades, viewing them as fifth columnists or playboys, but many (Joyce was a notable exception) came to accept their usefulness to the cause of an independent Ireland in providing a cultural basis for separatism.

The emerging coalition developed a synthetic and triumphantly eloquent cultural nationalism; it formulated a definition not only of Irish literature but of Irish culture and Irish nationality. Certain traditions, literatures, regional identities, and subcultures were championed and others disqualified, the champion frequently having to exchange his own identity and allegiances in the process. A faction of the Anglo-Irish made common cause with a faction of the Irish; the alliance required not only forms of self-denial, but alterations of the past and present, whether in life or literature. Certain unwelcome and inconvenient Irelands were ignored or misinterpreted: petty-bourgeois and small farmer Catholic Ireland that dominated the island in terms of population (and still does) and asserted itself with a vengeance after 1922, that Ireland known intimately, among others, to James Joyce, Brinsley MacNamara, D. P. Moran, and later Flann O'Brien and Patrick Kavanagh; the genuine Gaelic culture that had once flourished and had now a precarious grip on life in the west of Ireland; orthodox Anglo-Ireland, aristocratic, mercantile and clerical remnant of the Protestant Ascendancy that ended in 1800 with the Act of Union; and Protestant Ulster, the Nonconformist or Scots-Irish northeast of the island. All of this may have been unavoidable if a new and politically viable Ireland were to be fashioned; Ernest Renan said: "to forget, and I will venture to say, to get one's history wrong are essential factors in the making of nations." But I have implied that the particular, indisputable, and necessary nation-building and culture-building that were accomplished should be balanced by the damage that they may have inflicted on the island of Ireland in the domains of human happiness, cultural self-respect, and political stability.

Ultimately at stake during the Irish revival were the nature and identity of Ireland, and the extent of its legitimate power to define the nature and identity of the individual. The politics of the self was the revival's abiding concern and constitutes the key theme of my study.

Among the subcultures and even particular writers who dismayed the revivalists were those promoting individualism; the revival discouraged a sense of personal identity outside the jurisdiction of favored cultural forces. In the Free State (1922–49) and the Republic (1949–) that grew out of the revival (in both senses—as a plant grows out of a seed, and as a child grows out of his clothes), individualism continued to be discouraged, only this time by force of law and in service to a Catholic rather than pagan or romantic nation. Soon after the Free State came into being, Catholicism officially became, like the Irish language, an essential strand of cultural nationalism. Once this was done, the cultural nationalism of the Protestant revivalists began on hindsight to look like cultural unionism (or home colonialism) in disguise. But clearly in some real sense the Irish literary revival was a nationalistic movement and its anti-individualism as genuine as its nationalism.

It is, then, an irony both of the revival and of later events in Ireland that a handful of Catholic writers, notably George Moore, James Joyce, Gerald O'Donovan and Brinsley MacNamara, promoted self-realization. They esteemed, unwittingly except in the case of Moore, the individualism associated with the heritage of the Anglo-Irish writers who had repudiated that heritage in order to achieve the literary movement. These few writers had to liberate themselves from an ancient collective spirituality to which they were native—be it Catholicism or an elder superstitious paganism—by means of painful self-scrutiny and by holding a mirror up to Irish nature. If Moore is the largely unacknowledged father of Irish realism, Joyce is its stepfather, and it is on his early, influential and counter-revival work *Dubliners* that I have concentrated my attention when discussing him.

Moore and Joyce began the Irish fictional tradition of anti-clerical dissent (the Catholic Church was part of Ireland the Protestant revivalists tried to ignore), but Daniel Corkery was almost as influential in promoting a realism that was less antagonistic towards both the Church and nationalism. One of the aims of this book is to call attention to the neglected constituency of realism—dissenting or no—during the time of the revival. I offer the names of Moore, O'Donovan, Joyce, MacNamara, Corkery, Lysaght, O'Kelly, and—in a different mode—Ó Crohan (Catholics or ex-Catholics all) as representing a literary tradition alternative to the literary revival. Realism does not rival the more familiar tradition in quality or excitement. But nor can it be explained away simply by genre (the revivalists writing poetry, drama and experimental prose forms, the realists writing traditional fiction). It is true that the realists wrote Anglo-Irish fiction of the third type, or, as I prefer to put it, created Irish fiction proper: fiction written by Irish writers, self-consciously set in Ireland but for serious purposes and for any reader who cares to understand the Irish experience by which the writers embody in their work the universal. (In Moore we see a writer who follows Anglo-Irish fiction of the first type with, years later, Irish fiction proper.) However, it is in their perception of Ireland and their ideology, despite the expected ambiguities in tendency, that the realists and the revivalists are opposed, and the former have collectively suffered critical neglect and disarray.

Whether the dissident realists could or would have liberated themselves without the revival (to the debatable degree that they did) is problematical. In any event, the revival articulated for the twentieth century a cultural nationalism that inspired the politics of the Republic (and before that the Free State) and has held sway for many decades in much of Ireland, despite the efforts of the dissidents. This ideology is now at risk, though it has stiffened somewhat in the light of the freshly remembered threat by Ulster to the notion of a united, overwhelmingly Catholic Ireland. Some of the traditions excluded by the revival have begun to assert themselves (or have already asserted themselves) in defiance of the superior literary talent exhibited during the revival. For example, as compass point in the Irish imagination, North has begun to challenge West, with an Ulster literature emerging in the 1970s. Long before that, of course, the dream of the noble and the beggarman had been subjected to the solvent of hard times and actuality. It was with splendid perversity that AE wrote to Van Wyck Brooks in 1925: "We in Ireland are reacting against the idealism which led us to war and civil war and I fear we are in for an era of materialism." The chief fiction writers who followed the revival—from Frank O'Connor and Sean O'Faolain to John McGahern and Brian Moore—were realists, or would-be realists, who did not avoid petty-bourgeois Ireland (who could hardly do so without metamorphosis, being Catholics born of that Ireland) and were mostly anti-clerical dissidents, lonely maintainers of an anti-official ideology of individualism. When they were not, they were urbane writers who resuscitated the English novel in Ireland (Anglo-Irish fiction of the second type), an equally telling if politer retreat from the revival; mostly these were women, and mostly Catholic, but sufficiently middle-class to balance in literary historical terms the loss of Protestantism; they are the unsung talent in fiction during the Free State's existence—Elizabeth Bowen, Kathleen Coyle, Mary Lavin, M. J. Farrell (Molly Keane), Kate O'Brien.

The formidable accomplishments of the revival, even in prose, remain, and attacks on the movement do not worry the ghost of Yeats one whit. "Long ago," he wrote to Sturge Moore in 1929, "I used to puzzle poor Maud Gonne by always avowing defeat as a test—our literary movement would be worthless but for its defeat." But my argument to the contrary, it would not do, for any purposes whatsoever, to slight the literary achievements or to oversimplify the art and thought of the Irish literary revival, even if we restrict ourselves to a consideration of prose. The space I devote to that prose is, I hope, an earnest of my admiration for it and, by implication, my respect for (if neither sympathy nor agreement with) the ideology that underwrote much of it. I have sought to outweigh ideological anxiety with the responsiveness of a devotee of literature, not just of its significances but also its textures, not just its generalities but its localities. My argument has emerged from my reading of the literature, and not the other way round. As for the revival as a self-contained movement, I confess that at times I reify it more than close or comprehensive reading really sanctions. But a perspective must be reached. What is incontestable is that a great deal of the Ireland we live in (or choose not to live in) was fashioned, or fashioned anew, during the revival. This includes the examples of cultural retrogression I furnish alongside, and in problematical relation to, examples of the literary excellence I have intended to celebrate. *Fictions of the Irish Literary Revival* arises from this writer's Irishness in dialogue with the Irishness of those who made the Irish Renaissance (his fiction in dialogue with theirs, perhaps), and to that extent the book is about Ireland now as well as then.

JWF

Vancouver, 1987

Fictions of the Irish Literary Revival

The Coming of the Heroes
Versions of Saga and Heroic Romance

I

The heroes are coming; they are on the road.

—Standish James O'Grady

The Brightest Candle of the Gael
Cultural Interpretations of the Cuchulain Cycle

1

Uncovering the Heroic Past: The Cuchulain Saga

To English readers W. B. Yeats may have seemed extravagant when he recalled Patrick Pearse, outside the Dublin Post Office at Easter 1916, islanded amidst an ungovernable tide of British soldiery, summoning Cuchulain to his side. But he would not have seemed so to Irish readers, for whom life is rhetorical and literature a hazardous lever on the living, and for whom literary matters impinge on life in the way Matthew Arnold said enviously they did for the French. Pearse himself was acutely aware of the ancient Irish heroic tradition. He wrote two pageants, *Mac-Ghníomhartha Chúchulainn (The Boy-Deeds of Cuchulain)* and *The Defence of the Ford*—both adaptations from the *Táin Bó Cuailnge (The Cattle Raid of Cooley)*—which were presented in the grounds of Pearse's school, St. Enda's, in 1909 and 1913 respectively.[1] Nor did Pearse see any conflict between Christianity and the old heroic romances; indeed, he considered the *Táin* "like a retelling (or is it a foretelling?) of the story of Calvary."[2] And he thought that the famous words of Cuchulain, "I care not though I were to live but one day and one night, if only my fame and my deeds live after me" were compatible with those of St. Columcille, "if I die, it should be from the excess of love I bear the Gael,"[3] even though Cuchulain's would seem to express heroic egotism, St. Columcille's heroic selflessness. AE, for one, perceived an immense contradiction and was of the opinion that Christian obedience and selflessness were in Ireland merely the product of coercion by the priests. Christianity he took to task for robbing a nation of a pantheon of divinities and replacing it with but one divine man, and for removing the sacred realm to an exotic afterlife from the earth underfoot where it resided in pagan times. While giving Irishmen a choice between priest and hero (a choice rather lopsidedly expressed, one might think), AE fulminated: "we read in vivid romance of the giant chivalry of the Ultonians, their untamable manhood, the exploits of Cuculain and the children of Rury, more admirable as types, more noble and inspiring than the hierarchy of little saints who came later on and cursed their memories."[4]

It was heroism that was important, however, whether it was Christian or pagan, and Pearse would have agreed with AE that "whatever is not heroic is not Irish." Writing in 1917, Yeats saw no more difficulty in reconciling pagan with Christian heroism than did Pearse; the significant thing was that heroism and hero-worship permitted one to be other than what one was: "Some years ago I began to believe that our culture, with its doctrine of sincerity and self-realisation, made us gentle and passive, and that the Middle Ages and the Renaissance were right to found theirs upon the imitation of Christ or of some classic hero. Saint Francis and Caesar Borgia made themselves overmastering, creative persons by turning from the mirror to meditation upon a mask."[5] Although the pagan-Christian tussle in the Irish literary imagination remained alive, much of the fiction of the revival resulted from a search for ways of characterizing the heroic ideal and for the best narrative forms in which the old pagan romances might be recast for an awakening Ireland.

It is generally accepted that the Irish revival was in its beginnings what ethologists would call "displacement activity": energy that would have preferred to expend itself in politics expended itself instead in literature after the calamitous downfall of Charles Stewart Parnell in 1890; thwarted political nationalism took the consolatory form of cultural nationalism. "From that national humiliation," said Yeats in a 1932 lecture in the United States, "from the resolution to destroy all that made the humiliation possible, from that sacrificial victim I derive almost all that is living in the imagination of Ireland today . . . Everywhere I saw the change taking place, young men turning away from politics altogether, taking to Gaelic, taking to literature, or remaining in politics that they might substitute for violent speech more violent action."[6] Whether or not this interpretation is true, the cultural animation of the 1890s is undeniable.

It is also accepted that the revival is not to be explained entirely in terms of recoil and displacement. Before the revival got under way, there had been a nationalist wish to resurrect and commemorate Ireland's Gaelic past; that wish intensified throughout the nineteenth century[7] until in 1890 the Catholic Irish hero of William O'Brien's *When We Were Boys*—a novel set during Fenian times (the 1860s) and that does not really belong to the Irish literary revival—can tell the daughter of an Anglo-Irish landlord that "our conquerors have managed to make us a little bit ashamed of our fathers. They did the Irish a worse injury than stealing their lands and their lives—they wrote lampoons on their tombstones."[8] Ken Rohan, expecting to be ridiculed, believes that O'Sullivan Beara is as noble as Leonidas. Miss Westropp is not scandalized but sympathetic to the point of self-deprecation. Anglo-Irish and Catholic Irish writers and scholars, in concert with foreign scholars, would, a quarter of a century after the novel is set, attempt to right the historical balance, and do so by unearthing the Gaelic past as it lay neglected in manuscripts and unread scholarly translations. And the best part of all to unearth, it was felt, was the heroic.

The stories of the Mythological, Ulster, Fenian and Historical cycles preserved, among other manuscripts, in the *Book of the Dun Cow,* the *Book of Leinster* (both twelfth century), and the *Yellow Book of Lecan* (fourteenth century), represent a portion of "the oldest vernacular literature north of the Alps."[9] And since the oldest Irish narrative literature is in prose, we are speaking of the earliest prose fiction written down by Irishmen. We must say "written down" rather than "composed" since it is believed that this early Irish fiction had a long life in oral tradition before being commended to vellum. The trafficking between oral and written narrative was mutual and continuing, and in the case of medieval romances, for example, the written fostered oral variants.[10] Yeats claimed that the old literature "never ceased to be folk-lore even when it was recited in the Courts of Kings",[11] and whether true or not, such a comment suggests how consciously imitative during the revival was the symbiotic relationship between folklore and literature. This rather blurs the distinction I have drawn between the influence on revival fiction of heroic literature that I discuss in Part I and the influence on revival fiction of the folktale that I discuss in Part IV.

Of the four groups of stories, the Ulster cycle, also known as the Heroic, Red Branch, or Cuchulain cycle, is the most complete and homogeneous. "It exceeds the other Gaelic cycles in the fulness and orderliness of its conception," claimed Eleanor Hull, "as it exceeds them in dignity and in polish of style and sentiment,"[12] a claim that must nevertheless be set against the dignifying and ordering activities of the revival translators and editors. Hull like Lady Gregory was one of the staunch defenders and popularizers of the old heroic romances (both rounded on Robert Atkinson, "a gifted but cross-grained" English-born Professor of Comparative Philology at Trinity College Dublin, for accusing the old sagas of wanting idealism and imagination)[13] and Hull's claim that "Irish romance may take its place fearlessly beside the Arthurian legend, the French and Provençal romances, or the Northern sagas"[14] is not refuted by the fact that this precise claim of equality in epic production is, as we shall see, a motif in colonial cultural nationalism. What is more certain is that the Cuchulain saga depicts an Ireland of the so-called heroic period, before the fifth century and "at the earliest period of her known history"; Chadwick also believes that the major story in the cycle, the *Táin Bó Cuailnge* (probably composed in the eighth century but depicting an earlier way of life), "may be said to be the only European literature which gives us a picture of life in the Iron Age."[15]

The meanings of the *Táin,* composed so long ago, are not nearly so certain, as is demonstrated by the bizarrely different readings that have been offered. It has been seen variously as a struggle between priestly and warrior classes; a conflict between Celtic-Aryan father-dominance and pre-Celtic mother-dominance; an ancient ironic anti-feminist composition; an historical account of the invasion of Ulster by Uí Néill invaders from Leinster; and a disguised myth of solar regeneration.[16] The last is a reminder that despite the fact that revival nationalists preferred to see this story and the entire cycle as a masterwork of patriotic sentiment, the sagas' popularization in English around the turn of the century took place in the context not only of Irish cultural nationalism but also of the heroic age of British and American folklore and mythological studies.[17]

Both contexts, then, should be kept in mind when the prose fictions of the Irish literary revival, with their heavy dependence on folktale as well as on the old Gaelic literature, are read. In the meantime, what concerns me is the immediate impetus given to the fictions by the heroic literature in translation. Hull is probably not writing as a literary critic when she suggests that the plot of the Cuchulain saga "develops in the various tales with the regularity and sequence of successive chapters in a novel."[18] Recently Thomas Kinsella has allowed more soberly that even in a single story, in this case the *Táin,* "there is no unifying narrative tone: the story is told in places with a neutral realism, in places with an air of folk or fantasy."[19]

The very shortcomings of the sagas as fiction, as conceived by late Victorian and Edwardian Irish writers, was ironically one of the reasons they were picked up and re-shaped by the writers. Still, the stories are splendid things, by turns comic, tender, and awful, but always muscular, and it was on the best ones—"The Boy Deeds of Cuchulain," "The Wooing of Emer," "The Fate of the Sons of Usnach," *The Cattle Raid of Cooley,* "The Gathering at Muirthemne" and "The Death of Cuchulain"—

that the enthusiasm of Ireland's revival writers fastened. Since we sometimes speak of the Irish "Renaissance," it is fitting that as part of the cultural rebirth, the fiction writers should in search of models for their own work have turned—not entirely successfully, it transpired—to tales that like all such sagas and romantic legends were ancestors and prototypes of the modern novel and short story. It was as if Irish fiction, vaulting backwards over the Anglo-Irish and English novels, had to return to origins, like Irish literature and Irish culture at large, in order to seek the freedom of a fresh identity.

Many of the stories of the Red Branch cycle exhibit features of romance: heroic journeys; tasks and trials imposed on the hero; violated interdictions (mostly having to do with family or knightly solidarity); trickery and betrayal; nostalgia in exile; magic and enchantments causing all manner of transformations (humans into other humans, humans into animals); queens and maidens courted, loved, and lost; the return of the hero. A terser definition of the romantic tales is Alan Bruford's: "rambling episodic stories of battle and magic, sometimes loosely unified by a quest theme."[20] I mention these features for their own sake, since they illustrate the claim of A. H. Leahy that "the Irish epic form is Romance,"[21] but also because romance plays a large role in revival fiction. But in the Ulster cycle we are, strictly speaking, dealing not with tale but with saga, and the happenings are correspondingly darker. The sombre prophecy of Cathbad the Druid on the occasion of the birth of the ill-fated Deirdre could be a rough plot-summary of most of the stories: "There shall be jealousies, and strifes, and wars: evil deeds will be done: many heroes will be exiled: many will fall."[22] And the endings of the key stories are tragic in the manner of saga; some, especially the endings of "The Fate of the Sons of Usnach" and "The Death of Cuchulain," are moving and pathetic yet never sentimental like so much modern Irish fiction, but powerful, almost brutal.

Cuchulain was for the revivalists a magnetic figure. "The brightest candle of the Gael," as he is called in one manuscript, has the champion's portion of the cycle, a man for all seasons roaming Ireland and Scotland, now a romantic hero performing feats and surmounting obstacles, now a comic figure possessed of seven toes, three colors of hair, and seven pupils in each eye, and having to be dunked in a vat of cold water in order to have his ire cooled; now a terrifying figure, brooding and silent before exploding into brutal action. He is astonishingly versatile: "For Cuchullin was endowed with many perfections, such as centred not in any other one of his time: perfection of form, of swimming, of horsemanship, of chess-playing, of backgammon-play; pre-excellence in battle and in single combat; perfection of look-out, of eloquence, of counsel, of action, of inroad into strange borders."[23]

In the light of Cuchulain's versatility, it is appropriate that his name should come down to us in various forms: Setanta, Cuchullin, Riasthartha (The Distorted One), Cua (The Squinter), Cú na hAdhairce, and that his commonest name should be promiscuously spelled as Cuchulain, Cú Chulainn, Cuhoolin, Cuculain, Cucúlin, and Cu Chulaind. One of the recondite authorities on the occult that Yeats quotes illuminates perhaps the dim origins of a figure like Cuchulain: "A hero is a daemon, or good genius, and a genius a partaker of divine things and a companion of the holy company of unbodied souls and immortal angels who live according to their vehicles a versatile life, turning themselves proteus-like into any shape."[24]

Yet Cuchulain, whatever his origins and his status before redaction, is not a god in the cycle; he seems rather to be both superhuman and subdivine, a demi-god islanded between mortality and immortality (as romance is islanded between myth and fiction), and it is this ambiguity which explains the peculiar pathos, even tragedy, that softens the otherwise brutal existences of the Red Branch Knights and the Fianna. These are like men undeservingly failing to reach immortality, or sadly fallen gods, Titans doomed to war as though in punishment. Perhaps this ambiguity of existence which brings such suffering, as do all monstrosities, is characteristic of tragedy in general and attracted the revival writers (assuredly it did so Yeats) to the Fianna and Red Branch warriors.

Cuchulain's career—his disputed, semi-divine birth, his boy-deeds, his assumption of arms, his wooing of Emer, his guarding the marches of Ulster, his death in battle—is that of a culture hero, and follows the pattern observed in the careers of such heroes by Lord Raglan and Joseph Campbell.[25] Yet Cuchulain from the manuscripts reads like an Ulster rather than Irish culture hero, defending Ulster as he does against the men of Ireland. Indeed, Cuchulain's education makes it clear that he *is* in a sense the Ulster whose fertility and prosperity are vested in his welfare: "all the men of Ulster have taken part in my bringing-up, alike charioteers and chariot-chiefs, kings and chief poets," he tells Emer in a lapse from his usual modesty, "so that I am the darling of the host and multitude, so that I fight for the honour of them all alike."[26] In the hostilities between Ulster and Connacht, celebrated in the *Táin* from Ulster's point of view, we have an ancient and lingering expression of an east-west cleft in the Irish cultural psyche.

This cleft reappears during the revival, even though the revivalists sought to abolish it by making everything eastern submit ostensibly to the compelling westwardness of the cultural movement. Yet in the revival it takes low-key and sometimes oblique or metaphoric forms, such as the ancient but newly relevant separation between the folk (or, we might metaphorically say, western) and bardic ("eastern") imaginations, and the modern separation between rural ("western") and urban ("eastern") sensibilities, both separations nevertheless being denied explicitly or implicitly by the revivalists. James Stephens, however, provocatively claimed that any east-west distinction is really a north-south distinction: "East and west are merely geographical expressions: they have no national significance, for the east of a country is merely a prolongation of the north, and the west is as characteristically southern."[27] Whatever the merits of the observation as a cultural generalization, it makes sense for Ireland. The north-south distinction is there in the *Táin,* as well as the east-west distinction, even though the revivalists sought in their exploitation of the story and the cycle of which it is the centerpiece to "southernize" the saga (and much else besides in Irish culture) as they sought to "westernize" it (and much else besides). The mutual suspicion and dislike in the *Táin* between the Ulstermen and the men of Ireland is an odd thing to read in the light of the partitioning of Ulster from the rest of Ireland something over a millenium later.

To an extent, then, the Ulster cycle might be seen as a patriotic romantic epic belonging to one of the historic five provinces of Ireland. But when Cuchulain stood alone against the incursive army of Ireland, certain set apart, Irish cultural nationalists saw in him, in a transformation worthy of the saga itself, Ireland standing alone against the cultural imperialism of England, while more militant nationalists like Pearse saw in him the dwarfed numbers of rebel Ireland taking on the might of the imperial army. This hero, at whose birth Morann prophesied, "This child will avenge all your wrongs; he will combat at your fords; he will decide all your quarrels," could not but appeal to an aggrieved Ireland chafing under British rule.

Cuchulain: The Triumph and Eclipse of Self

Recovery of stories such as those in the Ulster cycle became synonymous with national loyalty and pride. "Patriotism," wrote Hull in the Introduction to her 1898 anthology of Cuchulain translations, "does not rest to any large degree upon a national pride in the physical beauty of the country that gave us birth, nor yet on a legitimate satisfaction in its commercial or industrial prosperity; it rests upon what we may call the historic imagination. It connects itself with certain events in the past history of our country, or with occurrences, sometimes of a semi-legendary character, that have stamped themselves upon the mind of the nation in a series of vivid mental pictures, and have fostered a just pride in the deeds and epochs of their fore-fathers."[28] Recovery of the legends was recovery of a heroic Ireland, and recovery not merely in the sense of unearthing but in the sense of vigorous convalescence, of enabling a rebirth. "If we will but tell these stories to our children," Yeats assured Lady Gregory's readers, "the Land will begin again to be a Holy Land, as it was before men gave their hearts to Greece and Rome and Judea."[29]

Not only the proportion but the nature of the assurance is astonishing: we speak of the Irish Renaissance, an ironic usage since Yeats and Standish James O'Grady and others desired nothing less than a return to a pre-Renaissance, pre-Greek, pre-humanist culture. And the Irish reality was held to justify the magnitude of the desire. "No other Aryan civilisation," claimed Alfred Nutt, "has developed itself so independently of the two great influences, Hellenic and Hebraic, which have moulded the modern world; nowhere else is the course of development less perplexed by cross-currents; nowhere else can the great issues be kept more steadily in view."[30] Above all, the old culture was pre-English and pre-conquest of Ireland, something that A. H. Leahy in his Introduction to his *Heroic Romances of Ireland* (1905) overlooked; the scholars, he noted innocently, "have been contented to ask for the support of that smaller body who for philological, antiquarian, or, *strange as it may appear, for political reasons,* are prepared to take a modified interest in what should be universally regarded as in its way one of the most interesting literatures of the world."[31] [My italics.]

The pursuit of *lof,* the praise and esteem of one's contemporaries, that motivates Beowulf also motivates Cuchulain, and this justified renown follows heroic action and achievement. That the heroic ideal of self-assertion personified by Cuchulain should appeal to the Irish nationalists is not surprising if Daniel O'Neil is correct in identifying the doctrine of self-reliance as a motif in anti-colonialism, balancing that of self-sacrifice.[32] However, the theme of self-assertion in the Ulster cycle requires qualification. The society of the cycle has been described as "essentially individualistic,"[33] but this is not quite correct.

First of all, Cuchulain is, as we have seen, as much an embodiment of Ulster as he is an individual. Indeed, through this Cuchulain was able to become a symbol of potency to the revivalists rallying Ireland to a resurgence. (And group rather than individual self-reliance is what O'Neil refers to.) But on this level Cuchulain is also a figure of impotence: he combines in himself the fertilizing power of the romance hero with the infertility of the romance king and his kingdom. In its tidal pattern of wastage and renewal, the saga is of course in a very real though metaphoric sense about potency and impotence, fertility and infertility. During the cattle-raid of Cooley, the Ultonians or Ulster warriors suffer a mysterious debilitation apparently through the agency of their women; in a sense they become as women in childbed for the duration of their enfeeblement. Twice Cuchulain himself loses his strength, once when by failing to knock birds out of the sky he cannot satisfy the women of Ulster who love him and who request the birds as love-tokens. That night he is visited by women of the sidhe who further debilitate him by enchantment at the request of Fand, the wife of the Irish sea-god, who desires him.

Cuchulain's subsequent journey to the land of the sidhe, after a year confined in bed, exploits the hazardous meeting of the mortal and the immortal (personified by the immortal goddess and the mortal, six-gifted Emer) that is a motif in the old Irish literature, but also recounts Cuchulain's recovery of military and (lightly disguised) sexual potency. That the stupefaction of the Ultonians and Cuchulain's occasional impotence could be used as a metaphor for modern Ireland's condition under English rule was not lost on the cultural nationalists. In an essay entitled "The Great Enchantment," Standish James O'Grady claimed that in a manner similar to that of the Ultonians, "The political understanding of Ireland today is under a spell and its will paralysed,"[34] though the modern Ultonians were for him not the select band of Catholic warriors of whom Pearse dreamed, but the Anglo-Irish landlord class. There is no evidence that any of the cultural nationalists were aware of the sexual cast either of their metaphor or of the Cuchulain saga; nor did they choose to interpret the strength and enfeeblement of Cuchulain and the Ulster warriors as that tussle between the triumph and eclipse of self that is nevertheless implicit in so much revival literature.

In a second qualification of the self-assertion theme in the Ulster cycle, we might note that the heroism in the stories, as distinct from the mere bellicosity and bravery of the hero, resides precisely in the hero's going under, in his acceptance of the denial of free action compelled by taboos, *geasa* (bonds), and obligations, in his belief that fame, honour, and reputation are the highest goods to which all else, including himself, must be sacrificed. Self-sacrifice (final submission to higher authority) was, in fact, promoted by the cultural nationalists as much as self-assertion of the group, and Daniel O'Neil, as I have said, has identified it, too, as a motif in anti-colonialism. Yeats's belief, then, that the hero "loves the world till it breaks him,"[35] that he makes his mask in defeat, is in accordance as much with the old stories and with the contemporary condition of Ireland as with the Yeatsian system.

Thirdly, although we glimpse in the Ulster cycle a larger Ireland of endlessly warring kinglets, the basic social unit of the cycle is not the individual but the élite corps of champions headquartered in Emain Macha and to whom through total loyalty each knight is subordinate. The idea of a native aristocracy, whose exploits were recited by schooled bards, appealed of course to Catholic nationalists who thought that native Irish society had been headless since the Flight of the Earls and who, though they might support republicanism in the present, enjoyed the contemplation of aristocracy in the past. Likewise, the legendary opulence of Heroic Ireland was perhaps in consoling contrast to the poverty of much of native Ireland. The aristocratic idea also appealed to some of the Anglo-Irish gentry who felt alienated from their mainland counterparts and, cut off half-willingly from the main stream of British aristocracy, thought to immerse themselves, at least while in their studies and libraries, in the even older mainstream of ancient Irish aristocracy.

And so Eleanor Hull, closer to the actual stories than most, tried to distinguish the barbarism of the saga's ideas and actions from the characters themselves "whose feelings are the feelings of gentlemen."[36] But these old stories were written down in and depicted a time before medieval chivalry. Of medieval Irish romance, one scholar has asserted that "the conventions of courtly love were never assimilated,"[37] and this holds true also for the conventions of war as we read of them in the prechivalric stories of the Ulster cycle. Certainly there is male camaraderie to a high degree in the saga, the culmination of which is the friendship of Ferdia and Cuchulain during their epic combat, as much an expression of love as of war. (In this combat, one cannot help but see a suggestive pre-figuration, perhaps source or model, of Pearse's near-mystical belief in male bonding in war, though considering the poetry of his English contemporary, Wilfred Owen, we might see Pearse in this regard as merely of his time.) Yet in the heroic romances barbarism balances interestingly and precariously their elements of chivalry, and this balance, uneven at times and frequently unpredictable, seems to me to be an enduring feature of Irish imagination and society.

These qualifications to the contrary, Cuchulain was seen by cultural and political nationalists (not always one and the same, as the career of Standish James O'Grady eloquently bears witness) as an individual and a rebel. Cuchulain's career not only provided a focus for the hope that

Ireland at the birth of the twentieth century might enjoy a second Heroic Period, it also reminded the more discerning that Irish leaders, like Achilles,[38] were fatally vulnerable in one respect. In the Irish case it is vulnerability to treachery and betrayal which gather their shape-changing forces around Cuchulain until he is hacked to pieces. He is disassembled by sword in a manner that emphasizes rather than diminishes his semi-divinity, for in his death is a representation of what Frye calls "*sparagmos* or the tearing apart of the sacrificial body, an image found in the myths of Osiris, Orpheus, and Pentheus," associated in literature with confusion and anarchy and an archetypal theme of irony and satire.[39]

Cuchulain's death, together with the superbly impassioned lamentations that punctuate the Ulster cycle, must have quenched the curious Irish thirst for defeat even of those in the vanguard of Irish resurgence during the revival, while his exploits and the catalogues of excellence that also punctuate the cycle, must have fed their simultaneous hunger for triumph. The ambiguous status of the cycle as both romance and ironic tragedy reflects a continuing Irish ambivalence in the face of last things, the Irish custom of seeing in fervent self-reliance the seeds of sacrifice.

Even in his acceptance of the unavoidability of his downfall, a motif in the career of culture heroes and one that seems to surface as a kind of death-wish in the careers of Irish insurrectionary leaders through succeeding centuries, Cuchulain is of course proud, and as Yeats insisted when thinking of Parnell, "A proud man's a lovely man." "Yet will I not for the world's lying vanities forsake my fame and battle-virtues," Cuchulain tells Dechtire and Cathbad, "seeing that from the day when first I took a full-grown warrior's weapons in my hand I never have shirked fight or fray . . . loath as ye be to dismiss me into danger and against my foes, there to encounter death and dissolution, even so cheerful am I that now go to have my side bored and my body mangled; neither knowest thou better than I myself know that in this onset I must fall."[40] This might be the prototype of the formula discourse of the Irish post-sentencing dock speech or eve-of-insurrection letter.

The lonely nobility of Cuchulain is beyond question and AE was right to detect in him the heroic spirit, though to call him "the redeemer in man," a different and preferable Jesus, is to go too far. Irish nationalists did indeed rather oversimplify the nature of Cuchulain's sacrifice and disregard the actual story. Cuchulain dies young not out of the perverse wilfulness of a modern Pearse but because the narrative necessity of a cultural epic—as tyrannical as any enemy—dictates that he bring the saga to its appropriate close. He dies young because his role as culture hero is fatally exhausting; by the end of the saga he has in his twenty-seven years lived several lifetimes and must succumb to the natural rhythm of spending and waning which is a precondition of renewal. He dies young because his birth and childhood predict that he will. He dies young because he yields to the blandishments of a false and beautiful woman (Badb in the guise of Niamh), and Cuchulain could never resist beautiful women, his other Achilles' heel. He dies young because he foolishly violates his *ges* (pl. *geasa*) by eating a dog—he, Culann's Hound, who must never eat of "his namesake's flesh." The death of Cuchulain is certainly "tragical", to borrow Hull's word, but it is a more complicated business than those who saw in him the nation's redeemer professed to acknowledge.

Limits of Self-Expression in Saga Literature

> My country is Kiltartan Cross,
> My countrymen Kiltartan's poor . . .
> —W. B. Yeats

Although we might speak of self-reliance and self-sacrifice in the stories of the Ulster cycle, there is in the old heroic romances little sense of what we moderns mean by self; there is small portrait of the hero's inner life, and almost no overt psychology. This, too, as it happened, was a decided attraction to those wishing to exploit the old stories. One student of the sagas remarks that "the characters are not made to say what they feel, but show it by a blow, a leap, or by the king at a moment of elation waving his crown in the air."[41] Such examples illustrate the formulaic and narrative exigencies as well as the ancient, pre-psychological conception of character to which the drawn figures of the romances submit. Perhaps this absence of psychology in the ancient stories metamorphosed, given the persistence among the people of the old manuscript and folk stories, into that aversion to psychology and that preference for a ritualistic approach to character (though the Church's distrust of psychology is probably a factor too) that are features of modern Irish literature and that have hindered the growth of a strong novel tradition. The problem became peculiarly evident when the revival writers decided to transform the old romances and sagas into modern fictions.

The importance of place in the sagas also influences the conception of character. The Irish are of course possessed by place. In part, such possession is a practical necessity, a way of distinguishing common and identical names by attaching them to a uniqueness of place: O'Sullivan of Beare, Johnston of Ballykilbeg. But even from the beginning, the self and the places it came from and inhabits are bound; biography is indistinguishable from geography, place from genealogy. "A notable characteristic of Irish tales," wrote Jeremiah Curtin, "is the definiteness of names and places in a majority of them. In the Irish myths we are told who the characters are, what their condition of life is, and where they lived and acted; the heroes and their fields of action are brought before us with as much definiteness as if they were persons of today or yesterday."[42] Indeed, "by the accretion of centuries," as Robin Flower has said, "there came into existence a large body of literature in prose and verse, forming a kind of Dictionary of National Topography, which fitted the famous sites of the country each with its appropriate legend."[43] Not merely the famous sites were so honoured. "There is hardly a bay, a plain, or a hill in Ireland," remarks Hull, "around which romance, pagan or Christian, has not woven some tale or legend."[44]

The high point of Irish placelore is *Agallamh na Senórach (The Colloquy of the Ancients)* from the *Book of Lismore,* a fifteenth-century vellum manuscript,[45] but in the *Táin* also is place, especially kind of place, important. In the chariotings of Cuchulain and his co-champions we have what Northrop Frye calls the centrifugal perspective of romance.[46] The wild and shaggy landscape through which they roam and which we glimpse appealed to the peculiar pastoralism of the Irish literary revival, as the courts of the cycle, such as Emain Macha, in which the champions headquarter, appealed to the aristocratic impulses of that pastoralism. The revivalists daydreamed of an Ireland even more rural than the Ireland of the end of the nineteenth century, an Ireland before even the rudimentary towns the Normans brought to the island, an Ireland of romantic forest and lake surrounding the feudal courts of local kings.

The sense of locality is powerful in the heroic romances, despite the centrifugal perspective, recording as they do a sacredness of place deriving from the association of places with local deities, of whom Cuchulain and his co-champions might well be vestiges. As the local deities gave way or were reduced to local heroes, so the latter gave way to local saints, but always the sacredness of locality was maintained. The worship of place (topolatry) that is evident in the Cuchulain saga became for cultural nationalists of the revival a love of place (topophilia) when the heroic tales were recovered, and just as Cuchulain the Ulster hero was enlarged into an Irish hero, so love of locality was expanded into love of Ireland. Localism and nationalism were simultaneous trends during the revival, both offsetting the despised urbanism and cosmopolitanism, and Standish James

O'Grady, for example, found no difficulty in reconciling them: "at some remote time, the bardic records were not national, but local, though perpetually tending in the direction of nationality. Every district in the island had its topical gods and heroes, and its local traditions embodying what was believed to have been their character and achievements . . . As intercourse increased between the various nations and septs, and as the bards passed to and fro, from assembly to assembly, the topical hero became of provincial, if not national importance."[47]

In its preoccupation with place as an unseverable aspect of self, revival literature is a descendant of the Irish myth and hero tales. Certainly "setting" is an inadequate word to describe the attention Irish writers from the adapters of the romances to our contemporaries lavish upon topography. What was sacred to the community in the old literature is sacred to the individual writer of modern literature, who tends to have almost totemic relations with one or more places. Yet one suspects that the revival passion for place—a passion that serves to limit freedom of self—derived not only from the example of custom and tradition but also from the fact that the Anglo-Irish leaders of the revival felt some unease about how profoundly they belonged to the places they chose to celebrate, and they to them. Overestimating in compensation the advantages of locality, they ignored the extent to which less privileged Irish (among whom are Joyce's Dubliners and MacNamara's Midlanders) felt themselves in thrall to their native places and against which in their struggle for freedom, economic survival, and selfhood they rebelled, often in a philistine or acquisitive fashion that earned them the contempt of the revivalists.

Revival fondness for place was not, then, provoked or satisfied entirely by the old literature. Curtin is careful to stress *definiteness* of place in the old stories; the fact is that in the old romances places exist not much more than in name alone, just as the heroes exist only in the externals of names, actions, and physical description. Names are very important in the heroic romances because the stories functioned, among other things, as genealogies and etymologies. The onomastic nature of the sagas is most vivid when the climax of a tale is used to explain the etymology of certain place-names, a formulaic code that often seems like the "point" of the tale. There are very few extended or specific descriptions of places; at most we find generic and hyperbolic descriptions of the heroes' living quarters, literally rhetorical commonplaces or *topoi*.

However dependent upon the heroic romances otherwise, revival fiction writers had to draw instead on the English literary tradition for detailed and evocative descriptions of the places they cherished. And they earnestly desired such descriptions, not merely because post-Romantic

European literature (of which they were a part whether they wished to be or not) demanded them, but also because nationalism demanded them. The sagas gave revival writers a fund of native words and place-names, but they did not give them sufficient local color or national texture, and these it was thought were ways of helping to distinguish Irish (that is, Anglo-Irish) literature from English literature. It is unlikely that the composers and early redactors of the old stories could have felt themselves under any comparable constraint, whether or not the literary methods and tradition of observing the constraint existed in their time. Jorge Luis Borges cites Gibbons' observation that there are no camels in the Koran, and remarks that the fact is enough to prove the authenticity of the work, since a modern composer, for example an Arab nationalist, would have had caravans of camels on every page, whereas Mohammed had no reason to know that camels were especially Arabian and knew he could be an Arab without them.[48] In folk and mythic literature of all kinds, including the Koran and the Irish saga which both function as expressions of the people or of a culture, whatever the origins of the works, men are never psychologically separated from nature in the fashion of modern urban men (for example, the Irish revivalists), but take their relationship to it for granted. We might say this is demonstrated by no compulsive need to describe nature in any but formulaic and generic ways.

Formula and convention govern the sagas. Throughout are set pieces, owing their existence equally to the originally oral nature of the narratives and the formal practice of bardic recitation. Many of these set pieces would, as far as the modern nonscholarly reader is concerned, answer one scholar's description of such set pieces in the later medieval Irish romances: "rhetorical purple passages, designed to sweep away the hearer in a sonorous wash of verbiage whose actual meaning was of little importance."[49] There are inventories and word games that the modern reader feels inclined to skip when he encounters them in literal, unedited translation. The most important set pieces are "runs": "set passages of florid description which are introduced by story-tellers into any hero-tale or *Märchen* where the appropriate action comes in—the hero putting on his armour, setting out on a voyage, being entertained at a feast and the like."[50] Various kinds of runs are found equally in the manuscript and oral tales—opening runs, battle runs, travelling runs, and dialogue runs. There are also rhapsodies, lays, and "kennings," the latter being an esoteric form of speech concocted by bards (a kenning "may be a mere form of erudite slang," Hull remarks)[51] and given to a character when there are those present who are not meant to understand him, such as Cuchulain when wooing Emer in front of his charioteer. Dialogue in any case promotes action rather than revealing character, but as often it stops action and emphasizes the ultimately formulaic and verbal nature of the narrative: it is language as much as people talking in the old romances. Speech is not self-expression but incantation, song, spell, pledge, or prophecy. The last provides a prior arrangement of the narrative and a mnemonic cue for composer and reciter (familiar resting places in the rhetorical itinerary), and the result is a form of narrative foreclosure very different from the modern, realistic—but not modernist—conception of fiction.

It is not surprising that in such narratives the will and individuality of the characters are thematically at the mercy of outside forces. The relationship between these forces can perhaps best be described by the physicist's phrase, "sympathetic resonance," of which the arch-waves of Erin that invariably roar in response to battle-strokes delivered against Conchobar's shield are merely the most vivid example that comes to mind.[52] The result is that the world of the sagas is a unified field that not even the brutal factionalism, nor even heroic solitude and enterprise that theme and character often illustrate, can fragment. How far it is a purely fictitious world, already anachronistic by the time the stories were given the shape in which we now know them, is difficult to tell. In any event, this world, real or imagined, was irreversibly disturbed by Christian interference centuries before it was refragmented and misinterpreted by the cultural revivalists in ways the next chapter will try to illustrate.

Yet through the epochs continuity of a kind persists. It is hardly matter for wonder that narratives dedicated to the persistence of their constituent parts (and in mutual transaction with a vigorous folk literature similarly dedicated) should themselves persist and reappear as an influence on modern Irish fiction, especially on the fiction of that self-regarding movement we call the Irish literary revival. The revivalists were to a debatable extent legitimate inheritors of the ancient narrative tradition, but they were even more so its conscious and artful imitators. The modern writers sought to avoid a literature of self-expression, and since the old stories, in which the heroic ideal was expressed, were impersonally and formulaically structured, the modern writers adopted them as models.[53] For some of those modern writers, attraction to the old literature went hand-in-hand with a disguising and transforming of their own racial, social, and cultural identities.

The Property of Discourse

Popular Translations and Redactions of the Cuchulain Cycle—P. W. Joyce, Lady Gregory, Eleanor Hull

2

Unity in Epos: The Finnish Parallel

The contribution of native bardic and folk material to the creation of an Irish fiction naturally became more significant during the Irish literary revival than it ever had been. Giving the Gaelic sagas and romances a new form of one kind or another, for example, represented a sizeable proportion of the literary revival's fictional effort. Cuchulain, Deirdre, Fergus, and other saga and romance characters became models for fictional heroes and the narratives themselves models and sources for fictional plots, structures, and motifs. This exploitation of the huge manuscript depository had a unifying effect on revival literature in general and revival fiction in particular. Yet the astonishing number of historical transformations the originally oral tales underwent even before the revival (be they redactions, copies, summaries, or abstracts), and the different processes to which the material was subjected during the revival (translation, editing, adaptation), resulted in a dispersal of revival energy. In the nineteenth century appeared literal translations of the manuscript versions of the tales by scholars without whom the Irish literary revival would have been virtually impossible and whose effort constituted its own kind of scholarly heroism: Kuno Meyer, O'Beirne Crowe, Eugene O'Curry, Ernst Windisch, Whitley Stokes, Heinrich Zimmer, M. d'Arbois de Jubainville, Rudolph Thurneysen. Only then did the editing, adapting, and novelizing for popular and highbrow consumption get under way. If at one end of the scale is the high aesthetic of the Cuchulain plays of Yeats (whose raw material was nevertheless the popular editions rather than scholarly translations), then at the other end is the meddlesomeness and sentimentalism of those, for example, who saw "the Fate of the Sons of Uisneach" as "the Deirdre story."[1] Between these extremes lies a great deal of Irish revival prose narrative.

The principles involved in the recovery and recasting of the heroic romances belong not to scholarly arbitrariness or literary whimsy but to a communal compulsion neither personal nor uniquely Irish. They follow, for example, those employed during the Finnish experience of cultural revival that largely preceded the Irish experience.[2] During a gathering revulsion to foreign rule, the Finns under Swedish and later Russian administration, like the Irish under English, came to view the "historic imagination" as an essential aspect of patriotism. The subsequent growth of romantic nationalism had the same roots as Irish romantic nationalism—German romanticism, especially Herder's concept of the national soul and of the national culture, national language, and folk poetry in which that soul is embodied. For the Finns, folklore research and romantic nationalism became synonymous. The Finnish predecessor of the Irish "culture-givers," Standish James O'Grady and Douglas Hyde, was Elias Lönnrot who collected the Finnish folk poetry and gave the Finns their unifying epic. In 1849 he produced his final version of the *Kalevala* in fifty poems and over twenty-two thousand lines. In early nineteenth century Ireland there was, of course, a cultural revival spearheaded by Eugene O'Curry, George Petrie, and John O'Donovan. Then there was the Young Ireland movement of the mid-century, and the work of Ferguson. What was achieved during these decades, relative to the national self-awareness, was not, however, comparable to the achievement of Lönnrot, and it was not until the Irish literary revival that the Irish Lönnrot, or Lönnrots, appeared. Like Hyde, Lönnrot collected in the field; like O'Grady, he composed fragments into a whole, albeit a whole more hypothetical than that of the Irish heroic romances which did, after all, already exist in rich manuscript form.[3]

The vital consideration for Lönnrot was that an epic should emerge from his transcribed oral fragments and that this epic should be unified. These were equally vital considerations for the Irish cultural nationalists, though the latter worked by compression and selection on a vast and ill-arranged original, while Lönnot worked by compilation and conjectural addition on vestiges and verbal shards. Unity for both camps was all, for ancient unity of epos, they thought, proved ancient unity of country. Alfred Nutt (though himself an Englishman) spoke of tales in the Ulster cycle "independent in themselves, but which allow of a chronological classification, and which fall into their place as component parts of a cycle."[4] Standish James O'Grady spoke of his "epic series" *(History of*

Ireland) "in which the literature has been toned and condensed into the uniformity and homogeneity of a single integral composition."[5] Yeats claimed that few of the old stories "really begin to exist as great works of the imagination until somebody has taken the best bits out of many manuscripts" and reunified them, as Lady Gregory had done in *Cuchulain of Muirthemne* that these words prefaced.

The unity of the *Kalevala* and the Ulster cycle was guaranteed in each case by the dominating presence of a hero, respectively Väinämöinen and Cuchulain, who embodied a pre-Christian age of national independence and passion and on whom could be centered a wish that such a golden age might return. Even the dispute among exclusive mythological interpreters, euhemerists, and exclusive historical interpreters which characterized Finnish romantic nationalism also characterized its Irish counterpart. To justify militarism in pursuit of a new golden age of independence, the Finns cited the militarism sung about in the old songs. The modern Irish were by and large not so militaristically inclined, though two lines of the *Kalevala* which entranced the Finns might easily have been written by Pearse:

> It's beautiful to die in war,
> Easy to die in the clashing of swords.[6]

The patriotic reader, Irish or Finnish, was meant by the cultural leaders to emulate the heroes of old, even to the extent when necessary of patriotic self-sacrifice; indeed, admiration for the heroes really entailed all along the patriot, caught up in nationalist passion, denying or forgetting himself. Lastly, just as Pearse, Lady Gregory, Yeats, and others ransacked O'Grady's versions of the old literature for subjects and inspiration, so the Finnish poets around the same time ransacked Lönnrot's *Kalevala,* producing, as William A. Wilson says in a remark that could (if we choose to define the literature of Young Ireland as propaganda rather than art) be made equally about the Irish literary revival, "an artistic period more nationalistic than any in Finnish history."[7]

There was a measure of justification for the liberties taken by those who, in rendering the Gaelic manuscripts into English, aspired to the spirit rather than the letter of the originals. After all, the monkish scribes had themselves been interested "in the historic rather than aesthetic value of the matter they recorded,"[8] and probably did ill-justice to the integrity of the oral originals. Were not the English translators who engaged in what A. H. Leahy called "a little judicious editing" in order to improve the literary quality of the tales not simply restoring their aesthetic shape? Furthermore, the literal translations of the scholars could not satisfy readers of literature, popular or serious, because, as P. W. Joyce pointed out, they were buried in scholarly journals, written in unreadable English (because literal translations), and undertaken not for literary but linguistic purposes.

Joyce claimed for his part that in *Old Celtic Romances* he had done his best "to tell the stories as I conceive the old shanachies themselves would have told them if they had used English instead of Gaelic."[9] Twenty-three years later, Yeats claimed that Lady Gregory was engaged in the same legitimate activity and that her own additions to the manuscript texts were no more indeed "than the story-teller must often have added to amend the hesitation of a moment."[10] His claim underestimates the extent of Lady Gregory's additions and confuses very different genres and media—recited, unattributed tales varied within strict limits by a storyteller, and written tales (such as Lady Gregory's) adapted from the recited tales but now attributable because the storyteller has, through print and the far less limited and formulaic changes of a quasi-novel, taken possesion of them. Since Lönnrot who arranged and supplied allegedly missing parts of the *Kalevala* was himself defended on the ground that he was not so much a collector or compiler of folk material as the last of the Finnish folksingers, this defence of literate meddling might well be a motif in the development of folklore and epic research undertaken by romantic nationalists.[11] However, the main interest for us in this matter lies in the fact that during the Irish literary revival, many writers, including the novelists, conceived of themselves as folk-writers and storytellers and that this led, particularly in fiction, to a great deal of generic confusion as well as creative experimentation.

The Versions of P. W. Joyce, Lady Gregory, and Eleanor Hull

O'Grady first brought the Red Branch cycle and related stories to a popular and literary audience. Since his use (or misuse) of the old literature is hard to distinguish from novelizations of the old literature, I will discuss him in the next chapter, where novelization is my subject. P. W. Joyce's *Old Celtic Romances* (1879) followed hard on the heels of O'Grady's first significant volume, *History of Ireland* 1: *The Heroic Period* (1878). After these came Eleanor Hull's *The Cuchullin Saga in Irish Literature* (1898), Lady Gregory's *Cuchulain of Muirthemne* (1902), L.

Winifred Faraday's *The Cattle-Raid of Cualnge* (1904), A. H. Leahy's *Heroic Romances of Ireland* (1905), J. Strachan and J. G. O'Keeffe's *The Táin Bó Cuailnge* (1912), T. W. Rolleston's *Myths and Legends of the Celtic Race* (1912) and Joseph Dunn's *The Ancient Irish Epic Tale Táin Bó Cúailnge* (1914).[12]

The more literary, less scholarly works of Joyce, Hull, Gregory, and Leahy, like those of O'Grady, rest on two largely unspoken premises: that the old stories should not merely be translated—for the scholars whom Joyce consults, Hull anthologizes, and Gregory plunders had already done that—but reshaped according to modern fictional criteria and expectations; and second, that the new-told tales (except perhaps in the case of Leahy who though he is an Irishman addressing English readers disavows nationalism) should promote the cause and redound to the glory of modern Ireland. This fictional transformation of an ancient form of narrative resulted in prototypes of which AE, James Stephens, Padraic Colum, W. B. Yeats, and Darrell Figgis, (and, for purposes of parody, James Joyce and Eimar O'Duffy) availed themselves in creating their own more modern fictions. Hull in choosing her selections, P. W. Joyce in consulting the translations of others as well as his own, and Gregory in creatively disguising the seams of her one-woman anthology by rewriting the whole—all strive to fashion unity out of the diversity of scholarly editions and translations. That unity is an essentially fictional one. Joyce, who claims his book "is the first collection of the old Gaelic prose romances that has ever been published in fair English translation,"[13] is not averse to making "a few transpositions in the order of the incidents" when "the narrative in the original is in some places very ill arranged." He has done his best, however, to render the tales "into simple, plain, homely English" because "the originals are in general simple in style," and to keep the narrative and incidents more or less the same, changing only phraseology. He does, though, lapse into the stiff English archaisms of "whithersoever," "fain" and "ye". Although he considers it hardly worth mentioning, he admits also to having divided the longer tales, such as "The Fate of the Sons of Usna," into chapters, "with appropriate headings," because "in the originals, the stories run on without break or subdivision." However the stories in recitation were divided by the *ollamh* (or bard), Joyce like those after him has by personal decision imposed on the Gaelic matter a modern fictional structure of opening and closure that creates a new rhythm and must slightly alter thematic emphasis. "The Fate of the Sons of Usna" reads like a cross between a hero tale and a novella.

In *Cuchulain of Muirthemne* Lady Gregory does for the Ulster cycle what she soon after did in *Gods and Fighting Men* (1904) for the Mythological and Fenian cycles. Her occasionally distinctive style and concentration on Cuchulain makes of *Cuchulain of Muirthemne* a whole to which *Old Celtic Romances* never aspires. She has cleverly interwoven various translations, and feels even freer than Joyce to transfer "a mere phrase, sometimes a whole passage from one story to another, where it seems to fit better";[14] she also felt entitled to use Scottish Gaelic versions. The same concern for narrative flow that occasions her wholesale transpositions also occasions her numerous omissions, additions, compressions and supplied transitions. More dangerous, perhaps, but necessary if the old literature were to become modern fiction, are her numerous *Motivierungen* ("I have sometimes tried to give the meaning of a formula that has lost its old meaning"),[15] conjectural or convenient explanations of incomprehensible details embedded in her narrative.

There is no doubt that several of Lady Gregory's written tales are triumphs, including her beautiful rendition of the fate of Deirdre and the sons of Usnach. This story is in any case a superb one, with the pathetic attempt of the heroine to circumvent known fate, with the folly of the heroes in mistaking their lack of fear for the absence of danger, and with its elements of prophecy, seductive beauty, flight, exile, vision, and treacherous enchantment. Lady Gregory wisely refrains (unlike James Stephens some years later) from making anything more than the story's swift acceleration of events demands, and is content to let it be merely a powerful episode. Yet although she retains the abundant invention, immense variety of incident and character, the lyrical outbursts, the supernaturalism and romanticism, all of which Yeats in his Preface saw as characteristic of the old romances, the result is something very different, even in spirit, from the manuscript versions. Hers is an English, turn-of-the-century redaction that sacrifices the dense cultural coding of the originals in its desire to achieve historical fiction, partly through a psychologizing of her characters. It is not the desire but the sacrifice that troubles: *Cuchulain of Muirthemne* demystifies its subject and, *pace* Yeats, denudes it of its "enigmatical symbols."

In the light of O'Grady's early works and Hull's book (to restrict ourselves to re-creations of the heroic age), Yeats was surely going too far in calling *Cuchulain of Muirthemne* "perhaps . . . the best book that has ever come out of Ireland." Lady Gregory was said by Yeats to have "discovered," and by an *Athenaeum* reviewer to have "invented" a new form of English, the first really faithful transcript of the speech of the Irish peasant as he thinks in Irish and speaks in English. Moreover, Yeats believed that Lady Gregory had found the language in which medieval Irish life might best be re-created, as William Morris had found in his prose romances the most suitable modern language in which to re-create medieval English life. The first claim is somewhat exaggerated and rather unfair to William Carleton and Douglas Hyde, but Yeats was clearly biased in favor of Sligo and Galway dialects. The second claim confuses the folk with the bardic, since he is praising Lady Gregory for rendering tales for bardic recitation into living folk speech. He recalled after Lady Gregory's death that when he first met her "she read the *Morte d'Arthur* continually, not for its stories but for its style," and also recalled that there were "at her side always *Arabia Deserta* and the *New Testament* in Gaelic; she never separated the discipline of religion from the discipline of style."[16]

Yeats's implicit defense of any resultant formality in his friend's prose is his claim that the speech of the country Irish is full of strange courtesy and aristocratic nobility. This may be true, particularly of the local dialects he had in mind around the turn of the century, but Lady Gregory's prose style is largely literary in inspiration, a style that effects a compromise between Irish dialect and the literary English thought by a turn-of-the-century writer to be fitting for historical romance. Irish idioms are there ("what place is?" for "where is?"; "from this out" for "from now on"; "it is what he said" for "this is what he said"), but they are few in number and are repeated often. The most concentrated effort at the idioms and grammar of western Hiberno-English is reserved for the ingratiating and patronizing dedicatory letter to the people of Kiltartan. Where Lady Gregory is most successful and affecting is in capturing (or generating, at least in their literary intensity) the undulating metrical cadences of western Hiberno-English that Synge soon after brought to literary perfection: "And Deirdre grew straight and clean like a rush on the bog, and she was comely beyond comparison of all the women of the world, and her movements were like the swan on the wave, or the deer on the hill."

That *The Cuchullin Saga in Irish Literature* by Eleanor Hull wants unity is in its favor, preserving as it does more of the shagginess of the various manuscript renditions. Like some of the scholars she anthologizes, Hull edits out unwanted passages, employing a modern narrative judgment in deciding what is florid and redundant, and she chapters and entitles, but generally the tales themselves take precedence over any attempt on her part to simulate historical fiction: the reader knows he is reading inconclusive translations of complex material from a vanished and mysterious society. Accordingly, there is no attempt at chronologizing Cuchulain's appearances in the tales to create, as Lady Gregory does, the unified story of a central figure whose biography the cycle seemingly is (and which it was not). When Hull's fashionable diffusionism and solar theory do not get in the way, her book is superior to Lady Gregory's. To adduce some evidence, we might look at their differing attitudes to the grotesque, the macabre, and the sexual.

A little way into her lengthy Introduction, Eleanor Hull accused monkish scribes of suppressing portions of the pagan tales, only later to admit that she too has suppressed certain "naturalistic expressions." But she is at least convinced that such expressions have nothing in common with "intentional grossness of idea and of speech," and continues: "though we have thought it well, in a book intended for general reading, to omit a few passages that might wound modern susceptibilities, we would have it to be understood that these passages are not only very few in number, but that they are generally the outcome of an ancient simplicity of life and thought, and seldom arise from any coarseness or indecency of design."[17] Hull is of course writing here as a cultural nationalist, but she is at least more forthcoming than Lady Gregory who in fact suppressed far more.

Take the question of Cuchulain's "paroxysm" or "demoniac rage" for which he was known as "the madman from Emain Macha" and "Riasthartha, or 'Distorted One'." Lady Gregory: "I have exchanged for the grotesque accounts of Cuchulain's distortion—which no doubt merely meant that in time of great strain or anger he had more than human strength—the more simple formula that his appearance changed to the appearance of a god."[18] This is the half-consciously naive and poetic thing she substitutes: "And it is then Cuchulain's anger came to him, and the flames of the hero light began to shine about his head, like a red-thorn bush in a gap, or like the sparks of a fire, and he lost the appearance of a man, and what was on him was the appearance of a god."[19]

Here is Standish Hayes O'Grady's literal translation, care of Hull, which I cannot resist quoting in full:

> Then it was that he suffered his *riastradh* or paroxysm, whereby he became a fearsome and multiform and wondrous and hitherto unknown being. All over him, from his crown to the ground, his flesh and every limb and joint and point and articulation of him quivered as does a tree, yea a bulrush, in mid-current. Within in his skin he put forth an unnatural effort of his body: his feet, his shins, and his knees shifted themselves and were behind him; his heels and calves and hams were displaced to the front of his leg-bones, in condition such that their knotted muscles stood up in lumps large as the clenched fist of a fighting man. The frontal sinews of his head were dragged to the back of his neck, where they showed in lumps bigger than the head of a man-child aged one month. Then his face underwent an extraordinary transformation: one eye became engulfed in his head so far that 'tis a question whether a wild heron could have got at it where it lay against his occiput, to drag it

> out upon the surface of his cheek; the other eye on the contrary protruded suddenly, and of itself so rested upon the cheek. His mouth was twisted awry till it met his ears. His lion's gnashings caused flakes of fire, each one larger than fleece of three-year-old wether, to stream from his throat into his mouth. The sounding blows of the heart that panted within him were as the howl of a ban-dog doing his office, or of a lion in the act of charging bears. Among the aerial clouds over his head were visible the virulent pouring showers and sparks of ruddy fire which the seething of his savage wrath caused to mount up above him. His hair became tangled about his head, as it had been branches of a red-thorn bush stuffed into a strongly fenced gap; over the which though a prime apple-tree had been shaken, yet may we surmise that never an apple of them would have reached the ground, but rather that all would have been held impaled each on an individual hair as it bristled on him for fury. His "hero's paroxysm" projected itself out of his forehead, and showed longer than the whetstone of a first-rate man-at-arms. Taller, thicker, more rigid, longer than mast of a great ship was the perpendicular jet of dusky blood which out of his scalp's very central point shot upwards and then was scattered to the four cardinal points; whereby was formed a magic mist of gloom resembling the smoky pall that drapes a regal dwelling, what time a king at night-fall of a winter's day draws near to it.[20]

The similes and conceptions of such a set piece are extravagant, grotesque, and ludicrous, and virtually alone among writers of the time, James Joyce did not put them out of countenance but swooped on them as matter for parody, for example in the Cyclops episode in *Ulysses* in which the real target is not the old Irish stories but the nationalist fanaticism that took seriously even the more playful elements of the stories. Yet they are, and were, I suspect, even at the time of recitation, a form of self-parody. Lady Gregory, half-deliberately, half-naively, misinterprets the probable function of such a set piece to awe, amuse, and hypnotize the listener as well as give the reciter a mnemonic cue and mental respite from the more difficult task of remembering the narrative. She instead avoided any element of the intentionally or unintentionally comic or grotesque.

The linguistic and figurative hyperbole and extravagance of the original match a gigantist conception of character, a gigantism that another romantic nationalist, AE—in the teeth of the old tales as we can here see—warned the Irish not to confuse with heroism, whereas in fact the ancient idea of the hero, unlike that of the cultural nationalists, included elements of the monstrous. In Lady Gregory's humorless biography, an exorbitant Ulster hero is forced into the mold of attractive culture-hero by a nationalist gentlewoman. Yeats, who played one role for his wealthy patroness and co-author and another for the real literary world, in his own plays made of Cuchulain's madness a tragic but still monstrous art while publicly praising Lady Gregory's innocent or misguided efforts.

In "Fate of the Children of Usnach," Lady Gregory has Deirdre commit suicide cleanly by stabbing herself with a knife after the killing of her husband Naoise and his brothers. Before she does so she throws herself on the body of Naoise and her mouth touches his blood. What Lady Gregory omits, like P. W. Joyce before her, are the two occasions, before and after her lay, on which Deirdre (in Whitley Stokes's literal translation that Hull used and Gregory consulted) drinks Naoise's blood. Hull notes that "this curious and horrible custom seems to have continued in Ireland into historical times," and directs us to Spenser's *A View of the Present State of Ireland* (1596).

Equally distasteful to Lady Gregory were overt sexual references. In this matter, as in the matter of the macabre and grotesque, her Victorian upper-class and Irish nationalist prejudices conspired to suppress an archaic feature of Irish literature that surfaced, against all attempts to censor it, in James Joyce. While parodying and mocking the Gaelic literature revived in translation by the revivalists, he was yet closer to it in spirit than were the cultural nationalists. It is diverting to track the passage of sexual references from the literal translations through Hull's editing of the literal translations to Lady Gregory's "creative" translations. These brief examples from "The Wooing of Emer" will suffice. In Kuno Meyer's translation in *The Archaeological Review,*[21] the men of Ulster are afraid Cuchulain will "ravish their maidens"; in Hull (who uses Meyer's revision for Hull of his own translation), their fear is that he will "spoil their daughters." In Lady Gregory we are informed that the men are jealous "for their women and their maidens loved him greatly." When the daughter of Donall the Soldierly falls in love with Cuchulain, he "refused to lie with her" (Meyer), he "refused her" (Hull) and in Gregory apparently does not have the opportunity either to accept or decline, luckily for him since in Hull her form is "very gruesome." In Meyer, Cuchulain at one point seizes Aife "by her two breasts"; in Hull he changes his grip to "under her two breasts" and in Gregory is content to take "a sudden hold of her." Too much for both Hull and Gregory are Uathach's magnanimous suggestion that Cuchulain sleep with her mother before he sleep with her, and Bricriu's malicious reminder that Conchobar has the right to deflower virgins and should therefore sleep with Emer before Cuchulain (the compromise solution is that she sleeps with Conchobar but chaperoned in bed by Fergus and Cathbad).

At first it seems odd that Meyer's translation in the august pages of

The Archaeological Review should in these respects be more entertaining as well as more honest than the two subsequent editions of Hull and Gregory, but then of course Meyer had no ideological or even literary purpose to serve. Of Hull and Gregory, it is the latter, clearly repelled by Cuchulain's promiscuity, who does greater violence to the spirit of the old romances when she sanitizes them for nationalist consumption.

The Clerisy in Revival Ireland

In their efforts to make Cuchulain at once more human, noble, historical, and godlike than he is in the original stories, those who dealt in English versions of the Ulster cycle were doing in one language what the bowdlerizers of Gaelic texts, in obeisance to "the Irish Catholic brand of Puritanism" and in pursuit of a "monstrous parody of the language," were doing in another. R. B. Walsh has claimed that the bowdlerizers were "incapable of understanding the character of the Gaelic culture which they were so anxious to claim as their heritage."[22] The same could be said of the anglicizers, among whom I do not include Hull or the scholars so much as the poetizers, novelizers, and mystics who stand the far side of Lady Gregory whose own Cuchulain is very definitely the "distorted one."

The Irish literary revival, dominated by such Anglo-Irish as Yeats, AE, Lady Gregory, Standish James O'Grady, and Douglas Hyde, was really what Michel Foucault has called a "fellowship of discourse" whose function it is "to preserve or to reproduce discourse, but in order that it should circulate within a closed community, according to strict regulations, without those in possession being dispossessed by this very distribution."[23] We can see the principles of constraint and exclusion this fellowship developed in reminding ourselves how it civilized and sophisticated the figure of Cuchulain, and how it ignored inconvenient folk versions of Cuchulain from parts of Ireland other than Ulster, such as the story of Cuchulain sulking to death, that cut the champion down to size. Along with provincial rivalry, localism was in the final analysis—and talk of Kiltartan and Sligo notwithstanding—sacrificed to the ideal of national unity. From the raw materials of a folklore and an ancient literature in another language, and the rudimentary processing carried out by the scholars in their literal translations, the *littérateurs* amassed what Foucault terms "the property of discourse." There was a class base for the phenomenon: highborn, patriotic, English-speaking Irish turned to Gaelic (at least in translation) as highborn, patriotic, Swedish-speaking Finns turned to Finnish. In colonizing and exploiting Gaelic literature the *littérateurs* imposed an urban discourse upon a rural (in the case of folklore), a modern upon an ancient (in the case of bardic literature), an English upon an Irish (in the case of both). And, we might venture to say, they imposed respectively, in real or metaphoric fashion, east upon west, south upon north.

That of the various kinds of old literature in Irish the revival writers were most attracted to the heroic romance is not surprising when we reflect how, in the words of Northrop Frye, "In every age the ruling social or intellectual class tends to project its ideals in some form of romance, where the virtuous heroes and beautiful heroines represent the ideals and the villains the threats to their ascendancy."[24] This is true of the original aristocratic patrons of the bardic literature, but it is perhaps even truer of the Ascendancy writers during the revival who felt it necessary to bring old stories—which are part-romance, part-saga, part-epic—into line with modern conceptions either of tragedy or romance. According to Frye one phase of romance has as theme "the maintaining of the integrity of the innocent world against the assault of experience";[25] this theme is not part of the Ulster cycle, so cultural nationalists used the medieval Irish voyage tales *(immrama)* and Tír-na-nÓg stories to supply this need.[26] They also considered the Fenian and Heroic cycles as the product of what it pleased them to call Ireland's heroic period. This idealized period was held to be Ireland's age of innocence before the assaults of Norman and English (even, intellectually, Judaeo-Christian) civilizations and value-systems, even though life as it is portrayed in many of the cycle stories is in fact nasty, brutish, and short.

The Irish literary revival vis-à-vis English literature was a triumphant art movement; vis-à-vis Gaelic literature it was frequently a philistine and instrumentalist movement. Superficially a reversion to Irishness, it was in reality a diversion *from* Irishness. Age, said Yeats, bestows authority on a language, thinking in his Preface to *Cuchulain of Muirthemne* of Hiberno-English, but the revivalists had their own way of bestowing authority; in two senses of the word did they "authorize" revival transformations of the old literature. For all the talk of bards and peasantry, they happily put their own signatures to adaptations of anonymous material, in so doing taking possession of matter in the public domain. Even when the theme of revival literature was selflessness, the assumed and collectively egotistic function of the revivalists was that of culture-givers. They stamped their imprimatur on new adaptations and collections. When Standish James O'Grady forfeited leadership in the revival by failing to follow his cultural premises to their political conclusion (he remained a Unionist) and their literary conclusion (he continued to believe that the heroic romances ought not to be dramatized), Yeats became his successor, inviting writers to change direction, indefatigably prefacing and introducing the works of others, bestowing his approval here, withholding it there.[27] Successively O'Grady and Yeats led a clerisy, whose social base was in the last analysis manorial, in which dissident voices as articulate as their own were remarkably few.

Transforming Down 3

Fictional Adaptations of the Cuchulain Cycle—
Standish James O'Grady, James Stephens

O'Grady's History of Heroic Ireland

Yeats acknowledged O'Grady's primacy when he wrote: "In his unfinished *History of Ireland* he had made the old Irish heroes, Finn, and Oisin, and Cuchulain, alive again, taking them, for I think he knew no Gaelic, from the dry pages of O'Curry and his school, and condensing and arranging, as he thought Homer would have arranged and condensed. Lady Gregory has told the same tales, but keeping closer to the Gaelic text, and with greater powers of arrangement and a more original style, but O'Grady was the first, and we had read him in our teens."[1] When he claims that "not even the rhythmic beauty of Lady Gregory's *Cuchulain of Muirthemne* and *Gods and Fighting Men* can take away from the splendour of Standish O'Grady's *History*,"[2] Ernest Boyd is like Yeats suggesting Gregory's greater artistry and O'Grady's greater (because prior) influence: "Standish O'Grady is the pioneer, beside whom his successors, in spite of their excellence, must seem of secondary importance." O'Grady's intrinsic merit as a writer seems hardly at issue. Even his strong antirepublican views are ignored in the general nationalist reverence for his status as cultural ethnarch.

As a pioneer in the popularization of the old romances O'Grady suffered initial ridicule; *History of Ireland* was laughed at a good deal and had to be printed and published at his own expense. Like all patriarchs his status was enhanced by his tendency to prophesy and vindicated by both the loneliness and rightness of those prophecies. The prediction in 1899 of an Irish military movement was his most famous prophecy, but even earlier he made a literary prophecy:

> when I consider the extraordinary stimulus which the perusal of [the bardic] literature gives to the imagination, even in centuries like these, and its wealth of elevated and intensely human character . . . I anticipate, with the revival of Irish literary energy and the return of Irish self-esteem, the artistic craftsmen of the future will find therein, and in unfailing abundance, the material of persons and sentiments fit for the highest purposes of epic and dramatic literature and of art, pictorial and sculptural . . .[3]

a prophecy fulfilled certainly in the short run of the succeeding forty years. The reference to "dramatic literature" may or may not contradict his later demand that Irish dramatists leave the Irish heroic romances alone (a demand AE respectfully rejected)[4] since, like so many in O'Grady, the phrase is ambiguous. If he means by the phrase "drama," then he came to change his mind either because he feared loss of his cultural autocracy through a diffusion of literary genres or because he came to dislike the crowds that attended theatrical performances.

History of Ireland 1: *The Heroic Period* (1878) and 2: *Cuculain and his Contemporaries* (1880) set in motion the literary revival that was to advance well beyond the scope of O'Grady's limited literary talents. In the pages of O'Grady, Cuchulain was reborn in the shape in which he was to dominate the Irish revival: chevalier, visionary, solitary, valiant, patriot. For him to be, in O'Grady's words, "the noblest character ever presented in literature," he had of course to be whited, chastened, and made modest, frequently against the evidence of the manuscripts. O'Grady's Cuchulain is, however, no rebel: that came later with the more nationalistic interpretations of the old literature. O'Grady's Cuchulain embodies an Apollonian pride and vaunt; it was Yeats who made of him (as James Stephens made of Deirdre) a Dionysian figure standing against the Apollonian figure of Conchobar. For the poet, Cuchulain was the active, passionate man bridling against laws in restraint of love and self-determination, and represented in this not merely a universal type but an active, passionate nation bridling against foreign rule.

Cuchulain was only one, albeit the chief, inhabitant of the imaginary epoch and kingdom O'Grady invented virtually single-handedly: Heroic Ireland. This age, which he desired to make "once again a portion of the imagination of the country, and its chief characters as familiar in the minds of our people as they once were,"[5] is an age which "breathes sublimity, and abounds with the marvellous, the romantic, and the grotesque,"[6] which in some respects is superior to ancient Greece, and beside which the early history of England is "a mere scuffling of kites and crows."[7] These "high nonsensical words" themselves exhibit a "filial devotedness" to the memory of the ancestral Irish which O'Grady attributed to his countrymen and which he did much to initiate as a trait in the psychology of the revival. Nonsense skirted his political as well as cultural pronouncements. The Irish had "never achieved a vital and stable political unity . . . But, that such was, from the remotest times, the ideal of the race, and the goal towards which the genius of the land ever impelled the country forward, is evident from the whole tenor of the bardic literature," one of the most striking features of which "is this dominant conception of the Irish race, as forming a single homogeneous nation, owing allegiance to a single sovereign, and governed by edicts issuing from one centre of rightful authority, namely, Tara."[8] He saw his countrymen, "through all the centuries . . . labouring to bring forth the Irish Nation, and that nation yet unborn."[9]

The sagas would seem to refute O'Grady, but more interesting here is that O'Grady could not or would not take the last obvious step towards a republican belief in Ireland's separation from Great Britain, but preferred to contemplate by some species of daydream the inchoate, never fulfilled unity of a purely legendary Heroic Ireland. Rightly did Lady Gregory call him a "Fenian Unionist," and others call him an aristocratic radical (he was the son of Viscount Guillamore), and he himself adopt the label "Tory democrat." He was an advocate of aristocracy, heroism, militarism, rank, order, hierarchical unity, personal property, landlords, patronage, martyrdom, and self-sacrifice. He repudiated commercialism, anarchy, nationalisation, materialism, centralization, bureaucracy, socialism, the middle class, philistinism, newspapers, unedifying literature, and crowds.

Many of his objects of hatred and desire were inherited by Yeats, including the Anglo-Irish landlords who for all their dereliction, cowardice, and corruption were "still the best class we have" and whose human hearts were "warmed yet by many a scarlet rivulet of the old heroic blood."[10] O'Grady's attacks on the landlords were really motivated by disappointment and love, and they are mirrored in D.P. Moran's attacks in *The Philosophy of Irish Ireland* (1905) on the ordinary Irish people whom he loved but excoriated for their lack of nationalist self-reliance and esteem. Long before independence, O'Grady gave an indulgent Irish landlord a prophetic choice between two Irish futures, both of which, as far as Yeats was later concerned, came to pass and out of which he made two kinds of poetry: "If you wish to see anarchy and civil war, brutal despotisms alternating with bloody lawlessness or on the other side, a shabby, sordid Irish Republic, ruled by knavish, corrupt politicians and the ignoble rich, you will travel the way of *Egalité*."[11]

O'Grady's alternative to *Egalité*, one repetitively dramatized in his fiction and lengthily explained in his essays, is a world in which the self is submerged within the group, be it the chieftainry or the peasantry, a world in which these groups and the nation itself usurp the role of the individual. The hero submits to the heroic code of honour, and everyone else to the hero, as, we are told, was the case in Heroic Ireland: "everywhere it was the custom that the weak should accept the protection of the strong and submit themselves to their command."[12] This desired and unequal world of heroic self-reliance and sacrifice and nonheroic submission and self-denial rested on the shaky foundation of wishful and undisciplined interpretations of a vellum and legendary past.

The anthropologizing of Ireland that went on throughout the revival and used Cuchulain and others as chief figurative devices, provided O'Grady with not only direction and shape but also a philosophy for his peculiar prose narratives. I hesitate to say his "fiction" since at the outset O'Grady did not believe he was in *History of Ireland* writing fiction. The fact that O'Grady assumed that the bardic literature, from which he created his *History*, yields historical evidence could be related to certain conditions of social psychology in Ireland. What Wilson says of the Finns could be said about the early revivalists: "when the Finns have faced a changed present or an uncertain future, they have tended to interpret [the *Kalevala*] historically, seeking in [it] evidence of a noble past and, at the same time, models on which to shape their lives and build the future."[13] But in his justifiable assumption that in the earliest written records literature and history, legend and fact are difficult to distinguish, O'Grady reversed the order of precedence we should have expected, and regarded as proper by the early Irish church, for whom Ireland entered history upon conversion (whereas for O'Grady Ireland entered history with Cuchulain during the heroic age). O'Grady is interested not in the historical events the legendary fiction succeeded to, but the historical events which promoted that fiction, and above all he is interested in the legendary fiction itself which he set about rewriting and popularizing. "Early Irish history," he held, "is the creation mainly of the bards,"[14] which is why England, devoid of bards, had the scantest early history.

Cuchulain, whom many, especially in the generation following O'Grady, regarded as mythological, was according to the elder writer a crucial and pivotal figure, an island situated in the transitional sea between fact and legend: "The floruit of Cuculain . . . falls completely within the historical penumbra"[15]; during his career Cuchulain "bears the weight of the vast epos into which the history of the times has resolved itself."[16] Cuchulain and his contemporaries, though not literary phantoms but historical characters, actual existences, are nonetheless "seen as it were through mists of love and wonder."[17] Once historical, they must now be viewed through the poetry of the bards, for in ancient Ireland "the history of one generation became the poetry of the next."[18] Further, historical fact is colored not merely by love but also by dream and aspiration: "The legends represent the imagination of the country; they are that kind of history which a nation desires to possess."[19]

O'Grady's notion of heroic romance as wish-fulfillment is in line with later Jungian thinking as practised by those critics who see the quest-romance as the search of the desiring self for a fulfillment.[20] We should, however, distinguish the Jungian concern with communal wish-fulfillment, which the revivalists practised, from the Freudian concern with individual wish-fulfillment, which the revivalists ostensibly did not practice. What O'Grady is saying about Heroic Ireland describes what went on during that Irish revival which O'Grady is setting in motion as he writes. Through the collective wish-fulfillment of the revival clerisy, recent and contemporary Irish history became literature of a legendary hue which in turn has been mistaken by post-revival readers for history, the history and literary legend of Parnell being the most obvious example. For O'Grady and the revivalists, history is essentially narrative and at some stage artistic. Even when historic event courses like a "slender and doubtful rivulet" from under "the rich and teeming mythus of the bards," the study of its coursing, scientific history, cannot destroy "the legend-making faculty": "Romance, epic, drama, and artistic representation are at all times the points to which history continually aspires—there only its final development and efflorescence. Archaeology culminates in history, history culminates in art."[21] Little wonder this circle, legend succeeding to history, history aspiring to legend, caused Irish historians trained in the English schools and English historians teaching at Trinity College, Dublin to laugh. But the laugh was on them, at least for the duration of the revival, for the literature of that movement usurped the role of history. O'Grady kindled with his words that Irish chronophobic imagination without which the cultural revival would have been impossible, and overthrew more decisively than Arnold could have anticipated "the despotism of fact."[22]

It would not have bothered O'Grady to reflect that in rewriting the bards in modern, "poetic" English he was filtering Irish history through the language of a distantly removed generation, that history, moreover, having already been filtered (purportedly) through the bardic literature. For O'Grady and the cultural nationalists he fathered, what had happened between the bardic rendition of the heroic period and the imminent recovery of this period at the close of the nineteenth century was a bad dream or a case of suspended animation; it did not in a sense happen at all. The well of Irish legendry had been capped by Christianity and successive philistine invasions and was now being reopened by a generation that could claim to be the bards' legitimate and even, where the imagination was concerned, immediate successors.

There is a modicum of truth in the claim, as the arrangement of the present study, with its leap from Old and medieval Irish literature to revival literature, implies. Despite successive colonizations, Christianization, the break-up of the Gaelic order in the seventeenth century, the Act of Union, and famine, the literary imagination of the bards does in a sense resurface during the revival and after; at least its key images and preoccupations do so, even if they are quickly modernized and superseded. (Though of course, as Carleton's work testifies, the time-capsule had not been hermetically sealed before O'Grady's appearance on the scene.) And so in rewriting the bards, O'Grady did not conceive of himself as writing historical fiction, the production of an imagination removed in time from the core of ascertainable fact around which it freely plays, but rather legendary history, an inspired and therefore time-sheltered interpretation of an already imagined bardic literature which was, of course, also bardic history. But although he imitated the bardic manner and thought of himself as a latter-day bard, O'Grady was from the outset writing fictionalized history.

Bardic legendary history, preserved for us in the various cyclical literature, O'Grady thought of as epic, though later writers and even O'Grady himself came to see it as romance rather than epic. The early conception of epic and his attempt to imitate the bardic manner account for the generally distended nature of O'Grady's *History of Ireland*. Everywhere is inflation: the exaggerated claims for the cultural status of Heroic Ireland and the quality of the bardic literature; the massive and unwieldy structure of multiple scenarios and poetic conjecture that is recognizably neither history nor novel; the gigantist conception of Cuchulain that is offset by no gift for the comic grotesquerie of the original. And of course the language: the epic similes, the hyperbole, the endless superlatives, the recondite vocabulary (anile, enure, litten, glaisin, aphelion, bratta, delver, glozing, corcur), some of it archaistic and all of it an attempt to re-create an ancient period, however unspecific. The impulse that leads O'Grady to use the old-fashioned English past-participles "drave," "wert," "brake" and "slang" helps to create a prose style really no closer to Old Irish than Lady Gregory's modern literary English laced with Hiberno-English idioms, and is part of the thrust of the revival towards anachronism, though the rodomontade to which O'Grady is prone is often punctured by the splendid actions of the narrative in which he cannot but help interest the reader. In order to imitate the Irish bardic manner O'Grady ironically drank from English and Scottish streams—the King James Bible, Malory, Carlyle, possibly Scott, Victorian sentimentalism, the historical novel, and "the bankrupt currency of nineteenth-century romantic verse"[23] as well as Sir Samuel Ferguson who might indeed be said to have dealt in that currency. The fevered and patrician voice even suggests an historical fiction of imperialist undertone, not so ironic when we consider that the Irish revival had in it a strain of cultural imperialism not to be confused with genuine cosmopolitanism. O'Grady's ambition, remarked Ernest Boyd, was "to capture the British Empire for the greater glory of Ireland;"[24] equally true would it be to say that O'Grady sought to create an imaginary native Irish empire whose "nations" (his word, but they were really septs) would resemble the nations of the American Indians.

The name of Carlyle appears in the list of influences on O'Grady courtesy of Yeats who tells us that O'Grady read Carlyle and that his prose style suffered as a result.[25] But we should have guessed at the influence in any case, and not merely on stylistic grounds. Carlyle was a key figure amid the nineteenth-century English clerisy of which the revivalists were at once an Irish chapter and rivals of a succeeding generation. If Carlyle on Odin resembles O'Grady on Cuchulain, it is not just in the exclamatory tone and apostolic fervor. O'Grady subscribed to Carlyle's Great Man theory of history outlined in *Heroes and Hero-Worship* (1841). Carlyle's belief that the hero is a bringer of light and the saviour of his epoch was also O'Grady's, but then it all went much further than the Scotsman and the Irishman. What Walter E. Houghton has to tell us about hero-worship among the early and middle Victorians is a reminder that in some respects the Irish revival was a late blossoming of Victorianism on the edge of the kingdom.

Houghton describes hero-worship as a nineteenth-century phenomenon, a major factor in English culture in the fifty years after 1830.[26] He draws our attention to the extraordinary popularity during this time of Greek myths and medieval legends, and especially of feudalism which for most Victorians derived from Scott and his heroic re-creations; but "Carlyle in particular took feudalism as his point of reference."[27] In O'Grady's summons of the Anglo-Irish landlords to knightliness is echoed Carlyle's summons of the English Captains of Industry to the same heroic condition. O'Grady's feudalism, promulgated during a period of land reform and political agitation, has political implications of a mid-Victorian familiarity. "In conservative-aristocratic circles," writes Houghton, "where the dread of bourgeois democracy was strongest, heroic literature acquired the value of a political symbol. Medieval romance in particular could be read as the image of a feudal society in striking contrast to the new order that was pushing it aside, and of an ideal which still might be revived."[28] Ruskin in 1869 detected a struggle approaching "between the newly-risen power of democracy and the apparently departing power of feudalism,"[29] and while he did so, "Carlyle could talk in the same way about the wisdom of restoring the aristocracy to power."[30] Victorians, it appears, were not always equal to the struggle. Houghton remarks on the recurring feeling of impotence and timidity, on "the ennui and frustration which accompanied the collapse of traditional belief."[31] One is reminded of O'Grady's Anglo-Irishry suffering, like the Red Branch knights on one occasion before them, a great and enfeebling enchantment. "Whatever its origin," Houghton continues, "the mood of weakness found the anti-self in the image of the hero, strong in both decisive force and mastery of circumstance."

Beside the antidemocratic, antibourgeois components of Victorian hero-worship we can set others: Froude's idea that hero worship could counter commercialism, the Protestant notion of the elect which Houghton believes to lie beneath Carlyle's hero-worship, the denial of a scientific conception of history as a vast and interrelated play of cultural forces, the pervasive anticosmopolitanism and English nationalism[32]; it all composes a picture familiar to students of the Anglo-Irish revival three and more decades later. At the center of the picture stood the hero. When he came to popularize his feudalism for the people, as Scott had done before him, O'Grady's energies converged on the figure of Cuchulain.

Cuchulain Revisited: O'Grady's Historical Romances

Cuculain: An Epic (1882) is a republication of those parts of *History of Ireland* that have Cuchulain as their central figure. Despite the narrower focus and tighter structure, the style, as the titular claim to epic forewarns, is that of the *History*. The delirious account of the combat between Cuchulain and Fardia (Ferdia in Hull) is drawn attention to by O'Grady as an example of his prose style which at such high moments, he writes, "is not quite that which is usually denominated prose."[33] But in fact the combat—powerful, choreographic and oddly impersonal in the literal translation—in O'Grady's version (he refers to Cuchulain's distortion merely as his possession by "war-demons," and omits the verbal repetitions of the Gaelic) resembles the overheated prose of adventure fiction: "Therewith then they fought, and Cuculain had no weapon save only his colg, for the Gae Bulg, the rude spear which he had fashioned, he dropped upon the shore, and Fardia discharged his javelins at the same time, for he was ambidexter, and quick as lightning, Cuculain avoided them, and they stuck trembling in the thither bank, and quick to right and left Cuculain severed the leathern thongs rushing forward. Then drew Fardia his mighty sword that made a flaming crescent as it flashed most bright and terrible, and rushed headlong upon Cuculain."[34] And so on.

If *Cuculain: An Epic* is at all significant, it is so because it reveals what was largely disguised in the role of the heroic romances in the revival: the search for a native form of the novel, the Anglo-Irish novel having been repudiated. It was an unfortunate irony that while inspiring the writing of longer fiction, the bardic literature actually hindered fulfillment of the novel form in Ireland by representing an already conceived and realized body of narrative too singular, remarkable and diffuse for the modern novelist to make over into a novel form other than historical romance. In his Preface to *Cuculain: An Epic,* O'Grady claims his book is neither novel nor romance; but historical romance is in fact what O'Grady and Lady Gregory were really aspiring to write, whether or not they knew it. But if he is not aware of how his epic ambitions have thus shrunk, O'Grady is at least aware that he is not, after all, engaged in history: "History it is not, at least as that term is conventionally employed, though I at one time thought that the signification of the word might be so enlarged as to embrace such a work as the present."[35] As though repeating the experience of the medieval Irish Christian redactors of pagan narratives, O'Grady is coming to separate history from legendry, a repeatedly necessary fission in Ireland where they interpenetrate so intimately and readily; legend-as-fact is succeeding to legend-as-fiction. But now O'Grady is separating also fiction from legendry; for the revival in choosing overtly to return to Irish legend rather than turning to English fiction became engaged in recapitulating the birth and development of fiction, a redundancy perhaps suggested in the very word revival, *living again what has already been lived.*

Cuculain: An Epic was followed a dozen years later by *The Coming of Cuculain: A Romance of the Heroic Age in Ireland* (1894). The latter continues the tendency of O'Grady's narratives towards the historical-romantic novel, a genre represented by his more conventionally historical and more plainly written fiction, *The Bog of Stars* (1893) and *Ulrick the Ready* (1908). In confining himself in *The Coming of Cuculain* to the hero's boy-deeds, O'Grady initiated the Ireland-childhood-heroism linkage that recurs in Irish revival literature. O'Grady apparently did not intend his novel to be read only by children, though, frankly, children would be his fittest readers; rather is precocious childhood held to be a fit subject for adult contemplation.

In his essay, "The Renewal of Youth" (1896), AE made the psychic or spiritual recovery of childhood a precondition of Irish nationhood. In his review of Lady Gregory's *Cuchulain of Muirthemne* he says something that is in *The Coming of Cuculain* turned from simile into literalness: "in spite of the bloodshed the heroes seem like children who fight steadily through a mock battle, but the night will see these children at peace, and they will dream with arms around each other in the same cot. No literature ever had a more beautiful heart of childhood in it."[36] If Frye is accurate in referring to "The perennially childlike quality of romance" (linked to its nostalgia and desire for a golden age),[37] then we might justifiably see revival delight in the childhood elements and childlikeness of the Ulster cycle as connected to the revival wish to romanticize the old stories. (And might we not see romance itself as the childhood of the novel, to which the Irish prose writers, under ideological impulse, were returning?)

But though AE might not have admitted it, childhood in the stories has its less romantic, more militaristic features in keeping with the stories' status as prechivalric saga and epic. O'Grady's loving and invented description in *The Coming of Cuculain* of the curriculum of the school at Emain Macha, circumstantially based on Cuchulain's boy-deeds and the adult Cuchulain's advice to a prince, might well have been a prototype for Pearse's vision of St. Enda's school in which disguised militarism had a role to play. We might think, too, of the children's military movements that sprang up in early twentieth-century Ireland—cadet versions of the adult insurrectionary army and modeled in part on fevered visions of Cuchulanoid Ireland (Synge's phrase). O'Grady's and AE's idea, that what goes on in the cycle is a species of child's play, is in fact not only distortive in interpretation of the stories but also highly dangerous in application to real Irish life in coupling insurrectionary and sectarian violence with the moral innocence of boyhood.[38]

O'Grady was reluctant to relax his grip on Cuchulain, and continued to subdivide the hero's story. *The Coming of Cuculain* began a trilogy that continued with *In the Gates of the North* (1901) and concluded with *The Triumph and Passing of Cuculain* (1917). All derive their incidents from *History of Ireland,* but the second and third volumes are directly indebted respectively to the second half and first half of *Cuculain: An Epic.* During his successive rewritings of the Cuchulain story, O'Grady abbreviated, simplified and unified in his search for an appropriate fictional form. He tried to retreat from the "amplitude and stateliness of diction" and "sonorous manner" which in his Introduction to *In the Gates of the North* he says his style exhibited in *History of Ireland.* He does not name his earlier work or self, but refers to a man he knew who wrote "some large sentences concerning Irish History in general;" he then quotes his earlier sonorous self as Introduction to *In the Gates of the North.*

Yet O'Grady thought that by so simplifying and accelerating he was sacrificing none of the story's mystery. His Introduction to *In the Gates of the North* warns, with a mingled *hauteur* and defensiveness he came to adopt towards his fiction, those "who endeavour to read the ensuing tale . . . that even if they afterwards learn to like it—and I know very well that some will—they must be prepared, in the beginning, to read it like a task, and pursue it at least through some initial chapters as if it were a severe mental exercise; so remote and unusual is the plane of thought and emotion, so unfamiliar the point of view, so strange are the characters and their manners and surroundings, while the very style is so different from that which is in common use to-day."[39] The swifter prose style is an improvement, but the overall result is yet not a satisfactory novel, and remains a wounded epic. Because he retains in his novels many features of the original romances, O'Grady cannot help but be readable, especially as the hero's predicted death nears in *The Triumph and Passing of Cuculain.* But on the whole, O'Grady demystifies, domesticates and prosifies the saga of an ancient and mysterious people.

The contrasting power of Yeats's Cuchulain plays might suggest that we are dealing in the prose interpretations with a mere insufficiency of genius and imagination, but it may also be a matter of the appropriateness of form. While it is true that all the prose retellings of the heroic romances suffer the originals to be, in the phrase of the electrical engineer, "transformed down," that is, having their imaginative voltage lowered as the current of retelling was stepped up (and this includes, because of the linguistic loss, the literal translations), the novel form had this effect especially. Ironically, Lady Gregory's unsatisfactory retellings, neither novels nor translations, and O'Grady's own fabulous histories, neither history nor fable, are yet finer accomplishments, not just in influence but intrinsically, than O'Grady's novels in which much is lifeless, mere gaudy stage property.

That O'Grady might have had youthful readers in mind as he had for some of his novels (for example, *The Chain of Gold,* 1895) cannot change our judgment. It is not that the bowdlerized retelling of myths and legends is misguided. Indeed, rewriting the old stories for children (see, for example, Eleanor Hull's *Cuchulain: The Hound of Ulster,* 1909, and *The Boys' Cuchulain: Heroic Legends of Ireland,* 1910) became a self-appointed minor task for revivalists, and produced an Irish equivalent of Victorian fiction for young boys of the Empire, G. A. Henty in saga form. But children demand above all the sense of mystery, which O'Grady sacrifices in diluting the Ulster cycle into novels. Rather than saying the heroic romances ought not to be dramatized, we can see by hindsight that on purely formal consideration O'Grady should have warned against their novelization, since the novel is ordinarily, though not in the extraordinary hands of Joyce, less implicative and presentational than drama and therefore less suited to recapturing the density of ancient stories mystified by the long passage of time.

But there was more at stake than genre in all of this. The use of the old stories by writers of the revival was debated in the pages of the Dublin *Daily Express,* and the debate published in 1899 as *Literary Ideals in Ireland.* John Eglinton (W. K. Magee), who opened the debate, hoped for an Irish national literature but wondered if a preoccupation with the "ancient legends" was the way to achieve it. "The truth is, these subjects, much as we may admire them in the modern world, obstinately refuse to be taken up out of their old environment and be translated into the world of modern sympathies. The proper mode of treating them is a secret lost with the subjects themselves."[40] He recommended Irish writers to study the old literature, merely hoping for some hint of "the forgotten mythopoeic secret" (p. 12). And if Cuchulain and Finn were to appear in the new literature, they were obliged "to take up on their broad shoulders something of the weariness and fret of our age" (p. 24), lest they be mere figures in belles lettres. The danger was that the legends would distract writers from "the facts of life" and cause them to remove poetry idealistically from reality, leaving intact the world of the philistines. He could not have foreseen that in 1916 Pearse proved that poetry and idealism could fatally rupture reality and without reality's permission; by proving Eglinton wrong, Pearse merely proved him right. In the new literature around him, Eglinton saw too much removal by the writer from his age and also "from himself": "In London and Paris they seem to believe in theories and 'movements,' and to regard individuality as a noble but 'impossible' savage; and we are in some danger of being absorbed into their error. Some of our disadvantages are our safeguards. In all ages poets and thinkers have owed far less to their countries than their countries have owed to them" (p. 13).

Eglinton was outnumbered in the debate by Yeats, AE, and William Larminie, but gave a good account of himself. In his replies Yeats offered the examples of Ibsen and Wagner as national writers availing themselves of ancient material, and thought that the Irish stories, in common with the Norse and German stories, would become universal like those of Greece and Rome. The old stories, he thought, led us back to a time "before men became so crowded upon one another, and so buried in their individual destinies and trades" (p. 18). Irritated that Eglinton, a theosophist,should adopt the stance he did, Yeats rejected realism alongside individualism, requesting artists, the new priests, to fill our thoughts "with the essences of things, and not with things." (p. 74) Sent packing, too, was Arnold's notion that poetry is a criticism of life, and supplanted with the notion that the arts should escape their age and lose themselves in beauty.

AE, ever the peacemaker, contrived to see no real quarrel between Yeats and Eglinton but was really more Yeatsian than Yeats. He saw developing around him a program of Irish writing: "To reveal Ireland in clear and beautiful light, to create the Ireland in his heart, is the province of a national literature" (p. 83); and this would accommodate individuality, he fancied, because in the moment a man "has attained to spiritual vision and ecstasy he has come to his true home, to his true self." (p. 53) O'Grady's Cuchulain would become to every Irish boy who reads his story "a revelation of what his own spirit is" (p. 87). Rather narrowly, AE saw no literary attitude in the Ireland of his day alternative to that of men like Edward Dowden of Trinity College who desired "to obliterate all nationality from their work" (p. 87). AE had missed Eglinton's point.

The Psychology of Epic: Stephens' **Deirdre**

Eglinton's views did not deter another writer with a much more sensitive awareness of the mystery of life, James Stephens, from trying to succeed where O'Grady had failed, namely, in turning the old heroic tales successfully into novels, though the task finally defeated him also. In his 1922 edition of *Ireland's Literary Renaissance,* Ernest Boyd entertained great hopes for Stephens' "new version of the *Tain Bo-Cuailgne,* of which the two first volumes, as yet unpublished, promise his masterpiece."[41] Boyd refers to *Deirdre* (1923) and *In the Land of Youth* (1924), typescript copies of both of which Stephens gave to Boyd in 1920.[42] Stephens, who conceived his project as early as 1918,[43] wished to delay publication of the first two volumes until the final three volumes of his projected five-volume series were written, but when it became clear that the plan would not advance beyond two volumes, he decided to publish. *Deirdre* and *In the Land of Youth* are retellings not of the *Táin* but of *remscéla* or pretales from the Ulster cycle leading up to the *Táin,* a measuredness of pace and breaking down of the vast original into manageable pieces that Stephens, like O'Grady before him, probably felt shortened the odds of his composing the fictional masterpiece that Boyd predicted. It was not to be, and *The Crock of Gold,* an earlier novel, remained his masterwork. But Stephens' was the most sophisticated of the attempts by revival writers to novelize the old stories, even if the result was not entirely satisfactory.

Between the time of Sir Samuel Ferguson's version of her story in the early nineteenth century and Stephens' 1923 novel, many writers were fascinated by the character of Deirdre: R. D. Joyce, Aubrey de Vere, Douglas Hyde, AE, Yeats, Eva Gore-Booth, Father Thomas O'Kelly, Alexander Carmichael, "Michael Field," William Graham, and John Millington Synge.[44] Deirdre was in her appeal the female counterpart of Cuchulain, and her tragic love story is a memorable one. Stephens' novel opens well with his refreshing and characteristically swift prose that on occasions has an Elizabethan dash and smart; the narrative is unfailingly buoyant and there is a drollery throughout. Alas—perennial pitfall for the writer handling such energetic material—*Deirdre* closes with a fifty-page account of the fight between the forces of Conachur (Conchobar) and the returning sons of Uisneac. This fight is a somewhat comic, superior *Boys' Own* version of the story, even down to the last ingenious description, that ought to have been harrowing, of Deirdre, Naoise, and his brothers swimming pathetically through an imaginary sea conjured up by Cathfa the magician. Perhaps Stephens felt such a protracted climax was necessary to distract the reader from the novel's preceding difficulties. Either way, the last few chapters of *Deirdre* counter the maxims he expressed later in *On Prose and Verse* (1928) but practised earlier in *The Charwoman's Daughter* (1912) and *The Crock of Gold* (1912): "Writing can be quite good, and yet have no violence whatever in it. It can be powerful on a very minimum of action."[45]

Stephens wisely follows the main incidents of a fine story, and mimics the bardic gift for the grotesque and macabre, but in *Deirdre* these are even jollier than they are in the original. "They were young," we are told of Naoise and his brothers, "but they had killed; and they rocked with glee as they told by what marvellous strategy they had got in the lucky blow, and how the champion had gone down never to rise again, and they had trotted home squealing and squawking with joy, with a head surveying the world from the top of a spear, and it grinning down on them as joyously as they chattered up at it."[46] Boys will be boys. Later, one of the three brothers recalls such heads: "'Very hairy, beardy, toothy kinds of heads . . . and they used to get hairier and beardier and toothier every second day. At last,' he explained to Deirdre, 'there wouldn't be any head at all, no face at all, only a mat of hair as long as a woman's, and it in knots, and a shiny grin among the knots.'" (p. 216)

Instead of trying to eclipse the legend he is retelling, Stephens in fact reminds us of it in several references, and though this disavowal of free invention reads now like a modernist device, it does mean that Stephens has relinquished some of his control as novelist. This is reinforced by Stephens' apparent acceptance, like O'Grady, of the legend as history. The narrator admits his ignorance, and the ignorance of the bards, of what is happening at certain moments of the story (for example, what became of Nessa or who actually killed the sons of Uisneac), and to admit ignorance is to imply that something theoretically ascertainable did really happen. For the same reason Stephens supplies us with several footnotes. Again, this reads nowadays like a modernist ploy, but we do not need to invoke the modernists to explain it. The surrender of rights of total invention and the ironic edge it can lend to a novel can both be found in the fiction of William Carleton whose natural, inventive, and untutored genius clashed, rather like Stephens', with that Irish belief that all the best stories, fact or fiction, have already been told. Hence, I think, the suggestion of tongue-in-cheek when Stephens wonders aloud: "How should I paint Naoise as Deirdre saw him, or show Deirdre as she appeared to the son of Uisneac? . . . When we endeavour to tell of these things words cannot stand the trial. It may be done by music, or by allusion . . . In these grave ways we may approach perfection, indicating distantly that which cannot be unveiled in speech." (pp. 70–71)

The talkative and busy word-spinner in Stephens does not believe for a moment that words cannot stand any trial (like the bards he believes implicitly in the magical omnipotence of words), but the romantic (or romantic ironist) in Stephens, a refugee from the Celtic Twilight, believed (or pretended to believe) that such was the case. Hence the repetition of decadent cult words like "delicious" and "joyous" in *Deirdre,* as though such repetition were the only defense against language's inadequacy. In the novel there is a coy turning away from the tale into quasi-romantic atmosphere very different from O'Grady's bullish rhetoric and confrontation. Unbardic too are the digressions and interpolations by the home-spun philosopher in Stephens, though they might possibly be regarded as equivalents to the bardic set pieces. They give all of Stephens' fiction a disconcerting narratorial egotism; he patronizes his characters incorrigibly, especially youths and women, and forces his readers to conspire with him in doing so. In *Deirdre* this has the unfortunate effect of suggesting parody by reducing on occasions the terrific power of a pagan legend to something resembling a fireside tale.

Stephens, then, both submits to and refuses to submit to the authority of *Longes mac n-Uislenn* ("The Fate of the Sons of Uisneac"). If he indulges his whimsy and salamandrine humor, he can also at rare moments sound like O'Grady, as in this comment on Conachur: "Not time nor thought could blunt the edge of his bodily or mental energy, so vast was it, and misfortune beat as unavailingly against him as the wind did against oaken Emania." (p. 154) He reproduces a fateful and captive world of the hero tales, a world of genealogy, prophecy and *geasa*. Having done so, he does not surprise us, except in the degree of youthful high spirits he portrays, by transforming Deirdre's and her companions' acceptance of ill-fate into a joyful occasion. Below this current of romantic heroism there is, as in all of Stephens' fiction, an undertow of essentially novelistic, often ironic, sometimes even cynical concern.

The cross-current so created is not entirely assuring. At one moment a bardic impersonator, at another moment Stephens is a modern narrator playing with the bardic material, with the reader and, one senses, with himself. Here is a typically chatty piece of exposition:

> As well as an aristocracy of birth there was in every Irish court an élite of excellence. Those who were foremost in learning, the arts, or the crafts, had the privilege of visiting the king equally with those whose merit rose from their fathers' graves or their skill at arms. A king was then close to his people, and he was by training and habit a connoisseur in many things which all could understand. A commonwealth of taste is the only one which can admit equality—it is democracy. (p. 159)

We recognize here O'Grady's notion of the ideal society with its various ranks cemented by the mutual fellowship between king and subject, a repeated ideal in revival literature which has as backdrop dissatisfaction both with contemporary Irish society and with English administration and royalty felt to be alien. Yet a hundred pages before, in apparently defending *droit de seigneur* in yet another talkative stopover, Stephens reminds us that there was no equality of birth in Ulster and in doing so introduces what would seem to be puckish irony:

> It is certainly a hardship and a tyranny if a neighbour should constrain a neighbour's wife to his own domestic uses, but it is only a hardship

> because the affair occurs between equals, among whom friendly observances are due, and between whom equal respect is grounded. Among equals anything that implies inequality is a punishable wrong: but there is no hardship when the superior takes what he carelessly desires. It is community of interests which makes equals, and the disturbance of this which makes enemies; but there is no community of interests between prince and the subject, and no man is aggrieved by an action which can only affect his honour by increasing it. Nevertheless, so illogical is the mind of man, and so uncompromising is the sense of property, that men could be found who would interrupt with a spear the careless pleasure of a prince; and there were some, blacksmiths mostly and cobblers, who would take a cudgel to the king's majesty itself and beat it out of a warm bed. (pp. 47–48)

Stephens' drollery and irony are often hard to gauge and sometimes, one suspects, are mere high spirits, but the attack on private property is as serious as Stephens could get and we will return to it in a later chapter. Furthermore, the drollery and irony are pressed into service of psychology that Stephens saw as the only science in the world and that "can only be attempted by a fully-conscious being."[47] As any good novelist would feel he had to do, Stephens supplied his epic characters with the inner lives missing from the original stories: out of what is *not* told in the Old and Middle Irish manuscripts arises the modern novel. This is Stephens' attempt to compensate for the dilution paraphrase inevitably entails. *Deirdre,* we might say, is a case of sustained psychological *Motivierung,* creative conjecture about character and motivation that used to be thought the soul of the novel. But this sits uneasily with the epic given, and Stephens' psychological interest remains anomalous.[48] Because in other respects the novel is rooted in the legend, and because even the psychological element is half-playful, *Deirdre* is a curious work, more fully emerged from legendry than the prose narratives of O'Grady and Gregory, closer to a novel and farther from an historical romance, yet ultimately dissatisfying even while shedding valuable light on revival fiction and revival psychology.

Subversion of the Heroic: **Deirdre** *Continued*

The psychological reading of events and characters in *Deirdre* is, as we shall see in a later chapter, something of a return to the psychological aspects of Stephens' first novel, *The Charwoman's Daughter,* and takes an interesting direction. Beneath the heroic self-sacrifice and stoic surrender to fate that follows, and indeed is an aspect of, the self-reliance that attracted O'Grady and Lady Gregory to the old heroes, Stephens detects, or chooses to detect, an ungovernable egotism that prevents self-mastery. In explaining the harsh treatment Lavarcham metes out to her foster-daughter Deirdre, sequestered by Conachur the king because dire consequences for Ulster are predicted by Cathfa upon her birth, Stephens writes:

> There are many people who can only do a particular thing on condition that they do it in two directions. They can repress themselves only when they are engaged in repressing some one else; for the thing we are doing outwardly and to others is always the thing that we are doing inwardly and to ourselves. If we treat others benevolently we are assuredly being kind to ourselves: if we mete out torment we will receive that measure and will writhe in it. A tyrant is ultimately one who is striving for self-mastery by the wrong method. (p. 104)

Lavarcham is a less harmful version of Conachur, "the slave to his ego," whom Stephens sees as a tyrant. Conachur is "masterful" in many ways but is given to jealousy ("All clever men are jealous," the narrator comments: "it is one of the forms of egoism"), and Deirdre's elopement with Naoise arouses a storm of jealousy. Both Conachur and Maeve, whose mutual enmity in the first part of *Deirdre* is carried on with an almost Jacobean passion for intrigue, represent powerful and thwarted wills which for Stephens merely proves their misguided attempts at self-mastery.

Kept out of sight of men, Deirdre on the other hand is at first demure and submissive; but in a way analogous to Stephens' assumption of the novelistic control he had surrendered at first to the ancient legend, Deirdre takes "conscious control" of her life once she encounters men; she develops an "intractable" and uncontrollable "mental greed": "her desire would swell about the world and banish all else from existence so that she could fashion the regal solitude in which so gigantic mystery might be contemplated" (p. 99). Beyond her sexual will Deirdre pursues what the narrator of *The Demi-Gods* (1914) believes in an astonishing passage his beautiful and apparently taintless heroine, Mary, is pursuing—"the Neuter" that Stephens was convinced the female "keeps up her sleeve."[49]

Addressing in a veritable paroxysm women in pursuit of power, the narrator of the earlier novel could almost be addressing Deirdre in the wake of the tragedy that befalls her and the sons of Uisneac: "No genius has yet sprung from ye but the Genius of War and Destruction, those frowning captains that have ravaged our vineyards and blackened our generations with the torches of their egotism."[50] These transports of malice that overtake Stephens' narrators (Stephens himself?) puncture, however, a genuine admiration, even affection for his heroines, and the result is a curious and emotional imbalance. Nor are the narrators sufficiently characters in their own right for us to attribute this emotional imbalance to *them* as complicated people rather than to the text.

Deirdre's relationship with Conachur, after she has met and fallen in love with Naoise whom she chooses over the king, resembles that of Antigone with Creon in Sophocles' play; in both cases inflexible power bears down on indomitable will and affection; in both cases the tragic hero is not the less dislikable heroine but the more dislikable king; and in both cases the king wins a Pyrrhic victory, though in *Deirdre* the implications of the duel are lost in the irrelevant duration of the physical combat.

Lavarcham, Maeve, Conachur, and Deirdre do not exhaust the egotism of the characters. Cuchullin is "forward" and proud, having refused Conachur first access to Emer and having refused to kill the sons of Uisneac should the king order it. Cuchullin is a minor figure in *Deirdre,* probably because he was being retained for prominence in the later retellings of the *Táin* proper, but one suspects also because there was a strong antiheroism streak in Stephens that caused him to have little conventional interest in the chief mythical hero of the revival. Conall likewise refuses to entertain the possibility of killing the sons of Uisneac should Conachur order it, and the king moodily contemplates him: "That man . . . has been hammered together stone by stone, and is no more than a petrified vanity. He loves nothing but his honour, which is that he loves himself" (p. 181). Even when filtered for us through Conachur's jealousy, the egotism of the chief characters remains intact. This egotism arises because each character is sundered from a spiritual and social entirety made impossible by Conachur, and this is most vividly imaged in Deirdre's banishment and in her broken family. All of Stephens' fiction charts the quest for renewed wholeness, and the broken family is his recurring social metaphor for this and his chief means of narratively exploiting the predicament. It is this quest that helps to make of Stephens a revival writer, for the family of Ireland, the revivalists believed, had been broken by cultural anglicization, and could only be reunited at the expense of individuality.

The psychological construction Stephens puts on the old tales is not in principle irreconcilable with the theme of fate he inherits from them, for in Shakespeare's tragedies fate and will contend in a relentless dialectic. But certainly in seeing the story of the sons of Uisneac as a clash of unquenchable egos, Stephens to some extent subverts the revival view of the Irish hero tales. First of all, not just the hero but everyone is egotistic. Second, egotism is not so much heroic self-assurance as unheroic vanity, and it is titillating to imagine how Stephens might have handled the vast heroic presence of Cuchulain; it is perhaps just as well Stephens never advanced as far as the *Táin* itself! Third, the egotism of the characters is at the service of no cause but their own, and this resembles a parody of the revival concept of Irish heroism that would place him in the Joycean rather than Yeatsian camp.

Yet, of course, Stephens' preoccupation with the self as a theme is very like the revival preoccupation with that same theme. And Stephens uses the fate of the chief characters in *Deirdre* to caution that self-mastery by the right method is necessary and desirable, and this connects with the revival advocacy of that mastery of self exhibited both by heroic self-possession and by the willing submission of those who are not heroes. "Self-expression is a great thing," Stephens told a poet in 1921, in the midst of preparing *Deirdre* for publication, "but self-mastery is a better," and self-mastery requires "a certain amount of 'transmutation'."[51] This is the key theme and activity of Irish revival writers.

Furthermore, Deirdre's and Naoise's joyful acceptance of death resembles the heroic choice of self-sacrifice (the ultimate self-transmutation) that the revival also established as an ideal. Ironically, the ideal from which there is depicted in *Deirdre* a falling off is an ideal claimed by the revivalists already to be expressed in the original tales which Stephens has deliberately reinterpreted, one might say misinterpreted, in order to justify his novel. In *Deirdre* Stephens sacrifices O'Grady's perception of the old heroes in order to fashion from his own jaundiced, novel, and anti-revival view of the heroes a moral that is in line with revival thinking and supposed by revivalists to be embodied in the lives and deaths of the heroes in the old stories!

It is perhaps a more acute version of that similar redundancy (dare one say authorial egotism masquerading as deference to ancient creation?) that haunts all of the revival rewriting of the old works, yet at the same time serves to remind us to what extent James Stephens was both an orthodox and heterodox revival writer. Revival orthodoxy, I realize, is something of an abstraction, trespassed against in any case by the best writers of the period who ultimately went their own self-expressive way, but a writer's attitude towards the heroic tales is nevertheless a fair gauge of orthodoxy, and in this matter James Stephens was, because of an inherently subversive imagination to which we will return, among the least orthodox and culturally nationalistic.

The Greek and Renaissance cast of Stephens' interpretation of the heroic romances, the tragic bent, removes him from Lady Gregory and Standish James O'Grady but places him closer to the Yeats of the Cuchulain plays. Where the lesser and more nationalistic writers seem content with the ultimate optimism of romance, Yeats, Synge and Stephens prefer to think of the old stories as tragic romances or else sagas from which tragedies can be extracted. The Ulster cycle can be seen as tragic to the extent that we regard it as the stories of Cuchulain and Deirdre who die premature deaths for which they can be held to some extent responsible. If we instead regard the cycle *as a cycle* then we will see it as saga. We can also regard the cycle as part of an even larger, less unified, and, until recently, living folk story in which the characters are not rounded enough to be interpreted as psychologically self-destructive and in which Cuchulain, in those tales, for example, where he meets Saint Patrick, is resurrected after having been torn to pieces. Then we are less likely to see it as tragedy and more likely to see it as romance with a happy ending. We are not sure which choice Stephens' novel *Deirdre* is making. The style and tone are unsettled, by turns serious and comic, didactic and lyrical, psychological and formulaic, bardic and novelistic.

I sense in *Deirdre* a certain tepidity of enthusiasm (it was written after though published before *In the Land of Youth*), a certain fatigue with the psychological approach and with the lack of comic enchantment and magical charm in the Ulster cycle stories compared with those of the Fenian and Mythological cycles. Perhaps Stephens abandoned the five-volume project because he grew to realize before all was said and done that the Ulster cycle was not his kind of material. Stephens, as *Deirdre* conveniently illustrates in capsule form, was as a novelist pulled in several directions with an entertaining but ultimately damaging perversity worthy of some of his own characters. He was protean enough to appeal both to Yeats, who no doubt found his liking for Blake and theosophy congenial, and to Joyce who perhaps fancied a fellow (though very different) Proteus whose language had the style of speech rather than written prose.

Stephens as nationalist, as mystic, and as writer was in conflict with himself. The solemnity of the bardic manner, the mischievous humor of the folk, the ironies and realisms of the novelist: all attracted him simultaneously. In this he might be regarded as the ideal revival writer because least self-possessed. Unlike Joyce he did not attempt a capacious work that would accommodate his warring inclinations; instead he remained something of a changeling. As such he was novelistically better equipped to recreate the folk and fairy world than to recreate the aristocratic world of the romance or epic hero, because the former is an even more magical and transformative world than the latter. *In the Land of Youth,* composed as I said before *Deirdre,* shows on Stephens' handling of the epic matter the lingering effects of *The Crock of Gold* and *Irish Fairy Tales* (1920) with their multiple enchantments. In its intricacy of structure *In the Land of Youth* is a fictional experiment in the direction not of the modern psychological novel as *Deirdre* was unwisely to be, but of narrative involution.

I will not treat *In the Land of Youth* at length because in a later chapter I will discuss narrative involution in other books by Stephens. Suffice it to say that although the world of the hero is undercut as effectively in *In the Land of Youth* as it is in *Deirdre,* it is done so not through psychological irony but rather thematically through the subversion of the sidhe. The two parts of the novel are entitled "The Feast of Samhain" and "The Feast of Lugnasa," references to the two occasions in the Celtic calendar when the gates to the land of the sidhe (fairies sometimes held to be the defeated gods, Tuatha de Danann) are thrown open and there is free and anarchic traffic between the worlds of men and immortals, when men and fairies alike can become changelings and normality is suspended. Stephens derives this framework for the book from *Echtra Nerai* ("The Adventures of Nera"), the first of the three *remscéla* leading up to the *Táin* that Stephens retells in his novel, the other two being *De Chophur in dá Muccida* ("The Begetting [or Quarrel] of the Two Swineherds") and *Aislinge Œngusso* ("The Vision of Aengus"). In such manner is the "male" and brittle universe of the hero contained within the "female" and protean universe of "faery," as indeed the concentrated epic magnificence of the *Táin Bó Cuailnge* is contained within the entire and multifarious Ulster cycle. The world of Faery was more congenial to Stephens' penchant for fantasy. In tackling heroism Stephens was patriotically dutiful; in giving rein to his comic fantasy, as he does in his earlier novels, Stephens was dutiful, as we shall take note, to his own sovereign gifts.

The Mirror and the Mask
Further Strategies of Self-Escape

II

I am joined to the "Irishry" and I expect a counter-Renaissance.

—W. B. Yeats

The Self-Ancestral
The Mystical Strategy—AE

4

Mysticism and Millenarianism

Early in his career AE was as fascinated by Cuchulain and Deirdre as were the other revivalists. He wrote a play, *Deirdre,* in whose production in 1902 the name "Cuchulain," it has been said, was spoken for the first time in an Irish theatre.[1] Before that, he co-authored with an American, James Pryse ("Aretas"), a retelling of the Ulster cycle tale given to us by Lady Gregory, several years later, as "The Only Jealousy of Emer." "The Enchantment of Cuchullain" was serialized in *The Irish Theosophist* (1895–96), and the place of publication rightly suggests that AE was claiming for occult philosophy the hero of the cycle. AE's retelling remains, of course, the story of how Cuchulain is enfeebled through enchantment by Fand, a woman of the immortal Tuatha de Danann who is estranged from her husband Manannan mac Lir, the Irish seagod, and who has fallen in love with the Ulster champion. AE depicts the jealous love immortals entertain for mortals, and the seduction of humankind by the sidhe, twin motifs in ancient Irish and revival literatures. More enthusiastically than Lady Gregory, he also depicts the war of the sexes that is waged throughout the Ulster cycle and that so engaged James Stephens. The sexual conflict encourages AE, anticipating Stephens' *Deirdre,* to cast his narrative and dialogue in the psychological and realistic manner of a novel, but the descriptive, visionary set pieces provoke, by almost Pavlovian reflex, an overwritten, bogus mysticism and mythology.

It is probable that AE preferred to contemplate the state of visionary excitement and physical impotence into which Cuchulain temporarily falls than to contemplate the unmystical state of bodily and martial vigor the hero normally inhabits. In his enchantment Cuchulain has the vision proper to a messiah who according to his foster-father, Fergus, "shall rule the souls of men." He envisions the titanic wars waged in the past by the succeeding waves of gods in Ireland, including the Tuatha de Danann. Another character recounts the history of the sidhe and an ancient prophecy which Cuchulain, centuries later, will help to fulfill when, we are meant to infer, he is reborn at the beginning of the twentieth century:

> "We came to Eri many, many ages ago," said Labraid. "from a land the people of to-day hold no memory of. Mighty for good and for evil were the dwellers in that land, but its hour struck and the waters of the oceans entomb it. In this island, which the mighty Gods of Fire kept apart and sacred, we made our home. But after long years a day came when the wise ones must needs depart from this also. They went eastward. A few only remained to keep alive the tradition of what was, the hope of what will be again. For in this island, it is foretold, in future ages will arise a light which will renew the children of time"[2]

For AE it is insufficient that Cuchulain be a romance hero. Although the basic motifs of AE's retelling are analogous to those of romance, they are really the motifs of solar and messianic mythology, as an observation by Frye might remind us: "the hero of romance is analogous to the mythical Messiah or deliverer who comes from an upper world, and his enemy is analogous to the demonic powers of a lower world."[3] "The Enchantment of Cuchullain" bathes in the solar mythology beloved of Alfred Nutt, and the battle waged by the sidhe against their demon enemies is seen as a battle against the powers of darkness by the forces of light. Both Cuchulain the mortal and Manannan the immortal are associated with the sun which is portrayed as working in an apocalyptic cycle rather than merely seasonal rhythm. For AE, Lug the Irish sun god and not the mortal Conchobar is Cuchulain's father and alter ego.

AE's interpretation of the Ulster tale is in tune with the millenarian and messianic aspects of theosophy in Ireland. Seven years after AE published "The Enchantment of Cuchullain," Annie Besant in a Dublin lecture spoke of revelation and clairvoyance as part of a long process of racial evolution out of which Ireland will emerge as Europe's spiritual mentor.[4] It was not AE alone but the mystical section of the revival (itself a section of contemporary British transcendentalism) who pressganged Cuchulain and other legendary Irish heroes into the service of theosophy and related occultisms. Yeats, for example, claimed Cuchulain as a petal of his far-off, secret and inviolate Rose:

> . . . him
> Who met Fand walking among flaming dew,
> By a grey shore where the wind never blew,
> And lost the world and Emir for a kiss

just as he claimed St. Patrick, who in "The Old Men of the Twilight," a story in *The Secret Rose* (dedicated to AE and prefaced by a poem from which I have just quoted), is Druid Patrick, one more miracle worker in an ancient Ireland in which miracles were such little things. The Yeats staking these claims is not just the artist but a founder member of the Dublin Hermetic Society, begun in 1885, one year before the Theosophical Society was formed in Dublin. (His definition of poetry as "a revelation of a hidden life" made membership in secret societies—especially against the background of a symbolist aesthetic—a not unnatural thing.)[5] Where O'Grady held that through emulation something like Heroic Ireland could be fashioned again, his followers of more mystical turn believed that Heroic Ireland lived on invisibly, as the Tuatha de Danaan lived on after their defeat, as the sidhe. Heroic Ireland could be witnessed in vision and, if the mystical effort were intense enough, reincarnated. But vision and the triumph of the spirit over the dead letter of common life required elaborate preparation as the mystical effort required coordination and cooperation; hence the need for the various ritual orders.

It is probable, it seems to me, that occult rites at the same time satisfied the cruder need of some Protestants for ritual discipline, a need satisfied for the less demanding by Freemasonry and for the more orthodox by High Church Anglicanism. (Not irrelevantly, Yeats noted that Irish country people "often attribute magical powers to Orangemen and Freemasons.")[6] With Catholics, Anglo-Irish Protestants shared a disdain for puritanism, for which unscriptural ceremony is corrupt, a disdain Yeats expresses in "The Curse of the Fire and of the Shadows," one of the stories in *The Secret Rose*. At any rate, the fact is that the most famous leaders of Irish literary transcendentalism were Protestant—W. B. Yeats, AE, John Eglinton (W. K. Magee), James Stephens, James and Margaret Cousins, Charles Johnston. According to Gretta Cousins, Charlotte Despard, an Englishwoman, "was one of the rare Catholics who were Theosophists."[7]

That the most responsive and intellectual members of a declining ruling social class, such as the Anglo-Irish Ascendancy at the beginning of the twentieth century, would turn to a mysticism ritually organized by rank (and one, moreover, that co-opted in spirit the hierarchical society of heroic Ireland) does not seem to me surprising. It was in part a withdrawal through unconscious pique into esotericism, in part—and this could be ventured, *mutatis mutandis,* of the whole Anglo-Irish revival—an attempt to regain leadership (intellectual and cultural where moral and social leadership had faltered) by concealing new symbols of power in cabbalistic language and gesture.[8] Perhaps too the mystical advocates of self-transcendence found peculiarly receptive listeners among Anglo-Irish Protestants. Stephens, AE, Yeats, Synge—all were preoccupied with the transience of the self and the natural order and with the need to escape both, though not through the heroic self-destruction, in the sole cause of patriotism, that attracted Pearse. It is possible that the themes of self-escape and self-denial reflected the uncertainty of the Anglo-Irish role in any new Ireland, perhaps a degree of Protestant guilt, even self-disgust.

The cultural conditions perceived, and to some extent created, by the revivalists were those shared by most messianic and millenarian eruptions: the sense that society is at a hazardous crossroads and that the native culture is endangered by an alien culture; a resulting feeling of crisis and emergency; social, political and cultural instability; a bewildering choice among cultures and lifestyles. The expressive features, too, fit the pattern of messianic movements: a nostalgia for a golden age which, it is predicted, will return imminently; a general abandon and self-forgetfulness (group and individual) that can even encourage notions of self-sacrifice; spiritual renewal and the rejection of the materialism of the alien culture; apocalyptic visions vouchsafed to certain individuals. It was believed by some of the Irish revivalists that a messiah or avatar would soon arrive to renew the life of the society. AE wrote to Yeats in 1896 regarding this avatar: "Out of Ireland will arise a light to transform many ages and peoples. There is a hurrying of forces and swift things going out and I believe profoundly that a new Avatar is about to appear and in all spheres the forerunners go before him to prepare. It will be one of the kindly Avatars, who is at once ruler of men and magic sage. I had a vision of him some months ago and will know if he appears."[9] Ireland was seen as a land of destiny. James Stephens wrote to Stephen MacKenna: "The more I think of ourselves & our history (for our history seems to me more glorious than that of any other nation in the world) the more I believe that Ireland is a land of destiny where the gods are brooding their great events & that Ireland will be the beloved of the world in a way that no other nation ever has been. For such a birth there must be a long gestation & a hard travail, but we will wave yet in the winds of the world & all the people will call us blessed—So!"[10] Had Stephens reflected that he was echoing AE eighteen years after, he might simply have been convinced that indeed a long gestation was required for such a miraculous birth as they both envisaged.

Some of these cultural conditions and expressions are of course features of many highly sophisticated, carefully engineered and nonmessianic revivals and revolutions, and that the Irish revival takes its place among such movements is perhaps shown by the way in which its members virtually invented the submerged culture said to be in jeopardy and to be an alternative to the predominant and "alien" culture. For example, the West in which the nature culture was said to be making its last stand was a largely fictional one; not in the actual, primitive, and indeed endangered West but in the sophisticated East was the revival really taking place. Yet the descriptions of apocalyptic visions that lace revival literature, fictional and nonfictional alike, suggest resemblances to those messianic movements that have struck primitive peoples, for example the North American Indians in the 1880s and the Melanesians in this century.[11] In all three cases there was an elemental and visionary religion, either native or foreign, from which the messianism could spring. In the case of Ireland, it was an evangelical Protestantism. Vivian Mercier has pointed out that many of the leaders of the revival were of Church of Ireland background and has identified the Evangelical movement in nineteenth-century Anglicanism as one of the root-strands of the Irish revival.[12] Enthusiastic cultural activity became for some Irish Protestants a substitute for "an intellectually insupportable evangelic fundamentalism," as another scholar has put it.[13] Protestant writers transformed the vestiges of Christian revival into the secular revivals of the Gaelic language and culture, Anglo-Irish literature, folklore, the occult, and, in the end, a spiritualized and encultured Irish nation.

Of course, the leaders of the revival cannot be regarded as the social equivalents of oppressively colonized Melanesians or endangered North American natives. Even those who felt most conscious of oppression by the English administration, Catholics such as William O'Brien, D. P. Moran, or Patrick Pearse, were educated representatives of a people and culture that did not face extinction. However, it is as if by a strange division of labour and cultural symbiosis the Protestant revivalists in their political decline supplied the visions for a relatively inarticulate but rising native Irishry.

The Interpreters: *A Novel Symposium*

In mysticism and millenarianism, then, can be seen one of the responses of revival writers to political and social flux in Ireland. There were others, though for several revivalists, notably AE, mysticism was the final and desirable response. Even if it is sometimes seen as monolithic (a view of which I may be guilty myself), the Irish revival was in fact a complex of attitudes and achievements, some of them sharing no more than a family resemblance, others engaged in downright contradiction. At its least nationalistic, the revival was an island chapter of mainland intellectual radicalism, the most graphic and succinct evidence of this that I am acquainted with being the joint autobiography of James Cousins, the Ulster poet and dramatist, and his wife, the Roscommon champion of women's rights, Margaret Cousins. *We Two Together* (1950) makes it clear how wide were the radical interests of the more advanced revivalists: the Cousinses were involved in astrology, theosophy and psychicism, in vegetarianism, agricultural cooperatives, mythology, Gaelic language revival, dramatic revival, the suffragette movement, poetry, anti-imperialist agitation, physical regenerationism, and anti-vivisectionism. But the book also unwittingly makes it clear that it was only the Dublin of a certain set (and a certain set apart, we may add) that wove this veritable nest of heterodoxies, and that the social and intellectual base of the movement was extremely narrow: the same names drop again and again when the supporters of this plurality of interests are mentioned. Moreover, to the advanced thinkers of the revival, the interests were by no means, in Louis MacNeice's phrase, "incorrigibly plural," and they set as their supreme goal realization of the ultimate and essential unity of the cosmos and of self-transcending existence. Little wonder, then, given the nature of the final objective and the comparatively small repertory company the revival represented, that the movement has seemed to succeeding generations a monolithic one, despite the fact that variety is its chief immediate characteristic.

Indeed, not even the Cousinses in their kaleidoscopic enthusiasm exhausted the total range of available revival attitudes, literary or social. Should further proof be required of the variety and experimentalism of cultural opinion abroad during the revival, I would direct readers to AE's *The Interpreters* (1922), itself a curious recruit to the ranks of fictional experiment, and a book AE thought his best prose work. Here, in more mature fashion than AE had previously achieved, are displayed the splintering philosophies of the revival and the simultaneous drive for philosophical, ultimately mystical unity. Here also is the preoccupation with the self—heroic, protean, needful of mastery and supersession, the whole stimulated by AE's meditation on the Easter Rising, the revival's key military event, turned emblem.

AE calls his work a "symposium," and it has some affinity with that classical form and with such a modern version of it as Dryden's *Essay of Dramatic Poesy* (1668). He had contemplated such a form as early as 1909 when he wrote to H. G. Wells, wondering that Wells had not thought of writing "a symposium upon science like the *Banquet* of Plato . . . one would require the slightest scenario."[14] There is, however, greater narrative and descriptive content in *The Interpreters* than in Dryden's work, and we may speak of it as something very close to a novel. It is set some centuries in the future, "so that," according to AE in the Preface, "ideals over which there is conflict today might be discussed divested of passion and apart from transient circumstance."[15] This was a forlorn hope, deliberately so or otherwise.

It is true that although the discussion takes place in a jail cell in the aftermath of an abortive insurrection, there is little that is clear in the reader's mind in the way of material events. What is said early on about these events as they strike the chief character, the poet-rebel Lavelle, extends to the novel's welter of ideas as they at first strike the reader: "Of the physical conflict in the arsenal the poet remembered little. It was blurred to his intellect by excess of energy or passion as objects are blurred to the eyes by excess of light" (p. 8). However, it could only have escaped the most sheltered of readers that AE had re-created in his own peculiar way the Easter Rebellion: "A world empire was in trouble. A nation long restless under its rule had resurrected ancient hopes, and this young man with many others was bent on a violent assertion of his right to freedom" (p. 2). The times are reproduced in detail—despite the poetic blur of AE's prose—down to the theosophical adventuring in which AE himself had been involved: "It was an era of arcane speculation, for science and philosophy had become esoteric after the visible universe had been ransacked and the secret of its being had eluded the thinkers" (p. 70). And, thinking no doubt of 1916 and subsequent events in Ireland that so angered Yeats, AE has one of his characters remark: "You will find . . . that every great conflict has been followed by an era of materialism in which the ideals for which the conflict ostensibly was waged were submerged. The gain if any was material. The loss was spiritual" (p. 136). The spiritual is AE's professed concern: "Those who take part in the symposium," he tells us in the Preface, "suppose of the universe that it is a spiritual being and they inquire what relation the politics of Time may have to the politics of Eternity" (p. vii). Equally might it be said that the symposiasts inquire into the role of the self in the spiritual and political systems of the universe.

Since the speakers as well as the setting can be fairly readily identified, *The Interpreters* can be called *roman à clef.* However, it is the ideas associated with or suggested to AE by the historical figures, and not the figures themselves (more than one of whom can in the novel inhabit the same fictional body), that are important. The plot too is mere scaffolding for the discussion. Lavelle's band of rebels commandeer a city arsenal, only to find that the unguarded gates were a trap. The band is captured and jailed. During the night, other rebel leaders are ushered into the jail cell. Over the city, airships, "winged shapes of dusk and glitter," maneuver to quell the insurrection, and we recognize in them not only futuristic airplanes but also the extraterrestrial winged beings that swarmed through AE's visions and paintings.[16] Meanwhile the captives argue, each speaker being given by AE and the others the opportunity of outlining without interruption his philosophy.

For most of the novel, Lavelle is recognizable as Patrick Pearse. He holds a spiritual theory of nationality which according to the sceptic rebel, Leroy, would lead to theocracy if implemented. This theory Lavelle has derived from the history of his nation "which began among the gods"; and from history (really mythology) he turned to literature and thence politics and insurrection. The "unity of character" and "national culture" of his country are traceable, almost uniquely among nations, back to the divine origin of things and today are vested especially in the peasant. Beside his country and his race he professes to account himself of little importance, except as a self-sacrificial helper in the national cause: "He was one of those who suffer on behalf of their nation that agony which others feel over personal misfortunes" (p. 33). It cheers Lavelle to think of the rebels dying for country, and he denies that the moment of death is the moment of self-extinction: "No, no . . . The self had already perished, for they had abandoned themselves to the genius of their race and it was captain of their souls. The last of life they knew was the rapture of sacrifice" (p. 102). The ancestral self is all.

At times Lavelle would seem to shade into Yeats. Like Yeats Lavelle believes that his country is unusual in not having to turn to other ancient cultures, such as those of the Greek and Jew, for its cosmogony, mythology, and culture. For the inhabitants of most countries "distant lands are made sacred, but not the air they breathe:" Milton's "Heaven-world," for example, "is rootless and unreal and not very noble phantasy" (p. 62), remarks that echo Yeats's sentiments and AE's own conviction that Christianity had robbed Ireland of a pantheon of native divinities and exported the sacred realm to an exotic afterlife. The revivalists considered themselves to be engaged in the task of repatriating Irish culture and spirituality after centuries of "exile" and of being displaced by foreign faiths and systems. And like Yeats, Lavelle is sadly aware of "how little high traditions move the people" (p. 13).

Certainly AE had Yeats rather than Pearse in mind when telling how the work of one of the captives, an imaginative historian, "had been followed by creative writers like Lavelle, in whom the submerged river of nationality again welled up shining and life-giving" (p. 41). Brehon the imaginative historian is Standish James O'Grady. (Brehon, Irish *breathamh:* an ancient Irish judge; Brehon law is the code of law which prevailed in Ireland before its occupation by the English. The ancient Irish connection between judge and bard is also implied in the name.)[17] Lavelle has come to believe (like AE himself, author of an essay entitled "The Hero in Man") that "The heroic is the deep reality in you and all of us," as he tells a fellow captive, and is implanted and reawakened through "the ennobling influence of heroic story" and of "the dream of the ancestors" that Brehon first made available to the poet's generation. Brehon is in jail because the authorities consider it better he be out of the way while the trouble continues (putting all the rebel luminaries together in one cell would seem to be an odd way of going about quelling the revolution), but, in fact, like O'Grady, "after his history had appeared, the historian seemed to take no interest in the great movement he had inspired. He became absorbed in more abstruse studies, the nature of which was known to but few among his countrymen" (pp. 41–42). Brehon's participation in the symposium is not only AE's salute to O'Grady, but also AE's reminder to the aloof historian that he bears some considerable responsibility for the events of 1916 and after.

As he is meant to do, the figure of Leroy blows a breeze of scepticism and cynicism through the proceedings. He is perhaps in part Oliver St. John Gogarty, but because he is a "fantastical humorist," he may also be in part James Stephens, as Henry Summerfield suggests, and because an individualist, perhaps too John Eglinton.[18] And being the greatest shape-changer in the novel, despite or because of his theory of individualism, he might also be in part James Joyce. Leroy has Joyce's self-possession, believing his vision to be as valid as the next man's, whatever institutional weight or theory of divinity lies behind the next man's, and he shares Joyce's parallactic and relativistic perspective. "You, if you dreamed," he tells Lavelle, "would see a vision so beautiful that you would imagine it was a vision of Paradise, but it would be no less of yourself than my fantasy" (p. 25). Leroy has taken part in the revolution despite himself, and this reminds us of the surprising militancy of Gogarty and Stephens, as well perhaps as of that residual patriotism that made Joyce fiercely and proudly Irish. In the aftermath of insurrection Leroy prefers reason to heroic passion and, Stephen Dedalus-like, considers it absurd to exchange the shackles of colonialism for the shackles of socialism or theocratic nationalism offered him by his fellow captives. "The cosmic consciousness I conceive to be an autocracy gradually resolving itself into a democracy of free spirits" (p. 69). His belief in freedom sustains his cynicism; in a prediction fulfilled by the fate of Yeats's poetry if not O'Grady's history, he tells Lavelle: "Your poetry and Brehon's History will be favourite studies in imperial circles in a few years" (p. 33). It also sustains an arrogance reminiscent of Stephen Dedalus': "You may think of me as a rebel angel . . . I am in revolt against Heaven" (p. 110). Leroy is the only interpreter who believes in the unadorned and freestanding self, and he entertains the notion of dying in the insurrection so that in the moments before death all his ideas and feelings would return to him "and I could be my entire self if but for a few seconds" (p. 103), a fate enjoyed symbolically and under different circumstances by Gabriel Conroy in Joyce's long story, "The Dead."

Very much in contrast to this hope, the somewhat sentimental socialist impulses of another captive, Culain, came into being when an old woman in the tenement where he was raised "wept a quarter of an hour or so before she died being unable to rise and give help to another. That self-forgetfulness when the self was passing from life seemed to me to be wonderful" (p. 86). He elaborates: "Whatever makes us clutch at the personal, whatever strengthens the illusion of separateness, whether it be the possession of wealth, or power over the weak, or fear of the strong, all delay the awakening from this pitiful dream of life by fostering a false egoism" (p. 89), an illusion shared outside the novel by O'Grady in his homage to strong heroes as well as by Culain's more evident opponents within the novel. Like Lavelle, Culain—James Connolly and Jim Larkin in thin disguise—believes in an ancestral self, but it is that of humanity and not just that of the individual race or nation. Culain is opposed to nationalism ("we would not be in this struggle merely to exchange world masters for nation masters," p. 37), but makes common cause with Lavelle as Connolly made common cause with Pearse at Easter 1916. His name has been chosen well. Culain is of course the smith whose watchdog young Cuchulain, when called Setanta, kills and replaces (hence Cuchulain, the Hound of Culain). "Smith" is a common name that sits well with Culain's socialism; a smith is also a manual worker of the kind championed by Culain (Connolly). Connolly had sympathy with the Gaelic Revival, and AE had a social, even socialistic interest in the old sagas, both of which make felicitous AE's use of the Cuchulain saga as a source of his socialist's name.

If Leroy is unique in his advocacy of self, Heyt is unique in his military imperialism. Heyt is "president of the Air Federation," whose airships now beleaguer the rebels (Heyt = height?), and has been arrested in error, conveniently for the symposium. In his anti-labor views and lofty arrogance (another kind of height), he conjures up the figure of William Martin Murphy, the industrial magnate and leader of the Employers' Federation against whom Larkin's strike during the Dublin lockout of 1913 was directed. Beyond Irish commercialism, Heyt is enlarged into British imperial power and the bureaucracy and centralization AE railed against in his essay, "Ideals of the New Rural Society."[19] And this is not all. Heyt's ideal society is the world state which "will absorb its romantics," like Lavelle, Culain, and Brehon, "and transmute emotion into wisdom" (p. 72). Whereas Leroy is for variety among individuals and Lavelle for variety among nations, Heyt is for total uniformity, and human evolution he sees as "the eternal revealing of the Self to the selves" (p. 73). In what seems to be a contradiction, Heyt upbraids Leroy for nourishing "a fantastic conception of freedom" while, according to Heyt, every cell in the sceptic's body and every atom of nature stirs with impulses beyond Leroy's control. Yet Heyt defines the will as power, as the self, "the king principle in our being." But the paradox is resolved: "The will," says Heyt, "grows stronger by self-suppression than in self assertion."

That the figure of Heyt does not prove an anomaly or imbalance in AE's symposium is due to the fact that where power and self-denial are concerned, Heyt speaks language Culain and Lavelle can readily understand. Indeed, AE himself believed that we must cultivate power and an unshakeable will if we are to scale the heavens, but that we must do so by purifying our being into selflessness so that the energy of the awakening power be not misdirected.[20] Heyt, on the other hand, cultivates power and will for unspiritual ends and suppresses others rather than suppressing himself. He threatens to take paradise by storm. Heyt, however, belongs philosophically and even spiritually in AE's world by being an object of that "inverted love that is hate" and a "perverted hindrance that is truly helpful," an enemy who like many enemies can be "dearer to you than ever your friend can be."[21] These are notions attributed to AE by James Stephens and in an earlier reminiscence Stephens recalled a belief of AE's that would suggest that a vigorous symposium like *The Interpreters* was a literary form especially congenial to AE: "It was his belief that we travel through life and time with our own company of friends and enemies. That there is a small clan of personages, and that this is the real family. The wives, husbands and children of such a person are almost unimportant, almost accidental."[22] And, interestingly enough, the family is not nearly so important in revival fiction as it is in post-revival Irish fiction, though Joyce and Stephens are important exceptions. Why not? One answer may be that the ideological and philosophical business of the revival precluded more mundane concerns, which may be, indeed, one reason why the revival did not produce a body of fiction recognizably novelistic.

The Interpreters *as Autobiography*

A virtual handbook of attitudes in revival Ireland, *The Interpreters* is, just as absorbingly, AE's philosophical autobiography, and as such more interesting in form than most autobiographies. For in the independent theories we can trace to real holders, AE contrived to reflect the various facets of his own complexity. In a very sincere fashion, he shared many of the attitudes of the fictional symposiasts with their real-life models. There is a good deal of AE in Leroy's shifting viewpoints, as well as in Leroy's championing of "the freedom of the local community" (p. 76), and in Leroy's intellectual remove, a version of which enables AE to re-create, rather fairly, contradictory, occasionally distasteful ideas. Culain's socialism is a heightened and urban equivalent of AE's involvement with the rural cooperative movement, while Culain's contempt for separateness and egotism accords with AE's blueprint for the ideal rural society: "The first thing to do," AE asserted, "is to create and realize the feeling for the community, and break up the evil and petty isolation of man from man."[23] AE supported the Dublin strike of 1913 in which Connolly was involved and spoke on behalf of it at a rally in the Albert Hall, London. We also see in Rian the architect something of AE the painter.[24]

The relationship with Brehon and Lavelle is more complex. Towards the end of the symposium Brehon, perhaps in his judicial role, is given thirty pages in which to sum up his philosophy, and in so doing he ceases to be O'Grady and becomes AE. He labors to harmonize the divergent views he has listened to, delivering himself of the judgment that only Leroy, the self-sufficing and anarchic man asserting absolute kingship over his own being, is on the true path, since only anarchy correctly founded guarantees justice—not only for the individual but for congregations of men, including nations: "The external law imposed by the greatest of states must finally give way before the instinct for self-rule which alone is consonant with the dignity and divinity of man" (p. 125). Yet Leroy *(le roi)* will not attain his full stature until he comprehends "the spiritual foundations on which other political theories rest, and can build on them as do the devotees of beauty or love or power" (p. 125). Once the spiritual ideal was a widespread reality during a Golden Age (O'Grady's heroic period, presumably) before it gave way to "the terrible and material powers ruling in the Iron Age" (p. 175), by which Lavelle seems to mean the "Anglo-Saxon" age of industry and the megalopolis. Now it is simply that, an ideal, but it must not on pain of loss be striven for or defended by material means such as those employed by the insurrectionists. The goal is psychic evolution towards self-fulfillment that sheds interest in the politics of time and awakens and attracts spiritual powers and elements akin to our expanding consciousness.

Although Lavelle earlier protested that "all distinctions of nationality seem to dissipate in a haze in this transcendentalism" (p. 143), he is finally converted to Brehon's position. Before the guards come to release Heyt whose side will be the probable winner of the material battle raging outside, Lavelle stands in Brehonic contemplation: "Everything was understood. Everything was loved. Everything was forgiven. He knew after that exaltation he could never be the same again. Never could he be fierce or passionate" (p. 177). The exaltation has caused him in the light of Brehon's transcendentalism to add a final section to a poem he had written before the rising and believed finished.

The poem, "Michael," a curious piece of over four hundred lines in four-beat couplets with stylistic elements from Wordsworth, Yeats, and Pearse and which has the same kind of importance for *The Interpreters* as has Stephen's villanelle for *A Portrait of the Artist,* is a verse *immram* (or voyage tale) and *fís* (or vision tale). Lavelle's title hero lives in the west of Ireland in a cabin where old tales are told, and embarks on a visionary voyage that closely resembles the voyages of *Immram Brain (The Voyage of Bran)* and *Immram Maíle Dúin (The Voyage of Maelduin),* both medieval tales. The journey amidst glimmering isles and cloudy seas filled with mythic forms is a spiritual pilgrimage on which Michael is vouchsafed a momentary sight of paradise. Since phrases from the journey echo phrases from the beginning of *The Interpreters* describing Lavelle's journey to the city, *Immram Michíl* (as we might call it) repeats (or prefigures) Lavelle's own spiritual journey in the course of the symposium towards the momentary and exalting vision of the spiritual destination and ideal provided by Brehon.

After his voyage, Michael can be found drudging in a dark, Dublin-like city; in the city he meets a Donegal Gaelic speaker, one of "The army of the Gaelic mind, / Still holding through the Iron Age / The spiritual heritage." In the company of Gaelic Leaguers he reads the old stories, including the one about he "who with his single sword / Stayed a great army at the ford"—Cuchulain. Then—for Lavelle's *immram* is set several centuries before in early twentieth century Ireland—Michael takes part in an Easter rebellion. Since this part of the poem was written before Lavelle's insurrection, the poet when he used the phrase about sacrificial rapture in describing the dying rebels outside the jail (p. 102) was quoting his own poem ("Yet Michael felt within him rise / The rapture that is sacrifice," 169), a rather Pearsian touch. In death, Michael has a last vision of the mystic isles he once saw momentarily and ends "afloat upon the heavenly seas."

The poem is a clever use of the *immram* and *fís* as a mold into which the content of Pearse's career is poured. But now, having heard Brehon (AE), Lavelle adds a harmonic new ending in which the slayer and the slain are pictured united and the be-all and end-all of life are seen as one spirituality "to which all life is journeying." In short, Lavelle becomes AE, that most myriad-minded and peacemaking of the revivalists. Having like some romance shape-changer shattered himself into the fragments of his diverse activities and beliefs, fleshed out as simulacra of real people, AE recomposes himself into a harmonic self-conception. It is as if in writing *The Interpreters* AE had kept in mind what Yeats wrote to him in 1898: "You are face to face with the heterogeneous, and the test of one's harmony is our power to absorb it and make it harmonious."[25]

But long before this letter, George Russell had taken for his pseudonym Aeon, the name of a mythical figure he later said "mirrored himself in chaos and became the lord of our world."[26] *The Interpreters* is a restatement of AE's mystical approach to the practical and intellectual world: the conception of himself and of Ireland at which he arrives is of a man and a nation whose self-fulfilment is self-transcendence, participation in the All. The temporal and the immortal, the human and the eternal are resolved; so too are politics and spirituality, Ireland and the universe of nations. It is a resolution of that conflict between self and alterity that underlay the Irish literary revival and for which the question of national identity was catalyst and metaphor. As a resolution it is as effective as that of W. B. Yeats in his later poetry and James Joyce in his fiction, if perhaps not as impressive because less fictional and imaginative, more philosophical.

For *The Interpreters* is not really a novel, as AE in his Preface admits. "I was not interested in the creation of characters but in tracking political moods back to spiritual origins." To do this he uses the symposium which seems an appropriate form for the democratic side of AE. It is AE who comes closest of all the revivalists to recalling, through an encyclopedic interest and refined concern for humanity, the ethos of Renaissance humanism. "Most of the Renaissance humanists," observes Northrop Frye, "show a strong sense of importance of symposium and dialogue."[27] However, Frye identifies symposium and dialogue as "the social and educational aspects respectively of an elite culture." For the form to accommodate AE's other side, the transcendentalist, was not so difficult, given the association of the symposium with Plato; but it did require AE to draw the characters into the unanimity of his own dominant voice, which, though it might be autobiographically satisfying, sacrificed (especially in the case of Brehon, who changes shamelessly from O'Grady into the author) any autonomy of character: It also sacrificed AE's humanism on the altar of AE's mysticism. *The Interpreters* at the end and upon a second reading becomes less a symposium than a transformation and imitation of the prehumanist *immram*. It is a spiritual and philosophical journey in which, until Brehon's high nonsensical words and Lavelle's exaltation on hearing them, various philosophical positions on a map of the intellect take the role of place in the spiritual landscape of the *immrama*. *The Interpreters* is a voyage tale where ideas, not places, are visited, but one that ends in a vision whose resemblance to the *fisi* is more literal. In that vision, contraries are harmonized in "the multitudinous meditation which is the universe."[28]

In the same year *The Interpreters* was published, Yeats wrote that AE was one of those men who cannot possess "Unity of Being" because "so far from seeking an anti-self, a Mask that delineates a being in all things the opposite to their natural state can but seek the suppression of the anti-self, till the natural state alone remains."[29] But unity in mystical vision AE certainly achieved and tried hard in *The Interpreters* to relay to us. His natural state was so various that it gave the appearance of a display of masks, even if these did not superimpose themselves into Yeats's ultimate Mask or Anti-Self. Yet despite the book's capacious inquiry, nowhere among the ideas can be found an unspiritual, realistic concept of nationality, let alone of that minority nationality that AE's native Protestant Ulster began to embrace during his lifetime. Further, there is no contemplation of a country's partition (even if it were contemplated only to be rejected) that was a fresh reality in Ireland the year *The Interpreters* appeared; nor of the inconvenient intractability of sectarian identity and conflict. Nowhere among the contraries can be found one that reflects the vividness of AE's own case: George Russell's Ulster, planter background and early development (the one self that is conspicuously absent as a candidate for interpretation) and AE's southern Irish, mystical, nationalist foreground and accomplishment.[30] It is the one contrary that is fairly crying out to be harmonized and destined under compulsion of the revival to cry in vain.

The Path of the Chameleon 5
The Symbolist Strategy—W. B. Yeats

I was lost in that region a cabalistic manuscript shown me by MacGregor Mathers had warned me of; astray upon the path of the Chameleon.

—*W. B. Yeats*

Hazardous Pursuits of Self-Transcendence: The Apocalyptic Stories

Despite Cuchulain's association with James Connolly in *The Interpreters,* it was the dream aspect of the Ulster cycle, the enchantments and visitations of the sidhe, more than the mortal heroisms, that appealed to the mystical revivalists, or rather to the mystical inclinations of writers who were in reality immensely versatile. Whereas Cuchulain for O'Grady stood for heroic manhood, for AE he generally stood for spiritual beauty and for Yeats creative joy separated from fear.[1] In their more mystical moments the writers preferred the stories of the Mythological cycle and the unearthly tales of the Fenian cycle to those of the Ulster cycle. The west of Ireland was closely associated with the supernaturalism of the ancient narratives, and it was in the west (on a lake isle) that Yeats, Maud Gonne, William Sharp ("Fiona MacLeod"), MacGregor Mathers, AE, and others planned to found an Order of Celtic Mysteries, a ritual conjunction of the mystical and the native Irish.

Of the fiction with which Yeats experimented from the late 1880s until 1904 (and this is the bulk of his unfairly neglected fictional output), this conjunction is especially evident in *The Secret Rose* (1897) and those stories at first meant to be a part of that volume—that is, the Red Hanrahan stories (removed from the volume in 1908 but published separately in any case in 1904), and the three formidable stories with which Yeats meant to bring *The Secret Rose* to a conclusion: "Rosa Alchemica" (the sole story of the three included in the 1897 volume), "The Tables of the Law," and "The Adoration of the Magi" (both of which the publisher of the 1897 volume disliked; they were privately printed together the same year).

Augustine Martin has made a strong case for *The Secret Rose* in its originally conceived and inclusive format (nineteen stories in all) being a unified work of art. The unities he perceives are those of theme (the theme Yeats announced in his dedication to AE, that is, the war of spiritual with natural order), historical perspective ("the book takes us progressively from pagan times to the end of the nineteenth century," says Martin), geographical focus (the west of Ireland), symbolism (the rose and the cross), and apocalyptic vision (in which each story and the projected volume as a whole culminate).[2] Even should Martin be right, there is still good cause for regarding "Rosa Alchemica," "The Tables of the Law," and "The Adoration of the Magi" as a compact trio, even trilogy; these remarkable stores are usually referred to as "the apocalyptic stories" in which the theme of apocalypse is, as Martin remarks, "overt and salient."

The events in the three apocalyptic stories form in the life of the narrator a chronological sequence, while the main events and characters of each story are referred to in the others. The plot is repeated from one story to the next: the narrator is reluctantly drawn into the vortex of the "Celtic Order of the Alchemical Rose" from which each time he emerges only half-initiated and half-illuminated but irrevocably altered. The ostensible protagonist in each story is an adept who tries to convert the narrator but ends the story exiled or dead. Through the trilogy the narrator's strength to resist the potent blandishments of the sect seems to increase, yet we sense that his alteration also increases. One theme of all three stories is the combat between Eleusis and Calvary, Celtic mysticism and Christianity, a combat which elsewhere Yeats resolved by absorbing Christianity into a larger mystical scheme of things. These two kinds of spirituality are in turn set over against the natural order, other complicating guises of this opposition being the tussles between the mythological and the heroic, the classical and the romantic, the Renaissance and the medieval. Spirituality, however, especially of the esoteric kind, is presented as extremely dangerous when one's pursuit of it is flawed, as is that of Michael Robartes and Owen Aherne.

The careers of these men seem to reenact "a familiar tragedy in occult history," as A. R. Orage called Nietzsche's career, that is, carrying into the occult world "the attachment and the desire that emphatically belong to the world of both Good and Evil" and attempting, in a variation of Heyt's flaw in *The Interpreters,* to take Heaven "by egotistic storm."[3] Precisely how far the narrator himself, occupying the hazardous condition of unfinished initiation, is threatened by this danger is left ambiguous, and this serves to make him the dominant character of the trilogy: the one for whom that which is at stake in the outcome of the stories—the maintenance of natural selfhood or the achievement of spiritual self-transcendence—is still in the balance by trilogy's end. Whereas *The Interpreters* and "The Enchantment of Cuchullain" are stories of successful self-transcendence, Yeats's three stories depict the peril of attempt and pain of incompletion. We witness the damage to a life dedicated to the pursuit, by magical rather than mystical means, of the Mask or Image.[4] Like the hero of Yeats's only novel, *The Speckled Bird,* the narrator of the apocalyptic stories is lost on the "path of the Chameleon" that leads to wisdom or bewilderment.[5] But that self-transcendence is a good, there is nevertheless no doubt.

Having been enticed into joining the Alchemical order that he had refused to join in Paris when he was a fellow student of Michael Robartes, the narrator of "Rosa Alchemica" takes a mysterious journey to the west of Ireland in Robartes' company. The narrator is still under the effects of Robartes' seductive invocations, and the west he sees is one continuous with his own inner tumult, "for the grey waves, plumed with scudding foam, had grown part of a teeming, fantastic inner life";[6] when they reach the Temple of the Alchemical Rose he is "possessed with the phantasy that the sea, which kept covering it with showers of white foam, was claiming it as part of some indefinite and passionate life, which had begun to war upon our orderly and careful days, and was about to plunge the world into a night as obscure as that which followed the downfall of the classical world" (p. 122). An apt site for revelation, Robartes' west, like that of the Irish cultural nationalists, is more specifically the abode of Ireland's pre-Christian spiritual presences. "The visions and speculations of Ireland differ much from those of England and France," Yeats wrote, "for in Ireland, as in Highland Scotland, we are never far from the old Celtic mythology."[7]

But the Dagda, Lug, Aengus, Bodb, and other "heroic children of Dana" cannot reign again, according to Robartes, "till there have been martyrdoms and victories, and perhaps even that long-foretold battle of the Valley of the Black Pig" (p. 124), a notion beside which we might set Pearse's later appeals for national sacrifice. Unlike Pearse and other nationalists, however, Yeats, AE, and the theosophists wanted to connect a nativist concern for Irish mythology with a concern for the universal, subterranean traditions of hermetic philosophy. Thus the Order of the Alchemical Rose was, we are informed, begun by six students "of Celtic descent," but this does not conflict with the arcana in the Temple library, since Yeats believed that "Ireland was not separated from general European speculation when much of that was concerned with the supernatural."[8] He thought too that there must once have been in Ireland many alchemists; he even claimed that "the seventeenth century English translation of Cornelius Agrippa's *De Occulta Philosophia* was once so famous that it found its way into the hands of Irish farmers and wandering Irish tinkers."[9] We might say that the west of Robartes is, to borrow the language of *A Vision,* an "antithetical" or aristocratic one imposed on the "primary" or democratic (or peasant) west, and we might easily extend this description to the west of Yeats himself and certain other revivalists.

Against this occult west is set the old Dublin in which the narrator lives when Robartes seeks him out. Robartes believes it is impossible to live except by forgetting oneself either in the bustle of the impure multitude of men (who compose the transient natural order) or amidst the pure multitude of those who govern this world (and compose the immortal spiritual order) and have their headquarters by the western waves. The narrator has done neither. His ancestors, who lived in the Dublin house and had made it "almost famous through their part in the politics of the city and their friendships with the famous men of their generations" (p. 106), including Swift "joking and railing" and John Philpot Curran "telling stories and quoting Greek," clearly chose the first way of life. The narrator is not an entirely worthy descendant. He has compromised by living in the house yet removing from his rooms the historical portraits, shutting out with peacock tapestries "all history and activity untouched with beauty and peace," and replacing them with exquisite aesthetic ornaments to passion and rapture.

The narrator has compromised in other ways. For his alchemy is a chemical reality but, beyond that, merely artistic metaphor. The "little work" he has written on the subject, *Rosa Alchemica,* is "a fanciful reverie over the transmutation of life into art, and a cry of measureless desire for a world made wholly of essences" (p. 106). But the narrator has surrounded himself with the mere vestments of mysticism; he is destitute, like some aesthete, of personal and spiritual conviction. He is merely ego, living a lie, holding himself apart by force of intellect and exercise of aesthetic taste, "individual, indissoluble, a mirror of polished steel" (p. 107). In his life he expresses not what the Upanishads according to Yeats call "that ancient Self" and what AE called "the self-ancestral" that the mystical revivalists sought, but instead individual intellect that those revivalists, in part because they sought to be truly Irish, considered an enemy.[10] It is as if Yeats is portraying a dilettantish version of himself, as is Joyce by creating Gabriel Conroy in "The Dead." The narrator's intellect will not allow him to forsake the definite world which he is of the opinion the minds of great men (such as Joyce, he might two decades later have instanced) reflect "with indifferent precision like a mirror." Even in his highest moments, he is "two selves, the one watching with heavy eyes the other's moment of content" (p. 108).

Robartes breaks in upon the narrator's unsatisfactory life. He causes the narrator to fall into a waking dream and sweeps him into the terrifying indefinite world barely contained or controlled by the mystical Order. The mirror, cries a disembodied voice, is broken into numberless pieces. "I was being lifted out of the tide of flame, and felt my memories, my hopes, my thoughts, my will, everything I held to be myself, melting away." (p. 118) It is after this he accompanies Robartes to the west and takes part in an initiation ceremony. He is robed and given a censer whose fumes induce a dream that brilliantly images the loss of identity the ceremony is meant to symbolize and achieve: "I put my hand to the handle, but the moment I did so the fumes of the incense, helped perhaps by [Robartes'] mysterious glamour, made me fall again into a dream, in which I seemed to be a mask, lying on the counter of a little Eastern shop. Many persons, with eyes so bright and still that I knew them for more than human, came in and tried me on their faces, but at last flung me into a corner with a little laughter; but all this passed in a moment, for when I awoke my hand was still upon the handle" (p. 131). Before the ceremony proper is over, he awakens also from the induced slumber of the ritual to hear the local people, for whom the members of the Order are idolaters, breaking down the doors of the Temple. The narrator escapes after failing to rouse Robartes and the others who are, we are permitted to infer, stoned to death.

If indeed he is killed, as Yeats in his poem "The Phases of the Moon" has Robartes claim he was meant to be, does Robartes thereby achieve one of the martyrdoms he believed necessary before the birth of the new dispensation can be induced? For "when we die," he had forecast, "it shall be the consummation of the supreme work" (p. 123); or was it needless death after all, the impotent result of arrogant folly and blind, yet wilful excess? The counter-Renaissance, counter-Christian order that Robartes predicts and desires the narrator comes to believe at the end of each of the three apocalyptic stories to be a creation of the devil, and he hopes fearfully that it may be an evadable one. We are meant, I think, to assume that the narrator's belief has been influenced by the instructive fate and opinions of Owen Aherne, central figure of "The Tables of the Law," a would-be repentant member of the Order broken by misery, incapable of escaping the spirits he has summoned forth, believing himself to have wickedly served Him whose name is legion. Certainly it would seem that neither Robartes nor Aherne can represent the way to truth, if only because one apparently dies an ignominious death while the other ends his days in misery and probable exile. Though we must not forget that ignominy and exile can for Yeats betoken spiritual triumph, nor that excess is a "vivifying spirit" primitive and Celtic in origin.[11]

The narrator in telling his stories is engaged in trying to dissolve the lingering influence of Robartes and Aherne; likewise of the three old, Gaelic-speaking brothers in "The Adoration of the Magi" who live on a western island reading classical writers and are able to converse in French. The brothers hear by disembodied voice of the death of Robartes and envision a dying female adept in Paris where they then journey—convinced nonetheless that they have been deceived by devils—to hear "secret powerful names" and revelations about the symbols of the sidhe. The narration in the three apocalyptic stories is, then, a species of exorcism. "I have let some years go by before writing out this story," the narrator informs us in "The Adoration of the Magi," "for I am always in dread of the illusions which come of that inquietude of the veil of the Temple, which M. Mallarmé considers a characteristic of our times; and only write it now because I have grown to believe that there is no dangerous idea which does not become less dangerous when written out in sincere and careful English" (p. 168). This exorcism is a kind of literary counter-ceremony and counterrevelation, but it is unclear how successful the exorcism is.

For although the narrator seems growingly confirmed in his opposition to the Order, he does not seek self-forgetfulness among the impure multitudes of common men as an alternative to union with the pure multitudes (that unappeasable host); indeed, he has become more reclusive even than before, and his writings, as he tells us at the opening of "Rosa Alchemica," "have grown less popular and less intelligible, and driven me almost to the verge of taking the habit of St. Dominic." (Yeats's own writings were during the eighteen-nineties becoming less popular, more inscrutable.) Moreover, the Catholicism to which the narrator now cleaves in a childish and superstitious manner (carrying his rosary beads as a man might carry garlic for fear of vampires) seems hardly the final answer, substituting as it does rule, custom, and a ceremony of sacrifice for the ecstasy that is supposed to accompany them; rather is it a way of "transforming down" the voltage of expected and unavoidable apocalypse.

At the close of "Rosa Alchemica" the narrator admits that the indefinite world, beside which Catholicism seems orthodox and definite, has lost only half its mastery over his heart; at the close of "The Tables of the Law" he admits he dare not pass Aherne's house for fear of the spirits possibly within; at the close of "The Adoration of the Magi" he admits without conviction he has turned "into a pathway which will lead me from [the old men] and from the Order of the Alchemical Rose." The narrator ends each story caught hazardously at the crossways between two multitudes, two dispensations, a spiritual centaur who hates his fixed and mirror-like self yet is only half-responsive to the prospect of radical change. And change, paradoxically, is essential if he is to be gathered into the artifice of eternity like doves into their dovecote or songbirds into a gilded cage. He is afraid that dissolving the self means dissolution (Robartes, we recall, resembles "something between a debauchee, a saint and a peasant," p. 110) and will not abase himself, as Robartes told him he must, in order to escape himself.

Although he is grappling with mystical quandaries universal in their nature and implications, Yeats wishes at the same time to convince us that they are more urgent and intense in Ireland than most other places, especially England and America, because Ireland is home to fanaticism, vision, and violence, a proposition that must have seemed the truer in the eighteen-nineties with its land war and hounding of Parnell and its vivid memory of the Phoenix Park murders. But the contemporary age was for Yeats only one catastrophic climax in an ancient and in some respects beneficial continuity. So far as this book is visionary it is Irish, he told AE in the Dedication to *The Secret Rose,* "for Ireland, which is still predominantly Celtic, has preserved with some less excellent things a gift of vision, which has died out among more hurried and more successful nations: no shining candelabra have prevented us from looking into the darkness, and when one looks into the darkness there is always something there." Vision because it is fed by unslakeable desire is perilous, and Robartes and Aherne fall victims to the peril.

Aherne's predicament when he visits the narrator and during his most delirious faith in Cabbala, is a more feverish version of the narrator's and is seen as quintessentially Irish: "He was to me, at that moment, the supreme type of our race, which, when it has risen above, or is sunken below, the formalisms of half-education and the rationalisms of conventional affirmation and denial, turns away, unless my hopes for the world and for the Church have made me blind, from practicable desires and intuitions towards desires so unbounded that no human vessel can contain them, intuitions so immaterial that their sudden and far-off fire leaves heavy darkness about hand and foot. He had the nature, which is half monk, half soldier of fortune, and must needs turn action into dreaming, and dreaming into action; and for such there is no order, no finality, no contentment in this world" (p. 144). (Like a less political John O'Leary, Aherne had returned to Ireland to endure "the fermentation of belief which is coming upon our people with the reawakening of their imaginative life," p. 145.) By "our race" the narrator means the Irishry, whether Anglo-Irish or "native" Catholic, since for Yeats both of these Irishries have a cloven psyche and unquenchable desires. It is tempting to quarrel with the easy identification (are we not speaking, among the tribe of the Anglo-Irish, only of the eccentric and romantic?) and to regard the Catholic Aherne as very much the creation of a *fin de siècle* Anglo-Irish writer.

There is no finality or contentment in this world for the narrator any more than for Aherne. The new order has not arrived, nor the old one died. But the pressure of historical progression would seem to make a climacteric imminent and inevitable, having been building since "men's minds," after the impure stability of the eighteenth century, "subtilized and complicated by the romantic movement in art and literature, began to tremble on the verge of some unimagined revelation" (p. 111). A new order is necessary, even though, paradoxically, it will be an order dedicated to dreadful freedom.[12] Morality and judgement are rendered irrelevant by historical necessity. Hence Yeats could treat with lofty equanimity the darker events in the Irish struggle for independence, and yet—because of the nature of universal antinomies, whereby thesis and antithesis progress simultaneously—could have his equanimity countered by occasional and painful self-questioning, a creative contradiction we see most vividly in poems such as "Easter 1916" (self-questioning giving way to the bardic obligation to recite euphonious names) and "The Man and The Echo," one of Yeats's several dialogue poems.

It is pointless, therefore, to claim that on the evidence of what happens to Robartes and Aherne that self, intellect, the natural order, science and Christianity are shown to be good; they seem so only because the advent of their opposites is terrifying even when desirable. The narrator remains painfully undecided, and if we wish to identify him in that respect with his creator, we might demonstrate a similar, equally compelled, but more creative ambivalence in the poet, a quarrel with himself out of which springs his poetry.

We know, for example, that Yeats despised "the pale victims of modern fiction" who passed for heroes, and preferred those who were placed by their creators "where life is at tension,"[13] be they benign heroes such as Cuchulain or somewhat demonic figures such as Robartes, as Oisin preferred hell with the Fianna to salvation with pale Christian converts. The sinful or heretical character is, because he is an agent of historical change, preferable to the orthodox. He may even be outside the normal spiritual and moral categories of sin and heresy, beyond good and evil. Aherne claims that Joachim of Flora taught in secret that certain people "were elected, not to live, but to reveal that hidden substance of God" (p. 154) and that the Pope was not their Father, who have "no father but the Holy Spirit." Of himself, Aherne claims: "in my misery it was revealed to me that man can only come to [the Heart of God] through the sense of separation from it which we call sin, and I understood that I could not sin, because I had discovered the law of my being, and could only express or fail to express my being, and I understood that God has made a simple and an arbitrary law that we may sin and repent!" (p. 160) And further: "I am not among those for whom Christ died, and this is why I must be hidden. I have a leprosy that even eternity cannot cure. I have seen the whole, and how can I come again to believe that a part is the whole? I have lost my soul because I have looked out of the eyes of the angels" (p. 161).

Discovery of the secret law of Aherne's being brings hardly bearable loneliness and alienation to him, apparently because it happens in his case to dictate self and not selflessness and because he is yet mortal: death, like historical change, does not always come when it is desired and there are periods of imminence and delay that cause misery and anxiety. (Aherne expresses a penitential sadness whereas Robartes expresses a noble ecstasy: he is Dowson to Robartes' Lionel Johnson.)[14] Robartes and Aherne are victims as much as instigators, as much out of control as in control, history's scapegoats and stalking-horses, unruly John the Baptists. The very flaws in the characters and circumstances of Robartes and Aherne prove rather than disprove the need for proper ritual to control as well as invoke spiritual reality. Self-transcendence remains a good but must be achieved correctly, an admonition that demonstrates Yeats's ability to distance himself to some extent, spiritually as well as artistically, from the mystical activity with which in real life he involved himself.

Realism and Restraint

The complexity of theme and perplexity of character in the apocalyptic stories would seem precociously in advance of their style which is characterized by a monotonous luxuriance. Although Robartes' excesses and the narrator's dreamy uncertainties are fittingly conveyed by the Celtic Twilight tone, what is wanted is a variety of rhetorics to suggest the essential ambiguity of the narratives. The theme might be the perilous and gradual distillation of the contents of the soul (which happens also to be the overarching theme and direction of Yeats's canon as well as the definition of alchemy given by the six students in "Rosa Alchemica"), but the writing does not enact it. It is true that in imitating ritual seduction, Yeats's sentences, with their languidly insistent and insinuating clauses that curve like smoke from a censer, are themselves seductive: "He leaned forward and began speaking with a slightly rhythmical intonation, and as he spoke I had to struggle again with the shadow, as of some older night than the night of the sun, which began to dim the light of the candles and to blot out the little gleams upon the corner of picture-frames and on the bronze divinities, and to turn the blue of the incense to a heavy purple; while it left the peacocks to glimmer and glow as though each separate colour were a living spirit" (p. 114). Yet for all the carefully inventoried vessels and instruments of the ritual order, missing from the stories are the scrupulous geometry and architecture of ritual and quest. Yeats confuses images with symbols and drowns his emerging symbolism in a surfeit of imagery and descriptive detail.[15]

With his characteristic attention to discarded masks, Yeats himself thirty years later preempted my criticism. In *Stories of Michael Robartes and his Friends* (1931), Yeats indirectly admits that in the trilogy of apocalyptic stories he "substituted sound for sense and ornament for thought."[16] The criticism is in fact Robartes'; Robartes has conveyed to John Aherne, Owen's brother, his bitterness over the style of the stories in which he appeared. In "The Phases of the Moon" (the verse dialogue between Robartes and Owen Aherne that follows the *Stories of Michael Robartes and his Friends* in *A Vision* in 1937), the former attributes the style of the apocalyptic stories to the influence of Pater. John Aherne, purportedly writing to Yeats, says he defended the stories to Robartes by appeal to literary history, a defense we may assume Yeats himself is making. "I said that you wrote in those tales as many good writers wrote at the time over half Europe, that such prose was the equivalent of what somebody had called 'absolute poetry' and somebody else 'pure poetry'; that though it lacked speed and variety, it would have acquired both, as Elizabethan prose did after the *Arcadia,* but for the surrender everywhere to the sensational and the topical; that romance driven to its last ditch had a right to swagger."[17] Robartes has the last word, replying to Aherne that "when the candle was burnt out an honest man did not pretend that grease was flame."

In such manner Yeats attacks and defends these early extravagant fictions and the *fin de siècle* sensationalism and Paterian elegance into which romanticism guttered. The couching of self-criticism in the minds of characters he has created is a typically brilliant ploy; it sows subliminal doubt in the reader's mind as to the relevance of this fictional criticism to actual stories Yeats wrote thirty years before; it distracts the reader from the earlier stories while ostensibly discussing them; it tries to obviate the criticism of those who might not be so distracted; and it salvages the discountenanced by absorbing it into the countenanced. Throughout his career Yeats had an arch-survivor's ability to turn adversity into advantage, and by the same token diversity into unity.

Stories of Michael Robartes is not just a critical ploy, of course, but a brief fictional experiment by which folktale characters, Huddon, Duddon, and Daniel O'Leary, are turned into fictional characters who then encounter fictional characters created by Yeats decades before. Yeats also turns himself into a fictional character receiving a letter from another character and takes the opportunity in that letter to have some of his poems discussed.[18] Unlike its apocalyptic predecessors, *Stories of Michael Robartes* is written in the dry, pseudofactual manner of a confident mystic who sees no call for poetic embroidery around visionary zeal. (One wonders if the contemporary master of metaphysical fiction, Borges, whose pared fictions are not dissimilar, though more playful, ever read *Stories of Michael Robartes.)* It is written in the confident manner also of the seasoned writer who has had the benefit of reading twentieth-century realistic novelists. But an early, realistic novella, "John Sherman" (1891), proved that in fact Yeats was early aware of the kind of fiction being written at the time over the other half of Europe.

The choice facing John Sherman (and, we might surmise, Yeats) between the values of London and those of Sligo (called Ballah in the novella), of city and village, of east and west, is conveyed largely in a restrained and unromantic prose. Indeed, so uncharacteristic is the style of the story, with its good-humored observations of the mundane, that it reads like an exercise, but this may be hindsight since we know that Yeats started the story partly in response to a challenge from his father to write something about real life.[19] But the lack of enthusiasm may derive from the story's title character. Like the figures of the apocalyptic stories, Sherman is suspended between loss of self and self-possession, each of which has desirable and undesirable versions. This theme, in its many forms and intensities, unifies Yeats's diverse fiction. It is, for example, the theme of "Dhoya," a shrill story begun in 1887 and published alongside the very different "John Sherman" in 1891. Like Cuchulain, the giant Dhoya is seduced by a woman of the sidhe. Through arrogance and folly he loses his immortal love and fails in his pursuit of a changeless self and ends the story astride a wild stallion that plunges into the western sea and into folklore, an ending very similar to that of "The Curse of the Fires and of the Shadows," a story from *The Secret Rose*. The flesh and blood John Sherman is a far less electric figure because there is in him no impulse towards self-transcendence and only a gesturing towards pursuit of the "self-ancestral." In psychic development Sherman is far behind Robartes or Aherne, even though like them he finds himself at a crossways. The style in which Sherman's story is told accords with the limitation of his psychic ambition; realism is used to promote a middling dream and the somewhat indulgent sense of selfhood Sherman achieves by leaving London and going back to Sligo. The more attractive spiritual excesses of Robartes and Aherne a few years later seemed to Yeats to necessitate a different and extravagantly romantic prose, itself later abandoned.

Stories of Red Hanrahan: *Patriotism, Selflessness, Immortality*

> Go, therefore; but leave Hanrahan,
> For I need all his mighty memories.
> —W. B. Yeats

"I have always known that love should be changeless," Robartes tells his assembled pupils in *Stories of Michael Robartes,* "and yet my loves drank their oil and died—there has been no ever-burning lamp."[20] "Dhoya" is a mythological version of this cruel paradox, "Rosa Alchemica" a ritual version; and where Robartes and Dhoya seek immutable love, Owen Aherne seeks immutable spiritual contentment; but the predicament of all three is at base the same. The search for a changeless self safe from the transient world, a search conducted with such passion that the passion consumes and transforms itself—this inescapable paradox along with the isolating flaws of recklessness and folly are elements in Yeats's romantic conception of the hero. Dhoya doomed to wander in exile across a folk sky, Robartes stoned by an irate crowd, Aherne wandering broken in Europe, the narrator of the three apocalyptic stories shrinking into a secret selfhood: all are outcasts through whom eternity chooses to reveal itself. "Bow down," commands the voice of Hermes chanting from the lips of one of the three old men at the bedside of the dying adept in "The Adoration of the Magi," and understand that when [the immortals] are about to overthrow the things that are to-day and bring the things that were yesterday, they have no one to help them, but one whom the things that are to-day have cast out." (pp. 172–173) "He meant, I think," says the youngest of the three, "that when people are good the world likes them and takes possession of them, and so eternity comes through people who are not good or who have been forgotten." (p. 174) The companionless—be they poets, peasants or aristocrats—are the chief heroes of Yeats's fiction and drama, yet hardly heroes: oracles, vortices, turbulent narrow channels, rather, through which the tide of eternity and flux is compelled.

More than any other revivalist, Yeats charges the romantic notion of the solitary with apocalyptic force. The solitary is seen as a kind of conductor of apocalyptic energy (found where life is at high tension, we might say). If this seems vividly the case with the dying Cuchulain lashed to a pillar and acting as a spiritual lightning rod, Yeats would have it equally true for himself, the poet conducting apocalyptic energy into the less hazardous art of poetry and into a rather mystical Irish nationalism, instead of into the more fearful "supreme art, the art which is the foundation of all arts" (p. 156) of which Owen Aherne speaks.

Conspicuous among Yeats's solitaries is the complex hero of the Red Hanrahan stories, the first of which were published in periodicals in 1892, and all six of which were revised and republished—but without a collective title—in *The Secret Rose* (1897). Publication of *Stories of Red Hanrahan* as a titled and self-contained suite took place in 1905, after changes in prose style, setting and the character of Hanrahan (called O'Sullivan in early versions of the stories). Hanrahan in the later versions is a human-sized Dhoya. His companions try to persuade him, through whiskey, song, and cards, to postpone his journey to his sweetheart. The third temptation is the one he cannot resist, and he foolishly repeats the giant's error of losing his sweetheart over a game. Although it is unclear if Hanrahan is under the spell of the sidhe from the very beginning of that fateful Samhain Eve, we are probably meant to assume the immortals have chosen the soul of an unstable fellow to tempt into their company, and that because he does not tread "in measured ways" (as poet or man), he cannot "barter gaze for gaze" with them.[21] Tricked and enchanted by the immortal gamester with whom he plays cards, he is led by a phantom hare to Slieve Echtge where he commits his second error, refusing to respond to the beauty of a sidhe queen and to question her four aged attendants as to the meaning of their talismans. He commits this error not out of strength but out of stubbornness and weakness, and by cutting himself off from the sidhe ("the lasting people") he is made to embrace his own mortality and yet in punishment is cut off likewise from his mortal fellows and deprived of the love of earthly women.[22]

Like Dhoya, Hanrahan is feckless and gullible and is driven half out of his wits; like Dhoya and Aherne he wanders in sorrow and "had never known content for any length of time"; and he shares Dhoya's prodigious and insatiable appetite for life and love and suffers occasional Cuchulainoid fits of passion. He becomes an outcast under the influence of native gods yet, half-remembering the classical learning he once imparted to children as a hedge schoolmaster, is suspended between the pure and impure multitudes, unhappy with himself because he has been touched by the otherworld and in a half-understood way searching for the true self, his purblind quest its own punishment.

Richard Finneran is correct, I think, in his assertion that in *Stories of Red Hanrahan* "Yeats had in mind a basic pattern of sin, suffering, repentance, and redemption."[23] In "Red Hanrahan" the sin against love and immortality is committed; in "The Twisting of the Rope" are suffering and loss; "Hanrahan and Cathleen the Daughter of Hoolihan" recounts a half-conscious repentance; Hanrahan propitiates the immortals by cursing old age in "Red Hanrahan's Curse"; in "Hanrahan's Vision" he witnesses the sidhe he repudiated; and in "The Death of Hanrahan" he apparently redeems himself by joining the sidhe in death. The implications of Hanrahan's "crime" or "sin" are not only personal but, as Finneran points out, are also national: "by rejecting the call of the immortal sidhe, Hanrahan has symbolically refused Ireland herself."[24] The old woman makes it clear that because of the repudiation of them by Hanrahan, who is their chosen one, "'Echtge, daughter of the Silver Hand, must stay in her sleep',"[25] the Silver Hand referring to Nuada, a king of the Tuatha de Danann, "a divinity of the sun and of light,"[26] whose daughter was a benevolent and fruitful goddess. Hanrahan, then, is a messiah or awakener who refuses the role, a failed light-bringer to ancient and, it is implied, modern Ireland, and he must suffer for his dereliction.

However, he is given opportunity to redeem himself and would seem to begin his patriotic conversion in "Hanrahan and Cathleen the Daughter of Hoolihan," wherein he sings "of Ireland and the weight of grief that is on her" (p. 229) and to complete it in "Hanrahan's Vision." But if Hanrahan is redeemed into love of Ireland (and into an awareness of true love: love of woman and love of country are not opposed in Irish nationalist mythology but synonymous), redemption is couched in the same ambiguity as the redemption of Owen Aherne; arguably, Hanrahan is among the Yeatsian incorrigibles and irredeemables. Terrified, aged, broken, Hanrahan is driven in the last story of the suite to accept the care of a wandering peasant woman, Winny Byrne, who is, an immortal voice tells him (speaking through her as it does through the dying prostitute in "The Adoration of the Magi"), one of the witless in whom along with the broken and dying "the lasting people" make their dwelling. Near death, Hanrahan asks the question about Winny's kitchen utensils—her big pot, her flat baking stone, her long knife and her long blackthorn stick, transformed by firelight into cauldron, stone, sword, and spear—that he should have asked about the sacred talismans. But whether his questions "What are they? Who do they belong to?" are prompted by delirium of fever and confused memory or belatedly but in the nick of time by mystical curiosity is not clear. Perhaps he becomes selfless and immortal (saved, as a Christian might be, but by nationalist conversion), and his soul taken by the aged Winny who insists she is a beautiful sidhe-woman, a crone capable of being transformed, like Cathleen Ni Houlihan (Ireland herself), from the haggardness of enforced servility (or colonial oppression) into the queenly beauty of sovereignty. But it may be equally true that the sidhe took Winny's wits, as the people believe, and that her self-delusion is matched by that of Hanrahan, who asks the necessary questions too late (certainly for this life) and whose terminal vision though moving is delusive and vastly ironic, reminding us of the horror of his errancy and the inadequacy of his nationalism. The ambiguity may well be intentional, for it accords with that of "Dhoya" and the apocalyptic stories; but the essential equation, patriotism-selflessness-immortality, remains intact.

Yeats's Symbolist Heroes

Hanrahan is a shanachie and bard, capable of reciting the story of Deirdre and the Sons of Usnach. We might argue that *Stories of Red Hanrahan* is among Yeats's "literature for the people," unlike the apocalyptic tales that were an attempt at an "aristocratic esoteric Irish literature . . . for the few," as Yeats described "Rosa Alchemica" to John O'Leary.[27] But Daniel Corkery's description of Owen O'Sullivan the Red (1748–84), an Irish Jacobite poet upon whom Hanrahan is in part based, as a "literary man singing for a literary audience" ("though it was in a tavern or in a farmer's kitchen that that audience assembled"), rather than a folk-poet "as the term is now understood,"[28] is equally applicable to Yeats's hero. In the early versions of one of the Hanrahan stories, "The Twisting of the Rope," the hero is "the last of that mighty line of poets which came down unbroken from Sancan Torpeist (whom the Great Cat well-nigh ate), and mightier Oisin, whose heart knew unappeased three hundred years of daemonic love."[29] The suite is of course set during the eighteenth century, but the *Gaelic* eighteenth century, thereby complementing the Anglo-Irish eighteenth century imagined in "Rosa Alchemica." That in his end is echoed the dissolution of the old Gaelic order (of which he is a last strayed reveller) and the end of a certain kind of Gaelic poetry is perhaps sufficient though only half-conscious cause of Hanrahan's unhappiness.

Corkery tells us that "after the terror of 1798, the *aisling* poem is heard no more,"[30] and Owen Roe O'Sullivan was famed for his *aisling* or vision poems. "The *Aisling* proper is Jacobite poetry," Corkery informs us,

> and a typical example would run something like this: The poet, weak with thinking on the woe that has overtaken the Gael, falls into a deep slumber. In his dreaming a figure of radiant beauty draws near. She is so bright, so stately, the poet imagines her one of the immortals. Is she Deirdre? or Gearnait? or is she Helen? or Venus? He questions her, and learns that she is Erin; and her sorrow, he is told, is for her true mate who is in exile beyond the seas. This true mate is, according to the date of the composition, either the Old or the Young Pretender; and the poem ends with a promise of speedy redemption on the return of the King's son.[31]

In the opening story of the early versions of Yeats's suite, the hero does not wait for the vision (the *Spéir-bhean,* literally "sky-woman") to appear but uses dark magic to conjure her up; in the opening story of the later version, Hanrahan does not question the vision. Each time, the poet-hero offends against the ceremony of inspiration and composition to be followed by the *aisling* poet, and this too must be seen as the hero's sinful dereliction and a cause of his subsequent unhappiness.

However, of greater significance is the fact that like the last romantics and *poètes maudits* of Yeats's own day, Hanrahan has envisioned immortality and is thereafter unhappy in the world of men.

> What portion in the world can the artist have
> Who has awakened from the common dream
> But dissipation and despair?

Yeats asks in "Ego Dominus Tuus." He might have been thinking of Johnson and Dowson, friends of his youth, "dissipated men, the one a drunkard, the other a drunkard and mad about women, and yet they had the gravity of men who had found life out and were awakening from the dream."[32] Aherne, the narrator of the apocalyptic stories, Dhoya, and Hanrahan are all men who have likewise awakened from the common dream into doubt, dissipation, or despair. It is art impelled by vision or dream that can redeem one so afflicted, but only if he is an artist and only if he pays the price of earthly happiness, even existence. Robert O'Driscoll when speaking of "Rosa Alchemica" has expressed the cruel predicament succinctly:

> It is only through the constant activity of art, not in merely surrounding oneself with works of art, that ecstasy can be experienced and a changing heart transmuted for a moment into a changeless work of art. But this transmutation is not a final alchemical act: as long as breath remains the artist must return to the material world from which during his moment of creative activity he has become transported. Life, therefore, when lived intensely, becomes an endless oscillation between spiritual vision and material life, and death becomes the consummation of the ecstatic process, for at death the weary human artist can become the weariless spiritual thing he has created: the poet can become the poem; the dancer can become the dance.[33]

And after death? As Aherne tells the narrator of "The Tables of the Law": "the world only exists to be a tale in the ears of coming generations" (p. 154). Escape from the self and the will, paradoxically through willful and concentrated self-sacrifice, became for Yeats a type of martyrdom comparable with the fatal patriotic gesture.

The turning of men into artists (even of an entire nation into a legion of artists), of artists into works of art (by means of folklore and legend), and of life itself into art (seeing politics, for example, as in the end aesthetic) was a constant aspiration during the Irish literary revival. In the reality in which artist-patriots such as Thomas MacDonagh and Pearse hoped their poetic dreams would issue, Ireland would itself become as a perfected work of art with their deaths; their philosophy and fate appealed to Yeats, according to whom a certain kind of artist—which Yeats himself was not—sought death as the ultimate aesthetic act.

In "The Crucifixion of the Outcast," Yeats takes the artist's pursuit of death to its logical conclusion. This is the fourth of eight stories in the 1897 edition of *The Secret Rose,* but in the 1908 *Collected Works* it is the opening story of the set. Its chief character, Cumhal, is a wanderer, outcast, pagan, poet, who is put to death by friars for having issued a bard's curse on them for their inhospitality. It is as if, however, in his Hanrahan-like, unappeasable pride, he courts his own persecution, thirsts for accusation, and his imitation of Christ on the cross is like an artistic reenactment. Yet it is far from clear that Yeats does not admire Cumhal as an ideal type.

This story is based on a twelfth century romance, *Aislinge Meic Conglinne,* but Yeats's adaptation springs from a context composed in part by O'Grady's notion of history as art. An epigraph, however, attached to *The Secret Rose* suggests the context was in part composed by others; it is a quotation from Villiers de l'Isle-Adam's *Axel* (which Yeats saw in Paris in 1894): "As for living, our servants will do that for us." For we are speaking, in the cases of Yeats's heroes and of the Irish poet-patriots, of the pursuit of symbolism, a pursuit remarkable in its intensity during the Irish cultural revival, and against which John Eglinton (unpopularly in literary circles) counselled.[34] Any adequate account of Yeats's fiction must take stock of its symbolist intent and elements. That literary-spiritual mood whose beginning Yeats ascribed to Poe was symbolism, and Poe's ideal to which Edmund Wilson draws our attention, "a suggestive indefiniteness of vague and therefore of spiritual *effect,* "became a symbolist ideal.[35] Yeats presents this ideal in the apocalyptic stories in which the confusion between the indefinite, spiritual world that is the heroes' goal and the definite, real world to which they are still bound is the author's own stylistic and thematic indefiniteness and ambiguity, an intimating rather than stating of things, to draw upon Wilson once again. And so, while dreams and hallucinations are symbolist features of the apocalyptic stories, these belong to the narrator and characters, not to the author. We can speak of the main characters as symbolist heroes (whose careers nevertheless prove the dangers, and perhaps cast grave doubt on the wisdom and even possibility of the symbolist life), but of Yeats as a symbolist artist only if we mean an artist who uses symbolist techniques and subject matter for his own ends and with a critical awareness, however imperfect. By the time his early fictional experiments were concluded (1904)—and experiments they were, in an analogously magic sense—Yeats had drawn away from symbolist atmosphere in his poetry, but if we are speaking of Yeats as a firm believer in and proponent of the symbolist life, the reaction had already set in by 1897 when *The Secret Rose* appeared.

It may be I am drawing a needless distinction here. Were not Villiers de l'Isle-Adam and others critical explorers (rather than exponents) of the symbolist life as well as practitioners of the symbolist discourse? In *Axel* is a dramatic record of the rewards, dangers, and ultimate impossibility of the sustained symbolist life, but the triumphant account of that impossibility represents the author's symbolist success. Yeats, perhaps, was true to symbolism even when he explored the hazards of the symbolist life. The difference may be that whereas Axel dies in rapture, Aherne and the narrator of the apocalyptic stories linger unhappily on.

Moreover, the failure of the symbolist hero need not detract from the inspired and necessary folly of his attempt, and Yeats in his postsymbolist career never lost admiration for him. The symbolist hero courts a Paterian and exclusive world of beauty, imagination, and spirituality, and risks being "thrown fatally out of key with reality," incurring "penalties which are not to be taken lightly."[36] What is interesting is that the experiment was later carried out in the most public of spheres by poet-patriots not entirely conscious of the fact that theirs was a political and nationalist version of the symbolist experiments of Axel, Marius, and Robartes. The difference is that they were the leading characters of their poetic drama as well as the dramatists, that the Easter Rising was both insurrection and attempted work of art, and that the dancer and dance in that fatal break with reality were very nearly indistinguishable. Several of the leaders of the Rising meant to die and they did. The Rising became a national and artistic icon and emblem, in the work of Yeats himself, for example.[37]

Were they then successful symbolist heroes in their own dream? Yes, if Axel was (their happy deaths and their assumption into legendry suggesting it), and if we accept their vision of Ireland as artistic and spiritual. But as prophets and evangelists of their gospel, in this case a nationalist one, they failed as Robartes seemed to have and as perhaps even Axel did, though he claimed to have left the world an example. Although the Easter Rising led eventually to Irish independence, it did not lead, in the part of the island that won independence, to the beauty, imagination, and spirituality Pearse and MacDonagh envisaged. As bringers of the desired life for others they failed, as surely as did Yeats's fictional heroes, for Irish independence has been, in comparison with their hopes, a squalid reality from which Yeats with one part of his being recoiled—he for whom the disparity between the hopes for independence and the fact must have been the more obvious and familiar because of his early exploration of the symbolist paradox and impossibility.

Robert O'Driscoll would place Hanrahan among the ranks of the failed symbolist heroes of Yeats's fiction; Hanrahan (unlike Axel) remains between the definite and indefinite worlds.[38] In partial contradiction and borrowing Wilson's distinction between symbolism and romanticism—the romantic hero is at war with society while the symbolist hero is in flight from it—Augustine Martin prefers to see a distinction between the romantic Hanrahan and the symbolist Robartes.[39] Yet I wonder if Yeats would have been happy with the exclusiveness of Martin's distinction.[40] An essential bond between Hanrahan and Robartes is the crossroads between the common and uncommon dream, mortality and immortality, at which they stand, and the burdensome self of which each wishes to be relieved. Moreover, Hanrahan is a wanderer on the edge of society while Robartes is against society, even if he is not always solitary in his stand like the romantic hero but is instead a member of a sect or a participant in a pact like the symbolist hero. And surely entrance into the company of the legendary which Hanrahan achieves by his life and death (Yeats's suite supposedly recounting the life and legend simultaneously) imitates a folk version of symbolism.

In any case, neither the romantic nor symbolist life is wholly achieved and lived, and, Virgil in hand, Hanrahan the hedge schoolmaster is tenuously bound, as was Yeats the writer, to classicism. Hanrahan fails, then, as the Easter Rising failed, and we are left with the account of the struggle against insuperable odds. In its quixotic revolt against England, was not the Rising then a romantic adventure as Hanrahan is in his lonely rebellion against society a romantic figure?

But when we speak of the wish of the poet-patriots in brotherly and secret pact, with or without revolution, to revive on the westernmost edge of Europe a Gaelic, pre-Renaissance, and comparatively esoteric society, to withdraw into a privileged Irishness from which large numbers of the Irish (unless they took "oaths" of allegiance, as many did, against their own cultural traditions) were excluded, we may legitimately draw an analogy with the themes and styles of literary symbolism. Wilson's distinction between romanticism and symbolism has limited application to Irish revival literature, in which nationalism of a peculiarly emblematic kind and a potent folklore cloud the issue, and in which symbolism and romanticism frequently coexist and commingle (as they do, for example, in the poetry and fiction of AE). Furthermore, it is not enough in Ireland to speak of the danger of failure and death in the symbolist hero, real or fictional. Yeats recognized that danger to Robartes, Aherne, Hanrahan, Cumhal, Dhoya, and others of his fictional characters, on hindsight to Dowson and Johnson, and equally on hindsight to the 1916 martyrs. He even came within hailing distance of condemnation. He reminded himself in "Easter 1916":

> Too long a sacrifice
> Can make a stone of the heart

But Yeats did not acknowledge the actual or potential danger and suffering to innocent others, the living and the unborn, caused by the quixotic or esoteric fantasies of these heroes. Did that play of his send out certain men the English shot? If it did not, it and other works and statements by Yeats, his entire early vision, helped to spin the fantasies he later attempted to attribute indiscriminately to all the Irish instead of to certain deluded individuals. If the Catholic Irishman, James Joyce, did not feed his heart on romantic nationalist fantasies that impinged on real life, why need Yeats (an Anglo-Irishman with much less reason to feel oppressed) have done so?

Certain Set Apart
The Romantic Strategy—John Millington Synge 6

. . . long travelling, he had come
Towards nightfall upon certain set apart
In a most desolate stony place,
Towards nightfall upon a race
Passionate and simple like his heart.

—*W. B. Yeats*

The Appeal of the Western Islands

The rewards and hazards of fantasy Synge explores in *The Playboy of the Western World* (1907). In that play, the title character is a caricature of O'Sullivan the Red, the wandering and dangerous poet. Disappointed by his story so far, Pegeen encourages Christy in Act One: "If you weren't destroyed travelling, you'd have as much talk and streeleen, I'm thinking, as Owen Roe O'Sullivan or the poets of the Dingle Bay; and I've heard all times it's the poets are your like—fine, fiery fellows with great rages when their temper's roused." At play's end, Christy is hounded from the shebeen by a mob, suffering the fate of Yeats's Hanrahan, but like him retreating in haughty eloquence. In Christy's rugged education as a storyteller and his discovery of his role in life are mirrored also something of Synge's own education as a Gaelic speaker and playwright that we find recorded in his account of his trips to the Aran Islands he took at the suggestion of Yeats. One somehow feels that it was not essential for Yeats to have been to the Aran Islands in order for him to proffer his famous advice to Synge in Paris in 1897, but Yeats had in fact been there with Arthur Symons the year before.

As usual, then, Yeats led the way, and it was two years after him that Pearse, AE (who was not impressed), Lady Gregory, and Synge travelled to the islands, from an outsider's point of view surely the islands' *annus mirabilis*. But in fact the western island appealed to cultural nationalists and revivalists long before 1896. Among the earliest of such visitors were George Petrie and John T. O'Flaherty, antiquarians who went to the islands in the eighteen-twenties. John O'Donovan, working on the first Ordnance Survey of Ireland, arrived in 1839. After these writers and scientists—many of them in pursuit of proof that Ireland had had a preconquest civilization—came philologists like F. N. Finck and Holger Pedersen, and folklorists like Sir William Wilde and Jeremiah Curtin, all four of whom Synge found remembered on Aranmor in 1898. "I have seen Frenchmen, and Danes, and Germans," one islander told Synge, "and there does be a power of Irish books along with them, and they reading them better than ourselves. Believe me there are few rich men now in the world who are not studying the Gaelic."[1] An exaggeration for which he can, I think, be forgiven: it must have seemed to him as if the entire civilized world were converging on his lonely island off the coast of Galway.

The west generally, of course, had assumed a special and potent significance for the national movement in the nineteenth century, if only because Ireland lay west of the hated England. Had not Thomas Davis ended his Young Ireland song, "The West's Asleep," with the promise of a triumphant rebirth?

> *The West's awake, the West's awake—*
> Sing, oh! hurrah! let England quake,
> We'll watch till death for Erin's sake![2]

It was from the island of Valentia that in 1867 the Irish Republic was to have been proclaimed. Later, as the Gaelic revival and new nationalism gained momentum, especially after the founding of the Gaelic League in 1893, the truer west of Ireland, particularly western islands such as the Blaskets and the Aran Islands, focused the place of impending awakening, providing a symbolic and, it was hoped, actual site where Ireland would be born again.

There were several reasons for the choice. The western island was, indisputably, as far away from England as it was possible for Irish soil to be. And the ruins and remains on the islands provided a sense of continuity with an unconquered Celtic Ireland, for even the Vikings made few permanent settlements in the west. That much of the medieval culture had been both Christian and pre-Reformation was not unwelcome to those who wished the new Ireland to be Catholic as well as Gaelic and free. Also, the islands formed the rich rim of the Gaeltacht, and the extent and purity of the Gaelic spoken on the Blasket and Aran Islands made them "to philologists a prized sanctuary of the Irish language, a place of pilgrimage for students of the ancient tongue."[3] When Pearse went to the Aran Islands in 1898, he inaugurated a branch of the Gaelic League at a meeting in a Kilronan schoolhouse and having done so was convinced that the Gaelic language would never die on the islands: "It will not be allowed to decay, but will be fostered until Aran is a college and a lantern of learning for the Gaels of Ireland once again, as it was in the old days."[4] As usual in the revival, the western island was a moveable feast (as it is to Gabriel Conroy's dismay in Joyce's "The Dead"). When he established his bilingual school in Dublin in 1908, Pearse named it after Enda, the patron saint of the Aran Islands.

It was also believed, at least popularly, that the western islanders were descendants of aboriginal or very ancient islanders and therefore constituted a genealogical link with preconquest Ireland preserved for centuries by protective seas, though according to anthropologists the islanders—at least on the Aran, Blasket and Gola islands—are in fact descended from comparatively recent mainland immigrants.[5] Lastly, it was often difficult to get on and off the islands, and the hardship involved in this, as well as simply existing on the islands, gave to a trip there the desired flavor of Christian pilgrimage. Until well into the twentieth century, the Aran Islands, for example, were rarely visited by ordinary tourists: a journey there was an earnest of one's cultural commitment to the new Ireland. It became almost obligatory for zealous patriots to turn their eyes, souls, and bodies westward, to cross a narrow threshold of mutinous Atlantic waves to be born again beside the holy wells, monastic ruins, military remains, and peasant cabins of the western islands.

What happened was that the cultural nationalists consciously and unconsciously began to attribute to real islands lying off the west coast of Ireland properties both of the mythological islands of Celtic imagination and of the real but transcendently imaged islands of medieval Christianity.[6] In short, the Irish cultural renaissance involved a new version of island mythology, a creation myth for an imminent new order. In taking this direction the cultural nationalists were engaging in primitivism, an aping of primitive thinking, for "to the 'primitive' mind," Mircea Eliade tells us, "all regeneration implies a return to the origins, a repetition of the cosmogony."[7] The western island became the chief setting for a communal, continuous, even on occasions lived fiction. It came to represent Ireland's mythic unity before the chaos of conquest: there at once were the vestige and the symbolic entirety of an undivided nation. Those who composed such a nation existed before selfhood, they inhabited mythic time before the advent of chronology and a mythic community before the coming of individuality. (One is reminded that James Connolly became fascinated by ancient Irish egalitarian principles of common ownership and democracy, ideas he learned about from Eoin MacNeill—who went often to the Aran Islands to speak Irish—and Alice Stopford Green.)[8]

The western island was not only the first island of Ireland, as it were, but also an appearing Tír-na-nÓg, an island lying off what was hoped would become an even larger "Land of Youth," as it had once been to those who had thought that Thule referred to Ireland, "the 'sacred island', or the poetic 'island of the Blest', in which the golden age of innocence and purity still continued to flourish, after all the rest of the world had become corrupt."[9] Patrick Pearse thought, priest-like, that in the children of Eire, innocent as yet of the knowledge of English oppression, lay the new Ireland's brightest hope. He believed that Ireland, because of the bondage in which she had dwelt, had remained morally and spiritually uncorrupted throughout the corruption of history, a fortunate island in the midst of an otherwise corrupt world. To that extent Ireland was an enchanted island, and the wellspring of the enchantment, of Ireland's privileged and essential mystique, lay, in the mythology and early literature, in the western island, at once the rudiment, vestige, and microcosm of free, Gaelic, Catholic Ireland.

Should all this seem fanciful on my part, listen to Sean O'Faolain in 1940, recalling three newly arrived professional Gaels whom he encountered on Great Blasket in 1920 and who were as elated as children:

> Twenty years ago when I first discovered the Gaeltacht myself I felt exactly the same sense of release. It was like taking off one's clothes for a swim naked in some mountain-pool. Nobody who has not had this sensation of suddenly 'belonging' somewhere—of finding the lap of the lost mother—can understand what a release the discovery of the Gaelic world meant to modern Ireland. I know that not for years and years did I get free of this heavenly bond of an ancient, lyrical, permanent, continuous, immemorial self, symbolized by the lonely mountains, the virginal lakes, the traditional language, the simple, certain, uncomplex modes of life, that world of the lost childhood of my race where I, too, became for a while eternally young.[10]

If it was a self without end, it was also without crude beginning. "And it may be a comfort in view of prevalent hypotheses," wrote George Sigerson feverishly in the 1890s, "that the stock of the Anthropoids never went through evolutions in this country. Whatever may have happened elsewhere, the beings who first leaped upon our shores must have been among the foremost in the developed attributes of manhood."[11] The laws of evolution were abhorrent not merely to the religious, but also to the patriotic and patriotic literary who believed instead in magical beginnings and marvellous transformations.

The Aran Islands: *The Search For Archaic Community*

Just as the cultural nationalists' interest in the western island sprang largely from the appearance there of a unified, preconquest civilization, so the interest of the Irish writers sprang largely from the appearance there of passionate community such as we had all composed before cities, industry, class, and warring systems—before, indeed, the separateness of self. In this regard the writers were primitivists. The flight from self and from modern society into primitive communion or archaic unity is an antihistorical, romantic tendency Synge came to share with other revival writers. In *The Aran Islands* (1907), on hindsight one of the most important prose works of the literary revival, Synge writes of the islanders' "strange archaic sympathies with the world," (p. 142) sympathies expressed partly through everyday implements and objects whose materials "to some extent peculiar to the island . . . seem to exist as a natural link between the people and the world that is about them" (p. 59), partly through the very carriage of the islanders who have preserved, by the absence of the heavy boot of Europe, "the agile walk of the wild animal" (p. 66). This world, peopled by "strange men with receding foreheads, high cheek-bones, and ungovernable eyes" who "seem to represent some old type found on these few acres at the extreme border of Europe" (p. 140, is a world innocent of the modern notion of time, where "it would be useless to fix an hour, as the hours are not recognised" (p. 115).

It is equally innocent, in a way that must have pleased Yeats, of the modern distinction between the natural and the supernatural, a psychology more ancient than the imitative psychology of the revivalists who were aware of the distinction but proclaimed a collateral belief in both. "My intercourse with these people," Synge writes, not without humor, "has made me realise that miracles must abound wherever the new conception of law is not understood. On these islands alone miracles enough happen every year to equip a divine emissary. Rye is turned into oats, storms are raised to keep evictors from the shore, cows that are isolated on lonely rocks bring forth calves, and other things of the same kind are common" (p. 128). Synge's interest in the supernatural was more than an eye for the droll, however, and before going to the Aran Islands he read Paulam's *Nouveau Mysticisme* and inquired into psychical literature.[12]

Not only the mind and physique of the islanders but also their sexuality assumes an older form: "The direct sexual instincts are not weak on the island," Synge writes of Inishmaan, "but they are so subordinated to the instincts of the family that they rarely lead to irregularity. The life here is still at an almost patriarchal stage, and the people are nearly as far from the romantic moods of love as they are from the impulsive life of the savage."[13] Work and play are full of sociability, and Synge believes it likely "that much of the intelligence and charm of these people is due to the absence of any division of labour, and to the correspondingly wide development of each individual" (p. 132), making of the individual something of a microcosm of the entire community. Likewise, at least on Inishmaan, are rank and class unapparent.[14]

The anthropological validity of Synge's observations is not at issue here, but rather his perception of the island life.[15] Medieval, prehistoric, pagan, illiterate: these are the recurring descriptions; most frequently does the word "primitive" occur: Synge came to see gradations of primitiveness on the islands, and came to hold in half-contempt the more "civilized" portions, those infected by bourgeois thinking, and sought the most primitive pockets, moving from Aranmor to Inishmaan for this purpose. When in 1905, three years after his final visit to the Aran Islands, Synge contemplated Great Blasket island, he wrote to Lady Gregory: "It is probably even more primitive than Aran and I am wild with joy at the prospect."[16] He was not disappointed; he found the Blasket Islands the most interesting place he had ever been and alive with a "singularly severe glory."[17] Perhaps the pursuit of unfamiliar primitive places played an unconscious role in Synge's abandonment of Aran in 1902.[18] What he seemed to crave was archaic community in isolation, by which he could flee the burden of self that he considered modern, bourgeois society lays upon one.

This fascination with a primitive people of the Celtic fringe we find equally in the works of Anatole le Braz which Synge read the year before he travelled to the Aran Islands.[19] The Bretons of which Le Braz wrote in such a work as *The Land of Pardons (Au Pays des Pardons,* 1894) are not unlike the Aran and Blasket islanders, being a legend-loving, credulous, yet humorous people, steeped in Catholicism and an elder paganism. And like Synge's islands, Le Braz' Brittany is a country of miracles amidst a world dedicated to fact and grey truth. One of Le Braz' descriptions of the Breton people could serve equally for Synge's western Irish: "that race of miserable souls, inured to trouble and hardship, the conditions of whose life have remained so precarious, and upon whom the long inheritance of suffering belonging to most of the Celtic communities has never ceased to press."[20]

The Land of Pardons is a loving account of several Breton pardons, festivals, and pilgrimages dedicated to local saints who in the distant past were substituted by Christianity for local pagan gods, as such saints had been in Ireland. Indeed, the pardons are very similar to the Irish "patterns" which, like their Breton counterparts, were acts of place-worship as much as of hagiolatry, although the religious banners of the Breton processionists bear an ironic resemblance to the banners of Orangemen. Le Braz stresses the medieval quality of the pardons, and this might well have reinforced Synge's perception of that quality of life on Aran. Like *The Aran Islands, The Land of Pardons* is a travel book, illustrated by paintings as *The Aran Islands* was illustrated by the sketches of Jack B. Yeats. In addition, Le Braz recounts the legends surrounding the various patron saints, the equivalent of which in *The Aran Islands* are the folktales Synge collected and inserts into his narrative. One of the legends in particular that Le Braz tells, that of King Gralon, is a remarkable story of medieval quality that has as one of its characters the last Druid, and it would not be out of place in a volume of stories by Morris or Yeats. During this pardon of the singers, Le Braz renewed acquaintance with Yann Ar Minouz, the Bard of Rumengol, a mercurial man "impatient of all control," wandering Brittany, having left his wife, making verses for unfortunate lovers and satires against miserly masters; in short, a willful outcast in the mould of Owen Roe O'Sullivan or Yeats's Hanrahan. One difference between *The Land of Pardons* and *The Aran Islands* is the unobtrusive part Le Braz plays in his own book, the crucial part Synge plays in his, and in this respect only *The Land of Pardons* more nearly resembles *The Western Island or The Great Blasket,* a much later work of island homage by Robin Flower.

Clearly Synge was greatly influenced by this and other books by Le Braz, and his view of the Aran islanders is in part a preconception framed by the outlook of the Breton writer.[21] A refrain in *The Land of Pardons* is Le Braz' fear of the extinction (at the hands of merchants, tourists, trains, machines, and other symptoms of bourgeois civilization) of age-old customs, beliefs, and communities. Yet in the interstices of civilized interference endures a way of life so old and unchanging that it creates in the writer "that feeling of being in a new-made land, a world scarce wakened out of chaos."[22] In Breton society are both changelessness and change, beginning and end.

Le Braz disapproves of modernization as strongly as Synge. One student of Breton nationalism has claimed that it was in order to shield

Brittany from the modernizing influences of French culture that members of the Breton clerico-aristocratic right were converted to the regionalist ideas which strengthened ethnic minority nationalism in Brittany around the time Le Braz was most involved in the affairs of his native region.[23] Unlike Le Braz, such Bretons were exclusively French-speaking, yet it was remarked as early as 1919 that "their lack of the language paradoxically heightens their sense of being threatened in their Bretonness."[24] A claim could be made that many exclusively Anglophone Irish revivalists similarly were political or cultural nationalists chiefly because they were enemies of capitalism and bourgeois industrialism, and not because of undiluted nationalist impulses.[25] Several of the revivalists, including Yeats and O'Grady, were, when they were political at all, right-wing and aristocratic in sympathy. (One notes the rightward bias in the political thinking of several major modernist writers whose modernism, ironically, might have had something to do with the antimodernization their work embodies.)

We would want to qualify generalizations about Synge's participation in aristocratic-rightwing tendencies in Irish revivalism, but the connection in his life and work between cultural nationalism and antimodernization remains intact. It is a connection that was surely reinforced through the influence of Le Braz, though, of course, Synge met Irish cultural nationalists before he read the Breton. Le Braz, as it happened, played a role in the Breton revival not unlike that of Douglas Hyde in its Irish counterpart. The recovery of the old language and of the region's submerged history and racial pride, and, for some, the maintenance of Catholicism, were all important in the Breton revival as they were in the Irish, but some Breton revivalists went further and encouraged separatism. Le Braz was the first director of the Union Régionaliste Bretonne, an avowedly nonpartisan and nonsectarian alliance between intellectuals and members of Brittany's upper classes, begun in 1898 "to develop by the revival of Breton sentiment all forms of Breton activity."[26] The following year—the year Synge himself visited Brittany and was reported by Yeats to be learning Breton in Paris[27]—Le Braz resigned as director of the URB when some members at the second annual congress attacked the Third Republic, just as Hyde resigned the presidency and his membership of the Gaelic League because of its espousal of Irish nationalism.

Besides the overt resemblances between Breton and Irish revivalism, there was a comparable millenarianism directed by intellectual prophets. What Jack E. Reece, drawing upon other social philosophers, has deduced from Breton millenarianism could also be said to some degree of the Anglo-Irish Protestant millenarianism of the Irish revival:

> In this respect Breton nationalism has differed little from earlier varieties of European nationalism that, especially in central, eastern, and south-eastern Europe, were largely the work of literary figures and other assorted intellectuals. This recurring pattern has led the British scholar Anthony D. Smith to theorize that a leading historical function of nationalism has been to resolve "the crisis of the intelligentsia."
>
> Such a crisis arises out of the threat to the social dependencies of a traditional order that is being undermined by modernizing currents. Among these dependencies the intellectuals, by virtue of their superior educational attainments and their broad cultural experience, are particularly cognizant of the peril in which they are placed by the conjunction of the old and the new. Indeed, their vulnerability is perhaps greater than that of any other dependent group. Long the most articulate exponents of the ideological world view that gave the traditional order its theoretical legitimacy, they had received substantial moral and material rewards from those whose interests they served. Such intellectuals thus find themselves doubly threatened: from above by the collapsing debris of the old order and from below by the builders of the new one, who are determined to sweep away all those whose fortunes are tied to the traditional holders of power. According to Karl Mannheim, the social thinker to whom Smith is most heavily in debt, these intellectuals may extricate themselves from their dangerous situation by following either of two courses of action. They may seek affiliation with one of the various groups that are struggling to dominate the emergent social order or, through scrutiny of their social moorings, they may seek to rise above their particular class interests and forge a new mission for themselves as the detached guardians of the moral and material objectives of the people as a whole.[28]

In the case of the Irish intellectuals, mostly Protestant, the collapse of the old order—be it the Ascendancy whose heyday was the century before the Act of Union or the landlord class dangerously corrupt by the late nineteenth century—exceeded in import the danger from builders of a new order, many of whom had been in recent history Protestants. Only after the Free State was achieved did the Anglo-Irish intellectuals come to realize that there was to be no place for them in the new petty-bourgeois Catholic state. As for the two methods of extrication from the predicament, both were attempted by the versatile leaders of the revival. The admiration of Yeats, AE, and Synge for aristocrat, peasant, and artist, for example, embodied several social options, and only from the petty-bourgeois class that emerged in strength later did they withhold all admiration and support. Unifying the various social adaptations and ploys was the desire of the chief revival writers to be the detached guardians of the moral objectives of the people as a whole. James Joyce, it might be said, did not feel the same need to extricate himself since he owed no more than dubious emotional allegiance to the old order and was in any case a Catholic; besides, he aligned himself with no social group and therefore felt far less the resonances of group and class peril.

The Aran Islands: *Return To The Sole Self*

While we might accept for purposes of argument that cultural nationalists rejoice in community and are willing to subordinate themselves to it, as Synge would seem to have tried to do while on the Aran Islands, but with mixed success, it is less easy to accept that writers do so wholeheartedly. The language and purpose of literature are rarely—even in times of cultural resurgence—those of cultural nationalism, and so it is hardly surprising that the Irish writers in their separate ways made of the western island a literary myth, related to but different from both Celtic and nationalist myth. When Arthur Symons described his trip to the Aran Islands with Yeats, for instance, he used the discourse of dream, fetched up out of symbolism, aestheticism, and the Celtic Twilight as well as the legendry of enchanted islands: "More than anything I have ever seen, this seashore gave me the sensation of the mystery and the calm of all the islands one has ever dreamed of, all the fortunate islands that have ever been saved out of the disturbing sea; this delicate pearl-grey sand, the deeper grey of the stones, and more luminous grey of the water, and so consoling an air as of immortal twilight and the peace of its dreams."[29] Symons is not distant from the "real" islands because he is an Englishman; he is certainly no farther removed than Yeats. To be sure, Synge came to know more about Aran than either of them (he acquired a fair amount of Gaelic), but even he used the rhetoric of romanticism, harsher but even more genuinely romantic than Symons's, for describing the islands, be they Aran or Blasket. Words suggesting the absence of community recur: desolate, lonely, singular, solitary, wild. For Synge too, "The whole sight of wild islands and sea"—in this case the Blaskets—"was as clear and cold and brilliant as what one sees in a dream," though at least Synge's dreams are hard-edged.[30]

Synge's romantic attitude to the Aran Islands derived in part from Pierre Loti's *An Iceland Fisherman (Pêcheur d'Islande,* 1886), a copy of which Synge carried on his first trip to Aran and which, he said in one typed draft of his Introduction to *The Aran Islands,* gave him his general plan for the book. Loti, he thought, treated "this sort of subject more adequately than any other writer of the present day,"[31] though whether Synge is referring to travel journals or to peasant societies is unclear. These references to Loti were crossed out, Synge apparently having changed his mind about the French writer. But although Synge says elsewhere in the unpublished typescript associated with *The Aran Islands* that Loti has erred in his treatment of a peasant society, it is not obvious wherein the error lay; he seems to be accusing Loti of having, like Emily Lawless, author of *Grania* (1892), a novel set on Aran, insufficient knowledge of the real lives of his fictional peasants, in which case it is not the two authors' possible romanticism that Synge found at fault.[32]

For despite reservations he came to have, Synge's book shares several features with *An Iceland Fisherman*. Loti's is the more evidently fictional, but both books have a strong documentary and folkloristic underpinning and attempt to convey the folkways and mind of an intensely local, coastal, and Celtic peasantry, a people presented as devout, shy, hardy, quietly heroic, loyal, proud, poor, superstitious, and, in their own way, passionate. The strangeness of the subjects, to writer and reader, is part of the charm of both books. We have in each, however, not just the appeal of remoteness to the traveler and folklorist, but also the appeal of exoticism to a romantic sensibility. In addition to its rejection of civilization (Paris denounced and Brittany lauded) and its flight into extremes of nature (the waters of Iceland), both of which it shares with *The Aran Islands, An Iceland Fisherman* is romantic in the marketplace sense by having a sentimental view of love, and this Synge may have come to suspect. Loti's we might call "soft" romanticism and Synge's "hard" romanticism. In any case there is a romantic suffusion in both books, and both authors have an acute sensitivity to impressions of the world around them. Loti's response when he first beheld the sea as a child is not unlike Synge's response to the Aran Islands: Loti, according to a compatriot, "felt a sadness unspeakable, a sense of desolate solitude, of abandonment, of exile."[33]

There is no doubt that the life of the Breton fisherman who seasonally ploughed the waters of Iceland was indeed a harsh and dangerous one, likely to appear as both romantic and tragic to the sensitive and sympathetic outsider. This was corroborated by Le Braz, who wrote that the families of the Iceland fishermen regularly swelled the ranks of the pilgrims. Reality, then, sustains but cannot entirely account for the romanticism of the writer, which overreaches it. Le Braz' own romantic description in *The Land of Pardons* of the Ouessantines, inhabitants of a "savage island," must surely have mingled with Synge's experiences on Aran (including the story he was told of the old woman seeing her dead son astride a living horse) to impel the making of *Riders to the Sea:*

> There is not one among these Ouessantines who from birth to death has not been destined to eternal weeping. They live in perpetual terror of that sea which robs them of their fathers, their lovers, their husbands, their sons. This is why they dress in mourning from the cradle to the grave. Black is the bodice, black the skirt and apron, black the covering worn over the stiff white cap. There is something priestly about this large angular head-dress, its falling flaps calling to mind the "Pschent" of ancient Egypt. No finery, no coquetry; even the hair, that pride of womanhood, crown of her sovereignty, hangs down the neck and cheeks in short straight locks. Everything—the sombre dress, the loose hair around the mournful faces, still more the melancholy lament that rises from their lips by way of prayer—all tends to sadden one's heart by calling up thoughts of death and desolation, till at length these women seem a troop of victims driven forward to their doom by some goddess of fate.[34]

And surely what an old woman on a pardon with her great-grandson said to Le Braz made a special impression on Synge: "This is the ninth Troménie I have been to! Yes, this path has seen me pass nine times, with my husband, my sons, and the sons of my sons. I have mourned every one of them, and have buried none. They are all in the cemetery that has no cross. This is the last remaining to me. I have a fancy that the sea will take him like the others. It seems very hard, but every one must work out his fate".[35] In *Riders to the Sea,* Maurya delivers herself of very similar sentiments, tallying the personal losses and deriving comfort from the very adversity of fate itself.[36] The author's connivance at this stoicism—more than that, this tragic joy—is as evident in *The Aran Islands* as in the play and it is in its intensity high romanticism.

In one regard *The Aran Islands* is more genuinely romantic than *An Iceland Fisherman,* and that is in the presence as hero of the author himself. For this to happen, Synge had to be conscious of his own apartness while on the islands, and in doing so he was little different from other Irish revival writers. It is difficult to tell how far the writers, under the influence of a late romantic and symbolist cult of isolation, were really pursuing a sense of their own separation from the islanders while seeming to seek, as participants in a Celtic renaissance, psychic and spiritual communion with them. Symons's attitude is perhaps the most ingenuous. When he summarizes the Aran islanders as "simple, dignified, self-sufficient, sturdily primitive people," he is, one imagines, bending from a lofty height to do so. More jarring is his description of the women as "placid animals on whom emotion has never worked in any vivid or passionate way,"[37] a remark, I suggest, that Symons's meagre knowledge of the islanders disqualified him from making. Yet how do Symons's impressions differ really from Synge's description of the islanders as curiously simple, primitive, and half-civilized, and of Connacht dwellers as half-savage? In depth rather than in nature of feeling, I suspect. Synge may have travelled to the islands ostensibly to express a life that had never found expression, and to garner material for writing to that end by achieving intimacy with the islanders, yet *The Aran Islands* is neither mere fieldwork for the plays nor mere record of a rural retreat, much less a manifesto of union with an archaic society. It is a romantic document in its own right.

What begins as Synge's apparent cultivation of the desolation of three islands becomes an awareness of his own desolation. The literary otherworld of the island, itself derived from the Otherworld of legend, becomes a private, profoundly experienced otherworld of the unadorned self. Reading *The Aran Islands,* we accompany Synge in the painful process of discovering himself, not as one with the islanders, as the pressure of the revival suggest he do (or suggest he assert), but as a man cut off from them as he is from his sophisticated fellows, a man whose stay on the islands merely confirms his feeling of ultimate and eternal isolation.

There is an intermediate stage when Synge sees the islanders as sharing some of the qualities of the advanced and the artistic, which must have pleased Yeats. The women, he thought, exist "before conventionality, and share some of the liberal features that are thought peculiar to the women of Paris and New York" (p. 143), a quality Symons, if he would have believed or seen it, must have been sorry to have missed. Of the islandman, Synge writes: "The danger of his life on the sea gives him the alertness of a primitive hunter, and the long nights he spends fishing in his curagh bring him some of the emotions that are thought peculiar to men who have lived with the arts." (pp. 132–33) And what are those emotions? "On the low sheets of rock to the east I can see a number of red and grey figures hurrying about their work. The continual passing in this island between the misery of last night and the splendour of to-day, seems to create an affinity between the moods of these people and the moods of varying rapture and dismay that are frequent in artists, and in certain forms of alienation." (p. 74)

But if the Aran islanders resemble artists, they also resemble at once aristocrats and wild animals, as this curious piece of social genetics informs us:

> Their way of life has never been acted on by anything much more artificial than the nests and burrows of the creatures that live round them,

> and they seem in a certain sense to approach more nearly to the finer types of our aristocracies—who are bred artificially to a natural ideal—than to the labourer or citizen, as the wild horse resembles the thoroughbred rather than the hack or cart-horse. Tribes of the same natural development are, perhaps, frequent in half-civilised countries, but here a touch of the refinement of old societies is blended, with singular effect, among the qualities of the wild animal. (p. 66)

By so thinking, Synge, like other revivalists, paid homage to the common people without in reality doing so. Synge's peasants are special and not to be confused with the proletariat: they are like kings and queens and poets in disguise and in exile, as in some fairy tale. Moreover, by so thinking Synge completes Yeats's ideal triumvirate: peasant, artist, aristocrat. (We recall that Pegeen Mike, who has the bulk of Synge's sympathy in *The Playboy,* seeks to transform the farmer's son, Christy Mahon, with his delicate feet and "quality name," into an aristocrat, an exiled potentate, as well as a poet.)

The alliance between Synge and the islanders on grounds of artistic sensibility, important though it is in *The Aran Islands,* does not survive. Synge writes of suffering exile as well as intermittent despondency, a half-involuntary exile which is clearly from the islanders as well as from the mainlanders. "In some ways," he confides, "these men and women seem strangely far away from me. They have the same emotions that I have, and the animals have, yet I cannot talk to them when there is much to say, more than to the dog that whines beside me in a mountain fog" (p. 113). They are lost together but feel and express that loss separately. One might, I suppose, argue that Synge's Anglo-Irish Protestant identity did not help much in his task of getting to know a people taciturn with mainlanders. Nor would island memories of his missionary ancestor who arrived there in 1851 and described himself as "surrounded by dirt and ignorance"[38] do much to dissolve the barriers, even if Synge was a very different kind of missionary, and indeed seemed to deserve, unlike his forebear, the label Le Braz affixed to himself, that of "literary pilgrim."

Perhaps more pertinent was Synge's initial difficulty with Gaelic that excluded him from so many of the delights of the island, though Declan Kiberd, whose observation this is, reminds us that throughout *The Aran Islands* Synge's confidence and ability as an Irish speaker grew.[39] (On this level the book is the pioneering record of attainment in summer courses in the Irish language of the kind on which Irish schoolchildren have been sent to the Aran Islands since independence.) Intellectuals other than Synge, and even Catholic nationalist intellectuals who were fluent Irish speakers, had difficulty in communicating with native Irish speakers. In "The Death of Synge," Yeats reproduces a diary entry of his that records a visit he had from one such: "MacDonagh called to-day. Very sad about Ireland. Says that he finds a barrier between himself and the Irish-speaking peasantry, who are 'cold, dark and reticent' and 'too polite.' He watches the Irish-speaking boys at his school [St. Enda's in Dublin], and when nobody is looking, or when they are alone with the Irish-speaking gardener, they are merry, clever and talkative. When they meet an English speaker or one who has learned Gaelic, they are stupid. They are in a different world."[40] That on Aran Synge was on the native speakers' own turf might then have helped to compensate for the cultural, social, and religious divide they clearly sensed.

To these considerations we can add the physical separation of the Aran Islands from the mainland which occasioned some unease on Synge's part. "If anything serious should happen to me I might die here and be nailed in my box, and shoved down into a wet crevice in the graveyard before any one could know it on the mainland" (p. 110), though perhaps there is a hint of bravado here. Then, too, there was Synge's natural shyness and penchant for solitude. To the islanders Synge was "so strange and silent that no one actually knew him,"[41] and "Michael" [Martin MacDonagh], the boy who helped him with his Gaelic, wrote to him from the mainland: "I am thinking there is no one in life walking with you now but your own self from morning till night, and great is the pity" (p. 112). Indeed, the birds of the island sometimes seemed to Synge closer than the islanders: "As I lie here hour after hour, I seem to enter into the wild pastimes of the cliff, and to become a companion of the cormorants and crows . . . Their language is easier than Gaelic, and I seem to understand the greater part of their cries, though I am not able to answer. There is one plaintive note which they take up in the middle of their usual babble with extraordinary effect, and pass on from one to another along the cliff with a sort of an inarticulate wail, as if they remembered for an instant the horror of the mist" (pp. 73–74).

The horror and the inarticulateness are in him, and one incident in *The Aran Islands* that begins with a Keatsian experience of disembodiment ends by approaching a dark night of the soul:

> I have been down sitting on the pier till it was quite dark. I am only beginning to understand the nights of Inishmaan and the influence they have had in giving distinction to these men who do most of their work after nightfall.
>
> I could hear nothing but a few curlews and other wildfowl whis-

> tling and shrieking in the sea-weed, and the low rustling of the waves. It was one of the dark sultry nights peculiar to September, with no light anywhere except the phosphorescence of the sea, and an occasional rift in the clouds that showed the stars behind them.
>
> The sense of solitude was immense. I could not see or realise my own body, and I seemed to exist merely in my perception of the waves and of the crying birds, and of the smell of seaweed.
>
> When I tried to come home I lost myself among the sandhills, and the night seemed to grow unutterably cold and dejected, as I groped among slimy masses of seaweed and wet crumbling walls. (pp. 129–130)

There is the romantic trajectory we know from the poetry of Keats: the seduction of the self from society by a simplified and intense nature (curlews and waves on a dark night) and, paradoxically, by the self's will to destruction; the highpoint of imagined self-transcendence and union with the natural symbols (the waves and crying birds); the emotional letdown with the return to the self (lost among sandhills but in a way that merely intensifies the self-suffering and consciousness).

It is a trajectory we find repeated in *The Aran Islands*. In the desolate islands, where the people were as intelligible as are whining dogs and crying birds, and all were as ultimately mute as bare rock faces, Synge found reflected his own terrifying loneliness of spirit—the islands were the habitat of his own soul, isolated and besieged by all that is other. It was a coincidence for Synge, happy artistically, less happy emotionally, that he found a people whose moods and way of life (their nocturnal activities, for example) were so complementary to his own—complementary yet inescapably other. It is noteworthy that Synge often becomes most painfully aware of himself at those times when he is most aware of the island, as he skirts the perimeter, conscious of the island as an inanimate and passive victim of antagonistic forces of being. It was Synge more profoundly than the islanders who was "certain set apart."[42] Synge received but what he gave, by pathetic fallacy projecting his feelings on to the islands, the islanders and the very birds (employing words like "solitary," "lonely," and "desolate" that are essentially ambiguous in their reference), unwarrantably at times, one feels, though it is a principle of the romantic imagination. "Seems" is one of his most-worked words. He writes of the loneliness, desolation, "pagan desperation," "passionate rage," even "pitiable despair before the horror of the fate to which [the islanders] are all doomed" that lie beneath the "daily trifles that veil from them the terror of the world" (p. 75). Synge approaches perversity when, watching high-spirited girls on the Blasket Islands, he recalls gloomily that "in spite of their high spirits it gave me a sort of grief to feel the utter loneliness and desolation of the place that has given these people their finest qualities."[43]

In Synge is a portion of that romantic willfulness we find in Yeats's Cumhal, Dhoya, Robartes, Aherne, Hanrahan, and, in lesser measure, the narrator of the apocalyptic stories. He records for us a dream he had on Inishmaan. In this dream he danced ecstatically until his will was threatened and he could barely tell the dancer from the dance, but at the last moment fell back from the enchanted precipice like Yeats's narrator:

> Last night, after walking in a dream among buildings with strangely intense light on them, I heard a faint rhythm of music beginning far away on some stringed instrument.
>
> It came closer to me, gradually increasing in quickness and volume with an irresistibly definite progression. When it was quite near the sound began to move in my nerves and blood, and to urge me to dance with them.
>
> I knew that if I yielded I would be carried away to some moment of terrible agony, so I struggled to remain quiet, holding my knees together with my hands.
>
> The music increased continually, sounding like the strings of harps, tuned to a forgotten scale, and having a resonance as searching as the strings of the 'cello.
>
> Then the luring excitement became more powerful than my will, and my limbs moved in spite of me.
>
> In a moment I was swept away in a whirlwind of notes. My breath and my thoughts and every impulse of my body, became a form of the dance, till I could not distinguish between the instruments and the rhythm and my own person or consciousness.
>
> For a while it seemed an excitement that was filled with joy, then it grew into an ecstasy where all existence was lost in a vortex of movement. I could not think there had ever been a life beyond the whirling of the dance.
>
> Then with a shock the ecstasy turned to an agony and rage. I struggled to free myself, but seemed only to increase the passion of the steps I moved to. When I shrieked I could only echo the notes of the rhythm.
>
> At last with a moment of uncontrollable frenzy I broke back to consciousness and awoke.
>
> I dragged myself trembling to the window of the cottage and looked out. The moon was glittering across the bay, and there was no sound anywhere on the island. (pp. 99–100)

Yeats quotes this passage approvingly in "J. M. Synge and the Ireland of his Time," possibly because it could, with rhetorical ornamentation, have appeared in "Rosa Alchemica."[44] Here, according to Yeats, was an outburst of hidden passion, the soul's will to express itself and refusing diversion into intense empathy for others (that can become, as I have suggested, pathetic fallacy). But that it happens in dream suggests that diversion is yet taking place and that the dramatic situation in which the narrator found himself at the climax of "Rosa Alchemica" was not in Synge's life a conscious possibility. Nor is self-release of a possessed and ecstatic kind quite the good (however dangerous) it is in Yeats's fiction. Perhaps it is the currency, and not the goal, of self-escape that is different in Yeats and Synge. The coinage of dream and reverie was more familiar and congenial to Yeats than the coinage of hard rock and ocean by which Synge sought to buy release from the self but which in fact secured for him a contrary state of affairs.

The Aran Islands *as Spiritual Autobiography*

The Aran Islands is a remarkable and closely observed travel book which emerged from notebooks crammed with impressions and anecdotes. Yet the book's suggestion of pilgrimage, its in-tales (the stories told to Synge and reproduced by him), even its structure: these somehow go beyond the journeyings and jottings of a traveler with both ears and both eyes open. *The Aran Islands* has as its goal a mortifying vision of primal unity before the emergence of the self. In these respects it bears a passing resemblance to the old Irish voyage tales, such as *The Voyage of Maelduin, The Voyage of the Sons of O'Corra* or *The Voyage of Bran.* Like them its documentary value is questionable. Although in his Introduction he denies he invented anything, Synge "admits" in the same breath that he has had nothing to say about the islanders that is not wholly in their favor, a defensive implication that he has omitted material that might have been construed as unfavorable to the islanders.

One scholar has recently told us that "Synge incurred the wrath of the islanders by publishing details of their life in April 1901."[45] We might see in the book a determination not to incur such wrath again; if so, Synge was foiled, for "their anger at Synge's disclosures was further increased by the publication of *The Aran Islands*. They commented sourly that it would have been a better book 'if Synge had spoken less of the people.'"[46] How ironic that he should share in this the fate of the Rev. Alexander Synge, though it might serve to remind us of the disguised missionary spirit with which many revival writers approached the west.

But however partial a record is *The Aran Islands* from an anthropological point of view, it is from the literary critic's point of view a profound spiritual autobiography whose landscape, like the landscape of the early penitential voyages, is utterly essential but ultimately emblematic, a spiritual projection. In the most honorable sense the book is fiction, by virtue of the transforming agency of Synge's subjective perception and narration. Under the fieldwork and documentary attentiveness exist a pattern and direction which develop as Synge abandons the more advanced, sociable and, in a metaphoric sense, "eastern" parts of the islands for the more primitive, isolated and "western" parts, all the while freeing the self from all social forces until at last it is at the mercy of the elements of existence. In *The Aran Islands,* the writer is his own romantic hero, and we might recall Frye's suggestion that "the most comprehensive and central of all Romantic themes . . . is a romance with the poet for hero."[47]

The romantic hero of the Irish literary revival is inseparable from the real or metaphoric west, and so Synge's autobiographical hero is the most romantic of all, inseparable as he is from a few wet but numinous rocks in the Atlantic in which are vested his most visionary moments. Synge returned to the mainland, but altered for good like Maelduin and the sons of O'Corra or, we might add, like Keats having followed his nightingale as far as is humanly possible. But perhaps in a sense he never returned at all, like Bran, the voyage out being all.

Beneath the apparent symbolism of primal unity and prehistoric community—a symbolism created or borrowed by the cultural nationalists—the western island was for Synge the pared habitat of the self. His lasting vision was not the reason that he travelled to the Aran Islands and the Blasket Islands; nor was it that of the sons of O'Corra, who found God, or of Maelduin, who found human companionship. It is not surprising that the island should during the revival combine contradictory meaning, since an island is by definition a visible portion of a submerged landmass yet at the same time cut off from the mainland. Students of archetypes favor Synge's implicit island symbolism since to them the island images the self emerging from selflessness,[48] while to Jung it represents a synthesis of the consciousness and will, a refuge from the menacing assault of the sea of the unconscious. Synge is the type of romantic writer for whom the revelation of one's solitariness is not a stage on the way to truth, as it is for Yeats's fictional heroes, but truth's sombre destination. He temporarily or nearly succeeds, having fled society, in achieving self-transcendence, whose emblematic site or vehicle is the island (as Keats's was on one potent occasion a nightingale). But he fails, and *The Aran Islands* is the eloquent record of the flight from and eventual return to his "sole self," a flight and return that leave him changed and dissatisfied, however grateful his readers might be for the artistry of the record.

Lavelle and Brehon in *The Interpreters* succeed where Synge fails, but then AE's is the more programmatic of the two works, less informed by actual experience, let alone experience of Synge's kind on Aran. The Synge of *The Aran Islands* resembles more closely Robartes, Aherne, and the narrator of the apocalyptic stories, but Synge's goal is less supernatural, his attempts at self-transcendence less ceremonial, his artistic record less symbolic and arcane, his ideal way of life less decadent; in most of these respects he is more like Hanrahan. But the same disparity between design and eventuality that is the chief irony in the lives of Yeats's heroes is there in *The Aran Islands*.

To speak, however, of writers rather than of fictional characters is to recognize that Synge sought to earn his sense of unity with Gaelic Ireland more honestly and painstakingly than most revival writers, and that paradoxically this makes him unusual among them. Moreover, such is the intensity of the failure, in which he brought back instead a profound and eloquent diary of the romantic self, that one cannot but suspect that, Yeats and AE and the revival to the contrary, Synge's search for the sole self outside the society of men has been all along his secret and unconscious impulse.

The Infinite Pain of Self-Realization *The Realist Reply*

III

I find in an old diary: "I think all happiness depends on the energy to assume the mask of some other life, on a re-birth as something not one's self, something created in a moment and perpetually renewed; in playing a game like that of a child where one loses the infinite pain of self-realisation."

—W. B. Yeats

I seriously believe you will retard the course of civilisation in Ireland by preventing the Irish people from having one good look at themselves in my nicely polished looking-glass.

—James Joyce
letter to Grant Richards concerning *Dubliners*

Hail and Farewell:
George Moore and Revival Ireland. Gerald O'Donovan

7

. . . only what my eye has seen,
and my heart has felt, interests me.

—*George Moore*

Preliminaries to the Affair

George Moore's promotion of the self—his abiding concern—was anything but secret, and Wilde's remark that his friend Moore conducted his education in public is celebrated. Moreover, that self was to be found inside rather than outside the society of men, and vocations are in his fiction the arena for the contest between personal and public morality. In 1909 (the year of Synge's early death), Moore remembered his passing desire nine years before to compose in Irish the play he was writing with Yeats: "but to do that one would have to know the Irish language, and to learn it, it would be necessary to live in Arran for some years."[1] His daydream of life on the Aran Islands is a kind of aesthete's pastoral evaporating into wistful realism. "A vision of what my life would be there rose up: a large, bright cottage with chintz curtains, and homely oaken furniture, and some three or four Impressionist pictures, and the restless ocean my only companion until I knew enough Irish for daily speech. But ten years among the fisherfolk might blot out all desire of literature in me, and even if it didn't, and if I succeeded in acquiring Irish (which was impossible), it would be no nearer to the language spoken by Diarmuid and Grania than modern English is to Beowulf." The acknowledgment of impossibility and defeat was as eloquent in Yeats and Synge as in Moore, but they were romantically nourished by it, whereas Moore in his disappointed romanticism embraced the offending reality, a reaction we will see displayed in the realist writers who came after him.

Yet for a short time Moore like Synge was recruited from France ("my own country") into the service of Ireland, and he told the assembled luminaries of the revival at the famous dinner in Dublin's Shelbourne Hotel in 1899 that it was the greatness of Yeats and the promise of the Irish Literary Theatre that achieved the recruitment.[2] His "Irish adventure" (John Eglinton's phrase) is recorded brilliantly in that memoir-cum-novel, *Hail and Farewell* (1911–14), and it can be variously dated.[3] After domiciles in Paris and London, Moore lived in Dublin between March 1901 and February 1911. But if in fact the end of the affair can be detected as early as 1902 when the rift with Yeats opened (it has been said that Moore's enthusiasm for the revival and his enthusiasm for Yeats were coterminous),[4] and made public in 1903 when *The Untilled Field* appeared or in 1905 when *The Lake* was published, the beginning can be sought as early as 1899 when Yeats and Edward Martyn told him of the Irish Literary Theatre, or 1894 when Martyn spoke longingly to him of the Irish language.[5] Indeed, Moore predicted the revival in 1885 when he was writing *A Drama in Muslin,* and when it came, the realist in him had to become involved in order, it seemed, to savor the disparity between romantic design and unromantic actuality. It is hard not to see Moore's revivalism as an elaborate piece of mummery and therefore doomed; but the speed of its doom argues a deeper fidelity to the lifelong agenda of the realist and ironist, an agenda, divorced from the adultery of Moore's motives, for which we in Ireland can be grateful.

Given the nature of Moore's work, especially that of the masterly *Hail and Farewell,* it is hardly trivial to register those unexalted motives for his crossing the Irish Sea and joining the Irish revival that Moore owned up to in his memoir: a wish to disrupt the monotony of his life in London ("by stripping myself of my clothes and running ahead a naked Gael, screaming Brian Boru," p. 111); a propensity "to have a finger in every literary pie" (p. 115); the desire of the realist writer, like a painter, to have models for "sittings."[6] *Hail and Farewell* fulfilled this last, despite the indignation with which Moore in that book recalled that at the Irish Literary Theatre lunch in 1900 at which he read his paper, "Literature and the Irish Language," "there were some cynics present, Gaelic Leaguers, who, while approving, held doubts, asking each other if my sincerity were more than skin-deep; and it was whispered at Edward's table that I had come over to write about the country and its ideas, and would make fun of them all when it suited my purpose to do so."[7] Realistic, sometimes witheringly so, about others, Moore was often deceiving (or deceived) about himself, and he would not acknowledge that the cynicism of the Gaelic Leaguers was prophetic realism. Moore suggested that he had a kind of dual personality, one self writing tragedy, the other living comic drama.[8] But *Hail and Farewell,* the transcript of a fundamentally and subversively comic life in Ireland during the heyday of the Irish revival, bears sufficient resemblances to his fiction proper for us to wonder about the divisibility of the personality and the separation of the comic self from the fiction which it surely colors.

Either way, the "self-consciousness" of the man (his own word) was inimical to the spirit and philosophy of the revival. Perhaps his temporary discipleship under AE rested on a hope that the latter's belief in the impersonal unity of the cosmos would make the troubling currents of his being as smooth as the Irish Sea, which he claimed had never a wave in it when he crossed.[9] Moore subscribed briefly to AE's pantheistic doctrine of "the extraordinary oneness of things," but he was truer to himself when later in the 1920s, back in England, he denied to John Eglinton any transcendental element in human experience and asserted his disbelief in all mysticism.[10] Moore's empiricism and materialism lay behind the naturalist's attention to heredity, environmental forces, and the accidents (or mutant events) of life.[11]

Moore, in short, was a prime candidate for the self-transcendence preached by the revival, but there were obstacles. His was an established reputation in 1899, and only Yeats among the lights of the revival (all of them save O'Grady younger than Moore) had one comparable; an excusable vanity might have got in the way, and did. Then there was his genealogy. That he came from an old landowning family, and in the west moreover, should have been an advantage to someone seeking to join the revival, but it was a Catholic family, and Yeats for one considered him a peasant (like Martyn, another landowning Catholic in County Mayo), but clearly no more a genuine peasant, because a landowner, than an authentic gentleman, because a Catholic.[12] The Moores, however, had turned Catholic only in the eighteenth century (conversion, then, was in the blood, we might say); in *Hail and Farewell,* Moore asserted that his father was Catholic "only of one generation"; Moore brings *A Story-Teller's Holiday* (1918) to a close by claiming his family for the Protestant Ascendancy, "a fact that must be borne in mind always—Irish Catholics being worthless."[13]

Moore himself discovered his own brand of Protestantism as early as his play *Martin Luther* (1879), yet in 1903 felt it necessary to renounce his Roman Catholicism publicly, in a way that paradoxically claimed his membership of that church until he was fifty-one. Whereas an unpracticed Protestantism aligned him with the revivalists, whose paganism he already shared, his vociferous anti-Catholicism assuredly didn't. Various reasons have been offered to explain Moore's anti-Catholicism, social, psychological, even sexual,[14] and it is clear that it bespoke a great unease in him. But the fact remains that the Protestant leaders of the revival were themselves anti-Catholic yet avoided open confrontation with the Catholic Church; theirs was a prudent realism where Moore's was a reckless and courageous realism. When clerical interference threatened the production of Yeats's *The Countess Cathleen,* Moore noted the playwright's apparent indifference. Yeats claimed to know Ireland better than did Moore and therefore was more patient; but he didn't, and lived to find out as a senator in the new Free State.[15] Moore's anti-Catholicism embarrassed the Protestant revivalists and offended Catholics who believed that Catholicism and Gaelicism were inseparable,[16] and it did not abate during his tenure as an enthusiast for the new Ireland. In fact, he claimed absurdly in *Hail and Farewell* that he returned to Ireland in the belief that he was the chosen instrument by which Ireland would be redeemed from Catholicism (pp. 353, 608), a mission that was not a plank in the platform of the revival, even if it logically should have been.

The suffocation of Catholic Ireland was one reason for Moore's early dislike of the island, and even if it was his family's fortunes rather than his own outlook that explained his early departure from it, it is nevertheless true that in his anticlericalism and Parisian exile he anticipated Joyce, just as in choosing France for his literary inspiration he anticipated Yeats. His dislike of Ireland returned after the revival adventure, and he claimed in 1923 that it bound him to the Ulsterman Eglinton who left Dublin in 1922 when the Free State came into being. Since his ancestral home, Moore Hall, had recently been burned by the Irish Republican Army, he had cause for outburst, though he had long predicted the end of this and other Big Houses and the social order at whose center they stood.

Moore's early dislike for Ireland culminated in *Parnell and His Island* (1887), and Douglas Hyde warned him when he arrived back in Ireland that the book would go against him with the Gaelic League.[17] That it was spiritually France rather than England for whom Moore had jilted Ireland did not help; it was the France not of Humbert and the 1798 expeditionary force to Mayo, but of Mallarmé, Verlaine, and Villiers de l'Isle Adam, and of the new painters with whom he became acquainted: Manet, Degas, Monet, Renoir. He remembered the reaction of the callous aesthete he was, or affected to be, in 1880 when agrarian disturbances in Ireland necessitated his return from Paris after seven years: "That some wretched farmers and miners[*sic*] should refuse to starve, that I may not be deprived of my *demi-tasse* at Tortoni's, that I may not be forced to leave this beautiful retreat, my cat and my python—monstrous! And these wretched creatures will find moral support in England—they will find pity. Pity, that most vile of all virtues has never been known to me."[18] This pose was later dropped, and though he recognized in *Hail and Farewell* that "love of cruelty is inveterate in the human being" (p. 220)—by way of excusing his own occasional malice—he also avowed that "without pity man may not live" (p. 187) (detecting in Yeats a lack of ordinary human sympathy) and is Joyce's kinsman in the avowal.[19] But his recurring aestheticism was held against him and unlike Yeats's (for Yeats too had had his symbolist phase) it proved unassimilable to Irish cultural nationalism.

Moore's aesthetic self survived *Flowers of Passion* (1878) and *Pagan Poems* (1881), and Eglinton claimed that "his mind had taken its permanent shape in the French language; his standards were French standards; the liberators and instructors of his spirit were those who held sway in Paris in the eighties."[20] As well as Moore the French symbolist there was Moore the French naturalist, the writer who wished to become "Zola's offshoot in England"[21] by observing realities and the commonplaces of life and following scientific methods, and who tried to do so in *A Mummer's Wife* (1885). But although Moore in time rejected naturalism while acknowledging its importance to him, and denied its theory of art, he did so because its materialism was impersonal. He spurned it not for the transcendentalism that characterized the Irish revival but for an individualist theory of art that would have found no favor with the Irish romantics, mystics, nationalists, and legendizers. After Moore the French naturalist came Moore the French realist under the sway of Balzac, and it was *Esther Waters* (1894) that established Moore as a major English novelist. The adjective ought not, however, to diminish the extent to which Moore anticipated the relocated experiments of the young Joyce who began to compose *Dubliners* a decade later and drew on realist and naturalist predecessors such as Moore; in doing so, Joyce estranged himself from the Irish revival as deeply as had his countryman, though in 1899 the older writer fondly thought, or pretended to think, that the estrangement was reversible.

English and Irish, Protestant and Catholic, gentry and peasant, landowner and aesthete, symbolist and naturalist, even male and female[22]—a simultaneity and succession of real and literary selves. Like the revivalists, Moore tried to unify these selves by transcendence, or, reversing the metaphor, by submerging and rebaptizing them in the deep lake of Irish nationality. But Moore's tergiversations, unlike those of the revivalists, were directed towards the realization of self, not its dissolution, and Ireland was hostile to this, whether it be the actual and passing Ireland of Ascendancy feudalism and Catholic torpor or the ideal or emerging Ireland of the revivals (of Gaelic nationalism, Catholic ascendancy, or cultivated pagan neofeudalism). "In Ireland," Moore wrote in *Hail and Farewell,* "men and women die without realising any of the qualities they bring into the world" (p. 58); if he really thought the revival would rectify this, he was soon disabused. Not for nothing do the chief figures of the revival parade before us in *Hail and Farewell* like players before a painted scene, theatrically out of key with Irish reality, comedians to the gay tragedians and proud Olympians Yeats later remembered as the dramatis personae of revival Ireland. One would want to acknowledge the very real changes that were taking place during Moore's stay, including the cooperative movement and the resuscitation of the native language. But amidst the renewal of Irish pride, the central reality of Irish life—inhibition of the individual—remained unaffected, as the young Joyce well knew.

An Earlier Breach: **A Drama in Muslin**

Moore briefly thought that he could satisfy the demands both of the individual and of nationality. When he gave up the attempt, a key direction for Irish literature (and Irish life) was lost. Thereafter, Irish literature played variations on the nationalist theme, the sorrowful legend of Ireland, or else, un-Moored, we might say, from Irish society, sought in perverse revenge an extreme and painful individuality, a subjectivity that began with Moore, continued with Joyce, and was passed from O'Connor and O'Faolain in the 1930s to John McGahern and Brian Moore three decades or so later.[23] The attempt was given up not once but twice in his career, for Moore's sojourn in Ireland was a resumption of the task he had postponed when he finished *A Drama in Muslin* (1886) and under the new circumstances he had in fact predicted in that novel. Although it is the later, eloquent surrenders *(The Untilled Field* and *The Lake)* that influenced Irish fiction, the earlier novel is well worth looking at, both as an anticipation of the later preoccupations and as evidence of Moore's stylistic development. To do so is to remind ourselves how much Ireland changed between 1886 and 1901, and the realism of the later works owes something, it should be admitted at the outset, to the revival discovery that there was matter for literature in aspects of Irish life hitherto ignored.

A Drama in Muslin: A Realistic Novel subjects to a scathing if undisciplined realism the life of the Anglo-Irish gentry (primarily Catholic, like Moore's own family) from 1882 to 1887, two years beyond the time at which Moore was writing. It concerned, he said, "the social and political power of the Castle in Modern Ireland,"[24] but it did so indirectly, by making the cruelty and frivolity of débutante life suggest the gaudy insolence of English power in Ireland and by concentrating on the inhabitants of a Big House in Galway. These gentlefolk are increasingly besieged by a restive peasantry incited by the Land League, yet they foolishly cast their eyes beyond the intervening reality to the marriage prospects offered by the Dublin season.

This "awful mummery in muslin"[25] is locally directed by Mrs. Barton of Brookfield, wife of an ineffectual amateur artist, mother of two daughters (one beautiful and featherbrained, one plain and intelligent), believer in the philosophy that "a woman can do nothing until she is married," who tells her daughters: "if you were Jane Austens, George Eliots, and Rosa Bonheurs, it would be of no use if you weren't married. A husband is better than talent, better even than fortune—without a husband a woman is nothing" (p. 137). Mrs. Barton has dedicated her life to amusing and flattering men and expects her daughters to do the same. The foibles of the Irish Belindas are set down with such pitiless relish and faithfulness to truth (Moore carried out field work for the novel during the winter of 1884–85) that the iridescent surfaces of their empty lives threaten to distract us from a second theme of the novel: the social conventions, as Moore put it, "that drive women into the marriage market."[26] Moore was justified in later claiming a pioneering affinity between his novel and Ibsen's *A Doll's House,* and he should receive credit for the punctuality of his feminism.

The Ibsenite heroine is young Alice Barton. She half-believes her mother's philosophy (which in one sense is an extreme realism, abject in acceptance of reality and incapable of conceiving changes in society), but she half-realizes "how men have bought women, imprisoned women, kept women as a sort of common property," decked them out "in innocence, virtue, and belief as ephemeral as the muslins we wear" (p. 101). It is the plain girl like Alice who is regarded as most pure, a stereotype that belies her real and unasserted self.[27] If she is falsified by the demands on her gender made by her decayed social class, she is falsified equally by the demands of her church, and the awful mummery in muslin is echoed in "the mummery of attending at Mass" when she no longer believes. In *Hail and Farewell,* Moore wrote that in Alice Barton he sought to represent "the personal conscience striving against the communal" (p. 275). Alice in other words is a "Protestant," but Moore does not, here or elsewhere, have the churchgoing subscriber to Protestantism in mind. For Alice's friend, Cecilia, after all, who wants the love of Alice and cannot have it, is a Protestant who turns Catholic at the end of the novel. Cecilia has discovered her real (and retrogressive) self to be "Catholic," as Moore's heroes, like Moore himself, discover their real (and progressive) selves to be "Protestant"—independent, individualistic, freethinking. In Moore's scheme of things (and my own in this study), Joyce could have been claimed as a "Protestant." Moore rebelled against the idea that once one was a Catholic, one was always a Catholic and that the most a freethinker could expect was to become a "bad" Catholic; he despised all imprisoning categories. To discover oneself a "Protestant" was simply to discover oneself; the creed of Protestantism that descended from Luther was in his opinion merely a stage in the evolution towards agnosticism.[28]

Cecilia is a mystic, idealist and man-hater, and she represents for Moore one form of late nineteenth century feminism, while Alice the agnostic and realist represents the other. Cecilia is rejected by Moore, as he later rejected her "mysticism and its adjuncts—foolish hope and wild aspiration" when he encc intered them during the revival. Alice turns from mysticism to "the natural duties and interests of life, its plain and simple rectitudes as she saw them revealed in the general history of mankind" (p. 187). She desires a husband, sexual intercourse, and a love that is founded on sympathy and collaboration between husband and wife. These she achieves (after years of retreating into herself, like the heroes of Irish novels long after her, "to escape the blinding and filthy rain of falsehood that swept in from all sides," p. 140); but she has had to lower her mother's standards that are a recipe for disaster (as the threat of spinsterhood hovering over the ageing ex-*débutantes* of her acquaintance shows). She becomes a writer, marries a doctor of the class beneath her, and goes to live in a London suburb. The novel ends with a self-conscious defense of suburbanism, provincialism, and "honest materialism"; but if this is a dubious hymn, and Alice has settled for something less than ideal, it is infinitely preferable to the fatuities and dangers of Ireland, a hymn to England only by default.

For the Ireland of 1882 is seen as the theatre of two kinds of drama, one comic, the other serious. The novel opens in an English convent school with the performance of a play that Alice has adapted from Tennyson's ballad of King Cophetua, and this play establishes the novel's central metaphor of mummery. The terrible acting of the play represents the thwarting of Alice's dramatic intentions by reality, just as the high hopes of the débutantes Alice and her friends are about to become will be cruelly dashed by the terrible reality that the glitter of the Castle balls disguises. In Alice's play, a king loves a beggar-maid, and the romantic idealism of this is scoffed at by the reality of life in Ireland during the 1880s: antilandlord disturbances orchestrated by the Land League; the Phoenix Park murders; the grim succession of Coercion Act, Arrears Act, and Crimes Bill; the clapping into prison of Parnell, Davitt and Dillon. The life of the gentry, who strive to ignore the turbulence, certainly to ignore its root causes, is more mummery. In one wonderful scene Moore has Mrs. Barton, while in her drawing-room politely dismissing the request of a penniless captain for the hand of her beautiful daughter, watching beyond the window "the pantomime that was being enacted within her view": her husband confronting his protesting tenants for whom "her eyes gleamed with hatred" (p. 127). When Mrs. Barton laments that "decidedly everything was going wrong," she may be referring to her daughter Olive's prospects, but Moore is referring to Ireland.

Moore has little sympathy for mortgaged landowners who mistook injustice for eternity: "An entire race, a whole caste, saw themselves driven out of their soft, warm couches of idleness, and forced into the struggle for life. The prospect appalled them; birds with shorn wings could not gaze more helplessly on the high trees where they had built, as they thought, their nests out of the reach of evil winds. What could they do with their empty brains? What could they do with their feeble hands? Like an avenging spirit, America rose above the horizon of their vision, and the plunge into its shadowy arms threatened, terrified them now, as it had terrified the famine-stricken peasants of Forty-nine" (p. 95). Alice early in the novel "had already begun to see something wrong in each big house being surrounded by a hundred small ones, all working to keep it in sloth and luxury" (p. 68), and by the end of the novel she has become sympathetic to the nationalist cause. But she cannot express both her nationalism and her individuality, and seeing the priority of the latter she leaves Ireland. In any case, by the autumn of 1882, the landlords have been saved, if bridled, by the Land Act, and the burden of terror has slipped from the landlords' shoulders on to the peasantry; for the gentry, the threatened revenge tragedy has reverted to the light comedy of yore, making exile for Alice a necessity.

In its bitter satire on the Irish gentry, *A Drama in Muslin* ought to have appealed to the architects of the revival, especially since it gave measurable offense to the right sort in Ireland. But writers of the revival preferred to ignore the doings of the gentry, and the serialization of Moore's novel in *Court and Society Review* would have suggested that it belonged more in a Loveresque than a Yeatsian universe of discourse. Similarly, the portrait of an independent-minded young woman ought to have appealed to a movement that found room for Kathleen Sheehy, Gretta Cousins, and Mary Colum, but Alice embodies the principle of individuality that finds itself expressed better in an eastward direction towards a London suburb than in that westward direction towards Galway that the revival would soon advocate. In his remarkably savage descriptions of Dublin in 1882 ("Never were poverty and wealth brought into plainer proximity") that drew upon his naturalist technique and of which some of Joyce's descriptions in *Dubliners* are reminiscent, Moore portrays a moribund city and country awaiting revival: indeed, he predicts it, seeing in Ireland "the inevitable decay which must precede an outburst of national energy" (p. 325). Yet when the outburst came, Alice Barton, in the guise of her creator, could not return to Ireland for good; the new nationalism proved as hostile to self-fulfillment as the old unjust feudal order.

A Drama in Muslin is an uneven blend of Moore's naturalism and aestheticism; both here are species of realism, one rarefied. Whereas the naturalism is reserved for the reality of Ireland, Moore exploits his familiarity with symbolism in re-creating the elegant superficiality of the gentry. Life for the women of the upper class, and by implication for everyone in the landowning class, is "arranged," a word that recurs. Marriages, outings and balls are arranged; people are likened to paintings and so too is nature; all is artificial and aspires to the picturesque; life is like one vast artist's studio. In one astonishing passage, the equivalent of which is Joyce's description of the feast-table in "The Dead," Moore orchestrates the painterly richness of apparel as a musical performance:

> Lengths of white silk clear as the notes of violins playing in a minor key; white poplin falling into folds statuesque as the bass of a fugue by Bach; yards of ruby velvet, rich as an air from Verdi played on the piano; tender green velvet, pastoral as hautboys heard beneath trees in a fair Arcadian vale; blue turquoise faille Française fanciful as the tinkling of a guitar twanged by a Watteau shepherd; gold brocade, sumptuous as organ tones swelling through the jewelled twilight of a nave; scarves and trains of midnight-blue profound as the harmonic snoring of a bassoon; golden daffodils violent as the sound of a cornet; bouquets of pink roses and daisies, charmful and pure as the notes of a flute. (p. 162)

But we are distracted from the satire and wallow in a wealth we are meant to deplore.

The novel is itself overarranged and, unwittingly or not, aligns itself with a view of life it wishes to reject. For Moore frequently objected to arrangement in life, and the equivalent of the way in which the life of the spoiled gentry was arranged was the way in which the Catholic church drew a circle around faith and morals, "arranging the Catholic's journey from the cradle to the grave as carefully as any tour planned by that excellent firm, Messrs Cook and Sons."[29] Moore streamlined the novel before reissuing it as *Muslin* in 1915, toned up its realism, though he retained the passage above. It was too late though to ingratiate himself with the Irish literati; nor, his Irish adventure being over, did he want to. Significantly, one passage he excised in the revision was the one that referred to the imminence of national revival; by 1915 he thought that in his terms it had failed or had not taken place at all, the moribund condition of the patient too advanced for reversal.

Ruin and Weed: The Untilled Field

Nevertheless, Moore's conversion to the revival occurred fifteen years after *A Drama in Muslin* appeared. If the first phase of his conversion was Yeats's founding of the Irish Literary Theatre—an event focussed by Martyn's telegram to Moore from Dublin in 1899: "The sceptre of intelligence has passed from London to Dublin"—the second was Moore's anti-British stand during the Boer War. He suddenly thought of himself as an Irishman rather than an Englishman, and found himself railing against English materialism and cosmopolitanism, coarse next to Ireland's spirituality and nationality. In "Literature and the Irish Language," he retracted the hymn to England that closes *A Drama in Muslin* and attacked "the universal suburb" which England was trying to make of the world.[30] He discovered a sentimental craving for Ireland and was absorbed by the legends of the country. His customary realism was forgotten, and in *Hail and Farewell* he remembered asking himself: "reality can destroy the dream, why shouldn't the dream be able to destroy reality?" (p. 120). It was suspiciously identical to a religious conversion (in one reading a subversive parody of the slower, quasi-religious conversions of his peers to cultural nationalism), and three times he heard a voice telling him to go to Ireland, or felt a presence forcing him to his knees.

Against the run of play, he was ready to pronounce "Salve" to Ireland. He had to overcome his aversion to Irish peasants ("creatures of marsh and jungle") and their language that frothed like porter. He had to put aside his distaste for the anthropomorphizing of Ireland ("a sort of Wotan who goes about—") that he noted among the new nationalists, his fear that Cathleen ni Houlihan like some vampire would get him after all, and would demand the surrender of his personality as surely as did the Catholic church:

> in a vision I saw Ireland as a god demanding human sacrifices, and everybody, or nearly everybody, crying: Take me, Ireland, take me; I am unworthy, but accept me as a burnt-offering. Ever since I have been in the country I have heard people speaking of working for Ireland. But how can one work for Ireland without working for oneself? What do they mean? They do not know themselves, but go on vainly sacrificing all personal achievement, humiliating themselves before Ireland as if the country were a god. A race inveterately religious I suppose it must be! And these sacrifices continue generation after generation. Something in the land itself inspires them. And I began to tremble lest the terrible Cathleen ni Houlihan might overtake me. She had come out of that arid plain, out of the mist, to tempt me, to soothe me into forgetfulness that it is the plain duty of every Irishman to disassociate himself from all memories of Ireland—Ireland being a fatal disease, fatal to Englishmen and doubly fatal to Irishmen. (p. 213)

He later remembered his enthusiasm as a "microbe" that destroyed his "former self" and permitted the emergence of his "new self." This new self did not forget that art and Catholicism were incompatible, but imagined that Ireland was "awaking at last out of the great sleep of Catholicism," so that perhaps less self-sacrifice was required than he feared. We can make sense of it all only by assuming that Moore welcomed his own euphoria that he might enjoy his disappointment, relish a deflationary realism and justify his previous anti-Irishness—unless he had a genuine and hidden longing to be at one with his native country strong enough to overrule temporarily his reason and instinct, which told him that even the new Ireland was no place for him.

In any event, not long after his arrival to take up residence in Ireland, he conceived the project of writing a volume of short stories about peasant life, after the manner of Turgenev's *A Sportsman's Sketches,* and in succeeding he established the Russian "feel" and connection in Irish fiction encouraged by Pearse and continued by O'Connor and O'Faolain. The stories were to be translated into Gaelic in order to plough and seed the "untilled field" of modern Gaelic literature and to answer his own call in "Literature and the Irish Language" for de-Anglicization, English being so debased that "bad Irish is better than good English."[31] In order to head off reflex aversion from Irish critics he would publish them in *The New Ireland Review,* edited by a Jesuit, Fr. Tom Finlay, and defended this apparent renegation to AE by suggesting that Gaelicization was the first order of business, anti-clericalism the second.[32] *An tÚr-Ghort, Sgéalta,* trans. Padraic O'Sullivan, appeared in 1902; it contained six stories and made no impression on readers of Irish. It was to be a private not public renovation of style that the stories were to accomplish. With the addition of fresh stories, it appeared in English the following year as *The Untilled Field*. The stories range widely in setting (Mayo, Galway, Dublin and environs) as well as in style and structure; whereas the prose is clean and not self-regarding like that of *A Drama in Muslin,* two of the stories written later, "A Play-house in the Waste" and "Julia Cahill's Curse", show the technique of narrative involution Moore brought to high degree in *Hail and Farewell* and *A Story-Teller's Holiday*.

In a later Preface, Moore identified *The Untilled Field* as Synge's linguistic inspiration.[33] While this claim is unfortunate, Moore might have with more justification claimed that his volume had anticipated a greater writer even than Synge, viz., James Joyce. The close observation, the interweaving of theme and character, and the master-themes of the volume—the bafflement of self-realization, anticlericalism, ruination—were later emulated in *Dubliners*. As composition progressed, Moore found his stories straining the alliance with Father Finlay, and in *Hail and Farewell* his recollection of composition slides effortlessly into detailed memories of his growing preoccupation with the incompatibility of literature and Catholic dogma.

But as in *Dubliners,* it is the observable results of clericalism in ordinary lives, not a theoretical objection to religious doctrine, that dominates. *The Untilled Field* is the realized version of the novel he dreamed in 1894 of writing and of calling *Ruin and Weed*.[34] Rural decay he had portrayed in *A Drama in Muslin,* but the hemorrhaging of the land through emigration, usually to America—a subject Moore did not invent, it is there in Carleton and has lingered as late as Michael McLaverty[35]—is shown here with a lack of clutter that does not characterize the west's "slattern life;" choked drains, empty cabins, fallen bridges: the untilled fields of Ireland. The "home sickness" that gives one story its title conveys the land's malady as well as the longings of a returned exile.

In offering an explanation, Moore rejects the conventional wisdom of nationalism: it is not the landlords but the priests who are the culprits. As composition proceeded, the anticlerical note got stronger, and what began as revival orthodoxy became heresy. Moore's Irish are submissive and debilitated, and "their pathetic submission was the submission of a primitive people clinging to religious authority" (p. 43). James Bryden, the returned exile, contrasts their acquiescence with "the modern restlessness and cold energy" of Americans, as Joyce was to contrast the grateful oppression of the Irish with the wealth and industry of Europeans. The priests are hostile to sensuality and, for a related reason, to art, as the story "Fugitives" offers to demonstrate.[36] The landscape empties as the Church drives away those who cannot afford to pay the priests for their weddings or those who want to marry for love.

The sexlessness of Catholic Ireland Moore had already depicted in *A Drama in Muslin* in which Alice Barton—anticipating the author of "The Dead"—imagines "the white bed of celibacy in which the whole country was sleeping. Yes; all were suffering alike, all were enduring the same white death!" (p. 100). Just as matriarchs arrange marriages among Moore's gentry, so priests arrange them among his peasantry, and as "Patchwork" and "The Wedding Feast" show, arrangements that discountenance the desire of the individual can occasionally unravel among the peasantry as painfully as among the gentry. What Moore indicts is the wrong *kind* of religion, and in "The Wild Goose" he is at pains to distinguish the priests from the faith they pervert.

It is not all gloom, and there is the fitful consolation of fantasy that is nourished on the deprivations of reality. Biddy McHale in "The Window" achieves a private life of vision within the physical, but outside the spiritual walls of the church; old Margaret Kirwin in "The Wedding Gown" retrieves at death and in fantasy the wedding-day sixty years before, which time and imagination have embroidered; Edward Dempsey in "The Clerk's Quest" hungers to death in pursuit of a woman he knows only through her heliotrope-scented checks it is his job to clear, and in death sees a star become her and lay its bright face upon his shoulder. These are stories told with a compassion that softens the savagery of indictment elsewhere, though Moore's implication is that such desperate subjectivity should not be necessary.

Nor are all of Moore's priests culpable, and in his desolate parish, Father MacTurnan racks his brains to find ways of stanching the flow of emigration. In "A Letter to Rome," his modest proposal is that the priests take wives, thereby adding forty thousand children to the birthrate. Behind the pathetic absurdity of his plan is his creator's apparently serious contention that the final Romanization of Irish Catholicism took place in the nineteenth century, and that rescission of the celibacy decree would help to localize, that is to nationalize, religion in Ireland. In separating the cosmopolitanism of the Roman church from its national ideal, Moore is seeking to separate cultural nationalism from a Catholicism that is responsible to Rome before Ireland.

MacTurnan is a lonely, ineffectual man and the Church ensures that his proposal goes nowhere, just as the government ensures that the roads he causes to be built as relief work benefit no one by going nowhere. But at least he secures five pounds from his bishop to enable two parishioners to wed and forgets his principle of a marriageable clergy amidst his satisfaction in bringing happiness to two individuals. In "A Play-house in the Waste" he has changed his mind about the principle and accepts emigration as evidence of the missionary spirit of the Irish in the service of the universal church. He does so in defeat, after the rural theatre he has erected to help stop emigration is damaged in a storm, three days after the mother of one of the young actresses has murdered and buried her daughter's illegitimate child, conceived after a rehearsal. Superstition is widespread, and when young Julia Cahill is driven from her home for consorting with boys ("an outcast Venus"), and in a curse condemns the parish to the loss of one roof every year and the departure of a family to America, the people believe that theirs is indeed an accursed countryside.

Few of Moore's characters resist the power of the priests: James Bryden, the returned American, does so in "Home Sickness," and so do Kate Kavanagh in "Some Parishioners" and "The Wedding Feast", the title character in "Julia Cahill's Curse," Lucy Delaney in "Fugitives". Three of these are women, embodiments for Moore of sensuality and independence, peasant versions of Alice Barton, and contemporaries of Synge's dramatic heroines. Their independence and sensuality come down to an instinct for self-realization, but not selfishness, though this vice, as "Almsgiving" demonstrates, is both redeemable and redemptive. Around them are "dupes of convention," as Father MacTurnan terms cardinals and government officials, human specters who are the real untilled fields of Moore's volume, those who live and die in Ireland without realizing the qualities they were born with.

Marriage looms large in *The Untilled Field* and is most often symptom and symbol of the imprisoned lives of Moore's figures, but in the volume's major story, "The Wild Goose," it has a meaning richly beyond this, while yet incorporating the idea of imprisonment. "The Wild Goose" in its length, complexity, and educated middle-class characters, bears the same and possibly influential relationship to the preceding stories that "The Dead" bears to the remainder of *Dubliners*.

Ned Carmady returns from America to the valley of the Liffey to write journalistic pieces on rural Ireland. Initially he is favorably impressed by the vestiges of ancient Ireland and by the contemporary Irish with their gifts for herdsmanship and horsemanship, but he is rather condescending, and of course is in quest of "sittings." He meets Ellen Cronin of Brookfield[37] who is a nationalist, a kind of prototype for Joyce's Molly Ivors. He is attracted to her but dislikes the way she has allowed her Catholicism to repress her sensuality or, on another level, the way she has made Catholicism an inseparable part of her nationalism; Ned wants to combine the expression of sexuality (that is, the self) with the expression of nationality. Nevertheless, he yields to her enthusiasm and they marry. He is absorbed by the heroic past evidenced in the legendary places they visit; he tries to learn the Irish language; he becomes involved in the political movement; and he even develops a pantheistic creed by which "there are not many things in the universe, but one thing divided indefinitely" (p. 253). In short, he becomes a revivalist. Ireland, via Ellen, or rather Ireland in the incarnation of Ellen, has beguiled him and in marrying her he has married Cathleen ni Houlihan.

But Ned grows more vocally anticlerical and begins a journal called *The Heretic,* resenting increasingly the "religious submission" of his wife—"soused in Catholicism", as she is crudely described by a character in the sequel story, "Fugitives." (Yet Ellen is not simply a pious Cathleen ni Houlihan; at the age of twenty-five she is being defeated by the imposed shortcomings of her gender, and Moore makes of her an indirect justification of feminism, as he had done more directly with Alice Barton fifteen years before, a woman suffering the double constraints on her desire for self-realization imposed by male clericalism and male chauvinism.) At last "the sensual coil that had bound them was broken; once more he was a free man" (p. 271). When Ned leaves his wife, he is leaving Ireland; "it was while writing *The Wild Goose,"* Moore remembered, "that it occurred to me for the first time that, it being impossible to enjoy independence of body and soul in Ireland, the thought of every brave-hearted boy is to cry, Now, off with my coat so that I may earn five pounds to take me out of the country."[38] Ned has become a modern wild goose, in service not of foreign armies but of himself. "If he had stayed," Ned muses at the story's end, "he would have come to accept all the base moral coinage in circulation," a metaphor Joyce put to considerable use when he wrote *Dubliners.*[39]

What we have in Carmady's return to Ireland, period of enchantment, and disillusionment is a version of Moore's own adventure with the revival, and it suggests that the adventure was over by the time the story was written. The three stages of Ned's involvement are those Moore later entitled "Ave," "Salve," and "Vale" when recounting his own story. Interestingly enough, they are the three phases of marriage, as Ned sees them: "a year of mystery and passion, then some years of passion without mystery, and a period of resignation." (p. 271). Moore's sojourn in Ireland was, then, a kind of marriage, somewhat calculatingly self-arranged yet not entirely volitional. Its end followed an inevitable course and was brought about not by those cases of adultery and abandonment that reach the divorce courts. Ned believes his marriage was necessary and useful and that his separation from Ellen will permit them a more intimate appreciation of each other. The three stages of marriage, in fact, are the three stages on the road to self-realization, and we will encounter another version of them in "The Dead." Despite "In the Clay" and "The Way Back," which show us Carmady about to take leave of Ireland, along with Rodney the sculptor and Harding the writer,[40] Moore felt that after *The Untilled Field* he still had something to say about the necessary pain of valediction suffered by those who sought personal fulfillment.

The Triumph of Self-Realization: The Lake

Between 1903 and 1905 Moore wrote a story he later believed should have been in *The Untilled Field* but which appeared separately as a short novel. Neither in style nor in theme would *The Lake* (1905) have been out of place in the earlier volume, but its orchestration is sustained over a greater distance and—at least in the novel's two revisions of 1905 and 1921—with a deeper subtlety. The Irish setting, a parish in Moore's part of Mayo, is of a piece with the stories in *The Untilled Field,* but its advocacy of self-realization was Moore's lifelong theme, though *The Lake* is unusual in the singlemindedness with which the theme is pursued. For Moore, self-realization meant five related liberties: the expression of sexuality and acceptance of the body; unbridled curiosity of thought; freedom of conscience; the satisfying of the aesthetic instinct; and relish of nature. The greatest threat in his world to these liberties he thought came from Catholicism, especially of the Irish variety, though some might argue that he libelled and caricatured Catholicism in his ruthless need for an incarnation of what he philosophically opposed. At any rate, to make a priest the hero of *The Lake* and have him seek self-realization at the expense of his vocation was to carry the fight into the enemy's camp and risk creating a straw man, merely intellectual offspring of his own dogma. But although I dissent from Richard Cave's judgment that *The Lake* is a great novel, I agree with him that "Moore's triumph lies in the subtlety with which he renders the slow process whereby Gogarty's consciousness works to heal its wracked condition so that [the] theme becomes an experience."[41]

"There is an unchanging, silent life within every man," Moore wrote at the end of "Home Sickness," "that none knows but himself." In his novel he gives this silent life form as Lake Carra in Father Oliver Gogarty's parish; "every man has a lake in his heart," Gogarty mysteriously realizes at the outset of the novel, which then develops in order that he might come to understand the meaning of the sentiment he repeats when his pilgrimage of self-discovery has ended (or begun). The lake is the repressed instinct for freedom and it has already begun to surface when the novel opens, for Gogarty has tired of Ireland's melancholy melody (the sorrowful legend), as has Ned Carmady towards the close of "The Wild Goose" when he actually hears that melody which Moore reproduces in notation. Gogarty's recollection of an incident with a woman explains how he has reached the stage of desiring exile from Ireland, but the bulk of the novel is given over to the incident's delayed aftermath, the time between the fatigue with Ireland's sad beauty and departure for America (which for Ned Carmady in "The Wild Goose" occupies only three pages). This suggests the intensive psychological realism with which Moore invests not merely the priest's autobiographical recovery of events and states of mind that have led him to tire of Ireland, but also the self-analysis he conducts to explain that fatigue and confront its implications. But in a sense all is in the past, present, and future simultaneously, for Gogarty is doing nothing else than discovering what has always been there (but concealed) and once discovered will change the present and dictate the future; the lake endures, seen or unseen.

We learn from Gogarty's memories in the opening chapter that his life has been, like Moore's, a history of "enthusiasms." But he does not suspect that what led him to become a priest was yet another enthusiasm, destined to be abandoned, though in accordance with an invisible pattern and unrecognized direction of real and psychological events. Already he has become the pantheist Ned Carmady and Moore himself became—"there is but one life, one mother, one elemental substance out of which all has come" (p. 33)—a belief midway in Moore's spiritual chronology between Christianity and the agnostic's (or "Protestant's") apotheosis of the self. Already he has accepted that the unity of things does not arrange our existence, and that we should accept the role of accidents in life (p. 5). The next stage will be to repudiate schemes and dogmas imposed on us in the name of heaven or some transcendent reality, an acceptance and repudiation that are aspects of Moore's realism as a writer.[42]

One such accident in Gogarty's life is the letter out of the blue from Father O'Grady in London, letting him know that Nora Glynn is alive and well. Nora was the schoolmistress in Gogarty's parish, a happy, independent, artistic, resourceful young woman (a combination of, say, Alice Barton, Esther Waters, and Kate Kavanagh) whom Gogarty had championed when her sexual vitality offended the parishioners but whom he denounced from the altar when she got pregnant. Her story repeats Father

Madden's treatment of Julia Cahill, and Father O'Grady's role that of Father Stafford, the compassionate priest who tries to temper Father Maguire's harshness in "Patchwork." Gogarty is conscience stricken about what happened and fears Nora may have drowned herself in the lake. His stricken conscience deepens the change in him that began when Nora vanished; even out of sight she is a catalyst, inducing alteration in him as Ellen Cronin did in Carmady, and when he writes to her and she replies, the process of catalysis quickens.

The bulk of *The Lake* is an exchange of letters between Nora and Gogarty, and through this epistolary device Moore externalizes and saves from monotony the interior monologue pioneered by his friend Dujardin (to whom the novel is dedicated) and controls the book's momentum and resolution of tension. Gogarty is a fine character, a decent, lonely, compassionate man like Father MacTurnan, driven gradually inward to discover the free currents and impeding dams of his own being. He slowly realizes himself, in the sense both of becoming self-aware and, having done so, of creating the conditions for future self-fulfillment out of Ireland (in New York) and out of the Church. Losing his faith, he comes to believe Mass (as did Alice Barton) "to be but a mummery" and that he has been in error, as he tells Nora, when "the priesthood seemed to offer opportunities of realizing myself, or preserving the spirit within me" (pp. 145–46). Orthodoxy is a sacrifice, and "we can sacrifice ourselves for a time, but we cannot sacrifice ourselves all our life long, unless we begin to take pleasure in the immolation of self, and then it is no longer a sacrifice" (p. 143). He is replacing his Catholicism with belief in nature, "a sort of pagan enchantment," and nature is the expression of instinctual fulfillment (he gets the idea of flight from his parish from watching a curlew). *The Lake,* which is a song of spring, is joyously full of blooms that silently reproach all habits, duties, prejudices, formulas and codes. And all hypocrisy, for Gogarty's "dead self" is a hypocritical one that denounced Nora under cover of religious authority but really out of jealousy; he then pretends that in correspondence with her he is trying to save her soul, but comes to admit that "he wanted her body as well as her soul." Release of the authentic self takes place not just in an appreciation of nature but also in the description of nature, for Gogarty is clearly, judging from his letters, a writer *manqué,* a rival in this respect to Walter Poole, the writer who is a tutor in life to Nora as Nora is to Gogarty. Poole plays the role that Harding played in *A Drama in Muslin,* but Poole is a thinker, Gogarty a creative writer in embryo.

Although at the end of the novel Gogarty believes that somehow Nora and he will merge, this is only a symbolic possibility. In one sense he cannot have her, or need not have her, as a woman, since she is his alter ego. At the same time, Nora is herself developing, in travel, by acquaintance with art, and under the tutelage of Poole.[43] She is both herself and Gogarty in his future guise; she is both a catalyst and an element capable of change in her own right; she both champions the self and is the embodiment of selfhood for Gogarty. "Each one must try to realize himself," she tells Gogarty, "I mean that we must try to bring the gifts that Nature gave us to fruition" (p. 133). She has gone into exile, like Moore before her, and like Gogarty after her. Moore had difficulty with her character, and she began her life in the novel as Rose Leicester; in his 1905 revision Moore deepened her character and in 1921 re-baptized her Nora Glynn. Revised, she is a better character, but she does not seem Irish (she is "of English extraction" in the revised 1905 text), and though this makes the point that Ireland tends not to breed independence of mind, it lessens the credibility of Nora as a Mayo schoolmistress, and qualifies, of course, Gogarty's triumph of self-realization by showing it happening under the English influence of Nora and Poole. (The Englishness is symbolic; Moore—a model combination of Nora and Poole—thought he could represent an 'English' or civilizing influence in Ireland and play tutor to his native country.) In the creation of Nora, Moore's own dogma threatens the instinctual process of characterization.

As instructress, Nora encourages Gogarty to travel and sings the praises of Italy which here, as in "Fugitives," represents the warm blend of liberties Ireland might have achieved without a series of unlucky historical accidents. She is encouraging him to change, and he comes to accept that "the law of change is the law of life," the paradoxical method of achieving the unchangeable state of self-realization. Willingness to change is willingness to accept that "there is no moral law except one's own conscience, and that the moral obligation of every man is to separate the personal conscience from the impersonal conscience" (p. 173). In other words, the novel is "Protestant" in Moore's terms, though Protestantism, as the rest of us use the word, is for Moore only a stage between the Catholicism it has advanced from and the neopaganism it will give way to, a paganism individuated and postreligious.[44] Change Gogarty does, and the novel ends when he stages his own suicide by drowning (following as it were the suicide he feared Nora had committed), but swims the lake by moonlight with his clerical clothes on the bank he leaves (the cast of his former self that he has killed) and lay clothes on the bank he reaches. We have to accept that Gogarty needs to swim the lake, which isn't necessary to stage a suicide, for Moore wishes to exploit the lake as a vast baptismal font. Gogarty's "baptism" is a secular or pagan alternative to the grotesque squabbling that goes on between Protestants and Catholics in his parish over the baptizing of an infant product of a mixed marriage and that ends up being baptized in both faiths but clearly, in Moore's and now Gogarty's understanding, is baptized in no genuine faith at all. Halfway across the lake, Gogarty is afraid he will fail in his swim, but he had earlier told himself that "he must put his confidence in Nature" (p. 136), and the lake is that "one mother, one elemental substance" that nevertheless permits her child fully to become himself. If the lake is the mother that cradles her infant, and the baptismal water in which he is wetted, it is also in the end a symbol of the child itself, allowed to develop towards the freedom of maturity.

In terms of Moore's historical perception, the individual note came into art, and, it would seem, the individual consciousness into being, when life declined in beauty at the Renaissance.[45] Individuality or self-awareness was a necessary evil we have rightly turned into a virtue to give our lives renewed value. Moore and Gogarty thought of the seventh and eighth centuries as the high point of Irish civilization when the appreciation of nature, art, and woman prevailed, when the close fabric of society did not necessitate the goal of self-realization, and when religion (a true Christianity, an ideal Catholicism) had not been perverted by its clerical custodians. Gogarty writes to Nora of this Ireland and quotes from the nature poetry of Marban, a cleric who lived the life of a hermit as Gogarty wanted to do before the Church ruined him spiritually and made necessary the pilgrimage away from his vocation towards the consolation of personal fulfillment. Marban's Ireland before the Danes came is celebrated by Gogarty, and at length by Moore in *A Story-Teller's Holiday* and *Hail and Farewell;* in each case the phrase "halcyon days" is used.[46] But in each case too, the celebration is an obituary. Gogarty comes to believe like Moore that the halcyon days are not recoverable, just as he comes to believe that the abbey whose roof he wanted restored ought perhaps to be left as a ruined memorial to a vanished era. That it was AE who told Moore about Marban, and Meyer's translations that he used in *The Lake,* is significant.[47] Moore regretted the Ireland that his countrymen wanted to revive, but he realistically saw that the way forward lay with individuality. As Moore saw it, a developed sense of beauty gave way in Ireland to a growingly authoritarian sense of faith. If a sense of beauty could be reinculcated in Ireland, then faith could be retrenched ("faith goes out of the window when beauty comes in at the door," Rose Leicester tells Gogarty in the first version of *The Lake*),[48] and aesthetics and individuality could be combined; indeed, as late as *A Story-Teller's Holiday* (1918), Moore thought this might happen.

But it was Moore's promotion of the self that got in the way; besides, his aesthetic appeals sounded like the habitual cries of a decadent, and his critics did not bother to examine them. Yet the revivalists would have done well to listen to him. Seemingly divisive in his personality and superficial doctrine, Moore is in fact a bridging figure. His signal importance is this: by changing the terms of the national argument, by translating Catholicism and Protestantism into states of mind (what he calls in *A Story-Teller's Holiday* "states of soul") rather than creeds, and by refusing to equate Roman Catholicism in Ireland with Catholicism or organized Protestantism with freedom of thought, Moore offered what is still the only hope of solution to the Irish problem. Although a difficulty with nomenclature remains, he attempted to metaphorize those odious and imprisoning terms, Protestant and Catholic, out of existence.[49] He offered his solution too early, too vividly, too captiously, but we are only beginning to catch up with the essence of what he meant, and few of his contemporaries are as relevant as he to the Ireland of today.

The Break with Dogma: Gerald O'Donovan's Father Ralph

According to Joseph Hone, Gogarty's swim across the lake, with his old clothes on one bank, his new awaiting him on the other, was suggested by a real incident. "There was a Protestant clergyman in Dublin, formally a Roman Catholic priest and at this time a conductor of Protestant missions among the poor, of whom the same story of escape was told."[50] John Cronin believes he has identified Moore's original as Rev. Thomas Connellan, whose story resembles Gogarty's.[51] In several respects, Connellan's resignation from the priesthood in 1887 resembles that of the hero of Gerald O'Donovan's novel, *Father Ralph* (1913). Ralph O'Brien like Connellan tastes "perfect peace" (the latter's phrase) when he leaves his parish, and travels to London with a literary ambition. Interestingly, Peter Costello has assumed that O'Donovan himself was the original for Moore's Oliver Gogarty. Before he was Gerald O'Donovan he was Father Jeremiah O'Donovan, a Galway priest of cultivation and intellect who ran afoul of church dogma and his superiors; when he left the priesthood in 1904 and went to London (changing his name like a suit of clothes), Moore gave him a letter of introduction of Fisher Unwin that praised O'Donovan's literary abilities. (As though in a signal of gratitude, O'Donovan names one of the few sympathetic priests in *Father Ralph* after the hero of *The Lake*.) Between 1913 and 1922, O'Donovan published six novels, of which *Father Ralph* is his first, and it is apparently a disguised autobiographical account of his break with Rome.[52]

Moore described *The Lake* as showing "the essential rather than the daily life of the priest," which Moore in any case could not have known.[53] *Father Ralph* shows with an insider's knowledge the priest's day-do-day life; O'Donovan is a realist not only in the reproduction of surfaces and appearances (his priests speak with colloquial accuracy, for example), but also in the revelation of unapparent motives and forces which impel institutions, in this case the Irish priesthood. He is concerned too with the practicalities of life and the significance of vocation. But he is a realist in Moore's additional sense: painfully conscious of the need for self-realization and the baffles placed in its way by Irish society. Despite its utilitarian prose, *Father Ralph* is a bitter and wounded performance, a valuable cultural document set down with integrity and feeling.

The essential life of the priest in *Father Ralph* is one of self-repression, not to speak of corruption and the repression of others, and the novel joins "The Wild Goose," *The Lake,* and *A Portrait of the Artist* (which Joyce was working on as O'Donovan was writing *Father Ralph)* as a chronicle of the lonely and besieged consciousness. Like them, it is a record of that moment in Irish cultural history (ironically the heyday of the Irish revival) when, calamitously, the sensitive consciousness and incorruptible conscience broke with dogma and convention and, alas, from social reality and possibility. Like them it is a portrait of the Catholic as a reluctant "Protestant"; in each case the realism of the hero and the author is the frank and painful acknowledgment that what passes for realism in Ireland is cynicism and expediency and the perception that true idealism is possible only out of Ireland. This is the central import of the tradition of fictional realism by lapsed Catholics begun by Moore, O'Donovan, and Joyce. In later decades exile is even more painful and damaging when it is an internal exile, when the citizen (writer or not) is an "inner émigré" inhabiting a Gorki of the mind.

Like Moore, Ralph O'Brien (and, we can assume, Father Jeremiah O'Donovan) had great hopes for the revival of Ireland a decade before the century's end. But his start is not auspicious. He is the son of a woman "bred, born, and reared on religious pap"[54] and is taught by his nurse to be anti-English and anti-Protestant. Like Stephen Dedalus he is nourished by guilt, and it is this, and the relentlessness of influence, that make him become a priest against the current of his real being. Ordained, he becomes a curate in a western locality, ridden by priests, not far from the Big House of his family that, like Moore's, is Catholic gentry. It is a time of apparent national resuscitation, and O'Brien is enthusiastic. He becomes involved in the cooperative dairy movement run by the Irish Agricultural Organisation Society, in the Gaelic revival, and in the Irish literary revival. He believes that these will be supported by the priests, and that the Church is itself being renewed through modernism and the separation of certainty from dogma.

This belief is in naive contrast to his experience as a student priest at the local seminary and at Maynooth, the chief seminary of Ireland. *Father Ralph* is a bitter assault from the inside on the seminary system in the late nineteenth century—its corruption, favoritism, laxity, and benightedness. Once ordained, Ralph finds himself among authoritarian, meddlesome, gluttonous priests "holding an ignorant laity in check through fear of eternal damnation" (pp. 264–65). These priests are hand-in-glove with the anti-IAOS "gombeen" men (corrupt wealthy shopkeepers and creditors) who grotesquely enough in O'Brien's parish represent an adulterated Land League. Priests and gombeen men prattle about Home Rule in a debased and hypocritical nationalism—the priests' primary allegiance is to Rome, while the gombeen men fear the cooperative movement as a genuine Home Rule of a local, practical kind. It is against the background of this entrenched clerico-capitalist alliance that O'Brien starts a club, a proto-union and civic organization, and sees it swiftly crushed in a way that makes a mockery of revival Ireland and appropriates it for right-wing purposes. Whereas in France and Italy the Church is renovating itself by loosening "the fetters of a medieval ecclesiasticism" (p. 264), in Ireland, "the home of obscurantism," it is hopelessly different with "autocrats, domineering over a sycophant clergy." "Love and pity had flown away with knowledge. A monstrous organization, self-seeking, material, thinking only of itself, had taken the place of the men of God whose lives manifested the God they experienced" (p. 318). There are good and kind priests in the novel, and there is evidence of real faith, but O'Donovan sees his own distinction between priests and the faith of which they are custodians as little more than academic (as it is in Moore) when the power of the priests in Ireland is ubiquitous and unretrenchable.

But the heart of the problem, as Moore knew, is Rome, and O'Brien comes to realize that "Roman absolutism and democracy are incompatible," that "by constant iteration and exercise of authority the Roman power had succeeded in persuading the simple millions that it was the sole guardian of faith" (p. 378). Rome publishes the decree *Lamentabili Sane* ("Life and growth and development were anathema. It was madness!" cries O'Brien, p. 450) and in 1907 the encyclical *Pascendi Gregis,* and it is the end of modernism and a vindication of the medievalism of the Irish church, a state of affairs that roused Moore to indignation.[55] Ordered to engage in a public act of self-criticism, O'Brien refuses. He believes that he will always be a Catholic, but a literary friend reminds him that he will be branded as a heretic once he removes the clerical collar. "I shall have the support of my conscience in any case," he replies, and goes into exile, a kind of Protestant by default. Conscience and selfhood are one and the same, and when O'Brien breaks with Rome he declares: "I have found myself at last." He has lost his mother, his mother church, and his mother country, but he has realized the nature of the nets that held him back and has at least laid down the conditions of a future fulfillment, if he trusts to conscience and instinct. There is a poignant moment when he cannot knot his tie because having worn a clerical collar for years he has forgotten how; but when he closes his eyes and trusts his fingers the knot is tied; it is what he must do in his future life. Instinct, of course, is inadequate without courage, and the courage of the realists, writers and heroes alike, facing an uncertain future outside the herd, lonely in their apostasy, even heresy, must never be forgotten.

Waking the Dead
The Young James Joyce, Dublin, and Irish Revival

8

Ireland is always Connacht to my imagination.
—W. B. Yeats

The Significance of "The Dead"

Daydreaming of escape from Ireland at the outset of *The Lake,* Father Gogarty thinks of England, but then reflects: "England was, after all, an island like Ireland—a little larger, but still an island—and he thought he would like a continent to roam in" (pp. 3–4). When Sean O'Faolain visited the Blasket Islands in the nineteen-thirties he was rather bored, unlike Synge, and later explained why. "D. H. Lawrence once wrote a lovely story, one of his very best, called *The Man Who Loved Islands*. This man, as he grew poor, went from larger islands to smaller islands, until he lived in the very smallest possible island on which any man could live. Lawrence's character was an incurable romantic. Any sensible man naturally goes from smaller to larger islands, and ends up with continents, which are also islands within the popular definition. I found I had been happier on the mainland, so I returned there. There was more adoing."[1] "The Man Who Loved Islands" begins: "An island, if it is big enough, is no better than a continent. It has to be really quite small, before it feels like an island; and this story will show how tiny it has to be, before you can presume to fill it with your own personality."[2] Lawrence takes delight in trying to show that the romantic self is an impossibility. There is no final victory over the elements that return in their eternal indifference to render the man's island—himself—unrecognizable. Pure self is impossible to sustain because it simultaneously summons forth the dissolution of self. The story ends with the man who loved islands watching the snow cover his earthly estate.

Despite its parable-like quality, "The Man Who Loved Islands" appears to be set, because of its references to "Celtic stillness" and a "Celtic sea," on western islands, perhaps the Hebrides. The story could even be a satire on island-lovers and romantic primitivists of the Irish varieties.[3] It is a provocative coincidence that writers and cultural revivalists tended to travel from larger to smaller islands. Ostensibly they were looking for archaic communities into which they might melt, but at least on occasions they were really seeking to fill the islands with their own powerful personalities.

Contrary to most revival manifestoes, there appears to have been at stake a good deal that was personal. Lady Gregory's unguarded account of her near encounter with Synge when she happened upon him on Aranmor displays, apparently without humor, a kind of territoriality. "I first saw Synge in the north island of Aran. I was staying there, gathering folklore, talking to the people, and felt quite angry when I passed another outsider walking here and there, talking also to the people. I was jealous of not being alone on the island among the fishers and sea-weed gatherers. I did not speak to the stranger, nor was he inclined to speak to me. He also looked on me as an intruder."[4] Synge's attitude is confirmed by this entry in his notebook: "With this limestone Inishmaan however I am in love, and hear with galling jealousy of the various priests and scholars who have lived here before me. They have grown to me as the former lover of one's mistress, horrible existences haunting with dreamed kisses the lips she presses to your own."[5]

The ending of Lawrence's story might recall for us the conclusion of "The Dead" by James Joyce, when Gabriel Conroy watches the snow falling on Dublin. This story has indeed often been read as though Gabriel were, like the man who loved islands, an egotist who foolishly refuses, until either the fatal end or the last possible moment, to recognize the forces of elemental being that Lawrence's character courts and to which he too is finally compelled to submit. Such readers, however, see Gabriel as an unromantic egotist and the elemental forces in "The Dead" as romantic forces bestowing life and passion on those who willingly submit to them, but death on those who do not. Since these forces appear in "The Dead" to reside most vividly in the west among the folk, the story has been interpreted as Joyce's reluctant admission that there is something after all to the cultural nationalists' orientation and that it is indeed in the west of Ireland that culture, passion, and life abide.[6] Viewed in this fashion, the story has been claimed for the canon of revival literature.

These readers fail to see the various targets of Joyce's irony in the story or his satire at the expense of romantic primitivism and what is in

Joyce's view the greater egotism of city-dwellers engaging in such a regressive movement. As an Irishman from a family whose fortunes were declining and an Irishman who had actually derived from the west in a profounder sense than had Protestant writers—Joyce's father claimed descent from inhabitants of Joyce's Country in Galway—Joyce rejected romantic primitivism, as did Catholic writers after him (such as Frank O'Connor, Patrick Kavanagh and Sean O'Faolain). Joyce's sense of irony and absurdity equalled Lawrence's; in "The Dead", it is more tellingly levelled against the forces that threaten Gabriel than against Gabriel himself. At the close of the story Gabriel does not come to love real islands: whatever islands lie beyond "the dark mutinous Shannon waves" belong to a visionary seascape beyond cultural myth, beyond east and west, island and continent, present and past.

A right interpretation of "The Dead" is desirable because of the signal importance of this story in *Dubliners* (1914), in Joyce's canon, and in the Irish literary revival. Even were it to stand alone, "The Dead" would be a splendid monument to Joyce's genius. But it is of course the last "acre" in the "Fifteen Acres" of *Dubliners,* at once crowning end-piece and an epitome of the entire masterly collection. And beyond this, in part because of its apparent wish to escape the neat confinement of the volume and to become an independent novella, "The Dead" hinges the fiction Joyce wrote before 1907, when the story was composed, and the longer fiction he went on to write. It has a more generous style than the earlier stories; the self-mortifying and "scrupulous meanness" of those stories comes to an end, something which as we shall see enacts the theme of "The Dead." The story also lies midway between the privacy of the small lives explored in the first fourteen stories of *Dubliners* and the publicity of the larger and more numerous lives explored in *Ulysses* (1922), which in fact grew out of *Dubliners*. "The Dead" displays features, vestigial, rudimentary, or perfected, characteristic of the Joyce canon. Here as both theme and hero is the proud and painfully conscious self beset by those cultural forces of Ireland and human society that create, inhibit, and sustain. And here as artistic response to these forces is a largely realistic, ironic, ambivalent, ultimately visionary, in sum Joycean treatment of contending elements. All in all, it would be difficult to contest Richard Ellmann's conclusion that "in its lyrical, melancholy acceptance of all that life and death offer, 'The Dead' is a linchpin in Joyce's works."[7]

We must not, however, overlook the story's partialities. Some of the forces that beset Joyce's characters were decried or ignored by the revivalists, but others they cheerfully promoted, including the lure and grip of place and past. And if in "The Dead" there are redeeming social and cultural forces (that offer Gabriel Conroy a second chance), they are not the forces that the revivalists championed. Most of Joyce's people cannot pick and choose among the forces that influence them, as could the Anglo-Irish writers, nor can they understand them, though they feel the enormous weight of them. For those who led the revival, to know who they were, to investigate, for example, the implications of their class, religious, cultural and racial identities, would have been a relatively easy business. To be themselves would have been harder, because of the declining fortunes of their class, religion, culture and race, and because of the distortions of identity wrought by colonialism—harder, but not impossible. How much more difficult it is for Joyce's lower and declining middle classes and O'Casey's working class—almost bereft of intellectual heritage—to know and be themselves. Identities imposed upon them by class, religion, and colonialism were rejected by the revivalists as hostile and unprofitable; similar identities, however, are even more hostile to Joyce's people because more insistent, authoritative, less understood and far less capable of being shrugged off.

Joyce may have fled Ireland (where the revivalists remained, choosing to find new identities there instead of abroad), but artistically he did not flee; rather he faced and analyzed the forces of Irish life through his literature. He has his most conscious heroes, Gabriel Conroy, Stephen Dedalus, and Leopold Bloom—on behalf of the less conscious inhabitants of Catholic Dublin—take stock, willingly or no, of the identities they have been given. *Dubliners* depicts the obstacles that impede the progress of his characters toward self-realization, yet provides in "The Dead," despite its title, a long deferred if impracticable victory. It is not, however, the victory of Irish nationalism, whether romantic, cultural, or political, for Joyce saw nationalism as a false promise, another obstacle, not the desired alternative to class, religion, and colonialism. But it had to be understood, as did they, and could be the matter upon which freedom could feed. You do not merely repudiate your heritage and assume another; you come to grips with it and exploit it, as Antaeus did the earth to gain mastery above it.

The Dances of the Dead

The jovial festivity of the "The Dead" that is rendered with such attentive realism was necessary to complete Joyce's portrait in *Dubliners* of his fellow citizens, a hitherto caustic portrait of idleness, perversion, hypocrisy, betrayal, prostitution (mainly figurative), and all manner of unscrupulous meanness. Having despised more than a little his native city for fourteen stories, he was uncharacteristically penitent, like the boy in "An Encounter." "I have not reproduced its ingenuous insularity and its hospitality," he acknowledged in a letter to his brother from Rome; "the latter 'virtue' so far as I can see does not exist elsewhere in Europe."[8] In nostalgic amends he allowed a little of this warmth of feeling to enter his fifteenth story, as Ellmann has observed, though "insularity" rings ironically before the story is over. "The Dead" is among many other things an exile's salute, through Joyce's remembrance of his great aunts' Christmas parties, to Irish generosity and hospitality, Dublin sociability, and the Irish family connection and its ritual and festive importance. Yet in their Joycean context, a somewhat frayed, rather philistine middle class, these were not quite the same features of Irish life the revivalists were wont to praise.

Besides, the festivity of the Misses Morkan's annual dance in their house on Usher's Island (near the center of Dublin, despite its name) would not be Irish without the element of folly, and reading "The Dead" with its large, potentially "Ulyssean" cast, one might have boarded a doomed ark of fools. That the dance takes place on Twelfth Night,[9] might reinforce our suspicion that Joyce is consciously observing the ancient Feast of Fools (or unconsciously observing its archetype) characterized by "licence and buffooneries," in this case Freddy Malins' drinking, Mr. Browne's risqué joking, and the feasting of all, brought alive by Joyce with more than a hint of pagan relish. Perhaps, too, Gretta Conroy's disclosure of a past love could only be made, and her husband's dampened desire for his wife rekindled, on this night when all that is untoward and uncustomary is possible, including the Conroys' staying overnight at the Gresham Hotel. One is tempted to go farther and to see Gabriel Conroy as the chief fool at this feast, the reluctant Lord of Misrule, especially, keeping in mind what he suffers at the hands of the dead Michael Furey, in the light of the fact that anciently in Europe the Christmas Fool was killed by his rival at the mid-winter Saturnalia.[10] Death is omnipresent in "The Dead" and undercuts the festive and redemptive setting, but it is strained through the irony of all manner of death being, at least for a time, humorous.

We do not need to invoke folklore to suggest that beneath the gaiety the Misses Morkan's party is a funeral ceremony with its ritual dancing, ceremonial feast, formal speech, and ritual singing. The corpse is played at one level of reference by all the named and unnamed dead, at another level by Aunts Julia and Kate, and at yet another level by all the guests themselves, who represent Joyce's lifeless Dublin in a lifeless Ireland. The guests perform the dances of the dead, a motif used by Joyce in the same early poem in which one of the story's crucial phrases, "distant music," occurs.[11] Gabriel's speech is a funeral oration over the "corpses" of the other guests, and the actual invisible corpses of the "dead and gone great ones." The toast and song to the hostesses are to a past that has already enveloped the partygoers and to the memory that the present has already become. *Arrayed for the Bridal,* which Aunt Julia sings for the company, is her own funeral dirge, her betrothal with the population of the other world she is soon to join. In this context the final and seemingly pointless series of goodnights has a plaintive and macabre effect, as though the living were exchanging farewells before their passage into death:

> —Well, good-night, Aunt Kate, and thanks for the pleasant evening.
> —Good-night, Gabriel. Good-night, Gretta!
> —Good-night, Aunt Kate, and thanks ever so much. Good-night, Aunt Julia.
> —O, good-night, Gretta, I didn't see you.
> —Good-night, Mr. D'Arcy. Good-night, Miss O'Callaghan.
> —Good-night, Miss Morkan.
> —Good-night, again.
> —Good-night, all. Safe home.
> —Good-night. Good-night.[12]

"The Dead" owes something, it would seem, to the *Danse Macabre* "wherein is lively expressed and shewed the state of manne, and how he is called at uncertayne tymes by death, and" (if we think of Gabriel, lustful in the Gresham Hotel) "when he thinketh least thereon."[13] At the same time, to turn a celebration of living Ireland into mourning for a dead Ireland, in however tongue-in-cheek a fashion, is a stroke of cultural realism since Irish hospitality in its strenuousness ("the tradition of genuine warm-hearted courteous Irish hospitality, which our forefathers have handed down to us," as Gabriel puts it) is, we might say, killing. This is perhaps why Joyce encased the "virtue" of Irish hospitality in inverted commas when writing to Stanislaus and why he has Gabriel refer to the guests as the "victims" of his aunts' generosity. And it is true that the festivities of the Irish often slide in the course of an evening from euphoria into nostalgia, remorse, and sentimentality (sometimes by way of dissension), from a sense of infinite possession and possibility into a sense of infinite loss and despondency. Detumescence is the obvious movement of "The Dead." It is also the movement of each of the fourteen preceding stories (whose brevity might make "coitus interruptus" the better metaphor) and a movement Joyce plotted in reaction perhaps to the optimism and expectant sense of apocalypse in a great deal of contemporary Irish literature. Under the surface sentimentalism, romanticism and symbolism of the story, a deflationary realism steadily advances, a narrative duplicity Joyce brought to perfection in "Ivy Day in the Committee Room" and the Cyclops episode of *Ulysses*.

Gabriel Conroy, Hero-Fool

The defeat, paralysis, and death that characterize his Dublin and his Ireland disqualify Joyce as a revivalist. Yet in the last story in Dubliners they are not ultimately triumphant, and for this we have to thank Joyce's unlikely hero, Gabriel Conroy, who suffers the pain of self-realization but attains a brief and powerful vision on the strength of it. Critics when willing to grant Gabriel's essential separation from the other guests at the party usually see it as a sad, even comic reflection upon his character. Certainly Gabriel exhibits some traits of the fool (and not the Yeatsian or Pearsean fool either), being foolishly dressed at first in galoshes and being the butt of others' irony, including Joyce's. He might even be regarded as a kind of proto-Bloom, a man not cast in the mold of heroic manliness depicted in the old romances and celebrated by the revivalists, a man whose ambivalent reaction to news of his wife's dead lover is a glimmering of Bloom's connivance at his wife's adultery.

At the same time Gabriel, if in some ways he resembles Leopold Bloom, is also as critics have pointed out what Stephen might have become had he remained in Ireland. (The dual likeness is another reason "The Dead" is a pivotal work in Joyce's canon.) Gabriel is without Stephen's artistic gifts (he writes book reviews rather than poems), a critic and an artist *manqué* who lacks Stephen's almost Faustian arrogance and who grows less articulate through "The Dead" as Stephen grows more so through *A Portrait of the Artist as a Young Man* (1916). Yet perhaps the creative ambition was once there, sterilized since by the besieging forces of the dead; and perhaps his crankiness and intolerance were once pride and single-mindedness. Either way, the folly of the hero in the twenty-six year old Joyce's astonishingly mature imagining of what might befall him (but will not: exile and composition of "The Dead" prevent it) has much in common with the folly of Stephen, though one hesitates, even given Gabriel's bewilderment before the facts of human existence, to compare it, as we might compare Stephen's, with the folly of Hamlet. Not quite the prince, yet neither is he quite Polonius.

Gabriel's eventual victory is like Bloom's (for which it paves the way) not so much a moral one as one of essential capacious humanity. It is tempting to say that Joyce's notion of heroism now seems better suited to the twentieth century than, say, Pearse's or even Yeats's, but of course no Joycean hero could ever win or defend political freedoms in short order. Let us merely say that Dedalus' highminded aestheticism, Gabriel's rational dilettantism and Bloom's daily expediencies offered those Irish readers who read Joyce, and even smaller number who understood and appreciated him, unpopular literary alternatives to the tragic heroism of nationalist legendry.

As hero-fool, Gabriel commands in the beginning only part of our sympathy, but it is still the lion's share if we read the scenes aright. For example, when he hands Lily a coin after their brief, embarrassing exchange, it may seem, as some have suggested, as though he were trying to reassert his social superiority by this hypocritical use of a tip or Christmas bonus.[14] Money of course plays a crucial role in most stories in *Dubliners,* and its use is realistic, since Joyce is mostly depicting those on the fringe of respectability and solvency, and also allegorical. In *Dubliners* money is the circulating medium of commerce by which love, marriage, family, friendship, religion, courage, and idealism are repeatedly traduced, usury a recurring metaphor for human relationships.[15] Thievery, betrayal, self-betrayal, dereliction, usury itself: all are metaphoric versions of "simony," the chief "mortal sin" of which Joyce's Dubliners are guilty and which, in these stories that are "gnomons" or registers of Dublin's moral life, issue in spiritual "paralysis."[16] Conroy, too, is a "simoniac," but what he is buying back from Lily is not so much his social superiority as a ritually defined and superficially comfortable relationship, a transaction in which he is misguidedly engaged most of the evening.

Ritual may be a way of avoiding reality, and Gabriel is later to repudiate his role in his family's Victorian social rites. But Lily's tactless and uncharacteristic outburst about the "palaver" of men ("she's not the girl she was at all," complains Aunt Kate) represents the other extreme, even though the outburst is to some extent vindicated by the evening's voluble proceedings. (Just as her contention that men are only after "what they can get out of you" is vindicated in a previous story by the behavior of the two "gallants" whose caddishness, it could be thought, is redeemed when Gabriel symbolically returns their ill-gotten gold coin to a different slavey.) The only thing Gabriel's aunts won't stand for from their help is "back answers." Lily answers Gabriel back, surely unjustifiably. But then, before the night is over life will have made Gabriel several back answers, just when he thought he had made its disorder obedient to his private rituals, and will have forced him to accept its mutiny before awarding him the wherewithal by which to comprehend it even as he falls before it.

In his altercation with Miss Ivors, Gabriel must shoulder more of the blame, but in part because his literal-mindedness—something he is destined to lose before the evening is out—does not equip him for parrying her ironies and banter. Miss Ivors is "a frank-mannered talkative young lady" apparently flirting with a man too absorbed with the appearance of dignity to recognize flirtation. And he is too conscious also, as he was with Lily, of his superiority as a man to see before him an equal being: after the encounter he refers inwardly to Miss Ivors as "the girl or woman, or whatever she was." Joyce in the figures of Gabriel and Mr. Browne is portraying the Irishman's traditionally patronizing, even contemptuous, at base fearful attitude to women beneath a chivalry the revivalists professed to admire in the old heroic romances. Gabriel exhibits palely this chivalry, but does not travesty it in the odious manner of Corley in "Two Gallants" (whose name, pronounced in the Florentine way, suggests the "whore" he really is) or of Gallaher in "A Little Cloud" (whose name suggests the Galahad he is not).

Gabriel foolishly mistakes Miss Ivors' mock-gravity and responds by "smiling at her solemn manner" before she quizzes him on the identity of G. C. and makes him color, just as he later and more seriously mistakes Gretta's sadness at the memory of Michael Furey for pity and pays too for that fresh example of his smug attitude to women. Yet although Gabriel appears foolish during their confrontation, we are meant to detect the foolish seriousness of Molly Ivors herself beneath her flirtatious guying of him. There is in this heavily coded scene a clash not only of personalities and private prejudices but also of public attitudes and principles.

By declining Miss Ivors' invitation to visit the Aran Islands, Gabriel discountenances the Irish literary and cultural renaissance. Miss Ivors does not represent the real west of Moore and O'Donovan, with its priests and untilled fields, but instead the newly-discovered west of the middle-class and Ascendancy cultural nationalists. Gaelic enthusiasm had a following among middle-class Irishwomen, for whom it was a fashionable and social cause and to which they had the leisure to devote themselves. Joyce in *A Portrait* has Father Moran refer to "the ladies" as "the best helpers the language has," and one of the most notable of these helpers was Kathleen Sheehy whom Molly Ivors has been taken to resemble.[17] If she is modeled on Kathleen Sheehy, then she is no mere do-gooder or profiteer, but a feminist and antigovernment militant. This gives an edge to her flirting, which is in one sense a blow struck on behalf of women's right to be assertive. Gabriel is better placed than Joyce's readers to wonder if she is really flirting at all when the moral strictness of the Gaelic movement, adverted to by Joyce's otherwise irrelevant remark that Miss Ivors "did not wear a low-cut bodice," would suggest the contrary. When she tells Gabriel who offers to see her home that she is "quite well able to take care" of herself, it is an independent young woman speaking. Unlike Irish peasant behavior, Gaelic enthusiasm was aggressively self-advertising, perhaps out of tactical necessity. As she departs, Miss Ivors shouts a blessing in Gaelic to the "West British" gathering, while "the large brooch which was fixed in front of her collar bore on it an Irish device," presumably the silver replica of the Cavan Brooch, symbol of Maud Gonne's organization, *Inghinuidhe na h-Eireann* ("Daughters of Ireland").[18]

During the revival, feminism was often associated with nationalism, and the association rested on membership of the middle class. The reality of the Irish language and culture of the west must be distinguished, then, from the nationalist versions of these. These versions were fashioned by those whose essential lifestyle differed hardly at all from those whom they considered West Britons. If in some sense Gabriel Conroy acknowledges the potency of the west at the close of "The Dead," it is decidedly not the "turas" west of Miss Ivors.[19]

Yet Joyce in depicting character never loses sight of the personal and human. Gabriel is not certain that Miss Ivors is a mere dogmatist. "Had she really any life behind all her propagandism?" he asks himself. (Is she an Alice Barton or an Ellen Cronin?) Neither Gabriel nor we know; probably Joyce himself had not decided. As a fiction writer he gives her the benefit of the doubt by leaving the question unanswered; as an anti-nationalist, in the sense of being someone for whom patriotism does not take pride of place among his beliefs, he manages to suggest a negative answer in the very formulation of the question. Molly Ivors seems in her energy and fervor, that are in contrast to the idleness of the others, to be quick among the dead, but it is only at this stage of the story that this is the case; and it is her energy and independence, not the nationalist cause they serve, that give her life. When she leaves, she too becomes one of the "departed."

For its part, Gabriel's personality serves his cause ill, for when he is reduced to silence by Molly Ivors it is less because his principles are threadbare beside hers than because he is a man easily harassed, unlike the mature Stephen Dedalus:

> —And why do you go to France and Belgium, said Miss Ivors, instead of visiting your own land?

—Well, said Gabriel, it's partly to keep in touch with the languages and partly for a change.

—And haven't you your own language to keep in touch with—Irish? asked Miss Ivors.

—Well, said Gabriel, if it comes to that, you know, Irish is not my language.

Their neighbours had turned to listen to the cross-examination. Gabriel glanced right and left nervously and tried to keep his good humour under the ordeal which was making a blush invade his forehead.

—And haven't you your own land to visit, continued Miss Ivors, that you know nothing of, your own people, and your own country?

—O, to tell you the truth, retorted Gabriel suddenly, I'm sick of my own country, sick of it!

—Why? asked Miss Ivors.

Gabriel did not answer for his retort had heated him.

They had to go visiting together and, as he had not answered her, Miss Ivors said warmly:

—Of course, you've no answer.

Gabriel's attitude is less simple than Miss Ivors' (she is here championing in clichés a fashionable cause), less amenable to instant declaration, and he is goaded into overstating his position, into proclaiming a redoubt when he is not possessed of Stephen's intellectual armament to defend it. What he wishes to tell Molly Ivors is that literature demands its own allegiance and is above and beyond politics, a view held by both Joyce and Yeats in opposition to politicians and cultural nationalists like Arthur Griffith who attacked Synge by claiming that "cosmopolitanism never produced a great artist nor a good man yet and never will."[20] In *A Portrait* Davin tells Stephen that "a man's country comes first. Ireland first, Stevie. You can be a poet or a mystic after."[21] This is an echo of Griffith's response to Yeats's suggestion that patriotism has its literary limitations: "He who is prepared to give up a great deal for his country is no doubt a good man, but unless he is prepared to give up all we do not deem him a nationalist."[22]

But it is doubtful if Gabriel, unlike Stephen, could have articulated the necessary reply to Miss Ivors. In any case, Gabriel does not really live his high-minded belief. Just as Molly Ivors does not represent the real west or peasant Irishry, so Gabriel does not represent cosmopolitanism and Europeanism but rather a provincial flirtation with these ideas, a reduction of them to cycling tours and brushing up one's conversational French. We find this provincial, titillated admiration for London and the Continent in other characters in *Dubliners,* Jimmy Doyle in "After the Race" and in "A Little Cloud" Ignatius Gallaher and Little Chandler, for whom bohemianism, gaiety, and energy are only found outside Ireland. The shallowness of Doyle's cosmopolitanism is exposed when under the influence of drink he reverts to the nationalist views his father held when a member of the petty bourgeoisie but modified when he became a "merchant prince." In turn, Doyle's nationalism is indistinguishable from provincialism because it arises only out of the pique of the colonized. Gabriel's Europeanism is not as shallow as Doyle's (though like Doyle's it is not so much a solution to, as a symptom of, colonialism), nor does he revert to Doyle's nationalism at the end of "The Dead." A much larger vision awaits the man who is not just the central character but the hero of the story.

The Crossroads of Irish Identity

We are treated in the scene with Miss Ivors to the spectacle of two middle-class provincialisms or insularities clashing, and for them Joyce feels comparable pity or contempt. But he does not feel equal pity or contempt for the respective realities and ideals they betray. The young foreigners whose company Jimmy Doyle courts may be idle and arrogant after the race, but the "wealth and industry" of the Continent are surely preferable to the "poverty and inaction" of "the gratefully oppressed" in Inchicore, even if one detects in Joyce's attitude to the losing Doyle a benevolent and disappointed contempt worthy of D. P. Moran. The malady which Joyce famously saw as Dublin ("I call the series *Dubliners* to betray the soul of that hemiplegia or paralysis which many consider a city")[23] assumes as many guises as does simony—from the syphilitic madness (or general paralysis of the insane) of Father Flynn in "The Sisters," through Tom Kernan in "Grace," paralytic from drink, and those frozen in piety, duty, routine, and timidity ("dupes of convention"), to Gabriel's vocal paralysis when taxed by Miss Ivors and his use of cliché and hyperbole during his speech, language paralyzed. When there is motion it is idle and usually circular: the characters circulate through the Dublin streets like the wind at the opening of "Two Gallants," mockeries of Yeats's and Synge's poetic wanderers.[24]

Very different is the portrait of Dublin that emerges from Yeats's letters of the period—a city that seems expectant and alive, that "is waking up in a number of ways and about a number of things," as Yeats wrote his sister in 1898, a mere handful of years before Joyce began *Dubliners*.[25] Most nationalists were agreed that Ireland during Parnell's career was culturally paralyzed but politically vital, that culturally it was sunk in

O'Grady's "great enchantment." Many considered the position to be reversed in the 1890s—political inertness, cultural movement. Joyce thought that the cultural paralysis had not been cured by the revival or by nationalism, though he may have been hostile to the new movement partly because he felt preempted by the ferment and realized that he could never rival Yeats's leadership of cultural Dublin.

There was a real and perhaps artistically necessary disagreement here between Joyce and Yeats. We must remember that Joyce is largely re-creating only the Dublin of the lower or descending middle class, classes peculiarly idle in Joyce's youth ("idle" is one of Joyce's favorite words in *Dubliners*.) According to Mr. Henchy in "Ivy Day in the Committee Room," the city lacked capital to revivify its moribund industries, and there is evidence for his opinion.[26] For members of these classes, the revival, when it meant anything or failed to antagonize them, meant a novel source of credit, be it money or respectability, a proposition to which "A Mother" is dedicated. In performing a biopsy on the diseased tissue of Ireland, Joyce fancied, at least in some early couplets, that he was fulfilling a necessary function for the revival, though he exaggerated its lowliness for satiric effect:

> all these men of whom I speak
> Make me the sewer of their clique.
> That they may dream their dreamy dreams
> I carry off their filthy streams
> For I can do those things for them
> Through which I lost my diadem,
> Those things for which Grandmother Church
> Left me severely in the lurch.
> Thus I relieve their timid arses,
> Perform my office of Katharsis.[27]

Instead of regarding Joyce, as many Irish readers of *Dubliners* did, as having betrayed Ireland by portraying a nation of betrayers, we might choose to regard Joyce as a revival writer in the ironic, paradoxical terms of these couplets—reluctant pennyboy for his enemies (a realist doing the dirty work for romantics)—not unlike the terms in which Gabriel Conroy comes to see himself. Or we may see Joyce as an accomplice of the revival, witting or unwitting, who deflates the pretensions of the social classes most likely to be hostile to the literary movement or for impure motives to be supporters of it. He wrote of *Dubliners:* "in composing my chapter of moral history in exactly the way I have composed it I have taken the first step towards the spiritual liberation of my country."[28] Was this not the aim of the revival?

Against this view of Joyce we might press the claims of those aspects of his work that seem to outlaw him from the movement: his urban and middle-class milieux (Ireland was always Dublin, not Connacht, to his imagination); his realism and naturalism; the democratic and gossipy promiscuity with which he deflates his characters who represent not just a citizenry but an entire nation. Then there is the idea we identified in Moore, that the moral and spiritual rot has gone too far to be reversed. Moore, O'Donovan, and Joyce initiated the modern Irish tradition of "pathological realism," a realism that demonstrates what makes acceptable reality in Ireland impossible. Several years before Joyce began to compose *Dubliners,* William Larminie in his contribution to *Literary Ideals in Ireland* (1899) wrote:

> It is clear that just as the meaning and seriousness of life shrink to nothing in the absence of transcendentalism, so does the value of the art shrink which deals with a life from which transcendental belief has disappeared. The life becomes aimless, corrupt, or both, the only point of interest remaining being the pathos of the spectacle of souls robbed of their heritage. But the men and women who are so affected yield no satisfactory material to the artist. The only way in which literature can deal with them at all is to give us realistic studies in pathology, of which the principal value will be for science, not for art; otherwise they only serve the purpose of the drunken Helot.[29]

This is a startling anticipation of *Dubliners.* It is true that Joyce did not intend to liberate his countrymen into a transcendental vision of life, and it is equally true that Larminie has diagnosed the empty lives of Joyce's Dubliners-to-be. But Joyce proved that his Dubliners were indeed satisfactory material to the artist and this was a thematic as well as formal triumph, for he implied (where Moore explained) that a positive alternative to transcendentalism is self-realization and that his men and women are material for art because they represent painful cases of repression and unwanted—not chosen—selflessness (and many of them drunken helots!).

There is also the fact that in his way of life as in his writing style and literary inspiration, Joyce preferred Europeanism and cosmopolitanism over the narrow and dogmatic demands of Irish nationalism, however weakly or illogically Gabriel expresses that preference. Joyce refused to shun the England of Shakespeare and the Europe of Ibsen for a bygone

Celtic Ireland, but if the championing of Ibsen might appear in the young Joyce as modish xenophilia, we should remember that in the long perspective it is not nationalism that is the Irish tradition or orthodoxy but instead Europeanism, exile, even heresy. Irish Christians of that period that profoundly influenced Joyce, the Middle Ages, were known across Europe for their "nomadic instinct or impulse," were frequently specimens of "*Hibernicus exul,*" and were regarded by Anglo-Saxon monks as heretical.[30] Joyce need not have invoked the names of Europeans to suggest the inspiration with which exiles and heretics provided him as he sojourned in Paris, Rome, and Trieste. In a sense, Joyce, the bringer of good news to Europeans concerning fictional possibilities, was as faithful to his forefathers as the sedentary patriots. It would, of course, be absurd to imply that Synge, Yeats, and AE were anything but men of international reading and interests, or that Yeats was not drawn to the heretics who disrupt the orthodox flow of historical orders. But these writers were willing to join a collaborative movement headquartered in Ireland and designed, in the short term, to change the face of the island.

Evidence of Gabriel's weakness and illogicality is his rushing to embrace the older generation, having been stung by Miss Ivors, a representative of the younger, nationalist-minded generation. Certainly a clash of generations is implied in "The Dead" and one that was acute during the time when the story is set and when Ireland was in political upheaval with the possibility of Home Rule.[31] The military metaphors and references in "The Dead" which culminate in the image of the Wellington Monument contribute to one kind of ambience in the story, a late nineteenth century "West British" imperial twilight whose faded gentility was a feature of the second city of the Empire, soon to be the first city of that lost empire of breakaway British colonies. The colonial attitudes of West Britonism comprise the story's third provincialism (alongside a provincial nationalism and a provincial Europeanism), and its ambience is later subverted by the ghostly presence of the "West Irish" in the image of Michael Furey, and the less dubitable presence of the young living nationalist, Miss Ivors, whose early departure from the party is an implied political gesture. But Gabriel is fooling himself, and senses it, in confusing an obscure nostalgia for empire with Europeanism or cosmopolitanism and in retreating into the camp of the older generation, even though one suspects beneath the irony the seductiveness for Joyce of Ireland's role in empire.

After his encounter with Molly Ivors, Gabriel decides to advert in a characteristically patronizing way to the clash of generations in his imminent speech. "He would say, alluding to Aunt Kate and Aunt Julia: *Ladies and Gentlemen, the generation which is now on the wane among us may have had its faults but for my part I think it had certain qualities of hospitality, of humour, of humanity, which the new and very serious and hypereducated generation that is growing up around us seems to me to lack."* He hardly believes this, for he immediately reflects: "Very good: that was one for Miss Ivors. What did he care that his aunts were only two ignorant old women?" Gabriel was wiser in keeping out of the guests' maudlin and self-indulgent palaver about dead opera singers which reduces Europeanism to a cult of the superiority of the past over the present, however much Joyce must have relished exploiting in this scene his love of music, and however much justification there is for the guests' nostalgia for a time "when there was something like singing to be heard in Dublin," as Mr. Browne laments.[32] And so most of the music heard in *Dubliners* is not in fact the high accomplishment of European composition but popular arias and ballads on the fringe of musical respectability as their singers and listeners are on the fringes of social respectability, good taste, or spiritual life; the songs ironically emphasize how far reality is from the characters' daydreams. Bartell D'Arcy as a member of the younger generation dismisses such nostalgia for bygone singers, while Miss Ivors had she been present would no doubt have advanced as evidence of current musical energy in Ireland the renaissance of folk songs from the west just then beginning and instigated by Douglas Hyde.[33]

Gabriel is unaware that he belongs neither to the older generation (he is, after all, one of the "hypereducated") nor to the new nationalist generation. He is suspended between two Irelands vying for supremacy. There is, on the one hand, a sentimentally recollected Dublin, the "spacious days" he hankers after (or believes he hankers after) and that are, though he does not realize it, of the early nineteenth century and a Protestant Ascendancy adjusting to the Act of Union. This Ireland is associated in "The Dead" with Phoenix Park, generous site of the Viceregal Lodge and in which stands the Wellington Monument. Wellington, with his Irish connections, hero of the empire, is the story's West Briton *par excellence*. By Joyce's day this Ireland is a fading dream, the reality being a shrunken and *déclassé* Dublin that in "After the Race" wears "the mask of a capital." It is a city falling deeper into provincialism and vividly represented in *Dubliners* in the decaying and constraining middle-class streets of the city. There is, on the other hand, a sentimentally imagined Gaelic-speaking west. Though they may be unaware of it, those who dream such a place are in reality party to a strange alliance between disaffected Protestants looking fondly back—in Yeats's case to an eighteenth century, pre-Act of Union Ireland, when they were masters in someone else's house—and restive Catholics owing their ambition to the nineteenth century and Catholic Emancipation engineered by Daniel O'Connell who along with Wellington is a statuesque presence in "The Dead." Wellington and O'Connell literally stand in this story for two opposing, consecutive, historically real social orders. Like his creator, Gabriel cannot belong to either yet is connected to both. Gabriel's way of resolving the dilemma is to espouse Europeanism, but if in his case this is somewhat bogus, Dedalus and Joyce translated it into authenticity.

Gabriel Conroy, then, represents the Irish identity at a crossroads, one made more immediate by the importunities of the cultural revival. He is the story's—and the culture's—crucial figure. His failure truly to belong both brands him as a man apart and is his saving grace, guarantee of a redeeming individuality more strongly marked in Leopold Bloom and Stephen Dedalus. He stands among the guests but not of them, not because his formal education is superior, his cultural horizons broader, his arrogance sterner, but because (contrary to appearances) only he has not finally or fatally settled into one unambiguous stance towards life. His problem is not, as many critics see it, to become one with those at the party who are "alive," but to escape all of them, for they are all without exception touched by death, directly or indirectly. But he must escape through them, not from them.

Their mortality is not just the caducity of flesh. It is, for example, the sterility of ritual and despotism of custom that exist by virtue of their own momentum and in which Gabriel participates before he sees himself as a dupe of convention and transcends in vision its demands. It is family and society reduced to a domesticity that stifles Eveline and so many others among Joyce's Dubliners and the larger cultural equivalent of which is provincialism and beyond that nationalism. It is Lily's self-abnegation because, presumably, of a bad experience. The celibate shrinking from the brute facts of life, later denied with ironic result by Gabriel's lust for his wife, is most starkly depicted by the monks discussed by the guests over dinner. In the case of the monks, celibacy is merely part of a total exaltation of the hereafter over the here-and-now, for the order of monks in question sleep in coffins in rehearsal for death. This renunciation of life entails a submission to authority, be it the monastic order, in the case of the coffined monks, or papal decree, in the case of the women turned out of church choirs in favor of boys, a decree briefly protested only by Aunt Kate. Then there is the required submission to one's forefathers. Implicitly championed in Miss Ivors' exalting of the Gaelic Irishry, these ancestors will not willingly release their grip on the living, as Gabriel discovers when he tries—with some snobbery—to rescue his wife Gretta from the demanding echoes of her Connacht background.

All of these are versions of forces and ideals by which Joyce felt threatened and stifled—religion, nationalism, class, history, provincialism, familism, and ancestor worship. They exact stern duty and routine and seek to subjugate the living self, and Joyce wove them into the nets Stephen Dedalus seeks to fly by in *A Portrait*. It has been argued that whereas Stephen is able to escape the nets, Gabriel is mortally entangled by them.[34] But this argument overlooks the story's final and liberating vision awarded by Joyce to Conroy and no other.

Gabriel's Subjunctive Self

> ". . . men may rise on stepping-stones
> Of their dead selves to higher things."
> —Tennyson, *In Memoriam*

The entire first "act" of "The Dead," events at the supper-dance, is strained by hollow politeness—"the rule of the order," to borrow Aunt Kate's defense of the coffined monks—in which all is mere gesture and rote. It is as empty of real communion with others as Mr. Duffy's life in "A Painful Case," a matter of mere encounters. The dead are in control and stifle any rebellious signs of life. Gabriel like the other guests is in collusion. His thinking during the party is ritualized (except during those moments when he wishes to flee) and is expressed in formulaic phrases, for example "thought-tormented," that are the language of the dead. Many of Joyce's Dubliners, including Gabriel, practice inwardly what is to be said outwardly. They are like artists incapable of improvising, mere phrase-mongers. They cannot adapt to life or express their true selves. Language, like life, is endlessly rehearsed instead of being practiced in the preferable sense of the word.

Gabriel's speech is his most blatant collusion with the dead. The premonition Gabriel has that his speech will be a failure because the product of an education superior to that of the other guests is not on the surface fulfilled; as it turns out, his homage to the waning generation is a studied, platitudinous, rather fake effort to deny any such superiority and any Continental bias, something of a handed coin to the assembly. It is also a hollow victory over the absent Molly Ivors. The "funeral oration," like that in "Ivy Day in the Committee Room," has an empty ring to it. To make matters worse, Gabriel in his speech pays lip service to "living duties and living affections" when what claim the strenuous endeavors of everyone at the party are not living but dead duties and affections.

Gabriel has a romantic and premature feeling of escape from these. Leaving the party with Gretta, he imagines that they have "escaped from their lives and duties, escaped from home and friends and run away together with wild and radiant hearts to a new adventure." Unknown to him, Gretta feels no such sensation of flight, she being preoccupied with thoughts of a dead lover, and so Gabriel's freedom and illusion of knightly valor end, significantly, when they pass from out-of-doors into the hotel. In the bedroom Gabriel tries to act as though he were indeed free from the clutches of the dead, but he is soon thwarted by the distant music of Gretta's past, distant both in time and space.[35] Gretta, like the others, is symbolically one of the living dead and as such beyond Gabriel's reach, beyond the scope and jurisdiction of truly living duty and truly living affections.

Gretta's disclosure about events in Galway summons at last the party's least punctual guest and the funeral celebration's least expected corpse—Michael Furey. How ironic that the man who prated to the guests about the virtue of Irish hospitality should now have to play host to the lover of his wife and be "acolyte" to a dead man, learning from him the mystery of love, as the boy in "The Sisters" learns the mysteries of the church by being "acolyte" to a dying priest. This revenant mocks the smug superiority of the living over the dead expressed by those around the supper table even as they pay homage to the departed. Gabriel is put in the shade by a shade, overshadowed and put upon by another, like so many of Joyce's Dubliners.

It is Furey who "embodies" in one ghostly figure the dead who haunt and crowd Gabriel and who will be acknowledged and admitted. He is a figure from the past ("whose fame the world will not willingly let die," as Gabriel unwittingly said when speechifying after dinner about the dead, the platitude returning to haunt him) and, as his name indicates, vividly enough to suggest irony, he was passionate, burning furiously in the way that Little Chandler (who might have daydreamed him) would like to but cannot because he cannot hold a candle to Byron or Mangan or the other real Romantic poets. Yet Furey's passion seems hardly Byronic, much less Cuchulainoid: he was passionate in a loyal, tubercular, even perverse way that might have appealed to the Pearse of *Iosagan and Other Stories*—in short, someone who took self-renunciation to the length of martyrdom.[36] He was, we might say, an incurable romantic, as Father Flynn is an incurable symbolist; the syphilitic priest dies paralyzed before the awesomeness of ritual secrecy, the consumptive is consumed by a self-denying passion. Moreover, Furey came from the west, the ancestral home of the Gael and the mythic locus of nationalist aspiration.[37] To his chagrin, Gabriel finds that the west is indeed awake. Amidst Gabriel's ordered life, Gretta's story is a chronicle of disorder, a story of the Wild West ironically different from the kind that offered escape to the boy in "An Encounter."

We are given Furey in the romantic outdoors, at the end of a garden like a would-be Red Hanrahan, but made ironic by rainfall and a job in the gasworks.[38] If Miss Ivors is a borrowed representative of Dublin cultural nationalism, Michael Furey is a borrowed creation from romantic primitivism. In making Furey such a formidable adversary for Gabriel, Joyce is acknowledging the powerful and fashionable alternative to his own complex attitude to Ireland that cultural nationalism and romantic primitivism represented. In Furey's Connemara we recognize the cradle of ancient forces that reach out from the Aran Islands via Nuns' Island to Usher's Island and even from Usher's Island to the "West British" refuge of the Gresham Hotel to threaten an educated, middle-class, emancipated Dubliner like Gabriel Conroy. We might recall the words of Standish James O'Grady that illuminate uncannily Gabriel's predicament: "Educated Irishmen are ignorant of, and indifferent to, their history; yet from the hold of that history they cannot shake themselves free. It still haunts the imagination, like Mordecai at Haman's gate, a cause of continual annoyance and vexation. An Irishman can no more release himself from his history than he can absolve himself from social and domestic duties. He may outrage it, but he cannot placidly ignore. Hence the uneasy, impatient feeling with which the subject is generally regarded."[39] Upon Michael Furey's ghostly advent, the dead can no longer be eulogized out of sight or concealed by euphemistic ritual. The dead must now be confronted.

This is to Gabriel's ultimate benefit, though he does not know it. Wrote Joyce elsewhere: "Giordano Bruno himself says that every power, whether in nature or in the spirit, must create an opposite power, without which it cannot fulfill itself, and he adds that in each such separation there is a tendency toward reunion."[40] That Furey is Gabriel Conroy's alter ego, his counterpart, his "subjunctive self," has been pointed out by a perceptive critic for whom Joyce's fiction is peopled by "negated possibilities" that "do not disappear entirely. They enjoy a ghostly half life, haunting his protagonists, no less vivid for their unreality."[41] "The dualism of the sublime Nolan" (Giordano Bruno) must have appealed to Yeats whose philosophy and even dramatic situation in the poem "Ego Dominus Tuus" illuminate "The Dead." Gabriel's subjunctive self is akin to the Yeatsian "anti-self" Ille wishes to conjure up.

> By the help of an image
> I call to my own opposite, summon all
> That I have handled least, least looked upon

Ille declares, and we can think of Gretta's image of a rain-soaked consumptive at the end of a garden that causes Gabriel to imagine, a little later, he sees "the form of a young man standing under a dripping tree." Furey "sank into his grave/His senses and his heart unsatisfied," like the Keats Ille describes. The unhappy man, the artist, sings his vision of reality while the happy man (and Gabriel until this evening has at least been smug about his lot) serves the world in the common dream of action. Here is one of several points of contact between Joyce and Yeats, for the theory of the other self may be rooted in an Irish hankering for the subjunctive, the otherwise.

In turn, this hankering may arise from a duality unsurprising in a colonial society. John Cronin has identified paired opposites in chief fictional characters as fundamental to Anglo-Irish literature. Such pairings oppose realism and romanticism, pragmatism and sentimentality, modern Ireland and its Gaelic past.[42] *Dubliners,* of course, is strewn with pairings: Mr. Duffy and Mrs. Sinico, Eveline and Frank, Little Chandler and Ignatius Gallaher, to name a few. They can suggest variously the relationships of master and disciple, master and servant, insider and outsider, ego and alter ego. All of them involve a struggle for power and expression, the weaker in each case representing the repressed self. The most vivid of the pairings in a social sense is that of Corley the police inspector's son and Lenehan the cadger. Lenehan is the outsider, satellite to Corley's planet. "Two Gallants" can be read as an allegory about colonial society that demands a petty over-bureaucratic infrastructure rewarding those "in the know" while penalizing those who aren't. The petty tyrants among Joyce's Dubliners who dominate others do so because they themselves are insignificant links in a chain of domination stretching from Dublin streets to Westminster, all counterparts of each other; Farrington bullies his son because he in turn is bullied by the Ulster (probably Protestant) head of the firm of solicitors for whom he works, and, on one evening at least, by the Englishman Weathers, English muscle in Ireland by proxy. Only with Gabriel Conroy does the weaker triumph over the stronger, and only after the appearance of defeat and the terrible irony of a dead man exerting more power than a living.

Although Joyce shared with Yeats the dualism of the Nolan, he did not wish to resolve it on behalf of heroism, strength, and deliberate sacrifice; the kind of man Gabriel is seems worthier of his final attention than the kind of man Furey is. Gabriel proves his Irishness by periodically imagining what would or might be the case, but at the end of the story the subjunctive gives way to the tenseless and tensionless vision which belongs to Gabriel. Once his wife is asleep, Gabriel calls to his opposite by the help of an image, and this is a stage in his own fulfillment. By releasing his repressed self, he absorbs his romantic anti-self and becomes a transcendent realist, a greater and different realist than he has been. His, like Bloom's, is in an "inward heroism," necessarily unimpressive beside the extravagant gestures of conventional heroism.[43]

When Gretta flings herself on the hotel bed sobbing, in a sense she is a martyr to the memory of her love for Michael Furey as he was to his love for her. The regret she feels (suggested by her name) ties her mortally to the past.[44] When Gretta and Michael "join" each other in loving "death," Gabriel is left looking out of the window, the vision beyond death ever closer. Only Gabriel, who like the others has conspired to pretend that death is life, is granted by Joyce indulgence to transcend his hypocrisy. In being thwarted in his desire for his wife and in yet feeling for her a "strange friendly pity" as he watches her asleep, he disproves Mr. Duffy's maxim in "A Painful Case" that "friendship between man and woman is impossible because there must be sexual intercourse." By proving Gretta's friend, as Bloom proved Molly's, Gabriel expiates Duffy's guilty error as he does the errors of the other Dubliners.[45] If "The Dead" on one level concerns the price death exacts from those who choose not to acknowledge with the fullness of their being its omnipresence, then when he looks out of the hotel window Gabriel has come close to setting right his account, though not in the shallow manner offered Mr. Kernan and his cronies in "Grace." Some truly tormented thought has been involved: how the phrase, "a thought-tormented age," so shallowly felt by Gabriel in his speech, echoes mockingly in this scene!

Yet Gabriel's is an initiation in no abrupt sense nor, as many critics have read it, a sudden rebirth. When Gabriel sees himself in the glass of outer weariness (to borrow from Yeats) as "a ludicrous figure, acting as a pennyboy for his aunts, a nervous well-meaning sentimentalist, orating to vulgarians and idealizing his own clownish lusts, the pitiable fatuous fellow he had caught a glimpse of in the mirror," he is not—any more than the boy in "Araby" gazing up into the reflecting darkness—seeing his real self, but instead the Gabriel who has acted up to then against the subliminal current of his real being, another false self to be repudiated.[46] The more authentic Gabriel is the man remembering the mirror image of himself in fool's mask, a man who in the terms of "Ego Dominus Tuus" is on his way to transcending rhetoric and sentimentalism into a vision of ultimate reality. By coming to know himself, Gabriel is transformed from the fool he appeared to be into the peculiarly Joycean hero he actually is. As in most of the stories in *Dubliners,* there is for the central figure a profoundly self-conscious, mortifying, even purifying awareness of humiliation, loss, and bewilderment. It is for Gabriel no mere comeuppance. Alone, as in glancing thoughts earlier in the evening he had ironically longed to be, ineloquent, gauche, haunted, Gabriel is suitably prepared in this "thought-enchanted silence" (Stephen's phrase) for the vision that has stalked him for hours and was denied his predecessors in *Dubliners* but whose surrogate he is.

In an important sense, then, Gabriel Conroy does move like the man who loved islands from larger to smaller islands, but only in the sense that "The Dead" gradually depopulates as Gabriel shrinks into his pure and desolate self (certain set apart!) which cannot, any more than Lawrence's character's, sustain its own individuality but must dissolve and become one with the rhythms of the universe. The outcome might be similar in both stories, but the means of getting there are precisely opposite. In "The Man Who Loved Islands," as in Synge's *The Aran Islands,* the real island becomes metaphorically the self. In "The Dead" the real self becomes metaphorically an island. To this extent Joyce's story could have been set anywhere. But of course the story is not "set anywhere" and so the nationalist reading of "The Dead" I mentioned at the outset of the chapter is not entirely mistaken. For if in no cultural sense, literal or symbolic, does Gabriel return to the west of Ireland at the story's end, for the bulk of the story he attempts unsuccessfully to deny that in terms of psychic genealogy he has come from there, to deny as it were one step of the dialectic. "This race and this country and this life produced me," Stephen admits to Davin. But he follows this up with: "I shall express myself as I am."

Certainly the forces of Irish nationhood, culture, language, religion and family ranged against Gabriel have made him what he is, and they have special associations with the west. In their combination they have helped to impose on him a false and fatuous self, an unsettling combination of Irish and "West British" identity, and in the course of the story he must renounce these forces and his falsity of self in order to find liberation. Gretta and Miss Ivors are calling him home, and this he is reluctant to admit and vexed to realize. When he manages at last to escape through the forces that threaten him, to turn paralysis into motion, Gabriel is apparently nothing as he drifts off among the rhythms of the universe.

Is Henry Grattan's eighteenth century challenge then unanswerable? "I laugh at those Irish gentlemen who talk as if they were the representatives of something higher than their native land," he sneered. "Let me tell those gentlemen, if they are not Irishmen, they are nothing."[47] Possibly, but only because Ireland wrongfully contrives to claim a man's every loyalty and to dominate his entire being. As Gabriel's predicament demonstrates, if the self is to grow, the authority of Ireland to govern the self must diminish. Yet Gabriel does live briefly in the present, free from the grip of an imprisoning Irishness, before Joyce hastens him on to a selfless exaltation, though in describing the epiphany as selfless we might remember that it was Stephen Dedalus' "old friend saint Thomas" who defined eternity as "the possession of one's self, as in a single moment."[48] Moreover, neither nationalism nor the west is an adequate destination for the human spirit. Gabriel acknowledges his own Irishness but not in a fashion likely to appease Grattan, for it is done in order to rise above it, the way Gabriel must acknowledge death in order to glimpse life.

The Journey Westward

> "The music of what happens," said
> great Fionn, "that is the finest music
> in the world."
>
> —James Stephens, *Irish Fairy Tales*

The quick feelings that helped to alienate Gabriel from the others all evening subside into emotional stasis. When he watches Gretta asleep he does so "unresentfully"; when he thinks of the small part he has played in her life he is "hardly pained"; and it is with "curious eyes" that he looks upon her. When emotion again suffuses him, it is pity rather than annoyance or lust or nervous fear: "as he thought of what she must have been then, in that time of her first girlish beauty, a strange friendly pity for her entered his soul."

For most of the story Gabriel has been—despite what critics say—the opposite of egotistic. He has allowed others to dictate his reactions; only now is he self-sufficient enough (egotistic enough, if you like) to afford unprovoked compassion toward another and to turn his self-consciousness from something crippling into something liberating. Now he has learned the dignity of altruism that MacCann told Stephen he had not done, and has expiated the snobbery felt toward their women by Mr. Duffy and by Bob Doran in "The Boarding House." He disproves Mr. Duffy's dictum: "We cannot give ourselves . . . we are our own." Like Stephen ("Dedalus . . . I believe you're a good fellow but . . .") Gabriel is not a bad fellow at heart. He weeps "generous tears": copious as well as pitying, but not self-pitying like those of Little Chandler. This harks back to Gretta's premature description of Gabriel as a "generous person" when he tells her of the pound he lent Freddy Malins whom he inwardly curses. (We recall too that he overtipped the cab-driver out of impatient lust rather than generosity). It harks back also to the newspaper remark Mary Jane quotes, that "the snow is general all over Ireland," a phrase Gabriel sleepily remembers at the story's end. Gabriel's pity, then, is an expansive emotion analogous to his growing sense of physical spaciousness.

Joyce considered important that note rare in Yeats—compassion. Indeed, he thought it was the greatest legacy of the European Renaissance. "All the modern conquests of the air, the earth, the sea, disease, ignorance, are dissolved, so to speak, in the crucible of the mind and are transformed into a drop of water, a tear. If the Renaissance did nothing else, it would have done much in creating in ourselves and in our art the sense of compassion for each thing that lives and hopes and dies and deludes itself."[49] When we read of the tears gathering in the eyes of a man who deluded himself for so long, does this remark of Joyce's not shed light on the end of "The Dead" which is also the end of *Dubliners?*

As well as being an expansive emotion, pity is a unifying emotion. Stephen in *A Portrait* defines pity for Lynch: "Pity is the feeling which arrests the mind in the presence of whatsoever is grave and constant in human sufferings and unites it with the human sufferer." The grave and constant thing in "The Dead" is ageing, the human sufferer in the last scene Gretta and then by degrees everyone. Gabriel's pity succeeds the "vague terror" which seized him a short time before when Gretta said that Michael Furey had died for her, and terror according to Stephen "is the feeling which arrests the mind in the presence of whatsoever is grave and constant in human sufferings and unites it with the secret cause." The secret cause in "The Dead" (secret because concealed by gaiety) is human mortality with which Gabriel is united by acknowledging, first Gretta's fading beauty, then Aunt Julia's imminent death, then the reality of Michael Furey's dying, and at last his own mortality.

Because sleep is a conventional euphemism for death, and because

Joyce writes that Gabriel's "soul had approached that region where dwell the vast hosts of the dead," some readers have assumed that at the close of "The Dead" Gabriel symbolically and deservedly dies, to stay dead or be reborn as a westward looking patriot. In this volume of stories about a paralyzed city, each of which seems for characters and readers alike to be a cul-de-sac, the last story is seen as the deadest of dead ends. But in fact, the stories are not cul-de-sacs but delayed avenues of escape. Nor does Gabriel "die." What is being mistaken for his "death" is his rehearsal for death but, unlike the coffined monks, it is by way of a vision which he experiences reluctantly only at the climax of the story's long pilgrimage.

There are literary precedents, including Irish ones, for such a vision. The models and sources offered by critics for the overall structure of "The Dead" have been bizarrely various, but Virginia Moseley is convincing in claiming that the eschatology of "The Dead" derives from Dante's *Divine Comedy*.[50] According to Moseley, Gabriel as Dante has to purge all perversions of love before the ultimate vision can be reached and these he does during the supper-dance that parallels Dante's *Purgatorio*. After this "purgative period," Gabriel "progresses through an illuminative one"—the journey from Usher's Island to the Gresham Hotel (with its infernal imagery of redness and flame) and the revelations in the hotel room concerning Michael Furey—"to parallel Dante's progression in rational mysticism." Upon his feeling of unity with both the living and the dead and his spacious vision of the snow, Gabriel accomplishes his Dantean final vision. "The three ways of Dante," as Moseley calls them—the purgative, the illuminative and the unitive—could be regarded as a spiritual version of that emotional and aesthetic dialectic which "The Dead" enacts. Gabriel, then, becomes a "soul," but like Dante an honorary soul, as it were, a privileged but reluctant witness to last things who will return upon waking to the realm of the living, at once punished, chastened, and delivered by what he has seen.[51]

The snow that during Gabriel's vision falls not only on the dead but on the living, not only on Dublin but on the Bog of Allen, on Oughterard, and all through the universe, cannot be the image of death some readers have taken it to be. Nor, for the same reason, can it be the "warm" image of passion as others have suggested, the passion of the west on which Gabriel has mistakenly turned his back. "A few light taps upon the pane made him turn to the window." This is an echo of Gretta's story of Michael Furey throwing gravel against her window in Nuns' Island and has suggested to some that symbolically Gabriel's soul is being summoned to judgment by the archangel Michael. Also, it has suggested to some that the dead Furey lives while the ostensibly living Gabriel is "dead". Oddly enough, "soft tapping on the window pane of the bedroom" is an omen of death on the Aran Islands where Molly Ivors wanted Gabriel to go, and this would support such a reading.[52] Yet I hear the tapping as an omen of impending vision, for at the dance Gabriel, thinking of the cool snow beyond, longingly taps the window in a gesture surely meant to echo in the story's last paragraph. We might read the later scene as Furey's imitation of Gabriel's tapping, as though the dead were answering the living in macabre code, but it makes greater sense to read in the tapping snow a signal for the vision that will be ignored no longer.

The vision is a descent, understandably since Gabriel is falling asleep. Death is certainly part of the vision and is seen as the descent of one's last end. (Like Fr. Gogarty's, Gabriel's old self is killed off.) But in Joyce falling frequently indicates epiphany rather than death. Joyce will sometimes forge a connection between falling darkness, falling asleep, and the physical sensation of falling as a metaphoric description of the spirit leaving its familiar moorings. There are other meanings in *Dubliners* of this important motif. There is the detumescent rhythm of the stories that I have already mentioned and that left his contemporary readers frustrated. Many of Joyce's Dubliners come to be disappointed or thwarted, often sexually, emotionally, or physically (in a way that is phallically mocked at the end of the volume by the Wellington Monument that looks back over Dublin and all the lives therein), though in any case their dreams or hopes suffer Joyce's disparagement. Many of the Dubliners, too, like the houses they inhabit, have experienced or are threatened by social descent. Yet these various descents do not disqualify Joyce's heroes as visionaries. For Joyce, as Gabriel, Bloom, and even Dedalus demonstrate, visionary moments belong to those whose souls are receptive. Whereas Yeats castigated the gentle and passive (we remember he dismissed Owen's poetry on the grounds of its passivity), Joyce did not, and his visions are given to those whose souls exhibit these qualities.

Above all, there is the falling snow. The faintly falling snow which Gabriel hears in imminent sleep fulfills the motif of distant music. It begins as mere eloquence in the phrase "thought-tormented music" that Gabriel with self-satisfaction recalls having used in his latest book review; becomes *fin-de-siècle* symbolism in the title, *Distant Music,* that Gabriel bestows on the imaginary picture his wife composes as she listens to D'Arcy singing; continues in the distant music of D'Arcy's song, *The Lass of Aughrim,* which is the music of grief and the sad passions of the west, and in the "distant music" of the love-words Gabriel recalls having written Gretta years before; and at last becomes the music of the spheres (the celestial music that Stephen Dedalus hears on occasion),[53] no longer distant but close and pervading. Thinking of the dissection of corruption that is *Dubliners,* we might remember that for the Pythagoreans the music of the spheres was the music of the incorruptible heard only by those sufficiently purified to hear the distant music of perfect harmony.

Some have taken the puzzling comment on Gabriel near the end of "The Dead"—"The time had come for him to set out on his journey westward"—as evidence of Gabriel's symbolic death as an inadequate patriot, since "going west" is in Celtic and other mythologies to die. Others see it as evidence of his renewal as a born-again patriot, which could find equal support in the mythology. The ambiguity, I suggest, is best resolved in terms of a third choice. Gabriel's pity for mankind, shading into Joyce's own acceptance of life and death, is a more powerful experience even than Furey's love and westbound passion, making Gabriel's "death" (or fatal punishment) unfair and his recovery of passion (or repentance) redundant. The west is accordingly the symbolic location both of death and of youthful passion transmuted into the symbolic location of vision.

The journey westward is the journey into vision immediately undertaken by Gabriel. Snow in the end of all is the weather not of paralysis but of vision. The vision is of universal motion, of the mutuality of death and life, of the "whatness" of all things, as Stephen calls it after Aquinas. The vision would have been impossible without self-awareness. A "journey westward" is the exact phrase Father Gogarty uses to describe his swim across the lake to freedom and spiritual renewal, and the phrase may have struck Joyce, who read *The Lake* at the time he sat down to write "The Dead."[54] These journeys westward are not to be confused with those made by the narrator of Yeats's apocalyptic stories, in the company of Robartes, or by the troop of cultural nationalists.

Vision, eschatology, the Otherworld, the journey west, self-transcendence and the whatness of the universe: Joyce shares an attraction to all of these with the revival. In what then lies the difference? In this: where the self is concerned, the mutuality of life and death does not render redundant or irrelevant the necessity for the safe passage of Joyce's lonely heroes through the dead. Gabriel's vision of the unity of the living and the dead is itself a spiritual triumph of the living over the dead, as the story is Joyce's triumph over the "dead" matter of Dublin he has transmuted into what Stephen calls "the radiant body of ever-living life." The vision is a reconciliation of opposing and diverse attitudes to Ireland and to life, but in rising above mere reconciliation is also a cancellation, a defeat of all the exclusive viewpoints in the story. Moreover, the vision is an instance of *rational* mysticism that has accepted and transcended the disorder of life, and it differs from the visions of Joyce's contemporaries who cheerfully courted the irrational and catastrophic.

A Transcendent Realism

Gabriel Conroy is the grown-up counterpart of the boy in the first three stories of *Dubliners*. Like them he is educated, intolerant, hypnotized by words, and haunted by duty. At the beginning of "The Dead," however, his maturity is nominal. *Dubliners* is a series of studies in precocious childhood or arrested adolescence, in thwarted attempts to cross the threshold into adulthood and independence. "Ugly, monotonous child's play" is how the boy in "Araby" thinks of his life, but the description could be extended to the lives of many of Joyce's Dubliners, who have been made infantile by various forces, ultimate among which are England and the Catholic Church.

A characteristic of childhood, and of repression, is a penchant for daydreaming and spinning unrealities. Instead of concentrating on the conversation of his worldly companions in "After the Race," Jimmy Doyle, "whose imagination was kindling, conceived the lively youth of the Frenchmen twined elegantly upon the firm framework of the Englishman's manner. A graceful image of his, he thought, and a just one." Not only is Doyle a true provincial and insular nationalist, but he is a Celt of the most stereotyped kind. So too is Little Chandler, who daydreamily desires to be the very thing that would clinch his oppression: a Celtic poet praised by the English. It is hard not to see in "A Little Cloud" a satire on the Celtic Twilight as well as on Chandler's travesty of it (or is it a travesty?), just as in "A Mother" we have a satire on the Irish revival as well as on the commercial exploitation of it. Fittingly, Little Chandler ends the story indistinguishable from his mewling infant. The impossibility of their imaginings being realized is an aspect of the Dubliners' grateful oppression, a condition in which every story in the collection is a study.

Gabriel, too, engages in dreamy imaginings at key moments, but if these are romantic, they are not of the passionate, out-of-doors, unruly and adventurous romanticism Furey parodies. Gabriel is really a "reluctant Indian" like the boy in "An Encounter," whose mind inclines inward and is at home with elaborate mystery. We remember Gabriel's response to finding his wife listening to Bartell D'Arcy singing:

> He stood still in the gloom of the hall, trying to catch the air that the voice was singing and gazing up at his wife. There was grace and mystery in her attitude as if she were a symbol of something. He asked himself what is a woman standing on the stairs in the shadow, listening to distant music, a symbol of. If he were a painter he would paint her in that attitude. Her blue felt hat would show off the bronze of her hair against the darkness and the dark panels of her skirt would show off the light ones. *Distant Music* he would call the picture if he were a painter.

This is an advance on the literal-mindedness of his response to Miss Ivors, but like studied elegance the search for symbolism in real life is a blinding confusion of artifice and reality. The answer to Gabriel's question is that she is a symbol of a woman who is thinking of a boy who loved her and who died of a disease she prefers to call love. It is rather a hollow mystery (at whose center is self-delusion) as so many are in *Dubliners*.

But the mysteries are always decorative in the manner of late Victorian decadence. Reading the passage above, we might think of the importance of painting to poets during the 1890s and the notion of life imitating art. We also might think of the boy's perception in "Araby" of Mangan's sister, a girl whose description associates her with Gretta and her name with a Furey-like romantic Irish poet, James Clarence Mangan. Mangan's sister is perceived by the boy in terms of that pseudo-religious imagery that would have come fairly naturally to a Catholic Irish writer but that also accords with the picturesque kind of Catholicism the aesthetes and Rhymers had in mind when they became converts:

> While she spoke she turned a silver bracelet round and round her wrist. She could not go, she said, because there would be a retreat that week in her convent. Her brother and two other boys were fighting for their caps and I was alone at the railings. She held one of the spikes, bowing her head towards me. The light from the lamp opposite our door caught the white curve of her neck, lit up her hair that rested there and, falling, lit up the hand upon the railing. It fell over one side of her dress and caught the white border of a petticoat, just visible as she stood at ease.

The narrators of the first three stories in *Dubliners* are, we might venture, ironically conceived symbolist heroes in embryo. (The elegantly ravelled and unravelled perversion in "An Encounter" permits us to include it among the trio.) That the boy in "The Sisters" is called a "Rosicrucian" by his uncle is telling but unnecessary evidence. The boy is fastidious yet fascinated by decay and corruption, secretive, given to flights of fancy, keeper of his own hooded counsel: qualities Gabriel has in reduced form, and Joyce himself in more creative measure. Amongst the guests at the Misses Morkan's annual dance, Gabriel resembles the boy in "Araby" who walks crowded Dublin streets hostile to romance, and Stephen Dedalus who also passes amid the common lives of his fellow citizens. All three imagine themselves apart from those who resemble the "impure multitude" of Yeats's apocalyptic stories. In *Stephen Hero* Daedalus wanders the streets of Dublin intoning phrases (as Gabriel is wont to do) and repeats to himself "The Tables of the Law" and "The Adoration of the Magi," ruminating on Aherne and Robartes, errants and outlaws who throw off the tyranny of the mediocre. The young Joyce not only read the apocalyptic stories (and praised them as "work worthy of the great Russian masters"), but read them in Marsh's Library in hopes of duplicating the terrified fascination of the narrator of "The Tables of the Law" when shown the heretical work said to be written by Joachim of Flora.[55] *Stephen Hero* more explicitly than *A Portrait* reveals the temptations that fanaticism, monasticism, heresy, esotericism, prophecy, and a secret sinfulness represented for the young Joyce.

Dubliners, whose period of composition overlapped that of *Stephen Hero,* bears traces of these temptations, stylistically as well as thematically. The inducement of mood, the epiphanies, the orchestration of motifs and images into a systemic elegance, the thought-out and painterly use of the city: these are some of the devices and characteristics of symbolism. So too are the particular motifs and images I have drawn attention to in "The Dead": darkness and light, snow, distant music. One student of symbolism has pointed out the symbolist use of the windowpane that separates the world of reality from the unpredictable nothingness of eternity, while Edmund Wilson referred to the symbolist love of synesthesia, "the confusion between the perceptions of the different senses."[56]

Joseph Voelker has directed our attention to Stephen's rejection in *Ulysses* of Joachim of Flora as a source of inspiration for the creation of beauty, and of Marsh's Library which "lends itself more readily to a Symbolist than a naturalistic description."[57] "Stephen's contemptuous avoidance of the evocative in his account of it," claims Voelker, "says more about Joyce's turning away from the career of a mystic than about the building itself." As an alternative to the symbolist tempters we are given the impure Bloom, "the prophet of sanity, realism, and a secular decency unsupported by dogma, and he passes his ministry on to Stephen." The resistance to the temptations of symbolism and the realist alternative are foreshadowed in *Dubliners*. As long as they prematurely turn life into symbol, people into portraiture, Gabriel and the boy in "Araby" are unhappy, self-deluding, and visionless. More obviously than the apocalyptic stories of Yeats, *Dubliners* is a critique of symbolism as a literary style.

Joyce's sense of reality punctures symbolist and romantic pretension and illusion. At its simplest, his sense of reality is an attention to fact and the finite realm of the actual and possible. Blunt fact and reportorial accuracy (which got the author of *Dubliners* in hot water with prospective publishers) Joyce perceived as elements in the fiction of Daniel Defoe, whom he called "the great precursor of the realist movement."[58] In many ways Joyce is a literary descendant of Defoe's, in his realism and in those preoccupations and themes we associate with realism: individualism, democracy, commerce, and rationalism. Some of the qualities he attributed to Defoe Joyce also attributed to Renaissance literature and the Renaissance mind: journalistic detail, local color, atavism, an appreciation of the circumstantial.[59]

Joyce's fiction, insofar as it shares these qualities, is an awakening from the vastly older Catholic mind that had for so long stood apart from the achievements of the Renaissance, a mind superficially imitated by the Protestant revivalists seeking pre-Renaissance, un-Protestant modes of thought and expression. Yet Joyce's work also exhibits the qualities he considered belonged to pre-Renaissance scholasticism (that the Protestant revivalists were less capable of imitating): the ideational, the formally perfect, the idly subtle. Joyce like Moore occupies a richly uncertain middle ground between Renaissance and pre-Renaissance ideals. Similarly, Gabriel Conroy is not unequivocally reborn as the individual we associate with the Renaissance, free of tyrannical duty and the absolutism of the collective and systematic mind, but he does transcend, by simplifying and dissolving them, the idle subtleties of Joyce's Dubliners.

According to Joyce, Defoe's realism does not share French realism's spiritual origin: "you will search in vain in the works of Defoe for that wrathful ardor of corruption which illuminates with pestiferous phosphorescence the sad pages of Huysman."[60] Joyce himself was, however, temporarily drawn to symbolism and neo-romanticism and fascinated by spiritual decay. Simultaneously he was drawn to naturalism and fascinated by social and bodily decay. Both fascinations are resisted by Stephen Dedalus in *Ulysses*. When he decides not to visit his Uncle Richie Goulding's house, Stephen reflects: "Houses of decay, mine, his and all. You told the Clongowes gentry you had an uncle a judge and an uncle a general in the army. Come out of them, Stephen. Beauty is not there. Nor in the stagnant bay of Marsh's library where you read the fading prophecies of Joachim Abbas."[61] Marsh's Library and the houses of decay have their equivalent in the "dark gaunt house on Usher's Island" (Come out of it, Gabriel) where the Misses Morkan live and where Gabriel's imagination kindles and spins graceful, unreal images.

Beauty comes out of the houses of decay and of Marsh's Library, even if beauty is not in them. In life such places are by themselves inadequate yet for Joyce are necessary, as in style are naturalism and symbolism. A synthesis is required, perhaps something akin to the achievement that Joyce attributes to Defoe: a realism that "defies and transcends the magical beguilements of music."[62] Through Gabriel Conroy, Joyce at once uses and discards the petty and self-regarding elaborations of symbolism.

Joyce abandons Gabriel's point of view at the end of "The Dead" when Gabriel's self dissolves in vision. "Yes, the newspapers were right: snow was general all over Ireland." Gabriel could not know this. It is the narrator who achieves on behalf of his hero that sense of spaciousness Gabriel longs for, genuinely and hypocritically, all evening. It is a spiritual spaciousness whose physical site is at first the plain of the Fifteen Acres (actually a couple of hundred acres) within the vast Phoenix Park that expands airily from the congested streets of Dublin, then Ireland from east to west (a visionary rather than nationalist or romantic orientation), and at last the universe. The closing lines with their delicate inversions and cadences read unsettlingly like the kind of thing Gabriel Conroy (or the youthful Yeats) would persuade himself is a very fine piece of writing, but the intention is clear. It is a transcendent realism—transcendent because it is musical and visionary and earns itself by assimilating the elements of a rival literature, realism because it is made possible by the infinite pain of Gabriel Conroy's self-realization. For Joyce, as for Yeats, the self must be splintered and dissolved before self-transcendence is achievable, but for Joyce, only dissolution of a real, humane, and authentic self makes transcendence desirable, and then only at surprising and unsolicited moments.

Betraying Presences
Fictional Tidings from Cork, Galway, and the Midlands—Daniel Corkery, Brinsley MacNamara, Edward E. Lysaght

9

Varieties of Contemporary Realism

While realism is neither the highest good nor the *terminus ad quem* of fiction, it is a desirable strain in a country's novel tradition viewed as a whole, especially in the light of realism's role in the history and development of the form. It is the more desirable in Irish fiction perhaps, given the potency and success of other styles and modes during a literary revival that played a crucial part in defining the identity of modern Irish literature and even of modern Ireland itself. My argument would be that the sense of actuality that realism can sponsor is and has been a much needed commodity in Ireland, and I make it in full awareness of the paradox that Irish writers, like certain South American and Indian writers, can be most realistic when they appear to be least realistic.

There can of course be found in fiction produced during the years of the Irish Renaissance by writers other than Moore, O'Donovan, and Joyce occasional expressions of an Ireland that bears the weight of worldly experience, that exhibits the logic and circumstantiality of that experience, and that is depicted faithfully, richly, or imitatively.[1] Shan Bullock's *Robert Thorne: The Story of a London Clerk* (1907), for example, is an interesting exercise in Edwardian realism replete with documentary details of the lives, at desk and hearth, of "pen-drivers," emasculated drudges beset by poverty, duty and routine. Thorne's deliverance at the end of the novel is by emigration to New Zealand, but the real answer lies in the "manliness" he might have achieved in his native Devon. But *By Thrasna River: The Story of a Townland* (1895) had already shown that whereas manliness is more likely in the countryside, its enemies there—in this case poverty, land-hunger, and an adverse climate—can be as fatally powerful as in London. In such Ulster novels as *The Squireen* (1903), *Dan the Dollar* (1905), and *The Loughsiders* (1924), Bullock combines (without real warmth despite the quirky humor) rural naturalism and mock-romantic melodrama. Though not entirely successful, in part due to a failure to handle point of view satisfactorily, Bullock's novels are valuable as social history and prove that realism was being written by Irish novelists during the years of the revival, even if Bullock owes little to that movement.

Very little more did the fiction of another Northerner, Forrest Reid, owe to the contemporary literary scene in Dublin, for like most Ulster Protestants he was culturally orientated towards England. He is remembered now as a gentle fantasist, author of the Tom Barber trilogy (1931–1944), but AE and Edmund Gosse considered him a realist. Certainly there are flashes of harsh realism in *The Kingdom of Twilight* (1904), Reid's first novel, and, say, *At the Door of the Gate* (1915), his sixth, a realism that is especially forthcoming when he wishes to portray the squalor of working-class Belfast. His best novel, *Peter Waring* (1937, a reworking of *Following Darkness,* 1912), combines realism and dream when deftly recreating a sensitive Protestant adolescence in the North of Ireland in the eighteen nineties. In this novel can be found convincing portraits of working-class tastelessness, lower middle-class shabbiness, and Ulster puritanism, all of which Reid the novelist generally fled into fantasy and personal myth.

It is not surprising that fictional realism during the years of the Irish Renaissance can be found in the North of Ireland where commerce and industry, and an associated middle class, as well as an urban working class, flourished. The novels of Bullock, Reid, and St. John Ervine cannot be accounted part of a literary revival that preferred romanticism to realism. Nor could the reality of the North of Ireland be accommodated by a cultural nationalism directed from Dublin. For these reasons I have dealt sketchily in this study with the Northerners.[2] Ulster writers, such as Bullock, went to England (or if they stayed at home, like Reid, wrote for English readers) or, like Ethna Carbery (née Anna Isobel Johnston), Alice Milligan, Seosamh MacCathmaoil (né Joseph Campbell), AE (né George Russell), and Moira O'Neill (née Nesta Higginson), they joined the romantic nationalist movement, in the process Gaelicizing or otherwise altering their identities. This they had to do, for the Protestant North, with its incorrigible nonconformism, industrialism, and political unionism, was not to be a part of the cultural revival.

A more eloquent flight from reality went on elsewhere in Ireland. I am thinking of those Southern writers and intellectuals whose Protestant heritage had rarely been depicted with seriousness or in depth and continued to be ignored, though pointedly now, during the revival. The social class with which Yeats, for example, was best acquainted was a Protestant middle class of merchants and parsons (a class in process of being economically superseded), but his influential preference was for an artistic and superstitious peasantry (thought to be nominally Catholic but *au fond* pagan) and a patronizing rural aristocracy, neither of which invited realistic scrutiny. As it happens, a fictional realism of the rural aristocracy appeared during the revival, but it came from the shared pen of two writers, E. Œ. Somerville and "Martin Ross" (Violet Martin), who had little truck with the nationalist movement and belong rather to the venerable and usually cavalier Anglo-Irish Big House tradition of fiction which on occasions they extend into a mature realism.

The Real Charlotte, for example, is an affirmative realism from the Anglo-Irish perspective written by two women who implicitly acknowledge their hereditary social position in Ireland. Somerville and Ross's novel was published in 1894, and it was in that year, as he tells us, that Moore daydreamed of writing a realistic novel of the western gentry but concluded that it was too late;[3] that the authors of *The Real Charlotte* did not consider it too late suggests the curious, nostalgic anachronism of their work. Yet the range of social classes depicted confidently in the novel is vast—from lords and ladies, English officers, and small landowners down to impoverished tenants and mendicants—and testifies to the authors' privileged grasp of contemporary social reality in Ireland.

The chief plot strand is spun by the title character who tries to upset the social equilibrium of her Galway community, but in a fashion (since she wants to better her position in the pecking order) that seeks to affirm it. Charlotte Mullen, a brilliantly wrought character, is willing through deceit to destroy others in pursuit of land, power, and social prestige. The authors reveal the real Charlotte and as realists undertake to disclose her true psychological as well as social self. The second plot strand concerns her impoverished young cousin from Dublin, Francie Fitzpatrick, whom Charlotte is willing to count among her victims. But besides being a perceptive study of Charlotte's pitiless ambition, *The Real Charlotte* is a study of Francie's punishment for her mingled naivety and artfulness. In the Galway of the 1890s, this "Dublin Jackeen" is more foreign even than an English soldier, and the degree to which Francie is responsible for her own death is the degree to which Somerville and Ross support, as realists of a tendentious kind, a stable social world to which they themselves belonged, in which people should stay true to themselves and, by dint of that, stay put. Reality for Somerville and Ross is in part the evident features of the life in Ireland with which they are familiar; reality is what they see, not what they wish to see. It is also in part the social origin of their characters; to their beginnings the characters ought to be faithful, for if they belie them, reality will return to punish them, its agency the avenging realism of their creators.

There are, however, fairly strict boundaries to the realism of Somerville and Ross. There are only sparse references in *The Real Charlotte* to the activities of the Land League during the early years of the 1890s, when the novel is set. Although there is a detectable suggestion that the Ascendancy is beginning to sway (Sir Benjamin Dysart's senility might be construed as the senility of the Ascendancy, a deafness and stupidity before a changing Ireland), it is quite muted. Somerville and Ross disqualified themselves from the Irish literary revival as realists and as Anglo-Irish writers who were unabashed participants in the soon-to-be *ancien régime*. If they were perfectly justified in ignoring the Gaelic past, which was not theirs, they were less justified, as realists, in ignoring a dissatisfied present in which nationalism had begun to be formidable rather than dismissibly quaint. Perhaps they were distracted by their awareness of the Englishness of their audience, and so played down the nastier realities of Ireland. The readers of *The Real Charlotte* are assumed to be English, and the authors go beyond merely interpreting exotic Ireland for these middle-class, English readers. Somerville and Ross seek to ingratiate themselves with their readers by explicitly confirming on occasions English prejudices against their engaging but incorrigible neighbors. Or perhaps the 1890s was the last decade in which the authentic Anglo-Irish perspective could claim to be a realistic one; if so, *The Real Charlotte,* a very fine novel in any case, gains significance from this possibility.

"Ulster realism" and "Ascendancy realism" would have been regarded as impertinences by the helmsmen of the literary revival. An equally interesting impertinence is the work of Canon (Patrick A.) Sheehan, who published a number of novels between 1895 and 1915. His novels amount to Catholic apologetics cast in fictional form, and we can set beside them in sharp contrast O'Donovan's *Father Ralph;* however, "Catholic apologetics" is a phrase which does Sheehan's novels an injustice. *Geoffrey Austin, Student* (1895) and its sequel, *The Triumph of Failure* (1899), follow a young man astray on the path of the Chameleon who must acquaint himself with degradation before finding God and donning the habits of the Carmelite brotherhood. If this sounds oddly reminiscent of Yeats's apocalyptic stories, with Geoffrey Austin a more orthodox Owen Aherne, that is because Yeats and Sheehan both inherited the *fin-de-siècle* theme of spiritual brinkmanship and were similarly fascinated by debauchery, dreams, and dark nights of the soul as necessary preludes to salvation. Sheehan in *The Triumph of Failure* quotes Francis Thompson's "The Hound of Heaven" and places Austin among the apparently irredeemable souls of a decade that represented the fag-end of romanticism with its subjectivist resistance to a materialistic century.

The Triumph of Failure is a strenuous, eloquent, and outright attack on the nineteenth century cultural forces that have seduced Austin: paganism, realism, materialism, German metaphysics, liberalism, and humanism. Despite the end-of-the-century parallels between Sheehan and the mystics of the Irish revival, Sheehan's novel by implication repudiates an Irish revival, opposed as it is to the notion of a clerisy, and depicting as it does an exclusively Catholic revival.[4] But in any case, the novel is set in the Dublin of the 1870s, and one character can say, without argument, "I know, for example, that there is no literary instinct just now in Ireland. I know we lack imagination. I know we shall never, for example, produce a great poet. We cannot. Our enthusiasm is not imagination . . . We ought to be the greatest dramatists or critics of the world. We never can be great poets."[5] Sheehan muses (prophetically) on the desirability of a Catholic theocracy in Ireland and proclaims the superiority of Catholic art and Catholic philosophy over their fashionable rivals, a preemptive strike, as it were, against the opposing view espoused by George Moore in *Hail and Farewell*.

Sheehan's programmatic approach, as priest and as novelist, does not exclude realism, however, and this is one of the most interesting aspects of *The Triumph of Failure*. He rejects the inductive system "and the corresponding influences on the arts and sciences which have found their lowest level in that which we call realism"; but he likewise deprecates the secular and pessimistic idealism of metaphysics, against which he pits what he calls "Christian realism": "a realism that comes down from the loftiest realms of speculative thought to the deepest abysses of human infirmity; a realism that searches with no profane curiosity into hidden places, but only seeks them to enlighten them; a realism that lays bare the wounds of humanity to heal them, the sins of humanity to forgive them, the wants of humanity to relieve them."[6] (He would have regarded *Dubliners* as a profane realism drained of altruism and spirituality, mere pathology.)

Since Protestantism is rejected in the novel, we had better call Sheehan's realism "Catholic realism." There are in the novel lowlife scenes among Dublin's slums (scenes stylized in the Victorian manner), but also unusual and finely observed scenes of life among Dublin's middle and professional classes, classes largely ignored by serious Irish novelists until after the revival. Despite Sheehan's huge clerical and middlebrow following, his Catholic realism and Catholic idealism were no match in literary terms for the revival that swept them aside, even if in social and political terms they triumphed in Ireland soon after the Free State was set up. Sheehan's importance is that he is the intellectual face of the Catholicism that the revivalists would not deign to regard as a serious rival but that dominated Irish culture once the romanticism of the revival had melted away.

Obstacles to an Irish Realism

> Resolve to be thyself: and know, that he
> Who finds himself, loses his misery.
> —Matthew Arnold, "Self-Dependence"

These essays in realism were few in number because certain enduring features of Irish life discourage the realism and moral inquiry that played a role in the development of the English novel. To see life steadily and see it whole: how effortlessly the Arnoldian prescription was adopted and quoted by English contemporaries of the Irish revivalists: by Lytton Strachey (in a letter to Virginia Woolf in 1908), by E. M. Forster (in *Howards End* and *Aspects of the Novel*), and by T. S. Eliot (in *The Sacred Wood*).[7] Arnold's seems an almost impossible prescription for Irish writers and critics; disinterestedness, curiosity, the study of perfection (not its quixotic pursuit), sweetness and light: how sportive and even undesirable these sound to an Irish ear.

Among the social and cultural features helping to create the Irish tradition is a suspicion of individualism fostered by Catholicism (a suspicion not of "character," which as Frank O'Connor pointed out passes in Ireland for individuality, but of genuine personality); and such a suspicion, if widespread, can militate against the writing of novels. George Orwell, sounding like an echo of George Moore, wrote in 1940: "Literature as we know it is an individual thing, demanding mental honesty and a minimum of censorship. And this is even truer of prose than of verse . . . The atmosphere of orthodoxy is always damaging to prose, and above all it is completely ruinous to the novel, the most anarchical of all forms of literature. How many Roman Catholics have been good novelists? Even the handful one could name have usually been bad Catholics. The novel is practically a Protestant form of art; it is a product of the free mind, of the autonomous individual."[8] These remarks help explain the finally unsatisfactory nature of the novels of as fine an intelligence as Sheehan's. But they have to be set beside the irony of Protestant writers abandoning their Protestantism and simultaneously the English novel, while a handful of (mostly "bad") Catholic writers, Moore, Joyce, O'Donovan, Corkery, MacNamara and Lysaght, kept the novel alive in Ireland, by exploring realistically the subjective consciousness. The "painful introspection" for which Joyce praised Ibsen was anathema to a Carlylean philosophy, which was a strand of revival thought, that recommended avoiding the misery of introspection and doubt.[9]

Sean O'Faolain in 1947 preferred to attribute the lack of realism in Irish literature not to Catholic anti-individualism but to the lack in Ireland of intellectual sophistication. This, in turn, he explained as a result of the overwhelmingly rural nature of Ireland where, even in Dublin, "an Anouilh, a Sartre or a Montherlant would be unthinkable."[10] We might mention in addition the absence of a vigorous, dominant, and enlightened bourgeois class, a class only nowadays in process of formation.[11] We might also remark on the notorious instabilities and polarities of Irish political life brought about by centuries of incomplete colonization and sectarian division. These instabilities interfere with any steadiness in point of view and wholeness of vision to which a potential realistic novelist might aspire. There is, too, the strong literary inheritance of the fantastic, verbose, and irrational which enrich and help to characterize Irish literature. In a sense the revival was an acknowledgment of native modes, a reversion rather than a revolutionary advance. The native prose tradition is a multifarious (and in its own way realistic) tradition of dream, fantasy, anecdote, folktale, romance, saga, and to this inheritance the Irish prose imagination turns when it begins to compose. This tradition the Anglo-Irish writers adopted in order to create an Irish literature in English that would be different from, even supersede, what was perceived as a declining English literature. When controlled through system and structure, the fantastic, verbose, and irrational can become in Irish fiction modernist artifice (as in the later work of Joyce and the work of Flann O'Brien and Samuel Beckett), but in the absence of control the result remains the sum of its parts. At best we have the richest and most ornate of imaginings, at worst a turning away through language from a more objective world into daydream, what one critic has called a "diseased subjectivity."[12]

Through a kind of law of the excluded middle, solipsism has seemed to be for the Irish mind and imagination the only alternative to the selflessness of myth and nationality. The excluded middle is realism, objectivity, and the proper marriage of self and society. That the alternatives often seem to resemble one another is one of the themes of "The Dead." Even the most self-conscious and would-be emancipated of Irish fictional heroes, such as Stephen Dedalus or Gabriel Conroy—whose predicament is precisely the wrong kind of self-consciousness—hears ghostly echoes of an archaic Ireland which must like his own unhealthy subjectivity be confronted and transcended. Conroy's victory—in self-perspective, then in a universal vision—is less satisfactory than Leopold Bloom's more mundane victory, less satisfactory because, unlike Bloom's, unbodied and unpracticed. The archaic imagination, through its expressive forms of tale, legend, proverb, anecdote, saga, and song, has continued, and properly, to exert great influence on the sophisticated art of Ireland. But the revival chose to strengthen this influence in the teeth of social and political evidence that a contrary influence was indicated. Realism, after all, is not, as Joyce showed, incompatible with myth or, as J. P. Stern suggests, with religion, but neither is permitted by realism to achieve an easy or uncontested victory.[13]

Margins of History: Corkery's **The Threshold of Quiet**

It was in the 1930s that the difficulties of achieving realism became insistent enough to constitute a crisis in the state of Irish fiction. O'Faolain and O'Connor wanted to write realistic novels and were much exercised by their failure. Hostile forces, among them clerical interference in secular affairs, including censorship, compelled the Irish writer, in O'Faolain's opinion, to turn inward: "for there alone in his own dark cave of self," he said in 1935, "can he hope to find certainty or reality."[14] This theme O'Faolain and O'Connor inherited from the Joyce of *Dubliners,* along with an apparatus of character, plot, and imagery. Yeats was wrong in announcing in 1932 that Joyce had not influenced Irish writers (whereas Synge had) and mentioning O'Connor to prove it.[15] The broken and dishevelled culture O'Faolain observed in 1935 had its antecedent in Joyce's post-Parnellite Dublin in which Joyce made fictional camp, exploiting its absurdities, disappointments and reversals. A long line of fiction that realistically depicts unrealistic lives on the periphery or in the interstices of society and that have been driven back upon resources of subjectivity stretches from Joyce to John McGahern, Edna O'Brien, Brian Moore, and Bernard MacLaverty. Moore, O'Donovan, and MacNamara stand in that line, but Joyce's influence is preeminent.

In *Dubliners,* lack of moral integrity is a function of cultural disintegrity; in turn the lack of cultural integrity is a function of Ireland's colonization (by Rome and London) and therefore provincialism. The nationwide provincialism perceived by Joyce is, when Ireland achieves the status of an independent country in 1922, scaled down accordingly to the local (in their case Munster) provincialism of O'Faolain and O'Connor. But in fact, these two writers were influenced as much by their Cork mentor, Daniel Corkery, as by Joyce, and Corkery was writing before the Free State came into being. Corkery's nativist affirmation of Irish reality is often contrasted with Joyce's dissent from it, but set within the whole picture of contemporary Irish literature, the Joyce of *Dubliners* has much in common with the Corkery of *The Threshold of Quiet* (1917). Like Joyce, Corkery knows best the lower middle class, though his clerks and commercial travelers are more upright than Joyce's idlers and spongers. Both are Catholics, one lapsed. They share the quietly observant eyesight of the realist. One's Cork is even more provincial than the other's Dublin, and like the island's capital, the provincial capital has seen better days, "the time there used to be great sport and life in Cork City."[16] Corkery's people as much as Joyce's live in a kind of limbo, and at one point in *The Threshold of Quiet* a clerk is fancifully seen as occupying the exactly middle ground between pirate and saint, "destined neither to damnation nor salvation" (p. 136). They languish without resemblance to the heroes and dramatic incorrigibles of revival literature. Even Cork is betwixt and between—a bustling regional capital for the summer visitor, a provincial town of quiet suburban hillsides for the residents among whom Corkery sets his novel.

The lives of these residents are lived on the margins of history; they are lives of quiet desperation, as the epigraph from Thoreau and numerous rephrasings of it throughout the novel tell us. On the far side of their despair is another kind of quiet; on the threshold of this Corkery's characters stand paralyzed by the thought that peace may not be worth achieving, so little joy it promises. What brings them to the threshold is middle age, but ostensibly the death of Frank Bresnan, a traveler for a tea-trade firm. Bresnan has made his quietus by drowning, and his companions spend a winter coming to terms with the unpleasant realization that their fellow of infinite jest could not bear the fardels of a weary life. His death brings to light the thwarted ambitions, bridled emotions, unfulfilled loves, or unsatisfied wanderlusts of his surviving friends. By what the psychologists would call displacement, they prefer to lose themselves amidst objects and minutiae than to admit the anguish that lies beneath their apparent repose: "With the present tense in the objective mood they thought to defeat all the other tenses in the subjective mood!" (p. 273). Chief among these bat-like souls is Martin Cloyne, trying to forge the uncreated conscience of the coterie. Pathetically, "he was not used to playing the principal part" (p. 291), and so, as with the others, "the spirit of quiet desperation was setting up his tabernacle in the heart of Martin Cloyne" (p. 172). Drifting in his air of lost connections, Cloyne is gently toyed with for three hundred pages until a second drowning and a lost, undeclared love induce him to cross that threshold into a passive, somewhat embittered peace.

I used the phrase "brings to light" advisedly, for as in "The Dead," the theme of paralysis in *The Threshold of Quiet* is enacted by the freezing of characters at certain moments into illuminated scenes resembling paintings or *tableaux vivants*. They are domestic interiors, as befits the internalized, privatized lives of the characters, and Corkery's artistic arrangement of his cast is occasionally shared by members of the cast themselves who, like those afflicted by certain nervous diseases, as the author tells us (and like Joyce's Dubliners), see themselves in characteristic attitudes, self-consciousness replicating itself. The passive gestures of disappointment these characters make, and the imagery of darkness and light by which we are given them, Corkery shares with the early Joyce and bequeathed to two generations of Irish Catholic novelists.[17] At times Corkery's realism melts into reverie and a lyrical twilight, into small epiphanies even more passive than Joyce's and very unlike the striking visions of AE, Synge, and Yeats. They are neoromantic epiphanies of self-worthlessness and failure and promote self-realization only in the sense that the characters realize that they can never fulfill their own potentialities. Whereas Corkery seems to deprecate this hopelessness (believing it an Irish vice), he makes shift to draw consolation—of a quietist and Catholic kind—from the claim that "when such souls quit our company it is the sweetness of their quiet spirits that remains like a fragrance in the air" (p. 310).

It is not easy to account for the desperation of Corkery's people. On the one hand, Corkery offers it to us as a universal affliction ("The mass of men lead lives of quiet desperation"—Thoreau): "It was curious enough, curious only, not striking—the same little dramas, as Martin told himself, are happening every day everywhere, bringing people together in a closer intimacy, as men in a sudden storm or in an outbreak of fire accost one another in terms almost of intimacy" (pp. 165–66). On the other hand, we have a grim portrait, not only of a town in winter, but a town suffering the effects of chronic emigration; Martin Cloyne is literally and figuratively keeping the home fires burning, but losing the struggle. And perhaps, as in *Dubliners*, the defeatism of Corkery's people evokes by implied contrast the heroism of Parnell and the collapse of hope and confidence his defeat began. It does seem odd that the novel should be set wholly out of sight and sound of the Irish cultural revival and militant nationalism, but this is in part a tactic. Corkery's apparently modest provincialism and realism were a deliberate recoil from the brilliance and—in terms of critical reception by foreign critics—centrality of revival literature. This critically central literature he judged with some justification to be—in terms of its expression of Irish reality—at best a disguised Ascendancy literature, at worst an exotic branch of English literature.

Corkery's provincialism was a quiet protest against the colonialist attitudes he thought underlay the revival's claim to be a national literature, quiet because he did not wish to be overheard by the "alien-minded" who ruled his island in the name of England or themselves. His local realism, like Joyce's in *Dubliners,* took him into narrow crevices of Irish life where the revivalists could not follow him, and was a counter-revival tactic. Whereas revival literature intended to express Ireland for the Irish (and in the intention differed from the Anglo-Irish literature that preceded the revival), in actuality it did not and could not do so. Corkery's provincialism was thus in reality nationalism, expressing itself in its apparent opposite; it was a fierce, almost conspiratorial pride in an Ireland largely hidden to Anglo-Irish eyes. Munster was not just a province in which he took local pride, but symbolically Ireland herself. His Ireland had to appear, in order to distinguish itself from Anglo-Ireland, unheroic, passive, and patient: one character in *The Threshold of Quiet* is "so much a piece of Ireland in his genial quietness, in his lack of ambition" (p. 168). The repression suggested in this—and which is the undeclared dimension of the novel's theme—was righted by Corkery after the revival, for the implication of nationalism in *The Threshold of Quiet* was made explicit and aggressive in his later work of criticism, *Synge and Anglo-Irish Literature* (1931).

The note of approval when Corkery contemplates his people distinguishes him from Joyce. So too does the use of provincialism as camouflage for nationalism. Corkery's hidden Ireland, like Joyce's, is a colonized Ireland, and the repression of his people, like that of Joyce's Dubliners, is that of Irish culture; his characters' lack of self-realization is their culture's. On this we can make Joyce and Corkery agree; Joyce, though, did not believe that any of the extant forms of nationalism (none of which accommodated individualism) was the cure to the paralysis of Catholic Ireland, and this was in part because the Irish had colluded with their oppressors and connived at their own exploitation for so long that a moral infection had set in.

Besides, Joyce identified two forms of colonialism in Ireland, English and Roman Catholic (Moore busied himself with the latter and did not exercise himself about the former), whereas Corkery was sure that Catholicism and nationality were desirably inseparable in Ireland. What is implicit in *The Threshold of Quiet* is, again, made plain in *Synge and Anglo-Irish Literature,* where Catholicism, nationalism, and love of the land are the qualifying attributes of Irishness. Corkery if he deepened the concept of Irishness also narrowed it; his definition of authentic Ireland disqualified much of Ulster as well as Anglo-Ireland (not to speak of James Joyce!). *The Threshold of Quiet* is to be praised as a deceptively demure reply to the extravagance of revival literature, and as a subtle exploration of lives that are unrealized. Only when we regard it as the implicit version of Corkery's argument in *Synge and Anglo-Irish Literature* does it appear worrisome. The later work of criticism sets out Irish literary history from a Catholic nationalist perspective that has prevailed in Southern Ireland since 1922 and which from the individualist's point of view represents no genuine alternative to the ideology of the Irish revival.

The Road of the Dead: MacNamara's **The Valley of the Squinting Windows**

> if way to the Better there be, it exacts
> a full look at the Worst
> —Thomas Hardy, "In Tenebris"

As we have seen, the reaction to revival euphoria set in fairly early, with *The Untilled Field,* followed by *Father Ralph, Dubliners,* and, before 1914, Yeats's own disenchantment with Paudeen. But it was not until Brinsley MacNamara wrote in 1916 *The Valley of the Squinting Windows* (1918) that a fully intimate fictional report from the neglected center of Ireland came in, and when it did it was of a kind unlikely to have commanded the stentorian defense of Yeats from the stage of the Abbey Theatre. Here was provincial reality so shockingly portrayed by someone who knew it inside out that the novel's author (whose real name was John Weldon) was driven from his native Westmeath, and the novel publicly burned. Even if the outraged were the same kind of people as those who attacked Synge and were to attack O'Casey, they could hardly be said to have been attacking the same kind of thing. Synge leaves his peasantry their poetry, MacNamara is not so charitable towards his villagers. And whereas Synge's drama, and even O'Casey's in its defiant rhetoric, somehow endorse the revival by censuring those who betray idealism, MacNamara flays so promiscuously that he proves idealism to be impossible in his time and place. By so doing he castigates those who have not earned their romanticism by first of all acknowledging fully the reality of his Midlands, the hard heart of Ireland.

MacNamara's indomitable Irishry are an astounding throng of drunkards, liars, thieves, eavesdroppers, blackmailers, and gossips who all display the "clayey villainies of earth." Charlotte Mullen would not be out of place in MacNamara's Garradrimna in the valley of Tullahanogue but rather would find stiff competition, though from those whose wickedness is less subtle than her own, just as MacNamara's novels are less polished, more strident performances than those of her creators. Malice towards all, charity towards none could be the civic motto of Garradrimna, and very nearly the motto of its satiric chronicler who requires for his unwholesome task a "sickening realism." The root of an action in MacNamara's world, with rare exception, "is always an amount of selfishness." The love of Mrs. Brennan for her son, for example, is "a selfish love, for it had mostly to do with the triumph he represented for her before the people of the valley,"[18] and John Brennan comes at last to recognize the "enormous selfishness" of that love. It would be difficult to think of anything more inimical than MacNamara's world to the selfless philosophies of Pearse, Griffith, and AE. If selfishness prevents selflessness, it also prevents the third and preferable state of self-realization, the infinite pain of which is MacNamara's paramount theme.

In his novels, MacNamara exacts from himself a full look at the worst, and he does not spare his characters, most of whom are driven by "the conjunctive thirsts of drink and gossip." The valley is full of fanged chroniclers of the countryside (to adapt John Montague), "vultures" whose routine character assassinations are almost surreal; the former schoolmistress, for example, is vilified in her absence by the police sergeant's wife, "reduced to little pieces and, as it were, cremated in the furnace of this woman's mind until tiny specks of the ashes of her floated about and danced and scintillated before the tired eyes of Rebecca Kerr" (p. 52). So intense and relishing is MacNamara's pursuit of uncharity, so preternatural the malice of his valley dwellers, that on occasions he anticipates the expressionism and black humor of Flann O'Brien who surely learned a great deal from him.

In gossip is the assumption that reality is secret, wilfully concealed by others but known to the gossipers who reveal it, often as an exhibition of power, always as a way of bringing others low. The assumption is frequently justified, for almost everyone in the valley hypocritically disguises the "amazing realities" of life there. The culprits, however, occasionally leave a "betraying presence" (like the empty can with slight traces of froth on the sides left outside the pub betraying the visit of bona-fide, "or rather *mala-fide*," travelers passionate for porter on the Sabbath). Indeed betrayal, of confidence or affection, is one of the numerous immoralities of the district, culminating in the novel in Marse Prendergast's shattering disclosure to John Brennan that he is Ulick Shannon's half-brother. It has been said that this novel originated the "squinting windows" school of Irish realistic fiction which depicts provincial narrowness, the narrowness of a society whose chief activities are surveillance and rebuke.[19] The description is two-edged, for MacNamara, like Somerville and Ross and Joyce before him, is "betraying" his characters as perseveringly as they betray others and themselves. "Were you unaware of his real character," he remarks of one figure in the novel, "you might foolishly imagine that he was thinking of high, immortal things, but he was in reality thinking of drink" (p.39). MacNamara is amazed at what he sees and overhears, like a visitor to the beach lifting a rock to uncover exotic, disgusting creatures, and finds himself in transports of revulsion against his creations. The price paid is the occasional suggestion of the narrator's naivety and righteousness and the novel as itself a species of gossip.

Realism is in the first instance imitation of the observable, and this is often (though not always) unprepossessing. Realism in the second instance is revelation of the disguised, and this too is often sordid. For example, there is a scornful portrait of a priest, Father O'Keeffe, who "had most discreetly used a seeming unworldliness to screen his advance upon the ramparts of Mammon" (p.128). O'Keeffe is from that division of the farmer class known as "grabbers" and who frequently put a son on for the church, in MacNamara's opinion, to atone for their avarice and to facilitate that very vice. In order to be fair, MacNamara balances the detrimental influence of Father O'Keeffe on John Brennan, the young student priest, with that of Father Considine who was "in spiritual descent from those priests who had died with the people in the Penal Days," a lonely custodian in Garradrimna of "the grandeur of Faith and Idealism" passed on from generation to generation.

Still, visible or not, reality is largely offensive and must be acknowledged. In one form or another it blights three budding romances: in the past between Henry Shannon and Nan Byrne (later Mrs. Brennan) and between Myles Shannon (Henry's brother) and Helena Cooper, and in the present between John Brennan and Rebecca Kerr. The heart of the story is Myles Shannon's plot to ruin John Brennan by having Ulick Shannon lead the student priest astray. The ne'er-do-well, literary Ulick, who is ignorant of his uncle's plan, is the bastard son of Henry Shannon and Nan Byrne who is unaware of her love-child's identity, the child having been taken away from her after birth. Myles hatches the plot to avenge Mrs. Brennan's part in the ending of his affair with Helena Cooper. John is particularly dear to his mother because she has dedicated her life to saving him (by encouraging him to become a priest) from the valley she believes lured Henry into dissipation. Mrs. Brennan, by interfering in the lives of Myles and Helena, was in turn avenging what she wrongly suspected to be Myles's hand in Henry's abandonment of her when she became pregnant.

These originally hopeful and decent people have been twisted by circumstances, their humanity having been replaced by a spitefulness that "like a malignant wind . . . warped the human growth within the valley's confines" (p. 78). Spitefulness visits ill upon its bearer as well as its victim, as Myles Shannon comes to realize. He is willing to sacrifice the life of his nephew Ulick in order to satisfy his desire for revenge, and indeed sacrifices his own humanity, as Mrs. Brennan has sacrificed hers before him. Encouraged by his uncle, Ulick seduces Rebecca who when she gets pregnant is driven from the village, abandoned by Ulick as Nan Byrne was by his father. John Brennan, in love with Rebecca, avenges her by murdering Ulick, only afterwards discovering that like Cain he has killed his own brother. The sins of the parents have been visited on the children, and John Brennan ends the novel in his mother's arms, emptied of humanity, spoiled as a priest, emotionally crippled. MacNamara writes early in the novel, foreseeing the conclusion of the story: "It was such a conflict, with such an anticipated ending, as had shaped itself inevitably out of the life of the valley. Where life was an endless battle of conflicting characters and antagonized dispositions it seemed particularly meet that a monumental conflict should at last have been instituted" (p. 79).

Romance in Garradrimna is either violently shattered by spite or like a candle gutters and goes out as it has for Marse Prendergast, the blackmailing postmistress, and a vindictive sense of reality is the withered changeling left in its place. Ulick shows Rebecca a copy of *The Daffodil Fields* by John Masefield:

> "It is a great tale of love and passion that happened in one of the quiet places of the world," he told her with a kind of enthusiasm coming into his words for the first time.
>
> "One of the quiet places?" she murmured, evidently at a loss for something else to say.
>
> "Yes, a quiet place which must have been like this place and yet, at

> the same time, most wonderfully different, for no poet at all could imagine any tale of love and passion springing from the life about us here. The people of the valley seem to have died before they were born." (p. 95)

As they talk they wander down a lane called The Road of the Dead. The name and Ulick's endorsement of it might put us in mind of Joyce's great story: "Around and about here they are all dead—dead. No passion of any kind comes to light their existence. Their life is a thing done meanly, shudderingly within the shadow of the grave" (pp. 95–96).

MacNamara no less than his chief characters is a realist because he is a thwarted romantic. For author and characters there is cold comfort in embracing the offensive so expansively, but their realism, because it is inverted romanticism, is hysterical and perverse, an Irish flight into extremity. For all its talk of reality, *The Valley of the Squinting Windows* as it proceeds increasingly borrows the plot structure and devices of romance—intercepted letters, trysts, frustrated love-affairs, illegitimate children, secret blood relationships, murder by evening shadow, white hero, dark villain. This may be MacNamara's final bitter irony, but I suspect it is his vestigial attraction to romanticism, and it undermines in its crudity his realism. The realities of the novel go beyond mere romantic antagonisms; MacNamara's romanticism is so frustrated that it denies its own possibility of fulfillment. Here is a recurring phenomenon in Irish fiction since *Dubliners:* realism as romantic feedback. Realism is not the preferred mode, but it is necessary because reality must be faced since it prevents the idealism and romance the writer actually desires. Yet the more squarely reality is faced, the farther from realization its opposite becomes. And the wildly unreal expectations and pretensions that in turn reality provokes are absorbed into it. It is difficult for hero, author, or reader to be even-handed, to encourage a salutary sense of equlibrium, where everything around him is disproportionate.

The Very Middle of Ireland: MacNamara's **The Clanking of Chains**

There was for the Irish reader of *The Valley of the Squinting Windows* in 1918 a measure of comfort. Idealism, poetry, and romantic nationalism, he was assured, existed, but in Dublin, not Westmeath. Ulick brings this message to Rebecca Kerr:

> He was fond of telling her about the younger Irish poets and of quoting passages from their poems. Now it would be a line or so from Colum or Stephens, again a verse from Seumas O'Sullivan or Joseph Campbell. Continually he spoke with enthusiasm of the man they called AE. . . . She found it difficult to believe that such men could be living in Ireland at the present time.
>
> "And would you see them about Dublin?"
>
> "Yes, you'd see them often."
>
> "*Real* poets?"
>
> "Real poets surely. But of course they have earthly interests as well. One is a farmer—"
>
> "A farmer!!!"
>
> This she found it hardest of all to believe, for the word "farmer" made her see so clearly the sullen men with the dirty beards who came in the white roads every evening to drink in Garradrimna. There was no poetry in them. (pp. 158–59)

The Dublin poets are the more real because Antaeus-like they grow strong through touching the earth; their unified sensibility is in appalling contrast to the collection of egotists who make up life on The Road of the Dead. If this passage suggests that MacNamara was a paid agent of the revival (he wrote successful plays for the Abbey Theatre between 1919 and 1945), scoring those who stood in the way of national resuscitation (rural equivalents of Joyce's Dubliners), the two novels he published in 1920 served to muddy this important issue.

The Irishman was published under the name of Oliver Blyth, possibly to protect MacNamara from the hostility provoked by his first novel, but more likely (since his other 1920 novel appeared under his usual pseudonym) because it was more autobiographical than the other two works and because the Irish revival is the object of some ringside satire. Martin Duignan, a small farmer and would-be writer, is the Irishman of the title. Among the influences preventing his self-realization is the Irish literary revival. Duignan becomes an actor with the Tower Theatre (the Abbey in flimsy disguise) and realizes the absurdity of the revival notion of the peasant, but cannot rectify it because the prior achievements of the revival stultify his work. A whole generation of writers, flailing to find snatches of available voice and scraps of subject-matter left by the revival, is immobilized and unrealized: "even as men had been caught in the cities of Pompeii and Herculaneum so had these young Irish literati been caught in the lava of their immense egotism, suddenly paralysed, as it were, by the great gestures of Yeats and Synge and 'AE.' And so, embedded in the failure of their execution, they had turned to spiteful, poisonous criticism,"[20] bohemian equivalents of the Westmeath peasants from whom Duignan sprang. Duignan manages at last to rise *de profundis* (from alcohol and fornication in Dublin, destitution in New York), not into Catholicism like Geoffrey Austin (Thompson's "The Hound of Heaven" sounds through MacNamara's novel as it did through Sheehan's), but into literature, but as a realist, not a revival romantic or pastoralist.

So Dublin and the revival are not a viable alternative to the provinces. *The Clanking of Chains* suggests this in political terms as *The Irishman* suggests it in literary terms, and Duignan, lone believer among his fellow small farmers in the Easter rebels whose insurrection marks the end of the novel and the beginning of his exile, bears some resemblance to the hero of the other novel. The pseudonymous Midlands town in which *The Clanking of Chains* is set is only marginally less vicious than Garradrimna, and more vicious than Glannanea in *The Irishman,* and yet we are told that "Ireland was nothing more than a bigger Ballycullen." If so, MacNamara's cultural prognosis in 1920 was a grim one.

Having dealt the idea of the noble Irish villager and countryman a telling blow in *The Valley of the Squinting Windows,* MacNamara now dealt the idea of the yeoman Irish patriot an equally telling blow in *The Clanking of Chains*. Their patriotic mouthings and gestures to the contrary, the inhabitants of Ballycullen have had, from a nationalist point of view, an unenviable record of behavior during the traumatic events of modern Irish history which are background to the novel—the Famine, the Young Ireland movement, the Fenian movement, the Land War, the Parnellite split, and the Boer War. The middle ground, made up of events occurring between 1913 and the aftermath of the Easter Rising, is occupied successively by the Larne gun-running, the rise of the Irish National Volunteers, the Howth gun-running, the First World War, Easter 1916, and the "Sinn Fein election." As foreground is played out the strange career of Michael Dempsey, a young man whose patriotism is seemingly too pure for the soiled patriots of Ballycullen.

Behind the hypocritical idealism of the townspeople stands the "dismal reality" of town life: hucksterism, opportunism, egotism, "mean, crushing gloom," "a drab crowd of facts and people," "cruelty and baseness . . . black uncharitableness." It is a "death in life," and the clanking of chains (cast-iron versions, one might say, of the nets that seek to inhibit the souls of Stephen Dedalus and Gabriel Conroy) is the most characteristic sound to the sensitive and the truly idealistic. The idea of Sinn Fein, "Ourselves," has ironically been interpreted by the townsfolk, as individuals and as a community, with egotistic literalness. Small wonder that Michael Dempsey's attempt at romance is crushed as finally as his attempt at an heroic nationalism; his girl, Mirandolina Conway, has been given her Christian nickname in the satirical and unChristian spirit of Ballycullen, satire being the preemptive strike reality makes against a budding idealism. On the nationalist front, Dempsey puts up a stiffer but no less doomed struggle.

Depicted in *The Clanking of Chains* are "the hopeless, dead, empty years which followed the death of Parnell."[21] Though the town had been "lukewarm in its support of the Chief," a very few citizens had been stalwart in their faithfulness to him, but their sons in this novel are unworthy successors. The remaindered Parnellites themselves are pathetic, lonely, ineffectual commemorators of the Chief's rise and fall, as the wife of one of them realized even when the memory of Parnell was greener:

> Then the sad look, falling like a mist upon her bright eyes, would show that she knew how this man she had married, in the prime of his patriotism, had spent his day with the others in some dark room at the back of one of the publichouses in Ballycullen talking about poor Parnell and telling them that his heart was in the grave in Glasnevin with his dear, martyred king, and striking the table and whispering fiercely the most dreadful things about the bishops and priests of Ireland. They would have achieved nothing by all this, for they were merely futile men drifting with their country down a dark tide. (pp. 41–42)

These forgotten men are reminiscent of Joyce's Joe Hynes and Mr. Casey. The rest of the opinionated in Ballycullen resemble the other characters in "Ivy Day in the Committee Room", mere hypocrites.

The fall of Parnell was in truth merely one more nail in the coffin of romantic, heroic Ireland, for the idleness of MacNamara's Ireland, and of Joyce's, began with the Act of Union. But what happened to Parnell is the equivalent of the Fall in twentieth century Irish myth: the Chief's martyrdom validated heroism at the moment of proving, in the fact of his premature death, the impossibility of a heroic way of life in Ireland. The deathly reality of an unromantic Ireland followed him; but before this, Parnell's late career confirmed the divisiveness of Irish life, and his disenchanted champions were forced to be realistic in accepting that fact. The post-Parnellite reality and the realism it compelled drove the idealists and romantics, by a kind of displacement, into solipsistic isolation. Michael Dempsey, like Oliver Gogarty, Ned Carmady, Ralph O'Brien, Gabriel

Conroy, and Stephen Dedalus, though they are otherwise very different, is a pioneering representative of the besieged and retreating hero of much Irish fiction in this century. This fiction has required a social realism in the depiction of the society that besieges and isolates the hero, and a psychological realism in the depiction of the self-consciousness society forces upon him. It might even be said that this Parnellite tradition in Irish fiction, continued by O'Connor and O'Faolain in the 1930s, has not been concluded even yet. It has embodied a recurring phenomenon since *Dubliners:* realism as nationalist feedback.

MacNamara's picture of Ballycullen is compatible with the revival detestation of the middle and lower middle classes and an Ireland of shopkeepers, but only if we ignore how widespread was the huckster and gombeen mind the revivalists fondly thought rare in Ireland. MacNamara knew how common in Ireland was everything the revival stood against, and his realistic acknowledgment of this, his disillusioning of readers, put him, like Joyce, beyond the revival pale. At the very least, Garradrimna and Ballycullen stand for the central bowl of Ireland, indeed for all of Ireland not celebrated by the more romantic nationalists, Ireland minus Dublin and Connacht; that is, the urban headquarters of the movement and its field laboratory. When we subtract from a revival view of Dublin as an intellectually fermenting capital Joyce's lower middle-class city, and from the revival view of the west Moore's untilled fields, the geography of revival delusion shrinks still further. It is the extensiveness of MacNamara's and Joyce's shoneen worlds that gives the lie to the revival view of the island.

When Joyce and MacNamara elect to be realistic in acknowledging so unflinchingly their worlds, they begin to resemble the shoneens of their fiction who also pride themselves on being realistic in acknowledging the romantic fatuity of a heroic nationalism, even when turned into reality. The shoneen attitude survived Easter 1916, as MacNamara convincingly shows in *The Clanking of Chains,* and even, as we know, the setting up of the Free State and the Irish Republic. The realism of MacNamara's shoneens is a self-congratulatory hardheadedness that is really callous opportunism, and it is difficult not to detect its equivalent in MacNamara's own attitude. Yet to read *The Clanking of Chains* is to be reminded of D. P. Moran who in *The Philosophy of Irish Ireland* (1905) likewise exposed sham idealism with the near-religious fervor of a frustrated pure nationalism; *The Clanking of Chains* resembles Moran set to fiction. The fervor is telling, as is the obsessive intimacy with what we are told (rather than shown) on every page is abhorrent. It is hard to gauge where exorcism leaves off and perverse homage begins. Like Joyce, MacNamara is half in love with what he scorns; it is a destructive love, but love nevertheless, and it thrives on an assumed rejection, a rejection proven to be more real in MacNamara's case, for his first novel was burned, than in the case of Joyce who left Dublin because he insisted on imagining the rejection before it actually took place.

It might be thought, then, that MacNamara sees contemporary heroism and idealism as possible only in distant Dublin. If we think of Ballycullen as a provincial town out of tune with momentous events in Ireland, then we can choose to see MacNamara serving the Yeatsian cause of lambasting Paudeen, an inconvenient obstacle on the road to a new Ireland. The epigraph to *The Clanking of Chains* is the "delirium of the brave" stanza from "September 1913," and there is an early reference in the novel to Ballycullen shopkeepers fumbling for their last halfpence in the greasy tills. But it is Dublin, not Ballycullen, that entertains the unreal perspective. "The feeble human breed in the Ireland of the time" is typified by the Ballycullenites. "There were moments in its history when Ballycullen appeared to be situated, psychologically as well as geographically, in the very middle of Ireland." (p. 184) Yeats, it is implied, got it more right in "September 1913" than he imagined, and whereas the poet recanted in "Easter 1916," the event celebrated in that poem comes and goes in MacNamara's novel, leaving only a ripple on the surface of life in Ballycullen.

The ambiguity continues when we consider the figure of Dempsey. It is Dempsey who attempts to bring the Revival and the philosophy of Sinn Fein single-handedly to Ballycullen and to recall the town to "the grandeurs of the ancient Gaelic civilisation," a young man for whom "it was a continuous battle between the romantic notions of his mind and the hard facts of all this cruel realism" (pp. 144–45). Is he the only pure idealist in town suffering the delirium of the brave and provoked into madness by the hypocrisy surrounding him? He suffers, like Pearse, from an "insane love of Ireland," and his mother fears that "this terrible thing called Ireland, which had ruined her man [Dempsey's Parnellite father], was now throwing its shadow over the life of her son" (p. 218). When Mirandolina tells him he has wasted his sweetness on the desert air, she sees him as some mute inglorious Milton, a village Pearse who might have come into his own and won fame in the end at Easter in Dublin.

But the frenzy of Pearse changed the course of Irish history, the frenzies of Cuchulain the course of Irish myth. Is Dempsey not instead a mere daydreamer, more kin to Little Chandler than to Padraic Pearse? He identifies himself with the rebaptized Fenians whom Pearse referred to in his speech over the grave of O'Donovan Rossa: "He was one of the generation for which Pearse spoke thus so proudly. He was a man of the age of Cuchullain and the Red Branch Knights, the Heroic Age of Ireland" (p. 157). Is this not mere self-delusion? The extent of his ignorance of how things stand not only in Ballycullen but also in most of Ireland suggests that it is: "He went on reading mostly about the Ireland of yesterday in its bearing on the Ireland of to-morrow, without fully realising the Ireland of his own day, or causing his own personality to bear upon it greatly. His mind was unable to grasp Ballycullen as the microcosm of that macrocosm" (p. 20). Since the novel begins with Dempsey's staging of a play, *Robert Emmet,* with himself in the title role (and Mirandolina as his Sara Curran), and since he entertains grand ideas about himself, we might even see him as a bit of a playboy (a playboy was an actor, an entertaining pretender, someone to be watched when truth or girls' honor was at stake), a Christy Mahon; Robert Emmet in Ballycullen, it seems, is as absurd as Owen Roe O'Sullivan in Pegeen Mike's pub, and provokes a justifiably realistic backlash.

It is difficult to decide, then, how far Dempsey is a fool, a melodramatist, a pretender dreaming miniature dreams of national liberation while the real thing is going on in Dublin (but only in Dublin), and how far he is the only pure disciple of Sinn Fein in Ballycullen, spanceled by circumstances and bayed about by grubbers and graspers. MacNamara's problem as a novelist is that he is confusing on point of view, a problem made worse by the discursive rather than presentational nature of his narrative and the lack of such a narrative system as the Joycean dialectic. At times an interpretation of Dempsey hinges on whether MacNamara or Dempsey is talking and it is often impossible to decide. Either way, there is little solace for those who from the perspective of Dublin would envisage a nation of rural and small town Pearses, rallying their hamlets to national resurgence.

Michael Dempsey ends the novel in more or less forced exile, like Rebecca Kerr and Martin Duignan. The alternative, MacNamara has made clear, is, like John Brennan and Mrs. Brennan, to conform outwardly to the warped values of the community while sublimating one's frustrated romanticism. In exile or out, romanticism and idealism are impossible. But exile at least permits, indeed compels, the open acknowledgment of unpleasant truth, a realism dissatisfying compared to romanticism but better than the expediency that passes for realism in much of Ireland. "He would have to be a realist dealing only with facts in whatever country he might go to," we are told, "and it was part of the irony of things that he could not be this same realist in his own country." (p. 236)

Realism and self-realization are connected, and we might think of Duignan, who wants "to make himself a man, rather than an Irishman, and to live in the world rather than in his native country, and so no narrow creed could quite shape itself affectionately to his mind."[22] MacNamara himself attempted to be a realist in his own country, but paid a double price. The first was a personal one, the revenge of those among whom he grew up. The second was artistic; his frustrated romanticism makes MacNamara exaggerate the ugliness of life in his Midlands and imbalances his realism. But his fictional tirade has a root accuracy and is endorsed in part by the fact that difficulties in the path of a resilient realism bedevilled later Irish writers. Joyce for his part decided he could only be a realist about his country if he left it and lived elsewhere; like MacNamara, the young Joyce believed that in reality not in dreams begin responsibilities.

Nationalist Realism: Lysaght's The Gael

The Valley of the Squinting Windows was published by Maunsel and Company, the revival's chief Irish publishing house that considered itself patriotic enough not to publish *Dubliners*. The chairman of Maunsel in 1917 (Maunsel was the middle name of the firm's founder, the biographer Joseph Hone), and reader of MacNamara's manuscript, was Edward E. Lysaght.[23] Lysaght—he later re-Gaelicized his name to MacLysaght—was himself a writer, and in 1919 he published a novel, *The Gael*, an interesting essay in what we might call "nationalist realism." O'Donovan and Joyce left Ireland in 1904, like Moore before them, exile being the Irish realist's escape hatch, a recourse after disappointed hopes. Moore and O'Donovan, unlike Joyce, had briefly believed that national and personal fulfillment could be synonymous, but realistically acknowledged their error. Corkery held the same belief but was patient in awaiting its justification; however, for him the Anglo-Irish revival was not the means of national fulfillment, nor was Catholicism a greater obstacle than colonialism, as Moore and O'Donovan believed. In *The Gael*, Lysaght bravely attempts to reconcile Corkery's rural, Catholic nationalism both with the tenets of the Anglo-Irish revival (using the Gaelic revival as a bridging enterprise) and with the individualist claims of Joyce, Moore, O'Donovan, and MacNamara.

Lysaght's is an affirmative realism, avoiding the pathological realism that justifies dissent and exile. The author of *The Gael* knows the practical life as well as O'Donovan, and he employs a comparably modest, utilitarian prose to confront difficulties in the way of achieving an independent Gaelic Ireland. Like *Father Ralph, The Gael* is full of discussion, workmanlike as a novel, fascinating as social testimony.[24]

The Gael of Lysaght's title is Con O'Hickie, raised in England but imbued with his father's Fenianism, though he himself is resistant to politics. He returns to Ireland in 1905 as a young man—reversing the direction of Joyce and O'Donovan—to buy back his ancestral house in County Galway (expropriated generations ago), for he belongs, like Father Ralph and Moore, to the Catholic gentry, that class neglected by history and literature. At first merely a farmer with some half-buried zeal for his Irishness, O'Hickie gradually becomes radicalized, and turns the novel's title from irony into a literal truth of some force. Despite a Land League as corrupt as it is in *Father Ralph,* and the class pressures exerted on him by a variety of shoneens and West Britons, O'Hickie discovers Hyde's Gaelic League and Horace Plunkett's cooperative movement. He entertains the Irish-Ireland hopes of a native, localized industrialism, but one "free from the horrors of British and American commercialism, with all its poverty and slums and sordidness."[25] Moreover, it would be a "godly" industrialism, for a liberal Catholicism is woven into the fabric of O'Hickie's vision, which we know to have been Lysaght's.[26]

O'Hickie is an idealist who believes it is possible to resuscitate the preconquest Gaelic code of law and society, which he sees as having been egalitarian, and to re-create "a Gaelic-speaking co-operative commonwealth," to inaugurate which he turns his ancestral Big House into a cooperative. It is in the vacuum created by Parnell's downfall that O'Hickie's radical program can flourish, for the Nationalist party is seen as inadequate; Gaelic communism requires republicanism, not Home Rule. Yet the revolution O'Hickie contemplates is not "armed insurrection, but rather the acceleration of a peaceful and gradual evolution towards a less imperfect state of society."[27] Unfortunately his program is interrupted by the Easter Rising, the guerrilla warfare against Britain, and British reprisals; these militarize the apolitical O'Hickie against his will, and the novel ends with him in an English jail, his communistic utopia intact but deferred.

Lysaght, then, is aware of right and wrong nationalisms. He himself would seem to have belonged to a nationalist tradition—pacifist, socialist and rural-industrialist—that was repressed in Ireland after 1916 by a more vivid tradition of militarism, capitalism, and right-wing Catholicism, a tradition the romantic revival opposed in theory and facilitated in practice. In *The Gael,* O'Hickie makes common cause with the physical-force tradition, as James Connolly did in 1916, even though he knows that "real freedom can be won not so much by political action as by laborious regeneration from within."[28] He wants to believe that militant nationalism and state politics will be shortlived, but the reader's knowledge of what transpired after 1918 permits him to see even the novel's cautious optimism as naive and to see O'Hickie's jail sentence as an exile more like that of O'Donovan and Moore than O'Hickie would admit.[29] The novel's weakness is its ending in which the account of O'Hickie's qualified conversion to militant republicanism is hurried and inadequate. Optimism betrayed by history is one thing, but the abandonment of realism and lapse in characterization are another. The effect of the ending is to provoke a perhaps unwarranted suspicion that behind O'Hickie's professed communism and pacifism may lurk bourgeois pastoralism and a rather reactionary Catholic Gaelicism.[30]

In *The Gael* national realization and the hero's self-realization are for a time one and the same, and the novel recounts O'Hickie's personal growth into confidence and effectiveness as he realizes his buried Irish identity. No doubt Lysaght's portrayal of the psychological effects of colonialism made appeal to Daniel Corkery who praised *The Gael* when he surveyed Anglo-Irish literature in 1931.[31] But the process of self-realization in *The Gael* is broken by politics at least partly of Irish manufacture. O'Hickie's story, we are told, "is the story of many Irishmen, drawn against their will into the vortex of destructive politics, deflected from constructive activity by the effects of the political system upon their lives as individuals."[32] O'Hickie has taken self-realization as far as anyone could while accepting the primacy of nationalism, militant or no, just as *The Gael* is a lonely translation of cultural nationalism into realism. These are the novel's achievements, but they are not unconnected to its shortcomings.[33]

IV

The Sorrowful Legend of Ireland
Folktale and the Escape from Environment

He has put me in wonderful grief,
The king of all, in many shapes.

—*Tuan Mac Cairill's Story to Finnen of Moville,* tr. Kuno Meyer

Who would know the national culture of modern Ireland must be aware of her folklore and folklorists.

—Richard Dorson

Visions and Vanities
Yeats, Lady Gregory, and Folklore

10

But stories that live longest
Are sung above the glass. . . .
—W. B. Yeats

Folklore and the Revival

During the revival, there were many temptations the realist had to resist. It was in defiance of contemporary Irish writers' interest in folklore, for example, that Joyce began his career with short stories that willfully orphaned themselves from folk parentage, as the stories of Moore and other European writers had done before them. Perhaps Joyce felt that many folk stories exhibited the imaginative incompleteness and senility of mind he identified in those collected by Lady Gregory in *Poets and Dreamers,* and therefore could not offer him an artistic model.[1] Not that the young Joyce escaped the influence of folklore entirely. We might claim that in "The Dead," for instance, he is quietly and ironically drawing upon the Celtic belief in "a race of fortunate beings who are immortal, ever beautiful, ever happy, and ever young, to whom men are nothing but 'the Dead,' whereas they themselves are 'the Living.'"[2] And since I have already connected the gravel Michael Furey threw against Gretta's window with Aran Islands lore, it is even more piquant to learn that Joyce used to sing a love song that contained the line "So I'll throw up a stone at the window."[3] Still, folklore in *Dubliners* is thematic, not formal or structural.

We could argue, of course, that far more folklore-as-content occurs in Joyce's works than we might at first think, if we agree with Moore that gossip is Dublin's folklore.[4] The young Joyce listened to and took note of his fellow citizens very much as a folk collector listens to and takes note of his informants, or as Synge eavesdropped on those peasant women in the room below. Then later on there are *Ulysses* and *Finnegans Wake*—history reduced to gossip, gossip raised to art. *Finnegans Wake,* Joyce claimed, was "written by the people I have met or known."[5] He implied that it could be heard as the voice of an entire race rather than of an individual; it is, we might say, a vast pseudo-folk narrative. Withal, the Joycean form remains that of art, aggressively so at the outset, in the manner of one who would flout the revival of folk Ireland.

The folklore movement like the heroic revival blossomed during the 1880s and 1890s, and in each case science—folklore studies and philology respectively—marginally preceded literature.[6] In search of lore, collectors went north, south, and west from Dublin—especially west, where Douglas Hyde, Jeremiah Curtin, William Larminie, W. B. Yeats, and Lady Gregory worked as folklorists. As early as Patrick Kennedy, whose *Legendary Fictions of the Irish Celts* (1866) offered Wexford material, writer-collectors in Ireland were associated with localities: when we think of T. Crofton Croker we think of Cork, Waterford, and Limerick; of Letitia McClintock, Donegal; of Hyde, Connacht; of Yeats, Sligo; of Lady Gregory, Galway and the Aran Islands.

Lady Gregory recalled in her compilation, *Visions and Beliefs in the West of Ireland* (1920), how the spur to her collecting was affronted local patriotism. "'The Celtic Twilight' was the first book of Mr. Yeats's that I read, and even before I met him, a little time later, I had begun looking for news of the invisible world; for his stories were of Sligo and I felt jealous for Galway."[7] From Kennedy onwards, but before a scientific interest in local variants and by-forms, lore was seen as the expression of the *genius loci* and not as mere variations of international patterns. The localism of the lore was evident from its use and explanation of place-names and topographic features and phenomena, in a manner similar to what we have encountered in the bardic literature.[8] All localities were not equal in purity or quantity of folklore, and the best rewarded collectors were those who worked in the Gaeltacht. But over the years a healthy competitive element in folklore collection has turned local patriotism to good account all over Ireland.[9]

During the revival local folklore collections were, like studies of the old sagas, placed at the service of nationalism. There was a nationalist counterpart of Lady Gregory's local pride; Hyde's industriousness, for example, was due in part to his recognition that Ireland was falling behind Scotland in collecting, and that no Irish collector rivalled Campbell of Islay.[10] Time was of the essence. The Irish folklore movement was a part of the British and European folklore movements of the late nineteenth century, that had their roots in European romanticism. Accordingly, folklore was regarded as an expression of cultural nationality and at the same time in decay because of hostile forces. In the Preface to his *Legend-*

ary Fictions, Kennedy bemoaned the fate of folktales at the hands of emigration and halfpenny journals and confessed to "the horrid thought that the memory of the tales heard in boyhood would be irrecoverably lost." This sentiment achieved the status of refrain in introductions to later folklore collections, suggesting that it might itself be something of a motif in such collections. "It is in many ways a mystery," Hyde claimed when musing on the genesis of the folktale, "part of the flotsam and jetsam of the ages, still beating feebly against the shore of the nineteenth century, swallowed up at last in England by the waves of materialism and civilization combined; but still surviving unengulfed on the western coasts of Ireland." A quarter of a century after Kennedy, Joseph Jacobs, referring to Irish storytelling, feared that "there are signs that its term of life is already numbered." J. H. Delargy announced in 1945: "The days of the folk-tale are numbered even in Ireland," while exactly one hundred years after Kennedy, Sean O'Sullivan wrote in his *Folktales of Ireland* that "Very soon, memories of Irish storytelling on the grand scale will be found only in recordings and in books such as this."[11]

Many of the folklorists of the revival were upper-middle-class Protestants. The attitude of these folklorists to their subject resembled that of an adult trying to recover the faintly recalled bliss of childhood. That in the Irish context it was not the childhood of *their* race did not faze the Anglo-Irish: indeed, their consciousness of dealing with another race was what made possible the folklore side of the literary revival. For the early folklorists the peasantry was exotic, and upper-class collectors had the outsider's curiosity, condescension, and brashness that resulted in a great quantity of data and that Catholic collectors of less exalted station could not in those days, out of shame, fear, and politeness, have mustered. Anglo-Irish collectors also had the leisure that Lady Gregory deemed a vital qualification of the field collector, along with patience, reverence, and a good memory.[12] Professionalism has since removed the necessity of leisure, as the Ediphone recording machine and later the tape-recorder have removed the necessity of a good memory.

But the Anglo-Irish from whom the folklorists drew their important figures were in some political and social difficulty by the time of the revival. It fell out that the romantic notion of a vanishing folklore, together with the romantic notion of a hidden peasant aristocracy (an idea to which I will return), accorded with the self-image held by the more perceptive landed gentry. Standish James O'Grady told the landlord class, of which he was a member, that unless it mended its ways it was finished.[13] In reading the history of folklore studies during the revival, one cannot avoid sensing members of one endangered species—the Ascendancy—seeking in imagination the fellowship of another endangered species—the Gaelic-speaking peasant. It was perhaps a measure of guilt and uncertainty that caused a few well-born Protestant nationalists to wish they themselves were peasants! James Stephens recalled hearing Yeats and AE actually express the desire to be reincarnated as such.[14]

If the folklorists tended to urgency and pessimism, some cultural nationalists were recklessly optimistic. They assumed that all the Irish had been, and could be again with effort and guidance, participants in the irreplaceable world and wisdom of the folk. They stressed the regenerative power of folklore over the merely preservative power of folklore studies. The writers, too, were optimistic and confident—though in a more respectful manner than their early nineteenth-century predecessors—that the folklore could be reborn as literature. (It must not be forgotten, of course, that the folklorist, cultural nationalist, and writer often coincided in the one revival figure.) In this regard, the attitude towards folklore during the revival duplicated the attitude towards the heroic romances.

Yeats and Folklore

Assessing the role of folklore in the Irish literary revival is a complicated business, involving questions about the revival concept of folklore and, in addition, the status of revival collections of folklore (as archives and as literature), the structural and thematic impact of folklore on revival literature, and the reaction against folklore by revival figures like Pearse and counter-revival writers like Joyce. At the center, radius, and circumference of these issues moves the restless, protean figure of Yeats, poet, playwright, fictionist, field-collector, anthologist, theorist of folklore, and student of matters spiritual. Characteristically, he was earlier into the field of folklore than his contemporaries, with two collections, *Fairy and Folk Tales of the Irish Peasantry* (1888) and *Irish Fairy Tales* (1892). These would be useful starting points for an investigation into the history of the relationship between folktale and fiction in Ireland. It is a relationship that involved exploitation of the folktale (and the peasant) before the revival, the folktale's attempt to shake itself free of fiction during the first phase of the revival, and the now complementary, now conflicting attempt of fiction during the second phase of the revival to reappropriate the folktale, though in a less arrogant way. As in the career of the heroic saga (though the chronology of their involvement is different), three kinds of writers engaged themselves with the folktale: the popularizer, the scholar, and the artist.

Yeats is a pioneering transitional figure. His early anthologies at once commemorate fiction's exploitation of folklore during the nineteenth century and try to undo some of the damage to folklore (and to Ireland) so inflicted. And these somewhat contradictory aims are carried out for the apparent purpose of popular entertainment, behind which lies a respect for the autonomy of lore. In a Note preceding *Irish Fairy Tales,* Yeats voiced the belief that this volume and its predecessor make "a fairly representative collection of Irish folk tales," but in fact in the two books, beside "folk tales," by which Yeats meant ghost stories, saints' legends, and tales about giants, we find also "fairy legends," "bardic tales" (snatches of saga and heroic romance), and poems about fairies by Allingham, Ferguson, Mangan, Yeats, and others. All are culled from writers, through whose diverse motives, literary rather than documentary in most cases, any genuine folklore is filtered. To offset this, Yeats shucks his often long-winded sources like a man searching oysters for pearls. Although in order to make books he was forced to relax his standards when choosing selections from Gerald Griffin, Samuel Lover, Standish James O'Grady, T. Crofton Croker, and William Carleton, which rub shoulders with the less corrupted lore published or collected by Lady Wilde, Patrick Kennedy, Hyde, and McClintock, Yeats is capable in his Introduction and Notes to *Fairy and Folk Tales of the Irish Peasantry* of shrewdly assessing his contributors and predecessors as folklorists. The two volumes, despite their entertaining variety, are given unity by Yeats's fundamental requirements and by his omissions and editing, which on occasion follow the demands of genuine folklore but more often follow those of the Irish revival in disguised, popular form.

For example, the revivalists had no interest in the ornate fictional frames the early nineteenth century Anglo-Irish writers felt they had to provide their folktales. And so Yeats rudely extracts the in-tales from stories such as Lover's "The White Trout—A Legend of Cong" and "King O'Toole and St. Kevin—A Legend of Glendalough." Titles are changed. Spellings of Irish pronunciations are altered, not because they are phonetically in error but because they are associated with certain attitudes and with a certain kind of literature: "sowl" reverts to "soul," "airly" to "early." The result is no closer to the oral style of genuine storytelling, though it is considerably closer to the unadorned plot of the true folktale.

Despite the violence Yeats visits, justifiably or no, on the nineteenth-century writers, he is still unable, for artistic and I suspect, class reasons, to condemn outright his literary predecessors. Indeed, he defends their apparent class snobbery on the grounds that it is at least preferable to the scientific approach:

> The various collectors of Irish folk-lore have, from our point of view, one great merit, and from the point of view of others, one great fault. They have made their work literature rather than science, and told us of the Irish peasantry rather than of the primitive religion of mankind, or whatever else the folk-lorists are on the gad after. To be considered scientists they should have tabulated all their tales in forms like grocers' bills—item the fairy king, item the queen. Instead of this they have caught the very voice of the people, the very pulse of life, each giving what was most noticed in his day. Croker and Lover, full of the ideas of harum-scarum Irish gentility, saw everything humorised. The impulse of the Irish literature of their time came from a class that did not—mainly for political reasons—take the populace seriously, and imagined the country as a humorist's Arcadia; its passion, its gloom, its tragedy, they knew nothing of. What they did was not wholly false; they merely magnified an irresponsible type, found oftenest among boatmen, carmen, and gentlemen's servants, into the type of the whole nation, and created the stage Irishman. The writers of 'forty-eight, and the famine combined, burst their bubble. Their work had the dash as well as the shallowness of an ascendant and idle class, and in Croker is touched everywhere with beauty— a gentle Arcadian beauty.[15]

Because his whole purpose was to dignify Irish folklore, Yeats substituted for the "comic folk" of these writers the "spirit folk" of his own specifications. It is in this that a seriousness of purpose can be seen to underlie the broad appeal of the anthologies, and in this that the apparently rescued autonomy of the lore can be seen as endangered once more. The scientific method was more offensive to Yeats than literary appropriation, perhaps because that method suggested to him a scepticism, at best neutrality, towards supernaturalism. Belief and poetry were to Yeats inseparable, and so he praised Hyde as a folklorist, not only because Hyde was an accurate worker but also because "he has not ceased to be a man of letters" who occasionally and legitimately alters his stories as a "sennachie must do perforce."[16]

The fact of a peasant's story being listened to and written down accurately in his own words was important to Yeats, but not sufficient: the peasant's belief was the more significant, perhaps even the more credible, for being poetic in conception and expression. It is not surprising, consequently, that Yeats is fitfully informative; in his two anthologies he names three informants personally known to him, but in his selections makes no effort to distinguish author from collector, author from storyteller, or short story from folktale. In this regard Lady Gregory was more scrupulous, to which *Visions and Beliefs* testifies. Her Galway and Aran Islands informants were personally known to her, and she interviewed them herself. When they are unnamed their occupation or status is supplied, and she claims that she is reproducing a faithful transcription of what they said to her. Whereas Yeats would never have become interested in motif and tale type indexes or in variant tabulation, one can imagine Lady Gregory doing so.

Yeats, then, made fresh literary demands upon folklore; he also made supernaturalistic demands upon it, though of course he would have been aware of no distinction between these demands. It is no surprise to find *Fairy and Folk Tales* "Inscribed to my mystical friend G.R." (AE?). Or to find that Yeats has tried to retrieve the folklore from its writerly accretions by arranging the selections in his two anthologies not according to author or collector but according to the class of creature about which the story is told, be it supernatural, fantastic, fairy, or human. If there is a theme in the two books, it is the supernatural, and the visions and metamorphoses that occur when the supernatural impinges on human affairs through the medium of the folk mind. In *The Celtic Twilight* (1893), Yeats distinguishes between "the darker powers" of sorcery and the arcane science (into which he delves in the "apocalyptic stories") and what we might call "the dim powers" of fairydom (into which he delves in *The Celtic Twilight* and these two anthologies of folklore). Angels, who characteristically inhabit broad daylight, complete the supernatural triangle with ghosts who inhabit the night and fairies who inhabit the twilight. Twilight releases "the fantastic and capricious,"[17] to which the Irish folk mind is drawn, an amoral kingdom of ever changing shapes. "This, then, is to be remembered," Yeats asserts in *Fairy and Folk Tales,* "the form of an enchanted thing is a fiction and a caprice."[18] Yeats's interest in enchantment is at base an interest in what elsewhere he calls "the power of imagination."[19] The danger and metamorphoses of enchantment are those of imagination and art which lie figuratively behind the ostensible concerns of the folklore anthologies.

Yeats and Lady Gregory: Visions and Belief

It was important to many revivalists to think of the peasant in closer touch with spiritkind than is the rest of humanity. That their interest in folklore had a spiritualist cast was due in part to a wider reaction in Europe to rationalism. As is evident from the two essays he appended to Lady Gregory's *Visions and Beliefs*—"Witches and Wizards and Irish Folk-

Lore" and "Swedenborg, Mediums, and the Desolate Places"—Yeats wanted to wire the fragmentary and relatively unsystematic beliefs Lady Gregory collected into a European intellectual circuitry of magic, alchemy, and the occult. The supernaturalist folk residing in the west are, it seems, inheritors of an alternative and even more venerable intellectual tradition driven underground by humanism and experimental science, a Yeatsian idea we have come across in an earlier chapter. Had Yeats succeeded in revitalizing the tradition he contemplated, it would have meant the end of folklore as the rest of us know it, with all its fugitive charms; folklore would have become the orthodoxy of the sophisticated and folk alike. That Yeats would have welcomed this suggests that he had little interest in folklore per se, but was interested in the power of folklore to keep alive ideas and symbols that had not always been, and ought not to be, in the exclusive possession of the peasantry, a class of people in whom, per se, he was likewise uninterested.

At the same time, the revival concern with the supernatural was probably also in part a turning away by the more sensitive members of the Anglo-Irish from the material world—the city, capital, industry, the bourgeoisie—in which they were in reputation and general fortunes faring ill. The interest has about it something of a rearguard action, and this might serve to explain Anglo-Irish enthusiasm for the past (nostalgia), for a perfect future (utopianism), for the west (primitivism), as well as that desperate rounding upon their own class forebears for their frivolousness and insensitivity in which O'Grady, Lady Gregory, and Yeats from time to time engaged. Then too there was revival pastoralism that detested mechanization. Peasants "have the spade over which man has leant from the beginning," said Yeats. "The people of the cities have the machine, which is prose and a *parvenu*."[20] At its most literary and lyrical, the recoil of the Protestant writers was from the mortal world itself: "For the world's more full of weeping than you can understand."

The spiritual world that the more poetic and mystical revivalists turned to for solace and escape was not one defined by their inherited Protestantism, but one defined by paganism, occultism, and the more mystical varieties of Catholicism. I have suggested that the Freemason element in Protestantism might have played a role in the fashion for the occult during the revival, and it was perhaps their Protestantism that allowed, even if it didn't encourage, revival enthusiasts to experiment with causes and beliefs. Nevertheless, it would hardly be going too far to describe the Irish literary revival, whether we are thinking of its Catholic or its Protestant writers and scholars, as an ostensibly anti-Protestant movement. The Protestant, after all, was too readily identified with the merchant as well as with the scientist and democrat. The indisputable paganism of the Irish peasant, lying as an elder faith beneath his adopted Catholicism, had another useful contribution to make to the revival. The revivalist who identified with it felt his Irishness had now a spiritual dimension, something which the Catholicism of his countrymen, in especial the candles of the Irish poor, had hitherto prevented him from feeling. Here was an ironic reversal of the soup-kitchen conversions of the Famine, in which Catholics became Protestants in exchange for food!

From his Introductions and appendices to *Fairy and Folk Tales* and *Irish Fairy Tales* it would appear that Yeats, like Lady Gregory, thought the Irish countryman believed in the supernatural the way all of us believe in the law of gravity, and that Yeats considered himself a fellow-believer, belief resting not just on the received wisdom of tradition and on theory, but on actual experience. But peasant belief has to be expressed, and in the expression arises a series of complications neither Yeats nor Lady Gregory took sufficiently into account.

To begin with, before scientific folklore studies developed, belief was conveyed by informants to sophisticated collectors, usually in Ireland of a different religious persuasion and of a vastly different social station. The informant must surely have tailored what he said to such a collector by playing the expected role and telling the collector what he wanted to know (in this case that the peasant believed intensely in the supernatural), taking advantage of the collector's earnestness and credulity and embroidering along the way so that he too might enjoy this peculiar occasion. It is absurd to claim with Elizabeth Coxhead that Lady Gregory was "a sympathetically received equal" in the lowly cottages she visited.[21] Coxhead admits that some of the tales Lady Gregory heard may have been bowdlerized for her ear (and had they not been, we can surmise from her treatment of the sagas and bardic tales that she would have done the bowdlerizing) and that she seems to have been told no stories of the wicked landlord "who loomed so large in peasant experience," an admission that flies in the face of the assertion that Lady Gregory entered the cottages as an equal. Lady Gregory cultivated her sense of identity with the Catholic, Gaelic-speaking, or bilingual peasants to an occasionally irritating degree, going so far as to remark in *Visions and Beliefs* that because of her contact with the country people and their lore she has lost "the practical side of memory that is concerned with names and dates and the multiplication table, and the numbers on friends' houses in a street,"[22] a faculty she imagined urban and therefore unpossessed by the peasant—he who could remember impeccably how much he paid for a pig years before! Yeats wisely never went as far as Lady Gregory in this, keeping somewhat aloof on their field trips (occasionally being mistaken for a priest), though both of them entered into some competition with the folk by hoping that the people would adopt some of their own inventions as folklore and in that way prove that they were in some sense folk themselves.

Certainly there was no conscious attempt by Lady Gregory to deceive her readers, and if the people deceived her a little, perhaps it was out of politeness and embarrassment; most of the deception was self-deception. Still, having written the above I came upon a passage in *We Two Together* in which James Cousins recalls an Englishwoman "keen on the Irish fairies" who came to Donegal and was initiated into fairy lore by her local host, one MacGarvey. "I stopped MacGarvey," Cousins remembers, "and asked him if he knew Mr. Russell (AE) who painted pictures of the countryside, and sometimes painted things that nobody saw but himself. 'Now *that's* a rale gentleman,' he replied, apparently as irrelevantly as I had asked the question, 'and I say so, although he never stud me a drink.' 'And what about the English lady and the fairies?' 'She knows the world and all about fairies.' 'Yes, but how much does she know herself, and how much have you told her?' 'Well, Mister Cousins, it's the way with us mebbe we say more than the God's truth, just to plaze people that want to know more than you know yourself.' 'And what do you know about the fairies? Have you ever seen one?' 'Damn the fairy or ghost or divil ever I've seen, or anything else worse than meself, thanks be to God.' "[23] The danger of distorted data lessened when local and Catholic folklorists took to the field and could not, and would not, be hoodwinked to the same extent.

A second complication arises from the fact that the Irish countryman, whose practical world is literal and devoid of humor, has a strong vein of playfulness, mocking, ironic, sometimes cruel, when it comes to the word. But this simply reminds us of the large element of play in traditional as well as sophisticated culture that Huizinga postulates in *Homo Ludens*. Any attempt to apply wholesale what Joseph Jacobs called "the anthropological method"—that is, taking stories and testimony of the folk as literal evidence—against which Jacobs cautioned interpreters in his *Celtic Fairy Tales* of 1892, is frustrated by this element of play that Yeats only occasionally acknowledged.[24] In "A Remonstrance with Scotsmen" *(The Celtic Twilight)* he remarks that a certain Sligo monster "is ardently believed in by many, but that does not prevent the peasantry playing with the subject, and surrounding it with conscious phantasies."[25] If the peasant's responses to the early collectors were sometimes playful, so too were his imaginative inventions and his very belief in them.

Thirdly, even if the belief is sincerely held, the countryman might still be thought of as holding by a kind of cognitive dissonance contradictory views—which become "views" and hence contradictory only during the reflection and explanation the collector demands of him. The formerly widespread sincerity of belief in the supernatural in Irish country districts is hardly in question. Were it nothing else, *Visions and Beliefs* would be an impressive demonstration of Irish rural belief in the supernatural around the turn of the century. Even so, the Irish country people might still be thought of as inhabiting two different worlds at once, one normally invisible, one visible. We might think of them as reconciling the two worlds by dividing the day and the calendar, their daily environment and even their habits and behavior, between them. Yeats felt at one with the peasant because vision, he was sure, was the basis of their respective systems of belief. But did not Yeats, mystic poet and cultural manager, exercise his own kind of cognitive dissonance, while failing to recognize the peasant's? In *Fairy and Folk Tales of the Irish Peasantry,* he adds a personal note to an anecdote by Letitia McClintock: "There is hardly a village in Ireland where the milk is not . . . believed to have been stolen times upon times. There are many counter-charms. Sometimes the coulter of a plough will be heated red-hot, and the witch will rush in, crying out that she is burning. A new horse-shoe or donkey-shoe, heated and put under the churn, with three straws, if possible stolen at midnight from over the witches' door, is quite infallible."[26] Does Yeats believe the last counter-charm is infallible or is he merely telling us it is believed to be so? Does he fully believe in the original charm? Perhaps he is merely reporting a belief as a folklorist, but he may also be writing as a sophisticated fellow-believer. Perhaps, again, he is writing as a poet. We know that folklore and the forms and content of supernatural belief enhanced the beauty and power of Yeats's poetry, but we do not know to what extent his own belief was a poetic one, sustained in aesthetic illusion for the sake of the poetry. In what sense did Yeats believe in, say, the complex system of *A Vision?* Is it primarily an intellectual artifact, complement to a poetic canon, an ultimate mask among masks?

Yeats himself would probably have refused to partition himself, where the supernatural is concerned, as folklorist, believer, or poet; he would no doubt have seen himself as all three, which is itself a poetic idea. Yet he preceded his commentators in acknowledging his epistemological ambivalence towards the mystical and supernatural. In his introduction to *The Wind Among the Reeds* in the *Collected Works* (1908), he spoke of moments of vision in sleep and waking, and of the images of a mystical language, but then, as Norman Jeffares recounts, "Being troubled by what was thought to be reckless obscurity he tried to explain himself in lengthy notes into which he put 'all the little learning I had, and more wilful phantasy than I now think admirable, though what is most mystical still seems to me the most true.' "[27]

The diluting of belief with scepticism can also be seen through the various editions of *The Celtic Twilight,* as Richard Finneran reminds us: "In later editions he increased his scepticism, but in the earlier editions he seems to be leaning towards agreement with the peasantry" in their belief in the fairies.[28] In "Belief and Unbelief," a chapter in *The Celtic Twilight,* Yeats writes: "It is better doubtless to believe much unreason and a little truth than to deny for denial's sake truth and unreason alike, for when we do this we have not even a rush candle to guide our steps, not even a poor sowlth to dance before us on the marsh, and must needs fumble our way into the great emptiness where dwell the misshapen dhouls. . . . When all is said and done, how do we not know but that our own unreason may be better than another's truth?"[29] Richard Ellmann describes Yeats as "latently sceptical by nature, but craving the irrefutable evidence of the supernatural which would finally lay his doubts at rest. . . . This attitude may be fairly described as a predisposition to believe and a desire to find fair evidence which would convince people lacking the predisposition."[30] "Yeats," claims Kathleen Raine, "was not more sceptical than AE; indeed all those from whose writings I have quoted [Douglas Hyde, Y. Evans-Wentz, Andrew Lang, William James, Carl Jung] were too subtle in their thought for scepticism. But he was more analytical, more aware that of 'facts of mind' there are many possible explanations."[31] In spite of his repudiation of science, Yeats, said Edmund Wilson during the poet's lifetime, "has always managed to leave himself a margin of scientific doubt . . . the romantic amateur of Magic is always accompanied and restrained by the rationalistic modern man."[32] "He believes, but—he does not believe," Wilson epigrammatizes, and his quotation of Yeats from *A Vision* might seem to answer the question I posed earlier: "Some will ask if I believe all that this book contains, and I will not know how to answer. Does the word belief, used as they will use it, belong to our age, can I think of the world as there and I here judging it?" "And he intimates," Wilson concludes, "that, after all, his system may be only a set of symbols like another—a set of symbols, we recognize, like the Irish myths with which he began."[33]

Something less problematic than the nature of Yeats's belief is the image of the Irish peasant, in Yeats and other revival writers, as inhabitant of a world primarily spiritual and magical. We are justified, I think, and not philistine, in demanding that this image, purported in folklore and autobiographical writings (which are like scaffolding around the brilliant incontestable structures of revival literature) to be verifiable, accord with the best evidence, including one's own experience, as far as that extends. I believe Yeats did not adequately take into account in fashioning his images of the peasant, on which so much of the revival depends, the playful, sceptical, and dramatic qualities of the peasant's testaments of belief with which Yeats endowed his own treatments—folkloristic, epistemological, poetic—of those testaments. Scepticism and distrust are a genuine aspect of the Irish countryman's make-up, but Yeats saw it as an uncommon attitude imported from the outside. In his Introduction to *Fairy and Folk Tales,* he writes:

> the Sceptic is [not] entirely afar even from these western villages. I found him one morning as he bound his corn in a merest pocket-handkerchief of a field. Very different from Paddy Flynn—Scepticism in every wrinkle of his face, and a travelled man, too!—a foot-long Mohawk Indian tattooed on one of his arms to evidence the matter. "They who travel," says a neighbouring priest, shaking his head over him, and quoting Thomas A'Kempis, "seldom come home holy." I had mentioned ghosts to this Sceptic. "Ghosts," said he; "there are no such things at all, at all, but the gentry, they stand to reason; for the devil, when he fell out of heaven, took the weak-minded ones with him, and they were put into the waste places. And that's what the gentry are. But they are getting scarce now, because their time's over, ye see, and they're going back. But ghosts, no! And I'll tell ye something more I don't believe in—the fire of hell;" then, in a low voice, "that's only invented to give the priests and the parsons something to do." Thereupon this man, so full of enlightenment, returned to his corn-binding.[34]

I have a sneaking regard for this curmudgeonly fellow. He is impertinent to his better and unaccommodating enough not to believe in ghosts; he has been presumptuous enough to have left Ireland, and even exhibits foolish pride in binding his corn in so diligent and self-absorbed a manner in his "merest pocket-handkerchief" of a field. (It is telling that the poet, foiled in his preconceptions, reverts to an irrelevant snobbery in recollecting the exchange.) But many a spalpeen or emigrant to America saved with his remittances many an Irish family from going the roads, and the energy required to leave Ireland, even for a short time, is not to be sneered at by someone who took the packet-steamer any time he felt like a change of company or a new project was brewing. The fellow may not even be a rationalist at all, merely perhaps having a sense of the difference between fact and fiction and between the occasions appropriate to each, and considering the binding of corn in the uncertain weather of the west far more pressing than any chat about ghosts with the idle gentry.

The curmudgeon rather deftly, I think, turns the upper-class chap's curiosity about folklore against itself by insulting the real gentry under cover of insulting the fairy gentry in whom he believes, apparently with some reluctance. Perhaps he rightly suspected that he was not the subject but the object of the curiosity. The fairies were, of course, called "gentry," as Yeats later informs us in his Introduction to *Irish Fairy Tales,* and he says it is "for politeness' sake."[35] He could be right if to the country people the real gentry were proper recipients of their politeness or if the fairies were regarded as the fled and defeated gods, the Tuatha De Danann who shrank physically in the imagination of the people as they faded in their historical memory. But many of the local legends and ghost stories of Ireland recount the doings of the real gentry, and not always favorably. If the fairies were thought of as fallen angels and mischievous creatures, then to call them "gentry" is, it could be argued, for impoliteness' sake. Since the mischievous fairies commanded respect on the one hand and fear and dislike on the other, the issue is a mixed one.

Lastly, as an obstacle to our applying the anthropological method too readily to oral folklore—as the revivalists, even the writers among them, tended to do—is the fact that the casting of a belief in narrative form would seem to change its order of existence. An experience or event becomes a first-person anecdote; thereafter it becomes a third-person anecdote and perhaps eventually a local legend. And a local legend may possibly, I suppose, become eventually a fairy tale or folktale proper. I suspect, too, there might be some devolution: a *Märchen* (or fairytale) is localized, a local legend is passed off to the outsider as personal experience. The transformation of personal experience into story does not mean that the original conviction or belief is rendered unfounded, insincere, or duplicitous; but it does mean that validity or sincerity or verifiability becomes irrelevant. The events of the story, as story, are independent of the credence of both storyteller and listener. In expression, an experience or event accrues or assumes motifs and formulas and passes under the jurisdiction of narrative laws of type and genre. At that point we have to make the distinction drawn by Douglas Hyde: "The *sgeal* or story is something much more intricate, complicated, and thought-out than the belief. One can quite easily distinguish between the two. One (the belief) is short, conversational, chiefly relating to real people, and contains no great sequence of incidents, while the other (the folk tale) is long, complicated, more or less conventional."[36] The transformations are not just from subject (or witness) to informant (or retailer) to anecdotalist or storyteller, but also from personal to impersonal modes of narration, and from local and specific place and historical and specific time to those conventional generalities of time and space we find in *Märchen*.

Lady Gregory was more aware of this process than was Yeats, and she recognized the possibility of devolution as well as evolution. However, she wished unlike Hyde to regard the reality of retailed experience as more important than its conventionalism. Instead of distinguishing Hyde's "belief" from Hyde's "story," she chose to distinguish Hyde's "belief" from "vision," an actual revelation of the supernatural. "It is hard to tell sometimes," she admits in *Visions and Beliefs*, "what has been a real vision and what is tradition, a legend hanging in the air, a 'vanity' as our people call it, made use of by a story-teller here and there, or impressing itself as a real experience on some sensitive and imaginative mind."[37] Because she has only one foot in the scientific camp, the other being in the Yeatsian camp, she does not quite clinch the necessary connection, which is that even a unique vision or supernatural revelation (or an experience believed to be such) must inhabit a category of experience. This category has been established long ago and is traditional, and tradition requires stories of *other* people's visions or revelations, in places and times other than here and how, though folk stories of the supernatural seem to prefer enough proximity to the alleged experience ("a few years ago," "in the next village," "a friend of my uncle's" etc.) to create the illusion of fact. There is, then, intimate traffic between direct and received experience, vision and belief, with the belief far outweighing the renewing visions. That the veil drawn between the visible and invisible worlds is an antique or categorizable one does not, of course, make the veil—which is a form of language after all—any the less thin or prevent it from being on privileged or unwelcome occasions transparent.

An appreciation of the conventional structures of oral lore, be it personal anecdote or hero tale, was possible only with the rise in Ireland of scientific folklore studies. Yeats had small interest in the formal properties of the authentic folktale or in the intricate conventions of storytelling. Having to compete against beliefs, anecdotes, local legends, and heroic romances, all chosen for an overt Irishness, the genuine *Märchen (seal-sgéal)* makes rare appearances in *Fairy and Folk Tales* and *Irish Fairy Tales*. Lover's "The White Trout; A Legend of Cong" was a truncated *Märchen* even in Lover's *Legends and Stories of Ireland*. "The Story of Conn-eda; Or the Golden Apples of Lough Erne," collected from a Gaelic storyteller by Nicholas Kearney, is a *Märchen;* so too is "The Horned Women" from Lady Wilde's *Ancient Legends, Mystic Charms and Superstitions of Ireland* (1887). "The Man Who Never Knew Fear," collected and translated by

Hyde, later published in *Legends of Saints and Sinners,* is a widespread international tale, listed as 326 in Stith Thompson's *Motif-Index of Folk Literature* and *The Types of the Irish Folktale* by Sean O'Sullivan and Reidar Th. Christiansen. O'Sullivan, like James Delargy, is a chief representative of the second generation, or post-revival, Irish folklorists—mostly local men, Catholics, inhabitants of no Big House or Georgian terrace, tutored by the Scandinavian pioneers—who have no personal system of belief to corroborate, no romantic image of a fey and credulous peasantry to project, little more desire than their contemporaries the New Critics to apply the anthropological method to texts. By the time they emerged, partly because they emerged, the Irish literary revival was finished.

The Death of Anshgayliacht 11

The Rise of Folklore Studies—Douglas Hyde, William Larminie

The Rescue of Folklore: Hyde's Beside the Fire

Although Yeats and Douglas Hyde were equally opposed to the "literary bantlings" (Lover's phrase) that passed for printed folktales before the revival, they were soon divided in their opposition. Praising Hyde in 1891, Yeats four years later was taking his influential contemporary to task for allowing his scientific bent to dominate his literary sensibilities.[1] It was not science Yeats sought but a new literature. Yet between 1888 *(Fairy and Folk Tales of the Irish Peasantry)* and 1920 *(Visions and Beliefs in the West of Ireland),* there appeared a number of books that are of interest to the literary critic: Hyde's *Beside the Fire: A Collection of Irish Gaelic Folk Stories* (1890) and *Legends of Saints and Sinners* (1915); Jeremiah Curtin's *Myths and Folk-Lore of Ireland* (1889), *Hero-Tales of Ireland* (1894), and *Tales of the Fairies and Ghost World* (1895); Edmund Leamy's *Irish Fairy Tales* (1890); Joseph Jacobs' *Celtic Fairy Tales* (1892) and *More Celtic Fairy Tales* (1894); William Larminie's *West Irish Folk-Tales and Romances* (1893); Seumas MacManus' *Donegal Fairy Stories* (1900); and Lady Gregory's *Poets and Dreamers* (1903), *The Kiltartan History Book* (1909), and *The Kiltartan Wonder Book* (1910). These are books to which the inquirer after prose fiction of the Irish literary revival should be directed; they constitute a prose fiction created by the cooperation of scholars and writers with the unlettered or barely literate, past and present. To them we might cautiously add Yeats's *The Celtic Twilight* and Synge's *The Aran Islands* since these include some folktales collected by the authors. I would also add a work that is speculative, annotative, monstrous, and yet wonderfully resourceful, a book in which history, folklore, and legendary fiction intermarry: W. G. Wood-Martin's *Traces of the Elder Faiths of Ireland: A Handbook of Irish Pre-Christian Traditions* (1902).

At the same time, these books are of interest to the folklorist, plotting as they do the escape of folklore as a discipline from the inhibiting patronage of nineteenth century literature.[2] In 1920 motif and tale type indexing and variant-tabulation were still in the future in Ireland, but at least by then folklore had as its primary tasks collection, transcription, translation, and investigation rather than editing, anthologizing, and exploitation. Literate meddling gradually diminished, the collector's own beliefs shrank in importance, and the reader as someone who wished to be entertained and to have his prejudices confirmed became of less account. It is an odd irony that the literary revival created national ideals which encouraged a professional ethnography, and that this ethnography in turn undermined those ideals. Especially did it undermine the notion that folklore is primarily a spiritual affair and that it expresses directly, or embodies the idealism of, a romantic peasantry, upon whom the emerging Irish nation was spiritually to rest. I have broached this irony already, but I would like to inspect it more closely using collections by Douglas Hyde and William Larminie, authors of two significant books in the above list.

Lady Gregory was inspired to rewrite heroic romances and translate folk testimony in the language she selected (the dialect of Kiltartan, a village in Galway) by the prose of Douglas Hyde's translations of folksongs in *Love Songs of Connacht* (1893) and of folktales in *Beside the Fire*. In translating Gaelic stories into English, Hyde innovatively employed Anglo-Irish idioms and word patterning used by English-speaking Irish of two classes: bilinguists whose first language was Gaelic and who mentally translated from Irish when speaking English, and speakers of English only whose dialect was Hiberno-English. His translations could not always be literal, therefore, and he gently chided Campbell of Islay for using literal translations of Gallic in order to achieve picturesqueness in the English product. To the extent that he avoided literalness, Hyde is an Anglo-Irish writer as well as Gaelic translator, but he keeps his freedom of translation on as tight a rein as possible, and any desire to pile up Anglo-Irishisms severely in check, with the result that the language of his stories does not smack of that condescension or gratuitous color that can mar Lady Gregory's Kiltartanese and even Synge's dramatic prose.

Hyde, who became a founder of the Gaelic League in 1893, knew Gaelic more thoroughly than either Gregory or Synge and this must have helped to curtail any urge to falsify or supplement. The prior commitment to Gaelic is evident from the fact that the folktales he collected were first published in Irish, in *Leabhar Sgeuluigheachta,* before appearing a year later in English, in *Beside the Fire*. Half of the stories in the English volume had not appeared in the Irish and their Gaelic originals face the English translations, the originals of the other half being available in *Leabhar Sgeuluigheachta*. The title of the bilingual volume recalls Kennedy's *The Fireside Stories of Ireland* (1870) which in turn recalls the Grimms' *Household Tales,* all three a reminder of the domestic circumstances in which folktales, unlike the bardic tales of the court, were told, irrespective of the highborn characters and distant settings of many of the stories.

The scientific rigor of Hyde's work was of a pioneering quality in Ireland. *Beside the Fire* has a long Preface in which Hyde assesses his predecessors and discusses Gallic parallels to his stories (some solar mythology and ethnocentric diffusionism here), the relation of bardic to folk tales, the distinction between native and foreign provenance, the narrators he encountered on his field trips in Roscommon, south Donegal, and Mayo and how best to make them talk, and the intention behind his own translations. Then follows the translations and some of the originals Hyde collected, with annotations, and a lengthy and characteristically speculative Postscript by the ubiquitous Alfred Nutt, intellectual midwife to British folklorists for many years. There is also a crucial section entitled "Where the Stories came from" in which Hyde makes good the promise of his Preface: "In the present book, as well as in my *Leabhar Sgeuluigheachta,* I have attempted—if nothing else—to be a little more accurate than my predecessors, and to give the *exact language* of my informants, together with their names and various localities—information which must always be the very first requisite of any work upon which a future scientist may rely when he proceeds to draw honey (is it always honey?) from the flowers which we collectors have culled for him."[3] Just as interesting to the future folklorist, Hyde attaches an "Index of Incidents" ("I use the word 'incident' as equivalent to the German *sagzug,* i.e., as connoting not only the separate parts of an action, but also its pictorial features"), an alphabetical list of motif catchphrases that Hyde was using alongside contemporary workers like Joseph Jacobs and Reinhold Köhler and in some deference perhaps to J. S. Von Hahn, and a prototype of the later motif index of Antti Aarne.

Hyde stands midway between, on the one hand, the largely diachronic concerns of British and European diffusionists, mythologists, and students of provenances, concerns which were nationalized by the more ethnocentric revivalists to show Irish supremacy in folk culture, and, on the other hand, the largely synchronic concerns of future students of motifs, tale types, variants, and narrative structures, concerns which were of little use to the revivalists. Hyde is among the first of the Irish folklorists to attempt a distinction between originally native and non-native elements in Irish folklore, a distinction that was not a priority for the more extreme nativists of the Gaelic and literary revival. Hyde claimed conscious genesis inside the shores of Ireland for all those later folktales that were "the detritus of bardic stories" such as the longer Fenian tales, and conscious genesis beyond the shores of Ireland for more antique folktales that bear traces of Aryan origin and solar mythology, together with that lore which most attracted Yeats and Lady Gregory: customs, beliefs, local legends, and anecdotes relating to fairies and the supernatural. "The King of Ireland's Son," included in *Beside the Fire,* belongs to the second category, "Bran," a Fenian story, to the first. After Hyde, when folklore theories abandoned a diachronic for a synchronic approach, internationality would be determined neither by elements of solar mythology nor by evidence of Aryan provenance, but by tale type, the presence or absence of motifs, and morphology. But Hyde at least was led, under the influence of Nutt and those European theorists Yeats and Lady Gregory tended to ignore, to avoid a totally ethnocentric and proprietary attitude to folklore in Ireland. Synge resembled Hyde in this respect. After one of the half-dozen folktales he includes in *The Aran Islands,* Synge identifies its two motifs and knowledgeably reminds us that they occur in stories from England, Scotland, Germany, Italy, Persia, and Egypt.[4]

Beside the Fire and its Gaelic predecessor restored Irish folktales to their rightful custodians, the people and their storytellers, and honored the language in which many if not all folktales in Ireland were first told. It was willful disregard of the language of storytelling in favor of plot skeletons that vitiated the interest of the earlier writers in folklore. The "largely-manipulated Irish stories" of Carleton and Lover, as Hyde deems them, were not offered as samples of folk fiction but were dragooned as contributors to the writer's sophisticated fiction, and the novel, claims Hyde, is very different from the folktale because it is the product of the novelist's individual brain. Appropriately, then, Hyde dedicates *Beside the Fire* "To the memory of those truly cultured and *unselfish* men, the poet-scribes and hedge-schoolmasters of the last century and the beginning of this who kept the lore alive" (my italics).[5] We know now that "sophisticated" fiction has its own conventional and traditional morphology (motifs, genre characteristics, linguistic structures, and patterns) over which the individual novelist has only partial control and which resemble some of the morphological features of the myth and the folktale. But Hyde's basic distinction between, on the one hand, oral, anonymous, collective, traditional fiction, and, on the other hand, written, attributable, original, invented fiction is sound, even if in the next two chapters we will find the distinction in some cases difficult to apply with any structural certainty.

Yet it is hard to see how Hyde escapes a peculiar paradox of folklore collection and publication. Once an oral tale is published, it becomes in its printed version literary fiction. Unless it is accompanied by variants the printed oral tale tends to assume canonical form, and this runs counter to folklore, which exhibits variation and conservation but in a dynamic interaction that precludes canons.[6] This was the case even as the poet-scribes and hedge-schoolmasters whom Hyde praised commended to manuscript stories that ipso facto took on something like canonical form.[7] And it is the case even though two contemporary experts have described Irish folktales as having fewer variants and more stylistic conventions than most European tales:

> Both the narrators themselves and their audience had as an intellectual background an ancient tradition which demanded of the storytellers that they should adhere to a style and manner determined by long established usage, literary in its origin and kept alive among people deeply conscious of their past. For theirs was a special way of thinking, a real culture, if, to all appearances, largely an illiterate one, but created and coloured by their respect for that ancient tradition, still pulsating with life in Irish-speaking country and which had impressed an Irish form on such ubiquitous international tales as Cinderella and the Dragon Slayer.[8]

Ironically, then, the folklorist who prints is allying himself with a medium that is the mortal enemy of the folktale. Yeats eloquently saw the peculiar vividness of the hostility in Ireland. "In Ireland today the old world that sang and listened is, it may be for the last time in Europe, face to face with the world that reads and writes, and their antagonism is always present under some name or other in Irish imagination and intellect."[9]

Hostile media do not have to appropriate folk material in order to damage it; nor do we have to imagine printed or filmed versions of folktales actually coming to the attention of storytellers and corrupting their stories (though we shall later see this happening in the case of *Beside the Fire*): the mere spread and intrusion of these media accomplish the damage and eventual displacement. Perhaps, too, to imbue storytellers and informants with a self-consciousness about their tales and lore and their own art of storytelling, as collectors must, is itself corrupting. If it is, then there is irony in Hyde's acknowledgment in *Beside the Fire* that the folktale is doomed and his claim that he is rescuing it from oblivion: the very act of rescue is another nail in its coffin. The dilemma of the Irish folklorists was an unenviable one: the greater the urgency to collect folktales before they vanished, the more (albeit fractionally) their departure was hastened. Yet we are grateful that the price was paid for salvaging for literate posterity such tales as are offered in *Beside the Fire,* tales that were doomed anyway (a fate in poignant contrast to the happy endings of the splendid tales themselves) and would have been extinguished without trace. And Hyde is not answerable for an intractable version of the paradox—that the most worthwhile folklore seems to attract exhaustive study as it itself grows exhausted and dies.

The folklorist as a preserver of lore in archival form was for the reader and student an unmitigated good, but he was not an essential part of the literary revival that discountenanced the purity of texts and actually preferred corrupted lore by which to further its own fictions, including its fictional image of the peasant. The folklorist as romantic revivalist and would-be preserver in the field (or rather, the writer and cultural nationalist as romantic folklorist) nursed for literary and even political purposes the hopeless ideals of revival and preservation. Hyde presumably knew that lore rarely survives translation into another medium or language, or removal outside its native environment, and so cannot be kept artificially alive, like a rare animal in a zoo, to be released later to replenish and increase its numbers in the wild. The more romantic nationalists were, as it has turned out, succeeded by unromantic tourist board bureaucrats in an independent Ireland who have speciously maintained for economic purposes the illusion of romantic revival in rural Ireland by advertising "zoo-bred" lore (subsidized cottage industries, brochured holidays among the folk, and the like) as the wild thing. It has been a fittingly ironic development of a revival whose romantic belief in the organic, the natural, and the primitive could become a differently romantic belief that these could be artificially maintained. Hyde expressed in his attitude to folklore the gist of both romanticisms, just as he combined the role of writer (establisher of canonical form, unliteral translator) with that of folklorist (literalist, student of variation) and, as folklorist, combined the aims and methods of science with those of cultural nationalism.

Beside the Fire: *Folk Aesthetic and the Revival*

The collections of living tales by Hyde and others became valuable specimens in a printed or manuscript folk museum and can still be studied by historians and analysts of texts, types, variants, and motifs. For when a folk form, such as the Gaelic folktale, dies, it can only be commemorated if it persists in an enduring medium; but it then becomes a different thing. In comparison with the living tale in its natural habitat, the printed tale is like a cast or discarded cocoon: it has the form, but it no longer has the living substance, of the tale. And yet in becoming a different thing, it accrues a different kind of value. The printed collections of Hyde and others have become folk literature, entertaining and repaying of study by readers and literary critics. For the literary student, unlike the folklorist, text and folktale become one and the same; the text is no longer merely one example of a hypothetical archetype or one variant among many variants: the notions of variant and type lose their relevance. The literary critic, because his appreciation is, like the artist's, of perfected form, likes to deal primarily with definitive or final texts, a preference for the very canonical form whose existence or desirability the folklorist denies. If the critic or literary scholar finds variants interesting, it is because they help to indicate the steps by which the perfected or definitive form of the work was approached. Unlike the folklorist, the critic prefers to know that there exists the text in holograph, for—at least until recently—[10] his ideal was to appreciate the masterpiece composed by a single, known hand. For the literary critic, Hyde's genuine, untouched-up folktales are an important part of the fiction dating from the years of the Irish literary revival, though because they stand outside ordinary history and literary culture they are not part of the revival in its ideological guise. The tales did influence revival fiction, as we shall see in the following chapters, but they are of too absorbing an interest and autonomous a value to be regarded merely as sources, models or prototypes.

Beside the Fire is a mixed bag of localized *Märchen,* pieces of saga, local legends, fairy stories, animal fables, and riddles. Some of the stories are as crafted and impressive as most authored work of the revival. All are of interest to the cultural historian, local and national, as well as to the linguist, folklorist, and literary critic. By grace of the scientific folklorist, the peasant storyteller is permitted to speak for himself, and yet the effect is rather of the storyteller speaking *by* himself for the people who composed the stories and entrusted him with them. He does so, however, in no entirely communal way. Many of his listeners know his stories—for the folk do not exhaust or consume their narratives as we tend to do—but they cannot recite them with sufficient flair. The storyteller in being able to recite the stories is in possession of a secret, albeit an open and shared secret, which he keeps in trust, like a banker, for the people. The secret bestows a certain power on the shanachie, and not just because the shanachie, through the median figure of the poet and satirist, is associated with the spellbinder and charmer. The power really resides in the story rather than the storyteller. This is evident from the fact that in many stories a tale is the object of the hero's search and which, when recited by the possessor, functions as an in-tale. Notable examples are "The Story of Bioultach" and "Morraha" given in *West Irish Folk-Tales and Romances.* In "Morraha," the hero is enjoined to fetch both the sword of light and news of the death of "Anshgayliacht," Larminie's phonetic rendering of the Gaelic phrase meaning "the storytelling." This idea of custody qualifies the romantic nativist notion of a peasantry expressing itself in an antique and unanimous voice. A deeper effect of *Beside the Fire* is of a people not entirely conscious of the narrative lore that is expressed through them but that only in a limited way expresses the people themselves.

Folk aesthetic is very different from both romantic self-expressionism and romantic primitivism and might be thought of as closer to medieval aesthetic, according to which Christian tradition is transmitted by gifted contributors whose aim is not self- but group expression. But while something like a medieval aesthetic appealed ostensibly to the revivalists, it cannot accurately be compared to folk aesthetic, even if the idea of the group is a mutual one. A cathedral built over centuries is built to express a governing idea and ideal, the glorification of God, and there is nothing comparable in consciousness in the folktale. The stories in *Beside the Fire* are often international narrative forms largely independent of local and expressive concerns and which have developed according to a mainly internal "genetic" program of motif and type. About this the revivalists were nervous since they wished—in accordance with the anthropological method—to understand the Irish peasantry as expressing itself locally and nationally with one voice through its lore. A story or belief found in Ireland, even should it be found and indeed have originated outside Ireland, is still Irish, of course (just as an Irish novelist, were he to live in Ireland writing novels set outside the island, would still be an Irish novelist), the more so when an international form has been localized. This was not enough for many of the revivalists, perhaps because much of the wider, non-folk culture, some of which we have seen represented in "The Dead" and which D. P. Moran and others attacked, was trying to divest itself of all traces of Irishness, out of colonial and provincial shame and aspiration. The neglect by Irish folklorists during the revival of international types and forms, except when Irish provenance was indicated, is paralleled by the revival's demand that the Irish writer reside in Ireland, set his work in Ireland, employ Irish themes and characters, and imbue his work with revival ideals. Joyce satisfied the second requirement, and then apparently only to mock it, and debatably the third, though his use of Irish characters was admitted more readily than his use of Irish themes. The traveled George Moore for a time acceded in peculiar fashion to all of the demands, except possibly the last. In folklore, if not entirely in literature, the bias has now been removed, and Ireland is now rightly proud of the eight hundred international folktales that have been found within its shores.[11]

The transmission of traditional narrative means that the storyteller's freedom of expression is limited and regulated. Motifs, runs, and other migratory formulas are not his invention, and their deployment should comply with the laws of folk narrative (which might through Anderson's law of self-correction put right any egregious error)[12] and with the overall structure of the particular tale archetype. One motif occurs in three of the stories in *Beside the Fire;* in "Paudyeen O'Kelly and the Weasel," "Leeam O'Rooney's Burial," and "The Hags of the Long Teeth," a black dog turns out to be a dead person. A common narrative formula closing both an episode and a day is employed three times in "The King of Ireland's Son" and is also used in "The Story of Bioultach," "The King Who Had Twelve Sons," and "King Mananaun," three of Laramie's stories. This is one version of it from Hyde's story: "they spent that night, one-third of it telling Fenian stories, one-third telling tales, and one-third in the mild enjoyment of slumber and of true sleep until morning" (p. 33). There is also a traveling formula that we find in Larminie's "King Mananaun," "The King Who Had Twelve Sons," and "The Nine-Legged Steed" and in Hyde's "The King of Ireland's Son" and "Guleesh Na Guss Dhu" ("Guleesh Black-foot"): "The cold winter's wind that was before them, they overtook her, and the cold winter's wind that was behind them, she did not overtake them. And stop nor stay of that full race, did they make none, until they came to the brink of the sea" (Hyde, p. 106; usually the March wind is specified in this formula). In addition there are formulaic nonsense endings, formulaic problems set the heroes and formulaic solutions, and battle runs, such as this from Larminie's "King Mananaun": "The two went to battle on board the ship. They began young like two little boys (and fought) until they were two old men. They fought from being two young pups until they were two old dogs; from being two young bulls until they were two old bulls; from being two young stallions till they were two old stallions. Then they began a battle in the shape of birds; and they were fighting as two hawks, and one of them killed the other."[13]

That the storyteller may on occasions fail to tell a story correctly entails as corollary the story's having an existence both typal and particular. The storyteller is aware he is telling not composing a story, and this relieves him of the need to justify what he is telling, though his own suspicion that he is not telling the story as well as it might be told could make him even less willing than usual to justify or clarify. This seems to be the case with the Roscommon storyteller, John Cunningham, who baffles Hyde's requests for clarification during a truncated and unsatisfactory rendering of the Fenian tale, "Bran," by shifting responsibility where all storytellers believe it belongs, with the story: *"(Who made a fawn of her? Oh, how do I know? It was with some of their pishtrogues.)"; "(And how could she catch the wild-geese? Wouldn't they fly away in the air? She caught them, then. That's how I heard it.)"* (pp. 17, 19). J. H. Delargy reminds us of a frequent ending formula: "*Sin é mo sgéal-sa! Má tá bréag ann bíodh! Ní mise a chúm ná a cheap é.* 'That is my story! If there be a lie in it, be it so! It is not I who made or invented it.' "[14]

The folklorist today, then, distinguishes the variant a storyteller gives him from the type to which the variant belongs, though it would be wrong to equate variation with local or even national contribution, much less with a storyteller's self-expression. Different tale types seem to permit different degrees of variation, for the possibilities of variation seem encoded in the type (as defined and identified by Aarne and Thompson in *The Types of the Folktale*) and not merely in the form (e.g., the fairy tale) which is as far as Vladimir Propp allowed himself to speculate in *Morphology of the Folktale* (1929). What the collector transcribes from the storyteller Propp calls a "text," wishing to distinguish this from the "tale" which is imperfectly represented in the text. The text may be the variant of a single tale or may include more than one folktale which the teller has sewn together. Hyde's "Paudyeen O'Kelly and the Weasel," for example, would even seem to be a text in which two kinds of narrative, a localized *Märchen* and a fairy story, are cleverly spliced.

More interesting than any splicing at work is the setting in this tale and others in *Beside the Fire*. The classic fairy tale, the strictest form of folktale, has only a few elemental and stylized settings, chiefly the cottage and hearth, the sea, the island, the forest, and the castle or palace. The closer the Irish folktale approximates the true *Märchen,* the fewer and more stylized the settings, with the cottage and hearth, the lake and river, the boreen and ditch, the *grianan* (sunny chamber), and the large house predominating. These have their obvious social significance, peculiar to Ireland, especially the cottage and large house which are where action ends, the others being chiefly connective settings. To this extent the Irish folktale can on occasions, but prudently, be held to reflect social reality in Ireland from a peasant point of view. In "Leeam O'Rooney's Burial,"

"Trunk-without-Head," and "Paudyeen O'Kelly and the Weasel," the large house (compare the castle of the fairy tale) is the Big House of the Irish Ascendancy, and the mystery of the Big House's inaccessibility and its many rooms surely accounts for its being the seat of enchantment and wealth in the tales, an aboveground counterpart of the inhabited rath of the fairy story. Between the reality of the cottage, with its wife, animals, and constant need for money, and the possibilities of the Big House, with its untold wealth and its flowing wine, the Irish folktale frequently plies. In "Paudyeen O'Kelly and the Weasel" and the very similar "Trunk-without-Head," the small farmer ends his days in the Big House, surely wishful thinking, and probably widespread. The *cluricaun* is a small fairy who frequents the cellar of the Big House and drinks the wine: such a figure seems to be another case of wishful thinking; the darkness of the cellar is an appropriate place for small figures to be mistakenly seen, but the desire to siphon off some of the wealth of the Big House in its most desirable and obvious guise no doubt encouraged the belief and the hallucination.

Many of Hyde's stories exhibit a triadic pattern of departure, trials and adventures, and return, a cast of hero, donors, villain, and maiden, and a modular structure of motifs, runs, and other formulas, all of which are characteristic of the folktale. "Guleesh Na Guss Dhu" is a very good, picaresque, and lengthy story (only twenty-four of whose sixty-odd pages, given in full in *Leabhar Sgeuluigheachta,* are reproduced in *Beside the Fire*), told to Hyde by Shamus O'Hart of Roscommon, that has elements of *Märchen,* fairy story, and local legend. The various settings, a Mayo cottage, a fairy rath, the Vatican, and the court of the King of France, suggest the story's picaresque wealth. The narrative style is equally eclectic. Beside a charming bardic expression, the rose and the lily fighting together in the face of the King of France's daughter, is this evocative description of the exit of the sidhe from their rath on Samhain, which I am sure James Stephens read, a description unusual in its original, realistic, and poetic portraiture of the western countryside:

> Guleesh accordingly went to the old rath when the night was darkening, and he stood with his bent elbow leaning on a gray old flag, waiting till the middle of the night should come. The moon rose slowly, and it was like a knob of fire behind him; and there was a white fog which was raised up over the fields of grass and all damp places, through the coolness of the night after a great heat in the day. The night was calm as is a lake when there is not a breath of wind to move a wave on it, and there was no sound to be heard but the *cronawn* (hum) of the insects that

> would go by from time to time, or the hoarse sudden scream of the wild-geese, as they passed from lake to lake, half a mile up in the air over his head; or the sharp whistle of the fadogues and flibeens (golden and green plover), rising and lying, lying and rising, as they do on a calm night. There were a thousand thousand bright stars shining over his head, and there was a little frost out, which left the grass under his foot white and crisp.
>
> He stood there for an hour, for two hours, for three hours, and the frost increased greatly, so that he heard the breaking of the *traneens* under his foot as often as he moved. He was thinking, in his own mind, at last, that the sheehogues [trooping fairies] would not come that night, and that it was as good for him to return back again, when he heard a sound far away from him, coming towards him, and he recognised what it was at the first moment. The sound increased, and at first it was like the beating of waves on a stony shore, and then it was like the falling of a great waterfall, and at last it was like a loud storm in the tops of the trees, and then the whirlwind burst into the rath of one rout, and the sheeh-ogues were in it. (pp. 122–23)

"In folk literature," remarks Kaarle Krohn, "man himself does not stand in contrast to his natural environment,"[15] and one proof of this is that the storyteller does not feel constrained to linger on natural descriptions, even in localized narratives, nature being largely taken for granted. In this respect folk literature resembles the heroic literature. Protracted descriptions of nature in folktales normally signal either impurification by local legendry or literate meddling. It is possible, though, that the combined narrative forms of "Guleesh Na Guss Dhu" and its picaresque linkage of settings and actions liberated O'Hart to some extent in his descriptive language.[16]

Folk Aesthetic and Larminie's West Irish Folk-Tales

William Larminie was of the opinion that the styles of the stories in *West Irish Folk-Tales and Romances,* which he collected and translated himself, differ "considerably from one story to another, and not so much in accordance with the narrator as with what he narrates" (p. xii). He rightly excepts from this generalization P. Minahan of Donegal, seven of whose stories Larminie reproduces. Minahan is a folk Hemingway whose narratives at the level of the sentence are laconic, sprightly, and oddly effective:

> When night came Jack and his master went out. They went to the field. Jack took one of the bullocks. He skinned the skin off it. He cut the flesh off the bones. He sewed the skin on the bullock again. They went home, and two loads of meat with them. They had enough that time. To make a long story short, they didn't leave a bullock in the field but they did the same to. When the last of the cattle was eaten, they began with the sheep. They played the same trick on the sheep.
>
> When the king thought it was time to kill a bullock he went to the butcher. They went to the field. When they went to look at a bullock, the bullock was barely able to walk. They were all like that. The king couldn't tell what happened them. They went to the field where the sheep were. They were in bad condition. There wasn't a sheep or a head of cattle that Jack and the tailor hadn't eaten the flesh off. (pp. 111–12)

As counterpart to the limited control and freedom exerted by storytellers and the limited localization that can take place to alter folktales is the limited identification with the hero of the folktale indulged in by the listener. The genuine folktale is a rather impersonal narrative form, whose events are often exotically distant from the experience of the listener. Whereas the myth tale is an important cultural code which the listener who belongs to the group whose myth it is can apparently break quite readily, the *Märchen* tends to be a diversion from the group's important activities. The listener to the folktale identifies with the hero during his trials and adventures, but does so only on the narrative plane.[17] Unlike those which may occur in the historic legend, the tensions are created and released within the story itself, and the less true this is of the story the less pure the *Märchen* with which we are dealing. Perhaps the revivalists sensed the impersonal and universal nature of the folktale and, since they wished to see folklore as the conscious expression of a unified and essentially Irish peasantry, showed relatively little interest in Irish versions of European narrative structures.

This is not to minimize the peculiarly Gaelic qualities of many of the folktales collected during the literary revival. Those qualities are perhaps even more evident in the Connacht and Donegal stories in Larminie's *West Irish Folk-Tales and Romances* than in Hyde's volume, and from the literary critic's point of view, Larminie's less miscellaneous compilation is superior. The "quiet domesticity" which Larminie perceives in some of the

Irish tales, and which reminds him of Grimms' household tales, is offset by an exotic unruliness that we encountered in the heroic sagas and which Larminie believes is shared by Highland tales. Some of the stories are filled with casual, even formulaic, yet often shocking murder, mayhem, sexual promiscuity, and cannibalism. This is by no means the sprightliest passage to be found:

> A young man was in the wood one day and a dog with him, and the dog took him to the place where the woman was; and the man saw the woman and the child there, and he went home and told the queen that there was a beautiful woman in the wood. And she went and took the dog with her, as if the dog was with George na Riell. She went in and found the woman and the babe, and she killed the babe and caught some of the blood, and mixed the blood and ashes up together and made a cake, and she sought to put a piece of the bread into the woman's mouth. And the woman dropped one tear from her eye; but the other went away home to her wedded husband, and she said to him that great was the shame for him to have children by that woman, and that she had had to kill her own child and eat it.
>
> ("Gilla of the Enchantments," p. 185)

For her pains the villainess is put up on a tree, hanged, and cast in a fire. There are whimsical tortures, such as molten liquid poured on enemies, and whimsically described combats that surely James Stephens must have relished: "Bioultach and the ragged green man went into the house, and when the giant saw them he was about to be away. The ragged green man caught him and threw him. Bioultach took hold of him and tied him tightly, and brought the five slenders together, so that the toes of his feet gave conversation to the holes of his ears, and no conversation did they give him but the height of mischief and misfortune" (p. 51). One tale, "Grig," is surmised by Larminie to be "a rather ghastly piece of mythology." The wilder reaches of archaic Gaelic imagination were as of little interest to the more ideological of the revivalists as were international tale types, since they tended to confirm the stereotypes of the comic Irish and the wild Irish. Certainly the impression one has after reading *West Irish Folk-Tales and Romances* is of an oral fiction dark, ancient, and exotic, pitched like many *Märchen* and much of the old saga literature between comedy and terror in a manner that keeps our modern emotional response on perpetual hold.

How we might account for the peculiar and potent effect of the tales is a task beyond the scope of this book, but the relationship of teller to tale might be one clue, after we acknowledge that the tales are translated from the Gaelic in which language they would presumably be more intelligible. The tales are old, and the storyteller is passing on something not even he finds entirely intimate or comprehensible. The tales show the narrative form and style of the *Märchen,* which bear the same relation to the form and style of familiar fiction that one mode of music bears to another, despite Larminie's claim that some of his stories resemble modern novels (p. 257). The ability of storytellers to memorize after one hearing novella-length tales and keep them in the memory for years until asked to recite them,[18] underlines how far the tales represented narratorial and auditory codes very different from the writerly and readerly codes of literature Roland Barthes has discussed in *S/Z* (1970).

The memories of the unlettered are probably better able to retain the spoken word than those of the lettered, and the storyteller's memory is probably in addition a distinctive gift. Both observations might account for the storyteller Delargy met who had learned his tales by eavesdropping when a boy on older tellers, a technique Synge adapted to his own purposes when gathering matter for dramatic dialogue when he was on the Aran Islands, though of course many writers are perpetual eavesdroppers. However, the memory of the unlettered was probably aided by the fact that a tale consists of a chain of formulas, motifs, and functions, with sparse formulaic settings and a small cast of typical characters. The listener (himself a future or present teller) perhaps used a mnemonic shorthand in remembering and retrieving the chain, or possibly once the early links of the chain had been well memorized, together with an overview of the story's total typal formula, the tale was "self-memorizing" in the sense that one link suggested the next not only by association but by a delimitation of sequential possibilities that grew increasingly severe as the tale progressed, rather in the way the possibilities for development become more clearly delimited and directed the older an organism becomes. (We might think of "teller" as a pun: to tell a story is to re-count it, to pay out the chain, beads, or currency of motifs.) The story carries as primary burden not meaning but interest, potential fulfilled (or unfulfilled) within the story itself.

The casual or indifferent nature of events in the folktale is characteristic of its impersonality. One of countless possible examples is the unruffled and unelucidated manner in which the wife in Hyde's story "Leeam O'Rooney's Burial" accepts the return of the husband she believed dead and buried. Little is explained or justified morally or psychologically in folktales, and if an element in them is artificially isolated or highlighted it is possible for the ignorant or ideological reader to take offense. Synge's play, *The Shadow of the Glen,* inspired by a tale told to him by the Aran Islander Pat Dirane, excited hostility in Ireland, but perhaps it did so for the casual and folktale-like indifference with which its adultery was depicted rather than for the adultery itself. In any event, adultery is common in folktales and is as casually and amorally depicted as all else, a reminder perhaps of how difficult it was during the revival to reconcile the true folktale with the moral intensity of the nationalist movement. This casualness of the folktale may be due to some extent to the fact that a storyteller has no personal investment in what he is telling.

Propp would no doubt tell us that it is due rather to the most characteristic feature of the fairy tale, the fact that what he calls "functions," actions and events, are far more important than characters. A folktale, he tells us, "often attributes identical actions to varied dramatis personae."[19] What folktale dramatis personae do is primary; who the dramatis personae are is secondary. Moreover, "the characters' will and intentions cannot be considered as the essential motives for their definition."[20] If so, then it is conceivable that over a long period of telling, a folktale might pare itself down to the essentials, in other words to the functions of which there are thirty-one possible, according to Propp, though all will not occur in a given tale. The moral and psychological, even cultural element in which actions, events, wills, and intentions live might tend to dissolve, and the distillation will be as enigmatic as it is pure, as high-proof liquor might bear no trace of its vegetable origins. Perhaps only a brilliant decoder like Levi-Strauss, armed with the relevant cultural knowledge and treating the narrative as a sustained occurrence of metonymy, can work backwards to recover the archetype. Such an archetype, in which the Irish revivalists showed scant interest, need not be in any special sense Irish.

Of Larminie's stories, Propp would have found "The Story of Bioultach" congenial, for there he would have discovered the character-types he calls heroes, villains, donors, helpers, and sought-for persons, and those functions he calls lack, mediation, interdiction, departure, first function of the donor, hero's reaction, guidance, struggle, provision, victory, initial misfortune liquidated, and return. Yet he would not have explained in this and other stories in Larminie and Hyde that dark eloquence too inscrutable to be of much use to the revivalists. It is the flesh of the story—its imagery, idiom, phrasing, vocabulary—provided by the storytellers over the generations that gives the skeletal structure power and movement. Propp leaves out of account language and the spirit that language breathes into any sequence of functions, and this omission must put into perspective his assurance that his functional analysis can be used on modern fiction as well as fairy tales. Nor is Propp interested in the living performance of the folktale (involving pace of delivery, inflection, gesture, dialect, audience reaction, place, time, and circumstances of narration) which is an essential part of each variant and of which the text is mere postscript. Somewhere between Proppian formalism and the special utilitarianism of the Irish literary revivalists we must find room and language to pay the Irish folktale due tribute.

The Mount of Transfiguration 12

The Writer as Fabulist—W. B. Yeats, James Stephens

I wish I could take out papers of naturalization as a dog or a hedge-hog or a cat. . . .

—*James Stephens*

Folklore into Art: **Stories of Red Hanrahan**

Yeats was the first major talent of the Irish revival to contemplate fiction's respectful emulation and appropriation of folklore, to let art vie with science and popularization in recognition of the productions of the peasantry. *The Celtic Twilight* was published in 1893 on the heels of his two anthologies of folklore, and fiction inspired by folklore, and is itself something of an anthology by one hand. In formal conception it lies midway between the miscellany of the anthologies and the shapeliness of *Stories of Red Hanrahan.* It is as if the notes that barnacle around the anthologies have floated free, released to become small comely essays and tales. A "handful of dreams," Yeats called them, but *The Celtic Twilight* is more substantial and various than that. Yeats gives us what he has heard (folk testimonies and traditions), what he has seen (firsthand experiences and visions), and what he thinks (commentary and speculation). The anecdotal testimonies to visions and experiences of the world of fairies and benign ghosts shade into the impersonal testaments of traditional beliefs, customs and narratives, including ghost stories, local legends, fairy stories, a fairly complete *Märchen* (in "Dreams That Have No Moral"), and poems.

Poets and storytellers (including AE, who is probably The Visionary in the chapter of that title) flit in and out among the pages of *The Celtic Twilight,* one of them being the allegedly last Irish gleeman (poet, jester, newsman of the people), one Michael Moran (Zozimus), a descendant—though in the chronology of Yeats's canon a precursor—of the medieval gleeman in "The Crucifixion of the Outcast," the direct connection being

Yeats's reference in "The Last Gleeman" to MacConglinne whose vision, recounted in *Aislinge Meic Conglinne* (twelfth century), was the basis for the story in *The Secret Rose*. For Yeats story is synonymous with either vision or belief, both of which are staples of *The Celtic Twilight*, and Yeats counts himself among these "tellers of tales," the fabulists who try to make all things perfect in their kind. *The Celtic Twilight*, if not perfect in its kind, is nevertheless a wonderful book and was more influential than the two anthologies that preceded it. More than the darker world of the apocalyptic stories (with their un-Irish associations with *poètes maudits* and heretical arcana), its twilight world helped in large measure to define the limits and scope of the early revival. In its conception it had a more formal influence on works of Irish folklore, particularly *Visions and Beliefs in the West of Ireland*, published twenty-seven years later, a book which categorizes testimony and belief more systematically, offers a wider variety of informants, demotes the author as artist and commentator, and is yet recognizably cousin to the poet's work.

Like the transformation of manuscript narratives into modern literature, the raising of folk testimony and tradition to art commanded a great deal of the attention of Irish revivalist writers. The nineteenth-century, pre-revivalist writers went about the task in a very different way and only with Yeats in *The Celtic Twilight* and *Stories of Red Hanrahan* did the task begin to be performed in a way satisfactory to revival and post-revival readers. Perhaps this was because Yeats's imaginative prose in these volumes genuinely aspired to the condition of folklore. This is made evident by the complicated history of the revisions and publications of the Red Hanrahan stories, unravelled by literary scholars and a testament to Yeats's seriousness about his fiction.[1] Around the turn of the century, Yeats was sufficiently ambitious as a fiction writer to specify the kind he would become: "I have an ambition," he said on the publication of *John Sherman and Dhoya*, "to be taken as an Irish novelist, not as an English or cosmopolitan one choosing Ireland as a background."[2]

From start to finish, effectively 1892–1905, the history of the Red Hanrahan stories involves three successive and distinct prose styles: Loveresque hibernicism (really a British literary argot and when used by an Irishman springs perhaps from a wish to ingratiate himself with potentially scornful English readers), standard literary English, and Kiltartanese. The last was achieved in 1901 in collaboration with Lady Gregory, and "Red Hanrahan," a fresh opening tale for the suite, was the first fruit of the collaboration. The syntactical characteristics of Kiltartanese that occur in *Cuchulain of Muirthemne* occur in *Stories of Red Hanrahan:* reordering of standard English parts of speech ("It is not of that I am thinking": the

Irish frequently put their verbs at the end of sentences); frequent impersonal use of "it" with the verb "to be" ("It was travelling northward Hanrahan was one time"), this characteristic, like the first one, allowing the writer to suggest archaism; heavy use of present participles, enhancing the effect of folk characters living, and events occurring, in an eternal present; equality rather than subordination of minor clauses, generally by use of "and" which enables sentences to be long yet loosely contrived in a formulaic way and suggestive of song or chant; frequency of colloquial, often metrical idioms.

The chief gains are a more insistent rhythm and the suggestion of a speaking voice, as is simply illustrated by the two versions of the opening sentence of the third story of the set: "After the twisting of the rope at Margaret Brien's, Owen Hanrahan the Red journeyed northward, doing odd jobs for farmers and telling tales at wakes and weddings, and then south again into Leitrim and so back in the direction of the Town of the Shelly River, through the Ridge of the Two Demons of the Air" ("Kathleen the Daughter of Hoolihan and Hanrahan the Red," 1897). "It was travelling northward Hanrahan was one time, giving a hand to a farmer now and then in the hurried time of the year, and telling his stories and making his share of songs at wakes and weddings" ("Hanrahan and Cathleen the Daughter of Hoolihan," 1905). According to Michael J. Sidnell, "In 1905, Yeats thought the [revised] stories had the 'emotion of folklore' and a 'beautiful idiom' and attributed these qualities to Lady Gregory. Later, Yeats was less enthusiastic, more ambiguous: 'If their style has merit now [1925] that merit is mainly hers.' "[3] It is possible that Yeats came in after years to find the language of *Stories of Red Hanrahan* somewhat precious and self-conscious, that he came to realize that the price for a poetically Irish prose was a certain quaintness that showed a vulnerability to time shared by the quaintness of Morris' "medieval" prose.

The stylistic transformation of 1905 was appropriate to (perhaps caused) the new exclusively western setting of the stories ("a ring round Sligo," as Sidnell puts it).[4] It must also have strengthened Yeats's desire to localize and better absorb into his tales his knowledge of folk ways and folk beliefs. For example, the crucial events in "Red Hanrahan" occur on Samhain Eve (Hallowe'en) when the sidhe are said to emerge from their subterranean abode, while the Galway mountain, Slieve Echtge (Aughty), is used because it takes its name from a sidhe legend that enables Yeats, as we have seen, at once to localize and nationalize his suite. The set is in form clearly meant to imitate an edited field collection of oral tales about a folk hero. Richard Finneran has rightly referred to at least three kinds of Yeatsian prose fiction: the fairy-folk stories (including the Hanrahan stories), the esoteric-occult tales (including the apocalyptic stories), and a realistic story ("John Sherman").[5] Thinking of the difference between "Dhoya" and *Stories of Red Hanrahan,* I would make it four, distinguishing a pseudo-mythic story like the former from pseudo-folk stories like the latter. The distinctions are not watertight, however, and the folkloristic in the Hanrahan stories shades into the mythic by virtue of the fact that the sidhe of whom Hanrahan runs afoul are the defeated gods, the Tuatha de Danann, and that the four old women of the sidhe hold talismans associated with Dagda, Lug, and Nuada. The ritual and occult nature of these talismans permits the mythic in turn to shade into the esoteric; Finneran points out that Yeats's revisions of the Hanrahan stories retrenched the fairy material (lessening, we might add, their value as "literature for the people") and increased the esoteric material (enhancing their value as "aristocratic . . . Irish literature . . . for the few").[6]

Perhaps more accurately *Stories of Red Hanrahan* could be described within the category of pseudo-folklore as pseudo-legend, in its creation of a legendary figure and in its use as underpinning of the Grail story. This is an underpinning suggested by one of Yeats's notes to Lady Gregory's *Visions and Beliefs in the West of Ireland* to the effect that the cauldron (one of the four talismans possessed by the old women) was thought by Alfred Nutt to be "the first form of the Holy Grail."[7] According to Jessie L. Weston, there is no Irish folk or hero tale corresponding to the Grail legend, despite the fact that "the four treasures of the Tuatha de Danann correspond generally with the group of symbols found in the Grail romances."[8] The stories of Red Hanrahan may well have been Yeats's attempt to fabricate an Irish Grail legend. Hanrahan fails to question the four old women and is punished, thereby repeating the fate of the hero in *Parzival:* "The punishment falls on the hero who has failed to put the question, rather than on the land."[9]

Historical figure (actual and alleged), legend, figment of Yeats's imagination: Red Hanrahan is richly all of these. Although some scholars have seen other historical figures as models for Hanrahan (including Carleton), there can be little doubt that the chief inspiration was Owen Roe O'Sullivan.[10] Yet in "The Tower," Yeats claimed: "And I myself created Hanrahan." Earlier, in *The Secret Rose* text of one Hanrahan story, he even attempted to palm Hanrahan off as an actual person, with a reference to "'Hanrahan's Rosary,' a book which is famous among Gaelic scholars,"[11] an interplay of fact and fiction we have already noted in *Stories of Michael Robartes.* Indeed, Yeats hoped that Hanrahan might be accepted as a once-historical figure and then, by way of Yeats's stories, pass into Irish legend and thence into folklore.[12] This attempted making of folklore, this weaving of history, folklore, and fiction were recurring tactics of the Irish literary revival. It is a curious dimension of literature's deference to folklore that the movement advocated.

Resurrected Forms: Stephens' Irish Fairy Tales

Yeats's relationship to folklore was altogether more purposeful than that of most of his contemporaries, who were content to retell traditional or manuscript stories in a language appropriate to a romantic revival. Alice Furlong in *Tales of Fairy Folks, Queens and Heroes* (1907)—dedicated to Hyde, Sigerson and Hull—turns episodes from the cycle stories into pleasant resemblances to folktales.[13] In *Celtic Wonder Tales* (1910), Ella Young performs the same feat; this handsome book, illustrated by Maud Gonne, celebrates all manner of wonders and transformations. While these volumes domesticate the wilder forms of the Gaelic imagination, they are forerunners of the finer work in this vein by James Stephens and Padraic Colum. Stephens' *Irish Fairy Tales* was published in 1920 but was first suggested to Stephens as an idea in 1913 and was written amidst his preparations for the *Táin* books. Even so, an earlier book of identical title that ought to be mentioned as a pioneer in such an enterprise is Edmund Leamy's volume of 1890.

That Leamy was, like William O'Brien before him, an M. P. and editor of *United Ireland* suggests the cultural and even political impulse that could lie behind the gathering of Ireland's lore.[14] Like several writers of the time, Leamy ostensibly wrote for children, but his *Irish Fairy Tales* is nonetheless a fine literary treatment of the plots and characters suggested by Irish bardic tales and fairy stories; Leamy, it was said at the time, "was by nature an improvisor."[15] Here are tales of enchantment and disenchantment, of love impeded and, by magical help, triumphant. Between 1890, when the book first appeared, and 1906 when it was reprinted, occurred the literary revival; according to T. P. G. (T. P. Gill?) in his introductory note, *Irish Fairy Tales* was reprinted for "a race of readers who have appeared since it was written and who ought to be in a mood more appreciative of such literature than the mood which prevailed in that day."[16] Gill reminds readers that Leamy published his stories before the formation of the Gaelic League and the Irish Literary Theatre, when only P. W. Joyce's *Old Celtic Romances* and the works of O'Curry were available for inspiration. There was early O'Grady, of course (as well as Yeats's *Fairy and Folk Tales of the Irish Peasantry*), but Gill opposes Leamy to O'Grady:

Leamy's "habitual mood was the exquisitely sensitive, the tender, playful, reverent mood. He was, in this, the antithesis of the 'cloudy and lightning' Standish O'Grady, whose temperament, equally Gaelic, is that of the fighting bard, delighting in battle, fierce, fuliginous, aristocratic, pagan, with the roll of Homeric hexameters in his martial style."[17]

The playful (if not always reverent) touch we find in Stephens' *Irish Fairy Tales,* a book in which the author grafts resurrected forms on to extant ones, at which operation none was more skilled. *Irish Fairy Tales* was misnomered as were Yeats's and Leamy's of identical title, but then Stephens was not a folk collector or even anthologist, though like many other patriots he went west, or at least southwest, to the Kerry *Gaeltacht,* possibly in 1916, to learn Irish. Rather Stephens imbibed stories by word of mouth or word of print and in retelling them was perhaps the nearest thing to a shanachie the Anglo-Irish revival produced. In *Irish Fairy Tales* we have his versions of Fenian and Mythological tales, some of which had already been versioned by Leamy and Young and by Lady Gregory, whose *Gods and Fighting Men* (1904) was, like *Irish Fairy Tales,* heavily indebted to Standish Hayes O'Grady's *Silva Gadelica* (1892), a seminal collection of old tales in both original and translated forms.

But in its particular sequence of tales and in its elements of pure modern artistry, Stephens was justified in calling *Irish Fairy Tales* "an original book."[18] The sequence, the importance of which Stephens stressed to his publisher, is not O'Grady's but his own, and it creates a complex arrangement I will comment upon later. What is original too is the way in which Stephens took manuscript material and infused it with the life and buoyancy of *Märchen.* He thought his book had been titled "nonsensically."[19] because it would suggest that the book concerned the doings of the wee folk, but maintained that it deserved its title in a more venerable fasion: "It is really not a book of fairy stories in the modern understanding of that term," he wrote to John Quinn. "But, I think, they are Fairy Stories in the ancient and authentic meaning. I claim that this is the first time real fairy stories have got into modern print, &, if the world likes them, there are plenty more where they came from."[20]

The claim, of course, is unjustified. Nor is *Irish Fairy Tales* a collection of authentic *Märchen.* Yet in his transformations of manuscript material into semblances of *Märchen,* Stephens was aided by the folk origins of the Fionn cycle, the contribution which Early Modern Fionn tales, such as *Eachtra Bhodaigh an Chóta Lachtna (The Adventures of the Churl with the Grey Coat,* translated by O'Grady as "The Carle in the Drab Coat"), laid folklore under and the living form of folktale which the Fenian cycle takes even today.[21] The Mythological and Fenian stories have a more

Märchenhaft quality than those of the Ulster cycle. When, for example, he diminishes the heroic in favor of the marvellous, Stephens is being faithful to the spirit of the Fionn cycle in which the marvellous plays a larger role than in the Cuchulain cycle. And the humor in *Irish Fairy Tales,* as when Fiachna Finn and his battalion are savaged and treed by venomous sheep in "Mongan's Frenzy," is Stephens' attempt to recover a humor native to the old tales but cowled by time, scholarship, and the revival popularity of the more tragic Ulster cycle.

Stephens agreed with the archangel Finaun in *The Demi-gods* (1914) that "Humour is the health of the mind" (p. 187), and when in "An Essays in Cubes," also published in 1914, he remarked that "humour may be defined as the last refuge of the intellectually destitute," he was not contradicting himself insofar as he was thinking of authors whose numbers would probably be swelled by the nineteenth-century Anglo-Irish writers, though he does not refer to them. In an earlier chapter we saw how Stephens humanizes the heroic by providing his romance heroes with flawed characters and psychological motivations. In *Irish Fairy Tales* he humanizes by humorizing and makes his heroes the butt of cosmic laughter, and this Stephens thought was justifiable, perhaps believing (in anticipation of Patrick Kavanagh) that the tragic and the heroic if allowed to ripen did so into comedy. The effect in Stephens is free both of the caddish tomfoolery of the pre-revival writers and of the domesticity of Lady Gregory. We see the approach also in *The Demi-Gods* where the bringing of angels down to earth is the source of the book's humor; in that book too we find a transvestite Cuchulain as a healthy, outrageous foil to the hero of Standish James O'Grady, Lady Gregory, and W. B. Yeats. Perhaps it was too late in the day for heroism, as Stephens seemed to suggest when chiding AE because the elder writer would set poets "to sing dead ideals, to hark back from this era of nineteen-hundred-and-ever-so-much to that year of dot-and-carry-one when the heroes ate raw enemies and drank the blood of whoever was handy."[22]

Stephens' humor had frequently an antidotal impulse, but in *Irish Fairy Tales* this is less the case since he had plots and characters to be reasonably faithful to if his title were to be justified. This is the purest and least didactic of his books, the spirit of which is best captured in the concluding and entirely invented (but formula-like) comment in "The Enchanted Cave of Cesh Corran" in which like most of the tales savage deaths are carelessly recited: "Nor is there any reason to complain or to be astonished at these things, for it is a mutual world we live in, a give-and-take world, and there is no great harm in it."[23] There is something of a realist acceptance here, and it derives from the sheer "whatness" of the world as it is portrayed in the old stories: the music of what happens is the finest music of all.

To these old stories Stephens brings the quickened pace and vocal presence of the modern storyteller, and he dilutes Hayes O'Grady's viscous narratives until they have the readerly flow and lucidity of modern fiction. He tends to curtail the descriptive runs in O'Grady, for example the splendid battle run when Finn enters the brawl at Allen.[24] Although on occasions he will invent his own formula, for example the traveling formula in the very amusing "The Carl of the Drab Coat": "Then he sprang up, and he took to a fit and a vortex and an exasperation of running for which no description may be found. The thumping of his big boots grew as continuous as the pattering of hailstones on a roof, and the wind of his passage blew trees down. The beasts that were ranging beside his path dropped dead from concussion, and the steam that snored from his nose blew birds into bits and made great lumps of cloud fall out of the sky" (pp. 190–91). His dialogue too tends in its swiftness to be rather that of modern fiction than that of the old tales. If Stephens in the liberties he takes with the old stories escapes our censure where lady Gregory invites it, it is because Lady Gregory asserted fidelity to, and privileged insight into the essence of, the old tales, because she changed and bowdlerized for ideological reasons, Stephens (at least in *Irish Fairy Tales*) chiefly for literary reasons, and because Stephens' changes are more in keeping with what I regard as the spirit of the old tales.

Stephens' liberties have their limits, in any event. The characters, plots and episodic structure of *Irish Fairy Tales* are those of the old stories. Stephens was in fact happiest when observing unconsciously the laws of folk narrative. It was to be his inclination toward the formulaic structure achieved by these laws that vitiated Stephens' attempts to capture the more crowded canvas of the Ulster tales in *Deirdre* which strains toward fairy tale as well as psychological portraiture. In 1915 Stephens expressed the desire to write "le Comedie Humaine of Ireland" *[sic]* on the Balzacian scale that would necessitate "dealing with large masses of people & events." But the kind of book he envisages, in which he would explore a slice of Irish time "with the particularity of a grub working through an apple, until I have attained to a consciousness of Ireland in all its dimensions,"[25] was to be published not by Stephens but by Joyce in 1922. Stephens sometimes comes across as Joyce *manqué,* and I believe Joyce thought that this was the basis of their later affinity. Not only did Stephens lack, as in the 1915 letter he confessed he might, the "knowledge of our bureaucrats, traders, farmers, thieves, prostitutes" needed for "the big job done bigly" ("I have tons of wisdom & no knowledge," he wrote in another letter),[26] but the whole thrust of his most inspired writing was towards a disqualifying duality;[27] he had none of Joyce's gift for the social and fictional middle ground, none of Joyce's ironic equipoise (perhaps Joyce's middle-class background helped) that the task required. Stephens' works, *Irish Fairy Tales* among them, swing unstably among fiction, saga, and fairy tale, but he would not be Stephens were it not so. Moreover, the disability had its own comic advantage, for the democratic effortlessness with which he could, more successfully than any other revivalist, convene the characters of saga, fiction, and folktale on the same page, most notably and comically in *The Demi-Gods,* fulfilled the revivalists' wish to make the Ireland of heroic saga and ancient folktale live again and at the same time showed subversively and not wholly intentionally the comic absurdity of the wish fulfilled.

Stephens' evident joy in creation imbues his work with a spirit of playfulness that is missing in that of the more serious revivalists and that is closer to the spirit of folklore than revival highmindedness playing at peasant naivety. It would not do, though, to underestimate Stephens' artistic ambitions. In a letter in 1914 to Stephen MacKenna, Stephens explained the curious title of "An Essay in Cubes": "like the Cubist pictures, its eye is sometimes on its knee & its ear on its shoulder."[28] The irreverent energy of Stephens' fiction, can be likened to that of folktale and Irish saga, but it can also be likened to that of cubist painting with its swift intersecting planes slicing across expected continuities. Yet before he was a nationalist (of an odd stripe) or a mystic or a literary theorist, Stephens was an author who wrote with an eye on that common reader whom Yeats and AE scorned, but rarely with an eye on the professor whom Joyce always wanted to engage. The price he pays is that his work seems frequently disrespectful towards the old stories, his imagination a seditious fertility that threatens to drive his native subject matter and nationalist sympathies into self-parody.

Like Joyce, Stephens writes from a vantage point of such confidence that he can happily make clichés, banalities, archaisms, and proverbs serve rather than hinder his purposes, though unlike Joyce he does not always protect himself behind the defense of point of view. He is especially partial to home-grown proverbs and epigrams: "most virtues are, on examination, the amalgam of many vices";[29] "We get wise by asking questions, and even if these are not answered we get wise, for a well-packed question carries its answer on its back as a snail carries its shell";[30] "A sword, a spade, and a thought should never be allowed to rust."[31] Given the high incidence of epigram in his work, I suppose we ought not to be surprised when we come across his admonition, voiced in a letter to *The Dial*

(1924): "Let the reader beware when he sees an epigram: 'tis the last refuge of an inferiority complex."[32] This contradicts itself and contradicts Stephens' own fiction. Stephens' epigrammatic bent makes of him the most quotable writer after Blake. I believe Stephens' epigrams, many of which define the relation between two variables, express the dualistic tendency of the Irish mind, but they also express the impatience of mind, Irish or merely Stephens', that prefers the shortest verbal distance between ignorance and wisdom and which he has the Philosopher in *The Crock of Gold* erect into a principle: "The healthy mentality should register its convictions and not its labours" (p. 86).

Stephens even thought that a novel could be constructed on the epigrammatic principle: he only sat down to write his first novel, *The Charwoman's Daughter,* when it dawned on him that a novel "can be wise on a very minimum of thought."[33] In Stephens we have the verbal trappings of the folk mind that "disappears with the development of contemplation," as one folklorist remarked,[34] and that still flourishes in Ireland. "The entire of their knowledge," said Stephens in 1949 of what he considered the vanished peasantry, "was cast in the form called proverbs."[35] Despite Stephens' preoccupation with wisdom, he is no philosopher in a modern sense (his sayings are like the traditional nuts of knowledge) which is perhaps why he parodies classical philosophy in *The Crock of Gold;* nor is he in any other than an instinctive way a psychologist, which is partly why *Deirdre* does not really come off. Like the Bloomian if not Dedalian Joyce he is demotic where Yeats and AE are esoteric, though on occasion he tries to infuse his sayings with the mystical force of Blake's; when this fails Stephens runs the risk of appearing, as the Northern Irish say of certain children, "oul-fashioned"—precocious, too winsome by half, ill-fitting.

It was folk speech rather than bardic or folktale conventionalism that Stephens wished to achieve. He described speech, by which he seemed to mean the best kind of talk, as "a much rarer, a much swifter, a very much more tangential thing than prose dares even to attempt, for prose must not move at any angle whatever from its subject, and the talk that doesn't do precisely that is no good."[36] Elsewhere he considered that "A writer may be judged by the variety of his matter and by the subjects he makes his characters talk about,"[37] a remark which, since it was written as early as 1914, explains in part the wandering eclecticism of Stephens' novels. Thirty-three years later he claimed that *Finnegans Wake* is all speech, "which moves at the speed of light, where prose moves at the speed of the alphabet . . . Now it is soliloquy; now it is dialogue; it becomes at times oration and tittle-tattle and scandal, but it is always a speech, and however it be punned upon by all the European and a few of the Asiatic tongues, it is fundamentally the speech that used to be Dublin-English."[38] Perhaps Joyce sensed in Stephens linguistic kin when he asked him to finish the masterwork should he himself be unable to. Like the later Joyce's, Stephens' prose has a "feminine" and protean ability to change shape and pace, to surround and infuse its subject. In a broadcast in 1946, "The James Joyce *I* Knew," Stephens called *Finnegans Wake* an attempt by Joyce to write "pure prose," by which he means what he elsewhere calls speech.[39] Unlike the realists Stephens detested, the Joyce of *Ulysses* and *Finnegans Wake,* like himself, passed the external world (which includes the actual speech one might hear in the street) through a mental crucible, digesting his vision before reprojecting it.[40] (The mixed metaphors are Stephens'.)

By commodious vicus of recirculation we arrive back at Stephens' highly literary style, a rhetoric that has the volatility of speech and the substance of prose, the pace of folktale and the punctuality of saga. Above all Stephens values energy ("all life and all greatness comes back to that word—Energy. Genius is energy controlled definitely.")[41] which his prose displays by its untiring sportiveness. I believe Stephens was more naturally gifted than any other Irish writer of his time and was more fluent and felicitous of phrase than even Joyce. His prose is a sprightly dance of quick and symmetrical motions. He writes rings round his subjects and most other writers. But he was unpossessed of Joyce's stamina and Joyce's willingness to strain at all costs against the boundaries of fictional form. His genius was self-congratulatory because eager for public acceptance and rested content with paradox and surprise. Moreover, there is a relentlessness about Stephens that requires the reader's cooperation to prevent it from issuing in what the popular mind would call blarney. We might find ourselves in reading him echoing now and again the jovial impatience of Dermod the high king of Ireland faced with a voluble cleric's lengthy story in "The Wooing of Becfola": "If you continue it," he said, "it will surely come to an end some time. A stone on a stone makes a house, dear heart, and a word on a word tells a tale" (p. 155). Stephens' complaint in "An Essay in Cubes" that Fielding chatters unceasingly is unintendedly ironic.

I am of course being unfair to Stephens, as he was to Fielding, once because *Irish Fairy Tales* is his best-paced book, twice because he is a storywriter, not a storyteller, and we can, unlike the poor Bloomsburyites entertained at first and bored into silence in the end by the Irish visitor to Garsington, choose our own speed of reading. If Stephens' superior energy leads him into that patronizing of characters to which I drew attention in an earlier chapter, it also leads him into whimsical narrative experiments, such as revealing himself fleetingly, anonymously, for no apparent reason, and to the MacCanns' ass alone, in chapter 32 of *The Demi-Gods,* like Alfred Hitchcock appearing unobtrusively and as a kind of signature in a scene of his film. Nor do I believe myself mistaken in glimpsing behind Stephens' chatter an Irish fear of silence that Stephens thought the most unnatural sound of all (*The Demi-Gods,* p. 25), the symbol of death that the Irish stave off, like Scheherezade, with the known words that fear inspires.

Irish Fairy Tales: *Varieties of Metamorphosis*

Surprise, which the narrator of *The Charwoman's Daughter* tells us is one of the commonest things in the world, we might define as energy abruptly changing the direction of its flow, and it is Stephens' chief ploy to counter narrative inertia. It can take the form of comic juxtaposition, in the way the Philosopher in *The Crock of Gold* can pontificate on bees and publicans in the same breath, or a dozen other forms, many resembling the formulaic surprises of fairy tales. All are expressions of the master motif in Stephens' work—transformation. "The law of life is change," we are told in "The Birth of Bran," a story in *Irish Fairy Tales,* "nothing continues in the same way for any length of time." (p. 96) Theme, character, setting: all obey the law.

True poetry, Stephens was fond of quoting AE as saying, has been written on the Mount of Transfiguration (not for nothing did Stephens entitle a volume of poems *Reincarnations*), and his prose fiction aspires likewise to this height. Accordingly, Stephens in *Irish Fairy Tales* recasts the Fenian and Mythological tales as wonder tales and filters both through a novelist's perception of form. In these tales, as in the fairy tales towards which he bends them, changes of character are more important than any heroic identity, and in the last story in the volume, "Mongan's Frenzy," we are surprised, except on reflection, to learn that Mongan is really Fionn, the protean genius of the collection. Disguise, impersonation, and zoomorphism abound. Tuiren is transformed into a dog in "The Birth of Bran"; in "Oisin's Mother," Saeve is at first a timid fawn; Mongan and his servant assume the shapes of the priest Tibraidè and his clerk. The characters ply between the perennial world of the sidhe and the mortal world of men. *Irish Fairy Tales* metamorphoses the Fenian and Mythological worlds into a strip cartoon-like world of transforming violence and brisk resurrections, wherein if nothing stays the same all can be restored before the next inevitable metamorphosis. The gruesome is even jollier and more innocent than it is in *Deirdre,* witness the careless dismemberment of the poets in "The Boyhood of Fionn." The machinations of faery attract Stephens because he is in tune with their demotic and Dionysian impulses. Faery represents a reversal in the normal ranks of society, categories of knowledge, modes of action, and personalities of people. It is as if the fairy story is the Dionysian mirror-image of the Apollonian hero tale; the sidhe belong to an underworld as the heroes belong to a world aboveground (and the gods to an upper world), and Stephens enjoyed the antiheroic idea of the world aboveground apocalyptically falling in upon itself.[42]

Like the sidhe, Stephens mischievously regards received heroes with a kind of envy (the envy of a diminutive man?) and his imagination is insurrectionary in face of them. Stephens' vision is democratic, and he tells us that he is "prepared to believe that everything whatever, including black beetles, is the noblest work of nature,"[43] though the democracy of his vision, as this echo of Blake suggests, has a hint of the mystical. (It is also an optimistic vision and for this reason his decision to retell Fenian tales, which lack the gathering pessimism of the Red Branch Cycle, was a felicitous one.) In the noble Fionn mac Uail,[44] Stephens is no more interested than in any other character, and his heroic identity is like others in these tales variously embodied through bizarre metamorphoses.

"The Story of Tuan mac Cairill," the oldest original of which is preserved in the *Book of the Dun Cow,* is almost as close as we can get to an Irish creation myth and swiftly charts the successive invasions of the island. The last transforming invasion recorded in the story is that of Christianity; the Abbot of Moville in Donegal is the somewhat comic converter of Tuan, a druid who is, for Stephens' purposes, Ireland's last pagan and first storyteller and custodian of the legendary past.[45] The Abbot Finnian reappears in the last story, "Mongan's Frenzy" (which Stephens would have adapted from Meyer's translation of the *Book of Fermoy,* a fifteenth-century manuscript), giving *Irish Fairy Tales* as framework the pagan-Christian succession. Finnian, we might say, plays Patrick to Tuan's Ossian. Tuan tells Finnian the story of Ireland's invasions, thereby transferring custody of Ireland's pagan lore to the Abbot who, writing the story down and filling up his manuscript boxes, represents the medieval Christian scribes who felt that "it would be a pity if the people who came after us should be ignorant of what happened long ago, and of the deeds of their fathers" (p. 259). The Fenian tales that follow "The Story of Tuan mac Cairill," although told by Stephens, are credited in their original form to Oisin (p. 132) who rather than Stephens might be the "I" who comments on "The Little Brawl at Allen" (pp. 171–72). "Mongan's Frenzy" brings the collection to a properly involuted conclusion. The story of Duv Laca of the White Hand is told by Mongan, a reincarnation of Fionn, but is contained within the story of Mongan told by one of his descendants, Cairidè, written down by the Abbot and the whole told to us by Stephens. The book ends with Cairidè having been told by Finnian that the one part of his story he dislikes is that in which Mongan makes game of a priest, and Cairidè is secretly gleeful (perhaps in revenge for the Christianization of Ireland) that the old stories have power to pain the priests.

The dynamics of storytelling fascinated Stephens, and storytelling, as it is in *Irish Fairy Tales,* is frequently a theme as well as narrative frame. Part Two of *In the Land of Youth* consists of Maeve's story of the Connacht sacking of the Shí (or sidhe) of Midir. Not only does the story illustrate the local or regional patriotism connected with Irish storytelling (the Connacht queen tells the story to humble the exiled Ulsterman Fergus and impress him with the wonderful happenings in the west), but it illustrates Stephens' notion of how long stories were actually told, with frequent interruptions and brief discussion until the momentum of the story is gathered and the listeners fall silent. This reflexive interest in the nature of storytelling is a feature of the Irish literary revival. It is this (in concert with a rejection, vigorous in Stephens, of both the romantic notion of art as self-expression and the overflowing of powerful emotion, and the realist notion of art as empiricism and representation) that enabled the best writers of the revival to function as modernist artificers as well as Irish revivalists.

The use of various narrators in a story and of in-tales denotes shifts in form analogous to those shifts of form frequently undergone by the characters of the old and revived stories. Tuan in Stephens' opening story is a witness to and a survivor of the earliest invasions. Like Ireland he had to change in order to survive, the changes in his case being zoomorphic: he recalls assuming successively the shapes and sensations of stag, hawk, boar, and salmon, the chief animals in the bestiary of Irish mythology and denizens of earth, sea, and sky. Throughout these metamorphoses he is himself and retains his human memory so that he can tell the Abbot centuries later of his adventures. But he is at the same time not himself—an entertaining dilemma in Stephens' world—and quite naturally slips into referring to himself in some previous zoomorphic guise as "he" as well as "I." As hero his identity remains through the vicissitudes of flight and concealment, but as quarry and eavesdropper, the first wood-kerne perhaps, his identity is splintered. He is in a sense Ireland herself: on the one hand the ancient and heroic nation, the Ireland of revival nationalists, keeping her purity of identity throughout the invasions and doomed always to remember ("I forget nothing of these things," says Tuan), on the other hand a comic, bright, and adaptive nation transmogrified by successive incursions, now fish, now fowl, her life "a ceaseless scurry and wound and escape" (p. 29).

How fitting that a modern literature whose theme and form was change should have arisen at a time when Ireland's identity was once more in a state of flux. We might in this regard consider as a masterpiece of the revival Joyce's *Ulysses* in which *la Comédie humaine* of Ireland is inspirited by change. However, the metamorphic aspect of *Ulysses* brought little in principle to Irish literature that was not already in Stephens and the old tales. Shape-changing as theme and form is an archaic feature of Celtic literature whose resuscitation the James Joyce of *Ulysses* and *Finnegans Wake* shared with the revivalists. It was in the beginning a Druid craft and necessity, which is to say a poetic craft and necessity. In its multitude of guises, flights, and masks, it is what defines the revival. Little wonder, then, that the versatile writers of the revival invade modernism, which is definable in terms of displacement, plurality, supererogation.

Tuan's transformations of self are analogous to those transformations of voice practiced here and elsewhere by a writer known variously as James Stephens, James Esse, Stephen James, Seumas James, Samuel James, and Shemus Beg.[46] Egotism, narcissism, massive self-revelation—these Stephens thought bad, and he was not quite sure that Yeats did not "too often hang around in his own poems, clank about in his own rhymes."[47] At the same time, he thought that there is a subtext which no author can keep out of his work, no matter how impersonal that work is, and which tells us a great deal about the author, but it should be the product of the kind of free and agile mind that Stephens thought Meredith and Hardy sorely lacked. The chief method of freeing the mind he explained like this: "The constant engagement of every artist is to dodge his own atmosphere: environment, which is everything to the historian and biographer, is poisoned air for an imaginative writer: imagination is in effect the escape from environment,"[48] an escape which he thought the Moore of *Esther Waters* and *Evelyn Innes* ("some other person's masterpieces") refused to accomplish, though an earlier Moore would in fact have agreed with Stephens' theory.[49] For a biographical explanation of Stephens' twin detestations of realism and self-revelation we might turn to his obscure and lowly origins in Dublin, an orphanhood (and perhaps illegitimacy) he wished to conceal; we might also turn to the anomaly of a poor Protestant upbringing in a Catholic city (something O'Casey, however, turned to a voluble account). Critically, we might explain the fictional expression of artifice and concealment in terms of a revival dedicated to self-trespass. Back of all is the Irish mind itself, which the revivalists at once inherited and affected.

There is, of course, a distinctive Stephens voice (later mimicked by Flann O'Brien), but in his ventriloquism Stephens comes closer to negative capability than to the egotistical sublime. For Stephens, genius resides in *Einfühlung,* in a changeling ability to enter one's characters, be they animal, vegetable, or mineral, and convincingly disperse one's presence among them. In *The Demi-Gods* Stephens can imagine not only the thoughts of a donkey but also the humanlike appearance items of food present to the donkey and the various noises they produce when eaten by him, an ingenious stroke of double anthropomorphism. The donkey in *The Demi-Gods* is one of my favorite examples of anthropomorphism in Stephens; others are the cats and sparrows on which the Philosopher discourses in *The Crock of Gold.* We might regard anthropomorphism as a vestigially mythopoeic device, and it is one that recurs in Irish literature and conversation.[50] It betokens a strain of wittily condescending anthropocentrism that runs through the Irish imagination. Even landscape can be imbued with human qualities, as in this passage from *The Crock of Gold:* "With every step along the curving road the landscape was changing. He saw and noted it almost in an ecstasy. A sharp hill jutted out into the road, it dissolved into a sloping meadow, rolled down into a valley and then climbed easily and peacefully into a hill again. On this side a clump of trees nodded together in the friendliest fashion. Yonder a solitary tree, well-grown and clean, was contented with its own bright company. A bush crouched tightly on the ground as though, at a word, it would scamper from its place and chase rabbits across the sward with shouts and laughter" (pp. 80–81). It is a short step from this to the invented, deliberately unconvincing landscapes of Flann O'Brien and Samuel Beckett that express at once the artifice of modernism and the Irish eschatological imagination.

The Charwoman's Daughter: *Realism or Romance?*

In *Irish Fairy Tales* we are entertained by various habitats and camouflages of the self, but none belongs to what we might choose to call the real world. By the time the book was written Stephens had decided he was uninterested in reproducing the real world, perhaps as a result of the mixed success of his first full-length fiction, *The Charwoman's Daughter* (1912) in which the real world is jostled by the hardier world of the fairy tale. That the author thought even gender a mere disguise and habitat of the self is evident from his remark about looking within himself before writing the book and there finding the character of the charwoman.[51] In this novel Stephens shares with his two title characters the self-trespassing power of imagination.

The elements of *Märchen* in *The Charwoman's Daughter* are many and obvious from the opening words ("Mary Makebelieve lived with her mother . . .") which mimic the fairy tale and introduce a heroine whose name resembles that of Snow White and Red Riding Hood. Stephens' maxims, clichés, and aphorisms function like formulas in folktales, and the risk the author runs in this regard we might easily think is amusingly alluded to in "Messrs Platitude and Gamble" (a firm of solicitors in the novel), were not the allusion a stroke of professional satire. There are also the frequent numerations, polarities, characters of functional anonymity (the policeman, the lodger), and metaphors and images drawn from the fund of the folktale (silk, gold, birds). Then there is a theme which is in part that of "Cinderella" for it has that fairy tale's Oedipal drama if not its problem of sibling rivalry. *The Charwoman's Daughter,* in short, is heavily indebted to the fairy tale, but to the international fairy tale, not the Irish fairy tale specifically. The probability is that Stephens had not yet read the native Irish material when he began to compose his first novel. He claimed he had not read the newer school, "Russell, Yeats, Colum, O Grady &c," when he began to write.[52]

Despite this debt to the fairy tale, Augustine Martin can still make the claim that *The Charwoman's Daughter* "is the first novel to deal with life in Dublin's slums."[53] The social realism that undergirds his fantasy and inventions, when he wishes it to, distinguishes Stephens from the nineteenth-century and revival writers who drew on folklore. *The Charwoman's Daughter,* for example, includes a portrait of a middle-class domestic interior as detailed as any description in Joyce or an English realist novel:

> There was a china shepherdess with a basket of flowers at one end of the mantlepiece and an exact duplicate on the other. In the centre a big clock of speckled marble was surmounted by a little domed edifice with Corinthian pillars in front, and this again was topped by the figure of an archer with a bent bow—there was nothing on top of this figure because there was not any room. Between each of these articles there stood little framed photographs of members of Mrs O'Connor's family, and behind all there was a carved looking-glass with bevelled edges having many shelves.

> Each shelf had a cup or a saucer or a china bowl on it. On the left-hand side of the fireplace there was a plaque whereon a young lady dressed in a sky-blue robe crossed by means of well-defined stepping-stones a thin but furious stream; the middle distance was embellished by a cow, and the horizon sustained two white lambs, a brown dog, a fountain, and a sun-dial. (pp. 41–42)

And so on. The dismalness is ironic, for the scene is meant to be viewed through the eyes of Mrs. Makebelieve, who chars in the house and who sees it from her lowlier social station as exotic and from her vantage point of superior pride as pretentious.

Apart from this episode, only the lives of the poor are seen at all clearly in the novel, and even they are misted up by the Makebelieves' habit of imagining. Stephens knows well the small domestic empire of the poor housewife, the daily trials of lodgers, shopping, housework, dressing, and children. One is reminded of a contemporary Ulster novelist, Forrest Reid, who was also a Protestant growing up in a city (though in far better circumstances than Stephens), in whose upbringing women too played an almost exclusive role, who early toyed like Stephens with realism—the passage I have quoted might easily have appeared in Reid's *Following Darkness,* also 1912, a novel which like *The Charwoman's Daughter* owes something to Edwardian realism—and abandoned it for fantasy, and who too adopted matrist values. But Reid had no interest in the young female characters that are Stephens' chief attraction, and into whose sexual psychology Stephens shows a great deal of insight.

Can reality and romance, realism and the fairy tale, coexist? Apparently, it would seem at first. The greenery of St. Stephen's Green and Phoenix Park where Mary seeks solace in the poverty of her adolescence is a kind of pastoral retreat where, in a wonderful passage, the very voices of children are tempered:

> In the great spaces the children's voices had a strangely remote quality; the sweet, high tones were not such as one heard in the streets or in houses. In a house or a street these voices thudded upon the air and beat sonorously back again from the walls, the houses, or the pavements; but out here the slender sounds sang to a higher tenuity and disappeared out and up and away into the tree-tops and the clouds and the wide, windy reaches. The little figures partook also of this diminuendo effect; against the great grassy curves they seemed smaller than they really were; the trees stirred hugely above them, the grass waved vast beneath them, and the sky ringed them in from immensity. Their forms scarcely disturbed

> the big outline of nature; their laughter only whispered against the silence, as ineffectual to disturb that gigantic serenity as a gnat's wing fluttered against a precipice. (p. 35)

Even in the city working people can be happy, transformed by sunlight in the way Mary and her mother transform their shabby lives by fulsome imagining. Yet the juxtaposition of fantasy and reality is disconcerting in *The Charwoman's Daughter,* even though that seems to be the novel's theme, and a theme that must result in one or both of two things. One, a fantasist's betrayal of realism in the sentimental notion that fantasy can overcome poverty, a betrayal aided and abetted by Stephens' poetic fluency in describing poverty (when a sense of painstaking adequacy is wanted) and which, like sentimentality, indicates insincerity. Or two, a realist's satire (here a gentle satire, more a smile of conspiracy) at the expense of Mary and her mother because of their foolish, however psychologically and socially understandable, imaginings. That Stephens seems to intend the second of these is suggested in the way Stephens subverts the form of the fairy tale and the theme of romance in the novel, something Stephens reversed in his fiction thereafter, when he came under the sway of the revival. Mary tells her mother of a dream she had of someone giving her a shilling, a dream she repeats the next night. "Her mother said if she had dreamt it for the third time some one would have given her a shilling surely." (p. 73)[54] But trebling is fulfilled only in the fairy tale, and Mary does not dream her dream a third night. There is a contest between modes which, soon into the novel, ironic realism seems to be winning. There is even a contest between genres. We call *The Charwoman's Daughter* a novel, but it is short enough and odd enough to be a tale, perhaps novella. The tension is there in the very first sentence, the fairy tale opening of which I have quoted and the realistic ending of which I now quote: ". . . in a small room at the very top of a big, dingy house in a Dublin back street."

Rather unexpectedly, fantasy and romance are in *The Charwoman's Daughter* expressions of egotism and self-indulgence. Mrs. Makebelieve weaves fantasies around her daughter that are not only protective but stifling, and her fairy tale descriptions of marriage cause Mary to fall for the first man she meets. The mother holds the growing daughter to herself: "If it had been possible she would have detained her daughter for ever in the physique of a child; feared the time when Mary would become too evidently a woman, when all kinds of equalities would come to hinder her spontaneous and active affection" (pp. 23–24). I am not sure how conscious Stephens was, in this novel or elsewhere, of the Electra complex as a theme to be explored. Stephens' attitude to his female characters is ambivalent in a way that is disturbing because it is at once over-and understated. Perhaps his love for and dependence on women masked some half-conscious resentment at their early power over him. At any rate, beneath the near sentimentality and gentle satire one senses a bitterer satire and a rougher compassion unexpressed. Less unconsciously, the outcome of the Electra conflict in his work is frequently generational inversion and surrogation where the female comes out on top: a sister becomes surrogate mother in *Deirdre,* a daughter becomes surrogate mother in *The Demi-Gods* and *The Charwoman's Daughter*. The conflict is the more vivid for taking place in a broken family (of which the mother is usually the survivor), a recurring initial situation in Stephens that may have biographical origins. Although Stephens, like several revivalists, supported female emancipation,[55] he tended to see the mere and familiar growth of a girl into a wife and mother as a growth into power, as it is in *The Charwoman's Daughter*. Mary (like her namesake in *The Demi-Gods,* and Deirdre) grows into an awareness that she can bend men to her will and into a wish to do so. Mary's expanding freedom from the possessiveness of her mother, who gets weaker in sickness as Mary gets stronger in imagined love, is an expanding freedom to exercise her own power; the egotism she inherits from her reluctant mother replaces bondage and submission. If indeed her growth into egotism is a kind of contrariness, Stephens might well have had in mind the nursery rhyme when he entitled the American edition of the novel *Mary, Mary*.

Romance in *The Charwoman's Daughter,* against the current of the literary revival, is the egotism and power of the other and it is very real in its effects. And so the policeman who seduces Mary takes over from her mother in feeding her the stuff of fairy tales, such as telling her about the phoenix after which he thinks (in error) the Dublin park is named, "a makebelieve bird, a kind of fairy tale" (p. 37). She falls for him and, raised on her mother's self-indulgent fantasies, seeks to absorb him into her own romantic dreams, delighting to think she could have power over such a large man. But she discovers him with another girl, a further step towards her maturity, while he discovers her charring for his aunt when her mother is ill, and thereafter treats her with the social superiority Stephens detested. Social superiority, like all superiorities, is its own kind of fantasy in Stephens, and the policeman's attempt to impose his upon Mary, when he decides after all he wants her, culminates in a long scene (chapter 30), which really belongs to some much longer, different novel, in which Mary, her mother, and her suitor engage in a strange contest of wills, a scene the more powerful for a muffled quality achieved by its having no direct speech. It is as if the policeman's social superiority pretends to a surrogate fatherhood, but he is expelled by the women from the Electra relationship because the female is stronger than the male, despite this sadistic daydream of the policeman's:

> He would gladly have beaten her into submission, for what right has a slip of a girl to withstand the advances of a man and a policeman? That is a crooked spirit demanding to be straightened with a truncheon: but as we cannot decently, or even peaceably, beat a girl until she is married to us, he had to relinquish that dear idea. He would have dismissed her from his mind with the contempt she deserved, but, alas! he could not: she clung there like a burr, not to be dislodged saving by possession or a beating—two shuddering alternatives—for she had become detestably dear to him. His senses and his self-esteem conspired to heave her to a pedestal where his eyes strained upwards in bewilderment—that she who was below him could be above him! This was astounding: she must be pulled from her eminence and stamped back to her native depths by his own indignant hoofs; thence she might be gloriously lifted again with a calm, benignant, masculine hand shedding pardons and favours, and perhaps a mollifying unguent for her bruises. Bruises! a knee, an elbow—they were nothing; little damages which to kiss was to make well again. Will not women cherish a bruise that it may be medicined by male kisses? Nature and precedent have both sworn to it. . . . But she was out of reach; his hand, high-flung as it might be, could not get to her. (pp. 100–101)

This should make us recall the early scene in which Mary, who feels "a terrible attraction about the idea of being hit by a man" (p. 18), asks her mother if a man ever struck her and her mother collapses in tears, which imply that someone, perhaps her husband, had. This is a bit of working-class realism, but Mary's masochistic fantasy is a counterpart of the policeman's contemplated sadism, and this painful complementarity is an aspect of the male-female relationship in Stephens. In spite of his popularity as a writer of fairy stories, Stephens had a near pornographic interest in bondage and sado-masochism; for a scene comparable to the above, we might think of that in *The Crock of Gold* in which the Thin Woman momentarily abases herself sexually before the Third Absolute. When the male in Stephens is merely masculine and egotistic, as is the policeman in *The Charwoman's Daughter,* the female can unexpectedly defeat him, just as the courage possessed by the lodger, who wins Mary and is beaten by the policeman, is finally and unexpectedly stronger than mere strength (and as Ireland is stronger than her English master). Mary who has escaped the thrall of her mother's fantasies is not likely to submit to the policeman's threadbare social and sexual fantasies.

Stephens intends Mary to grow out of her mother's tyrannizing fantasy and her own egotistic fantasy into real and self-transcending relationships. The public is to succeed the private life, the social the domestic. "The only subject in which a competent writer should engage," Stephens wrote in 1914, "is one showing the growth of a soul to some maturity," adding in distaste—as though in explanation of Mary's not actually getting married at the end of *The Charwoman's Daughter*—"the subject chosen by almost all novelists has been the progress of some male or female person towards matrimony. They have never heard of the Mount of Transfiguration; and if they had heard of it, they might not have understood what it meant. Their whole conception of life is physical."[56] Besides, matrimony of this kind is clearly a goal, whereas progress, Stephens maintained in "An Essay in Cubes," "is not towards a goal, but towards an experience." This does not satisfactorily happen in *The Charwoman's Daughter* because the problem and the solution really belong to conflicting kinds of fiction. Bettelheim might be right in claiming "socialization" of the hero or heroine as the goal of the fairy tale, but it is achieved in the fairy tale along consistent lines, in its case symbolic, whereas Mary's "socialization" is not consistently achieved. By the time the climactic scene in chapter 30 is reached, for example, Mrs. Makebelieve is an entirely incongruous figure. And while we can accept the policeman as filled with "self-love," it is harder to accept him as evil, as Stephens directs us to do. The clear distinction between good and evil belongs in the fairy tale, which in *The Charwoman's Daughter* Stephens seemingly parodies in his beginning but reinstates in his ending. The policeman is needed, not only as a catalyst in Mary's development but because "next to good the most valuable factor in life is evil" (p. 127), a Blakean epigram that the realism of the novel cannot justify. Psychologically the policeman is even rather pathetic.

The policeman is of course a recurring and hated figure in Stephens' fiction. He represents the detested law, but in his brittle arrogance he is like a modern version of the old hero of whom Stephens was so suspicious, a vestige from the heroic saga that makes, as we have seen in *Deirdre,* a strange bedfellow for the modern novel. In *The Charwoman's Daughter,* the policeman more realistically (if confusingly) is also a member of the Dublin Metropolitan Police, an agency of the alien British Empire which as a military and commercial entity must have seemed to

Stephens to be egotism writ large. The policeman's rival in love, the lodger, is on this plane an equally realistic figure, an Irish nationalist whose views could be, and possibly are meant to be, Pearse's:

> Of Ireland he sometimes spoke with a fervour of passion which would be outrageous if addressed to a woman. Surely he saw her as a woman, queenly and distressed and very proud. He was physically anguished for her, and the man who loved her was the very brother of his bones. There were some words the effect of which were almost hypnotic on him—The Isle of the Blest, The Little Dark Rose, The Poor Old Woman, and Caitlin the Daughter of Houlihan. The mere repetition of these phrases lifted him to an ecstasy; they had hidden, magical meanings which pricked deeply to his heartstrings and thrilled him to a tempest of pity and love. (p. 107)

The lodger too is a fantasist (a forerunner of MacNamara's Dempsey), and the fate of Ireland he weaves into a fairy tale or heroic romance:

> Of England he spoke with something like stupefaction: as a child cowering in a dark wood tells of the ogre who has slain his father and carried his mother away to a drear captivity in his castle of bones—so he spoke of England. He saw an Englishman stalking hideously forward with a princess tucked under each arm, while their brothers and their knights were netted in enchantment and slept heedless of the wrongs done to their ladies and of the defacement of their shields. . . . "Alas, alas and alas, for the once proud people of Banba!" (p. 107)

The lodger is ironically presented, the irony extending to the nationalist fanaticism of real life. Fairy tale romance as the butt of irony is a disguised form of realism. Yet even the lodger's beating by the policeman hardly brings him squarely to earth since after it he is extolled by Mary and her mother "until he glowed again in the full satisfaction of heroism" (p. 120)—another example of make-believe as well as of the somewhat masochistic Stephensian conjunction of heroism and victimization. The lodger's heroism is meant to be one of the "experiences" towards which the novel has moved, but it is a rather fairy tale experience. Moreover, the *deus ex machina,* the legacy from an American uncle, which Stephens lamely justifies by a defense of the unexpected in life, firmly returns the novel to the realm of the fairy tale in which transformation is independent of the rooted forces of environment. This sets the psychological insights at naught and betrays realism into the damp hands of sentimentality that corrupts modern fairy tales. Remembering Stephens' epigram, we might say that in *The Charwoman's Daughter* there is the wrong kind of minimum thought, though the novel at least gestures towards the symbolic intensity shared by the classic fairy tale and Blake's poetry and to which Stephens aspired. Perhaps Stephens envisioned a sequel (the endnote is from the old tales: "Thus far the story of Mary Makebelieve") in which reality could be less swervingly confronted, but it never came.

In any event, Mary does not achieve self-transcendence because the novel's polarities—man/woman, hunger/fullness, good/evil—are not properly reconciled. The golden mean is rejected as a reconciliation: "As to the golden mean—let us have nothing to do with that thing at all" (p. 126). We hear Blakean echoes in this of roads of excess, and states in their extremity becoming their opposites. The solution according to Stephens is not compromise but an apocalyptic synthesis, a golden age that might even arrive after the independence crisis: "the regeneration of Ireland and of Man?" (p. 126) A second and indisputable golden age is that which Mary Makebelieve has left behind, and the successive existence of two golden ages is, according to Stephens, also a Blakean idea. "He postulates two golden ages: one in the beginning when each of these states [Power, Intellect, Love, Spirit and Matter] was separate and untroubled by the others, and the second the golden age of brotherhood and reconciliation."[57] *The Charwoman's Daughter* attempts to lift Mary out of the first golden age and deposit her on the threshold of the second, leading directly into Stephens' next novel.

The Crock of Gold (1912) was written on the heels of the first novel and is a philosophic if not narrative sequel in which Stephens at its end claims an apocalyptic synthesizing of the true and ultimate Self splintered in the beginning along Blakean lines. "In this book," he said, "there is only one character—Man—Pan is his sensual nature, Caitilin, his emotional nature, the Philosopher his intellect at play, Angus Óg his intellect spiritualised, the policeman his conventions and logics, the leprecauns his elemental side, the children his innocence."[58] Not satisfied with this subdivision in the interests of ultimate unity, Stephens has oppositions proliferating throughout the book that would gladden the heart of the Proppian analyst or the more literal structuralist: knowledge/wisdom, fullness/hunger, head/heart, fatness/thinness, god/man, adulthood/childhood, wisdom/love, mind/matter, spirit/flesh, thought/emotion, righteousness/holiness, ice/fire, marriage/bachelorhood, motion/changelessness. Most of the characters, too, form opposing or complementary pairs. "Everything," as the narrator tells us, "has two names, and everything is twofold" (p. 120). The energy of opposition is a good, whereas "finality," we have already been told in *The Charwoman's Daughter,* "is the greatest evil which can happen in a world of movement" (p. 99), even though, ironically, Stephens insisted in a letter to his publisher that "the last sentences of [*The Charwoman's Daughter*] were calculated to produce an effect of finality."[59]

Stephens could not quite make up his mind about this, or perhaps he thought that self-contradiction would produce its own synthesis, thereby illustrating his fondest theory. The Philosopher in *The Crock of Gold* informs Meehawl MacMurrachu that "the merging of opposites is completion" (p. 53) and his wife that "finality is death" (p. 27), but then this is before the Philosopher is converted by Pan and then by Angus Óg, gods who reject the inexorable and logical progression the Philosopher has in mind. It is in some doubt, then, whether Stephens really wished to see come to pass one kind of completion mooted in *The Crock of Gold*—the final return of Heroic Ireland that the novel promises and envisages and that is in Stephens' fictional imagination closer, as a result of the book's concluding apocalypse, than in *The Charwoman's Daughter.* The doubt gathers on hindsight when we consider what Stephens actually did to Heroic Ireland in *Deirdre* when it presented itself to him in ancient guise.

The Blakean philosophy is one thing, the formal and thematic problems facing a fiction writer using it while working in the context of the Irish literary revival, are another. *The Charwoman's Daughter* was an erratically brilliant false start, a confused and unsynthesized book neither wholly fairy tale nor novel, realism nor fantasy. Stephens made a choice after writing it, and except for usually incongruous aspects of later works, he turned away from the penetrating urban realism some parts of his first novel exhibit. It was a crucial and possibly erroneous decision for Stephens, if not for Irish fiction. He no doubt believed that in making the choice he did he could still address all the varieties and oppositions of human experience. But unlike Joyce he did not earn the philosophical synthesis of reality and imagination through a hard apprenticeship in attention to the continuities of experience. Blake's influence was early, persistent and, I believe, in the long run calamitous, as it often produced reheated Blake and discouraged Stephens from doing other than handling oppositions cleverly and schematically. Unlike Yeats, Stephens found Blake (who without doubt was an important influence in the Irish literary revival) indigestible. The antirealistic, extremist thought of the revival, the admiration for Yeats, and the greater, less wise admiration for AE, all aided and abetted the influence of Blake and seduced Stephens in the direction of those alliterative forms, fantasy, fable, and fairy tale, when much of his work reveals an ironist and realist struggling to get out. When he left Ireland in 1925, the influence of Blake and AE was insufficient fodder for his imagination and when he should have been (like Joyce, a fellow exile) building on earlier work, he was effectively silent in fiction thereafter, though he lived for a further quarter century. Still, both *Irish Fairy Tales* and a novel we must look at presently, *The Crock of Gold,* are masterpieces in Stephens' chosen mode.

Language and Parody in Stephens

Perhaps the hardness of life in rural Ireland can be more readily transformed by a poetic imagination than the hardness of life in Irish slums. (Synge's seems a less real world than O'Casey's, even though his observations seem as careful.) For example, there is a good deal of reality in Stephens' picture of tinker life in *The Demi-Gods* (1914), yet it merges easily into fantastic mock-eschatology and into extensive parody of Yeats, AE, and their theosophizing (in which Stephens seems never to have been a wholehearted or earnest participant). Stephens is incapable of staying still: *The Demi-Gods,* which is a fine and amusing book, even includes a parody of English drawing-room fiction (chapter 33) in the scene set in an Irish Big House whose lives within are not recognizably Irish. There is far less reality in *The Crock of Gold* in which poverty is seen through the soliloquizing of an old woman lifted from the dramatic revival; perhaps she is Yeats's Cathleen ni Houlihan; certainly she is the Shan Van Vocht (Ireland personified as the Poor Old Woman): "Ah, God be with me! an old creature hobbling along the roads on a stick. I wish I was a young girl again, so I do, and himself courting me, and him saying that I was a real nice little girl surely" (pp. 89–90). There is also a parody of *The Playboy of the Western World:*

> "I wonder," said the first man, "what it was gave you the idea of marrying this man instead of myself or my comrade, for we are young, hardy men, and he is getting old, God help him!"
>
> "Aye, indeed," said the second man; "he's as grey as a badger, and there's no flesh on his bones."
>
> "You have a right to ask that," said she, "and I'll tell you why I didn't marry either of you. You are only a pair of tinkers going from one place to another, and not knowing anything at all of fine things; but himself was walking along the road looking for strange, high adventures,

> and it's a man like that a woman would be wishing to marry, if he was twice as old as he is. (p. 102).[60]

Stephens' parodies reveal the confidence of what we might call the second generation of Irish revivalists, to which Joyce belonged, and its impiety towards the first generation. The hazardous use of leprecauns in *The Crock of Gold* may be parodying the interest of Yeats and Lady Gregory in the perennial ones, as well as the puerility of nineteenth-century Irish writers who exploited corrupted folklore. Then there are the journeys of the Philosopher and the Thin Woman in search of Angus Óg, the Irish god of youth, love, and beauty whose kingdom, from which he has been exiled over the head of our egotism, is Tír-na-nÓg; the adventures they have recall the old Irish *echtrai,* while the vision that concludes the book, witnessed by Caitilin and Angus, recalls the *immrama* and *fisi*. The unleashing of the power of the gods, Pan, Angus Óg, and the shrunken divinities of the sidhe, is a plunge by Stephens into mythology, regulated by a Blakean scheme and the whole brought to an apocalyptic close that transcends parody and makes of *The Crock of Gold* ultimately a serious work, neither mere tragic pathos nore mere comedy.

Parody and impiety in Stephens deserve pause. Both are as old as Irish literature,[61] though they were in abeyance during the sober, manifesto years of the revival. They accompany a self-consciousness about language and literary tradition that encourages irony and humor, a self-consciousness (the precise opposite of self-expressiveness) that Joyce brought to its highest pitch in *Ulysses*. One critic has explained Joyce's linguistic virtuosity—his ambiguity, irony, paradox, parody, mimicry, and multiplicity of viewpoints—in terms of Joyce's innate scepticism, a Pyrrhonism that prevented him from cleaving to one mode of thought or expression or to one system of belief.[62] This is probably true, but there must be a larger explanation that fits equally Joyce's virtuoso contemporary, James Stephens, and his descendant, Flann O'Brien.

Is it possible that the linguistic virtuosity of the Irish is promoted by a sense of linguistic orphanhood? Stephen Dedalus in *A Portrait of the Artist as a Young Man* considers English to be a foreign tongue, but it is the language he must use because, he tells Davin, his ancestors threw off their own language and took another when they allowed a handful of foreigners to subject them. He refuses to pay in his own life and person the debts they incurred. Gaelic is a pawned racial heirloom neither Stephen nor Gabriel Conroy—who tells Miss Ivors that Irish is not his language—will redeem. If Irish writers other than Joyce feel, however obscurely, that

English is the borrowed furniture of expression—and the possibility places Joyce in the ranks of the revivalists who felt that Irish was the mother tongue carelessly disowned in the past by her sons—then perhaps they also felt, as Joyce seemed to feel, no filial obligation to the English language any more than to the Gaelic. This may have given them license to experiment, their orphanhood a freedom and adventure. We need not see in other Irish writers Stephen Dedalus' concern to fly by the net of inherited language, a concern that seemed to be Joyce's when he generated the "Joycespeak" of *Finnegans Wake,* a tongue that transcends national boundaries and racial heritages. We can rest content to see in such an Irish writer as James Stephens a good-humored quarrel with the English language, much like the quarrel Carleton's mother thought the Irish tune of "The Red-haired Man's Wife" had with its English words, more of a quarrel between spouses than between foes.

Yet we may want to go further and see an obscure and unarticulated desire for revenge in the Irish writers's overfamiliarity with English, a curious attempt by the colonized, using captured weaponry, to colonize the colonizer in return. The *need* for revenge became more apparent with the Gaelic revival which revealed the extent to which Gaelic had been lost and which recalled Irish people—unsuccessfully as it proved, but seductively enough to be heard in sympathy by George Moore (for a time), Yeats, Stephens, Synge, and others—to a living awareness of the ancestral speech. The renewed *possibilities* for revenge became apparent with the literary revival when attention was drawn to the uniqueness and inventiveness of authentic Irish-English. However, there was a price: the perennial temptation away from self-awareness into impersonation, since for few of the revivalists was Irish-English, let alone Gaelic, the mother tongue.

The Road to Apocalypse: **The Crock of Gold**

The familiar is parodied and exploited in many of the characters in *The Crock of Gold.* Caitilin Ni Murrachu, the heroine, is the familiar sequestered daughter of Stephens' own fiction, of the fairy tale, and of the early Irish tale (she resembles Deirdre), whose growth into sexuality is the spine of the story. Once again, as in *The Charwoman's Daughter,* the daughter of a broken home searches for wholeness and ends by making the transition from a family to a marital relationship. The Philosopher is a composite of familiar figures in Irish culture. In the scheme of the novel he represents "the petrifactions of intellect".[63] He expresses a superficial self in the most literal way, by opening his mouth and uttering thoughts of a dry brain in a dry season, just as Pan expresses in the novel a sensual self in the most shameless way, through his body. Beyond this we might hear in the Philosopher an echo of those pedantic Irish storytellers so beloved of unlettered listeners for a "hard Irish" *(crua-Ghaoluinn)* that was barely comprehensible. We might also be reminded of the scholars and priesteens Carleton parodies, for example in "Denis O'Shaughnessy Going to Maynooth," whose pedantry is in inverse ratio to the knowledge of his listeners, and of whom Stephens could easily have been thinking when he characterized talk that isn't on the wing: " 'tis on the ground, it has become pedestrian, the nightingale is dead, and instead of the Bird of Arcady, the good old clumping donkey is braying great sesquipedalian hehaws."[64]

Ireland, of course, has a standing army of such bores as the Philosopher and in Stephens the bore often, as he does in *The Crock of Gold,* and as he was to do in Flann O'Brien, assumes the guise of that most experienced of interdisciplinary students, the policeman. In *The Crock of Gold,* in one comic scene, the Philosopher and Shawn, one of the arresting policemen, engage in flyting (what old jazzmen would have called a "cutting contest") which the Philosopher wins hands down. The Philosopher talks in unstoppable floods of prose and although he answers Stephens' demand that a good talker be not "consecutive" but be rather various,[65] he is surely meant to represent the bad talker. The Philosopher's speech is a series of set pieces—there is a splendidly comic one on the subject of water in Book I, chapter 3—and this is an Irish characteristic (decorating the folktales and sagas but hindering, in literature and life, genuine thinking and self-realization) that Stephens the fictional narrator, critic, and broadcaster shares.

The Philosopher is no mere comic figure. His ultimately purgatorial progress is analogous to that of Caitilin, of Mary Makebelieve, and even of Gabriel Conroy whom we might see as dimly figuring the pedant of Irish fiction. In each case the repressed and true self must be first expressed and then transcended. Like Caitilin, who is seduced by the goat god, the Philosopher is converted to pantheism, not by argument but by seeing the beautiful girl naked among goats. Immediately he feels hungry, and hunger, actual and figurative, is a staple of Pan's philosophy. "Every person who is hungry is a good person," he claims, "and every person who is not hungry is a bad person. It is better to be hungry than rich." (p. 67) This is a tenet put forward in *The Charwoman's Daughter* in which hunger "is life, ambition, good will and understanding" (p. 126), and in *The Demi-Gods* in which hunger is said to override the rights of property (p. 267). The recurrence of the idea suggests that Stephens regarded himself, in a special sense, as a pantheist.

Because Pan is against self-repression and self-sacrifice, he helps the Philosopher as well as Caitilin to reach stage two in their progress towards the self-transcendence he cannot, however, deliver as can Angus Óg (Angus the Young). The Philosopher rediscovers his body as he knew it in the childhood that Angus also promotes and that is a recurring ideal in Irish literature. Pan is the sensual side of man that must make its appearance in puberty; the Philosopher rediscovers sexual desire (he soon after flirts with a married woman), and deprives his mind of its hegemony. However, he is now merely sensually complete, and his encounters with three kinds of women—the flirtatious woman, the poor woman (the Shan Van Vocht), and the possessive woman (closely resembling Eileen ni Cooley in *The Demi-Gods*)—are only stages in a journey.[66]

In Pan's cave, the two gods contend for Caitilin's fidelity. Both claim to be Joy and Love, and both command the goddess of the earth (Pan commands Demeter, Angus Dana), but Pan cannot rise like Angus above the promiscuous earth into the air of imagination. Although he disports himself in sunshine and brings sunlight to the dark wood (Coilla Doraca) in which the Philosopher and his wife the Thin Woman live, Pan lives in a cave, unlike Angus who lives atop a mountain. Pan is essential and represents an advance, but he has his crucial limitation: he does not know the end of wisdom. Angus, who has the secret to wholeness, does: it is the divinity of imagination. Angus is the more youthful of the two, having, unlike the busy and promiscuous Pan, slept without ageing for centuries. Pan has permitted Caitilin's accession to the Tree of Knowledge, but around it is a wall barring her from the Tree of Life. She instinctively wishes to scale the wall but cannot because her instinct has been schooled in "the science of unbelief" (p. 108). Angus believes with the Yeats of *The Celtic Twilight* (and with Pearse and AE) that they shall be among the divine who have kept their natures "simple and passionate"[67] (credulous like children of poetic things) and who have not wearied themselves "with 'yes' and 'no,' or entangled their feet with the sorry net of 'maybe' and 'perhaps.'"[68]

Moreover, Pan is a seducer who does not act or feel out of real need—he is a self-sufficient egotist. Caitilin leaves Pan for Angus because the Irish god needs her and Pan does not; for just that reason Mary Makebelieve rejected the egotistic policeman (a kind of Pan) in favour of the young lodger (a kind of Angus, youthful, more native than the policeman because he does not work for the enemy and is a nationalist) whose love is need rather than demand. (We might think here of Gabriel Conroy, filled with egotistic lust outside the Gresham Hotel. Gretta "leaves" him in the hotel bedroom for the memory of Michael Furey, an Angus Óg who needed her. Joyce, however, awards ultimate victory to a repentant Pan, a Gabriel who learns compassion and need.) Stephens' recipe for feminine happiness might, despite his support of female emancipation, jar today, but it is in line with the revival precept of self-repudiation. In *The Charwoman's Daughter* Mary comes to believe that "the quest of a woman was to find the man who most needed her aid, and having found, to cleave to him for ever" (p. 85), and it seems as though the narrator shares her belief. A similar ambiguity of perspective is shared by a scene in *The Crock of Gold* in which Caitilin gazes upon Pan's wonderful, sad, grotesque face and the narrator comments that "no woman can resist sadness or weakness, and ugliness she dare not resist. Her nature leaps to be the comforter. It is her reason. It exalts her to an ecstasy wherein nothing but the sacrifice of herself has any proportion. Men are not fathers by instinct but by chance, but women are mothers beyond thought, beyond instinct which is the father of thought. Motherliness, pity, self-sacrifice—these are the charges of her primal cell, and not even the discovery that men are comedians, liars, and egotists will wean her from this" (p. 43).

The Thin Woman later acknowledges these feminine attributes, but teaches her daughter Brigid how to circumvent men (as she teaches her son Seumas how to circumvent women):

> Women . . . should love all other women as themselves, and they should hate all men but one man only, and him they should seek to turn into a woman, because women, by the order of their beings, must be either tyrants or slaves, and it is better that they should be tyrants than slaves. She explained that between men and women there exists a state of unremitting warfare, and that the endeavour of each sex is to bring the other to subjection; but that women are possessed by a demon called Pity which severely handicaps their battle and perpetually gives victory to the male, who is thus constantly rescued on the very ridges of defeat. (p. 203)

These opinions, which may not be exceptionable to as many people today as they were meant to be in Stephens', are delivered before the Thin Woman is redeemed in the presence of Angus Óg, and Stephens does not condone the war of the sexes, though his fiction would be thin fare without it. To the maleness of egotism and self-sufficiency Stephens prefers the femaleness of creative insufficiency and need, which was his preference for the daily capricious over the brittlely heroic, the wonder tale over the hero tale, the underground passages of imagination over the ramparts of reason, pity over strength.

Still, the chief quest in Stephens' fiction is in search of true marriage, the "matrimony of minds" (*The Crock of Gold,* p. 120), for most of the poles in Stephens' various polarities have a gender which must be risen above in the unity of opposites. Thus there is point to the frequent transsexuality, often comic, in Stephens' novels: a mortal having a guardian angel of a different sex, and Cuchulain in female attire, both in *The Demi-Gods,* Maeve calling herself a man and telling a love story in a manly fashion in *In the Land of Youth.* Transsexuality is a blow against the egotistic security of the self. It is to be remembered that Stephens has a symbolic scheme in mind in which his heroines represent Blake's Pity. Yet Stephens intends his heroes and male figures to accept psychologically—as did Joyce beneath his own comic and symbolic transsexuality in *Ulysses*—the womanly part of themselves, as Gabriel Conroy accepts Gretta and his own previously hypocritical and unexercised capacity for pity.

The place where all opposites unite and all sexualities are joined and crossed is the home from which Angus Óg is exiled because the Irish have forgotten him—Tír-na-nÓg, which is charted for us in *In the Land of Youth* and *The Crock of Gold* and appears as Mary's visionary green island (p. 84) and the lodger's Isle of the Blest (p. 107) in *The Charwoman's Daughter.* The idea that sexuality and the divisive pains associated with it can be overcome in vivid memories of childhood ("nothing is worth remembering but our childhood," says the Philosopher, p. 138), memories mythicized by the culture into Tír-na-nÓg, and promoting a reversion to presexuality, is a recurring one in Irish literature. Nor is Stephens wholly satiric in his employment of it. Pan fails to secure the Philosopher's and Caitilin's commitment to the present because Angus (whose unadmitted commitment, like revival Ireland's, is to the past and the future), and not Pan, is the native god. The past and the future are the dimensions in which the Irish tend to live, which might explain a lack of enthusiasm for realism in art and explain (or be explained by) there having been no important middle class dedicated to the present with all its immediate fulfillments. Of Pan, the Philosopher informs Meehawl that "there is no record of his ever having journeyed to Ireland, and, certainly within historic times, he has not set foot on these shores" (p. 51). Stephens' playful disturbance of history records yet another invasion of Ireland to add to the impressive list Tuan tallies up for St. Finnian, but he may also be suggesting that Ireland needs at least an inoculation of pantheism and sensuality if Angus Óg is to be appreciated, and Pan finally guarded against.

If the three writers of the period in whose fiction Pan is a character—Stephens, Forrest Reid, and Lord Dunsany—were Protestants, that might signify a willingness on the part of Protestants, especially on the part of Protestants such as Reid and Dunsany who were not really revival writers, to countenance Greek ideals generally if not hedonism in particular. In any event, Stephens slaps gently Irish nationalism when he has Caitilin's father Meehawl prefer his daughter to be abducted by a native rather than a foreign god on the grounds that "the devil you know is better than the devil you don't know" (p. 53). But the satire like the comedy is skin deep, for *The Crock of Gold* is an ultimately serious work on the need for the rehabilitation of the old native gods and an expulsion of the foreign idols the Irish worship. When Angus saves Caitilin from Pan, it is Ireland being saved from foreign domination. Caitilin is Cathleen ni Houlihan, the girlish counterpart of the Shan Van Vocht, and she ends the novel in a fairy tale manner, as a queen with the walk of a girl, the Shan Van Vocht redeemed into beauty as she is in Yeats's play. Pan is England, with her immoral and promiscuous ways, by whom the beauty and mind of Ireland have been temporarily beguiled.

It is hard to know how revolutionary in a political sense Stephens means to be; I suspect to an even lesser degree than the early Yeats. Interestingly enough, he uses the Irish revolutionary motif of the "eve of rebellion" (a motif we find, for example, in the song "The Rising of the Moon") when he has the Philosopher being given coded messages by Angus for the three men he is to meet on his return to Coilla Doraca—Mac Cúl and his children (that is, Finn MacCool and the Fianna), MacCulain (Cuchulain) and MacCushin (Oisin); his message to Cuchulain is that "The Grey of Macha had neighed in his sleep and the sword of Laeg clashed on the floor as he turned in his slumber" (p. 134). Heroic Ireland has slumbered in the "Caves of Sleepers"—caves not unlike Yeats's "Spiritus Mundi" or Plato's "Cave of Essences"—until such time as Ireland needs it and is worthy of it. Its hour come round at last, Stephens envisages the scope of the apocalypse required to announce Heroic Ireland's incarnation. But Stephens' Heroic Ireland is not O'Grady's or Yeats's or Pearse's: its chief qualities are kindness, equality, and happiness. When he witnessed the abortive rising at Easter 1916, four years after *The Crock of Gold* appeared, Stephens believed he was witnessing the end of the beginning for Ireland, an inspiration; but in contemplating the future at the end of *The Insurrection in Dublin* (1916) Stephens wrote of the need not of new Cuchulains or Irish aggrandizement but of local politics and Irish self-counsel.

Before the apocalypse, to be worthy of it and even in a sense to enable it, the Philosopher must be purged of his inadequacies. He is arrested by four policemen on suspicion of murdering the other Philosopher and his wife, the Grey Woman; he is rescued by the leprecauns; and then he gives himself up, claiming—with a philosophy that would have enlisted no favor with the militant nationalists outside the covers of Stephens' book—that "a man should always obey the law with his body and always disobey it with his mind" (p. 173). While his body languishes in the barracks, he hears two stories from unseen inmates of neighboring cells. The first is a darkened and romanceless version of Mrs. Makebelieve's experience, a story about a man suffering drudgery, illness, injustice, and enforced exile. The story is Irish insofar as these are the wrongs associated with colonialism, but it is also existential and resembles *Bartleby the Scrivener*. In the second story the teller is himself mostly to blame, his vanity, folly, and desire having driven him into a life of theft.

Together, these stories, which function as in-tales in Stephens' novel, are detonations set off by Stephens below the social system, as though Blake had been prosified by Dostoevsky. The subject of the first story would seem to be the missing husband of the wife in Book V, chapter 14 who cannot control her animal-loving son (possibly a fanciful portrait of Stephens as a boy), and so the in-tale is neatly folded into the larger narrative. When the subject of the first story imagines himself in hell, we are reminded that Stephens intends his jail scene to be a vision of hell (where the convicted are the damned) and of purgatory (where the Philosopher awaits conviction), yet another revival equivalent of the medieval Irish *fis*. But the Philosopher is saved by the Thin Woman's embassy to Angus Óg on his behalf. The people's amnesty that follows Angus Óg's intervention and renewed apotheosis might call to the reader's mind the storming of the Bastille. But Stephens chooses an Irish folk motif, the hosting of the sidhe, as the setting for his apocalypse, and those whose shackles have bound the inmates are of the professional and middle classes, not of the aristocracy, thereby placing the ending of the book firmly within the context of the Irish revival.

Kilmasheogue, the hill of the fairies, where the last scene takes place, is the Hill of Vision celebrated in Stephens' volume of poetry of that title published the same year as *The Crock of Gold*.[69] Four years later, when the apocalypse came to Dublin at Easter, it was no hosting of the sidhe, but a brutal farce that turned into tragedy. Stephens kept a journal of his observations during that fateful week, a brilliant work full of incongruity, rumor, silence, query—the very opposite of chronicle or war commentary, let alone epic. And the fitful advance of the writing in *The Insurrection in Dublin* suits perfectly its master theme: the absence of revelation. "Prose," said Stephens in a broadcast, "is piecemeal and informative, it is not revelatory."[70] But he nevertheless struggles hard to disprove his own maxim at the close of *The Crock of Gold.*

The ultimate vision of the novel belongs to Caitilin. It is Caitilin who is most aware of the changes she has undergone:

> Never again could the gratification of a desire give her pleasure, for her sense of oneness was destroyed—she was not an individual only; she was also part of a mighty organism ordained, through whatever stress, to achieve its oneness, and this great being was threefold, comprising in its mighty units God and Man and Nature—the immortal trinity. The duty of life is the sacrifice of self: it is to renounce the little ego that the mighty ego may be freed; and, knowing this, she found at last that she knew Happiness, that divine discontent which cannot rest nor be at ease until its bourne is attained and the knowledge of a man is added to the gaiety of a child. Angus had told her that beyond this there lay the great ecstasy which is Love and God and the beginning and the end of all things; for everything must come from the Liberty into the Bondage, that it may return again to the Liberty comprehending all things and fitted for that fiery enjoyment. (p. 221)

On one level Caitilin has grown into marriage and a readiness for motherhood. On a higher level gender itself must be overlooked in the achievement of collective freedom. "Growth is not by years but by multitudes," we are told (p. 221): "Through the many minds [of the hosting sidhe] there went also one mind, correcting, commanding, so that in a moment the interchangeable and fluid became locked, and organic with a simultaneous understanding, a collective action—which was freedom" (p. 226). Here is reflected Stephens' interest in AE's cooperative scheme and his sympathies with the working classes, a socialism that encouraged him to speak in *The Demi-Gods* of "the solidarity of man" that must be forged before "the great Ethic of Possession" can be escaped (p. 53). Yet Stephens' was an odd socialism, and it is not surprising to learn that Stephens broke with James Connolly after years of agreement. Secular socialism was clearly inadequate to Stephens' philosophical needs; in *The Demi-Gods* he has Patsy MacCann, like no good socialist, learn to scorn worldly possessions entirely. In *The Crock of Gold* socialism is a female mode of thinking called "Illusion" in Tír-na-nÓg; it must be mated with male philosophy ("Delusion" in Tír-na-nÓg) before it can bear fruit. Later, in *Irish Fairy Tales,* it is his peculiar brand of socialism that requires Stephens to insist that one of his heroines, Becuma, share her evil with everyone, since "to insist on other people sharing in our personal torment is the first step towards insisting that they shall share in our joy, as we shall insist when we get it" (p. 244), a conclusion surprisingly drawn from the less exceptionable view that the sense of separateness is a "vanity" and "the bed of all wrong-doing."

Clearly Stephens' socialism was a fairly spiritual affair, though he adopted AE's homely notion of one's own crowd (enemies as well as friends), a notion that might have been in his mind when he created the inflamed multitude at the close of *The Crock of Gold.* The notion is borrowed again in a later talk: "There is a sense, of course, in which one should not be either a person or a self; one should be one's own crowd perhaps, and nothing else, and neither think nor imagine outside the fears and hopes that belong to our order."[71] That order in Stephens' case was rich and various, and it was an expression in many ways of the Irish literary revival. Caitilin's is not a homely vision, however. Watching the hosting sidhe, the revival of heroic, fairy, and mythic Ireland happening within sight of Dublin (the Town of the Ford of Hurdles), Caitilin glimpses a truth expressed elsewhere by a writer other than AE, though the man who combined mysticism and marketing, farms and fantasy, could as easily have expressed it. "Thus the Mythologies of the world," wrote James H. Cousins, "are but the personalities of the indestructible Ego [Stephens' "mighty ego"] which, passing from each to each, is enriched by the individual, tribal, or race-consciousness of its personalities, and will one day gather itself and them into one simple conscious expression of the Divine Word."[72]

Caitilin's journey with Angus to Kilmasheogue has been only the first of two journeys, and on the second journey they will be led by Caitilin's son, the Scaler of the Wall, unborn at novel's end. The first journey ends in a vision of Ireland's spiritual emancipation. Wholeness and right marriage are in *The Crock of Gold* metaphors for Irish unity, and unity for Stephens is freedom. (Freedom in unity, in a more remarkable equation common to Stephens and the revival, is imagination itself, an idea which provides the aesthetic underpinning of the movement's cultural nationalism.) The second journey will end in a vision of the whole world's spiritual emancipation. Ireland freed will unchain by example, possibly by influence or even ascendancy, a waiting and captive world. Stephens reviewed the book from which I have taken Cousins' words, *The Wisdom of the West,* in April 1912, the same month in which he wrote his agent that he had almost completed the manuscript of a new novel. The new novel appeared in October as *The Crock of Gold.*

The Kingdom of Fantasy 13

The Writer as Fabulist II—George Moore, Padraic Colum, Darrell Figgis, Eimar O'Duffy, Lord Dunsany

George Moore's A Story-Teller's Holiday

In the Spring of 1917, Stephens found himself in the slightly awkward position of reading for purposes of stylistic emendation parts of the manuscript of George Moore's imminent new book, *A Story-Teller's Holiday* (1918). He was asked to "heighten the colour" of the portions of the script written in Hiberno-English, to "sprinkle the idiom over the story"[1]—an odd request from a writer who believed that the language of *The Untilled Field* gave Synge his start. Stephens was helpful but demurred when the word "collaboration" was mentioned. There is, however, some overlap between Moore's book and *Irish Fairy Tales*. At moments, Moore's shanachie, Alec Trusselby, quickens into the racy language and fantastic incident of Stephens and his predecessor Synge, into, in other words, the rhythms of the ancient Irish comic tradition, of which these Anglo-Irish writers were heirs and imitators. And Moore prides himself on his mimicry (the book includes a parody of Pater), an ability he may well have admired in the many-voiced Stephens. In turn, Stephens as he approached the task of *Irish Fairy Tales* was perhaps stimulated as much by Moore's Irish stories as by the theory and practice of storytelling in which Moore's book engages and in which Stephens had already proven his own deep interest.

Among the eleven stories recounted during *A Story-Teller's Holiday* are four told by Trusselby, who learned them from his grandfather who in turn learned them from his father "or from the old writings in the National Libraries in Dublin."[2] The National Library, with the help of Richard Best and John Eglinton, is where Moore got the gist of these stories, even though he represents himself as one learning in the field the virtuous patience of "the folk-lorist." For example, the story of the doomed poet-lovers, Liadin and Curithir, Moore got from Kuno Meyer's *Selections from Ancient Irish Poetry* (1911).[3] The other three tales come under the heading, borrowing the title of one of Hyde's collections, of local legends of saints and sinners. The stories of Marban and Scothine push the clerical virtue of resisting temptation to its logical and comic conclusion and are told with relish, explicitness, and an almost malicious glee. In referring to them, Moore mentioned Rabelais, while one critic has talked of an Irish Boccaccio.[4] The story of Moling is startling. The elderly hermit comes down from the crags to confess the nuns of Cuthmore; in order to appease one young nun who demands a sign from Jesus, her bridegroom-to-be in heaven, Moling impersonates the savior on His cross, comes down to embrace the young nun, Ligach, and gets carried away. Ligach conceives, miraculously she thinks, and gives birth to God's grandson. Under pretext of solving the theological problem posed by having extended the trinity to a quaternity, Moling returns to the wilderness. The heresy is stifled when years later three old hermits arrive—in comic parody of the Epiphany—to tell the real story Moling has confided to them. They disappear, young Martin, God's "grandson," goes in search of them to disprove a story that casts aspersions on his mother, returns to find her dead, and goes off to Germany where he founds a religion that is itself, Trusselby thinks, "no better than a whore."

In *A Story-Teller's Holiday,* then, Moore shows a revivalist's concern for traditional stories and the revivalist's desire, not entirely respectful in his case, to turn the old stories to modern fictional account. (He had broached this desire in *The Untilled Field,* which included "The Wedding Gown," a story that resembles a folktale.) Moore meditates on the impersonality of the folk story and on the difference between "eye stories" and "ear stories." Moore's holiday in Ireland, whose beginning and end frame the narrative, turns out to be a busman's holiday: instead of finding respite from storytelling, Moore (by his own contrivance and volition, of course) imagines a deeper immersion in the principles and practice of a craft venerable in the ancient Ireland the revivalists wished to resuscitate. And so the opening journey from Euston Station to Mayo reenacts the return to Ireland remembered in *Hail and Farewell.* Standing by the ruins of Dublin in the aftermath of the Easter Rising, Moore, in a reversion to his Parisian self, seeks their picturesqueness and in the moonlight thinks of Pater; but in Mayo he tells Trusselby that his story of the nuns of Cuthmore has revived his own interest in "the Celtic Renaissance" and decides (though surely with some malice) to tell it to dear Edward on his return to Dublin.

But of course it is a parody of *Hail and Farewell,* itself a wittily satiric reminiscence. As if on the principle of once bitten, twice shy, Moore invents more decisively here than the facts permitted him to do in *Hail and Farewell* the traditional Ireland he pretends beguiles him. Trusselby is an entirely fictitious character, just as on the train from Euston to Holyhead, Moore is both himself and the passenger who tells a story from Moore's own past.[5] In an impressive feat of literary impersonation, Moore is both the sophisticated, professional fictionist on holiday and the shanachie against whom he competes in an informal storytelling contest, "Ballinrobe cock against the Westport rooster." The eleven stories range from slight, autobiographical anecdotes through amplified and reshaped legends to a virtual novella concerning Albert Nobbs, the lonely lifelong transvestite, that Moore thought one of his best things and that might have sprung from the pen of one of the Edwardian realists, or, indeed, from that of the author of *Esther Waters.* After he tells it, he makes Trusselby admit: "I'm bet, crowed down by the Ballinrobe cock."[6] Moore's treatment of Trusselby's legends is novelistic, and he interrupts the shanachie with the realist demands of vivid characterization, to which Trusselby (Moore is thinking no doubt of his English readers of modern fiction) complies.

Above all, Trusselby's "folk" stories do not come under the heading of "Any Other Business," but are carefully prepared items in Moore's literary agenda. They concern temptations of the flesh, especially of forbidden sex, woman being "the temptation of the temptations" (Moore claimed to have introduced adultery into the English novel). *A Story-Teller's Holiday* is something of a counterblast to the "Christian" folk stories of Hyde's *Legends of Saints and Sinners,* which rather cleans up the old stories by omission.[7] Sexuality is forbidden by convention and decree, habit and prejudice that separate Liadin and Curithir as surely as they do Gogarty and Nora Glynn ("a lake come to divide us!" exclaims Liadin when they awake to a watery mist after a night of lovemaking). The battle between authority and desire, which is one of Moore's master themes, is that between the false and realized self. Moore has the realist's relish for the world of appearances, but the realist's deeper interest in the reality that lies beneath appearance, one form of which is the hidden, sensual self unacknowledged or tardily acknowledged by Gogarty, Marban, Scothine, Moling, and the nuns of Cuthmore. The most visible Irish symbols of psychological repression are priests and nuns, and Moore plays a joke on his invented shanachie by having the good Catholic tell stories against the clergy. But Trusselby does so only because the priests and nuns of his stories belong to the twelfth century and are as exotic to him as druids and druidesses. Moore's clerics deny the claims of the flesh, and are reprehensible for that, but in doing so with such perilous intimacy they exhibit the fearlessness and earthiness of Irish Catholicism, as Moore sees it, before it imported a Continental puritanism. *A Story-Teller's Holiday* is *in toto* what "The Wild Goose" and *The Lake* are in part, a lament for Ireland between the seventh and twelfth centuries—sensual and aesthetic at once, alive to the beauties of woman and of art, those "halcyon days," as Moore calls them, echoing his earlier creation, Father Gogarty. Those days are gone and are incapable of being revived in an Ireland in the grip of a Catholic Church whose forseeable invincibility the Anglo-Irish revivalists dared not admit.

Of Moore's characters in this book, it is women who are most responsive to their real and sensual selves. Ultimately, though, it is not a question of gender. Anthony Farrow has pointed out that Liadin "is at base 'Protestant' in the sense in which Moore uses that word, relying rather on personal integrity than on external discipline as a test for her action."[8] (Certainly Liadin joins the ranks of Moore's independent women.) And trouble for Moling begins when Ligach, like a Protestant, can pray only to Jesus and not to His mother. As we have noted, Moore's belief in the sovereignty of the self (his own psychological brand of Protestantism), like his public embracement of the Reformed church, disqualified him from full participation in the Irish revival. *A Story-Teller's Holiday* ends with a valediction to Ireland, as did *Hail and Farewell,* and without the author visiting Moore Hall, embodiment of an Ascendancy Ireland destined to pass away like the halcyon Ireland of the twelfth century. Its closing assertion of the Protestantism of Moore's family and of modern Irish literature and thought seems needlessly petulant. Yet it is prophetic. Seven years later Yeats made much the same claim, and made it sound almost as petulant, in the changed circumstances of an Irish Free State Senate introducing yet another Catholic law into newly-independent Ireland.

Tales within Tales: Colum's **The King of Ireland's Son**

> All the way to Tir na n'Og are many roads that run,
> But the darkest road is trodden by the King of Ireland's Son.
>
> —Nora Hopper

There is a connection, then, between the extent to which Moore in *A Story-Teller's Holiday* appropriates by impersonation traditional matter and the extent to which the book is a feinting blow against the revival. It is a highly literary performance, whose ancestor, like that of *The Untilled Field,* is Turgenev's *A Sportsman's Sketches* (the Russian writer is the subject of the book's last story), but also Lover's *Legends and Stories of Ireland* (1831). Lover's narrator is on a trip through the west of Ireland and is told stories by peasants, each tale framed by the narrator's exposition and encounter with the storyteller. Against the advice of Stephens, Moore retained the device of Trussleby speckling the story with "your honour" (Trusselby is in turn a "peasant" uninteresting outside of his storytelling), and this is a reminder that Moore never forgot his Ascendancy and landlord beginnings and that as well as being a nineteenth-century naturalist and aesthete he was also a nineteenth-century Anglo-Irish writer, heir of Lover as well as of Zola and Pater.

But it is Moore's realism that poses a problem for Yeats's suggestion in a letter in 1905 to Florence Farr that the writers of Ireland who come from the mass of the people "have more reason than fantasy. It is the other way with those who come from the leisured classes."[9] It is a hazardous formula and one which the fiction of James Stephens would also seem to disprove. It is arguable that the strain of antiromance and antifantasy in *The Charwoman's Daughter* was truer in biographical impulse than Stephens' later pursuit of its opposite. But what are we to make of Padraic Colum who frequently adapted or imitated the fantastic mode in traditional Irish literature, a Catholic who was acquainted with the inside of a Longford workhouse (albeit as the Master's son) and who knew rural lowlife as well as Stephens knew urban?

Actually, Colum's work, like Stephens', early exhibits a contest between reason and fantasy. Yeats had been thinking of Colum, among others, when he wrote of the working and leisured classes, and would have had in mind Colum's early dramatic exercises in peasant realism for the Abbey Theatre and not the bent of mind that later produced *The King of Ireland's Son* (1916), the revival prose work perhaps closest to the book it preceded, Stephens' *Irish Fairy Tales*. Colum seems to have tried in prose fiction to reverse Stephens' direction, for the brilliant folk fantasy of *The King of Ireland's Son* was followed by a realistic narrative of nineteenth-century Irish life, *Castle Conquer* (1923), that is still attracted to folklore and legend, a work that is part historical fiction, part heroic romance. Despite the achievement of this novel and of the much later novel, *The Flying Swans* (1957), it is probable that Colum's children's stories, consistently fanciful, will survive his adult fiction.

There are parallels between Stephens and Colum other than the rival claims reason and fantasy make in their work. Both were founder staff-members of *The Irish Review;* both flirted with the occult and frequented the Hermetic Society. Both were taken up as promising revivalists by Yeats and AE. They were close associates in Dublin before Colum left for America.The names of both writers, who were perhaps unsure at first of their real identity and best direction, underwent transformations; Colum was variously Patrick, Pádraig, and Padraic, Colm, Colum and Collumb. This seems the more fitting since so much of the Irish revival, so much of the folk imagination that inspired Colum, and so much of *The King of Ireland's Son* are concerned with metamorphosis.

Colum's biggest change was his removal in 1914 to the United States where *The King of Ireland's Son* was written and where he lived for most of his life. In the United States, the Irishness of his concerns was diluted by the contractual obligations of a professional writer, Colum delivering to Macmillan on order rewritings, usually for children, of Greek, Scandinavian, Hawaiian, and other national epics and myths. Whereas Colum's diversity of interests—in plays, essays, children's literature, folk adaptations, travel books, poems, novels, and biographies—might have befitted a new and Irish "Renaissance," it seemed to betray a promiscuity, a basically journalistic impulse and career.

To this charge, Colum might have replied that the variety of his prose work was the result of his pursuit of good stories wherever they were to be found. Like Stephens, he usurped in print the role of the traditional storyteller, many of whose stories concern, in plot or form, transformation and identity. Yet one hesitates to see disguised in these stories Colum's own search for new selves, one reason being that his choice of children as readers for many of his books reined his powers of self-expression. To an extent he was following in this a tendency of cultural revivals to turn saga and folk material into children's literature after it has been adapted for adults. Despite its scientific apparatus, Jacobs' *Celtic Fairy Tales,* for example, was intended for "the young ones." It was Patrick Pearse who was most aware of the educative powers of revival; he maintained that the "philosophy of education is preached now [1910], but it was practised by the founders of the Gaelic system two thousand years ago. Their very names for 'education' and 'teacher' and 'pupil' show that they had gripped the heart of the problem. The word for 'education' among the old Gaels was the same as the word for 'fostering'; the teacher was a 'fosterer' and the pupil was a 'foster-child.'"[10]

Colum came under the influence of Pearse's educational theories and occasionally lectured at Pearse's two schools in Dublin. It is appropriate, then, that the story of the King of Ireland's Son is told by Colum's narrator to an unidentified "foster-child," and in *Story Telling New & Old* (1927) Colum suggests (debatably) that the folktale teaches the need for kindliness and adventure, an aspect that presumably should not counteract what he also sees as the necessary element of "reverie" in folktales.[11] But Colum's children are the children of the world and not merely, as Pearse's were, the children of the Gael; when he wrote that the lasting patterns of the folktale belong to "the deeper consciousness of the race," Colum had the human, not just Irish race in mind.[12]

Stephens for his part had to insist that *Irish Fairy Tales* was "not a book for children at all,"[13] yet fiction that lent itself to the kind of illustration associated with children's literature—as his did, along with Colum's and Lord Dunsany's—could easily have its intended readership mistaken. In Colum's case there was rarely any mistake, for he became, and intended to become, primarily a children's author. This did not prevent striking work. *The King of Ireland's Son* is ostensibly a children's book that is also a structural masterpiece, exceeding in ingenuity of plot even Stephens' *Irish Fairy Tales*. Without the brilliant surfaces, witticisms, and twists of phrase of *Irish Fairy Tales,* Colum's book compensates with a narrative intricacy beyond the conscious appreciation of children. Nor could children (and most adults, for that matter) be expected to see the political meanings of *The King of Ireland's Son* that lie less visibly behind the structural delight than they do in Stephens' book.

There are two major tales in *The King of Ireland's Son:* the King's Son's search for Fedelma, the Enchanter's daughter, and the Gilly's search for his mother and father. The ravelling and unravelling of relationships of love and of kinship are common themes, of course, in folktales. Around and within these two tales are woven a score of others, the tapestry of tales being brought to a satisfying and simultaneous conclusion.

It is reasonably easy to ascertain the affinities the stories in *The King of Ireland's Son* have with authentic folktales, even if we cannot be sure that they all came directly from storytellers and not from published collections, or that none of them was invented by Colum. It is worthwhile establishing these affinities, but only after noting the unerring pace with which the stories are told, and the transparent prose style enlisted for their telling. Colum told Zack Bowen that he began as literary folklorist "by telling the stories I remembered from my grandmother's house in *The King of Ireland's Son.*"[14] About his later books of folklore, he claimed: "I didn't get it wrong you know—I looked it up and consulted the authorities in the libraries and so on." It is probable that he also researched before writing *The King of Ireland's Son* even if he had been told some of the stories while at his grandmother's in County Cavan.

Colum quite likely drew upon published versions of his two major tales. There are resemblances between Colum's first major tale and "Beauty of the World," "Morraha," and "The Nine-legged Steed" in Larminie's *West Irish Folk-Tales and Romances,* "Fis fá an aon Sgeul" in Kennedy's *Legendary Fictions of the Irish Celts,* "The King of Ireland's Son" in Hyde's *Beside the Fire,* "The Son of the King of Erin and the Giant of Loch Léin" in Curtin's *Myths and Folk-Lore of Ireland,* and "Beswarragal" in Lady Gregory's *The Kiltartan Wonder Book.* "Morraha" shares with *The King of Ireland's Son* the sword of light as an object of the hero's search, and the tasks set the hero because he loses a card game, including the discovery of a certain tale. The beginning of the second half of the "Unique Tale" that the King's Son must find in Colum's book is identical to the tale that the king's son seeks in "Morraha." Curtin's story, like Larminie's and Gregory's is a variant of Aarne-Thompson tale-types (AT) 313 and 400. From "The Son of the King of Erin" or "Beswarragal," Colum may well have borrowed the king's son's concealment of the maiden's clothes (swanskin in Colum's book) while she is swimming and the three tasks the giant imposes on the hero.

Colum's other major tale, of Flann (the Gilly of the Goatskin), may derive from "The Pursuit of the Giolla Dacker and his Horse" in P. W. Joyce's *Old Celtic Romances,* a story differently translated in Hayes O'Grady's *Silva Gadelica* and in Colum's own, much later book, *The Frenzied Prince, Being Heroic Stories of Ancient Ireland* (1943), and from "Gilla na Chreck an Gour" in Kennedy's *Legendary Fictions of the Irish Celts,* reprinted as "The Lad with the Goat-skin" in Jacobs' *Celtic Fairy Tales.*[15] Into this tale Colum weaves a variant of AT 1525 (The Master Thief) which Colum could have derived from a number of Irish sources,[16] and also a variant of AT 451 (The Maiden Who Seeks her Brothers). The stories of Flann and the King's Son form a double helix, and so they invade each other's tale-type: it is Flann, for example, who has his memory restored by the Little Red Hen when according to AT 313 it ought to be the King's Son. Similarly, the tasks set the King of Ireland's Son and his fight with the King of the Land of Mist resemble elements in "Gilla na Grakin and Fin MacCumhail" in Curtin's *Myths and Folk-Lore of Ireland,* a story that in turn resembles versions of the *Giolla Deacair* (the troublesome Gilly); but then the Gilly is really Flann, son also of a king.

Colum's debts are of course difficult to prove since he is offering versions of tales in the oral as well as literary tradition. *The King of Ireland's*

Son is a printed source for Ó Súilleabháin and Christiansen in their compilation, *The Types of the Irish Folktale,* which means that they regard the versions of tales they find in it authentic, even if they are listed under "no provenance," meaning the versions have no known county or provincial origin. Nor do we know whether Colum's own sources were oral or printed, or, if the latter, which published versions he drew upon. In any case, Ó Súilleabháin and Christiansen find in *The King of Ireland's Son* variants of three tale-types, AT 313, 451, and 1525, but in fact it includes variants and elements of others, including AT 222, 400, 410 (Sleeping Beauty), 510A (Cinderella), 650, 670, 956C, 1000, 1007, 1889H, and the tale-type Ó Súilleabháin identifies as type 27 in the Irish Finn cycle, the quest of *An Claidheamh Soluis* (The Sword of Light).[17] In addition, *The King of Ireland's Son* exploits many folk motifs, the functions Propp has analyzed, and various Irish folk characters, including the *Gobán Saor* (the mythical builder), the *gruagach,* Mananaun, Fergus, the Old Woman of Beare, Crom Dubh, *An Giolla Deacair,* the King of Ireland's Son *(Mac Rí Éireann),* and the Spae-woman (the prophecy-woman).

But the involuting of the in-tales in Colum's book is more complex than in any of the texts Propp analyzes and may serve to realize Propp's hope that his analysis of fairy tales could be extended to "sophisticated" works of fiction, of which *The King of Ireland's Son* is one. The craft with which Colum has laced his variants together is more important than the provenance of those variants. Below is a chart of the various stories in *The King of Ireland's Son,* many of which are recognizable folktales. These stories do not always correspond to Colum's chapters or episodes. The chart is meant merely to suggest the book's complex layering of narrative. The indentations indicate Colum's system of in-tales (stories within stories). The story of the sixth layer (story 20) is told within a story of the fifth, which in turn is told within a story of the fourth, and so on. Stories of the sixth and fifth layers are told by characters, stories of the fourth, third, and second are told by the narrator, and the whole is told by Colum.

Narrative Layering in *The King of Ireland's Son*

1 2 3 4 5 6

1. *The King of Ireland's Son,* told by Colum to his readers
    2. "The King of Ireland's Son," being the adventures of the King of Ireland's Son and Gilly of the Goatskin, told by the narrator to an unidentified "foster-child"

1 2 3 4 5 6

3. 'The Adventures of the King of Ireland's Son,' told by the narrator
    4. 'The King of Ireland's Son's Search for the Enchanter's Dwelling-place and for the Hand of Fedelma,' told by the narrator
        5. "The Ass and the Seal," told by the King's Son to Fedelma
        6. "The Sending of the Crystal Egg," told by Fedelma to the King's Son
        7. "The Story of the Young Cuckoo," told by the King's Son to Fedelma
        8. "The Story of the Cloud Woman," told by Fedelma to the King's Son
    9. 'The King's Son's Search for Fedelma (and for the Sword of Light and the Unique Tale),' told by the narrator
        10. "When the King of the Cats Came to King Connal's Dominion,"[18] told by Art, King Connal's Steward, to the King's Son
11. "The Adventures of Gilly of the Goat-skin," told by the narrator
    12. 'The Theft of the Crystal Egg,' told by the narrator
    13. 'The Churl of the Townland of Mischance', told by the narrator
        14. The first part of the "Unique Tale" (or 'The Enchantment of Sheen's Brothers'), told by Gilly to the King's Son
    15. 'Gilly, the Master Thief,' told by the narrator
        16. The second part of the "Unique Tale" (or 'The Theft of the Gilly by the Enchanter and Crom Duv'), told by the Enchanter and the Maid of the Green Mantle to the King's Son
    17. 'The King's Son's Killing of the King of the Land of Mist,' told by the narrator
    18. 'Flann's Escape from Crom Duv,' told by the narrator
        19. "The Story of Morag," told by Morag to Gilly (Flann)
            20. "The Story of the Fairy Rowan-Tree," told by the King of Senlabor's Councillor to Morag

1	2	3	4	5	6
			21. (=14) 'The Disenchantment of Sheen's Brothers,' told by the narrator		
			22. 'The Enchantment and Disenchantment of Flann,' told by the narrator		

In *The King of Ireland's Son* the in-tales frequently double back to explain, continue, or precede (in narrative chronology) previous tales. For example, Gilly's pursuit of the Crystal Egg (story twelve in the above chart) is a continuation of story six (though with a different narrator, as the two parts of the "Unique Tale" have different narrators) by a device we might call "narrative looping." Many of the stories interlock in such fashion. Just as love relationships and identities must be unraveled, given final form, so the separate stories in *The King of Ireland's Son* must be unraveled and given final form, plot and structure thereby complementing each other. It is all done in a marvelously wrought form and makes the book an ornament of the Irish literary revival.

The King of Ireland's Son *and Cultural Nationalism*

However, *The King of Ireland's Son* is a work of the revival for more than its emulation of folktale. His first major tale Colum describes as bardic ("the deeds of one are in the histories the shanachies have written in the language of the learned")[19] and the second as folk ("the deeds of the other are in the stories the people tell to you and me"), a distinction that Colum would have difficulty in maintaining in terms of provenance but somewhat less so in terms of the book itself and its political thrust. That thrust was hinted at by Zack Bowen, but it has taken a recent student of Colum's work to measure it.[20]

The King of Ireland's Son is a champion who would be at home in the heroic romances; despite his adventures and misadventures across a wide landscape, he belongs by right and acknowledgment to "the courts and cities, the harbors and the military encampments" (p. 316) over which he is given sway at the end of the book. Gilly of the Goatskin, the hero of the other major tale, by contrast begins life as a poor servant who does not know who his parents were. Gilly is at home in "the waste places and the villages and the roads where masterless men walked" (p. 316), and he is given authority over them when the rule of Ireland is divided at the end of the book between Gilly and the King of Ireland's Son. Gilly represents the peculiar heroism of the Irish peasantry which Colum once said was the underlying motif of his work,[21] a heroism that demonstrates itself by the skills of survival and self-protective cunning. He is a hero in Colum's book presumably because the author felt that the revival concept of Irish heroism, an Anglo-Irish and aristocratic concept, was insufficient even if necessary, and had to be expanded to include the peasantry, their earthiness and folly. In fact Colum, as a revivalist himself, has it both ways, for Gilly is discovered to be in reality Flann, also a king's son. The discovery repeats the notion of the Irish peasantry's submerged nobility, entertained by Yeats and others.[22] Such a notion in theory enables the revivalists and the peasants to make common cause, in literature and in politics, and Colum makes doubly sure of this by revealing towards the book's end that Flann and the King of Ireland's Son are stepbrothers. The "orphaned" Irish peasantry through travail accedes to its ancient and noble birthright.

The optimism of *The King of Ireland's Son* may be an ancient wish fulfillment of the kind expressed by Nora Hopper in the short poem, the first couplet of which I have quoted as epigraph to this discussion of Colum. This poem, reminiscent of Kipling's "En-dor," Colum presumably knew, and it portrays the King of Ireland's Son as a pursuer of dreams and shadows whom nothing can daunt. Perhaps, too, an Irish writer like Colum is attracted to the unconstricted times and places of folktales as a subliminal expression of an age-old Irish desire for freedom. Beneath the folktale's apparent freedom of action, setting, and narrative are the structural complications and constraints along with the themes and formulas of capture, disguise, and mistaken identity, all coded and perhaps attractive to a national mind conspiring for independence. That conspiracy was highly wrought indeed in 1916, the year *The King of Ireland's Son* appeared, and the picture of Ireland as "the Island of Destiny" ruled by native rulers, by peasant and aristocrat, must have seemed to the politically aware Colum as something more substantial than wish fulfillment.[23] In the veritable "conspiracy" of tales that composes his book, Colum was clearly in pursuit of a new national if not a new personal self.

Gilly's identity as a dispossessed prince is only revealed through completion of the "Unique Tale" of which the King of Ireland's Son is in search. In other words, the key to Gilly's identity is within a folktale. For Colum, folklore and national identity are closely bound; in telling the stories that constitute *The King of Ireland's Son,* he is furthering the cause of Irish cultural nationalism. The "foster-child" to whom they are told can now be identified as Ireland herself who will not mature until she hears and remembers the old stories. (By contrast, Joyce's Dubliners—*his* multiple symbol of his country—will not mature until they refuse to be characters in the oldest native story of all: the sorrowful legend of Ireland.) Moreover, to transmit the tales is to participate in the conspiracy to achieve the political reality symbolized in the tales, even when the teller is unaware of that symbolism. The allegory of *The King of Ireland's Son* is a political version of the cultural coding we find in myth tales, and it signals the book's literate (and eloquent) meddling with a narrative form, the Irish folktale, that is not normally political or allegorical.[24] The book in its political guise is perhaps closer to Irish street ballads that contain covert political and revolutionary symbolism and even to *aisling* poetry; it belongs in part to the Irish tradition of disguised protest and revolutionary literature.[25]

There is one other respect in which *The King of Ireland's Son* commands our attention. Larminie saw a connection between one of his stories and "many a modern novel,"[26] but such a resemblance begins to ring true only with the advent of modernist fiction, despite the political allegory, psychological motivation, and moral heroism, all of them familiar to readers of realistic fiction and all of which Colum injects in small but expert doses into the folk tissue of *The King of Ireland's Son*. Colum himself made no practical distinction between authentic and imitation folk narratives: for him, story was all. Similarly, he was aware that changing circumstances necessitated the closing of the gap between the writer and the traditional storyteller. In *Story Telling New & Old* he instances oral storytelling for children in American libraries and his own attempt to reshape folk stories so that they can be read off the pages to children.[27] He thought that the modern writer could avail himself profitably of the structures and formulas of the folktale:

> It would be well if the modern and metropolitan story-teller could do what that story-teller's art permitted him to do—to make certain descriptions purely conventional—the description of a ship sailing the sea, for instance; the description of a castle or of a lonely waste. By such conventionalizations he was able to get what every one who undertakes to tell a story of some length has to try to get, points of rest, passages that are relief in the narrative. When he set his ship sailing upon the sea, when he set his hero wandering through a wilderness, the audience rested and the story-teller rested, not because there was nothing happening, but because what was happening was regular and anticipated.[28]

To the extent that Irish revival fiction writers learned from traditional narratives, we can identify a convergence of sorts between revivalism and that modernist impulse to return to, for purposes of renewal, earlier and more clearly conventional patterns of fiction.[29] A rereading of *Ulysses* in this light will show Joyce—revivalist or no—using the conventionalizations and ploys of the storyteller that Colum directs us to, in addition to holding in modernist fashion a verbal mirror up to literature. Narrative involution and structuring is an Irish fictional forte and takes the place of that moral engagement and genius for registering social experience we find in the English novel.

Sub-heroic Days: Figgis and O'Duffy

Stephens and Colum were not alone when they sported in a modern manner with bardic and folk tales in order to further the aims of the revival. In 1923 appeared a fine book under the pseudonym of Michael Ireland. It was rumored that *The Return of the Hero* was written by Stephens, but a 1930 edition, for which Stephens supplied an Introduction as disclaimer, revealed that the author was the hapless Darrell Figgis, whose wife shot herself the same year the novel first appeared and who gassed himself in Bloomsbury two years later.[30] In this odd novel Figgis shares Stephens' penchant for epigram amidst a playfully purple prose, but a close reading would have ruled out Stephens as the author. Since, however, *The Return of the Hero* is unlike anything else Figgis had written, the surmisers were confounded.

As Stephens points out in his wary Introduction (he does not actually praise the book), he himself had already published *Irish Fairy Tales* in 1920, which also turned characters and incidents from the Fenian cycle into wonder tales, though he drew on the first half of the saga, whereas Figgis drew on the more modern Fionn tale, *Agallamh na Senórach* ("The Colloquy of the Ancients"). "Will Usheen ever come again?" Ned Carmady wonders in Moore's "The Wild Goose." *The Return of the Hero* as if in answer has Oisin as the last representative of Heroic Ireland, come back from Tir-na-nOg to search for his comrades, the Fianna, and discovering that two hundred years have elapsed and that Ireland is in the hands of Patrick and the "hierarchy of little saints" whose memory AE libelled. There ensue a tale-telling contest and debate that represent the battle for supremacy between Christianity and paganism in early Ireland. This theme recurs in revival literature, with the revivalists renewing the claims of a mystical paganism (Moore's paganism is less exalted), and Figgis' sympathies are clearly with Fenian Ireland more than with the "sub-heroic days" of Oisin's listeners.

In the end, Oisin rejoins his comrades by vanishing into legendry when it becomes obvious that the Christians will not alter their opinion that the Fenians are in hell. Hell or no, "it is a good place," Oisin had said, "wherever they are": better with the Fianna in hell than without them in heaven.[31] And this refusal of adaptation is the most obvious contrast Figgis' version of the old matter bears to Stephens' *Irish Fairy Tales*. Figgis employs Oisin to defend selfhood: "For no man can go outside his own skin, and no man can depart from his destiny" (p. 118); whereas Stephens wanted in jest to take out naturalization papers as a dog or hedgehog, Oisin insists: "I do not want to be a dog, and I do not want to be an angel. Oisin I am, and Oisin the son of Finn I would remain, whatever happens" (p. 123). Although it is tempting to read into this the disguised autobiographical despair of the future suicide ("a man may escape all things, but there is one thing he cannot escape, and that is himself," p. 53), Figgis is celebrating the heroic, not sub-heroic or ordinary self. And the revivalists, who repudiated the sub-heroic self, saw an heroic, implacable identity as the only alternative to the protean, conspiratorial self Stephens and Colum celebrated and to which heroism throughout Irish history has had periodically to resort.

The Return of the Hero re-expresses the Anglo-Irish fascination with the old literature, especially that of Heroic Ireland before Christianity (that is, Catholicism) redefined Irishness too narrowly for Protestant nationalists like Figgis. Since the book was written in 1918–19, when the author was active in the war against the British, and despite one character's remark, "Directly I suspect a story to have a secret meaning, I desert the teller of the story at once" (pp. 172–73), it is hardly fanciful to see the novel as a summons to heroism in twentieth century Ireland or to see mirrored in the colloquy of the ancients the fierce struggle in the nineteenth century between Fenianism and a Church that would condemn it. "Be of good courage," Oisin exhorts the absent spirit of Finn. "The fruits of victory are to the strong, and the ripe fruits to the brave . . . So we will fight on, O captain. It is better to be tortured than to bend the knee. For victory comes at last to the unbreakable will" (p. 209). At the end of the novel, Patrick and his bishops are not just the medieval church or even just an anti-Fenian church, but an occupying military power whose opponents will not admit defeat. In one sense an impressive retelling of an old tale, in another *The Return of the Hero* is one more attempt to recolonize real Ireland with the heroic spirit of a fictitious, pre-Catholic, pre-Colonial past.

In the year *The Return of the Hero* was published, Eimar O'Duffy began the first volume of a trilogy that the unwary reader might think is in the revival vein of updating ancient matter to educate an emerging, reheroized Ireland. Nothing could be further from the truth. If in the first volume, *King Goshawk and the Birds* (1926), O'Duffy like Stephens and Figgis before him turns saga into prose fantasy, he does so for bitterly satirical purposes and impelled by deep disillusionment: his novel is the first exploitation of the old literature in the wake of the Irish Civil War and partition, and after such knowledge there is little forgiveness. *King Goshawk and the Birds* is the fantasy equivalent of MacNamara's novel length recriminations and shares with them a dark and desperate energy. Where MacNamara's novels are aggressively explicit realism, O'Duffy's satire is realism disguised but no less savage for being so. By casting Cuchulain in his mock-epic, O'Duffy satirizes not only the mock-heroic (the reality which falls below the heroic) but also the heroic (which ill-serves the legitimate demands of reality).

At the request of a poor Philosopher in Dublin (O'Duffy might be parodying Stephens), Cuchulain returns from Tir na nOg to redeem man "from the course of wickedness and folly by which he was travelling to destruction."[32] Satirized here is the revival notion that man is degenerate and requires redemption through heroic example, but it is satirized only in its underestimation of how far the degeneration has gone; O'Duffy's Swiftian awareness of the depth and ubiquity of this degeneracy puts him, like MacNamara, beyond the revival pale, even though he believes that redemption is indeed in order, though hardly by heroic example, as the plot demonstrates. Cuchulain is so disgusted by what he sees that he returns whence he came, though not before taking a mortal wife in order to produce a son; this hero (Cuandine, the Hound of Man), because he is half-mortal, has the stomach as well as the spirit to continue the job of redemption. He finds himself scorned in Ireland, however, by the press, public, and professors, and proceeds to England; there he is turned into a celebrity, before revealing his purpose on earth and being reviled. Frozen out of England, he intervenes successfully in a one-sided dispute between a powerful dictatorship and a small nation, after the League of Nations has abjectly failed to confront the erring big power: "Thus far the account of the Wolfo-Lambian war; and here endeth the first part of the ancient epic tale of the deeds of Cuandine."

O'Duffy sets his novel in the future (since in it is celebrated the centenary of Shaw, who is claimed by warmongers and millionaires, we can suppose the 1950s) and narrates it from an even more distant future. As in *1984,* the future in *King Goshawk and the Birds* is the present disguised (now masquerading as then) and functions like Swift's far-flung geography in *Gulliver's Travels* (here disguised as there). O'Duffy's Ireland is a squalid place of petty electioneering between two indistinguishable parties (the Yallogreens and the Greenyallos), outcomes of a civil war fought over whether Ireland should rejoin the British Empire and which involved the invasion of Ireland by the British in order to restore the Republic as an independent state! But Ireland is just the world writ small. A world war has resulted in victory for monopoly capitalism headquartered in "America, the Great, the Renowned, the Progressive, the Uplifted, to whom all nations bow" (p. 275). O'Duffy wrote his book during the heyday of American plutocracy and the attempts to weaken the power of corporate giants and industrial magnates through anti-Trust and anti-Monopoly laws. O'Duffy envisages a world where all anticapitalist forces have been repelled and this has been the grim result:

> children working for a living, and adults with nothing better to do than dance, flirt, play ball, and ride-a-cock-horse; children starving, and adults shortening their lives with overeating; middle-aged women doctoring their complexions by bathing in cream, and children fed on the skim; millionaires, sick with idleness and high living, ordered holidays and change of air by their doctors, and broken-down clerks, sick with undernourishment and overwork, dosed with coloured stuff out of bottles; millionaires' wives, surfeited with pleasure, recuperating on tropic beaches, and poor men's wives hard at work a week after childbirth; mansions and vast estates inhabited by idle sterile couples, and teeming families crammed into a single room; a millionaire buried in a silver coffin, and children stifled in the womb for lack of the money to bring them into the world . . . men that asked for a better and a wiser world scorned as madmen or locked up as dangerous. (pp. 176–77)

Cuandine's symbolic task is to defend the freedom of the earth's songbirds which have been ordered captured and made his private property by King Goshawk, the American billionaire and Wheat King, a figure more powerful than any monarch or statesman. O'Duffy's is a violent, socialist attack on the monopolistic tendency of private enterprise and on the notion of private property itself. Capitalism is seen as a ruthless power that absorbs, appropriates, coopts and domesticates everything in its path; it is in O'Duffy's eyes what totalitarianism is in Orwell's eyes; indeed, it is a species of totalitarianism but organized from the land of liberty (whose welcoming monument has been renamed the Statue of Efficiency) and requiring for its success not terror but the degradation of taste.

While waging his attack on American capitalism, O'Duffy hits lesser targets, some of them topical, such as psychoanalysis, inoculation, and advertising, as well as, above all, newspapers. That O'Duffy worked for a time on an American newspaper in Paris is doubly revealing; at any rate, he adds an international dimension to the nationalist concerns of the revivalists, and is capable of praising England while pretending to the Irish (his real target in one instance) to satirize it. Likewise, he adds a genuinely socialist dimension to the usually fanciful notion of brotherhood entertained by the Anglo-Irish writers. At the same time, one suspects that his socialism is an angry resort in the face of what he came to regard as the failure of nationalism; he wrote *King Goshawk and the Birds* after he left Ireland to reside in England, having become disillusioned with the Easter Rising, a disillusionment chronicled in the very different novel, *The Wasted Island* (1919).[33] One wonders, too—given his onslaught on contraception in *King Goshawk*—if his socialism may not have a streak of reaction in it, if he is not on occasions attacking aspects of advanced liberal thought in his day by exaggerating them into a fascist future.

Yet O'Duffy's is a remarkable work that demonstrates a powerful and innovative use of an ancient literature that had tempted earlier Irish writers into nationalist euphoria and disguised class reaction. By turning Cuchulain material to political account, the novel grants a significance to the old literature beyond that which it enjoys in Stephens' *Deirdre,* which turns it to psychological account. The internal forms of Irish saga are here—the pillow-talk, the runs, the in-tales, the catalogues. But these are barely distinguishable from the internal forms of modernist encyclopedic fiction, with its collagistic set pieces, tables, lists, newspaper extracts (parodied here), deliberate use of cliché and voices, and the entire act of a play (a Shavian comedy of manners and ideas). *King Goshawk* belongs beside *Ulysses,* or, rather, beside Dos Passos' *USA,* since neither the American nor O'Duffy has Joyce's genius for the seamless warp and weft.

Modernism does not in itself lift a writer clear of the revival, as I have implied before. However, O'Duffy's tough realism (reinforced in his case by a socialist conscience, a fearless satire, and an internationalism of political outlook) puts him in another tradition, that of Moore, Joyce, MacNamara, O'Donovan, Austin Clarke, Flann O'Brien, Patrick Kavanagh, and John McGahern. This tradition of unfazed disenchantment maintained by Catholic-born, patriotic, but not narrowly nationalistic writers is one twentieth-century alternative to the Irish literary revival.

A Dreamer's Tales: The Stories of Lord Dunsany

On the whole, Yeats's formulation—from the leisured classes, fantasists, from the mass, realists—has much to recommend it, especially if we mean by "leisured classes" (as Yeats no doubt meant) the Anglo-Irish or well-off Protestants and by "the mass" Catholics or native Irish.[34] A writer who seems to fit Yeats's formula to perfection is Lord Dunsany whose gift for fantasy was in no wise trammelled by social or cultural commitment of a nationalist kind. Colum praised him as "that rare creature in literature, the fabulist . . . One can hardly detect a social idea in his work. There is one there, however. It is one of unrelenting hostility to everything that impoverishes man's imagination."[35] Dunsany himself distinguished the imagination or inspiration of his stories from the intellect he used when playing chess,[36] yet that he was a chess champion seems fitting since his stories and novels have a pure inventiveness we associate with highly-skilled games. And this fantasist was an aristocrat, of the kind Yeats could seek as a revival patron and participant and, if Gogarty is to be believed, envy:

> It would be a mistake to think that the rivalry between Dunsany and Yeats was a literary one. Far from it. Yeats had no rival to fear among contemporary poets. It was not so much rivalry on Yeats' part (shocking to say it before it can be explained) as it was envy. Yeats, though his descent was from parsons, dearly loved a lord. He was at heart an aristocrat, and it must always have been a disappointment to him that he was not born one. Not by taking thought could he trace his descent from the year 1181 . . . This then was at the bottom the cause of the failure of friendship between Dunsany and Yeats. Dunsany sensed some sort of opposition, real and imaginary for some of the forms it was reputed to have taken were probably part of an over sensitive suspicion.[37]

Dunsany's wealth and title were troublesome. Stephens' early praise of his stories, "The Hashish Man," "Poltarnees" and "Blagdaross," expressed in letters in 1910 and 1911, might appear fulsome by his desire to secure Dunsany's patronage for *The Irish Review:* "I do believe you are one of the greatest living writers," Stephens told him in 1910, "& are going to do amazing things."[38] The following year he wrote: "I do believe that you & I are the only writers doing real stuff, the artist seems to have died out of English prose & the Jerry builders reign in his stead."[39] Long after the question of patronage, however, as late as 1938, Stephens wrote praisingly to Dunsany whom he continued to admire.

Despite Yeats's efforts to coax Dunsany into his revival circle ("claiming you for Ireland"),[40] Dunsany was reluctant to think of himself as a member. He cared little for Irish sagas and folktales and did not especially draw on them as models or sources for his fantasies; he felt with commendable honesty that Irish folklore did not truly belong to him.[41] Associating culturally with revivalist Protestants desperately seeking new identities, Dunsany persisted in associating socially with unliterary Protestants, the vast majority of whom foolishly refused to adapt at all to a changing Ireland. Occasionally his literary and social worlds collided, as on the evening before World War I when he ferociously defended England in defiance of Colum's German sympathies.[42] This double life led one of Dunsany's biographers to wonder if he was a writer who shot or a shooter who wrote. Dunsany's social class stretched unbroken across the Irish Sea, and though he was proud to be a Meath man, it was to England that he owed his birth (in London), his education (at Cheam, Eton, and Sandhurst), his title (a British baronage), his marriage (to an Englishwoman), and his final resting place (near the family's second home in Kent).

There is something close to admirable, however unwise, in Dunsany's unflinching loyalty to lineage and proven values. Here was a man who in the teeth of arms collections by authorities and terrorists, of fire and counterfire, literally as well as figuratively stuck to his guns, a giant hunting on Irish bogs with genial sang-froid. Perhaps his experiences with the British Expeditionary Force in France made Ireland, even during the Civil War, seem small beer. His fiction was equally unaltered by political convulsion; nor was it altered by the withering of the revival, suggesting that even in its heyday that movement hardly molded his work. Literature was outside his life; it was in both senses a fantasy (a handicraft, some critics implied), where the revivalists sought a mutuality of life and letters. (If he sought in his fables an escape from environment, it was a temporary escape and not for nationalist or even cultural, much less social reasons.) It is appropriate, then, that if today Dunsany's fiction after years of eclipse is undergoing resuscitation, that resuscitation has nothing to do with the revival. He is seen in the United States as a master of "adult fantasy" and shelved alongside J. R. R. Tolkien, C. S. Lewis (another Irishman), and H. P. Lovecraft, a few Dewey decimal points, as it were, from the science fictionists and ghost story writers. Dunsany is a beneficiary of the current expansion of the boundaries of "legitimate" fiction to accommodate science fiction, adult fantasy, and children's literature.

Dunsany shares with Tolkien the contrivance of entire imaginary cultures and kingdoms. In his work can be found invented theogonies, geneses, legends, and dynasties—mock-myth, epic, and romance rolled into one. Ancient Irish literature and tradition contribute little to the synthesis. Nor does the real Ireland figure commonly in the early stories; the real world when it is present ("the fields we know") is more often a Georgian English landscape half-remembering its medieval ancestry. However, after his dream journey down the river Yann that traverses so much of Dunsany's invented geography, the narrator of "Idle Days on the Yann," from *A Dreamer's Tales* (1910), fancifully recalls his Irish homeland and "those hazy fields that all poets know, wherein stand small mysterious cottages through whose windows, looking westwards, you may see the fields of men, and looking eastwards see glittering elfin mountains, tipped with snow, going range on range into the region of Myth, and beyond it into the kingdom of Fantasy, which pertain to the Lands of Dream."[43] Myth, fantasy, dream: these are regions progressively distant from the workaday world; they are Dunsany's successive goals as a storyteller and they half-exist already, it is suggested, at least in this story, in the living Ireland.

Perhaps it was the rare mention of Ireland in "Idle Days on the Yann" that caused Yeats to find seductive this dream journey through imaginary places nectared with Dunsanian exoticism: Goolunza, Kyph and Pir, Mandaroon whose inhabitants sleep because when they awake the gods will die, Astahahn whose inhabitants "have fettered and manacled Time, who would otherwise slay the gods," and Perdóndaris with its immense city gate alarmingly carved out of one solid piece of ivory, cities revisited by the narrators of "A Shop in Go-by Street" and "The Avenger of Perdóndaris" from *Tales of Three Hemispheres* (1919). Yeats's praise is ambivalent: "Had I read the *Fall of Babbulkund* or *Idle Days on the Yann* when a boy I had perhaps been changed for better or worse and looked to that first reading as the creation of my world; for when we are young the less circumstantial, the further from common life a book is, the more does it touch our hearts and make us dream. We are idle, unhappy and exorbitant, and like the young Blake admit no city beautiful that is not paved with gold and silver."[44] Idleness is a recurring condition in Lord Dunsany's stories, but never does it have the social implications of Joyce's depressed lower middle-class Dublin; occasionally we cannot avoid thinking of the vast leisure men of Dunsany's class enjoyed, though Dunsany as a writer was anything but idle. The idleness is of a kind that Yeats had to throw over before he could activate a literary revival and had to outgrow as a prescriptive theme before his own work could mature. The influences that operate on Dunsany's early fiction include those that operate on the revival as well as those repudiated by the revivalists, yet the suggestion in Yeats's praise of a sigh of relief after a close shave is unavoidable.

Among those influences might seem to be a *fin-de-siècle* preoccupation with narcotic and sensuous environments of spices, tapestries, and incense. Like writers of the nineties, Dunsany "occultivates" such environments but in an artificial and conventional way appropriate to fantasy. Aleister Crowley praised in a letter "The Hashish Man" from *A Dreamer's Tales* but chided the author knowledgeably: "I see you know [hashish] by hearsay not by experience. You have not confused time and space as the true eater does."[45] Incidentally, Dunsany's use of drugs and dreams to half-explain his heroes' fantastic voyages threatens to violate what according to Tolkien is a principle of the fairy tale, that "it cannot tolerate any frame or machinery suggesting that the whole story in which [marvels] occur is a figment or illusion." Hyde too claimed that the strange happenings in Irish folktales are never explained in terms of dreams.[46] The oriental elements in Dunsany's fiction derive from a Victorian curiosity pricked by empire, and the promiscuous invention of imaginary kingdoms we might even interpret as transposed imperialism. Given that Dunsany was a well-traveled man, as hunter and soldier, it was appropriate that Sir Richard Burton was a relative and Kipling a friend. In contrast we might think of AE, a genuine mystic who had been to India, but by transmigration of soul, for he had never set foot there.

The Irish literary revival had to produce its own alternatives to empire and orientalism, but Dunsany's fiction played small part in the attempt. William Morris was useful to Yeats in his efforts at a literary revival, and because Dunsany's stories seem to have an affinity with, if they do not owe a direct debt to, Morris' prose romances, we might insist on seeing Dunsany as a revivalist writer. At first glance Dunsany's pseudo-medievalism seems part and parcel of the medieval revivalism of the Irish Renaissance. That revivalism had its distant roots in the romantic medievalism of Keats, in Pugin's Catholic and Ruskin's Protestant gothicism, in the Pre-Raphaelite Brotherhood and the Morris circle.[47] On one level the Irish movement simply added new sources—the Celtic sagas and heroic romances—to the sources already plundered by nineteenth century British romantic medievalists who shared both a detestation of the European Renaissance and a longing for a changeless world. The quests, imaginary kingdoms, dream atmospheres, and pseudo-medievalism of Morris' prose romances, *The Wood Beyond the World* (1894) and *The Well at the World's End* (1896), suggest the utopianism of a decayed romanticism, though they were probably meant to imply condemnation of an industrial, capitalist, puritan, Whig present, a condemnation Yeats, who was no socialist, could echo from an assumed aristocratic vantage point.[48]

Divided by perspective, Morris and Yeats shared their objects of hatred; they met, moreover, in their admiration for high craftsmanship and their nostalgia for an anachronistic medievalism; they met, too, in their desire for a vigorously objective art that would avoid "the little doubtings, and little believings, and little wonderings" of introspective art.[49] The influence of Morris on Yeats is well-attested,[50] but it may be worth remarking on the variety of medievalisms in the Irish movement, including those of O'Grady and all those who drew inspiration from Middle Irish literature, Synge (life on the Aran Islands was thought to be medieval), Joyce (very different, his medievalism from the others'—a theology and pedantry doubly fossilized in Ireland and Stephen Dedalus), and of course Yeats. Morris' influence is detectable in the stories of *The Secret Rose* and mingles with that of Poe, another romantic medievalist. In his Preface to *Cuchulain of Muirthemne,* Yeats admitted that his early fiction was an attempt to find an equivalent of Morris' prose in his medieval romances, that he had failed but that Lady Gregory had now succeeded with Kiltartanese. He made the admission in 1902; the previous year he had already planned the revision of his Hanrahan stories with Lady Gregory's help. Moreover, Morris with his poetic voyages among wondrous isles and his real voyage to Iceland had already gone over some of the ground the Irish revivalists were to tread.

Lord Dunsany occupied in fact the aristocratic vantage point Yeats occupied in principle. His stories share with Morris' prose romances the quests, imaginary kingdoms, dream atmospheres, and pseudo-medievalism I already mentioned, as well as archaisms and dialect words, and a vigorous pictorialism. Despite Morris' radicalism and historical knowledge, C. N. Manlove has called Morris' prose romances, and Dunsany's, "escapist" in order to distinguish them from the "imaginative" fantasies of Charles Kingsley, George MacDonald, C. S. Lewis, J. R. R. Tolkien, and Mervyn Peake.[51] Certainly Dunsany's are escapist and testify to the limitations of pure story devoid of the mystery of tradition as well as of the relevance to life. Dunsany's stories also exhibit what Manlove terms a sense of enclosure: however well-written, their impersonality is not just that of fantasy but also of well-staged entertainment. There is a comforting impression of properties being moved around. Gods, kings, magicians, and princesses are his cast, unicorns, gargoyles, centaurs, hypogriffs, and dragons his bestiary, cities, deserts, mountains, and woods his geography.

There is a strong sense of compound and facsimile in the folk form of his work. Not only is there no didacticism, but there is little of what Tolkien calls "applicability" to life, certainly no strong personal sense of revelation or *Sehnsucht.* This indulgent conventionalism, even if superbly exploited, prevented Dunsany from being active in the Irish literary movement. The same qualities, AE claimed, put Morris beyond the interests of revivalists. "I find it curious," he wondered, "that Yeats, who so often speaks of passionate literature when he is generalising, loves in fact the romances of William Morris, the least passionate inventions in English literature, more perhaps than any other imaginative works. He himself is endlessly speculative, while the works of Morris are without speculation. . . . I suppose an intellect which is so restless must be envious of a spirit so content with its vision."[52] It was indeed the "contentment" of *The Well at the World's End*—Yeats's word to describe his apparent favorite among the prose romances that he thought Morris' highest artistic achievement—that early attracted Yeats, a quality not unlike that of idleness which attracted him to Dunsany's romantic tales. Perhaps it was a question of masks, of unlike poles attracting, as AE implied.

But Dunsany if he is not speculative is at least inventive, and it is inventiveness that sharpens his fantasy. The splendidly titled quest romance, "The Fortress Unvanquishable, Save for Sacnoth," from *The Sword of Welleran and Other Stories* (1908), is one of Dunsany's best stories, full of felicitous and imaginative strokes. The hero Leothric sets out on a journey perilous to destroy the fortress of the evil magician Gaznak, who has sent bad dreams to plague Leothric's village of Allathurion. The fortress is unconquerable except by the sword Sacnoth that protects the spine of the metallic monster Tharagavverug which can only be killed by starvation. Tharagavverug, having been slain (emitting dying breaths that resemble "the sound of a hunt going furious to the distance and dying away"), is melted down "till only Sacnoth was left, gleaming among the ashes." Gaznak has conjured his fortress and its inhabitants into existence: the pinnacles and spires are in fact marble dreams, and dreams also are the beautiful women whose eyes are little flames and the Queens wearing jewels, each one of which has an historian to itself who writes no other chronicles all his days. The combat between Leothric and Gaznak is reminiscent of the Irish sagas: until Leothric severs his opponent's uplifted hand, Gaznak escapes the sword Sacnoth by clutching his head by the hair, lifting it aloft while the sword cleaves thin air, and replacing it on his shoulders. Upon Gaznak's death the dream-fortress and the dreams that plague Allathurion vanish.

Lord Dunsany's stories rarely achieve the sense of "spontaneity" that Stephens admired in them, though certainly Dunsany composed spontaneously, dashing off on frequent occasions a story or play, in almost finished form, between tea and dinner. The best of them, however, manage, as does "Sacnoth," to transcend contrivance; they include "In the Land of Time," from *Time and the Gods* (1906), in which an army invades what is believed to be the country of Time but loses men to old age in the campaign and returns unavailing to its native city to find it delapidated and the inhabitants wizened; "Of the Gods of Averon," from the same volume; "Poltarnees, Beholder of Ocean," from *A Dreamer's Tales;* the superb "Idle Days on the Yann"; and "The Probable Adventure of the Three Literary Men," from *The Book of Wonder* (1912). Dunsany's conventionalism denotes a reflexive interest in stories and storytellers that sometimes reminds me, in the nature of its inventiveness, not so much of Irish writers, past or present, as of that more speculative fantasist, Borges. Borges knew Dunsany's work and was, I suspect, influenced by his stories.[53] The historians of jewels in "The Fortress Unvanquishable"; the stories exacted from travelers as a toll in "The Idle City" from *A Dreamer's Tales;* the fearful tales told by the Wanderers in "Idle Days on the Yann"; the "poems of fabulous value" kept in the Golden Box that is the object of the quest in "The Probable Adventure of the Three Literary Men"—all must sound familiar to readers of the Argentine.

There is in the fiction of Lord Dunsany an absence of that self-consciousness we discovered in fiction of the revival. The selflessness of his work is of no urgently personal or patriotic kind; indeed, there is very little presentation of the self at all, few heroes with whom he or we can identify save on a purely narrative level and through the technical device of point of view. We might account for the composure of Dunsany's fiction in terms of his imagination which, Colum's opinion to the contrary that Dunsany has "the *mind* of a myth-maker,"[54] seems to me to lack the *Einfühlung* which Stephens' imagination had in abundance and which is the basis of mythopoeia. Stephens, Blake, and Lawrence seem to me essentially mythopoeic writers, creators of myth; Tolkien, Dunsany, Morris, even Joyce, seem to me formally mythopoeic writers, users of myth. Yeats stands between, a maker of legends. Of course, the conventions of fantasy (like those of the folktale) are impersonal ones, highly suitable for authors who wish to create selfless worlds without the pain of transcending the self through various forms of self-expression.

But we might also take into account, and possibly could do so in the cases of Lewis and Tolkien as well as Dunsany, a social self-confidence. Lord Dunsany, whose social station and sense of self seem to have been so closely entwined, apparently considered no reason for self-questioning to exist. Perhaps we could see in his double life, fantasy and literature on the one hand, snipe-shooting and safaris on the other, the Irish law of the excluded middle, or in his fashioning of otherworlds an Ascendancy longing for social security (dreaming his fracturing world intact), yet his English literary affinities suggest otherwise. If he and his literature are

Irish, they are so in a peculiar and negative way, which might, after all, be said equally of the orthodox Ascendancy during the Irish struggle for independence. Colum chose to see Dunsany's imaginings as socially innocent. But surely there is a connection between, firstly, Dunsany's ignoring of Irish folk and bardic material and the purity of his fantasy, and, secondly, the conservatism of his mind (he detested modern poetry, for example) as well as of his politics. His freedom from self-questioning and political anxiety released his imagination from the demands of social reality. The social ideas are there in his work, but like nineteenth century landlords, are detectable by their absenteeism.

The Indifferent Cairn
The Peasant Voice in Revival Prose

V

. . . let me who am neither Brendan
Free of all roots nor yet a rooted peasant
Here add one stone to the indifferent cairn.

—Louis MacNeice

Hidden Ireland

Real and Imagined Peasantries

Patrick Pearse, James Joyce, Seumas O'Kelly

14

Peasants and Gentlefolk

The importance of the peasant to writers of the revival is well-known. Peasant Quality was a necessary ingredient not just in Abbey plays but in revival ideology generally. It was usually factitious. For example, certain upper-class Irish, mostly Protestant, believed they shared with the peasant a disdain for worldly possessions—they who, unlike the peasants, already enjoyed the possessions they disdained. This was a shallow and self-deceiving notion, and to some extent a counterpart of the notion that Ireland's heroic age was an entirely chivalrous one. The peasant may not have worldly goods, but he certainly wants them, though generations of poverty may have taught him to tell others in self-compensation that the opposite is the case.

This is not to say that the peasant was not more spiritual, in Yeatsian terms, than the rest of his compatriots; no doubt he was (he was certainly more superstitious), but this did not cancel out his normal human cupidity. Nor was there any sustained intention to be spiritual, at least in a pagan sense, at the expense of material well-being. And I am not denying that the countryman loses a great deal of his irreplaceable lore when he graduates into the middle class or into the city or into the age of technology and print. But I would certainly deny an idea current among revivalists, that a member of the upper class has any natural affinity with the peasant and his lore. Yeats thought that both the peasant and the aristocrat were free from the anxieties associated with acquisitiveness and could thereby cultivate a spiritual existence. We have already remarked, in an earlier chapter, on the difficulties such thinking arouses. The fact is that the Irish gentry were as believers in folk systems of expression and belief even farther from the peasantry than were and are the Irish middle classes, which emerged in comparatively recent times and which have, added to the normal anxieties associated with possessiveness, that anxiety attending the vivid remembrance of poverty, a poverty associated in their minds with the folklore that even in the city they remember and try to forget. Middle-class disdain for peasant lore rests as much on close and uncomfortable succession in time, and sometimes proximity in space, as on difference in class, wealth or attitude. What I described as Gabriel Conroy's ambivalence towards the west and the peasantry could be described as Joyce's bourgeois discomfiture.

In any case, well-off Irish Protestants who discovered and collected peasant lore were frequently black sheep among their families and delinquents among their class—one thinks of Lady Gregory and Douglas Hyde—and not entirely representative of the gentry. If the peasantry of the revivalists was an imaginary one, so too were their gentlefolk. According to some, the affinity between gentry and peasantry rests on what we might call a half-historical, half-legendary conviction that the latter, or at least the seers and storytellers among it, held in protective custody the memory and art of a native aristocracy dispersed with the overthrow of the Gaelic order, an idea given most vivid expression in Daniel Corkery's *Hidden Ireland* but prefigured in Yeats's equation of peasant, artist, and aristocrat, the three angles of his ideal triangle. All three, said Yeats, create beautiful things, enjoy long tradition, possess a special kind of knowledge or wisdom, and are above (in the case of the aristocrat), beneath (in the case of the peasant) or beyond (in the case of the artist) merely materialist concerns.[1] It is clear too that he believed that each denies the sovereignty of the self. If we think of the bard as the poet of the aristocracy, then we are dealing here with three kinds of artist—the bard, the shanachie, and the modern artist. Moreover, the peasantry was viewed by some of the revivalists as itself a secret aristocracy driven west or underground by successive invasions, and for the revivalists culture and class were faster bonds of sympathy and identity than race.[2] At the very least the peasant could be regarded as an aristocrat in the impressive though largely anonymous genealogy of his artistic tradition. "Folk-art," said Yeats, "is, indeed, the oldest of the aristocracies of thought."[3]

The Stories of Patrick Pearse

> The Poet who could merely sit on a chair, and compose stanzas, would never make a stanza worth much. He could not sing the Heroic warrior, unless he himself were at least a Heroic warrior too.
>
> —Carlyle, "The Hero as Poet"

Yeats's rural aristocracy was one imagined peasantry among several of the time. Patrick Pearse's peasantry was another. Like Yeats's, Pearse's peasantry was western. Creators and custodians of the folklore, embodiments of the past, the Irish peasantry became of interest to the revival proportionate to their distance westwards from Dublin. Yet this generalization has to be qualified in the case of Pearse. For Pearse, as for many revivalists, usually Catholic, the old language of Gaelic was to be the new language of the coming Irish utopia. But this did not mean that writers in Irish should submit to the authority of the old achievements in Gaelic. In 1903 Pearse called for a fresh start in Gaelic literature. Writers in Irish thenceforth should express themselves (and by doing so, Ireland) and not merely the conventions of the Gaelic folktale which he regarded, unlike many of the Irish collectors and writers, as universal in basic structure and therefore insufficiently Irish or distinctive. Save on the subject of blood-sacrifice for Ireland, Pearse was a reasonable, progressive, and, as his letters prove, hardheaded thinker, of which his sense of the basic internationality of the folktale gives some hint. His own stories were published in two volumes, *Íosagán agus Sgéalta Eile (Iosagan and Other Stories)* (1907) and *An Mháthair agus Sgéalta Eile (The Mother and Other Stories)* (1916). It has been claimed that modern literature in Irish begins with these stories and with the stories of Padraic Ó Conaire.[4] Unqualified before either writer's fiction in Irish, I want to discuss Pearse's stories in translation because of Pearse's immense significance in Irish history and Irish thought. In 1917 Joseph Campbell translated Pearse's stories for the volume he edited, *Plays, Stories, Poems* by Patrick H. Pearse.[5]

The stories were presumably meant to answer Pearse's own summons to writers in Irish, though one might hope—as far as one is entitled to through reading translations—that they did not in fact satisfactorily do so. Failure in practice need not, of course, damage the theory. Suffice it to say that in opposing the sway of the folktale and the eighteenth century Munster poetic tradition (later beloved of Daniel Corkery) as literary models, Pearse had to combat Gaelic language "hardliners" such as Patrick Dineen and Richard Henebry who spoke witheringly of "Revival Irish" written by those for whom, the Dublin-born, half-English Pearse included, Irish was not the language of the nursery. Answering Henebry's criticism of one story, "Íosagán," for its third-person omniscient viewpoint when it ought to have had, according to its critic, a chronicler's voice and point of view, Pearse claimed that "It was meant as a standard of revolt . . . the standard of definite art form as opposed to the folk form."[6] Certainly his stories lack many of the formulas of the Gaelic folktale that Henebry demanded, for example the introductory genealogy of the hero, but in their simplicity, a damaging simplicity, they are in fact closer to the corrupted folktales of printed tradition than to the European short story whose form Pearse imagined he was smuggling into Gaelic fiction. We can see, even in translation, a muted struggle to wrest a modern fictional narrative out of folk narrative, and fictional character out of folk typology, but the struggle is an unequal one because Pearse simply does not have the literary or psychological equipment for the job.

"The folktale is an echo of old mythologies, an unconscious stringing together of old memories and fancies: literature is a deliberate criticism of life. . . . Why impose the folk attitude of mind, the folk convention of form on the makers of literature?"[7] Pearse slights the folktale here, but he is basically correct in his distinction, even if in *Iosagan and Other Stories* there is neither adequate form nor adequate character, one respected critic's view to the contrary that Pearse's short stories "are presented with uniform severity; the phrasing is gem-like, and the final impression is of a most disciplined and perceptive mind."[8] Ironically, Pearse's question could easily have been posed later by Stephen Dedalus to revival writers, while *Dubliners* and *A Portrait of the Artist* could be regarded as the most effective reply that art form made to folk form during the Irish literary revival. Pearse again: "The evangels of the future will go forth in the form of light, crisp, vivid, arresting short stories. Gorki rather than Dickens suggests the style."[9] This is yet another admirable and prophetic, or perhaps influential, distinction, as we shall see in the next chapter (it certainly anticipates the Russian connection in Irish fiction forged by Frank O'Connor and Sean O'Faolain), even if it is left unclear how Russian influence can help create a distinctive Irish literature.[10] There is irony—not to Pearse's discredit—in his desire for writers in Irish to follow sophisticated models while Irish writers in English were turning to folk models. Pearse at first thought the new Anglo-Irish literature a retrograde step and an antinationalist impertinence that should be speedily checked, but like Griffith he changed his mind. Perhaps he sensed that what the two fledgling literatures had in common was a wish through fresh forms to instate fresh or revived awarenesses, new literatures that would aid in creating new men and women for the struggle ahead.

Pearse's prescription of art form is unfulfilled in his own stories; or at least, such form does not survive translation. And despite his admirable abhorrence of sentimentality,[11] several of the stories recall the more sentimental moments of the English Boz. They do not exhibit the "nervous vigour, vividness, pathos, passion" he desired in Gaelic fiction, nor "the plain straightforwardness, the muscular force of what is best in medieval Irish literature" that he said should, alongside the style and form of the Continental short story, claim the attentions of Gaelic fiction writers (as they were already, though he does not acknowledge it, claiming the attentions of Irish writers in English).[12]

Pearse bowdlerizes in his imagination the old Irish fictions even more drastically than the Anglo-Irish writers, viewing them through the triple veil of puritanism, nationalism, and an urban sensibility: Tír-na-nÓg, for example, is reduced in one story, "Eoineen of the Birds," to a Christian heaven borrowed from the most sentimental Victorian fiction. In trying to re-create what he imagined as a simple and ageless Ireland still alive in the twentieth-century west, he achieved merely a posed naivety. We cannot even defend the stories on the ground that they are meant for youthful readers. Only "Eoineen of the Birds" and "Barbara" (a doll-story praising emotional self-sacrifice, likewise sentimental and Victorian) are true children's stories in which the narrator evens his wit to his young readers. The other stories are informed by an adult's views and as such are revealing of the mind of "this most famous of Irishmen."[13]

The stories cherish the notion of a blessed and enchanted west, site of a poverty and simplicity that induce miracles. "Putting these stories in order . . . I see before my eyes," wrote Pearse in his Foreword to *Íosagán agus Sgéalta Eile*, "a countryside, hilly, crossed with glens, full of rivers, brimming with lakes; great horns threatening their tops on the verge of the sky in the north-west; a narrow, moaning bay stretching in from the sea on each side of a 'ross,' the 'ross' rising up from the round of the bay, but with no height compared with the nigh-hand hills or the horns far off; a little cluster of houses in each little glen and mountain gap, and a solitary cabin here and there on the shoulder of the hills. I think I hear the ground-bass of the water-falls and rivers, the sweet cry of the golden-plover and curlew, and the low voice of the people in talk by the fireside."[14] Unfortunately there is little description as evocative as this in the stories themselves in which the west, as in folktales, is a given, signposted only by references to roads, cabins, and hearths.

The four stories in *Iosagan* have children as major characters, presumably because Pearse agrees with the priest in one story who speaks of "the cleanest and most beautiful thing that God created—the shining soul of the child"; the title of "The Priest" refers, it turns out, to a small boy who anticipates his calling by mimicking the priest at Mass. For a contrasting, contemporary view of children we might recall the three opening stories of *Dubliners* in which the child-hero is introduced to and contaminated by various forms of perversion. Many of Pearse's stories concern innocence, in the sense either of wrongful accusation or of blissful ignorance. Childhood and innocence culminate in the title story of Pearse's first volume in which an elderly apostate is seduced back into the arms of Mother Church by a love of children that has preserved his spiritual innocence intact throughout his apostasy (as Ireland has had her innocence preserved through centuries of occupation), a love that focuses on the infant Jesus (Íosagán is an affectionate Gaelic diminutive of Jesus) reincarnated, with some racial favoritism one might have thought, as a beautiful Irish peasant boy. Again for contrast we might think of Joyce's fiction which demonstrates, in the undeclared cause of a profounder innocence, Ireland's prodigious capacity for hypocrisy, treachery, and cruelty.

Submission and self-denial are Pearse's theme and practice. He submits himself as a fiction writer to naive narrators, purportedly natives of Connemara, and thereby deprives his fiction of irony without bringing himself closer to the real west. And like his adult characters, he submits himself in theme and philosophy to childhood.[15] His fiction conveys no inner sense of character, no psychology: his scenes are devotional tableaux, and because of this his characters have no inner sense of worth, no realized self to be denied. They submit to everyone and everything—poverty, the landscape, the priest, the family, fate itself: everything against which Joyce has Dedalus rebel. Especially do they submit to the Mother, the dominant figure in the stories of *An Mháthair* and in Pearse's imagination and who is herself a symbol of submission in addition to being, as her guises of Mother Church and Mother Ireland suggest, a symbol of hegemony.

In "The Mother," title story of the second volume, a peasant woman is childless. She tries many remedies, including self-mortification: "Once she drew blood from her shoulder-blades with blows she gave herself with a switch. Another time she stuck thorns into her flesh in memory of the crown of thorns that went on the brow of the Saviour."[16] Because of her intense love of children, she is visited on Christmas Eve by the Virgin Mary and the baby Jesus, blessed, and delivered later of a child. The husband is significantly absent from the story and the intended or unintended suggestion is of an immaculate conception. Though the reader might be forgiven for thinking that the Almighty takes an inordinate interest in Ireland, we have here the re-Incarnation theme and Vision motif we already noticed in "Iosagan" and that recurs in "The Roads" in which a runaway girl sees the suffering Christ on the journey to Calvary. This theme is not unconnected with the belief of the more Christian mystic nationalists that Ireland would undergo a Celto-Christian rebirth, a belief that made it natural (or supernatural) for people to call the 1916 Dublin insurrection a resurrection, the "Easter Rising." The peasant woman in "The Mother," named Maire, is not merely visited by the Virgin Mary but is clearly meant to *be* the Virgin Mary, a Mother Ireland made fruitful by divine dispensation or, more specifically, a barren, post-Famine west quickened into life by divine (or revival?) intervention. For Joyce, on the other hand, Ireland's fecundity was alarming and even self-defeating—the old sow eating her farrow was, despite the depopulating effect of the Famine, an apt metaphor for a country of teeming and impoverished families.

Selflessness and endurance, then, are something of a ploy, disguising as they do the pretense of Pearse's Irish peasants to a quietly triumphant divinity which is also Ireland's triumphant divinity. "Those who look in these pages for a vision of Pagan Ireland, with its pre-Christian gods and heroes," warns the Introduction to the *Plays, Stories, Poems* (significantly date-lined "Maynooth" one year after Easter 1916), "will be disappointed. The old divinities and figures of the sagas are there, and the remnants of the old worship in the minds of the people are delineated, but everything is overshadowed by the Christian concept, and the religion that is found here centres in Christ and Mary. The effect of fifteen centuries of Christianity is not ignored or despised. The ideas of sacrifice and atonement, of the blood of the martyrs that makes fruitful the seed of the faith, are to be found all through these writings; nay, they have even more than their religious significance, and become vitalizing factors in the struggle for Irish nationality." These remarks have a dual purpose. They take to task the (mostly Protestant) revivalists who demoted Christianity in favor of paganism, and they claim Pearse for Catholic rather than secular nationalism.[17]

Pearse and Heroism

It was notably but not exclusively Pearse who saw Ireland's cultural and political resurgence in terms of Christian myth and ritual. His versions of the Irish struggle that we find in his letters, speeches, and literary works are often at the same time versions of Christian—and especially Christ's—experience: baptism, mortification, miraculous vision, martyrdom and blood sacrifice, salvation, resurrection and redemption.[18] It is historical orthodoxy now that these notions played a central role in Pearse's political philosophy and that Pearse regarded his work as something akin to a ministry. It was not just a question of metaphor. For assuming that the national struggle and the Christian struggle were one and the same, Pearse was branded a heretic by the late scholar-priest, Fr. Francis Shaw.[19] Before returning to this charge, we should perhaps distinguish two kinds of Christianity in Pearse's life and works. The Christianity of the short stories is not the muscular variety Pearse exploited in his political speeches. He exalts in the stories a Christian heroism often associated in Ireland by urban intellectuals with the peasantry, a heroism characterized by anonymity and community, innocence, poverty, passive endurance, and self-abnegation. Such heroism is quietist, "feminine" rather than "masculine," and stresses suffering and patience: " 'tis women that keep all the great vigils," Pearse has a character state in his play *The Singer*. This has had its political version in Ireland, most memorably expressed by Terence MacSwiney, the Lord Mayor of Cork who starved himself to death in Brixton prison in 1920 and who claimed that victory went not to those who inflicted the most but to those who endured the most. In one of the two genuinely readable stories in Campbell's selection, "The Keening Woman" (the other is "The Dearg-Daol"), Pearse attempts to reconcile this heroism with the more militant heroism he also and more famously admired and elsewhere thought of as likewise Christian.

"The Keening Woman" is the story of a Connemara youth wrongfully accused of assassinating a visiting absentee landlord outside Oughterard (Co. Galway) during the nineteenth century agrarian disturbances. He is convicted and sent to jail in Galway for life where he dies an unsung patriot martyr, despite the attempts of his pious mother—once again the father is conspicuously absent—to save him. "The Keening Woman" has a real sense of time and place, and the account of the mother pleading her son's cause in Gaelic to a bemused Queen Victoria outside her palace is rather moving. But on plot and motivation Pearse was usually weak. "The Keening Woman" fails because whereas the circumstantial evidence against the martyr would convict him in any court, we are apparently meant to divine his innocence; besides, no motive is imaginable for a government agent killing a landlord in order to frame an obscure country boy. Despite his claim that literature should be a criticism of life, a story like "The Keening Woman" proves that Pearse's first allegiance was not to literature but to cultural ideal. What makes the story interesting is something secondary but telling. Between the narrator's father and mother there is that curious division of family labor we find time and again in Irish literature. The mother counsels against violent reaction, advocates passive acceptance of oppression, and in general looks after the Catholic welfare of the family. The father stands for nationalist indignation. In this way, through the metaphors of gender and family, are Christian piety and Irish nationalism equally accommodated, indeed married.

The heroism that inspires Pearse's militant nationalism is characterized by valor, fame, and a "masculine" self-assertion. Such an ideal is pagan, yet Pearse associated it in speech and drama with the Church militant, an apocalyptic Christianity in which the need for struggle against tyranny is accompanied and encouraged by glimpses of the vast remunerative world beyond (in nationalist terms, free, Gaelic, Catholic Ireland) that we must strive to recreate on earth: "God has spoken through the voice of his ancient herald," Pearse wrote in *The King*, a morality play, "the terrible, beautiful voice that comes out of the heart of battles." The heroic assertion implied here is capped, not diminished, by the hero's ultimate self-sacrifice. Mary Colum remembers Pearse saying: "We may have to devote ourselves to our own destruction so that Ireland can be free."[20] This was part of an entire nationalist vision, not merely a military tactic; his patriotic ideal was a "love and a service so excessive as to annihilate all thought of self, a recognition that one must give all, must be willing always to make the ultimate sacrifice."[21] At St. Enda's, Pearse inculcated these twin ideals of manliness and self-sacrifice, and tried himself to live them. His verse judgement on his part in the Easter Rising, for example, deliberately echoed the Cuchulain motto of St. Enda's:

> The memory of my deed and of my name
> A splendid thing which shall not pass away.[22]

It is only just to remark that Pearse was no outcast in his more alarming notions. First of all, that he did not invent an Irish tradition of patriotic self-sacrifice is clear from the fact that it was practiced by a long line of patriot martyrs before him; even the expression of the idea in its pseudo-poetic and quasi-Christian clarity was not unique in Irish literature.[23] Such an attitude as Fr. Shaw's might even, unless kept within strict theological bounds, require us to indict the Irish imagination itself, which is drenched in a Catholicism that traditionally accorded primacy to eschatology, and readily appropriates for its self-expression, be it religious or secular, Catholic language and imagery.[24] Secondly, whereas Pearse's belief that an ascetic struggle and self-sacrifice were required lest the Gael become extinct may be distinctive in its articulateness, I have already cited Daniel O'Neil to the effect that self-sacrifice is one of three basic motifs in the quite impersonal pattern of twentieth century anticolonial revolutions. Thirdly, Pearse inherited a Catholicism quite capable of fostering remarkable visions. If we place him in the context created by Canon Sheehan's *The Triumph of Failure*, [25] he loses some of his unique fanaticism. Sheehan's novel depicts "a great religious revival" among Dublin Catholics in the 1870s, a movement led by a charismatic lay reformer whose fiery sermons are very different from the scholastic symmetries that terrify Stephen Dedalus in *A Portrait of the Artist*. Sheehan's hero, Geoffrey Austin, is reconverted to his Catholic faith by three consecutive visions as powerful and ornate as any in the pages of AE or Yeats. There was, then, an evangelizing, apocalyptic Catholicism to which Pearse was heir and which he might have displaced into nationalist fervor as the Protestant writers displaced an inherited Evangelicalism into cultural fervor.

The "feminine" element in Pearse's Irish hero is, I think, essential. (It can be readily studied in "The Wandering Hawk," a long and apparently unfinished story uncollected in Pearse's lifetime.[26] This is the only fiction Pearse composed in English. It is an interesting attempt to transpose the spirit of the Cuchulain and Fenian stories into a modern romance, set as it is in Connacht—but among educated schoolboys and their masters—during the Fenian disturbances of the 1860s.) This "feminine" element enables Pearse's hero to submit, like all his people, to the leadership of a greater hero, while his "masculine" element permits him in turn to exert authority over lesser heroes and the general populace. Leadership is all. It was his total belief in the near-mystical nature of leadership that allowed Pearse to believe naively that the British would grant amnesty to all the Easter rebels in exchange for his one life.[27] The dangers of such a conception of heroism and leadership are clear, and in it we might see foreshadowings of Fascism. The "feminine" element was marked in Pearse himself, in a psychological way rather than in the imaginative way we have seen instanced in other Irish writers. Nor could it be said that the two elements are satisfactorily synthesized in Pearse's psychology or philosophy, much less transcended. His courage is undeniable, but in his planning of the Rising one might see a "feminine" desire, beneath the "masculine" recklessness, for the opportunity for submission almost certain defeat offered.

Bat-like Souls: Joyce and the Peasantry

In Pearse, then, self-denial links a pagan-Christian heroism of warrior nationalism to a Christian heroism of peasant nationality, even though in one case the self-denial is deferred, in the other welcomed from the outset. The idea was not likely to appeal to Joyce. For a brief time, Joyce was a pupil in one of Pearse's Irish language classes. When Joyce ceased attending, it may have been, beyond a clash of personality, Joyce's lack of commitment to the Gaelic language and all in Pearse's visionary eyes it entailed. But in any case, the youthful Joyce was not the aptest of pupils and in *A Portrait* and *Ulysses* he questioned the role of disciple, one he may have felt uncomfortably close to that of servant, there being in each case a master. By the time the earlier novel was written, he had already repudiated the cultural authority of Yeats, nor did he involve himself in those occult societies in which mastery and discipleship were crucial. The two most prominent masters he repudiated were, of course, the British Empire and the Roman Catholic church. But the career of Parnell may have early cured him of belief in that other authority in a colonial society, the charismatic native leader who promises freedom to his followers, the figure Pearse became.

Discipleship entailed an unacceptable submission. When during the cultural revival the peasant and the west were invested with authority and promoted as the figure and locus of triumphant self-suppression, Joyce reacted. Unlike Pearse and other revivalists, he preferred as a writer to operate from a middle-class, urban milieu and with a concern for ethical, rational, and individual man in society. As we have already seen, Joyce at the close of "The Dead," having entertained the west against his will, as it were, buries it in a shroud of snow. There was to be no easy or decisive victory for the romantic primitivism of the revival. Five years after he wrote "The Dead," Joyce went to the Aran Islands and published a brief account of the trip in *Il Piccolo della Sera*, a Trieste newspaper.[28] Despite the absence of Dedalian scorn in "The Mirage of the Fisherman of Aran," I cannot because of my interpretation of "The Dead" agree with Richard Ellmann that the trip was a realization of Gabriel Conroy's sleepy resolution to go westward. Nor do I see the Trieste article as an expression of Joyce's embracement of "Ireland's primitivism" that according to Ellmann Joyce himself predicted in "The Dead." Although the stories of St. Brendan and the sunken islands appealed to him, as did traditional island hospitality, the account of the trip, even considering the foreign readership for whom it was intended and to whom Joyce would never have run Ireland down, is written in a factual manner one can only call diplomatic. Joyce came at least to respect, at last to absorb Celtic mythology and legends, but in 1912 the encounter of writer and islands, it would seem, was rather polite than cordial, rather an opening round of matchmaking than a romantic tryst.

"We Irish cannot become philosophical like the English," Yeats approvingly quoted an Irish poet (or was it really himself?), "our lives are too exciting."[29] Yeats saw no excitement in the only Ireland Sean O'Faolain came to see as real: the Catholic, English-speaking, democratic, petit-bourgeois world created by Daniel O'Connell in the nineteenth century; this Ireland was a wave of Yeats's "filthy modern tide."[30] I say world rather than nation or culture for neither of these was O'Connellite Ireland. We see it vividly in Joyce's middle-class and lower middle-class versions as a "throughother" affair. Its literature and music and received wisdom are scrappy, half-English, half-Irish, handed down from above and beyond. It is a world without cultural, moral, or spiritual integrity, at once inchoate and vestigial. Its center is its reflex Catholicism or perhaps merely its volubility, its entertaining, consoling, hollow eloquence; all else is precarious and piecemeal. What order it possesses is that of routine and empty ritual. It is, to borrow from *A Portrait*, a "sabbath of misrule," the unruly reality Dedalus intends to capture with a realist art while imposing on it his aesthetic order. Gabriel Conroy tries to impose on Irish life a social as well as aesthetic order but merely becomes, ironically, Twelfth Night's Lord of Misrule. Mr. Duffy in "A Painful Case" "abhorred anything which betokened physical or mental disorder," but his abhorrence, like Gabriel's, is set at naught.

Joyce's exploitation of the unruliness of Irish life, opposing as it did the uncaring tidiness of imperialism, Catholicism, nationalism, and socialism (and Yeatsian feudalism), distanced him from the revival. Joyce lamented the incompleteness of his characters' lives but did not advocate the recovery of wholeness along revival lines. Mr. Duffy may be right to describe Dublin workmen as "hard-featured realists" (i.e. materialists and self-seekers), just as he is right to describe the Dublin middle class (which Joyce will scrutinize in "The Dead" a few stories on) as "obtuse," but he is wrong to imagine that his socialist purity, a cloistered virtue, is superior to the workmen's materialism. To acknowledge the reality of Ireland that lies below "isms" is the first step toward realizing Ireland and, after that, oneself. (But of aesthetic necessity, to achieve artistic order, Joyce's acknowledgment had to be *in absentia*.) In Joyce's agenda, if it can be called that, self-realization had to come first and independence from England take its place alongside independence from a variety of foreign and home-grown forces, all "counterparts" of each other and equally imperious. Realize the self (as Mr. Duffy fails to do) and independence follows, but independence (and the history of free Ireland proves him right) does not guarantee self-realization.

In wishing to envision Ireland as a distinctive integrity, the revivalists ignored or attacked the sprawling and inconvenient reality of O'Connellite Ireland, but Joyce is its chief laureate. (Equally, and disastrously, did they ignore its Ulster Protestant counterpart: yet these are the only two Irelands that matter today, and their horns are locked.) The center of O'Connellite Ireland was middle- class and lower middle-class Dublin, and, not far beyond MacNamara's Westmeath, its periphery gave out before the impoverished west was reached. That the west was not a vigorous part of O'Connellite Ireland enabled the revivalists to impose with some success their cultural will upon the west and to create out of it a literary iconography. (What on earth could Pearse or Yeats or AE have done with Mr. Henchy or Freddy Malins or Corley, the gallant?) Joyce was relatively ignorant of western reality and this accounts for the ambivalence he showed towards peasant Ireland, the rest of his ambivalence being accounted for by his antipathy towards the revivalists' literary image of the west, an image that contradicted his own goals as a writer.

The ambivalence is offered to us almost emblematically in several places in *A Portrait of the Artist as a Young Man* and more vividly than in "The Dead." To Davin, his colleague, an enthusiastic young nationalist and follower of Michael Cusack (the founder of the Gaelic Athletic Association and parodied in *Ulysses* as the Citizen), Stephen attributes a "rude Firbolg mind." Davin worships "the sorrowful legend of Ireland," a myth "upon which," Stephen believes, "no individual mind had ever drawn out a line of beauty."[31] Davin is a mock-Fenian or, as Stephen tells him, one of Ireland's tame geese (a stay-at-home or armchair warrior). Yet Davin alone is close enough to Dedalus to call him by his first name, an intimacy reciprocated by Stephen's references to Davin as a "peasant," "a jesting name between them."[32] Davin's reluctance of speech half-expresses (he is, after all, a former not a genuine peasant) "the hidden ways of Irish life," the dark simplicity that fitfully haunts Stephen and is illustrated in Davin's beguiling anecdote of the young married woman in County Limerick who entreats him without success to stay the night, "a type of her race and of his own," Stephen reflects, "a bat-like soul waking to the consciousness of itself in darkness and secrecy and loneliness and, through the eyes and voice and gesture of a woman without guile, calling the stranger to her bed" (p. 183). Stephen associates himself with this peasant woman, for both stand on the threshold of racial consciousness. The threshold is literal as well as metaphoric, for the young woman seeks to draw Davin over the threshold of her cabin, and Stephen later stands on the threshold of the National Library watching flying birds and thinking of Daedalus. At the end of *A Portrait*, Stephen goes forth to create a racial self-consciousness, but even should he succeed as bringer of light to his benighted people he will not have done so by entering and portraying the dark cabins of the poor. Should the peasant gain awareness of himself, it will not be through the fiction of Stephen or Joyce. Davin's peasant woman reminds Stephen of the similar woman he once saw at the half-door of a cottage in Clane.

When he saw her he longed "to sleep for one night in that cottage before the fire of smoking turf, in the dark lit by the fire, in the warm dark, breathing the smell of the peasants, air and rain and turf and corduroy. But O, the road there between the trees was dark! You would be lost in the dark. It made him afraid to think of how it was" (p. 18). Among the things that Stephen fears, even as a young man, are "country roads at night." Like Gabriel Conroy, Stephen has issued in some way from these women, from peasant Ireland, but estrangement from them has created fear and consternation and made of peasant Ireland for them both a dark and mysterious thing.

Even Davin the nationalist cannot, or will not, penetrate the mystery of the peasant. That the young Limerick woman fails to draw him over the threshold of her cabin suggests that despite his nationalist fervor, indeed perhaps because of it (he will no doubt absorb her into the sorrowful legend of Ireland), Davin cannot help her consciousness come to birth. Far less hope has Stephen. He feels the thoughts and desires of "the race to which he belonged flitting like bats across the dark country lanes, under trees by the edges of streams and near the pool-mottled bogs," (p. 238) but unlike Davin "him no woman's eyes had wooed." Besides, it is too late. To attempt to bring a consciousness to birth requires an intimacy that Stephen contemplates in sexual terms; without this intimacy, the attempt would be an affectation and pretense. But these peasant women have already been known. Just as Davin sensed that the young Limerick woman was carrying a child within her, so the woman Stephen remembers seeing at the half-door of a Clane cottage had a child in her arms. Stephen, if he wishes to do something for the consciousness of his people, would seem best equipped to take as material the Irish he knows best. This is what his creator did in *Dubliners*. In that volume of stories, all of which depict varieties of reversion and childishness, Joyce grapples with a consciousness already born but arrested in figurative childhood or adolescence.

These peasant women are representative not only of the peasantry but also of womanhood, and at times Stephen in revival fashion sees Ireland, the peasantry, and womanhood as a mysterious (but for him untrustworthy) trinity. And so he thinks of Emma in the identical terms he thinks of Davin's seductress, as "a figure of the womanhood of her country, a bat-like soul waking to the consciousness of itself in darkness and secrecy and loneliness," (p. 220) a girl unfaithful to him as the peasant women, already pregnant or mothers, were "unfaithful" to Davin and himself. Davin and Stephen are recruits to the ranks of Joyce's husbands and lovers, including Leopold Bloom and Gabriel Conroy, who are wronged or who believe themselves wronged, and who banish themselves, or are banished, from the intimacy of their women, which is the intimacy of Mother Ireland (including the Mother Church and the mother tongue), a mother who is also—like Yeats's Cathleen Ni Houlihan—a sweetheart. Although Joyce shares with Yeats and other revivalists an interest in the love triangle—another vivid version of it is the Naoise-Deirdre-Conchubar triangle—his larger sympathy tends to reside with the man who for higher cause forsakes Ireland or is forsaken by her.

In the journal that closes *A Portrait*, Stephen expresses more of these unsettling feelings towards the Irish peasantry, this time uncomplicated by the question of gender.

> *April 14*. John Alphonsus Mulrennan has just returned from the west of Ireland. European and Asiatic papers please copy. He told us he met an old man there in a mountain cabin. Old man had red eyes and short pipe. Old man spoke Irish. Mulrennan spoke Irish. Then old man and Mulrennan spoke English. Mulrennan spoke to him about universe and stars. Old man sat, listened, smoked, spat. Then said:
> —Ah, there must be terrible queer creatures at the latter end of the world.
>
> I fear him. I fear his red-rimmed horny eyes. It is with him I must struggle all through this night till day come, till he or I lie dead, gripping him by the sinewy throat till . . . Till what? Till he yield to me? No. I mean no harm.

This is not really in the style of a diary; it is highly wrought as befits a tyro author, concise not to save time and space but to convey irony and parody. There is an ironic slap at the ethnocentricity of Irish nationalism and revivalism ("European and Asiatic papers please copy") and a parody of AE, Yeats, and Synge, not only in the old man's reply but also in Mulrennan's disquisition for the old man's benefit, determined as he seems to be in seeing the old man as a romantic or mystic who contemplates the universe and stars.

Yet almost balancing Stephen's disdain for the west and for romantic primitivism, a disdain not unlike Gabriel's, is what would appear to be Joyce's mockery of his hero's overcharged and Jacobian version of his dilemma ("gripping him by the sinewy throat")[33] and Stephen's awakening from this feverish exaggeration ("No. I mean no harm.") It seems at first as if fear will make Stephen fight the old man as Gabriel ought perhaps to have closed with the ghost of Michael Furey, but no, Stephen is as apparently irresolute as Gabriel, though in reality both are as wise in this regard as their creator. Neither will engage these threatening figures from the west on their native grounds; instead, he will coexist with them, defeating them by absorbing them into a vision greater than primitivist enthusiasm or cynical repudiation, an absorption half conscious in the case of Gabriel, more conscious in the case of Stephen, wholly conscious in the case of Joyce himself. Ironically, fulfillment of the vision requires physical exile (to which Gabriel's out-of-the-body experience is tantamount): the shortest way to Tara, Stephen tells Davin, is eastwards, via Holyhead, but of course each has a different Tara in mind.

When Stephen writes of struggling with the old man, we sense a psychic and even archetypal combat. Estranged from the Mother, he must become estranged from the Father too, be he the actual father (Simon), the fathers of the Church, or, in this instance, the Peasant Ancestor. Synge, who paid homage to the Mother, dramatized in *Playboy* an unsuccessful attempt to destroy the father, and the son's final and amicable succession to the estate of his father, that resilient and unslayable figure. Dedalus too promises succession to his father's estate, only his father is not the Peasant Ancestor but the fabulous artificer; the son Icarus becomes his own father, Daedalus.

In the struggle with the old man, we also sense a literary combat, the clash of two literatures, two ways of perceiving and ordering the world.[34] Yet Joyce could not or would not see the peasant in terms of his accustomed realism, but tended like other Irish writers of the time to see, however ironically, a literary, emblematic west. In his verse he even indulges a poetaster's feeling for the "desolate places" of the west beloved of Yeats and others. In his diary entry for April 14th, Stephen seems on the verge of distinguishing the reality of the old man (whatever that might be) from revivalist iconography, but he could not really do so because Joyce's acquaintance with cabin dwellers fell short even of the contrived acquaintance of Yeats and Lady Gregory. At best, the old man is an ancestral ghost, half comic, half alarming, an old father whom Stephen will not ask to stand him in good stead.

Epic Realism: O'Kelly's The Weaver's Grave

More convincing portraits of the peasantry can be found in the pages of those whose relationship to the revival was at best uneasy. The stories in Corkery's *A Munster Twilight* (1916) are a grim counter to Yeats's Celtic Twilight.[35] Set mainly on the west Cork coast or in the shadowy Kerry mountains, they portray untilled fields ("desolate treeless hills" . . . a "dispeopled land") for whose inhabitants the breath of life is an obscure memory of injustice. If Corkery's people are mythic in gesture, myth is no liberating enactment of antiquity but a dark force to which they are in thrall, and Corkery's realism lies in his recognition of that thraldom. *A Munster Twilight* joins *The Untilled Field* and *Dubliners* to complete a trio of short story collections as seminal in theme as in form. The title of one story, "The Spanceled," resounds through the volume. Gripped by a vindictive past and prevented from realizing themselves, a widow and a land-grabber's nephew love in order to spite their jailers (their friends and neighbors, self-appointed custodians of the past): "And so they leaped from their pit of sorrow, as the spanceled will until time be over; in no other way is it possible for them—this is their sorry philosophy—to revenge themselves on fortune, to give scorn for scorn." It was poor Ireland's sorry philosophy too, driven inwards upon itself, feeding upon an ingrown passion that, oddly, Corkery saw as remediable, even benign, when in his criticism he later translated it from twilight into the light of day.

Among the half-dozen novels praised by Corkery in *Synge and Anglo-Irish Literature* for their grasp of rural Ireland is Darrell Figgis' *Children of Earth* (1918).[36] But although there is plenty of reality in this novel of a western island, *Children of Earth* is full of romantic device and extravagant vision and places Figgis, as does his later book, *The Return of the Hero*, among the revivalists. Figgis in *Children of Earth*, with its Syngean dialogue, does not escape Martin Duignan's stricture on his literary predecessors in *The Irishman*: "They had all attempted to express the Irish peasant through the medium of his talk, in what he said rather than in what he did."[37] Duignan sees this as a literary convention as tyrannical as any that preceded the revival; even the language obsession of the Gaelic League was culpable, since it was "an organised attempt to give language an importance greater than the life for which, at the fullest stage of its development, it could never be more than an ornament." If Duignan succeeds at the end of MacNamara's novel in being a rural realist, it is by refusing to let the power of language hide "the power of the clay."

Seumas O'Kelly, the Galway poet, novelist, short-story writer, playwright, and journalist, gloomily acknowledges the power of the earth in his novel *Wet Clay* (1922). Brendan Nilan, an Irish-American, returns to Ireland at the close of the Land War and when the Land Purchase Act of 1903 is breaking up the estates and creating a population of smallholders. Although he has "no hankering after the heroic, in this flight to the pastoral life of the country of his parentage,"[38] he has a rather romantic notion of peasant proprietorship. He notes as an "observant American" the meagre life "of a land whose pulse beat had gone down" with its "naked poverty" and "domination of the hovel," yet becomes something himself of a "strange peasant." Like Lysaght's O'Hickie (and unlike Joyce's Conroy), O'Kelly's Nilan upon landing in Ireland travels westward to Galway to become a Gael and tries to reconcile romanticism with practicality. O'Kelly, like Tynan in *A Girl of Galway*, records with nationalist glee the end of the power of the land-agents, instruments of a tottering oligarchy and seekers in their own right after class conquest, behind which stands "a burning racial hatred" of the mere Irish. Nilan transforms himself like O'Hickie into a practical man and wants to encourage the emergence of a locally independent rural Ireland, this "phoenix from the clay."

Nilan's practical nationalism has his creator's sympathy, but O'Kelly reveals some romantic frustration when Nilan recognizes around him a want of idealism and a distaste for a wider cultural revival in Ireland. Yet if O'Kelly's thwarted romanticism echoes MacNamara's, so too does his suspicion of the idealism that is lacking. Nilan is aware of the deep forces of conservatism on the land (a reverse idealism that refuses modernization and machinery) but romantically underestimates their power, and in the end he is destroyed by them. The brutal marriage of the woman he loves (who chooses to remain in that marriage) symbolizes a reality in Ireland no Land Act can alter. Martha fails to become the Ibsenite heroine Nilan reads about, and Nilan is sacrificed in the failed cause of her self-realization, ending the novel face down, clutching in a death-grip the wet clay that has been his undoing.

Wet Clay is an interesting but quite ordinary novel that labors with realism and flirts with melodrama. It is hard to believe that the man who wrote it also wrote *The Weaver's Grave* (1919), a novella James Stephens rightly said "is about as close to greatness as anything in our time."[39] The plot is of the simplest and achieves epic stature with an almost insolent ease. A widow enlists the aid of an ancient nail-maker, Meehaul Lynskey, and an ancient stonebreaker, Cahir Bowes, to find the grave of her deceased husband, Mortimer Hehir, the ancient weaver, that he can be buried in Cloon na Morav (the Meadow of the Dead) and claim the penultimate grave in this antique cemetery. The three are accompanied by youthful twin gravediggers, but the grave remains unfound until Malachi Roohan, the ancient cooper—upon whose death the ultimate grave will be filled—is consulted. During this brief but epic search, the young widow is attracted to one of the twins, and this spellbinding novella ends with their kiss by the side of her husband's yawning grave.

Cloon na Morav is a monument to human vanity undermined by the vengeful contrariness of time:

> Plain heavy stones, their shoulders rounded with a chisel, presumably to give them some off-handed resumblance to humanity, now swooned at fantastic angles from their settings, as if the people to whose memory they had been dedicated had shouldered them away as an impertinence. Other slabs lay in fragments on the ground, filling the mind with thoughts of Moses descending from Mount Sinai and, waxing angry at the sight of his followers dancing about false gods, casting the stone tables containing the Commandments to the ground, breaking them in pieces—the most tragic destruction of a first edition that the world has known.[40]

This disintegration is the reality, these essays in immortality the illusion; indeed, according to Malachi Roohan the reality is that human existence is itself a delusion, a dream that ends with our extinction, from which we dead do not awaken. Likewise, any attempts on the part of the approaching visitor to make sense of Cloon na Morav by thinking of *Hamlet* or Gray's "Elegy" are doomed by the "sabbath of misrule" within its walls. Only religion and mythology can contemplate the disorder and antiquity of the graveyard, and then hopelessly. "The mind could only swoon away into mythology, paddle about in the dotage of paganism, the toothless infancy of Christianity." (p.6)

O'Kelly's graveyard is archetypal, like Shakespeare's in *Hamlet*. But its "haze of antiquity" is surely that of Ireland itself, whose history is confused and overlaid, the whole island an unruly burial ground. Mortimer Hehir in his lifetime cherished the traditional rights of the weavers as "great authorities and zealous guardians of the ancient burial place," a fanatical historian of Ireland in microcosm. "Cloon na Morav was the grand proof of his aristocracy" (p. 34); he has battled to keep "alien corpses out of his own aristocratic pit" (p. 34); his heart has been in Cloon na Morav "and the sweet, dry, deep, aristocratic bed he had there in reserve for himself" (p. 35). Behind the weaver's "truculent egoism" is a view of Ireland—historical, genealogical, racial, nationalistic—that prevailed during the time O'Kelly wrote *The Weaver's Grave*, and it is shown to be unequal to the reality of Cloon na Morav, or of Ireland itself: "But these ancient vanities," O'Kelly writes of the graveyard's aristocratic monuments, "only heightened the general democracy of the ground." Democracy is a disorder that flouts myth, religion, literature, and monumentality (as "The Dead" reminds us). Its favorite device is irony, and so Mortimer Hehir, who failed to make his knowledge of Cloon na Morav democratic, looked forward to a royal funeral whereas "instead of t at they had no more idea of where to bury him than if he had been a wild tinker of the roads" (p. 36). Democracy is also realism; after death comes the wake, which is "a grand review of family ghosts" during which a "woman with a memory speaking to the company from a chair beside a laid-out corpse carries more authority than the bishop allocuting from his chair" (p. 32). "The wake," adds O'Kelly, "is realism."

The weaver's young widow hates genealogy, traditional rights, and the impersonalizations of her husband's mind, but she is compelled by duty to find the weaver's grave. At first she is unmoved by the handsome gravediggers because "the first grave-digger spoiled the illusion of individuality in the second grave-digger" and "there is nothing more powerful, but nothing more delicate in life than the valves of individuality" (p. 61). But "that most subtle and powerful of all things, personality" enables her to distinguish one twin from the other and to receive in the end his spring across the grave to her. Padraic Colum in his Introduction to the 1965 edition of the novella refers to the widow's "unrealized life," but she awakens into the first stage of self-realization and does so, like Gabriel Conroy, by means of an epiphany that gives fresh and hopeful meaning to Malachi Roohan's dream-theory of human existence.

The subversion in *The Weaver's Grave* of vanity, aristocracy, and tradition, and all other tyrannies of order, by transitoriness, democracy, and individuality, and all other rebellions of disorder, is rehearsed in the triumphant artistry of the story's telling. The bitter competition between the nail-maker and stonebreaker to find the weaver's grave swells into epic contest, and Meehaul Lynskey and Cahir Bowes themselves into creations of the impersonal centuries. Cahir Bowes is "so beaten down from the hips forward, that his back was horizontal as the back of an animal" (p. 5) . . . "his face hitched up between his shoulders, his eyes keen and grey, glint-like as the mountains of stones he had in his day broken up as road material" (p. 11) . . . "He was one of the great destroyers, the reducers, the makers of chaos, a powerful and remorseless critic of the Stone Age" (p. 12). Meehaul Lynskey is a slender, warped figure that drifts along while he casts his eyes over the ground—"eyes that were small and sharp, but unaccustomed to range over wide spaces. The width and wealth of Cloon na Morav were baffling to him. He had spent his long life on the lookout for one small object that he might hit it" (p. 10).

The jaunty mythopoeia of Stephens is detectable here, the same instantaneous collapse of epic into mock-epic. For O'Kelly's realism undermines his own epic pretensions, not least through phrasing and figuration so concisely brilliant as to be comic. Bowes and Lynskey are desperate fellows, by turns pitiable, admirable, and detestable, with "all their little bigotries," materialists in reality, unreliable middlemen, pretenders to tradition and rank, as reprehensible as the spurious aristocracy they serve—epic heroes, mock-epic butts, clowns, discomfiting drawings from real life. To the unwary they might resemble Synge's beggarly poets and philosophers, but in a passage that echoes MacNamara's remark of one character in *The Valley of the Squinting Windows* (see above, p. 188), the widow realizes that Meehaul Lynskey is no more poet or philosopher than (we might interject) the old man John Alphonsus Mulrennan met: "She knew then that Meehaul Lynskey was not thinking of any great things at all. He was only a nailer! And seeing the Evening Star sparkle in the sky he had only thought of his workshop, of the bellows, the irons, the fire, the sparks, and the glowing iron which might be made into a nail while it was hot! He had in imagination seized a hammer and made a blow across interstellar space at Venus! All the beauty and youth of the star frolicking on the pale sky above the slash of vivid redness had only suggested to him the making of yet another nail! If Meehaul Lynskey could push up his scarred yellow face among the stars of the sky he would only see in them the sparks of his little smithy" (pp. 59–60).

O'Kelly's mythic realism makes him in an Irish context kin to James Stephens, one of the fabulists, and when satirical, kin to Brinsley MacNamara.[41] But if his old men are enslaved by the impersonal past, by myth, they are enslaved equally by the impersonality of the modern world that makes machines of us; Meehaul Lynskey, indeed, had "put up a tremendous but unequal struggle against the competition of nail-making machinery" (p. 10). The dreamlike quality of event in *The Weaver's Grave* is indistinguishable from its contrivance, its shamelessly mechanical presentation of character and action. (O'Kelly, we remember, was a playwright.) The "fabulous artifice" of *The Weaver's Grave* makes it a forebear of the fiction of Flann O'Brien and Samuel Beckett and other postmodernists. Such artificial mythmaking crossed with an unshrinking realism issues at times in the monster of grotesquerie. In the descriptions of Cahir Bowes in a taking of remembrance of where the weaver's grave is (the maker of fragments triumphs over Meehaul Lynskey, the maker of wholes) or of Malachi Roohan, the bedridden cooper, in a daily performance of his own resurrection, it is hard not to think of Molloy or Malone:

> The mummy on the bed came to life. And, what was more, he did it himself. His daughter looked on with the air of one whose sensibilities

> had become blunted by a long familiarity with the various stages of his resurrections . . . He turned over on his side, then on his back, and stealthily began to insinuate his shoulder blades on the pillow, pushing up his weird head to the streak of light from the little window . . . Up he wormed his shoulder blades, his mahogany skull, his leathery skin, his sensational eyes, his miraculous beard, to the light and to the full view of the visitor. At a certain stage of the resurrection—when the cooper had drawn two long, stringy arms from under the clothes—his daughter made a drilled movement forward, seeking something in the bed. The widow saw her discover the end of a rope, and this she placed in the hands of her indomitable father. The other end of the rope was fastened to the iron rail of the foot of the bed. The sinews of the patient's hands clutched the rope, and slowly, wonderfully, magically, as it seemed to the widow, the cooper raised himself to a sitting posture in the bed. There was dead silence in the room except for the laboured breathing of the performer. The eyes of the widow blinked. Yes, there was that ghost of a man hoisting himself up from the dead on a length of rope reversing the usual procedure . . . There he was, sitting up in the bed, restored to view by his own unaided efforts, holding his grip on life to the last. It cost him something to do it, but he did it. It would take him longer and longer every day to grip along that length of rope; he would fail ell by ell, sinking back to the last helplessness on his rope, descending into eternity as a vessel is lowered on a rope into a dark, deep well. (pp. 41–42)

Bowes and Lynskey, stonebreaker and nail-maker, Hammer and Nail—they are precursors of Beckett's Hamm and Clov. Yet they are meant to be secondary actors only in this unforgettable tale of a widow's seizure of real life and real love in a dream of death and decay. The gravedigger's leap breaks the spell antiquity has woven about the widow. She answers him in a voice "fresh, like the voice of a young girl." However, she is no Cathleen ni Houlihan, her girlhood redeemed by male patriotic self-sacrifice, but a woman awakening through love of a man (not of a country) to her own reality, bearing witness against all the impersonalities of this world.

The Island Man
The Rise (and Fall) of the Peasant Author—Tomás Ó Crohan

15

> This is not landscape, full of the somnambulations
>   Of poetry
> And the sea. This is my father or, maybe,
>   It is as he was,
> A likeness, one of the race of fathers: earth
>   And sea and air.
>
> —Wallace Stevens, "The Irish Cliffs at Moher"

The Islandman: *Archaism into Selfhood*

Joyce's peasantry—dark and exotic, half-contemptible, half-ominous—takes its place beside other imagined peasantries of the revival. Pearse's peasantry is innocent, childlike, submissive, Catholic; Synge's romantic, primitive, artistic; Yeats's and Lady Gregory's mystical, other-worldly, traditionalist; Colum's and Stephens' bright, adaptive, quick-witted. All of these bar Joyce's are rooted, naturally aristocratic, self-denying or self-transforming. All sought to displace the comic and credulous peasantry of Lover and other nineteenth century writers—that peasantry which survived less stagily in the fiction of Jane Barlow (1857–1917), Seumas MacManus (1868?–1960), and Lynn Doyle (1873–1961)—yet are all literary and cultural inventions.

Recognizably real peasants walk the pages of O'Kelly, Lysaght, MacNamara, and Corkery, but until after the revival (and in a sense despite the revival), perhaps William Carleton is as close as we get to a peasant author committing himself, his upbringing, ambitions, and inner feelings, to paper, and the Ulsterman Carleton thought of himself as of the yeomanry, not peasantry. The peasant had scant access to sophisticated means of self-expression, so others put words in his mouth and thoughts in his head. It is telling, for example, that Yeats when he advised Synge assumed that the hitherto unexpressed life on the Aran Islands would find tongue in the literature of a middle-class, Rathfarnham Protestant residing in Paris, not in the productions of the islanders themselves. Live on the islands, Yeats told him, *"as if you were one of the people themselves."*[1] It was not until the revival had virtually ended that autobiographies and fictions written by the remote countryman himself appeared. When they did, they came, remarkably enough, from one small western island but not one of the Arans.

An t-Oileánach by Tomás Ó Criomhthain was the first book of its kind and was completed in 1926. It appeared in Irish in 1929 and then in English as *The Islandman* in 1934. *Fiche Bliain ag Fás* by Muiris Ó Súilleabháin appeared in 1933 and came out the same year as *Twenty Years A-Growing,* with a Foreword by E. M. Forster. *Machtnamh Seana Mhná* by Peig Sayers was published in 1939 and later translated as *An Old Woman's Reflections* (1962). These books represent an astonishing output from one tiny island in the smother of the western sea, as Tomás Ó Crohan (Ó Criomhthain's Anglicized name) described Great Blasket. They are of immense documentary interest, in combination giving us firsthand accounts of the Blasket Islands' way of life from roughly 1860 until the 1930s, but also giving us traditional and hearsay accounts of life on the islands long before Ó Crohan's birth in 1856. The first and best of them initiated an Irish literary genre, the Gaelic peasant autobiography, of which there have since been a handful of examples, though the genre is obviously incapable of longevity. *The Islandman, Twenty Years A-Growing,* and *An Old Woman's Reflections* are all in part elegies and obituaries as well as celebrations and thefts from time. "Since the first fire was kindled on the islands," Ó Crohan wrote, "none has written of his life and his world. I am proud to set down my story and the story of my neighbours."[2] A few sentences earlier he had delivered himself of the soulful remark that brings to mind Hamlet's judgement of his dead father and the last line of Yeats's "Beautiful Lofty Things," a remark that became famous enough to be parodied by Flann O'Brien in *The Poor Mouth (An Béal Bocht:)* "I have done my best to set down the character of the people about me so that some record of us might live after us, for the like of us will never be again." It was prophetic: the Blaskets were abandoned in 1953.

Although *The Islandman, Twenty Years A-Growing,* and *An Old Woman's Reflections* form a compact trio—a "striking tryptych," one scholar has called them[3]—they are different both in form and genesis. The bulk of *The Islandman* was written as a series of letters to Brian O'Kelly who handed them over to a Mr. Sugrue (Pádraig Ó Siochfhradha) for whom Ó Crohan wrote the remainder of the book. This method of composition accounts for the book's haphazard quality, a quality which, as it happens, reflects a way of life that was full of surprises and incidents, governed as much by serendipity as by predictable simplicity. A similar quality marks *An Old Woman's Reflections,* for Peig Sayers dictated her memories to her son, the oral equivalent, one might say, of Ó Crohan's letters. There are more traditional stories in Sayers' than in Ó Crohan's book and less autobiographical matter, though what autobiographical matter there is is more personal than Ó Crohan's. *Twenty Years A-Growing* appears to have been conceived as a book, and it resembles more familiar and sophisticated autobiographies, despite Forster's rather sickly reference to it as the newly-laid egg of a seabird. Maurice O'Sullivan's book has been usefully called "soft" primitivism to distinguish it from the "hard" primitivism of *The Islandman*.[4] The English translation was immediately successful and some of Ó Crohan's relatives believed it stole the thunder of Robin Flower's translation of *An t-Oileánach*.[5]

In Seán O'Tuama's opinion, "the author of *An t-Oileánach,* Tomás Ó Criomhthain, had very few of the natural literary gifts of Ó Súilleabháin or Peg Sayers. Imaginativeness, humour, inventiveness, natural storytelling ability—all these he seemed to lack to a degree. Yet, paradoxically, his book is reckoned—and rightly so—to be the masterpiece of *Gaeltacht* literature."[6] According to Riobárd P. Breatnach, *An t-Oileánach* when it appeared came to Gaelic-speaking readers and scholars as "a blinding revelation"; here were "the real facts of Irish life, of the Hidden Ireland, we might say, in the mother tongue for the very first time."[7] No less of a revelation, artistic as well as cultural, must it have been to English-speaking readers when it appeared as *The Islandman*.[8] Written at the tail-end of the revival, translated well after the revival, *The Islandman* itself commemorates three "ages" as Ó Crohan sees them: the "savage age" before the 1850s (known to Ó Crohan through hearsay and legend), the "heroic age" of Ó Crohan's childhood and youth (roughly 1856–75), and the "age of decline" (roughly and ironically the decades of the revival). The historical shadow and spread of the book, from Blasket legendry to Ireland in 1934, is therefore vast. Of the first age Ó Crohan speaks with awe, of the second with laconic fondness and nostalgia, of the third with genial scorn and stoic gloom.

It would have been difficult for *The Islandman* to have matched George Moore's momentary daydream in *Hail and Farewell* of a genius arising, "completely unequipped," on a western island. "If such a one were to write a book about his island he would rank above all living writers, and he would be known evermore as the Irish Dante."[9] But Ó Crohan, who had to learn to write his native Irish before attempting his autobiography, comes as close to unequipped genius as it is reasonable to expect. In both Irish and English versions, *The Islandman* is one of the ornaments of twentieth century Irish literature. Its majesty is its mystery: it is the utterance of a singular and ancient voice speaking to us in understandably muffled tones across intervening centuries that have not in fact passed at all. Yet if we listen carefully, the voice sounds ambiguous. It is not just that of archaic man but, less assured, that of modern Irish man awakening, in a remote pocket of existence, from archaism into selfhood. All is equivocacy and a dangerous passage. Twentieth-century Ireland, herself in the period costume of the literary movement, disturbs the sleep of the island; time disturbs timelessness; place placelessness; fact legend.

The Islandman, claims O'Tuama, "is more the biography of an island community than of a single islander."[10] On a first reading we are likely to agree, as we accompany the islanders in their communal though often competitive pursuits: salvaging, house-building, fishing, hunting, talking, hard drinking—their rugged commensalism. Here are peasants expressed in what they do. But they cannot be taken without qualification to represent the west. Despite the frequent and sometimes heroically maiming factionalism (for the hand is lifted readily and even fellow-islanders can be callously cast adrift on the open sea), the Blasket islanders knew themselves to be different from outsiders, to be "certain set apart." "We had characters of our own," writes Ó Crohan, "each different from the other, and all different from the landsmen . . . we are not to be put in comparison with the people of the great cities or of the soft and level lands." (pp.242–43) The islanders close ranks against mainlanders, and spirited battles with rival mainland fishermen and salvagers, or with hapless tax collectors, fights grown legendary in island memory, enliven Ó Crohan's narrative. Inexorably, however, centralized authority with (in times of island defiance) its superior firepower and, after Home Rule, a new altruistic, even more damaging mandate, exerts an intrusive power and influence. So does the outside world, at first merely Dunquin, Ventry, dimly Tralee, rarely Valencia, and at the end Dublin, England, Scandinavia, and the western world in comparison to which the island shrinks and discovers itself.

That there is in *The Islandman* no sense of the island's distinctive if minimal landscape might be attributed to Ó Crohan's fidelity to his role as the island's amanuensis, a role in part awarded by his mentors from the mainland, in part self-assumed. Since countrymen, especially those of the Irish west, pay little aesthetic attention to a begrudging landscape, neither, we might say, does Ó Crohan. O'Sullivan's attitude to island landscape is closer to Synge's romantic appreciation than to Ó Crohan's indifference, and *The Islandman* stands in chastening and refreshing contrast to the romantic pastoralism of the revival. Ó Crohan's mute Catholic faith, accompanied without conflict by an elder superstition, is likewise in marked contrast to the militant Catholicism of Pearse and Joseph Mary Plunkett, and seems the firmer for it. Certainly it seems to have contributed to the stoic repose, devoid of Pearse's Victorian Christian sentimentality, with which Ó Crohan faced his personal tragedies: "Well," he says smartly, after recounting the death of the first of several children, "those that pass cannot feed those that remain, and we, too, had to put out our oars again and drive on" (p. 186).

The Islandman is the authentic inside information, social observation and documentary realism revival writers would have required to write a genuine rural fiction of the west, but mostly did not possess, bar possibly Synge who was of the opinion that "to write a real novel of island life one would require to pass several years among the people . . . ."[11] Nor could they have come into its possession without, as Synge did, disrupting in however slight a degree the fragile equilibrium of island life. But I think O'Tuama's observation that *The Islandman* is the biography of an island is only half the story. By subtler signals than Ó Crohan's personal hardship and tragedy have we the impression of a man set apart from his fellows. In the early chapters we meet a boy who is bold and lively, a schoolfriend of the future island "king," the best scholar at the school, a precociously deft speaker. When he recalls his passionate fondness for the tales of a neighbor, Bald Tom, we have an image of the apprentice tale-teller, future custodian of the people's lore. This boy will become special, not because he can bring ill-luck with a satiric verse like the island-poet Dunlevy—who makes Ó Crohan his misgiving amanuensis and in whose power the islandman fervently believes: "a gust of the ill wind had always been blowing against me ever since the day the poet and his songs kept me from cutting the turf" (p. 117)—but because he is a sharp-tongued and sharp-witted observer.[12] (And unlike the poet Dunlevy, Ó Crohan is an island Renaissance man of Crusoe-like versatility—as several western islanders were, Synge and Flower tell us—fine dancer, hunter, fisherman, singer, house-builder, poet, swimmer, turf-cutter, storyteller.) There is a circumspection, a sternness in Ó Crohan, a moralistic detachment most evident when he is islanded in vigilant sobriety during the Blasketmen's epic drinking bouts. He is almost, it seems, the self-appointed conscience of the island, a primitive forerunner (actually elder contemporary) of Joyce. On occasions he even uses this unique opportunity to pay off old scores against those who failed to reach his exacting standards of loyalty, as Joyce sometimes used his fiction. In *The Islandman*, then, is an emerging integrity and individuality of hero and voice that go against the grain of revival philosophy and are expressively autobiographical in tenor.

The Islandman: *Folklore into Fame*

A duality analogous to Ó Crohan's status as an islander is exhibited by the form and style of *The Islandman*. It has a pronounced oral accent and intentionally avoids, Flower tells us in his Foreword, literary formality. "He has told me that, in writing this book, he aimed at a simple style, intelligible to every reader of Irish, using none of the 'cruadh-Ghaoluinn,' the 'cramp-Irish' of the purely literary tradition. This aim he has achieved. For the narrative runs easily in the ordinary language of the island, with only an occasional literary allusion of a straightforward kind" (p. ix). The book is also strewn with scraps of legendry and folklore, including many references to traditional songs. Ó Crohan delivers himself of numerous proverbs whose dexterous use in Irish-speaking communities is a sign of learning and eloquence. There is an easy reference to the death of Owen Roe O'Sullivan. And Ó Crohan can several times toss off a quotation from the Finn sagas (oars are "tough, sweet-sounding, enduring, white, broad bladed"), and, pace O'Tuama, Flower assures us in his Foreword of Ó Crohan's prowess as a tale teller, presumably *Sgéalaí* to Bald Tom's *Seanchaí*.

We are treated to a hint of Ó Crohan's ability with the long tale in his account of his combat with a beached seal which, as O'Tuama rightly says, takes on "the proportions of an epic act of Achilles."[13] Indeed, J. V. Luce, the Irish Greek scholar, has in fact tried to show analogies between life and literature on Great Blasket and the Homeric epics and early Ionian way of life.[14] Communal self-reliance, a simple and virile humanism, a heroic way of life, a precapitalist economy: these are features of early Ionian way of life Luce finds echoed in the life of the Blasket Islands. The predominance of simile and metaphor, humanistic descriptions of nature, concentration on preliminary description rather than on decisive moments in the action, wit and eloquence of dialogue: these are features of Blasket literature analogies to which Luce finds in Homer. Here is a piece of Ó Crohan's account:

> As she turned towards the sea, I gave her a blow, six blows one after the other, but she paid no more attention to any of those blows with the haft than if it had been this pen in my hand that had struck her: and with one of them I broke the haft of the fork in two. I gave her a whack across the snout with the bit left in my hand, but she caught it in her mouth and chewed it, and made bits of it. All I had then was a stalk of the weed, and I showered blows on her with that as fast as I could, but I was doing her no harm, only that I was hindering her from getting to the

> water, which was not far from her by this time. In the end, when I was worn out, and she was too, I managed to bang her on the top of the head with a lump of rock from the shore, and the blow turned her belly upwards, but she soon came to her senses again.
>
> At last I thought she was dead, and I was still whacking away at her with a stalk of weed, when, what do you think? I went too close to her, and she had a shot at taking a bite out of me. And she managed it, too! She bit a huge lump out of my calf. As much as her four front teeth could get a grip of—all that she tore out of my leg. I didn't give in, though blood was flowing out of it in torrents, just as it was out of the seal.
>
> Well, I'd finished the seal at last, and the seal had pretty well nearly finished me, too, and it was like to be my last day when I looked closely at my leg and saw the lump out of it and the fountain of blood spurting. The last drop had nearly left my heart; I had to strip off my little vest and twist it round my leg, binding it with the cord from my waist. The water was coming up with the rising tide and the seal was not far from the edge, so that I was terrified that the sea would carry her off again from me after all my trouble; there was not a soul coming next or nigh me. It was the middle of the morning by now, and, as I thought the thing over, I cast a glance now and again at my leg, which was spouting a stream of blood. (pp. 75–76)

Later, some islanders travel to the neighboring island of Inishvickillaun to kill a seal that a dollop of its flesh might be fastened to the bitten leg, for some remembered this drastic and simple measure having been successful in the past.

But if Ó Crohan's account of his combat with the seal suggests some ancient narrative, it also exhibits the particularity of Defoe, as Ó Crohan the seal fighter exhibits the initiative of Crusoe. Just as O'Tuama regards *The Islandman* as the biography of an island rather than of a single islander, so Virginia Woolf thought that *Robinson Crusoe* "resembles one of the anonymous productions of the race itself rather than the effect of a single mind."[15] Like Crusoe, Ó Crohan is never entirely free from "the troubles of the world." Set against the elemental background of an island, those troubles seem nearly symbolic of human misfortune which Ó Crohan accepts as unflinchingly as Crusoe. Both books glorify self-sufficiency. Both heroes dislike idleness and ingratitude. Neither Crusoe nor Ó Crohan is emotionally forthright and their wives are dismissed in a few sentences. Crusoe and Ó Crohan are kinds of Everyman, yet supreme individualists. Their individuality requires realism and particularity of expression, a preoccupation with facts and things highlighted by their similar necessity to beachcomb and salvage. The rage for fact is strong in Ó

Crohan because, despite his individuality, he saw his task as telling "how the Islanders lived in the old days" (p. 245) and setting down "the character of the people about me" (p. 244). Folklore could not be a primary model in form or content. "I have set down nothing but the truth," he claims, "I had no need of invention, for I had plenty of time, and have still a good deal in my head" (p. 242).

Out of a primitive mentality and archaic sense of time, Ó Crohan can be seen in *The Islandman* wresting history and objectivity. It is a birth and a forgetting. Ó Crohan's dating is fitful to a degree. The first sentence of *The Islandman* tells us he was born "on St. Thomas's day in the year 1856," but this is chiefly to explain his Christian name, and thereafter his sense of history is haphazard. (The attentive reader can date to the year twelve out of Ó Crohan's twenty-five chapters.) Ó Crohan's sense of history is chiefly provided by the various customs that died out during his lifetime, the eating of seal meat, sobriety at wakes, the eating of gannets, the use of seal-oil lamps, and by the positive changes, such as the introduction of paraffin and cups and saucers. He recalls more startling innovations: the first tea (found as salvage and thought to be a dye by the islanders and used as such), the first spectacles (thought to be worn by a man from hell by the schoolchildren) and the first steamship (misunderstood as a sailing ship on fire by the islanders who fruitlessly pursued it by oar).[16] The islanders tumble to their errors, and waken to the facts of the matter; Ó Crohan's observation, too, achieves a difficult independence from convention and customary perception.

As well as winning chronology and fact by putting in abeyance a traditional understanding, Ó Crohan was constrained by his adviser, Brian O'Kelly, to tell a life *story,* and we can read his somewhat painful efforts through some primitive chapter linkage to cast his life into a narrative. But the pull of the book, with its brusque pace and incidental structure, is towards independent tales, be they the ghosts of voyage or wonder tales, *echtrai* or *Märchen*. His anecdotes about accidentally netting a shark (a "monster") and on another occasion an unidentified and immense "sea beast" (a whale?) closely resemble the sea-monster legends collected by Lady Gregory in Galway and on the Aran Islands and reproduced in *Visions and Beliefs in the West of Ireland*. On such occasions we see fact and rudimentary (and vestigial) legend combine. Since the facts concern Ó Crohan's life and since the suggestion of folk anecdote in his telling of them remains, we might describe *The Islandman* as an extended memorat, a form of personal tradition the recording of which Lady Gregory, by encouraging her informants to talk about themselves, helped pioneer in

Visions and Beliefs.[17] In such a tradition the content of personal experience is poured into the conventional mold of folk expression.

To be his own hero through an extended narrative goes against the grain of the traditional storyteller, and Ó Crohan takes understandable refuge in anecdote, and when he feels he must comment on himself does so with an engagingly self-deprecating humor. There is, however, a sufficiently shaped and sustained awareness of self for us to call *The Islandman* a genuine autobiography, newly emerged from folk information and the memorat. Flower refers to the distinctive personality of Ó Crohan's prose style. Though he may write in the ordinary language of the island, "the style is none the less unmistakably his own, and to those who have known the man his whole figure and character is implicit in the manner of his writing" (p. ix).[18] But neither the style nor the self-portrait is romantic, and we may read *The Islandman* as a counterbalance to Synge's *The Aran Islands* in which a romantic selfhood wears a mask of factual concern.

The Islandman is a further crucial transition in the gradual emergence from obscurity of the folk teller or informant and, in fact, the Irish peasant. In the early and middle nineteenth century, the storyteller and informant were anonymous or, at best, distorted as comic raconteurs. During the revival they gradually gained respect, due partly to the awakening appreciation of them as performers.[19] Yeats's Biddy Hart and Paddy Flynn, Larminie's Pat Minahan, Synge's Pat Dirane (Lady Gregory's Old Deruane in *Visions and Beliefs*)—all prefigure Sayers, Ó Crohan, and O'Sullivan. These last three finally achieve independence from their mentors and notaries by having acknowledged their personalities as well as performance and fund of traditional material; at the end they become writers themselves whose fame outstrips that of their literary cicerones.

Waking the Dead: **The Islandman** *and the Revival*

But there is some silent irony in the fact that although it salvages folkways and folklore from the smother of the past, *The Islandman* itself, in conception and effect (it was conceived as literature, not oral testimony), was part of what helped to kill the traditional oral lore of the Blasket Islands. Ó Crohan recalls procuring his first books during the Irish language revival and remarks with his customary dispassion: "Very soon I had a book or two, and people in this island were coming to listen to me reading the old tales to them, and, though they themselves had a good lot of them, they lost their taste for telling them to one another when they compared them with the style the books put on them. It would be long before I tired of reading them to them, for I was red-hot to go ahead" (p. 223). The men who encouraged Ó Crohan to read books were those who bemoaned the loss of the oral literature because of the incursive tyranny of print. The irony escaped them, as it escapes Synge when in *The Aran Islands* he tells us that in his cottage a young islander is reading Douglas Hyde's *Beside the Fire* (presumably Synge's own copy). "A few years ago," Synge remarks, "this predisposition for intellectual things would have made him sit with old people and learn their stories, but now boys like him turn to books and to papers in Irish that are sent them from Dublin"; and further, when the young islander quarrels with Hyde's English: "It is curious to see how his rudimentary culture has given him the beginning of a critical spirit that occupies itself with the form of language as well as with ideas."[20]

The western islands were undergoing damaging changes in their traditional way of life in any case during the years of the revival; island life was at a dangerous crossroads around the turn of the century. The introduction of modern implements, customs, and points of view accelerated, causing dissatisfaction, sloth, and emigration among many. Internal problems caused by peculiar inheritance and marriage systems, and such acts of God as alterations in the migration habits of fish shoals, grew more acute. Flower recalls major changes in the agricultural and social pattern of settlement that Great Blasket underwent between 1910 and 1930, changes more numerous in his opinion than in all the previous years of the island's existence.[21] Flower's first visit in 1910 coincided with the beginning of the transition from the medieval common field system to "striping," a system supervised by the Congested Districts Board. Meanwhile there were the tax men, the First World War, foreign fishing fleets, and the Home Rule crisis, all impinging on island life. Synge for his part noted significant changes in the life of the Aran Islands around 1898: the emergence of class, rank, and division of labor; the advent of prosperity; the appearance of the criminal mind (which, having told the story that inspired *The Playboy of the Western World,* Synge blames on the introduction of police); and the decline of Gaelic.

These changes the scholars and enthusiasts of the revival quickened. They waked the dead in an opposite fashion to Joyce: they aroused and celebrated the west on purpose but helped to bury it unintentionally. The conscious attempt at revival was, ironically, another nail in the coffin of the traditional island way of life. The continuation of those features for which the west was lauded, variously described as primitive, archaic, prehistoric, medieval, and pagan, depended precisely upon western life remaining incompatible with grandiose revivalist notions espoused in the native colonialism that was the cultural renaissance. Those notions were sometimes resisted by the islanders, as Synge found when one man talked scathingly of the Gaelic Leaguers who began a branch on the Aran Islands and taught "a power of Irish for five weeks and a half"—an allusion, presumably, to Pearse's visit in 1898.[22] This man had no use for the Leaguers and thought, like a second man, that Irish would remain alive without its interference. Others, Synge found, especially older islanders, had no particular affection for Gaelic. Still others, however, welcomed the League and its activities and thought them necessary. Ó Crohan himself became involved in the Gaelic revival but had some private reservations.[23] He recalls the arrival of the language experts, including "the Norseman Marstrander" (Carl Marstrander) "about the year 1909," followed soon after by Tadhg O'Ceallaigh and Robin Flower; it was O'Ceallaigh who helped Ó Crohan compile an island thesaurus in Gaelic for Marstrander.[24] Synge, of course, had visited the Blasket Islands four years before Marstrander, but Ó Crohan does not mention him though his son later did.[25]

The continuation of features of island life revivalists thought desirable depended on the incompatibility of those features even with those amenities the visitor took for granted in his own life. Synge fails to see the irony in his generous gift of a clock to Aran islanders who had no clock and worked by hunger and shadow: "when I tell them what o'clock it is by my watch they are not satisfied, and ask how long is left them before the twilight."[26] Now, thanks to Synge, they became acquainted with the petty tyranny of chronometric time. Clearly the revivalists could not have their unreformed west and their revival too. These western islands attracted the revivalists chiefly because of an isolation that was in fact more complete under the neglect of English rule than under the solicitude of Home Rule fervor. "I often told the fishermen," Ó Crohan remembered, "that Home Rule had come to the Irish without their knowing it, and that the first beginning of it had been made in the Blasket now that the yellow gold of England and France was coming to our thresholds to purchase our fish, and we didn't give a curse for anybody" (p. 155). It would be difficult to imagine a notion of independence more removed from the mystical nationalism of Pearse.

The economic motive weakens the pull of nationalism on the Blasket islanders. The goals of security and profit are to the fore throughout the successive economic systems that *The Islandman* adumbrates. In Ó Crohan's childhood and youth the islands endured an absentee landlordism enforced by bailiffs, rent collectors, and other middlemen, a system under whose negligence the islanders were primarily salvagers, precarious farmers, and hunters. In the early chapters we have a portrait of a Crusoe-like precapitalist, prespecialized culture. With the coming of the foreign fish-buyers, the islanders enjoyed a measure of economic self-sufficiency and profitable private enterprise, something at odds with the paternalism of the Congested Districts Board that gave way to the more thorough paternalism of the Free State. National independence was a system that militated against individualism in the way nineteenth century landlordism and the middleman system had done before it. Under the various systems the Blasket people tried to assert their own economic identity, at the very least as islanders, ideally as individuals. *The Islandman,* with the growth of its writer into economic awareness, is a record of that attempt. When Robin Flower is setting out in a curragh from Dunquin bound for Great Blasket, one of the oarsmen cries, "Say your farewell to Ireland."[27] These islanders thought of themselves as a breed apart, as many local communities in Ireland must have done.

I suspect that some of the revivalists were not happy with this kind of attitude and wanted paternalistically to change, not preserve, contemporary island life in accordance with their picture of the noble communal past of the island, one vastly different from Ó Crohan's "savage age." I suspect too that other revivalists realized that revival, even preservation, was impossible. Revival midwives such as Flower were, it might be thought, engaged in inducing a cultural rebirth on the islands, but the feverishness of their activities suggests they sensed that island life and lore were doomed and felt that they should be recorded, even if in the process the doom was hastened. There was a birth, certainly, we have evidence and no doubt, but it was like death and it was those who were visited, such as Ó Crohan, not the journeyers, who were no longer at ease in the old dispensation. In a double irony, the revival helped articulate a self-consciousness that was incompatible with revival ideals; but as for the archaic western island, as it expressed itself it succumbed, like some lowly species of animal for whom death and reproduction are one and the same.

According to Flower, "it would probably never have occurred to Tomás to write his life, had it not been for Mr. Brian O'Kelly of Killarney, who encouraged him to set about the work, and read over part of Maxim Gorki's autobiography to him to show the interest of that kind of writing" (p. x). As a matter of fact, there is little resemblance between *The Islandman* and Gorki's *My Childhood* (1915), except perhaps the role of poverty and the backdrop of decline, of a family in Gorki's case, an island community in Ó Crohan's. I see also one formal resemblance, presumably coincidental: both books create a world seen through a narrator's vivid but blinkered eyes. In Gorki this is deliberate; the narrator of *My Childhood* is an adult recollecting the world as he saw it as a child, and consequently the reader does not see beyond the family and can only guess at the wider social context. In Ó Crohan it is not deliberate. The elderly narrator of *The Islandman* simply has little perception of mainland society beyond Dingle, and this lends the book a muted, myopic quality shared by *My Childhood.*

It appears that O'Kelly also read to Ó Crohan Pierre Loti's *An Iceland Fisherman*. Perhaps O'Kelly's choice of this book was occasioned by Synge's fondness for it, and his choice of Gorki by Patrick Pearse's advocacy of the Russian to Gaelic fiction writers. But once again the differences are vast. There is some documentary value in Loti's novelistic account of the Breton cod-fishermen, and presumably it was for this that O'Kelly read Loti to Ó Crohan, but the sweeping geography of *An Iceland Fisherman* and, more importantly, its dilute neo-romanticism (despite which the novel is still a fine one) dintinguish it sharply from *The Islandman*. It is revealing of revival thinking, however, that O'Kelly should read a sophisticated primitivist author to Ó Crohan from whom he wished to solicit a primitive account. Although *The Islandman* is entirely Ó Crohan's (as it has been suggested *Twenty Years A-Growing* is not entirely O'Sullivan's),[28] the fact remains that Ó Crohan was exposed to highly crafted and self-consciously literary works before writing his book. Part of the mysterious charm of *The Islandman* may be due to its being a hybrid of traditional and sophisticated influences.

Literary affines are probably more illuminating in this case than literary stimuli. I am thinking of the autobiographies of American Indians to which Sean O'Tuama has to draw our attention since, in his own estimation, the Gaelic autobiographies "by common European standards are *sui generis*."[29] There are several similarities between *Black Elk Speaks* (1932), for example, and *The Islandman;* the two illustrate an interesting case of correlative evolution, social, psychological, and literary.

Black Elk and Tomás Ó Crohan were near contemporaries (the former born in 1863, the latter in 1856) and members of societies regarded as backward by outsiders and endangered by incursion. Both were articulate spokesmen for their people and provided from the inside valuable documentary and historical data during a crucial period of social breakdown. Both had their words listened to by important European scholars and thinkers (by Jung in the case of Black Elk, Marstrander and Flower in the case of Ó Crohan) interested in "undeveloped" modes of thought and life and were encouraged to write their stories by strangers.[30] Both infused their recollections with a personal and cultural sense of an ending. Both were convinced that the past was superior to the present, a conviction the more justified in the case of Black Elk whose people, the Oglala Sioux, faced not merely change but extinction. Although the Blasket islanders too ceased to be, Ó Crohan's is the more formulaic charge, that the men of his youth were "twice as good as the men of today." Yet Ó Crohan does not aggrandize the island the way Pat Mullen, in late revival euphoria, was to aggrandize the Aran Islands in *Man of Aran* (1934) and *The Hero Breed* (1936). Ó Crohan's melancholy certainty that "the like of us will never be again" has its equivalent in what Seán Ó Conaill (born 1853), another Kerry storyteller, said to James Delargy: "The people who had the old tales are all gone now and the world is changed since I was young. Soon I too shall follow them."[31] And in what Peig Sayers said: "We'll be remembered when we have moved into eternity. People will yet walk above our heads: it could even happen that they'll walk into the graveyard where I'll be lying, but people like us will never again be there. We'll be stretched out quietly—and the old world will have vanished."[32]

Such sentiments carry more weight coming from the mouths of natives than they would coming from the pens of folklorists, and beside them we might set the words of Black Elk: "I, to whom so great a vision was given in my youth—you see me now a pitiful old man who has done nothing, for the nation's hoop is broken and scattered. There is no centre any longer, and the sacred time is dead."[33] Black Elk, like Ó Crohan, is aware that something has vanished in the character of his people, and his attempt to voice it might nearly be Ó Crohan's: "I looked back on the past and recalled my people's old ways, but they were not living that way any more. They were travelling the black road, everybody for himself and with little rules of his own."[34] It had to happen. Petty selfishness is the undesirable aspect of that growing individuality that helped to kill a close-knit community but also permitted these spokesmen to voice their laments and have them heard in the capitals of the wide world. However, what Ó Crohan lamented (and in this he implicitly challenges revival thinking about the west) included the loss of an elder individuality of life, doomed at the hands of a political nationalism he barely understood.[35] Another difference between the fate of the Oglala Sioux and that of the Blasket islanders is that the Indians died through cultural claustrophobia when the white man, as Black Elk repeatedly reminds us, penned them up "in little islands," whereas Ó Crohan's real islands were increasingly exposed to an outside world that parasitically drew the finite energies of the islands to itself.

Black Elk's sense of an ending is the more poignant since he was a holy man who when he was nine had an apocalyptic vision of the ultimate triumph and rebirth of his people. His failure to translate this vision into reality is the core and chief interest of *Black Elk Speaks*. In the case of Ireland, it was the revivalists, not the peasants, who had the visions. ("The centre cannot hold," said Yeats in words similar to Black Elk's.) The peasants through long decades of hardship seem to have become too spiritually debilitated to have apocalyptic visions, too removed from the medieval Christianity that once imagined their islands. Nor had they that millenarian sense of nation or race that frequently inspires such visions. But they did at least and at last, and in a fashion that undermines for us the visions of their "betters," grow into an awareness of their cultural and personal identity.

The End of the Beginning

If *The Islandman* can be regarded as protohistory and protogeography, it can also be regarded as protonovel, not only in its fitful similarities to *Robinson Crusoe* but in having its beginnings in letters as though in imitation of some eighteenth century epistolary fictions. There are some blatantly fictional techniques, for example the re-creation of scenes, complete with dialogue, at which Ó Crohan was not in fact present, or Ó Crohan's ironic view of himself as "the scrapings of the pot," "an old cow's calf," a late and spoiled child in whom roguery showed itself early, a view held not just by a humble man but by one with an eye on persona and effect.

It was inevitable that the islanders should begin to dramatize and distance themselves, to see themselves the way outsiders saw them. Pat Mullen, the Aran islander who was Robert Flaherty's go-between when the American film maker was making *Man of Aran,* has, in his book of the same title, recounted how during the making of the film—which in any case fictionalized life on the islands for cinematic purposes—some of the islanders saw themselves as characters (which is no doubt how Flaherty saw them), and began to act as Flaherty islanders off-camera. Amusingly, one woman said of another: "'Well, Pat, did you ever hear the likes of that—Noreen Shawn thinking that she knows as much about film work as I do. How proud she is sure enough this hour of her life. But all the same,' she added, 'I'll say she knows a little about it. I noticed for the past week that she was walking very heavy in herself. Yes, I'd say she has a touch of that drama thing.'"[36] In this way, Flaherty's "screen-islander," a filmic version of the stage Irishman, began to walk the real earth. (Another woman neatly turned art back into life when she wouldn't allow her daughter to appear in the film for fear her relatives in America would consider the islanders' traditional red flannel dress a poor apparel.) What we have here is a crude version of a process already begun in *The Islandman* by which the more creative islanders fictionalized themselves and their fellows, a process brought to a stage of great sophistication by the Aran islander Liam O'Flaherty. Yet as long as they stayed close to the hard life on the rocks, these islanders never falsified their life in the manner of the revivalists.

The fictional possibilities of island life were grasped more firmly by Maurice O'Sullivan than by Ó Crohan. From his comparatively crafted autobiography, *Twenty Years A-Growing,* I would refer merely to one example of O'Sullivan's powers and purpose as a fictionist. In an early chapter there is a charming and well-known scene in which young Maurice falls asleep and dreams that he and his friend Mickil are in a meadow gathering flowers and sit down because they are tired. Mickil falls asleep and Maurice sees a butterfly coming out of the sleeper's mouth, walking over his body and fluttering down the meadow until it comes to the skull of a horse. The butterfly enters the skull through the eye-sockets, emerges and returns up the meadow to re-enter Mickil's mouth. Mickil then awakes. He tells Maurice he has dreamed of going astray while gathering the flowers and ending his journey in "a big bright house" from which he found it difficult to escape, but did so at length and returned to the meadow. Then the dreaming Maurice is awakened by the real Mickil. The scene is a fine insight into the bizarre connections between dream and waking experiences, but it is more. The idea of the butterfly as a soul that can leave the sleeper and return is a widespread one that is met with inside and outside Ireland. It is found in a story, virtually identical to that in *Twenty Years A-Growing,* collected by Seosamh Ó Dálaigh from Peig Sayers in 1943 and presumably known to O'Sullivan.[37] In his autobiography O'Sullivan appropriates it and offers it to the reader, without reference to the folktale, as a dream he had. Folktale is stealthily absorbed into fiction.

Other writers, not always islanders, were quick to see the fictional value of the western island as a social and political microcosm. The documentary resemblance between *The Islandman* and Peadar O'Donnell's *Islanders* (1927) is the more remarkable because as far as I know O'Donnell wrote his novel of life on a Donegal island without knowledge of Ó Crohan's finished but yet to be published work. This being so, we cannot say on direct evidence that *Islanders,* a much more plotted work than Ó Crohan's, is an example of the raising of "low" forms (in this case, the Gaelic peasant autobiography) that formalists have identified as a typical method of literary regeneration.[38] But it seems to me that the observation could be applied nevertheless to revival fiction that benefited from the saga and folktale and to post-revival fiction that benefited from the peasant autobiography. *The Islandman* itself is a startling example of what we might call self-raising literary form, for it enacts the early development of the novel almost two centuries after it occurred. The existence of *The Islandman* is triple, then, and not merely dual as I have implied—it is folklore, it is history and autobiography, and it is fiction. It "begins" as folk form and "ends" with the promise of fiction.

We might risk similar observations about social theme. Because they were already established in rural Irish fiction since Carleton, the themes of rural decline and individual dissatisfaction with life on the land are foreground in *Islanders*. In *The Islandman,* a book aspiring to the novel, they are only potential foreground. To become dissatisfied with island shortcomings, as Ó Crohan dimly begins to do, is to become aware of the island as island. *Islanders* lends substance to this change in island psychology and makes the Irish civil war a factor in the damaging and beneficial exposure of island life to the scrutiny of a wider world. In the *immrama* the western Irish are orientated towards the sea, and it is in the infinite west that the imaginary islands were to be found. *The Islandman* is still a portion of that mythology, but it also charts an inclination towards the east, away from the sea. For the islanders the east is an otherworld whose shallow mystery they will inevitably penetrate, as Liam O'Flaherty's novels demonstrate, losing in the process their ancient identity. Between these two orientations Tomás Ó Crohan stands Janus-faced. Out of the dilemma emerges the self (like the dead awakening) which the island comes to symbolize: a self suddenly vulerable, unmoored from familiar and age-old beliefs, launched on a lonely search to understand and weigh the exotic values of the world.

But it was not as the revivalists thought; this sense of self could only be achieved at the expense of the island as revival artifact. For the revivalists the island meant underlying unity of nation, of race, of being: in short, the assimilation and submergence of self. It meant, paradoxically, that "mainland" of Irish identity and continuity preserved in its fragments, be they the offshore islands of the Gaeltacht or the heroic distinction and self-possession of the Gaelic champion. Gael and hero were not just "part of the maine" but its noblest manifestations. This perception, on occasions apocalyptic, of the changelessness and unity of Irish culture, demanded from many, particularly the Anglo-Irish, an extraordinary and at times penitential transformation of identity and self-mortifying cultural separation from their tribe. (Luckily the island in its perversity is a symbol that can accommodate this and other revival paradoxes. It is, after all, part of the continent pretending to be cut off.) While the revivalists struggled eloquently to escape themselves, some of the "mere Irish," in partial imitation, struggled to discover themselves and find appropriate tongue. For them, what became primary about the real and metaphoric island, or at least had to be acknowledged, was not its sunken connection with the mainland but rather its proud, embattled, and costly isolation, the fact of its being "intire of it selfe." This too is an ancient significance.

Gabriel Conroy and Joyce were, like Ó Crohan, caught between two orientations that were counterparts of but more sophisticated than his. It is as if Ó Crohan as hero begins the long trek that ends for our purposes with the Catholic, middle-class Dubliner Gabriel Conroy, haunted by echoes of his dim origins in the west, or as if Ó Crohan as writer begins the long trek that ends for our purposes with Joyce, the ex-Catholic, ex-middle-class, ex-Dublin author of "The Dead." We might even see Tomás Ó Crohan as the old man John Alphonsus Mulrennan met, a figure whom Stephen Dedalus fears and yet with whom he sympathizes, both batlike souls awakening to consciousness and one the disowned father of the other. (However, Ó Crohan in awakening to a twentieth-century consciousness of himself, shrugs off the role of father or ancestor and becomes, as it were, his own son, just as Dedalus, in acceding to *his* individuality, becomes his own father.) To these extents *The Islandman* is a literary coelacanth, a contemporary forerunner. That the realization of self is as brief in *The Islandman* (considering the imminent extinction of the islanders) as Gabriel's in "The Dead" (before the self-transcending epiphany) is irrelevant; the trek itself and the symbolic accession are all. Besides, in so far as *The Islandman* encouraged Peig Sayers and Maurice O'Sullivan to record almost for the first time the feelings and thoughts of Irish western peasants, Ó Crohan was a pioneer, an unqualified precursor. The Irish literary revival drew to a close when Irish writers, led in their vastly different ways by Ó Crohan and Joyce, became conscious of the loneliness and responsibility of the individual. In a final paradox, such consciousness was made possible by the revival, whose peculiar variety of prose fictions reflects a bewilderment over national and personal identity. It is a movement to which all Irish writers since have been indebted, even when—especially when—they have queried those and others of its fictions.

Notes

Chapter 1—The Brightest Candle of the Gael

1. Raymond J. Porter, *P. H. Pearse* (New York: Twayne Publishers, 1973), 95–96.
2. From a 1912 lecture on Cuchulain, quoted in Porter, 102.
3. Porter, 44.
4. "Priest or Hero?" *The Irish Theosophist* 5 (1896–97): 149.
5. "Anima Hominis," *Per Amica Silentia Lunae,* in *Mythologies* (New York: Collier Books, 1969), 333–34.
6. "Modern Ireland: An Address to American Audiences, 1932–1933," *Massachusetts Review* 5.2 (Winter 1964): 258.
7. Part One of William Irwin Thompson's *The Imagination of an Insurrection: Dublin, Easter 1916* (New York: Oxford University Press, 1967) is an excellent discussion of the wish and its fulfillment.
8. William O'Brien, *When We Were Boys: A Novel* (London: Longmans, Green, 1890), 148.
9. Nora Chadwick, *The Celts* (Harmondsworth: Penguin Books, 1970), 255.
10. Such trafficking is the subject of Alan Bruford's *Gaelic Folk-Tales and Mediaeval Romances* (Dublin: The Folklore of Ireland Society, 1969).
11. In his Preface to Lady Gregory's *Cuchulain of Muirthemne* (London: John Murray, 1903), ix.
12. *The Cuchullin Saga in Irish Literature* (1898; rpt. New York: AMS Press, 1972), xxxiv.
13. Hull, xxxvi; Lady Gregory, *Gods and Fighting Men* (London: John Murray, 1919), 461–62. The description of Atkinson is that of W. B. Stanford and R. B. McDowell, *Mahaffy* (London: Routledge & Kegan Paul, 1971), 108. The sagas became the prize in a tug-of-war between "West British" scholarly detractors and nationalist champions. J. P. Mahaffy, Provost of Trinity College, shared Atkinson's bigoted view that Irish literature was silly when it was not indecent; in 1899 he and Douglas Hyde locked horns over the issue.
14. Hull, xl.
15. Chadwick, 266.
16. The first four readings, by Alwyn and Brinley Rees, Heinrich Zimmer, Frank O'Connor, and T. F. O'Rahilly respectively, are summarized by Thomas Kinsella in his

Introduction to his translation, *The Tain* (London: Oxford University Press, 1970), xii; the fifth is that of Alfred Nutt in "Cuchulainn, the Irish Achilles," *Popular Studies in Mythology, Romance and Folk-Lore* 8 (London: David Nutt, 1900), 38–42.

17. See Richard M. Dorson, *The British Folklorists, A History* (London: Routledge & Kegan Paul, 1968) for an account of this heroic age.

18. Hull, xxxv.

19. Kinsella, xiii. Daniel Frederick Melia, however, refers to the "structural narrative characteristics" of Irish saga; he identifies in the *Táin* a small number of narrative units repeated within one elaborate overall structure, albeit a structure more typical of oral than of written literature: "Narrative Structure in Irish Saga," Diss. Harvard University 1972: 13, 29, et passim.

20. Bruford, 1. It should be remembered that Bruford is discussing late medieval and later romances found in Irish manuscripts from the fifteenth to the nineteenth centuries.

21. A. H. Leahy, *Heroic Romances of Ireland* (London: David Nutt, 1905), I, x.

22. "The Fate of the Sons of Usna," in P. W. Joyce, trans., *Old Celtic Romances* (Dublin: The Talbot Press, 1961), 287–88.

23. Hull, 131. Harrison Butterworth identifies twenty-one characteristics of Cuchulain in his "Motif-Index and Analysis of the Early Irish Hero Tales," Diss. Yale University 1956.

24. John Heydon, quoted by Yeats in a note to Lady Gregory's *Visions and Beliefs in the West of Ireland* (Gerrards Cross: Colin Smythe, 1970), 346. That Cuchulain was originally a mythic figure is suggested by the fact that in some accounts he is the reincarnation of the god Lug, and by the intimation of incest in his mysterious birth.

25. See Lord Raglan, *The Hero* (1936) and Joseph Campbell, *The Hero With a Thousand Faces* (1949).

26. Hull, 67. Joseph Dunn in the introduction to his translation, *The Ancient Irish Epic Tale Táin Bó Cúailinge* (London: David Nutt, 1914), xiii–xiv, maintains that no racial clash can be read into the *Taín,* the cycle's centrepiece, that it is simply the story of a cattle-raid, but this seems too cautious a reading.

27. *Letters of James Stephens,* ed. Richard J. Finneran (London: Macmillan, 1974), 325.

28. Hull, xi.

29. Preface to Lady Gregory's *Cuchulain of Muirthemne,* xvii.

30. "Celtic Myth and Saga," *Archaeological Review* 2 (1889): 137.

31. Leahy, v.

32. Besides the "self-sacrifice theme" and "the self-reliance theme" O'Neil discusses "the exploitation theme," *Three Perennial Themes of Anti-Colonialism: The Irish Case,* University of Denver *Monograph Series in World Affairs* 14, 1 (1976).

33. Chadwick, 267.

34. *Selected Essays and Passages* (Dublin: The Phoenix Publishing Company, n.d.), 174.

35. "Anima Hominis," *Per Amica Silentia Lunae,* in *Mythologies,* 337.

36. Hull, xlv. Cf. Nutt's claim that "The Gael is a better gentleman than the Greek," in "Cuchulainn, The Irish Achilles," 36.

37. Bruford, 26.

38. Alfred Nutt, as we have noted, dubbed Cuchulain the Irish Achilles. In his Preface to *Beside the Fire: A Collection of Irish Gaelic Folk Stories* (London: David Nutt, 1910), xxxvii, Douglas Hyde attributes to Sir John Rhys the identification of Cuchulain with Hercules (both being sun gods). Herbert Howarth sees in the revival figure of Cuchulain the

Irish equivalent of Siegfried: *The Irish Writers, 1880–1940* (London: Rockliff, 1958), 26. According to AE, "Cuchulain represents as much as Prometheus the heroic spirit, the redeemer in man," in John Eglinton, W. B. Yeats, AE, and W. Larminie, *Literary Ideals in Ireland* (1899; rpt. New York: Lemma Publishing Corporation, 1973), 51.

39. Northrop Frye, *Anatomy of Criticism: Four Essays* (Princeton: Princeton University Press, 1971), 148, 192.

40. Hull, 247–48.

41. Butterworth, 122.

42. *Myths and Folk-lore of Ireland* (1890; rpt. Detroit: Singing Tree Press, 1968), 11.

43. Quoted by Sean O'Sullivan, *The Folklore of Ireland* (New York: Hastings House Publishers, 1974), 11–12.

44. Hull, xii.

45. A translation can be found in Standish Hayes O'Grady's *Silva Gadelica* (1892; rpt. New York: Lemma Publishing Corporation, 1970). Seán Ó Coileáin also directs us to the *Dinnshenchas* (The Lore of Famous Places) "which set out the traditions relating to the famous places in Ireland," "Irish Saga Literature," in *Heroic Epic and Saga,* ed. Felix J. Oinas (Bloomington: Indiana University Press, 1978), 179.

46. Frye, 58.

47. *Selected Essays and Passages,* 83–84.

48. "The Argentine Writer and Tradition," *Labyrinths: Selected Stories and Other Writings,* eds. Donald A. Yates and James E. Irby (New York: New Directions, 1964), 181.

49. Bruford, 37.

50. Bruford, 36.

51. Hull, 290.

52. An earlier example, from Irish mythology, would be the case of the four magical treasures belonging to the chieftain-gods of the *Tuatha* (the cauldron of the Dagda, the spear of Lug, the sword of Nuada, and the Stone of Fál) which cried out aloud when stepped on by the lawful king of Ireland: see John X. W. P. Corcoran, "Celtic Mythology," in *New Larousse Encyclopedia of Mythology* (New York and London: Prometheus Press, 1968), 227.

53. The use of these models and the self-evasion they helped to effect accorded, not entirely by coincidence, with that modernist belief T. S. Eliot put succinctly when he famously described poetry as an escape from personality. It could be argued that Yeats and Joyce, divided in their early careers by their romanticism and realism respectively, were somewhat closer in a mutual and later modernism. I have discussed this aspect of the Irish Renaissance in "Romantic Revival, Modernist Prescription: An Irish Case-Study," in *Modernism and Modernity,* eds. Benjamin H. D. Buchloh, Serge Guilbaut, and David Solkin (Halifax, Nova Scotia: Press of the Nova Scotia College of Art and Design, 1983), 65–80.

Chapter 2—The Property of Discourse

1. This example of the attitude of those he calls "literate sentimentalists" is offered by Alan Bruford, *Gaelic Folk-Tales and Mediaeval Romances* (Dublin: The Folklore of Ireland Society, 1969), 103. The story in question has been given various titles in translation. *Longes mac n-Uislenn* has been titled "The Fate," "Tragical Death," and "Exile" of the Sons (or Children) of Usnach (or Uisneach or Usnech or Uisliu or Usna or Uisneac).

2. An experience recounted by William A. Wilson, *Folklore and Nationalism in Modern Finland* (Bloomington: Indiana University Press, 1976). See also Felix J. Oinas,

"The Balto-Finnic Epics" in *Heroic Epic and Saga,* ed. Oinas (Bloomington: Indiana University Press, 1978), 286–301.

3. Yeats was aware of the *Kalevala* and discussed it in his 1902 essay, "The Celtic Element in Literature," *Essays and Introductions* (New York: Collier Books, 1968), 173–88. But we are speaking not so much of imitation or emulation or even direct influence as of a pattern of literary and cultural revival that can be traced at some period of the nineteenth and twentieth centuries in, among other places, Finland, Estonia, Poland, Brittany, Hungary, Czechoslovakia, and Ireland. National epics are originally products of an ascendant culture, but in the nineteenth century were frequently revived or re-composed by or on behalf of suppressed cultures attempting to regain self-respect. In epic revival, a noble past was asserted, a people spiritually reunified, and a vernacular language legitimized. Frequently and ironically, epic revival was made possible by sympathetic, scholarly representatives of the alien culture enjoying cultural ascendancy over that culture the epic originally adorned. We can interpret such sympathy in terms not only of romantic enthusiasm for the aboriginal, oppressed, and folkloric, but also of revenge by the sympathizers against their ancestral culture (in the Anglo-Irish case, England) from which they are exiled and half-distant; out of a sense of rivalry rather than oppression, they set up a culture-source alternative to, and closer than, the metropolis (in the Anglo-Irish case, London).

4. "Cuchulainn, the Irish Achilles," *Popular Studies in Mythology, Romance and Folk-Lore* 8 (London: David Nutt, 1900), 23.

5. *Selected Essays and Passages* (Dublin: The Phoenix Publishing Company, n.d.), 88.

6. Quoted by Wilson, 89.

7. Wilson, 60.

8. Gerard Murphy, *The Ossianic Lore and Romantic Tales of Medieval Ireland* (Dublin: Colm O Lochlainn for the Cultural Relations Committee of Ireland, 1955), 61.

9. *Old Celtic Romances* (Dublin: The Talbot Press, 1961), vii.

10. Preface to *Cuchulain of Muirthemne* (London: John Murray, 1903), viii.

11. Wilson, 55–56.

12. Faraday claimed her book as the first translation and printing (as distinct from analysis) of the *Táin.* She does not mention Lady Gregory's *Cuchulain of Muirthemne,* published two years before. I might have added to my list J.M. Flood's *Ireland: Its Myths and Legends* (1916), a readable paraphrase of the major episodes from all the cycles.

13. Joyce, vii. The subsequent quotations are likewise from Joyce's Preface to *Old Celtic Romances,* vii–ix.

14. *Cuchulain of Muirthemne,* 359.

15. *Cuchulain of Muirthemne,* 355.

16. "Modern Ireland: An Address to American Audiences, 1932–1933," *Massachusetts Review* 5.2 (Winter 1964): 259. I am not, of course, the first to have reservations about Lady Gregory's style and method in *Cuchulain of Muirthemne.* Stephen J. Brown in *Ireland in Fiction* (1919) is scornful and shows an anti-peasant, anti-folklore bias; he quotes Fiona MacLeod (William Sharp) who is perhaps a fairer judge: "Fiona McLeod says very well of the style that it is 'over cold in its strange sameness of emotion, a little chill with the chill of studious handicraft,' and speaks elsewhere of its 'monotonous passionlessness' and its 'lack of virility.' Yet to the book as a whole he gives high, if qualified, praise": *Ireland in Fiction* (rpt. New York: Barnes and Noble, 1969), 119. Synge's high praise was less qualified than MacLeod's, but he warned of omissions and unevenness of diction, and I detect some strain in his praise; he was much less enthusiastic, however, about Leahy's translations: see J. M. Synge, *Collected Works* 2: *Prose,* ed. Alan Price (London: Oxford University Press, 1966), 367–73.

17. *The Cuchullin Saga in Irish Literature* (1898; rpt. New York: AMS Press, 1972), xlii.

18. *Cuchulain of Muirthemne,* 355.

19. *Cuchulain of Muirthemne,* 237–38.

20. Hull, 174–76.

21. *The Archaeological Review* 1 (1888): 68–75.

22. "Aspects of Irishness," in *Literature and Folk Culture: Ireland and Newfoundland,* eds. Alison Feder and Bernice Schrank (St. John's: Memorial University of Newfoundland, 1977), 19, 21.

23. *The Archaeology of Knowledge,* trans. A. M. Sheridan Smith (New York: Harper & Row, 1976), 225.

24. *Anatomy of Criticism: Four Essays* (Princeton: Princeton University Press, 1971), 186.

25. Frye, 201.

26. I discuss the revivalists' use of *immrama* in "Certain Set Apart: The Western Island in the Irish Renaissance," *Studies: An Irish Quarterly Review* 66 (Winter 1977): 261–74.

27. One writer from whom Yeats withheld his approval was James H. Cousins, whom Yeats, as an historian of Irish drama has put it, "firmly detached" from the theatre movement: Robert Hogan in *Dictionary of Irish Literature,* ed. Hogan (Westport: Greenwood Press, 1979), 176.

Chapter 3—Transforming Down

1. "The Trembling of the Veil," in *Autobiographies* (London: Macmillan, 1955), 220–21.

2. Ernest Boyd, Introduction to Standish James O'Grady, *Selected Essays and Passages* (Dublin: The Phoenix Publishing Company, n.d.), 6–7.

3. O'Grady, *Selected Essays and Passages,* 47.

4. AE, "The Dramatic Treatment of Legend," *Imaginations and Reveries* (Dublin and London: Maunsel & Company, 1915), 7.

5. O'Grady, *Earlier Bardic Literature* (1879; rpt. New York: Lemma Publishing Corporation, 1970), 17.

6. *Early Bardic Literature,* 28–29.

7. *Early Bardic Literature,* 32.

8. *Selected Essays and Passages,* 82.

9. Introduction to *The Triumph of Cuculain, or In the Gates of the North* (Dublin: The Talbot Press, n.d.), vii.

10. *Selected Essays and Passages,* 258.

11. *Selected Essays and Passages,* 228.

12. *The Coming of Cuculain* (London: Methuen, 1894), 41.

13. William A. Wilson, *Folklore and Nationalism in Modern Finland* (Bloomington: Indiana University Press, 1976), 87.

14. *Selected Essays and Passages,* 23.

15. *Early Bardic Literature,* 28.

16. *Selected Essays and Passages,* 88–89.

17. Preface to *The Coming of Cuculain,* i.

18. *Early Bardic Literature,* 6.

19. *Early Bardic Literature,* 27.

20. See Northrop Frye, *Anatomy of Criticism: Four Essays* (Princeton: Princeton University Press, 1971), 193.

21. *Selected Essays and Passages,* 42.

22. O'Grady uses the Arnoldian phrase "unyielding despotic fact" when he endorses the artist-historian's "escape from the actual": *Selected Essays and Passages,* 42. It would be hard to overestimate O'Grady's early influence on Yeats, a writer who strove throughout his life to create legend; that is, figures and events pitched midway between mythology and actuality.

23. The phrase is David Wright's; he uses it when deploring attempts to render *Beowulf* into poetic diction through the employment of such words as "fain" or "blithe": *Beowulf,* trans. David Wright (Harmondsworth: Penguin Books, 1957), 23.

24. Introduction to O'Grady's *Selected Essays and Passages,* 17.

25. Introduction to *Fighting the Waves,* repr. W. B. Yeats, *Selected Criticism,* ed. A. Norman Jeffares (London: Pan Books, 1976), 208.

26. Walter E. Houghton, *The Victorian Frame of Mind, 1830–1870* (New Haven and London: Yale University Press, 1957), 305, 310.

27. Houghton, 319.

28. Houghton, 325. Malcolm Brown has written: "One of the strands running through O'Grady's thought is easily identified as the Carlyle-Froude critique of the Irish gentry for its incompetence in scourging the restive canaille," *The Politics of Irish Literature: From Thomas Davis to W. B. Yeats* (Seattle: University of Washington Press, 1973), 299.

29. Quoted by Houghton, 327.

30. Houghton, 328.

31. Houghton, 332–33.

32. Houghton, 317, 306, 313, 324.

33. Preface to *Cuculain: An Epic* (London: Sampson, Low, Searle, Marston & Rivington, 1882), ii.

34. *Cuculain: An Epic,* 236.

35. Preface to *Cuculain: An Epic,* ii.

36. "The Character of Heroic Literature," *Imaginations and Reveries,* 3.

37. *Anatomy of Criticism,* 186.

38. To this day, volunteers of the Irish Republican Army are referred to by sympathizers as "the lads."

39. Introduction to *The Triumph of Cuculain, or In The Gates of the North,* xii.

40. John Eglinton, W. B. Yeats, AE, and W. Larminie, *Literary Ideals in Ireland* (1899; rpt. New York: Lemma Publishing Corporation, 1973), 11. Subsequent quotations from this book are followed by page numbers in parentheses.

41. *Ireland's Literary Renaissance* (New York: Barnes & Noble, 1968), 418. Stephens consulted Joseph Dunn's 1914 translation.

42. *Letters of James Stephens,* ed. Richard J. Finneran (London: Macmillan, 1974), 255.

43. Hilary Pyle, *James Stephens: His Work and an Account of His Life* (London: Routledge & Kegan Paul, 1965), 93.

44. In a series of articles published in *Eire-Ireland* in the 1970s, Herbert V. Fackler discussed Deirdre as she appeared in the pages of Ferguson, R. D. Joyce, and Aubrey de Vere. Graham's *Deirdre and the Sons of Uisneach, A Scoto-Irish Romance of the First Century A.D., Compiled from Various Sources* (1908) claimed to be the first "united and popular form"

of the full narrative concerning Deirdre. Graham confessed himself ignorant of Gaelic and relied on O'Curry and P. W. Joyce for translations. Incidentally, Stephen J. Brown lists a scholarly edition of *The Fate of the Children of Uisneach,* edited by Richard J. O'Duffy in 1898 for the Society for the Preservation of the Irish language, based on an 18th century manuscript. "Michael Field" was the pseudonym of Katherine Bradley and Edith Cooper, whose plays Yeats admired.

45. "On Prose and Verse," in *A James Stephens Reader,* ed. Lloyd Frankberg (New York: Macmillan, 1962), 404.

46. *Deirdre* (London: Macmillan, 1923), 73. Subsequent quotations are from this edition of the novel, with page numbers in parentheses.

47. "An Essay in Cubes," *The English Review* 17 (April–July 1914): 88; repr. *Uncollected Prose of James Stephens,* ed. Patricia A. McFate (London: Macmillan, 1983), 2: 115–25.

48. However, according to Pyle (*James Stephens,* 101), Stephens before writing *Deirdre* consulted *Táin Bó Fraich,* one of the pre-tales of the *Táin Bó Cuailnge* and which O'Beirne Crowe translated in 1870, Kuno Meyer in 1902, and Alan O. Anderson in 1903. The translation Jeffrey Gantz published in his *Early Irish Myths and Sagas* he described as "neither mythic nor heroic so much as literary and psychological. More attention is paid to motivation here than in any other early Irish story": *Early Irish Myths and Sagas* (Harmondsworth: Penguin Books, 1981), 114.

49. *The Demi-Gods* (London: Macmillan, 1914), 65. Stephens wrote to W. B. Blake in 1916: "Certainly the world is shouting just now with a masculine bellow, and it does seem that the baby is being born of the father instead of the mother; but for me I redoubt exceedingly the female gender and the neutre [*sic*] that she keeps up her sleeve," *Letters of James Stephens,* ed. Finneran, 184–85. That was written not long after he published *The Demi-Gods.* Not long before he published *Deirdre,* he wrote to John Quinn in 1920: "Fantastic as it may seem I think that something of the masculinity of man has been submerged, and this 'something' has rendered us all less sensitive and more touchy. I am inclined to call it feminism for want of a better definition. . . . You would know how to describe its effects in the political sphere, but in poetry I describe it thus: the male sensitive quality is dead," *Letters,* 250.

50. *The Demi-Gods,* 66.

51. *Letters of James Stephens,* 274.

Chapter 4—The Self-Ancestral

1. Henry Summerfield, *That Myriad-Minded Man: A Biography of George William Russell "A.E." 1867–1935* (Gerrards Cross: Colin Smythe, 1975), 113.

2. *The Irish Theosophist* 4.6 (March 1896): 103.

3. *Anatomy of Criticism: Four Essays* (Princeton: Princeton University Press, 1971), 187.

4. James H. and Margaret E. Cousins, *We Two Together* (Madras: Ganesh & Co., 1950), 75.

5. In John Eglinton, W. B. Yeats, AE, and W. Larminie, *Literary Ideals in Ireland* (1899; rpt. New York: Lemma Publishing Corporation, 1973), 36.

6. "Witches and Wizards and Irish Folk-Lore," an essay appended to Lady Gregory's *Visions and Beliefs in the West of Ireland* (Gerrards Cross: Colin Smythe, 1970), 302.

Perhaps the country people had some justice in their attribution, since Freemasonry and occult societies have been perceived as having had links: see Frances A. Yates, *The Occult Philosophy in the Elizabethan Age* (London: Ark, 1983), 169. Maud Gonne joined the Order of the Golden Dawn when Yeats was a member, but began to suspect that its ritual was tainted with Freemasonry: see Joseph Hone, *W. B. Yeats 1865–1939* (London: Macmillan, 1965), 85–86. The Pollexfens, who were the in-laws of Yeats's father, were, incidentally, "loyal Protestants and active Freemasons," Hone, 29. AE, it seems, was opposed to the Golden Dawn, believing it to represent magic rather than mysticism: Hone, 72.

7. *We Two Together*, 170. According to Mary Colum, however, Charlotte Despard, the sister of Lord French, Viceroy of Ireland, was of an Irish family; the confusion is telling. Mrs. Despard's suffragette and nationalist activites are mentioned in Mary Colum's *Life and the Dream* (London: Macmillan, 1947), 149, 284.

8. Cf. Desmond Bowen's remark that it was the culture of the Anglo-Irish after Disestablishment in 1870, and not the culture of the Gael, that became the *real* Hidden Ireland: *The Protestant Crusade in Ireland 1800–70* (Dublin: Gill and Macmillan, 1978), 305.

9. *Letters from AE*, ed. Alan Denson (London: Abelard-Schuman, 1961), 17.

10. *Letters of James Stephens*, ed. Richard J. Finneran (London: Macmillan, 1974), 143.

11. *Black Elk Speaks* (1932) is the autobiography (as told through John G. Neihardt) of a survivor of the spiritual revival of the Sioux that culminated in Wounded Knee in 1890. See also Peter Worsley's *The Trumpet Shall Sound: A Study of 'Cargo' Cults in Melanesia* (1968).

12. "Victorian Evangelicalism and the Anglo-Irish Literary Revival," in *Literature and the Changing Ireland*, ed. Peter Connolly (Gerrards Cross: Colin Smythe, 1982), 59–101.

13. Terence Brown, "The Church of Ireland: Some Literary Perspectives," *Search* 3.2 (1980): 14.

14. *Letters from AE*, 68. AE seems to have been inspired by Wells' tract-novels, *romans-à-clefs*, and romances, including *A Modern Utopia* (1905), *The New Machiavelli* (1911) and *The World Set Free* (1914). *The Interpreters* is distantly related to science fiction and has its Wellsian colorations.

15. *The Interpreters* (London: Macmillan, 1922), viii. Subsequent quotations are followed by page numbers in parentheses. The scenario was not completely original. In 1908, *When the Dawn is Come* was produced in Dublin, a play by Thomas MacDonagh (one of the Easter rebels) about an insurrection in Ireland set fifty years in the future.

16. Science fiction and the Irish question had been combined before AE wrote *The Interpreters*. Tom Greer's bizarre novel, *A Modern Daedalus* (1887), purports to be the reminiscences of one John O'Halloran, whose discovery of the means of flight enables him to lead the Irish to total victory over the English in 1886, interrupting Parnell's parliamentary struggle to do so. The wish-fulfillment of O'Halloran's physical-force nationalism and his introduction to Ireland of guerrilla warfare (learned from the Boers) sit strangely with Greer's Anglophile Preface and the confessed unionism of O'Halloran himself. According to Stephen J. Brown, Greer was a County Down man and Liberal Home Ruler who unsuccessfully contested North Derry in 1892. The novel is anti-Tory and pro-Parnell but otherwise unstable in political viewpoint.

17. According to George Sigerson, a revival scholar, poets were judges until their incomprehensible technical language forced princes to add laymen to the court: "Irish Literature: Its Origin, Environment, and Influence," in Charles Gavan Duffy, George

Sigerson and Douglas Hyde, *The Revival of Irish Literature* (1894; rpt. New York: Lemma Publishing Corporation, 1973), 74.

18. *That Myriad-Minded Man,* 212.

19. *Imaginations and Reveries* (Dublin and London: Mausel & Company, 1915), 93–111.

20. *The Candle of Vision* (New York: University Books, 1965), 137–42.

21. *James, Seumas & Jacques: Unpublished Writings of James Stephens,* ed. Lloyd Frankenberg (New York: Macmillan, 1964), 120.

22. *James, Seumas & Jacques,* 113.

23. "Ideals of the New Rural Society," *Imaginations and Reveries,* 101.

24. Summerfield sees in Rian something of the young Yeats and perhaps John Hughes the sculptor: *That Myriad-Minded Man,* 212. Rian promotes aesthetic harmony, even uniformity, as Lavelle, Culain, Heyt and Brehon (as AE) respectively promote its national, socialist, imperialist and transcendental equivalent. (*Rian* in Irish means order, arrangement, system.)

25. *The Letters of W. B. Yeats,* ed. Allan Wade (London: Hart-Davis, 1954), 294.

26. *The Candle of Vision,* 75.

27. *Anatomy of Criticism,* 59.

28. Preface to *Imaginations and Reveries,* x.

29. "The Trembling of the Veil," in *Autobiographies* (London: Macmillan, 1955), 246–47.

30. However, that AE sprang from parents who were both devout members of the Church of Ireland and attracted to evangelicalism (*That Myriad-Minded Man,* 3) might—in the light of Mercier's findings—suggest that the contradiction was more apparent than real.

Chapter 5—The Path of the Chameleon

1. Cf. Hone, *W. B. Yeats 1865–1939* (London: Macmillan, 1965), 137, 473.

2. Augustine Martin, "'The Secret Rose' and Yeats's Dialogue with History," *Ariel* 3.3 (July 1972): 91–103.

3. A. R. Orage, *Readers and Writers (1917–21)* (New York: Alfred A. Knopf, 1922), 107. When Heyt claims that "The will in itself is power" (*The Interpreters,* 92), he echoes Nietzsche's formula that "This world is the will to power." AE's biographer, Henry Summerfield, does not mention the German, nor does the editor of AE's letters, Alan Denson. AE would, of course, have been familiar with Nietzsche's ideas (even if only via Yeats) when he sat down to write *The Interpreters.* Orage makes his remarks about Nietzsche in the course of discussing AE's *The Candle of Vision.* Orage calls Nietzsche's preoccupation with the problem of power "an occult exercise"; he sees AE as "full of warning against the quest of power," but adds that AE realizes that "without power the student of the occult can do nothing."

4. In his life of Yeats, Hone makes a useful distinction between magic and mysticism, between Yeats's and AE's method, respectively, for achieving vision: Hone, 72.

5. Since Yeats worked on *The Speckled Bird* between 1896 and 1902, it belongs to the period of Yeats's experiments in fiction writing. However, I have chosen not to discuss the novel because it exists only in incomplete versions, because it travels much the same philosophical ground as the apocalyptic stories (if in a more realistic style), and because its

drafts to me promise no final artistic success comparable to that of the apocalyptic trilogy. Readers can judge for themselves by consulting *The Speckled Bird: With Variant Versions,* annotated and edited by William H. O'Donnell (Toronto: McClelland and Stewart, 1976).

6. "Rosa Alchemica" in *The Collected Works of William Butler Yeats* (Stratford-on-Avon: The Shakespeare Head, 1908) 7: *Rosa Alchemica, The Tables of the Law, The Adoration of the Magi, John Sherman and Dhoya,* 122. Subsequent quotations from the apocalyptic stories (with page numbers in parentheses) are from this edition. I have also consulted *The Secret Rose, Stories by W. B. Yeats: A Variorum Edition,* eds. Phillip L. Marcus, Warwick Gould and Michael J. Sidnell (Ithaca: Cornell University Press, 1981).

7. "Witches and Wizards and Irish Folk-Lore," in Lady Gregory's *Visions and Beliefs in the West of Ireland* (Gerrards Cross: Colin Smythe, 1970), 302.

8. "Witches and Wizards and Irish Folk-Lore," 302.

9. "Swedenborg, Mediums, and the Desolate Places," a second essay appended to Lady Gregory's *Visions and Beliefs,* 332.

10. Yeats uses his phrase in "A General Introduction for My Work," *Essays and Introductions* (New York: Collier Books, 1968), 525.

11. Yeats's essay, "The Celtic Element in Literature," written in 1897, discusses the desirable Celtic dimensions of exile and excess, *Essays and Introductions,* 173–87.

12. According to Robartes, an age of necessity, truth, goodness, science, democracy and peace might well be about to give way to one of freedom, fiction, evil, art, aristocracy and war: "Stories of Michael Robartes and his Friends," in *A Vision* (New York: Collier Books, 1966), 52.

13. For the reference to pale victims, see Peter Faulkner, *William Morris and W. B. Yeats* (Dublin: Dolmen Press, 1962), 22. I take the phrase "where life is at tension" from John Aherne's description of the wanderings of his brother Owen and Michael Robartes in Ireland, "Stories of Michael Robartes and his Friends," *A Vision,* 53.

14. The description of Dowson and Johnson occurs in "Modern Poetry: A Broadcast," *Essays and Introductions,* 493. Those whom Yeats thought Johnson typified would be at home in the pages of the apocalyptic stories: "souls turned from practical ends become contemplative but not yet ready for the impress of the divine will, an unendurable burden" (quoted by Hone, *W. B. Yeats,* 117).

15. Edward Hirsch would have it that Yeats's commitment to the minimal degree of realism fiction demands was undermined by his commitment to rendering spiritual and supernatural experiences. Hirsch believes that the problem was solved by fiction writers after Yeats, and that Yeats is a transitional figure between romanticism and modernism, as the poet's fiction is a bridge between his early verse and his later visionary poetry. Hirsch does not examine in sufficient detail the revelatory capabilities of 19th century realism or the realism of 19th century romanticism to convince me that Yeats's fiction was an historical failure in mode rather than a tactical failure in style. See Edward Hirsch, "A War Between the Orders: Yeats's Fiction and the Transcendental Moment," *Novel: A Forum on Fiction* 17 (Fall 1983): 52–66.

16. *A Vision,* 55.

17. *A Vision,* 55.

18. However, Richard Finneran is reluctant to admit *Stories of Michael Robartes and his Friends* among Yeats's prose fiction proper, on the grounds that this material is too intimately connected with Yeats's philosophical system of *A Vision;* see *The Prose Fiction of W. B. Yeats: The Search for 'Those Simple Forms'* (Dublin: Dolmen Press, 1973), 37, note 49.

19. Hone, *W. B. Yeats,* 58.

20. *A Vision,* 40.

21. I take these phrases from Yeats's early poem, "To Ireland in the Coming Times."

22. Losing the love of women is the price those in touch with unearthly powers often pay, as the Druid implies in Yeats's early poem, "Fergus and the Druid."

23. "'Old lecher with a love on every wind': A Study of Yeats' *Stories of Red Hanrahan*," *Texas Studies in Literature and Language* 14.2 (Summer 1972): 354.

24. Finneran, 354.

25. "Red Hanrahan" in *The Collected Works of William Butler Yeats* (Stratford-on-Avon: The Shakespeare Head, 1908) 5: *The Celtic Twilight and Stories of Red Hanrahan*, 208. Subsequent quotations from the Hanrahan stories (with page numbers in parentheses) are from this edition.

26. Sir John Rhys, a philologist and folklorist contemporary with Yeats, quoted by Finneran, 354.

27. *The Letters of W. B. Yeats,* ed. Allan Wade (London: Hart-Davis, 1954), 286.

28. Daniel Corkery, *The Hidden Ireland: A Study of Gaelic Munster in the Eighteenth Century* (Dublin: Gill and Macmillan, 1967), 212.

29. This quotation is from the 1892 version of "The Twisting of the Rope" (with the hero called O'Sullivan the Red) that appeared in the *National Observer;* it is reprinted in Michael J. Sidnell, "Versions of the Stories of Red Hanrahan," *Yeats Studies* 1 (1971): 119–74; the reference to Seancan Torpeist, a seventh-century Irish poet, occurs on page 138.

30. Corkery, 142.

31. Corkery, 129.

32. "Anima Hominis," *Per Amica Silentia Lunae,* in *Mythologies* (New York: Collier Books, 1969), 331.

33. "*The Tables of the Law:* A Critical Text," *Yeats Studies* 1 (1971): 88–89.

34. See one of Eglinton's contributions to *Literary Ideals in Ireland* (1899; rpt. New York: Lemma Publishing Corporation, 1973), 45–46.

35. The mood Yeats referred to was that "which Edgar Poe found in a wine-cup . . . passed into France and took possession of Baudelaire, and from Baudelaire passed to England and the Pre-Raphaelites, and then again returned to France." These words, from the *Savoy,* April 1896, are reproduced in Robert O'Driscoll's "*The Tables of the Law:* A Critical Text," 90. Wilson's remarks can be found in *Axel's Castle* (New York: Charles Scribner's Sons, 1931), 13.

36. Wilson, 34.

37. See William Irwin Thompson's *The Imagination of an Insurrection: Dublin, Easter 1916* (New York: Oxford University Press, 1967) and my own article, "Yeats and the Easter Rising," *The Canadian Journal of Irish Studies* 11.1 (June 1985): 21–34. In the latter article, I try to show the rich ambiguity of Yeats's response to the Rising, an ambiguity not unrelated to that which we find in the apocalyptic stories.

38. "*The Tables of the Law:* A Critical Text," 89.

39. Martin makes the distinction in his article, "'The Secret Rose' and Yeats's Dialogue with History": see note 2 above.

40. For example, Yeats wrote a poem entitled "O'Sullivan Rua to Mary Lavelle"; O'Sullivan Rua (or the Red) was a model for Red Hanrahan; subsequently Yeats retitled the poem "Michael Robartes Remembers Forgotten Beauty," which would suggest some telling confusion of identity. See A. Norman Jeffares, *A Commentary on the Collected Poems of W. B. Yeats* (London: Macmillan, 1968), 67. Elsewhere, however, Yeats wrote that "Hanrahan is the simplicity of an imagination too changeable to gather permanent impressions, or the adoration of the shepherds; and Michael Robartes is the pride of the imagination brooding upon the greatness of its possessions, or the adoration of the Magi" (see Jeffares, 55).

Chapter 6—Certain Set Apart

1. J. M. Synge, *Collected Works* 2: *Prose,* ed. Alan Price (London: Oxford University Press, 1966), 60. Subsequent quotations from *The Aran Islands* are from this edition and are followed by page numbers in parentheses.

2. *Songs and Ballads of Young Ireland,* ed. Martin MacDermott (London: Downey, 1896).

3. The words belong to R. L. Praeger, *The Way That I Went* (Dublin: Allen Figgis, 1969), 380.

4. "Cuairt ar Arainn na Naomh," *Fainne an Lae* (November 19, 1898), 155. (Translated for me by Dr. Patrick O'Neill of the University of British Columbia.)

5. "In these islands," wrote Michael MacDonagh, "you find the pure and undiluted Celt, descended without any intermixture of foreign blood, from 'the mere Irish,' who got from Cromwell the alternative of banishment to these inhospitable regions or eternal misery down below, when he uttered his historical exclamation to the Catholics—'to h— or Connaught,'" "Life in Achill and Aran," *The Westminster Review* 134.2 (1890): 166. Post-revival thinking from outside the Republic is that the population of the Aran Islands was genetically modified, ironically, by Cromwell's soldiers themselves, many of whom chose to stay in the region when their comrades departed: see John C. Messenger's study of the Aran Islands, *Inis Beag: Isle of Ireland* (New York: Holt, Rinehart & Winston, 1969) and the section on these islands in Kenneth McNally, *The Islands of Ireland* (New York: W. W. Norton, 1978). For the descent of the Blasket islanders, see Robin Flower, *The Western Island or The Great Blasket* (Oxford: The Clarendon Press, 1944); for Gola, consult F. H. A. Aalen and Hugh Brody, *Gola: The Life and Last Days of an Island Community* (Cork: Mercier Press, 1969).

6. I discuss the islands of Celtic mythology and of Irish Christianity in "Certain Set Apart: The Western Island in the Irish Renaissance," *Studies* 66 (Winter 1977): 261–74.

7. *Myths, Dreams and Mysteries* (London: Harvill Press, 1960), 161. In this book, Eliade discusses several topics of interest to students of the mythology of the Irish revival, including the nostalgia for paradise, the myth of the noble savage, and the relation between secret societies and spiritual regeneration.

8. Donal McCartney, "Gaelic Ideological Origins of 1916," in *1916: The Easter Rising,* eds. Owen Dudley Edwards and Fergus Pyle (London: MacGibbon and Kee, 1968), 46.

9. W. G. Wood-Martin, *Traces of the Elder Faiths of Ireland: A Handbook of Irish Pre-Christian Traditions* (London: Longmans, Green, 1902) 1: 209. George Sigerson believed that Ireland was Ogygia to which Ulysses came and where Calypso welcomed him: in *The Revival of Irish Literature* (1894; rpt. New York: Lemma Publishing Corporation, 1973), 65.

10. *An Irish Journey* (New York: Longmans, Green, 1943), 144.

11. In *The Revival of Irish Literature,* 64.

12. David H. Greene and Edward M. Stephens, *J. M. Synge 1871–1909* (New York: Macmillan, 1959), 64. When he came to write *The Aran Islands,* Synge wisely resisted, however, Lady Gregory's suggestion that he make his book dreamier and add more fairy belief: see Greene and Stephens, 120–21.

13. *Collected Works* 2: *Prose,* 144. A very different set of explanations for the islanders' subordinate sexuality is offered by the anthropologist John C. Messenger, who has written about the Aran Islands under the guise of "Inis Beag." Messenger interprets the subordination as repression, and he suggests as its primary causes the traditions of monastic, Augustinian, and Jansenist Catholicism, and the prevalence of the Oedipal complex (including the

controlling figure of the mother). See "Sex and Repression in an Irish Folk Community," in *Human Sexual Behavior,* eds. Donald S. Marshall and Robert C. Suggs (New York: Basic Books, 1971), 3–37.

14. Synge found inequality emerging on Inishere, the south island: *Collected Works* 2: *Prose,* 140. Cf. Yeats: "In the great cities we see so little of the world, we drift into our minority. In the little towns and villages there are no minorities; people are not numerous enough. You must see the world there, perforce. Every man is himself a class," "Village Ghosts," an essay in *The Celtic Twilight: The Collected Works of William Butler Yeats* (Stratford-on-Avon: The Shakespeare Head, 1908) 5: *The Celtic Twilight and Stories of Red Hanrahan,* 17.

15. However, one cultural geographer has quoted Synge's observations with approval: T. W. Freeman in his survey, *Ireland: A General and Regional Geography* (London: Methuen, 1972), 424.

16. *Some Letters of John M. Synge to Lady Gregory and W. B. Yeats,* ed. Ann Saddlemeyer (Dublin: Cuala Press, 1971), 14.

17. *In Wicklow, West Kerry and Connemara,* in *Collected Works* 2: *Prose,* 248.

18. Declan Kiberd believes Synge may have abandoned the Aran Islands in part because his relations with the islanders had deteriorated; he also cites Nicholas Grene, who believes that Synge left the islands because he was losing interest in the homogeneous, closely-knit community, though this hardly squares with Synge's joy in 1905 at the prospect of Blasket primitiveness. See Declan Kiberd, "Synge's Studies in the Gaeltacht," *Maynooth Review* 4.2 (1978): 16. According to the editor at Maunsel's publishing house, George Roberts, it was Synge's fear of what the Aran Islanders would think of the *Playboy* riots "that stopped him from visiting his beloved islands again": quoted by W. R. Rodgers in his *Irish Literary Portraits* (London: BBC, 1972), 113; however, the riots took place five years after Synge left the islands for good. Synge's failure to return to the islands in 1904 was more immediately due to rumours of smallpox there: *Some Letters of John M. Synge to Lady Gregory and W. B. Yeats,* 8.

19. Greene and Stephens, 64.

20. *The Land of Pardons,* trans. Frances M. Gostling (London: Methuen, 1906), 5.

21. One minor example would be the way in which Synge thought the women of Inishmaan had "some curiously Mongolian features, rather resembling the Bigoudennes of the south coast of Brittany," in "The Last Fortress of the Celt," an article in *The Gael* (1901), reprinted in Padraic Colum, *A Treasury of Irish Folklore* (New York: Crown Publishers, 1964), 463.

22. *The Land of Pardons,* 129.

23. Jack E. Reece, *The Bretons against France: Ethnic Minority Nationalism in Twentieth-Century Brittany* (Chapel Hill: University of North Carolina Press, 1977), 52.

24. Maurice Marchal, quoted by Reece, 29.

25. Yeats has his young hero, justifying his Irish nationalism, exclaim: "England is the modern world, one wishes to get rid of the modern world," *The Speckled Bird,* ed. William H. O'Donnell (Toronto: McClelland and Stewart, 1976) 45. Later, Yeats famously characterized the modern world as a "filthy modern tide."

26. Quoted from the URB charter by Reece, 54.

27. *The Letters of W. B. Yeats,* ed. Allan Wade (London: Hart-Davis, 1954), 314.

28. Reece, 39–40.

29. *Cities and Sea Coasts and Islands* (London: Collins, 1918), 326.

30. *In Wicklow, West Kerry and Connemara,* in *Collected Works* 2: *Prose,* 248.

31. *Collected Works* 2: *Prose,* 48n.

32. *Collected Works* 2: *Prose,* 102n.

33. Jules Cambon, Introduction to *An Iceland Fisherman* (New York: Collier, 1902), xviii.

34. *The Land of Pardons,* 116.

35. *The Land of Pardons,* 237.

36. However, Lord Dunsany believed he had discovered the source of Maurya's defiant lament in Kipling's 1890 poem, "The Gift of the Sea," the second verse of which runs: "But the mother laughed at all. / 'I have lost my man in the sea, / 'And the child is dead. Be still,' she said, / 'What more can you do to me?'" See Hazel Littlefield, *Lord Dunsany: King of Dreams* (New York: Exposition Press, 1959), 20.

37. Symons, 310–11.

38. Quoted by Greene and Stephens, 75.

39. "Synge's Studies in the Gaeltacht," especially 8–9. This is one of a series of articles by Kiberd in this journal, later absorbed into his book, *Synge and the Irish Language* (London: Macmillan, 1979).

40. *Autobiographies* (London: Macmillan, 1955), 505–6.

41. Maurice Bourgeois, *John Millington Synge and the Irish Theatre* (New York: Benjamin Blom, 1913), 80.

42. We might recall other words of Yeats's. Synge, he wrote, "had that egotism of the man of genius which Nietzsche compares to the egotism of a woman with child . . . He had under charming and modest manners, in almost all things of life, a complete absorption in his own dream . . . For him nothing existed but his thought . . . He was too confident for self-assertion": "The Death of Synge," *Autobiographies,* 511–12.

43. *In Wicklow, West Kerry and Connemara,* in *Collected Works* 2: *Prose,* 253.

44. *Essays and Introductions* (New York: Collier Books, 1968), 332–33.

45. Kiberd, "Synge's Studies in the Gaeltacht," 16. In particular, Martin MacDonagh was offended to see a letter he had written Synge reproduced in Synge's article, "The Last Fortress of the Celt." Synge used five of MacDonagh's letters in *The Aran Islands,* but felt free to reverse the order in which they had been received (Greene and Stephens, 103–4) and to alter them for artistic or other purposes. As further evidence of the shaping spirit at work in *The Aran Islands* there is the observation Synge made in the typescript: "In arranging my chapters I have, of course, used a good deal of freedom, bringing kindred things together and keeping jarring things apart": *Collected Works* 2: *Prose,* 48n.

46. Kiberd, 17. Kiberd, however, may be rather harshly interpreting Bourgeois's observation: Bourgeois, 79.

47. *A Study of English Romanticism* (New York: Random House, 1968), 37.

48. See, for example, Lee M. Whitehead, "The Island-Mountain in Myth: Some Notes Towards the (un)Natural History of an Image," *The Human Context* 7 (Summer 1975): 212–27.

Chapter 7—Hail and Farewell

1. This and the following quotation are from *Ave,* the first volume of Moore's autobiographical trilogy, *Hail and Farewell,* ed. Richard Cave (Gerrards Cross: Colin Smythe, 1976), 255. Further quotations from the trilogy will be from this omnibus edition, with page numbers in parentheses. *Ave* appeared in 1911, *Salve* in 1912, and *Vale* in 1914. The date of 1909 in my text refers to the year in which Moore was writing *Ave.*

2. *Hail and Farewell,* 137.

3. For Moore in revival Ireland, see also Joseph Hone, *The Life of George Moore* (London: Gollancz, 1936), Chapters VI and VII; Malcolm Brown, *George Moore: A Reconsideration* (Seattle: University of Washington Press, 1955), Chapter 7; *George Moore in Transition: Letters to T. Fisher Unwin and Lena Milman, 1894–1910,* ed. Helmut E. Gerber (Detroit: Wayne State University Press, 1968).

4. Anthony Farrow, *George Moore* (Boston: Twayne Publishers, 1978), 122, 135.

5. Moore opens *Hail and Farewell* with a memory of Martyn's remarks made in 1894; but in a later Preface to *The Untilled Field,* reproduced in the edition published by Colin Smythe in 1976, Moore dates Martyn's remarks as probably made in 1899.

6. "Sittings" is Moore's own word: *Hail and Farewell,* 69.

7. *Hail and Farewell,* 235.

8. *Hail and Farewell,* 114.

9. See *Hail and Farewell,* 140–42, 272–304, for accounts of the early stages of the friendship with AE.

10. John Eglinton, *Irish Literary Portraits* (1935; rpt. Freeport, New York: Books for Libraries Press, 1967), 126–27.

11. AE, of course, denied the theory of organic evolution, a theory as we have noted unpalatable to the revivalists. (AE's denial is recorded in *Hail and Farewell,* 287.) In the 1920s, Moore told Eglinton that life was no less wonderful for the materialist ("for Darwin, if you like") than for the transcendentalist: *Irish Literary Portraits,* 126–27.

12. "Dramatis Personae," extracted in *W. B. Yeats: Selected Prose,* ed. A. Norman Jeffares (London: Pan Books, 1976), 105–6.

13. *A Story-Teller's Holiday* (London: Cuman Sean-eolais na hEireann, 1918), 345. For Moore's complicated family background, see Hone's *The Life of George Moore* and *The Moores of Moore Hall* (London: Jonathan Cape, 1939); Moore's brother's account of their father, *An Irish Gentleman: George Henry Moore* (London: T. Werner Laurie, 1913); Elizabeth Harris, "George Moore: 'The Little Catholic Boy of that Name'," *Eire-Ireland* 15.1 (1980): 64–85.

14. Moore may have been rebelling against class associations of Catholicism with the peasantry; he may have been rebelling against the Catholicism of his father's nationalism; he may have been rebelling against a church that threatened his sexual expression (or that he thought caused what was rumored to be Moore's impotence). See Harris, though she does not include the rumor in her discussion of the sexual element in Moore's anti-Catholicism.

15. *Hail and Farewell,* 116, 126.

16. That Catholicism and Irishness are inseparable is an old idea. Within the scope of this book, it received rhapsodic expression in William O'Brien's novel, *When We Were Boys* (London: Longmans, Green, 1890), 136–37; it was the belief of Edward Martyn (see *Hail and Farewell,* 235) and T. P. Gill (*Hail and Farewell,* 123); James Stephens attributes it to Joyce, "The James Joyce *I* Knew," in *James, Seumas & Jacques: Unpublished Writings of James Stephens,* ed. Lloyd Frankenberg (New York: Macmillan, 1964), 149; it was the view also of Daniel Corkery. How far such an idea is a defensive one and a basically social and political one, rather than a religio-racial one, is difficult to gauge.

17. *Hail and Farewell,* 266.

18. Quoted in Hone's *The Life of George Moore,* 80.

19. In *A Story-Teller's Holiday,* he inveighs against cruelty to animals, including unnecessary confinement; the latter is blurrily associated in his mind with the imprisoning nature of Catholicism: 14–15, 43–44, 53, 174.

20. *Irish Literary Portraits,* 97.

21. A letter to Zola, quoted by Hone, 101; the succeeding definition of naturalism is Hone's (96).

22. Moore several times drew attention to the feminine elements in his make-up.

23. Moore's attempt was resumed by such Irish women novelists as Kate O'Brien, Kathleen Coyle, and Mary Lavin, but their gender consigned them historically (if wrongly) to perceptive but marginal social analysis.

24. In a letter, quoted by Hone, 107.

25. *A Drama in Muslin: A Realistic Novel* (London: Walter Scott, 1918), 99. Further quotations will be from this edition, with page numbers in parentheses.

26. Preface to *Muslin* (London: William Heinemann, 1915), viii.

27. In *Hail and Farewell,* Moore recounts his attempts to discover the real selves of those he encountered: two examples are T. P. Gill (who rarely reveals "his real self, his cheerful superficial nature," 310) and Father Tom Finlay (who dare not uncover himself in an autobiography for fear of offending his Jesuitical identity, 339–41).

28. *Hail and Farewell,* 362.

29. *Hail and Farewell,* 362. The literary equivalent was the kind of arranged plot he disliked in Hardy, with coincidence substituted for accident.

30. "Literature and the Irish Language" appeared in the *New Ireland Review* and then in *Ideals in Ireland,* ed. Lady Gregory (1901; rpt. New York: Lemma Publishing Corporation, 1973), 45–51. In reprinting Moore's paper, Lady Gregory adds a couple of sharp dissenting footnotes.

31. *Hail and Farewell,* 320.

32. *Hail and Farewell,* 343-4.

33. While claiming that he wrote his first stories in English rather than in Hiberno-English (or "Anglo-Irish"). The Preface is reproduced in *The Untilled Field* (Gerrards Cross: Colin Smythe, 1976), from which edition I take my quotations of the stories. It is Richard Cave, in one of his valuable notes to *Hail and Farewell,* who identifies Padraic O'Sullivan and not Taidgh O'Donoghue as the translator of Moore's stories, an error Moore makes once again in his later Preface to *The Untilled Field: Hail and Farewell,* 715, n. 83.

34. See *Hail and Farewell,* 58–74.

35. Carleton is the unidentified "rudiment" Moore refers to in *Hail and Farewell* (57), in dismissal of Irish literature before himself.

36. "Fugitives" appeared in 1914 as a fusion of two stories in the 1903 edition, "In the Clay" and "The Way Back".

37. Moore re-uses the name of the Big House in *A Drama in Muslin* to suggest how the gentry, whose heyday was the eighteenth century, has "happily fallen" to become the middle class of the late nineteenth century.

38. *Hail and Farewell,* 349.

39. For both it was only half metaphor; Moore claimed that Balzac was the first to discover that in the nineteenth century civilization means money: cited by Farrow, 32.

40. Harding is the writer who encourages Alice Barton in *A Drama in Muslin.*

41. Richard Cave, "Afterword" to *The Lake* (Gerrards Cross: Colin Smythe, 1980), 191. My quotations from *The Lake* will be from this edition of the 1921 revised version of the novel, with page numbers in parentheses. I recommend Cave's substantial Afterword for discussion of the psychological subtleties of the novel, of the nature of the revisions Moore made in 1905 and 1921, of autobiographical elements in the novel and the real-life models of Moore's characters, of stylistic influences on *The Lake,* and of the Wagnerian aspects of the whole. See also Cave's *A Study of the Novels of George Moore* (Gerrards Cross: Colin Smythe, 1978), Chapter 9.

42. The notion that every man has a lake in his heart has come to Gogarty apparently by accident. In *A Story-Teller's Holiday,* Moore remembers how the story of *Esther Waters* was given to him by chance in the single sentence of a newspaper (207–208). These accidents, of course, are revelations of an unseen and underlying reality that, if we are open, we can gradually approach, but it is psychological rather than mystical reality and can be felt before it is seen. Protestantism appealed to Moore because it admitted the "accident" of revelation and eschewed unnecessary schema and dogma.

43. Poole's name—in the unrevised novel he was called Ralph Ellis—suggests a body of water in which Nora is "re-baptized"—like Gogarty, of whom she is spiritually in advance; the lake of the novel's title is called a pool after Gogarty swims it to spiritual freedom. Metaphorically, Gogarty does drown when he kills off his old self; on this level he was ironically correct when he thought Nora had drowned in the lake.

44. See Moore's remarks on change and creed in *A Story-Teller's Holiday,* 49–50. Richard Cave points out that in *The Brook Kerith* (1916), Moore made St Paul represent the Catholic temperament (assertive, ungenerous, obstinate) and Christ the Protestant temperament (curious, compassionate, flexible): *Hail and Farewell,* 718, n.106. Moore's own occasional malice and cruelty can, then, be seen as a half-compelled, half-willed expression of the "Catholic" side of his mixed temperament: regrettable but necessary in the dialectic of his spiritual development. Also, Edward Martyn's reluctance to change (see *Hail and Farewell,* 186) is connected by Moore to his Catholicism. Moore's smug attitude to Martyn is difficult to swallow, but it is made easier if we realize that Moore is being smug to a projected version of himself, that Martyn is Moore's alter ego, as Nora is Gogarty's. But if Nora is Gogarty's better half, Martyn is Moore's worse half. Martyn is Catholic, landowning, bourgeois, and respectable—an incarnation of the decencies Moore wanted to preserve that he might enjoy offending against them. Martyn is a haunting, not entirely defeated, troubling reminder of the self Moore could kill off only through the vehicles of his fictional characters.

45. "Literature and the Irish Language," in *Ideals in Ireland,* 50.

46. *The Lake,* 43; *A Story-Teller's Holiday,* 97; *Hail and Farewell,* 289.

47. As appendix to *The Lake,* Cave reproduces Meyer's translations which Moore plagiarized and extracted.

48. See Cave's Appendix A to *The Lake,* 252.

49. There is a recurring contest in Moore's thinking between an almost superstitious belief in the power of names (his symbolism) and a recognition that there is a sometimes belying reality behind names (his realism).

50. *The Life of George Moore,* 247.

51. "George Moore's *The Lake:* A Possible Source," *Eire-Ireland* 6.3 (1971): 12–15.

52. The other novels are *Waiting* (1914), *Conquest* (1920), *How They Did It* (1920), *Vocations* (1921) and *The Holy Tree* (1922). Costello has valuable pages on O'Donovan in *The Heart Grown Brutal: The Irish Revolution in Literature, from Parnell to the Death of Yeats* (Dublin: Gill and Macmillan, 1977), 58–64.

53. Preface to *The Lake,* x.

54. *Father Ralph* (London: Macmillan, 1913), 388. Further quotations will be from this edition, with page numbers in parentheses.

55. Hone, *The Life of George Moore,* 281. "A Western Tibet" Moore called an Ireland indifferent to the great theological debates of Europe. Ralph O'Brien is much influenced by Maurice Blondel's 1893 Sorbonne thesis in which the Catholic philosopher decried the concentration of the Church on external signs and arguments. Blondel directed attention to action as a way of preventing man's powerless cry for the transcendent and the answering imposition of dogma from without. "Nothing," he wrote, "can enter man unless it proceeds

from him and in one way or another corresponds to a need for development": quoted by T. M. Schoof, *A Survey of Catholic Theology 1800–1970* (New York: Paulist Newman Press, 1970), 52. Blondel's concept of action is in contrast to the transcendentalism of the revival, yet its attempt to square action with belief has its specific equivalent in AE's attempt to square transcendentalism with the cooperative movement in which Ralph O'Brien becomes involved. The enthusiasm with which the Church in Ireland welcomed Rome's vicious assault on modernism as the "sum total of all heresies" destroyed an opportunity for the Church to participate in the renewal of Ireland from within (since many priests were engaged in various revival activities) and reduced the practical efforts of the revival to symbolism in the hands of Protestant idealists. (Moore had in a minor way predicted this lost opportunity in his portrayal of Father MacTurnan in *The Untilled Field.* Note too the dominance of *inaction* in Joyce's portrait of contemporary Ireland.) The Church in Ireland maintained its conservative course and when the revival came to an end in the 1920s it was left in uncontested control of belief (and even political action) in much of the island. This unfortunate crossroads in Irish cultural history occurred while the revivalists remained oblivious or indifferent. See Schoof, 45–69, for an account of modernism; Rome seemed to smell traces of Protestantism and socialism in the modernist movement.

Chapter 8—Waking the Dead

1. *An Irish Journey* (New York: Longmans, Green, 1943), 145.
2. "The Man Who Loved Islands" can be found in *The Complete Short Stories* of Lawrence (London: Heinemann, 1955).
3. However, it was Compton MacKenzie who saw in Lawrence's story a portrait of himself and objected, causing Lawrence to make changes.
4. The first half of this passage is quoted in David H. Greene and Edward M. Stephens, *J. M. Synge: 1871–1909* (New York: Macmillan, 1959), 81; the second half is quoted in Elizabeth Coxhead, *Lady Gregory: A Literary Portrait* (London: Macmillan, 1961), 54.
5. Synge, *Collected Works* 2: *Prose,* ed. Alan Price (London: Oxford University Press, 1966), 103n.
6. I have discussed a variety of interpretations of the story in "Passage Through 'The Dead,'" *Criticism* 15.2 (1973): 91–108.
7. *James Joyce* (Oxford: Oxford University Press, 1983), 252. Readers should consult Ellmann's chapter, "The Backgrounds of 'The Dead.'"
8. Quoted by Ellmann, 245.
9. The Epiphany date was first suggested by Julian B. Kaye in "The Wings of Daedalus: Two Stories in 'Dubliners,'" *Modern Fiction Studies* 4 (1958): 37. According to a Celtophile in Richard Power's novel *The Land of Youth* (1964), the proper Celtic date for the celebration of Christmas is Twelfth Night.
10. Information on the Christmas Fool is available in Frazer's *The Golden Bough* (1890) and Gertrude Jobes' *Dictionary of Mythology, Folklore and Symbols* (1961).
11. The poem is quoted by Ellmann, 82.
12. This quotation and other quotations from *Dubliners* are from the edition published in New York by the Viking Press in 1968 and edited by Robert Scholes. Since I am quoting from short stories, I have omitted page references.

13. This definition from Lydgate can be found in the *Oxford English Dictionary,* s.v. "Macabre."

14. The American formalist critics, with their distrust of subjectivity, have taken a dim view of Gabriel, seeing in him irredeemable egotism: see my article, "Passage Through 'The Dead.'"

15. Joyce's adoption of money as the base currency of Irish life was perhaps inspired by the downfall of Parnell, during which the leader cried to his followers: If you wish to sell me, at least demand a decent price.

16. These are the three words, of course, that fascinate the boy in the opening story of *Dubliners,* "The Sisters." As well as being an astronomical indicator, a gnomon is a geometrical figure, which Joyce may be using to suggest the incompleteness of his Dubliners' lives.

17. By Conor Cruise O'Brien, Kathleen Sheehy's son: see his *States of Ireland* (St Albans: Panther Books, 1974), 79–80, 103–104.

18. In *Life and the Dream* (London: Macmillan, 1947), 107, Mary Colum describes the dress affected by women enthusiasts of the Irish revival (ordinary Dubliners called them "Irishers" in contempt, just as Sean O'Casey—the Protestant John Casey—was dubbed "Irish Jack" by fellow tenant-dwellers for learning Gaelic).

19. The "turas" or open-air excursion was part of the program of the Gaelic League, as was the Summer College for the learning of Irish, "usually in a wild part of the country, planted in the midst of an Irish-speaking population": Diarmid Coffey, *Douglas Hyde, President of Ireland* (Dublin and Cork: Talbot Press, 1938), 163.

20. Griffith is quoted by F. S. L. Lyons, *Ireland Since the Famine* (London: Fontana, 1973), 242. I attribute this view to Joyce despite the fact that in the aftermath of the *Playboy* riot at the Abbey Theatre which occurred in February 1907 and which distracted Joyce from starting work on "The Dead," Joyce sided with Griffith and the nationalists against the literary men. Ellmann remarks that Joyce's "position was mostly an airing of resentments. He refused to take this theatrical dispute seriously and preferred to consider it a Donnybrook of contending pettinesses, in which he wanted to see the established writers beaten and so would not acknowledge that in the battle with censorship he had common cause with them": *James Joyce,* 240. The same perverse attitude of the homesick exile's surface agreement with the nationalists, the literary man's underlying agreement with the exalters of literature, and the fiercely solitary and expatriate writer's ironic removal from both informs "The Dead" which Joyce began on the heels of the *Playboy* affair. For an excellent discussion of nationalism and cosmopolitanism during the revival, see "The Battle of Two Civilisations," a chapter in Lyons' *Ireland Since the Famine.*

21. *A Portrait of the Artist as a Young Man* (Harmondsworth: Penguin Books, 1960), 203.

22. Quoted by Lyons, 242. Ironically this is what Yeats has Cathleen ni Houlihan tell the Gillanes in his 1902 play.

23. Letter to C. P. Curran in 1904, quoted by Ellmann, 163. I have silently restored the correct spelling of hemiplegia, misspelled in Ellmann's 1983 revision of his 1959 biography. For a discussion of Fr. Flynn in "The Sisters" as a syphilitic, see Burton A. Waisbren and Florence L. Walzl, "Paresis and the Priest: James Joyce's Symbolic Use of Syphilis in 'The Sisters,'" *Annals of Internal Medicine* 80 (1974): 758–62.

24. In the light of the movements of Corley and Lenehan in "Two Gallants," which include the area of Stephen's Green, it might be apt to quote this passage by Seumas O'Sullivan: "And there is another wind which visits Dublin, and a very curious wind it is—

very hard to identify, for it does not blow directly from the direction of any of the city's boundaries, but seems to rise, as it were, within the railings of St. Stephen's Green, and moves in a small circle between that and the Ballast Office in Westmoreland Street": *Essays and Recollections* (Dublin and Cork: Talbot Press, 1944), 80. O'Sullivan goes on to recollect Joyce and his "curiously continental air," of which Lenehan and other characters in *Dubliners* are rather inauthentic possessors (parodies of Joyce's own youthful, fake Europeanism). *Dubliners* is full of depressing circulations, of which Gabriel's story of Johnny the horse is one example, suggesting the oblivious circularities of the Irish through history.

25. *The Letters of W. B. Yeats,* ed. Allan Wade (London: Hart-Davis, 1954), 306. Before *Dubliners* appeared, Yeats had changed his mind about his "blind and ignorant town."

26. The year *Dubliners* appeared, a Government Housing Commission in its report classified half of the population of Dublin, 169,736 out of 305,000, under the heading of "Indefinite and unproductive class": see David Krause, *Sean O'Casey: The Man and His Work* (New York: Macmillan, 1975), 5–6.

27. "The Holy Office." To read Krause on the condition of plumbing and sewerage in O'Casey's (and Joyce's) Dublin is to make Joyce's metaphor apt indeed: Krause, 5–6.

28. Quoted by Ellmann, 221. The phrase "of my country" I have taken from the 1965 OUP edition of *James Joyce;* the revised edition gives "in my country," which looks like a printer's error.

29. *Literary Ideals in Ireland* (1899; rpt. New York: Lemma Publishing Corporation, 1973), 63.

30. H. Zimmer, *The Irish Element in Mediaeval Culture* (New York and London: G. P. Putnam's, 1891), 49, 57.

31. John V. Kelleher dates the action of "The Dead" in "the early 1890s" with the latest date "the Christmas season of 1892," and supplies evidence from *Ulysses* and *A Portrait:* "Irish History and Mythology in James Joyce's 'The Dead,'" *The Review of Politics* 27 (1965): 417. This creates a problem with Bartell D'Arcy's reference to Caruso, who did not make his debut until November 1894; moreover, D'Arcy's casual mention of Caruso seems to assume the guests' knowledge of him, and Caruso did not sing outside Italy until 1902. Donald Torchiana dates the story after 1903, since he suggests that Gabriel's speech is derived from Browning's *Asolando;* he claims the story takes place on Wednesday, January 6, 1904: "James Joyce's Method in 'Dubliners,'" in *The Irish Short Story,* eds. Patrick Rafroidi and Terence Brown (Gerrards Cross: Colin Smythe, 1979), 129, 138.

32. Mary Colum in *Life and the Dream* (102–3) confirms that though Dublin during the revival was not lacking in musical appreciation, there was little first-rate European music to be heard there, save for some opera. By contrast, it has been claimed that Dublin was a centre of musical activity when Shaw was a boy (1860s–70s), a period Mr Browne and the Misses Morkan might be recalling: the claim was made by Lady Hanson, a friend of the Shaw family, in W. R. Rodgers, *Irish Literary Portraits* (London: BBC, 1972), 124.

33. Mary Colum remembers the islandwide interest in the *Feis Ceoil* (Music Festival) and the excitement created by Hyde's *The Love Songs of Connacht* (1893): *Life and the Dream,* 102, 113–14.

34. In support of such a view, Kelleher shows that during the course of the evening Gabriel violates taboos associated with Ireland, but I disagree with his conclusion that these are tragic errors for which Gabriel must pay. Stephen violates many similar taboos without incurring the wrath of Joycean gods; Gabriel violates the taboos of the dead, not of the living, and the claim that the dead vindictively press is, as the hotel scene demonstrates, unrightful.

35. Here in the encounter with a third woman, his wife, Gabriel perhaps hears the third of the "three blasts" of Michael, archangel of the Last Judgement, of which Father Arnall speaks in *A Portrait,* the first two blasts being the encounters with Lily and Molly Ivors. The three blasts, according to Father Arnall, signify "Time is, time was, but time shall be no more," and this is the sequence of temporal meaning in "The Dead." Like Fr. Flynn in "The Sisters," Gabriel suffers a third "stroke," but it turns out there is hope for him as there isn't for Fr. Flynn.

36. Though Furey's name also evokes the vengeful spirit he unwittingly is years later in the room of the Gresham Hotel. His Christian name suggests the archangel.

37. Which makes it fitting that Adaline Glasheen should hear an echo in Gretta's reply to Gabriel's question, "And what did he die of so young, Gretta? . . . I think he died for me," of the old woman (Ireland) in Yeats's *Cathleen ni Houlihan,* who, asked what brought yellow-haired Donough to his death, replies "He died for love of me." Glasheen is cited by Ellmann, 248n.

38. Yet three more associations—besides those with yellow-haired Donough and the archangel Michael—contrive to give significance to Furey. Stephen Dedalus imagines himself standing in a moonlit garden with a rejecting lover; Furey's predicament is the ironic reality: *A Portrait,* 63, 71. During this time, Parnell is much in young Stephen's mind, and we might compare Gretta's description of Furey below her window with this account of Parnell's last days: "The end was near. When he mounted the platform at Creggs [in Furey's Galway!] to speak bareheaded in the pouring rain, he was already in the last stages of exhaustion": Joan Haslip, *Parnell: A Biography* (London: Cobden-Sanderson, 1936), 392. Furey is like Parnell a romantic lover, a Romeo beneath Gretta's window; there is a picture of the balcony scene in *Romeo and Juliet* in the Misses Morkan's drawing-room.

39. *Early Bardic Literature, Ireland* (1879; rpt. New York: Lemma Publishing Corporation, 1970), 33.

40. "The Universal Literary Influence of the Renaissance," in *James Joyce in Padua,* ed. Louis Berrone (New York: Random House, 1977), 20.

41. Joseph C. Voelker, "'Proteus' and the *Vaticinia* of Marsh's Library: Joyce's Subjunctive Selves," *Eire-Ireland* 14.4 (1979): 133. Gabriel himself is one of Stephen Dedalus' negated possibilities, as I have suggested.

42. John Cronin, *Gerald Griffin (1803–1840): A Critical Biography* (Cambridge: Cambridge University Press, 1978), 135–37.

43. The phrase is Joyce's, applied in a letter to Ibsen: Ellmann, 86.

44. According to Ellmann (247n), Joyce borrowed Gretta's name from Gretta (Margaret) Cousins, wife of James Cousins. Since Gretta Cousins was a nationalist, this adds another dimension to Gretta Conroy's connection with Furey.

45. At this point, Joyce softens his attitude toward marriage. In the early stories marriage suggests captivity, but in "The Dead" it is absorbed within a larger scheme of possibility. The same change of attitude occurs between the early stories of Moore's *The Untilled Field* and "The Wild Goose." When marriage becomes a relationship that accommodates the self instead of an institution that imprisons the self, it becomes benign to these two writers.

46. Gabriel might be thought at this point to represent the Irish, gazing uncomfortably into Joyce's nicely polished looking-glass. Joyce hoped (or, seeking the publication of *Dubliners,* pretended to hope) that the Irish once seeing themselves undistorted might release their collectively repressed personalities.

47. Quoted by Malcolm Brown as epigraph to *The Politics of Irish Literature* (1972).

48. Yeats is quoting Villiers de l'Isle Adam quoting Aquinas: "Swedenborg, Mediums, and the Desolate Places," in Lady Gregory's *Visions and Beliefs in the West of Ireland* (Gerrards Cross: Colin Smythe, 1970), 315. Compare AE above, page 66.

49. "The Universal Literary Influence of the Renaissance," *James Joyce in Padua,* 23.

50. Virginia Moseley, "'Two Sights For Ever a Picture' in Joyce's 'The Dead,'" *College English* 26 (1965): 426–33. Models and sources offered by critics for the overall narrative structure of "The Dead" include Homer's *Odyssey, Togail Bruidhne Dá Derga* ("The Destruction of Da Derga's Hostel," an Old Irish saga), the events of Passion Week, Aristotelian tragedy, the Epiphany offices of the Roman Catholic church (the marriage at Cana, the visit of the Magi, the Baptism of Christ), and the myth of Orpheus and Eurydice. This is not to speak of the literary sources it is said Joyce drew upon for images, scenes, names, or motifs, including a song by Thomas Moore, a novel by George Moore *(Vain Fortune),* the *Iliad,* a novel by Bret Harte, a story by Anatole France, a volume by Browning; nor should we overlook the influence of Ibsen, including the play the young Joyce reviewed in 1900, *When We Dead Awaken.*

51. Dante was himself anticipated by the medieval Irish *Fís Adamnán (The Vision of Adamnán)* in which the soul of "the High Scholar of the Western world" departs from his body and is shown by his guardian angel those regions where dwell the vast hosts of the dead, the sevenfold Kingdom of Heaven, and also Hell with its fiery torments and throngs of the sinful that read familiarly after Father Arnall's sermon in *A Portrait.* After the revelations Adamnán returns to his body and is enjoined to rehearse for his countrymen the rewards of Heaven and the pains of Hell. See C. S. Boswell, *An Irish Precursor of Dante: A Study on the Vision of Heaven and Hell Ascribed to the Eighth-century Irish Saint Adamnan, with Translation of the Irish Text* (London: David Nutt, 1908). Joyce need not have known this tale: he shares the medieval eschatological inclination of the Catholic mind that has survived stubbornly among the Irish. (Yeats would have preferred to see it as evidence of a Celtic mind: in "The Celtic Element in Literature," he quotes approvingly Ernest Renan to the effect that the framework of the *Divine Comedy* is Celtic: *Essays and Introductions* [New York: Collier, 1968], 185.)

52. John C. Messenger, *Inis Beag: Isle of Ireland* (New York: Holt, Rinehart & Winston, 1969), 99.

53. "The vast cycle of starry life bore his weary mind outward to its verge and inward to its centre, a distant music accompanying him outward and inward," *A Portrait,* 103.

54. Ellmann, 234.

55. Joyce's praise of the apocalyptic stories is quoted by Hone in *W. B. Yeats 1865–1939* (London: Macmillan, 1965), 175. His adventures in Marsh's Library are recounted by Voelker, 135.

56. Edward Engelberg, *The Symbolist Poem* (New York: E. P. Dutton, 1967), 32; Wilson, *Axel's Castle* (New York: Charles Scribner's Sons, 1931), 19.

57. Voelker, 135.

58. In a lecture, reproduced in *Daniel Defoe,* ed. from Italian manuscripts and translated by Joseph Prescott (Buffalo: State University of New York, 1964), 13.

59. In "The Universal Literary Influence of the Renaissance," *James Joyce in Padua,* 21–22. Like Moore, Joyce regrets the passing of pre-Renaissance beauty, but considered individuality and compassion as necessary and adequate compensations.

60. *Daniel Defoe,* 23.

61. Voelker directs our attention to this passage, 134.

62. *Daniel Defoe,* 22.

Chapter 9—Betraying Presences

1. These are identified as realist characteristics by J. P. Stern in *On Realism* (London: Routledge & Kegan Paul, 1973).

2. Discussions of Reid, Bullock, and Ervine can be found in my earlier book, *Forces and Themes in Ulster Fiction* (Dublin: Gill and Macmillan, 1974). Ulster had its own chapter of the Irish revival, but largely because of Yeats's distaste for Ulster people (he later embraced the partitionism the literary revival had always secretly espoused), cultural relations between Belfast and Dublin were strained.

3. *Hail and Farewell* (Gerrards Cross: Colin Smythe, 1976), 58–74.

4. Chief among the philosophers Austin follows before repudiating are Kant and Fichte, and as Ben Knights has shown, both philosophers were important resources for the clerisy of the nineteenth-century: *The Idea of the Clerisy in the Nineteenth Century* (Cambridge: Cambridge University Press, 1978), 18–21. Austin also comes to repudiate Carlyle, another key figure among the nineteenth-century clerisy. Sheehan's rejection of a clerisy is an implicit rejection of a literary and cultural revival of the Anglo-Irish sort.

5. *The Triumph of Failure* (London: Burns Oates & Washbourne, 1935), 143.

6. *The Triumph of Failure,* 378, 379.

7. Joyce used Arnold's phrase before all of these, when praising Ibsen: see *James Joyce: The Critical Writings,* eds. Ellsworth Mason and Richard Ellmann (New York: The Viking Press, 1964), 65.

8. "Inside the Whale," in George Orwell, *A Collection of Essays* (New York: Doubleday & Company, 1957), 246.

9. For Joyce's praise of Ibsen, see *The Critical Writings,* 64. For Carlyle's opposition to introspection, see Houghton, *The Victorian Frame of Mind* (New Haven and London: Yale University Press, 1957), 311.

10. *The Irish* (Harmondsworth: Penguin Books, 1969), 130.

11. In William Carleton (1794–1869) and many later Irish novelists we have a travesty of a middle class—gaugers, land-agents, gombeen-men, bailiffs—that was instrument to the often invisible or absentee real power of the Ascendancy.

12. Seamus Deane uses the phrase in his review of my book, *Forces and Themes in Ulster Fiction,* in the *Education Times* 15 Aug. 1974.

13. Stern, 46–47.

14. Quoted by John Nemo, *Patrick Kavanagh* (Boston: Twayne Publishers, 1979), 57.

15. "Modern Ireland: An Address to American Audiences, 1932–1933," *Massachusetts Review* 5.2 (1964): 263.

16. *The Threshold of Quiet* (Dublin & Cork: Talbot Press, 1944), 53. Further quotations from the novel will be from this edition, with page references in parentheses.

17. Among this "dark fiction," I would include Sean O'Faolain's *Bird Alone* (1936), Frank O'Connor's *Dutch Interior* (1940), John McGahern's *The Dark* (1965), and Edna O'Brien's *A Pagan Place* (1970) and *Night* (1972).

18. *The Valley of the Squinting Windows* (New York: Brentano's, 1919), 16. This is the edition from which I will quote, with page references in parentheses.

19. By Andrew E. Malone, quoted disapprovingly by Michael McDonnell in the *Dictionary of Irish Literature,* ed. Robert Hogan (Westport, CT: Greenwood Press, 1979), 418.

20. *The Irishman: A Novel* (London: Eveleigh Nash Company, 1920), 215.

21. *The Clanking of Chains* (Dublin and London: Maunsel and Company, 1920), 35. Further quotations will be from this edition, with page references in parentheses.

22. *The Irishman,* 292.

23. For Lysaght's involvement with MacNamara's novel, see *Changing Times: Ireland Since 1898* (Gerrards Cross: Colin Smythe, 1978), 59. Lysaght published this book of memoirs under the name of Edward MacLysaght.

24. Various shades of opinion are entertained in *The Gael,* and the novel reads occasionally like a down-to-earth version of *The Interpreters.* Lysaght worked with AE on preparing the Irish Convention of 1917–18, and AE's dispassionate analysis of political positions in Ireland may have influenced Lysaght and prepared AE himself for the writing of *The Interpreters.*

25. *The Gael* (Dublin and London: Maunsel and Company, 1919), 201.

26. Lysaght discusses his beliefs in *Changing Times.*

27. *The Gael,* 262.

28. *The Gael,* 336. The repressed tradition included Tom Kettle, Francis Sheehy-Skeffington and Francis Cruise O'Brien. Lysaght's notion of renewal from within through action (of a peaceful kind) bears comparison with the contemporary modernist movement in Catholicism, and beside it Pearse's nationalism, culminating in Easter 1916, was a kind of dogma imposed from without and which Lysaght came to accept.

29. According to Lysaght, the Civil War ended his hopes for true language revival in Ireland: *Changing Times,* 135.

30. Lysaght attributed his own conversion to political nationalism to the Easter Rising: *Changing Times,* 55. He refers to himself as "conservative by nature" with a "leaning towards Socialism of a mild and Fabian type" (*Changing Times,* 138). During the Convention he was an informal Sinn Fein spokesman, yet he became an admirer of Collins during the Civil War and accepted the Treaty with England. He admired in their turn Moran, AE, Plunkett, Hyde, De Valera, Griffith, and Collins; he seems to have been a man of promiscuous nationalist enthusiasms. One form his Gaelicism took was his expertise in Irish pedigrees and he published *The Surnames of Ireland* in 1969.

31. Corkery in *Synge and Anglo-Irish Literature* (New York: Russell, 1965), 21, praises *The Gael* as a novel written above Lysaght's accustomed pitch, which Corkery attributes to the author's close engagement with the land. *The Gael* also illustrates those psychological effects of colonialism Corkery discusses with insight before suggesting that consciousness of the land can be an anticolonial force.

32. *The Gael,* 335.

33. Lysaght published a later novel in Irish, *Toil Dé* (1936), about the Black-and-Tan War. No novel seems to have been written indicting the Irish social and political forces that betrayed the ideals entertained in *The Gael.*

Chapter 10—Visions and Vanities

1. Joyce reviewed *Poets and Dreamers* in the Dublin *Daily Express* in March 1903; it is reprinted in *James Joyce: The Critical Writings,* eds. Ellsworth Mason and Richard Ellmann (New York: Viking, 1964), 102–5.

2. Kenneth Hurlstone Jackson, *A Celtic Miscellany: Translations from the Celtic Literatures* (Harmondsworth: Penguin Books, 1971), 142.

3. As reported by Padraic and Mary Colum, *Our Friend James Joyce* (New York:

Doubleday, 1958), 34. Nor is "Clay" fully comprehensible without knowledge of the rural Irish custom and belief from which Joyce borrows his saucer of earth; I stumbled on a description of the custom and belief in Eibhlís Ní Shúilleabháin's *Letters from the Great Blasket* (Dublin and Cork: The Mercier Press, n.d.), 60.

4. Richard Cave, Introduction to his edition of Moore's *Hail and Farewell* (Gerrards Cross: Colin Smythe, 1976), 26.

5. Joyce said this to Eugene Jolas: see Richard Ellmann, *James Joyce* (Oxford and New York: Oxford University Press, 1983), 6.

6. To place the Irish folklore movement within a larger context, consult Richard M. Dorson's indispensable book, *The British Folklorists: A History* (London: Routledge & Kegan Paul, 1968).

7. *Visions and Beliefs in the West of Ireland* (Gerrards Cross: Colin Smythe, 1970), 15.

8. See, for example, the tale entitled "The Court of Crinnawn" in Hyde's *Beside the Fire: A Collection of Irish Gaelic Folk Stories* (1890).

9. By 1964, the manuscript collection of the Irish Folklore Commission totaled a million and a half pages: see Sean O'Sullivan's Introduction to his *Folktales of Ireland* (Chicago and London: University of Chicago Press, 1966), xxxv. As early as 1892, Joseph Jacobs in his Preface to *Celtic Fairy Tales* said that whereas the problem he faced with an earlier volume of English fairy tales was one of collection, the problem with his Irish volume was one of selection; the plenitude of Irish tales necessitated, and the sales of the first volume warranted, a sequel to *Celtic Fairy Tales* in 1894.

10. *Beside the Fire* (London: David Nutt, 1910), xvi.

11. Kennedy, *Legendary Fictions of the Irish Celts* (Detroit: Singing Tree Press, 1968), vii; Hyde, *Beside the Fire,* x; Jacobs, *Celtic Fairy Tales* (London: The Bodley Head, 1970), 4; Delargy, "The Gaelic Story-teller," *Proceedings of the British Academy* (London: Oxford University Press, 1945), 187; O'Sullivan, *Folktales of Ireland,* xxxvii. Twelve years before Kennedy, Mrs. S. C. Hall lamented the disappearance of beliefs in and anecdotes about fairies: "It is now-a-days almost impossible for the traveller in Ireland to obtain any stories concerning them . . . the old have departed and the young become sceptical." See her Introduction to John O'Neill's *Handerahan, the Irish Fairyman and Legends of Carrick* (London: W. Tweedie, 1854), 7. As well as fitting the pattern of collectors' laments, this might suggest that the revivalists, a half century after Hall, were going against the grain of the people in demanding stories about fairies, unless, which is likely, lore was simply being concealed from members of the Ascendancy.

12. *Visions and Beliefs,* 15.

13. This is the burden of his essay "Ireland and the Hour," reprinted in *Selected Essays and Passages* (Dublin: Phoenix, n.d.).

14. "A.E." in *James, Seumas & Jacques,* ed. Lloyd Frankenberg (New York: Macmillan, 1964), 113.

15. Yeats's Introduction to *Fairy and Folk Tales of the Irish Peasantry:* this anthology and its sequel, *Irish Fairy Tales,* have been combined to form *Fairy and Folk Tales of Ireland;* the quotation appears on pp. 6–7 of the Macmillan, Colin Smythe, and Picador editions.

16. Yeats, *Uncollected Prose,* 2 vols. (New York: Columbia University Press, 1970) 1: 188. These words occur in an 1891 review by Yeats of Hyde's *Beside the Fire.*

17. The phrase occurs in "The Sorcerers," a chapter in *The Celtic Twilight,* in *The Collected Works of William Butler Yeats* (Stratford-on-Avon: The Shakespeare Head, 1908) 5: *The Celtic Twilight and Stories of Red Hanrahan,* 48.

18. *Fairy and Folk Tales of the Irish Peasantry,* in *Fairy and Folk Tales of Ireland,* 135.

19. The phrase occurs in "Witches and Wizards and Irish Folk-Lore," in Lady Gregory's *Visions and Beliefs,* 303.

20. *Fairy and Folk Tales of Ireland,* 5.

21. Foreword to *Visions and Beliefs,* 7.

22. *Visions and Beliefs,* 16.

23. James H. and Margaret E. Cousins, *We Two Together* (Madras: Ganesh, 1950), 141.

24. Although he mentions Yeats's first anthology only once (and gets the title wrong), Jacobs extracts from Croker, Lover, Carleton, and others several stories Yeats extracted four years before him, and retitles them identically.

25. "A Remonstrance with Scotsmen for Having Soured the Disposition of their Ghosts and Faeries," *Collected Works,* 5: 150.

26. *Fairy and Folk Tales of Ireland,* 138.

27. *A Commentary on the Collected Poems of W. B. Yeats* (London: Macmillan, 1968), 48.

28. *The Prose Fiction of W. B. Yeats* (Dublin: Dolmen, 1973), 14.

29. *Collected Works* 5: 7–8. In "Enchanted Woods," also in *The Celtic Twilight,* Yeats writes that only those with neither simplicity nor wisdom deny the existence of spirits: *Collected Works* 5: 87.

30. Yeats: *The Man and the Masks* (New York: W. W. Norton, 1978), 196–97.

31. Foreword to *Fairy and Folk Tales of Ireland,* xv.

32. *Axel's Castle* (New York: Charles Scribner's Sons, 1931), 48.

33. *Axel's Castle,* 57.

34. *Fairy and Folk Tales of Ireland,* 6. In the Macmillan edition of this book (and its Picador impression), the phrase reads "seldom come holy"; in his *W.B. Yeats: Selected Prose* (London: Pan, 1976), 161, Jeffares gives the phrase, surely correctly, as "seldom come home holy." Yeats takes his revenge on this sceptic (who is referred to again in "Belief and Unbelief") in "The Man and his Boots," a chapter in *The Celtic Twilight.*

35. *Fairy and Folk Tales of Ireland,* 301.

36. Quoted by Raine in her Foreword to *Fairy and Folk Tales of Ireland* (New York: Macmillan, 1973), vii.

37. *Visions and Beliefs,* 15.

Chapter 11—The Death of Anshgayliacht

1. See Yeats's review of Hyde's *The Story of Early Gaelic Literature,* reprinted in *Uncollected Prose,* 2 vols. (New York: Columbia University Press, 1970) 1: 358–59.

2. How storytelling and collecting could be confused is evident from Jacobs' Preface to *Celtic Fairy Tales.* "I have endeavoured to include in this volume," he wrote, "the best and most typical stories told by the chief masters of the Celtic folk-tale, Campbell, Kennedy, Hyde, and Curtin . . . I have only been enabled to do this by the courtesy of those who owned the copyright of these stories," including Lady Wilde, author-compiler of *Ancient Legends, Mystic Charms, and Superstitions of Ireland* (1887). Collectors told the stories they collected, and held copyright on those versions. Once the notion of variation became widespread, it became less easy for writers to drive folktales from the public into private domain. Meanwhile, Jacobs, because he knew no Gaelic, felt at liberty to do what Yeats praised Hyde for doing: modifying the translations; his defense of this liberty was the same as

that made by Yeats on behalf of Hyde (and duplicates that made of "creative" redactions of the saga material): "I have tried to put myself into the position of an *ollamh* or *sheenachie* familiar with both forms of Gaelic [Irish and Scots], and anxious to put his stories in the best way to attract English children." Jacobs was not an Irishman, but an Australian folklorist and historian of the Jews. His volumes of Celtic stories were for a young English readership. The Saxons had conquered the Celt, but the Celt reconquered the Saxon "in the realm of imagination." Jacobs' anthologies were not meant to further Celtic, much less Irish, political or even cultural nationalism, though this may have been their unwitting effect. They were meant to achieve between Saxon and Celtic children "a true union of hearts" within, of course, the political reality of the Union.

3. *Beside the Fire: A Collection of Irish Gaelic Folk Stories* (London: David Nutt, 1910), xvii. Future quotations from this book are from this edition, with page numbers given in parentheses.

4. *Collected Works* 2: *Prose,* ed. Alan Price (London: Oxford University Press, 1966), 65. For this kind of internationalism, Synge was attacked by Arthur Griffith: see F. S. L. Lyons, *Ireland Since the Famine* (London: Fontana, 1973), 241–42.

5. We might place beside Hyde's praise of the early collectors Seán Ó Coileáin's praise of early scribes who preserved the saga literature: "It is difficult now to fully appreciate this wholly unselfish and traditional frame of mind," "Irish Saga Literature," in *Heroic Epic and Saga,* ed. Felix J. Oinas (Bloomington: Indiana University Press, 1978), 181.

6. For a theoretical statement of this idea, see J. Barre Toelken and John Wilson Foster, "A Descriptive Nomenclature for the Study of Folklore," *Western Folklore* 28 (1969): 91–111.

7. Incidentally, it was with the manuscript miscellanies of the late 19th century, compiled by small farmers who succeeded the poor scholars, that the Gaelic literary tradition which began with the literature we looked at in Chapter One, exhausted itself and died: see J. H. Delargy, "The Gaelic Story-teller," *Proceedings of the British Academy* (London: Oxford University Press, 1945), 202.

8. Seán Ó Súilleabháin (Sean O'Sullivan) and Reidar Th. Christiansen, *The Types of the Irish Folktale, Folklore Fellows Communications* 78.188 (1963): 7. Compare Propp's belief that "the entire store of fairy tales ought to be examined as a chain of variants," *Morphology of the Folktale,* ed. Svatava Pirkova-Jakobsen, trans. Laurence Scott (Bloomington: Indiana University Press, 1958), 103.

9. Quoted by R. B. Walsh, "Aspects of Irishness," in *Literature and Folk Culture: Ireland and Newfoundland,* eds. Alison Feder and Bernice Schrank (St. John's, Newfoundland: Memorial University, 1977), 11.

10. Structuralists and semioticians prefer to discuss cultural codes of which a writer and his work are conveyers rather than originators.

11. See Sean O'Sullivan's Introduction to *Folktales of Ireland* (Chicago and London: University of Chicago Press, 1966), xxxvi. O'Sullivan tells us that forty-three thousand versions of these tales were recorded up to 1956.

12. Walter Anderson's law is discussed by Stith Thompson in *The Folktale* (Berkeley: University of California Press, 1977), 437.

13. William Larminie, *West Irish Folk-Tales and Romances* (Totowa: Rowman and Littlefield, 1973), 82. Quotations from this book are from this edition with page numbers in parentheses.

14. Delargy, 194.

15. Kaarle Krohn, *Folklore Methodology,* trans. Roger L. Welsch (Austin and London: University of Texas Press, 1971), 26. Kaarle's father Julius was a disciple of Elias Lönnrot

and made a lifelong study of the *Kalevala*. In turn, Kaarle's disciple was Antti Aarne, pioneer of the tale-type index. (See Thompson, *The Folktale,* 396–97.)

16. It should not be overlooked, however, that Hyde confesses of this story: "I had only taken notes of it, and not written down the whole as it fell from [O'Hart's] lips" (173). It is difficult to gauge, then, the degree of any falsification that may have occurred.

17. I am aware of Bruno Bettelheim's reading of fairy tales in *The Uses of Enchantment* (1977), based on a theory of the young listener's psychological identification with the hero of the tale. The tensions and resolutions in the narrative are helpful metaphoric versions of those within the child. However, those resolutions are not achieved outside the intimate listener-tale (that is, child-hero) identification whereas, Bettelheim believes, the listener to a myth as story (cf. the Cuchulain stories) is an adult who is to emulate the hero, thereby exporting the tensions and resolutions of the narrative into society.

18. See Delargy, 194, 199, 201.

19. Propp, 18.

20. Propp, 74.

Chapter 12—The Mount of Transfiguration

1. See chiefly Michael J. Sidnell, "Versions of the Stories of Red Hanrahan," *Yeats Studies* 1 (1971): 119–74; Richard J. Finneran, "'Old lecher with a love on every wind': A Study of Yeats' *Stories of Red Hanrahan,*" *Texas Studies in Literature and Language* 14.2 (1972): 347–58.

2. Quoted by Richard Finneran in his edition of *John Sherman and Dhoya* (Detroit: Wayne State University Press, 1969), 25.

3. Sidnell, 167.

4. Sidnell, 119.

5. *The Prose Fiction of W. B. Yeats* (Dublin: Dolmen, 1973), 9.

6. *The Prose Fiction of W. B. Yeats,* 27.

7. *Visions and Beliefs in the West of Ireland* (Gerrards Cross: Colin Smythe, 1970), 357. As Finneran reminds us in his article, "'Old lecher with a love on every wind': A Study of Yeats' *Stories of Red Hanrahan*" (353), Yeats suggested the Irishness of the Grail legend in his essay "The Celtic Element in Literature" (1897).

8. *From Ritual to Romance* (New York: Doubleday Anchor Books, 1957), 77. Against this should be set Kathleen Coyle's claim in her autobiography that in Norman Ireland "the Irish basic themes of Tristram and the Grail and Joseph of Arimathea flourished. Either they had originated in Ireland, *or* the Irish version of them was the most popular": *The Magical Realm* (New York: E. P. Dutton, 1943), 290.

9. Weston, 19. Finneran doubts if Yeats drew consciously on the Grail story and prefers to see in the Hanrahan stories "a unique Irish legend created by Yeats himself." In his 1912 book, *The Wisdom of the West: An Introduction to the Interpretative Study of Irish Mythology* (London: Theosophical Publishing Society), 58–61, James H. Cousins, whose approach to Irish myth and legendry resembled AE's, considered the Cauldron of the Dagda, Cuchullin's Cauldron, and the Holy Grail to be variants of the same archetype.

10. Richard J. Finneran in "'Old lecher with a love on every wind'" (350) discusses the resemblances between Owen O'Sullivan the Red and Red Hanrahan, and credits Thomas Whitaker with first making the connection. Both Whitaker and Finneran refer us for a description of O'Sullivan's character to *Reliques of Irish Jacobite Poetry* (1844) by John O'Daly

and Edward Walsh, but a more accessible source is Daniel Corkery who in *The Hidden Ireland* (Dublin: Gill & Macmillan, 1977), 184–221, might frequently be describing Hanrahan when he describes O'Sullivan. Finneran suggests that the poet William Dall O'Heffernan might also have been in part a model for the figure of Hanrahan. In "'The Secret Rose' and Yeats's Dialogue with History," *Ariel* 3.3 (1972), Augustine Martin offers William Carleton as a possible model. Ole Munch-Pedersen in "Some Aspects of the Rewriting of W. B. Yeats's 'Red Hanrahan's Song About Ireland,'" *Orbis Litterarum* 36 (1981) combatively adds yet another name to the list: Timothy O'Sullivan the Gaelic. Not to be outdone, I will add my own twig to this bonfire. In 1854 appeared a Loveresque book of rather corrupted fairy lore collected by John O'Neill (a reformed drunkard), entitled *Handerahan, the Irish Fairyman and Legends of Carrick* (see note 11 to chapter 10 above); much of this lore concerns the title figure whose name resembles that of Yeats's hero, though Yeats insisted that he took the name from a Galway shop: see William H. O'Donnell, *A Guide to the Prose Fiction of W. B. Yeats* (Ann Arbor: UMI Research Press, 1983), 38. Handerahan was an eighteenth-century figure (born 1710); he was thought to have become an "intermediate being" (35) under the influence of the fairies; he insulted the fairies by rejecting the fairy princess in favor of a mortal woman and suffers at the hands of the fairies thereafter. One of the kinds of fairies Yeats describes in his "Classification of Irish Fairies" appended to *Irish Fairy Tales* is "The Far Darrig (Ir. *Fear Dearg,* i.e. red man)": *Fairy and Folk Tales of Ireland* (New York: Macmillan, 1973), 385. According to Joseph Jacobs, "Red-haired men in Ireland and elsewhere are always rogues," *Celtic Fairy Tales* (London: The Bodley Head, 1970), 314. In "The Devil's Book" and "The Book of the Great Dhoul and Hanrahan the Red," early versions of the same early Hanrahan story, the roguish Hanrahan teaches English to schoolboys from *The Lives of Celebrated Rogues and Rapparees.* (Cf. Swift's remark in *Gulliver's Travels* about the Yahoos, who are on one level the Irish—"the red-haired of both sexes are more libidinous and mischievous than the rest!")

11. Finneran, "'Old lecher with a love on every wind,'" 351.

12. See Finneran, 353.

13. The date is Robert Hogan's and is given in *Dictionary of Irish Literature* (Westport, CT: Greenwood, 1979). No date appears in the Browne and Nolan copy I have inspected, but Brown in *Ireland in Fiction* (1919; New York: Barnes & Noble, 1969) gives 1909.

14. The 1906 reprint of Leamy's book promises a Preface by J. E. Redmond, but I have yet to locate this Preface.

15. T. P. G.'s Note to 1906 reprint (Dublin: M. H. Gill), xii.

16. *Irish Fairy Tales,* v.

17. *Irish Fairy Tales,* xi. There is a hint here of that male/female, bardic/folk, hero/survivor, self-assertion/self-effacement contest that recurs in Irish revival literature.

18. *Letters of James Stephens,* ed. Richard J. Finneran (London: Macmillan, 1974), 253.

19. *Letters of James Stephens,* 257.

20. *Letters of James Stephens,* 258–59.

21. At least up until 1955, the year Gerard Murphy's *The Ossianic Lore and Romantic Tales of Medieval Ireland* appeared and on which I have drawn in my comments on folklore and the Fionn cycle.

22. *Letters of James Stephens,* 50.

23. *Irish Fairy Tales* (New York: Macmillan, 1968), 218. Further quotations will be from this edition, with page numbers in parentheses. Cf. Yeats in "Dreams that have no Moral," a chapter in *The Celtic Twilight:* "The story, which I am going to tell just as it was

told, was one of those old rambling moralless tales, which are the delight of the poor and the hard driven, wherever life is left in its natural simplicity. They tell of a time when nothing had consequences, when even if you were killed, if only you had a good heart, somebody would bring you to life again with a touch of a rod, and when if you were a prince and happened to look exactly like your brother, you might go to bed with his queen, and have only a little quarrel afterwards" (173). Stephens relishes the amorality of this world far more than does Yeats.

24. *Silva Gadelica: A Collection of Tales in Irish,* 2 vols. (1892; rpt. New York: Lemma Publishing Corporation, 1970) 2: 383.

25. *Letters of James Stephens,* 153–54.

26. *Letters of James Stephens,* 151.

27. Or triplicity: cf. his 1913 book, *Here Are Ladies,* which he thought of calling *Triangles* (*Letters,* 53); this book celebrates what the folklorists call the Law of Three. Triplicity is a recurring formation in ancient and traditional Irish literature, and there was even a poetic form, Triads, upon which Kuno Meyer wrote. In 1914, Stephens told Stephen Mackenna that he was becoming interested in mathematics (*Letters,* 129).

28. *Letters of James Stephens,* 129.

29. *The Charwoman's Daughter* (Dublin: Gill and Macmillan, 1972), 87. Future quotations from the novel will be from this edition, with page numbers in parentheses.

30. *Irish Fairy Tales,* 64.

31. *The Crock of Gold* (New York: Macmillan, 1974), 9. Quotations from this novel will be from this edition, with page numbers in parentheses.

32. *Letters of James Stephens,* 301.

33. *On Prose and Verse,* in *A James Stephens Reader,* sel. Lloyd Frankenberg (New York: Macmillan, 1962), 404.

34. Kaarle Krohn, *Folklore Methodology,* trans. Roger L. Welsch (Austin and London: University of Texas Press, 1971), 26.

35. "No More Peasants," in *James, Seumas & Jacques: Unpublished Writings of James Stephens,* ed. Lloyd Frankenberg (New York: Macmillan, 1964), 275.

36. "Talk," in *James, Seumas & Jacques,* 104.

37. "An Essay in Cubes," *The English Review* 17 (1914), 85–86.

38. *"Finnegans Wake,"* in *James, Seumas & Jacques,* 161.

39. *James, Seumas & Jacques,* 154.

40. The mixed metaphors are Stephens': "An Essay in Cubes," 86.

41. "Irish Idiosyncrasies," *Uncollected Prose of James Stephens,* ed. Patricia McFate. 2 vols. (London: Macmillan, 1983) 1: 70.

42. One of Stephens's sources for *Irish Fairy tales* was Kuno Meyer's scholarly edition, *The Voyage of Bran, Son of Febal* (1895–97), which includes as Appendix an edition of the story of Mongan. In the second volume appears an essay by Alfred Nutt, "The Celtic Doctrine of Re-birth"; in this essay, which Stephens would have known, Nutt makes connections between the Celtic notion of reincarnation and metempsychosis and a Celtic Dionysian cult—the frenzy "wherein bonds of individuality are loosened, wherein the fixed and settled outlines of nature by which man is controlled and confined shift and transform themselves and accommodate themselves to his directed energy. Life viewed from this ecstatic standpoint is not a series of individual manifestations rigidly confined within irremovable limits, but is a plastic essence the infinite potentialities of which are accessible to whoso knows the means of attaining and mastering them" (138).

43. *James, Seumas & Jacques,* 275.

44. Hilary Pyle rounds on Stephens for calling the hero Fionn the son of Uail instead of the son of Cumhail: *James Stephens: His Work and an Account of His Life* (London: Routledge & Kegan Paul, 1965), 97. However, Gerard Murphy informs us that "in certain ancient references the father's name is given as Umall (not Cumall), and Umall may be the original form," *The Ossianic Lore and Romantic Tales of Medieval Ireland* (Dublin: Colm O Lochlainn for the Cultural Relations Committee of Ireland), 7.

45. Stephens' Abbot is probably meant to be St. Finnian, a sixth-century bishop who founded a school of learning and whose disciples included St. Columba and St. Brendan. St. Finnian, however, is associated with the Abbey of Movilla in County Down, not with Moville in County Donegal.

46. See Richard J. Finneran, Appendix A to *Letters of James Stephens,* 418.

47. *James, Seumas & Jacques,* 92.

48. "An Essay in Cubes," 90.

49. Joseph Hone quotes from Moore's *Impressions and Opinions* (1891): "The vulgar do not know that the artist makes but little use of his empirical knowledge of life, and that he relies almost entirely on his inner consciousness of the truth": *The Life of George Moore* (London: Gollancz, 1936), 173.

50. It may be relevant, however, that the neuter pronoun is not found in modern Irish.

51. *On Prose and Verse,* in *A James Stephens Reader,* 406.

52. *Letters of James Stephens,* 111.

53. Introduction to *The Charwoman's Daughter,* 4.

54. Cf. these lines from Yeats's *The Countess Cathleen:* "But dream of gold / For three nights running, and there's always gold." A folk belief is involved.

55. See Pyle, 58; consult Pyle, too, for what is known of Stephens' early life. An account of the suffragette movement and its connection with the Irish literary revival can be found in *We Two Together* by James and Margaret Cousins.

56. "An Essay in Cubes," 86.

57. Stephens discusses Blake while reviewing James H. Cousins' *The Wisdom of the West: Irish Review* 2.14 (1912): 100–102.

58. Quoted by Augustine Martin in *James Stephens: A Critical Study* (Dublin: Gill & Macmillan, 1977), 38, from Birgit Bramsback's *James Stephens, A Literary and Bibliographical Study* (1959); Bramsback is in turn quoting Stephens' note on the flyleaf of the first edition of *The Crock of Gold.*

59. *Letters of James Stephens,* 26.

60. Pyle reminds us that in *The Charwoman's Daughter* Stephens had already caricatured George Moore, AE, Yeats and Synge: Pyle, 47.

61. See Vivian Mercier's *The Irish Comic Tradition* (1962).

62. Hugh Kenner in his book, *Joyce's Voices* (1978).

63. The phrase occurs in "An Essay in Cubes," 93.

64. "Talk," in *James, Seumas & Jacques,* 104.

65. *James, Seumas & Jacques,* 104.

66. The intellectual Gabriel Conroy likewise encounters three women on his journey towards enlightenment.

67. The phrase occurs in "Enchanted Woods," *The Collected Works of William Butler Yeats* (Stratford-on-Avon: The Shakespeare Head, 1908) 5: *The Celtic Twilight and Stories of Red Hanrahan,* 88.

68. "The Untiring Ones," *Collected Works,* 5: 109.

69. Among the poems in *Nineteen-Sixteen: An Anthology* (Dublin: Browne and Nolan, 1935), ed. Edna C. Fitzhenry, is one by Dermot O'Byrne (the English composer Arnold Bax) entitled "Kilmasheogue—1916."

70. *James, Seumas & Jacques,* 91.

71. *James, Seumas & Jacques,* 270.

72. *The Wisdom of the West,* 18.

Chapter 13—The Kingdom of Fantasy

1. The first quoted phrase is from a March 1923 letter from Moore to Stephens in which Moore remembers Stephens' aid: quoted by Finneran in his edition of *Letters of James Stephens* (London: Macmillan, 1974), 211. The other phrase is from a 1917 letter from Moore to Stephens, quoted by Joseph Hone, *The Life of George Moore* (London: Gollancz, 1936), 336. Stephens in his replies seems uncertain which tone to adopt towards his famous elder; Moore later credited Stephens with more input than the latter, out of politeness or no, was willing to acknowledge.

2. *A Story-Teller's Holiday* (London: Cumann Sean-eolais na hEireann, 1918), 145.

3. See Hone, 335; also, Gareth W. Dunleavy, "George Moore's Medievalism: A Modern Triptych," in *George Moore in Perspective,* ed. Janet Egleson Dunleavy (Naas, Kildare: Malton Press; Gerrards Cross, Bucks.: Colin Smythe; Totowa: Barnes & Noble, 1983), 85–87.

4. See *Letters of George Moore,* ed. John Eglinton (Bournemouth: Sydenham & Co., 1942), 44, and Brendan Kennelly, "George Moore's Lonely Voices: A Study of his Short Stories," in *George Moore's Mind and Art,* ed. Graham Owens (Edinburgh: Oliver & Boyd, 1968), 161.

5. The Society for Irish Folklore *(Cumann Sean-eolais na hEireann)* that published *A Story-Teller's Holiday* in limited edition was, according to Hone, a fictitious outfit: Hone, 343.

6. Moore praised the story when writing to Eglinton: *Letters of George Moore,* 62. "Albert Nobbs" found a new and later home in Moore's *Celibate Lives* (1927). Moore's victory in the storytelling contest is reversed in *Ulick and Soracha,* the 1926 novel that was published alongside *A Story-Teller's Holiday* in a 1928 two-volume edition of the latter. In *Ulick and Soracha,* Moore has himself admit: "The Ballinrobe cock is outdone, and the crow is to the Westport rooster!"

7. As a glance at Whitley Stokes' translation, "The Birth and Life of S. Moling," with its pedophilia, adultery, and indecency, will show: *Revue Celtique* 27 (1906): 257–312.

8. Anthony Farrow, *George Moore* (Boston: Twayne Publishers, 1978), 147. Farrow also suggests that Marban's defense when he is overcome by desire for the youngest nun, that his intention was good, is a "Protestant" argument. Moling, too, offers this to himself in self-defense.

9. *The Letters of W. B. Yeats,* ed. Allan Wade (London: Hart-Davis, 1954) 464.

10. *The Letters of P. H. Pearse,* ed. Séamas Ó Buachalla (Atlantic Highlands, NJ: Humanities Press, 1980), 153. Colum dedicated his book of poems, *Wild Earth,* "To A.E., who fostered me".

11. *Story Telling New & Old* (New York: Macmillan, 1968), 14–15.

12. *Story Telling New & Old,* 21.

13. *Letters of James Stephens,* 256.

14. Zack Bowen, *Padraic Colum: A Biographical-Critical Introduction* (Carbondale: Southern Illinois University Press, 1970), 125. The young Colum heard stories both from his grandmother, Anne Connolly, and from one Charlie MacGauran: see Colum's reminiscence, "The Tradition that Existed in My Grandmother's House," *The New Yorker* 23 Dec. 1967: 28–31. But in an interview with Bowen, Colum referred to the stories he wove into the first part of *The King of Ireland's Son* as "translations" of Irish stories, but translations of what he doesn't say: *Journal of Irish Literature* 2.1 (1973): 25. And in a memoir, Colum claimed that the opening of *The King of Ireland's Son* "does not come out of any particular story that I have heard," *JIL* 2.1: 65.

15. Jacobs cites Alfred Nutt's belief that The Lad with the Goat-skin is the original of Parzival: *Celtic Fairy Tales* (London: The Bodley Head, 1970), 313.

16. See Ó Súilleabháin and Christiansen, *The Types of the Irish Folktale, Folklore Fellows Communications* 78.188 (1963): 261.

17. Seán Ó Súilleabháin, *A Handbook of Irish Folklore* (Hatboro, PA: Folklore Associates, 1963), 595.

18. A slightly different version of this tale appears in Colum's *The Fountain of Youth: Stories to be Told* (1927), a selection of his stories made by himself. In this chart, titles in double quotation marks are Colum's own; those in single marks are mine.

19. *The King of Ireland's Son* (London: George G. Harrap, 1920), 316. Subsequent quotations will be from this edition, with page numbers in parentheses.

20. Bowen, *Padraic Colum,* 138. For a discussion of political and other aspects of *The King of Ireland's Son,* and of the connections between this and other prose works by Colum, see Kay Diviney MacLaine, "Elements of the Folk Hero-Tale in the Fiction of Padraic Colum," diss., U of British Columbia, 1984.

21. K. D. MacLaine refers us to a passage in Richard J. Loftus, *Nationalism in Modern Anglo-Irish Poetry* (Madison: University of Wisconsin Press, 1964), 319–20: "Colum told me in January 1961," notes Loftus, "that the underlying motif of his work has always been the heroism of the peasantry. At a seminar at the National University of Ireland, Dublin (U.C.D.), in February, 1961, Colum while talking of heroism used the phrase, 'Plutarch lied,' by which he meant to suggest that Plutarch was wrong in identifying heroism with great and noble men."

22. MacLaine shows the persistence of this notion in Colum's later fictions, *Castle Conquer* (1923) and *The Flying Swans* (1957), and reveals the sequence of functionally comparable heroes, Gilly, Gillick, Ulick. She refers to "Colum's double vision of Irish heroism in *The King of Ireland's Son*" and adds that "the romantic heroism of the King's Son and the peasant heroism of Gilly, each by itself an insufficient model for the heroism of New Ireland, together form a unifying vision of Irish character as well as of what may be considered heroic in Ireland": MacLaine, 152, 153.

23. Colum's political awareness is revealed in *My Irish Year* (1912) wherein he discusses the possibility of Irish independence.

24. Perhaps political allegorizing is suggested by the recurrence of subjection as a primary feature of fairy tales.

25. Colum discusses "Secret songs" or "Treason songs" in *My Irish Year* (New York: J. Pott, 1912), 72–74, and likens them to symbolist poems.

26. *West Irish Folk-Tales and Romances* (Totowa: Rowman, 1973), 257.

27. *Story Telling New & Old,* 1–2.

28. *Story Telling New & Old,* 5–6.

29. One assumption of the revival was that English literature had become exhausted, giving Anglo-Irish literature a chance for development; it was a literary version of the older political maxim that England's difficulty is Ireland's opportunity.

30. Peter Costello in *The Heart Grown Brutal: The Irish Revolution in Literature from Parnell to the Death of Yeats* (Dublin: Gill and Macmillan, 1977) gives the date of Mrs. Figgis' suicide as 1924 (266). Costello rather oddly insists that Figgis was a failure (98, 264), despite the fact that he wrote *The Return of the Hero,* not to speak of four other novels and a quantity of verse and criticism, took a leading part in the Howth gunrunning, and drew up the Constitution of the Irish Free State.

31. *The Return of the Hero* (New York: Charles Boni, 1930), 47. One is reminded of the epitaph Black Elk (another last representative of a dying order) provided for Crazy Horse (the Sioux Finn): "It does not matter where his body lies, for it is grass; but where his spirit is, it will be good to be," *Black Elk Speaks* by John G. Neihardt (London: Sphere Books, 1974), 107.

32. *King Goshawk and the Birds* (London: Macmillan, 1926), 23. The later volumes in the Cuandine trilogy were *The Spacious Adventures of the Man in the Street* (1928) and *Asses in Clover* (1933).

33. For a brief account of O'Duffy's life and an introduction to his works, see Robert Hogan's *Eimar O'Duffy* (Lewisburg: Bucknell University Press, 1972).

34. Indeed, Yeats equates "the mass of the people" with those "who come from Catholic Ireland." He mentions Colum and Edward Martyn on the Catholic side; realizing that Martyn's father came from a very old family, he maintains that Martyn has inherited his temper of mind from his mother, whose family was of no account: *The Letters of W. B. Yeats,* ed. Wade, 464.

35. Introduction to *A Dreamer's Tales and Other Stories* (New York: Boni & Liveright, n.d.), xvii. Colum's Introduction is dated August 1917.

36. Cited by Hazel Littlefield, *Lord Dunsany: King of Dreams* (New York: Exposition Press, 1959), 49.

37. Quoted from an unpublished essay by Gogarty in Mark Amory, *Biography of Lord Dunsany* (London: Collins, 1972), 75. In *Hail and Farewell,* ed. Richard Cave (Gerrards Cross: Colin Smythe, 1976), 540, Moore, with his characteristic two-edged irony, tells AE's anecdote: "one day whilst Yeats was crooning over his fire Yeats had said that if he had his rights he would be Duke of Ormonde. AE's answer was: I am afraid, Willie, you are overlooking your father—a detestable remark to make to a poet in search of an ancestry; and the addition: We both belong to the lower-middle classes, was in equally bad taste. AE knew that there were spoons in the Yeats family bearing the Butler crest, just as there are portraits in my family of Sir Thomas More, and he should have remembered that certain passages in *The Countess Cathleen* are clearly derivative from the spoons."

38. *Letters of James Stephens,* 15.

39. *Letters of James Stephens,* 26.

40. Letter from Yeats to Dunsany, quoted by Amory, 78. However, Yeats reserved the category of associate membership of his Irish Academy of Letters for those Irish writers, whether or not they resided in Ireland, who did not set their work in their native island, such as Stephen MacKenna and Lord Dunsany; Dunsany was offended by what he considered a slight: see Amory, 231. Yeats's prejudice has lingered in the Irish literary scene.

41. In his book *My Ireland,* Dunsany contrasted himself with Francis Ledwidge (the poor poet who was his neighbor and whom Dunsany befriended and helped) on the ground that Ledwidge shared with his other neighbors "a golden hoard of folk-lore" that he, Dunsany, merely glimpsed: *My Ireland* (London: Jarrolds, 1937), 59–60.

42. Reported by Stephens to a correspondent, *Letters of James Stephens,* 161.

43. "Idle Days on the Yann," in a miscellaneous collection of Lord Dunsany's stories, *At the Edge of the World,* ed. Lin Carter (New York: Ballantine Books, 1970), 117.

44. Quoted by Amory, 78, and by Colum, Introduction to *A Dreamer's Tales,* xv–xvi.

45. Quoted by Amory, 72.

46. Tolkien is quoted by C. N. Manlove, *Modern Fantasy: Five Studies* (Cambridge: Cambridge University Press, 1975), 6. Hyde's observation appears in *Beside the Fire,* 189.

47. See Graham Hough, *The Last Romantics* (Oxford: University Press, 1961), 83–102.

48. The differences between Yeats and Morris may not be so great as first appears: according to Walter E. Houghton, the medieval focus in the art of Morris and Burne-Jones on knights and saints "had its roots in the Anglican-aristocratic tradition": *The Victorian Frame of Mind* (New Haven and London: Yale University Press, 1957), 326.

49. The phrases are from a contemporary commentator on Morris, quoted by Houghton, 336.

50. See Peter Faulkner, *William Morris and W. B. Yeats* (Dublin: Dolmen Press, 1962).

51. Manlove, 11. However, although Dunsany seems not to have been a religious man, he might with profit be linked to the Protestant fantasists, George MacDonald, C. S. Lewis, Charles Kingsley, and Charles Williams, the first three of whom Manlove discusses. Manlove does not, however, openly consider fantasy as transposed theology or as a mode particularly attractive to Protestants. The parallel between the fantasies of Manlove's subjects and the Celtic writings of the Protestant revivalists may be worth pursuing.

52. Quoted by Faulkner, 14. Moore's reaction to Morris is not unexpected: "In Wales, whilst staying with Howard de Walden, I read some Morris, *The Well at the World's End* and *The Wood Beyond the Well* [*sic*], and at the end of the week felt like one who had been poisoned. I would sooner go to the galleys at once than write like Morris, but I wish I knew the language as well as Topsy. Topsy seems to have been able to write that language spontaneously. All the same, nobody ever did, and nobody ever will, read the stories he wrote in it, except perhaps W. B. Yeats": *Letters of George Moore,* ed. Eglinton, 55.

53. Borges refers to Dunsany at the close of "Kafka and His Precursors," in *Other Inquisitions, 1937–1952,* trans. Ruth L. C. Sims (New York: Simon & Schuster, 1968) 108.

54. Introduction to *A Dreamer's Tales,* xvii.

Chapter 14—Hidden Ireland

1. "Poetry and Tradition," in *Essays and Introductions* (New York: Collier, 1968), 251.

2. Cf. Mary Colum: "many of the country people had every traditional aristocratic attribute—fearlessness, courtesy, a high sense of honor, ease of manner, pride and charm, delicate and beautifully formed bodies, fine silken hair, and long slim hands," *Life and the Dream* (London: Macmillan, 1947), 76–77.

3. In "By the Roadside," an essay in *The Celtic Twilight,* in *The Collected Works of William Butler Yeats* (Stratford-on-Avon: The Shakespeare Head, 1908) 5: *The Celtic Twilight and Stories of Red Hanrahan,* 191.

4. By Seamus O'Neill in "Gaelic Literature," an entry in the *Dictionary of Irish Literature,* ed. Robert Hogan (Westport, CT: Greenwood Press, 1979), 62.

5. Ó Conaire (1883–1928) has also been translated; see, for example, *The Woman at the Window and Other Stories,* trans. Eamonn O'Neill (Dublin: Talbot Press, 1921). The title story is an impressive one; in translation at least, Ó Conaire seems to be an immeasurably finer fiction writer than Pearse.

6. Quoted by Raymond J. Porter in his *P. H. Pearse* (New York: Twayne, 1973), 79. I have drawn in these pages on Porter's book for statements by Pearse and facts about him.

7. Quoted by Porter, 47.

8. Eavan Boland, "Aspects of Pearse," *The Dublin Magazine* 5.1 (1966): 51. Boland is assessing the stories only in translation.

9. Quoted by Porter, 47.

10. However, it has been claimed by Seamus O'Neill that Ó Conaire was the first Gaelic writer, and even Irish writer, to seek Russian influences in his fiction: the *Dictionary of Irish Literature,* 62.

11. Boland quotes from Pearse's "The Murder Machine": "One scarcely knows whether modern sentimentalism or modern utilitarianism is the more sure sign of modern decadence," "Aspects of Pearse," 47.

12. Porter, 47, 49.

13. The phrase is Boland's, uttered however in the heat of Easter Rising commemorations in 1966.

14. Translated by Joseph Campbell and given in the Appendix to *Plays, Stories, Poems* (Dublin: Talbot Press, 1958).

15. Childhood itself Pearse ideally saw in terms of "struggle, self-sacrifice, self-discipline," though he also wished to encourage in schools "the fostering of individualities." Education should address itself to "the child's worthiest self" yet make provision "for maintaining the suzerainty of the common weal." Pearse set out his (educationally radical) views on the self in human development in 1909 in his school review, *An Macaomh,* reproduced in part by Padraic Colum in his Introduction to *Poems of the Irish Revolutionary Brotherhood,* eds. Colum and Edward J. O'Brien (Boston: Small, Maynard, 1916), xvi–xxi.

16. *Plays, Stories, Poems,* 132.

17. The Introduction was written not by Joseph Campbell but by P. Browne (presumably Father Paddy Browne, the nationalist priest who edited a slim anthology of poems about the Rising in 1917, *Aftermath of Easter Week*).

18. Pearse's wish to redeem the shameful history of Ireland is precisely opposite to Stephen Dedalus' refusal in *A Portrait* to redeem that same history.

19. Father Shaw does so in the course of an essay whose title suggests its theme and scope: "The Canon of Irish History—A Challenge." This essay was written in 1966, the year in which the fiftieth anniversary of the Easter Rising occurred, but it was judged too inflammatory to publish until 1972, after Father Shaw's death, in *Studies* 61 (1972): 113–53. This courageous reclamation of Catholicism from physical-force republicanism, this repudiation of the received tradition of phobic nationalism in Ireland, of which Pearse was a chief perpetuator, is one of the most important documents of the Irish twentieth century.

20. *Life and the Dream,* 280.

21. Quoted from Pearse's "The Murder Machine" by Joan Towey Mitchell, "Yeats, Pearse, and Cuchulain," *Eire-Ireland* 11.4 (1976):61.

22. From the poem "To My Mother," written in custody after the Rising.

23. See Father Shaw, also G. F. Dalton, "The Tradition of Blood Sacrifice to the Goddess Éire," *Studies* 63 (1974): 343–54.

24. For example, whereas Pearse saw the nationalist struggle in terms of Christianity (specifically Catholicism), Joyce borrowed Christianity (transubstantiation, martyrdom etc.)

in order to express the artistic struggle. Joyce might seem the more disrespectful for draining Christianity of its substance and using only its forms, but he did not *identify* art and Christianity as Pearse identified physical-force nationalism with Christianity.

25. Without apparent allusion to Sheehan, Ruth Dudley Edwards subtitled her recent book on Pearse, *The Triumph of Failure* (1977).

26. It can be found in *The Literary Writings of Patrick Pearse,* ed. Séamas Ó Buachalla (Dublin and Cork: Mercier Press, 1979).

27. See Pearse's Court Martial Statement, reproduced in *The Letters of P. H. Pearse,* ed. Séamas Ó Buachalla (Atlantic Highlands, NJ: Humanities Press, 1980), 379. Cf. Christ's request to the Pharisees: "If I am the man you want, let these others go," St. John, 18: 8.

28. The article is reproduced in translation in *The Critical Writings of James Joyce,* eds. Ellsworth Mason and Richard Ellmann (New York: Viking, 1964), 234–37.

29. Introduction to *The Oxford Book of Modern Verse* (Oxford: Clarendon Press, 1936), xiv.

30. O'Faolain is cited by Terence Brown, "After the Revival: The Problem of Adequacy and Genre," *The Genres of the Irish Revival.* ed. Ronald Schleifer (Norman, OK: Pilgrim Books, 1979), 160.

31. *A Portrait of the Artist as a Young Man* (Harmondsworth: Penguin Books, 1960), 180. Further quotations will be from this edition, with page references in parentheses.

32. Mary Colum wrote that she never heard the word "peasant" in her childhood: *Life and the Dream,* 65. In *Wet Clay,* Seumas O'Kelly has a character reply to the returned American calling himself "a peasant": "We never call ourselves peasants. It was always The People." Stephen may be mocking the romantic, outsider's, revival attitude to country people.

33. Stephen's dream-struggle with the old peasant is reminiscent of Jacob's struggle with the angel, as a result of which Jacob discovers his real name, Israel. Jacob is, as Dedalus wishes to be, the father of his race, but Dedalus wishes to be the spiritual-artistic father rather than nationalist patriarch. In each case a mythic figure must be fought (on this level the actual fathers, Isaac and Simon, are irrelevant).

34. Hugh Kenner remarks that Joyce in *Ulysses* recalled his 1902 meeting with Synge in terms of St. Patrick's meeting in the forest with Ossian whom it is his destiny to supersede: Kenner is quoted by Herbert Howarth in *The Irish Writers, 1880–1940* (London: Rockliff, 1958), 240.

35. *A Munster Twilight* (Cork: Mercier Press, 1963) is a later edition.

36. *Children of Earth* (Dublin and London: Maunsel, 1918).

37. Oliver Blyth [Brinsley MacNamara], *The Irishman* (London: Eveleigh Nash, 1920), 277–78.

38. *Wet Clay* (Dublin: Phoenix, n.d.), 22. This novel was published in 1922 by Talbot in Dublin and Unwin in London.

39. *Letters of James Stephens,* ed. Richard J. Finneran (London: Macmillan, 1974), 247–48. Joyce poured scorn on O'Kelly's earlier stories in *By the Stream of Killmeen* (1906) for their portrait of romantically pure Connacht girls and romantically handsome Connacht men, but he had great admiration for *The Weaver's Grave:* see Herbert Gorman, *James Joyce* (New York: Rinehart, 1948), 181. There are indeed two aspects of O'Kelly: his nationalism that compromises his literature and his dark and comic realism that undermines his nationalism to the benefit of his literature.

40. *The Weaver's Grave* (Dublin: Allen Figgis, 1965), 8. Further quotations will be from this edition with page references in parentheses. This novella first appeared in *The Golden Barque and The Weaver's Grave* (1919).

41. In a non-Irish context, Colum evokes the names of Russian storytellers, including Gogol, when introducing *The Weaver's Grave*.

Chapter 15—The Island Man

1. Preface to the First Edition of *The Well of the Saints*, in *Essays and Introductions* (New York: Collier, 1968), 299 (my italics).
2. *The Islandman*, trans. Robin Flower (Oxford: The Clarendon Press, 1951), 245. Further quotations will be from this edition, with page references in parentheses.
3. The phrase is Riobárd P. Breatnach's, from his Foreword to his translation of Conchúr Ó Síocháin's 1940 memoir, *Seanchas Chléire: The Man from Cape Clear* (Dublin: Mercier Press, 1975), ix. Ó Síocháin's book also belongs to the genre of Gaelic peasant autobiography.
4. Breatnach, x.
5. See Eibhlís Ní Shúilleabháin, *Letters from The Great Blasket* (Dublin and Cork: Mercier Press, n.d.), 24–25. Ní Shúilleabháin was Ó Crohan's daughter-in-law, having married Sean Ó Crohan, and it is his sentiment I am noting.
6. "The Other Tradition: Some Highlights of Modern Fiction in Irish," in *The Irish Novel in Our Time*, ed. Patrick Rafroidi and Maurice Harmon (Lille: Publications de L'Université de Lille III, 1975–76), 38.
7. Breatnach, viii.
8. There has been disagreement among scholars about Flower's translation. According to Seán Ó Lúing, Myles na gCopaleen (Flann O'Brien) thought it "miserably botched": "Robin Flower (1881–1946)," *Studies* 70 (1981): 131. Máire Cruise O'Brien believes Flower translated Ó Crohan "perhaps somewhat unevenly": "*An tOileánach:* Tomás Ó Criomhthain (1856–1937)," in *The Pleasures of Gaelic Literature*, ed. John Jordan (Dublin and Cork: RTE/Mercier, 1977), 25. Ó Lúing, however, thinks it "a worthy and by no means unsuccessful effort to match the dignity of the original." Daniel A. Binchy considered Flower's translation "masterly": "Two Blasket Autobiographies," a review of *The Islandman* and *Twenty Years A-Growing*, *Studies* 23 (1934): 549.
9. *Hail and Farewell*, ed. Richard Cave (Gerrards Cross: Colin Smythe, 1976), 75.
10. O'Tuama, 39.
11. *Collected Works* 2: *Prose*, ed. Alan Price (London: Oxford University Press, 1966), 102n.
12. Daniel A. Binchy, who met him, saw a "somewhat ironic detachment" in Ó Crohan the man, "Two Blasket Autobiographies," 547.
13. O'Tuama, 39.
14. "Homeric Qualities in the Life and Literature of the Great Blasket Island," *Greece & Rome*, Second Series 16 (1969): 151–68.
15. Quoted by J. Donald Crowley in his Introduction to his edition of *Robinson Crusoe* (London: Oxford University Press, 1972), vii.
16. T. H. Mason furnishes another example of misunderstood innovation in his chapter on the Blaskets in his delightful book, *The Islands of Ireland* (London: Batsford, 1936): when Lindbergh's plane passed over the island, the boys below thought it was an eagle: Mason, 102. Regarding my first example from Ó Crohan, cf. tale-type 1339C, "Woman Unacquainted With Tea," Ó Súilleabháin and Christiansen, *The Types of the Irish Folktale*.

17. Richard Dorson, Foreword to Sean O'Sullvan's *Folktales of Ireland* (Chicago: University of Chicago Press, 1966), xix.

18. Binchy agrees, calling Ó Crohan's style "entirely self-formed . . . in the most literal sense of the phrase, *le style est l'homme*" (552). O'Tuama, however, sees in Ó Crohan's language "little of his own personal stamp: it is the colloquial community language": O'Tuama, 39.

19. There is a vivid portrayal of the Gaelic storyteller in action by Tadhg Ó Murchú and quoted by J. H. Delargy in his 1945 lecture to the British Academy, "The Gaelic Story-Teller," *Proceedings of the British Academy* (London: Oxford University Press, 1945), 190.

20. *Collected Works* 2: *Prose,* 133.

21. See Flower's *The Western Island or The Great Blasket* (Oxford: The Clarendon Press, 1944). For an older account of the Blaskets, fueled by Catholic and nationalist indignation over Protestant proselytism on the islands in the nineteenth century, see Patrick Foley, *The Ancient and Present State of the Skelligs, Blasket Islands, Donquin and the West of Dingle* (Dublin: An Cló-cumann Teoranta, 1903).

22. *Collected Works* 2: *Prose,* 150.

23. Binchy thought that Ó Crohan's "private views on the relative merits of Irish and English" would not "commend themselves to Gaelic League orators. As for the swarms of Gaelic enthusiasts—some of them equipped with far more enthusiasm than Gaelic—who invade his territory annually, good manners and self-interest alike dictate a friendly reception to them, but he is secretly puzzled by their zeal": "Two Blasket Autobiographies," 559.

24. Ó Lúing dates Marstrander's first visit to 1908: Ó Lúing, 124.

25. See *Letters From The Great Blasket,* 53–54.

26. *Collected Works* 2: *Prose,* 66.

27. *The Western Island,* 6. Binchy writes: "Tralee, Cork and Dublin are almost as 'foreign' to the Blasket Islander as London or Glasgow. Indeed, by a curious irony of circumstance, they are much more remote from him than Springfield, Mass., where so many of his kith and kin are congregated": "Two Blasket Autobiographies," 558–59.

28. The suggestion is Binchy's. Binchy quotes the translators of *Twenty Years A-Growing,* Moya Llewelyn Davies and George Thomson, on the influence of Synge's Hiberno-English on their translation; see the Translators' Preface to the 1933 Viking Press edition, x. *Twenty Years A-Growing,* we might say, is a book of the revival, *The Islandman* a book of realism written under the unwitting auspices of the revival.

29. O'Tuama, 36.

30. Caution has to be exercised in the comparison, as it is difficult to estimate the contribution to *Black Elk Speaks* of John G. Neihardt, "through" whom Black Elk tells his story.

31. Delargy, 186.

32. Quoted by Bryan MacMahon, "Peig Sayers and the Vernacular of the Story-teller," in *Literature and Folk Culture: Ireland and Newfoundland,* ed. Alison Feder and Bernice Schrank (St. John's, Newfoundland: Memorial University, 1977), 108.

33. *Black Elk Speaks* (London: Sphere Books, 1974), 188.

34. *Black Elk Speaks,* 153.

35. Binchy remarks that Ó Crohan knows little of political wrangling in Ireland, and adds provocatively: "almost as little as he knows of that political nationalism which owes its introduction to the descendants of English colonists and its progress to the spread of the English tongue": see "Two Blasket Autobiographies," 559.

36. *Man of Aran* (London: Faber, 1934), 76.

37. Reproduced in Sean O'Sullivan, *The Folklore of Ireland* (New York: Hastings

House, 1974), 126–27. For an Irish belief in the soul as a butterfly, see also Yeats, *Fairy and Folk Tales of the Irish Peasantry,* in *Fairy and Folk Tales of Ireland* (New York: Macmillan, 1973), 117–18; for the belief in witchery, see Yeats's essay, "Witches and Wizards and Irish Folk-Lore," in Lady Gregory's *Visions and Beliefs in the West of Ireland* (Gerrards Cross: Colin Smythe, 1970), 303–4.

38. Robert Scholes, *Structuralism in Literature: An Introduction* (New Haven and London: Yale University Press, 1974), 176. Originally published by Jonathan Cape in 1927, O'Donnell's *Islanders* was republished by Mercier Press in 1963.

Select Bibliography

I have departed from the customary division of "primary" and "secondary" and chosen a chronological division: work published during (or before) the revival and work published after the revival. This is because translations, compilations, manifestoes, letters, even criticism written during the revival function in a "primary" fashion. So too does the occasional work published after 1930. Where the first cited work of an author appeared before 1930, I have included the works published after that year in the "Works Before 1930" section. I have listed a few works that I found helpful but did not have occasion to cite.

WORKS BEFORE 1930

AE [George William Russell). *The Candle of Vision*. 1917. New York: University Books, 1965.

———. *Imaginations and Reveries*. Dublin and London: Maunsel, 1915.

———. *The Interpreters*. London: Macmillan, 1922.

———. *Letters from AE*. Ed. Alan Denson. London: Abelard-Schumann, 1961.

———. "Priest or Hero?" *The Irish Theosophist* 5 (1896–97): 127–31, 148–52.

AE and Aretas [James Pryse]. "The Enchantment of Cuchullain." *The Irish Theosophist* 4 (1895–96): 32–35, 50–54, 72–75, 83–89, 101–8.

Barlow, Jane. *Irish Idylls*. London: Houghton & Stoughton, 1892.

Boswell, C. S. *An Irish Precursor of Dante: A Study on the Vision of Heaven and Hell ascribed to the Eighth-century Irish Saint Adamnan, with Translation of the Irish Text*. London: David Nutt, 1908.

Boyd, Ernest. *Ireland's Literary Renaissance*. 1916, 1922. New York: Barnes & Noble, 1968.

Brown, Stephen J. *Ireland in Fiction: A Guide to Irish Novels, Tales, Romances, and Folklore*. 1919. New York: Barnes & Noble, 1969.

Bullock, Shan F. *By Thrasna River: The Story of a Townland*. London: Ward, Lock & Bowdon, 1895.

———. *Dan the Dollar*. Dublin: Maunsel, 1906.
———. *The Loughsiders*. London: Harrap, 1924.
———. *Robert Thorne: The Story of a London Clerk*. London: Laurie, 1907.
———. *The Squireen*. London: Methuen, 1903.
Carlyle, Thomas. *On Heroes, Hero-Worship and the Heroic in History*. 1841. London and New York: Macmillan, 1897.
Colum, Padraic. *Castle Conquer*. New York: Macmillan, 1923.
———. *The Fountain of Youth: Stories to be Told*. New York: Macmillan, 1927.
———. *The King of Ireland's Son*. 1916. London: Harrap, 1920.
———. *My Irish Year*. New York: J. Pott; London: Mills & Boon, 1912.
———. "A Padraic Colum Number." Eds. Zack Bowen and Gordon Henderson. *Journal of Irish Literature* 2.1 (1973).
———. Introduction. *Poems of the Irish Revolutionary Brotherhood*. Eds. Padraic Colum and Edward J. O'Brien. Boston: Small, Maynard, 1916. ix–xxxvi.
———. *Story Telling New & Old*. 1927. New York: Macmillan, 1968.
———. "Thomas MacDonagh and his Poetry." *The Dublin Magazine* 5.1 (1966): 39–45.
———. "The Tradition that Existed in My Grandmother's House." *The New Yorker* 23 Dec. 1967: 28–31.
———, ed. *A Treasury of Irish Folklore: The Stories, Traditions, Legends, Humor, Wisdom, Ballads and Songs of the Irish People*. 1954. New York: Crown, 1962.
Corkery, Daniel. *The Hidden Ireland: A Study of Gaelic Munster in the Eighteenth Century*. 1924. Dublin: Gill & Macmillan, 1977.
———. *A Munster Twilight*. 1916. Cork: Mercier, 1963.
———. *Synge and Anglo-Irish Literature*. 1931. New York: Russell, 1965.
———. *The Threshold of Quiet*. 1917. Dublin and Cork: Talbot, 1944.
Cousins, James H. *The Wisdom of the West: An Introduction to the Interpretative Study of Irish Mythology*. London: Theosophical Publishing Society, 1912.
Cousins, James H. and Margaret E. Cousins. *We Two Together*. Madras: Ganesh, 1950.
Curtin, Jeremiah. *Hero-Tales of Ireland*. 1894. New York: Benjamin Blom, 1971.
———. *Myths and Folk-lore of Ireland*. 1890. Detroit, MI: Singing Tree Press, 1968.
Duffy, Charles Gavan, George Sigerson, and Douglas Hyde. *The Revival of Irish Literature*. 1894. New York: Lemma, 1973.
Dunn, Joseph, trans. *The Ancient Irish Epic Tale Táin Bó Cúailnge*. London: David Nutt, 1914.
Dunsany, Lord. *At the Edge of the World*. New York: Ballantine Books, 1970.
———. *The Book of Wonder*. London: Heinemann; Boston: John W. Luce, 1912.
———. *A Dreamer's Tales and Other Stories*. 1910. New York: Boni & Liveright, n.d.
———. *Fifty-One Tales*. 1915. London: Elkin Mathews, 1919.
———. *The King of Elfland's Daughter*. 1924. New York: Ballantine Books, 1969.
———. *My Ireland*. London: Jarrold's, 1937.
———. *The Sword of Welleran and Other Stories*. London: George Allen, 1908.

———. *Tales of Three Hemispheres*. Boston: John W. Luce, 1919.
———. *Time and the Gods*. London: Heinemann, 1906.
Eglinton, John [W. K. Magee]. *Irish Literary Portraits*. 1935. Freeport, NY: Books for Libraries, 1967.
Eglinton, John, W. B. Yeats, AE, and William Larminie. *Literary Ideals in Ireland*. 1899. New York: Lemma, 1973.
Faraday, L. Winifred. *The Cattle-Raid of Cualnge (Táin Bó Cuailnge): An Old Irish Prose-Epic*. 1904. New York: AMS Press, 1972.
Figgis, Darrell. *Children of Earth*. Dublin: Maunsel, 1918.
———. *The Return of the Hero*. 1923. New York: Charles Boni, 1930.
Flood, J. M. *Ireland, Its Myths and Legends*. Dublin: Talbot, 1916.
Foley, Patrick. *The Ancient and Present State of the Skelligs, Blasket Islands, Donquin and the West of Dingle*. Dublin: An Cló-cumann Teoranta, 1903.
Furlong, Alice. *Tales of Fairy Folks, Queens and Heroes*. Dublin: Browne & Nolan, [1907].
Graham, William, comp. *Deirdre and the Sons of Uisneach: A Scoto-Irish Romance of the first Century A.D.* Edinburgh: J. Gardner Hitt, 1908.
Greer, Tom. *A Modern Daedalus*. 1887. New York: Arno Press, 1975.
Gregory, Lady Augusta. *Cuchulain of Muirthemne: The Story of the Men of the Red Branch of Ulster*. 1902. London: John Murray, 1903.
———. *Gods and Fighting Men: The Story of the Tuatha de Danaan and the Fianna of Ireland*. 1904. London: John Murray, 1919.
———. *The Kiltartan History Book*. 1909. London: Unwin, 1926.
———. *The Kiltartan Wonder Book*. Dublin: Maunsel, [1910].
———. *Poets and Dreamers: Studies and Translations from the Irish by Lady Gregory Including Nine Plays by Douglas Hyde*. 1903. Gerrards Cross: Colin Smythe, 1974.
———. *Visions and Beliefs in the West of Ireland: With Two Essays and Notes by W. B. Yeats*. 1920. Gerrards Cross: Colin Smythe, 1970.
———, ed. *Ideals in Ireland*. 1901. New York: Lemma, 1973.
Hull, Eleanor. *The Boys' Cuchulain: Heroic Legends of Ireland*. New York: Thomas Y. Crowell, 1910.
———. *Cuchulain: The Hound of Ulster*. London: Harrap, 1909.
———, ed. *The Cuchullin Saga in Irish Literature*. Translated from the Irish by Various Scholars. 1898. New York: AMS Press, 1972.
Hyde, Douglas. *Legends of Saints and Sinners: Collected and Translated from the Irish*. 1915. New York: Frederick A. Stokes, n.d.
———. *A Literary History of Ireland from Earliest Times to the Present Day*. London: Unwin, 1899.
———, ed. *Beside the Fire: A Collection of Irish Gaelic Folk Stories*, 1890. London: David Nutt, 1910.
Jacobs, Joseph. *Celtic Fairy Tales*. A one-volume reprinting of *Celtic Fairy Tales* (1891) and *More Celtic Fairy Tales* (1894). London: The Bodley Head, 1970.

Joyce, James. *The Critical Writings*. Eds. Ellsworth Mason and Richard Ellmann. New York: Viking, 1964.
———. *Daniel Defoe*. Ed. from Italian manuscripts and translated by Joseph Prescott. Buffalo: State University of New York, 1964.
———. *Dubliners*. 1914. Ed. Robert Scholes. New York: Viking, 1968.
———. *Finnegans Wake*. 1939. New York: Viking, 1959.
———. *A Portrait of the Artist as a Young Man*. 1916. Harmondsworth: Penguin Books, 1960.
———. *Stephen Hero*. 1944. St. Albans, Herts.: Triad/Panther, 1977.
———. *Ulysses*. 1922. London: The Bodley Head, 1960.
———. "The Universal Literary Influence of the Renaissance." *James Joyce in Padua*. Ed. Louis Berrone. New York: Random House, 1977.
Joyce, P. W., trans. *Old Celtic Romances*. 1879. Dublin: Talbot Press, 1961.
Kennedy, Patrick, ed. *Legendary Fictions of the Irish Celts*. 1866. Detroit: Singing Tree Press, 1968.
Larminie, William, trans. *West Irish Folk-tales and Romances*. 1893. Totowa: Rowman, 1973.
Lawless, Emily. *Grania: The Story of an Island*. 2 vols. London: Smith, Elder, 1892.
Leahy, A. H. *Heroic Romances of Ireland*. 2 vols. London: David Nutt, 1905.
Leamy, Edmund. *Irish Fairy Tales*. 1890. Dublin: M. H. Gill, 1906.
Le Braz, Anatole. *The Land of Pardons*. 1894. Trans. Frances M. Gostling. London: Methuen, 1906.
Loti, Pierre. *An Iceland Fisherman*. 1886. New York: Collier, 1902.
Lysaght, Edward E. [Edward MacLysaght]. *Changing Times: Ireland Since 1898*. Gerrards Cross: Colin Smythe, 1978.
———. *The Gael*. Dublin and London: Maunsel, 1919.
MacDonagh, Michael. "Life in Achill and Aran." *The Westminster Review* 134.2 (1890): 165–71.
MacManus, Seumas. *Donegal Fairy Stories*. 1900. New York: Dover, 1968.
———. *Through the Turf Smoke: The Love, Lore, and Laughter of Old Ireland*. New York: Doubleday & McClure, 1899; London: Unwin, 1901.
MacNamara, Brinsley. *The Clanking of Chains*. Dublin and London: Maunsel, 1920.
———. [Oliver Blyth]. *The Irishman*. London: Eveleigh Nash, 1920.
———. *The Mirror in the Dusk*. Dublin and London: Maunsel & Roberts, 1921.
———. *The Valley of the Squinting Windows*. 1918. New York: Brentano's, 1919.
Meyer, Kuno, ed. and trans. *The Voyage of Bran Son of Febal*. 2 vols. London: David Nutt, 1895.
———. "The Wooing of Emer." *The Archaeological Review* 1 (1888): 68–75, 150–55, 231–35, 298–307.
Moore, George. *A Drama in Muslin: A Realistic Novel*. 1886. London: Walter Scott, 1918.
———. *Hail and Farewell: Ave, Salve, Vale*. 1911, 1912, 1914. Ed. Richard Cave. Gerrards Cross: Colin Smythe, 1976.

———. *The Lake*. 1905. Gerrards Cross: Colin Smythe, 1980.
———. *Letters of George Moore*. Ed. John Eglinton. Bournemouth: Sydenham, 1942.
———. *Muslin*. London: Heinemann, 1915.
———. *A Story-Teller's Holiday*. London: Cumann Sean-eolais na hEireann, 1918.
———. *The Untilled Field*. 1903. Gerrards Cross: Colin Smythe, 1976.
Moran, D. P. *The Philosophy of Irish Ireland*. Dublin: James Duffy, 1905.
Morris, Lloyd R. *The Celtic Dawn: A Survey of the Renascence in Ireland 1889–1916*. 1917. New York: Cooper Square, 1970.
Neihardt, John G. *Black Elk Speaks: Being the Life Story of a Holy Man of the Oglala Sioux,* as told through John G. Neihardt. 1932. London: Abacus, 1974.
Nutt, Alfred. *The Celtic Doctrine of Re-birth*. Vol. 2 of *The Voyage of Bran Son of Febal to the Land of the Living: An Old Irish Saga*. Ed. and trans. Kuno Meyer. London: David Nutt, 1895, 1897.
———. "Cuchulainn, the Irish Achilles." *Popular Studies in Mythology, Romance and Folk-Lore* 8. London: David Nutt, 1900.
O'Brien, William. *When We Were Boys: A Novel*. London: Longmans, Green, 1890.
Ó Conaire, Padraic. *The Woman at the Window and Other Stories*. Trans. Eamonn O Neill. Dublin: Talbot Press, 1921.
Ó Crohan, Tomás. *The Islandman*. 1929 (in Irish), 1934 (in English). Trans. Robin Flower. Oxford: Clarendon Press, 1974.
O'Donnell, Peadar. *Islanders*. 1927. Cork: Mercier, 1963.
O'Donovan, Gerald [Jeremiah O'Donovan]. *Conquest*. London: Constable, 1920.
———. *Father Ralph*. London: Macmillan, 1913.
———. *The Holy Tree*. London: Heinemann, 1922.
———. *How They Did It*. London: Methuen, 1920.
———. *Vocations*. London: Martin Secker, 1921.
———. *Waiting*. London: Macmillan, 1914.
O'Duffy, Eimar. *King Goshawk and the Birds*. London: Macmillan, 1926.
———. *The Spacious Adventures of the Man in the Street*. London: Macmillan, 1928.
———. *Asses in Clover*. London: Putnam's, 1933.
O'Grady, Standish Hayes, ed. and trans. *Silva Gadelica: A Collection of Tales in Irish With Extracts Illustrating Persons and Places*. 1892. 2 vols. New York: Lemma, 1970. Vol. 2: Translation and Notes.
O'Grady, Standish James. *The Bog of Stars and Other Stories and Sketches of Elizabethan Ireland*. London: Unwin, 1893.
———. *The Coming of Cuculain: A Romance of the Heroic Age in Ireland*. London: Methuen, 1894.
———. *Cuculain: An Epic*. London: Sampson Low, Searle, Marston & Rivington, 1882.
———. *Early Bardic Literature, Ireland*. 1879. New York: Lemma, 1970.
———. *History of Ireland: The Heroic Period*. London: Sampson Low, Searle, Marston & Rivington, 1878.

———. *History of Ireland: Cuculain and His Contemporaries*. London: Sampson Low, Searle, Marston & Rivington, 1880.
———. *Selected Essays & Passages*. Dublin: Phoenix, n.d. [1918?].
———. *The Triumph and Passing of Cuculain*. Dublin: Talbot Press, 1917.
———. *The Triumph of Cuculain or In the Gates of the North*. 1901. Dublin: Talbot Press, n.d.
O'Kelly, Seumas. *The Weaver's Grave*. 1919. Dublin: Allen Figgis, 1965.
———. *Wet Clay*. 1922. Dublin: Phoenix, n.d.
O'Neill, John. *Handerahan, the Irish Fairyman and Legends of Carrick*. London: W. Tweedie, 1854.
Ó Síocháin, Conchúr. *The Man From Cape Clear*. 1940. Trans. Riobárd P. Breatnach. Dublin and Cork: Mercier Press, 1975.
O'Sullivan, Maurice. *Twenty Years A-Growing*. Trans. Moya Llewelyn Davies and George Thomson. New York: Viking Press, 1933.
Pearse, Padraic H. [Patrick]. *Plays, Stories, Poems*. 1917. Trans. Joseph Campbell. Dublin: Talbot Press, 1958.
Pearse, Patrick. "Cuairt ar Arainn na Naomh" ["A Visit to Aran of the Saints"]. *Fainne an Lae* 19 Nov. 1898: 154–55.
———. *The Letters of P. H. Pearse*. Ed. Séamas Ó Buachalla. Atlantic Highlands, NJ: Humanities Press, 1980.
———. *The Literary Writings of Patrick Pearse*. Ed. Séamas Ó Buachalla. Dublin and Cork: Mercier Press, 1979.
Reid, Forrest. *At the Door of the Gate*. London: Edward Arnold, 1915.
———. *Following Darkness*. London: Edward Arnold, 1912.
———. *The Kingdom of Twilight*. London: Unwin, 1904.
———. *Peter Waring*. London: Faber, 1937.
Rolleston, T. W. *Myths and Legends of the Celtic Race*. London: Harrap, 1912.
Ryan, Frederick. *Criticism and Courage and Other Essays*. Tower Press Booklets 6. Dublin: Maunsel, 1906.
Ryan, William Patrick. *The Irish Literary Revival: Its History, Pioneers and Possibilities*. 1894. New York: Lemma, 1970.
Sayers, Peig. *An Old Woman's Reflections*. 1936. Trans. Seamus Ennis. London: Oxford University Press, 1962.
Sheehan, Canon. *Geoffrey Austin, Student*. 1895. Dublin: M. H. Gill, 1908.
———. *The Triumph of Failure*. 1899. London: Burns Oates & Washbourne, 1935.
Somerville and Ross [E. Œ. Somerville and "Martin Ross"]. *The Real Charlotte*. 3 vols. London: Ward & Downey, 1894.
———. *Some Experiences of an Irish R.M.* London: Longmans, Green, 1899.
Stephens, James. *The Charwoman's Daughter*. 1912. Dublin: Gill & Macmillan, 1972.
———. *The Crock of Gold*. 1912. New York: Collier, 1967.
———. *Deirdre*. London: Macmillan, 1923.
———. *The Demi-Gods*. London: Macmillan, 1914.
———. "An Essay in Cubes." *The English Review* 17 (1914): 83–94.

———. *Here are Ladies*. New York: Macmillan, 1913.
———. *The Insurrection in Dublin*. 1916. Gerrards Cross: Colin Smythe, 1978.
———. *Irish Fairy Tales*. New York: Macmillan, 1920.
———. *James, Seumas & Jacques: Unpublished Writings of James Stephens*. Ed. Lloyd Frankenberg. New York: Macmillan, 1964.
———. *A James Stephens Reader*. Sel. Lloyd Frankenberg. New York: Macmillan, 1962.
———. *Letters of James Stephens*. Ed. Richard J. Finneran. London: Macmillan, 1974.
———. *Uncollected Prose of James Stephens*. 2 vols. Ed. Patricia McFate. London: Macmillan, 1983.
Strachan, John and J. G. O'Keeffe, eds. *The Tain Bo Cuailnge from the Yellow Book of Lecan With Variant Readings from the Lebor Na Huidre*. Dublin: School of Irish Learning; Hodges, Figgis, 1912.
Synge, John Millington. *Collected Works* 2: *Prose*. Ed. Alan Price. London: Oxford University Press, 1966.
———. *In Wicklow, West Kerry, The Congested Districts, Under Ether*. 1910. Boston: John W. Luce, 1912.
———. *Some Letters to Lady Gregory and W. B. Yeats*. Sel. Ann Saddlemyer. Dublin: Cuala Press, 1971.
Weston, Jessie L. *From Ritual to Romance*. 1920. New York: Doubleday Anchor, 1957.
Wood-Martin, W. G. *Traces of the Elder Faiths of Ireland: A Handbook of Irish Pre-Christian Traditions*. 2 vols. London: Longmans, Green, 1902.
Yeats, William Butler. *Autobiographies*. London: Macmillan, 1955.
———. *The Collected Works in Verse & Prose*. 8 vols. Stratford-on-Avon: The Shakespeare Head, 1908. Vol. 5: *The Celtic Twilight and Stories of Red Hanrahan*. Vol. 7: *The Secret Rose, Rosa Alchemica, The Tables of the Law, The Adoration of the Magi, John Sherman and Dhoya*.
———. *Essays and Introductions*. 1961. New York: Collier, 1968.
———. *The Letters of W. B. Yeats*. Ed. Allan Wade. London: Hart-Davis, 1954.
———. *John Sherman & Dhoya*. 1891. Ed. Richard J. Finneran. Detroit: Wayne State University Press, 1969.
———. "Modern Ireland: An Address to American Audiences, 1932–1933." *Massachusetts Review* 5.2 (1964): 256–68.
———. *Mythologies*. 1959. New York: Collier, 1969.
———. *The Secret Rose, Stories by W. B. Yeats*. A Variorum Edition. Eds. Phillip L. Marcus, Warwick Gould, and Michael J. Sidnell. Ithaca and London: Cornell University Press, 1981.
———. *Selected Criticism*. Ed. A. Norman Jeffares. 1964. London: Pan Books, 1976.
———. *Selected Prose*. Ed. A. Norman Jeffares. 1964. London: Pan Books, 1976.
———. *The Speckled Bird*. Ed. William H. O'Donnell. Toronto: McClelland and Stewart, 1976.

———. *Uncollected Prose.* 2 vols. New York: Columbia University Press, 1970. Vol. 1: *First Reviews and Articles.* Ed. John P. Frayne.
———. *A Vision.* 1925, 1937. New York: Collier, 1966.
———, ed. *Fairy and Folk Tales of Ireland.* 1888 *(Fairy and Folk Tales of the Irish Peasantry),* 1892 *(Irish Fairy Tales).* New York: Macmillan, 1973.
Young, Ella. *Celtic Wonder Tales.* Dublin: Maunsel, 1910.
Zimmer, Heinrich. *The Irish Element in Mediaeval Culture.* New York and London: Putnam's, 1891.

WORKS AFTER 1930

Aalen, F. H. A. and Hugh Brody. *Gola: The Life and Last Days of An Island Community.* Cork: Mercier Press, 1969.
Amory, Mark. *Biography of Lord Dunsany.* London: Collins, 1972.
Bettelheim, Bruno. *The Uses of Enchantment: The Meaning and Importance of Fairy Tales.* 1976. New York: Vintage Books, 1977.
Binchy, Daniel A. "Two Blasket Autobiographies." Rev. of *The Islandman* by Tomás Ó Crohan and *Twenty Years A-Growing* by Maurice O'Sullivan. *Studies* 23 (1934): 544–60.
Boland, Eavan. "Aspects of Pearse." *The Dublin Magazine* 5.1 (1966): 46–55.
Bowen, Desmond. *The Protestant Crusade in Ireland, 1800–70: A Study of Protestant-Catholic Relations Between the Act of Union and Disestablishment.* Dublin: Gill & Macmillan; Montreal: McGill-Queen's University Press, 1978.
Bowen, Zack. *Padraic Colum: A Biographical-Critical Introduction.* Carbondale and Edwardsville: Southern Illinois University Press, 1970.
Brown, Malcolm. *George Moore: A Reconsideration.* Seattle: University of Washington Press, 1955.
———. *The Politics of Irish Literature: From Thomas Davis to W. B. Yeats.* Seattle: University of Washington Press, 1972.
Brown, Terence. "After the Revival: The Problem of Adequacy and Genre." *The Genres of the Irish Revival.* Ed. Ronald Schleifer. Norman, OK: Pilgrim Books, 1979. 153–77.
———. "The Church of Ireland: Some Literary Perspectives." *Search* 3.2 (1980): 5–19.
Bruford, Alan. *Gaelic Folk-Tales and Mediaeval Romances.* Dublin: The Folklore of Ireland Society, 1969.
Butterworth, Harrison. "Motif-Index and Analysis of the Early Irish Hero Tales." Ph.D. diss. Yale University, 1956.
Campbell, Joseph. *The Hero with a Thousand Faces.* 1949. Cleveland: World, 1956.
Cave, Richard Allen. *A Study of the Novels of George Moore.* Gerrards Cross: Colin Smythe, 1978.
Chadwick, Nora. *The Celts.* Harmondsworth: Penguin Books, 1970.
Coffey, Diarmid. *Douglas Hyde, President of Ireland.* Dublin and Cork: Talbot Press, 1938.

Colum, Mary. *Life and the Dream*. London: Macmillan, 1947.

Colum, Mary and Padraic Colum. *Our Friend James Joyce*. New York: Doubleday, 1958.

Corcoran, John X. W. P. "Celtic Mythology." *New Larousse Encyclopedia of Mythology*. New York and London: Prometheus, 1968. 222–44.

Costello, Peter. *The Heart Grown Brutal: The Irish Revolution in Literature, from Parnell to the Death of Yeats, 1891–1939*. Dublin: Gill & Macmillan; Totowa: Rowman, 1978.

Coxhead, Elizabeth. *Lady Gregory: A Literary Portrait*. London: Macmillan, 1961.

Coyle, Kathleen. *The Magical Realm*. New York: Dutton, 1943.

Cronin, John. "George Moore's *The Lake:* A Possible Source." *Eire-Ireland* 6.3 (1971): 12–15.

———. *Gerald Griffin (1803–1840): A Critical Biography*. Cambridge: Cambridge University Press, 1978.

Cross, Tom Peete and Clark Harris Slover, eds. *Ancient Irish Tales*. 1936. New York: Barnes & Noble, 1969.

Dalton, G. F. "The Tradition of Blood Sacrifice to the Goddess Éire." *Studies* 63 (1974): 343–54.

Daly, Dominic. *The Young Douglas Hyde*. Dublin: Irish University Press; Totowa: Rowman, 1974.

Delargy, J. H. "The Gaelic Story-teller: With Some Notes on Gaelic Folk-Tales." *Proceedings of the British Academy*. London: Oxford University Press, 1945.

Dorson, Richard M. *The British Folklorists: A History*. London: Routledge & Kegan Paul, 1968.

———. Foreword. *Folktales of Ireland*. Ed. Sean O'Sullivan. Chicago and London: University of Chicago Press, 1966. v–xxxii.

Dunleavy, Janet Egelson, ed. *George Moore in Perspective*. Naas, Co. Kildare: Malton; Totowa: Rowman, 1983.

Eliade, Mircea. *Myths, Dreams and Mysteries*. London: Harvill, 1960.

Ellmann, Richard. *James Joyce*. Oxford and New York: Oxford University Press, 1983.

Engelberg, Edward. *The Symbolist Poem: The Development of the English Tradition*. New York: Dutton, 1967.

Farrow, Anthony. *George Moore*. Boston: Twayne, 1978.

Faulkner, Peter. *William Morris and W. B. Yeats*. Dublin: Dolmen Press, 1962.

Feder, Alison and Bernice Schrank, eds. *Literature and Folk Culture: Ireland and Newfoundland*. Proc. of the Ninth Annual Seminar of the Canadian Association for Irish Studies. 11–15 Feb. 1976. St. John's, Newfoundland: Memorial University of Newfoundland, 1977.

Finneran, Richard J. "'Old lecher with a love on every wind': A Study of Yeats' *Stories of Red Hanrahan*." *Texas Studies in Literature and Language* 14.2 (1972): 347–58.

———. *The Prose Fiction of W. B. Yeats: The Search for "Those Simple Forms."* Dublin: Dolmen, 1973.

Flower, Robin. *The Western Island or The Great Blasket*. New York: Oxford University Press, 1945.
Foster, John Wilson. "Certain Set Apart: The Western Island in the Irish Renaissance." *Studies* 66 (1977): 261–74.
———. *Forces and Themes in Ulster Fiction*. Dublin: Gill & Macmillan; Totowa: Rowman, 1974.
———. "Passage through 'The Dead.'" *Criticism* 15 (1973): 91–108.
———. "The Plight of Current Folklore Theory." *Southern Folklore Quarterly* 32 (1968): 237–48.
———. "Romantic Revival, Modernist Prescription: An Irish Case-Study." *Modernism and Modernity*. Eds. Benjamin H. D. Buchloh, Serge Guilbaut, and David Solkin. Proc. of a Conference on Modernism and Modernity. 12–14 March 1981. Halifax, N.S.: Press of the Nova Scotia College of Art and Design, 1983. 65–80.
———. "Yeats and the Easter Rising." *The Canadian Journal of Irish Studies* 11.1 (1985): 21–34.
Foucault, Michel. *The Archaeology of Knowledge*. Trans. A. M. Sheridan Smith. New York: Harper & Row, 1976.
Freeman, T. W. *Ireland: A General and Regional Geography*. London: Methuen, 1972.
Frye, Northrop. *Anatomy of Criticism: Four Essays*. 1957. Princeton: Princeton University Press, 1971.
———. *A Study of English Romanticism*. New York: Random House, 1968.
Gantz, Jeffrey, trans. *Early Irish Myths and Sagas*. Harmondsworth: Penguin Books, 1981.
Greene, David H. and Edward M. Stephens. *J. M. Synge: 1871–1909*. New York: Macmillan, 1959.
Harris, Elizabeth. "George Moore: 'The Little Catholic Boy of That Name.'" *Eire-Ireland* 15.1 (1980): 64–85.
Harrison, J. F. C. *The Second Coming: Popular Millenarianism 1780–1850*. London: Routledge & Kegan Paul, 1979.
Hirsch, Edward. "A War Between the Orders: Yeats's Fiction and the Transcendental Moment." *Novel: A Forum on Fiction* 17.1 (1983): 52–66.
Hogan, Robert. *Eimar O'Duffy*. Lewisburg: Bucknell University Press, 1972.
Hogan, Robert et al., eds. *Dictionary of Irish Literature*. Westport, CT: Greenwood, 1979.
Hone, Joseph. *The Life of George Moore*. London: Gollancz, 1936.
———. *W. B. Yeats 1865–1939*. 1943. London: Macmillan, 1965.
Hough, Graham. *The Last Romantics*. 1947. Oxford: Oxford University Press, 1961.
Houghton, Walter E. *The Victorian Frame of Mind, 1830–1870*. New Haven and London: Yale University Press, 1957.
Howarth, Herbert. *The Irish Writers, 1880–1940: Literature Under Parnell's Star*. London: Rockliff, 1958.

Jackson, Kenneth Hurlstone, trans. *A Celtic Miscellany: Translations from the Celtic Literatures*. Harmondsworth: Penguin Books, 1971.

Jeffares, A. Norman. *A Commentary on the Collected Poems of W. B. Yeats*. London: Macmillan, 1968.

Kiberd, Declan. *Synge and the Irish Language*. London: Macmillan, 1979.

Kiely, Benedict. *Modern Irish Fiction: A Critique*. Dublin: Golden Eagle Books, 1950.

Knights, Ben. *The Idea of the Clerisy in the Nineteenth Century*. Cambridge: Cambridge University Press, 1978.

Kinsella, Thomas, trans. *The Tain: Translated from the Irish Epic Taín Bó Cuailnge*. London: Oxford University Press, 1970.

Krause, David. *Sean O'Casey: The Man and His Work*. New York: Macmillan, 1975.

Krohn, Kaarle. *Folklore Methodology*. 1926. Trans. Roger L. Welsch. Austin and London: University of Texas Press, 1971.

Littlefield, Hazel. *Lord Dunsany: King of Dreams. A Personal Portrait*. New York: Exposition Press, 1959.

Loftus, Richard J. *Nationalism in Modern Anglo-Irish Poetry*. Madison and Milwaukee: University of Wisconsin Press, 1964.

Luce, J. V. "Homeric Qualities in the Life and Literature of the Great Blasket Island." *Greece & Rome* 2nd ser. 16 (1969): 151–68.

Lyons, F. S. L. *Ireland Since the Famine*. 1971. London: Fontana, 1973.

Lyons, J. B. *Oliver St. John Gogarty: The Man of Many Talents*. Dublin: Blackwater, 1980; Atlantic Highlands: Humanities Press, 1981.

McCartney, Donal. "Gaelic Ideological Origins of 1916." *1916: The Easter Rising*. Eds. O. Dudley Edwards and Fergus Pyle. London: MacGibbon & Kee, 1968.

MacLaine, Kay Diviney. "Elements of the Folk Hero-Tale in the Fiction of Padraic Colum." Ph.D. diss. University of British Columbia, 1984.

McNally, Kenneth. *The Islands of Ireland*. New York: Norton, 1978.

Manlove, C. N. *Modern Fantasy: Five Studies*. Cambridge: Cambridge University Press, 1975.

Martin, Augustine. "Apocalyptic Structure in Yeats's *Secret Rose*." *Studies* 64 (1975): 24–34.

———. *James Stephens: A Critical Study*. Dublin: Gill & Macmillan, 1977.

———. "'The Secret Rose' and Yeats's Dialogue with History." *Ariel* 3.3 (1972): 91–103.

Martin, F. X. and F. J. Byrne, eds. *The Scholar Revolutionary: Eoin MacNeill, 1867–1945, and the Making of the New Ireland*. Shannon: Irish University Press, 1973.

Mason, Thomas H. *The Islands of Ireland: Their Scenery, People, Life and Antiquities*. London: Batsford, 1936.

Melia, Daniel Frederick. "Narrative Structure in Irish Saga." Ph.D. diss. Harvard University, 1972.

Mercier, Vivian. *The Irish Comic Tradition.* Oxford and London: Oxford University Press, 1962.

———. "Victorian Evangelicalism and the Anglo-Irish Literary Revival." *Literature and the Changing Ireland.* Ed. Peter Connolly. Gerrards Cross: Colin Smythe; Totowa: Barnes & Noble, 1982.

Messenger, John C. *Inis Beag: Isle of Ireland.* New York: Holt, Rinehart & Winston, 1969.

———. "Sex and Repression in an Irish Folk Community." *Human Sexual Behavior.* Eds. Donald S. Marshall and Robert C. Suggs. New York: Basic Books, 1971.

Mitchell, Joan Towey. "Yeats, Pearse, and Cuchulain." *Eire-Ireland* 11.4 (1976): 51–65.

Mullen, Pat. *Man of Aran.* London: Faber, 1934.

Murphy, Gerard. *The Ossianic Lore and Romantic Tales of Medieval Ireland.* Dublin: Colm O Lochlainn for the Cultural Relations Committee of Ireland, 1955.

Ní Shúilleabhaín, Eibhlis. *Letters from the Great Blasket.* Dublin and Cork: Mercier, [1978].

O'Brien, Conor Cruise. *States of Ireland.* St. Albans, Herts.: Panther, 1974.

O'Brien Maíre Cruise. "*An tOileanách:* Tomás Ó Criomhthain (1856–1937)." *The Pleasures of Gaelic Literature.* Ed. John Jordan. Dublin and Cork: RTE/ Mercier, 1977.

Ó Coileaín, Seán. "Irish Saga Literature." *Heroic Epic and Saga: An Introduction to the World's Great Folk Epics.* Ed. Felix J. Oinas. Bloomington: Indiana University Press, 1978.

O'Connor, Ulick. *A Terrible Beauty is Born: The Irish Troubles 1912–1922.* London: Hamish Hamilton, 1975.

O'Donnell, William H. *A Guide to the Prose Fiction of W. B. Yeats.* Studies in Modern Literature Series. Ann Arbor: UMI Research Press, 1983.

O'Driscoll, Robert. "*The Tables of the Law:* A Critical Text." *Yeats Studies* 1 (1971): 87–118.

O'Faolain, Sean. *The Irish.* 1947. Harmondsworth: Penguin Books, 1969.

———. *An Irish Journey.* New York: Longmans, Green, 1943.

O'Grady, Hugh Art. *Standish James O'Grady: The Man and Writer.* Dublin: Talbot Press, 1929.

Ó Lúing, Seán. "Robin Flower (1881–1946)." *Studies* 70 (1981): 121–34.

O'Neil, Daniel J. *Three Perennial Themes of Anti-Colonialism: The Irish Case.* Monograph Series in World Affairs 14.1. Denver: University of Denver, 1976.

O'Rahilly, Thomas F. *Early Irish History and Mythology.* Dublin: Dublin Institute for Advanced Studies, 1946.

Ó Súilleabhaín, Seán [Sean O'Sullivan]. *The Folklore of Ireland.* New York: Hastings House, 1974.

———. *A Handbook of Irish Folklore.* Hatboro, PA: Folklore Associates, 1963.

———, ed. and trans. *Folktales of Ireland.* Chicago and London: University of Chicago Press, 1966.

Ó Súilleabhaín, Seán and Reidar Th. Christiansen. *The Types of the Irish Folktale. Folklore Fellows Communications* 78.188 (1963): 1–347.

O'Sullivan, Seumas. *Essays and Recollections.* Dublin and Cork: Talbot Press, 1944.

O'Tuama, Sean. "The Other Tradition: Some Highlights of Modern Fiction in Irish." *The Irish Novel In Our Time.* Ed. Patrick Rafroidi and Maurice Harmon. Lille: Publications de L'Université de Lille III, 1975–76.

Owens, Graham, ed. *George Moore's Mind and Art.* Edinburgh: Oliver & Boyd, 1968.

Patch, Howard Rollin. *The Other World According to Descriptions in Medieval Literature.* Cambridge, MA: Harvard University Press, 1950.

Porter, Raymond J. *P. H. Pearse.* New York: Twayne, 1973.

Propp, Vladimir. *Morphology of the Folktale.* 1929. Ed. Svatava Pirkova-Jakobson; trans. Laurence Scott. Indiana University Research Center in Anthropology, Folklore, and Linguistics 10. Bloomington: Indiana University Press, 1958.

Pyle, Hilary. *James Stephens: His Work and an Account of His Life.* London: Routledge & Kegan Paul, 1965.

Raglan, Lord. *The Hero: A Study in Tradition, Myth, and Drama.* London: Methuen, 1936.

Reece, Jack E. *The Bretons Against France: Ethnic Minority Nationalism in Twentieth-Century Brittany.* Chapel Hill: University of North Carolina Press, 1977.

Rodgers, W. R. *Irish Literary Portraits.* London: BBC, 1972.

Seymour, St. John D. *Irish Visions of the Other-World.* London: SPCK, 1930.

Schoof, T. M. *A Survey of Catholic Theology 1800–1970.* Trans. N. D. Smith. Paramus, NJ: Paulist Newman Press, 1970.

Shaw, Francis. "The Canon of Irish History: A Challenge." *Studies* 61 (1972): 113–53.

Sidnell, Michael J. "Versions of the Stories of Red Hanrahan." *Yeats Studies* 1 (1971): 119–74.

Skelton, Robin. *The Writings of J. M. Synge.* Indianapolis: Bobbs-Merrill, 1971.

Stanford, W. B. and R. B. McDowell. *Mahaffy: A Biography of an Anglo-Irishman.* London: Routledge & Kegan Paul, 1971.

Stern, J. P. *On Realism.* London: Routledge & Kegan Paul, 1973.

Summerfield, Henry. *The Myriad-Minded Man: A biography of George William Russell "A.E." 1867–1935.* Gerrards Cross: Colin Smythe, 1975.

Thompson, Stith. *The Folktale.* 1946. Berkeley: University of California Press, 1977.

Thompson, William Irwin. *The Imagination of an Insurrection. Dublin, Easter 1916: A Study of an Ideological Movement.* New York: Oxford University Press, 1967.

Voelker, Joseph C. "'Proteus' and the Vaticinia of Marsh's Library: Joyce's Subjunctive Selves." *Eire-Ireland* 14.4 (1979): 133–44.
Wilson, Edmund. *Axel's Castle: A Study in the Imaginative Literature of 1870–1930.* New York: Charles Scribner's Sons, 1931.
Wilson, William A. *Folklore and Nationalism in Modern Finland.* Bloomington and London: Indiana University Press, 1976.

Index

Major references to authors and works are in **boldface** type.

FICTIONS OF THE IRISH LITERARY REVIVAL
was composed in 10 on 12 Galliard on a Mergenthaler Linotron 202
by Coghill Book Typesetting Co.;
printed by sheet-fed offset on 50-pound, acid-free Glatfelter Antique Cream
and notchbound with paper covers
by Maple-Vail Book Manufacturing Group, Inc.;
with paper covers printed in two colors
by Johnson City Publishing Co., Inc.;
designed by Victoria M. Lane;
and published by
SYRACUSE UNIVERSITY PRESS
Syracuse, New York 13244-5160

IRISH STUDIES

Irish Studies presents a wide range of books interpreting important aspects of Irish life and culture to scholarly and general audiences. The richness and complexity of the Irish experience, past and present, deserves broad understanding and careful analysis. For this reason an important purpose of the series is to offer a forum to scholars interested in Ireland, its history, and culture. Irish literature is a special concern in the series, but works from the perspectives of the fine arts, history, and the social sciences are also welcome, as are studies which take multidisciplinary approaches.

Irish Studies is a continuing project of Syracuse University Press and is under the general editorship of Richard Fallis, associate professor of English at Syracuse University.

IRISH STUDIES Richard C. Fallis, *ed.*

An Anglo-Irish Dialect Glossary for Joyce's Works. Richard Wall
Caught in the Crossfire: Children and the Northern Ireland Conflict. Ed Cairns
Children's Lore in "Finnegans Wake." Grace Eckley
The Drama of J. M. Synge Mary C. King
Fictions of the Irish Literary Revival: A Changeling Art. John Wilson Foster
Finnegans Wake: A Plot Summary. John Gordon
Fionn Mac Cumhaill: Celtic Myth in English Literature. James MacKillop
Great Hatred, Little Room: The Irish Historical Novel. James M. Cahalan
Hanna Sheehy-Skeffington: Irish Feminist. Leah Levenson & Jerry H. Natterstad
In Minor Keys: The Uncollected Short Stories of George Moore. David B. Eakin & Helmut E. Gerber, *eds.*
Intimidation and the Control of Conflict in Northern Ireland. John Darby
Irish Life and Traditions. Sharon Gmelch, *ed.*
Irish Literature: A Reader. Maureen O'Rourke Murphy & James MacKillop, *eds.*
'Ireland Sober, Ireland Free': Drink and Temperance in Nineteenth-Century Ireland. Elizabeth Malcolm
The Irish Renaissance. Richard Fallis
The Literary Vision of Liam O'Flaherty. John N. Zneimer
Northern Ireland: The Background to the Conflict. John Darby, *ed.*
Old Days, Old Ways: An Illustrated Folk History of Ireland Olive Sharkey
Peig: The Autobiography of Peig Sayers of the Great Blasket Island. Bryan MacMahon, *tr.*
Selected Plays of Padraiċ Colum. Sanford Sternlicht, *ed.*
Selected Short Stories of Padraic Colum. Sanford Sternlicht, *ed.*
Shadowy Heroes: Irish Literature of the 1890s. Wayne E. Hall
Ulster's Uncertain Defenders: Protestant Political, Paramilitary, and Community Groups and the Northern Ireland Conflict. Sarah Nelson
Yeats. Douglas Archibald
Yeats and the Beginning of the Irish Renaissance. Phillip L. Marcus